Contents

Microsoft®
OLE DB 1.1
Programmer's Reference and
Software Development Kit

Microsoft Press

PUBLISHED BY
Microsoft Press
A Division of Microsoft Corporation
One Microsoft Way
Redmond, Washington 98052-6399

Library of Congress Cataloging-in-Publication Data
Microsoft OLE DB Software Development Kit and Programmer's Reference /
    Microsoft Corporation.
        p.   cm.
    Includes index.
    ISBN 1-57231-612-8
    1. Database management.   2. OLE (Computer file)   3. Computer
software--Development.   I. Microsoft Corporation.
    QA76.9.D3M5735   1997
    005.74--dc21   97-7697
                                                            CIP

Printed and bound in the United States of America.

1 2 3 4 5 6 7 8 9   QMQM   2 1 0 9 8 7

Distributed to the book trade in Canada by Macmillan of Canada, a division of Canada Publishing Corporation.

A CIP catalogue record for this book is available from the British Library.

Microsoft Press books are available through booksellers and distributors worldwide. For further information about international editions, contact your local Microsoft Corporation office. Or contact Microsoft Press International directly at fax (206) 936-7329.

Acquisitions Editor: David Clark
Project Editor: Maureen Williams Zimmerman

Contents

Part 2 OLE DB Reference 171

Contents

Part 3   Appendixes 507

About This Manual

The OLE DB specification is a set of interfaces that expose data from a variety of data sources using the OLE Component Object Model (COM).

Organization of This Manual

This manual is divided into the following parts:

- **Part 1** *Introduction to OLE DB,* providing conceptual information about OLE DB
- **Part 2** *OLE DB Reference,* containing syntax and semantic information for all OLE DB interfaces
- **Part 3** *Appendixes,* containing technical details

Audience

This manual assumes the following:

- A working knowledge of the C or C++ programming language
- Knowledge of COM

In addition, a general knowledge of databases and SQL is helpful.

Document Conventions

This manual uses the following typographic conventions.

Format	Used for
WIN.INI	Uppercase letters indicate file names, SQL statements, macro names, and terms used at the operating-system command level.
`#include <io.h>`	Sans serif font is used for sample command lines and program code.
argument	Italicized words indicate information that the user or the application must provide, or word emphasis.
IRowset	Bold type indicates that syntax must be typed exactly as shown, including method names.

About the Code Examples

The code examples in this book are designed for illustrative purposes only. Because they are written primarily to demonstrate OLE DB principles, efficiency has sometimes been set aside in the interest of clarity. In addition, whole sections of code have sometimes been omitted for clarity. These include the definitions of non-OLE DB functions and most error handling.

Acknowledgements

OLE DB represents the work of many people over several years. Although the contributors are too numerous to mention, we attempt to list those who have made significant contributions. Our apologies and thanks to any we have missed.

OLE DB started as an idea from Adam Bosworth, who wanted a way to retrieve all types of data in an OLE COM environment. With support from David Vaskevitch, he formed a task force that wrote the original OLE DB specification. Seth Pollack carried this work forward and the result was refined by a group headed by Naveen Garg. A subset of this was released as the Data Binding interfaces in Microsoft® Visual Basic®.

Realizing the importance of OLE DB, Tanj Bennett and Goetz Graefe redesigned key aspects of the specification, improving the component model and creating a rowset model that allowed consumers to efficiently share data and work in a disconnected environment such as the Internet.

José Blakeley and Mike Pizzo, with assistance from Renato Barrera, led the final work on the OLE DB specification. They resolved numerous design issues and worked with many people inside and outside Microsoft to ensure that OLE DB would fill the needs of consumers and providers alike. Leading the development of the OLE DB Software Development Kit (SDK) and keeping the entire team focused was M. Alam Ali.

The Development team wrote the first OLE DB provider—the ODBC Provider—both to provide access to relational databases, and to test the OLE DB specification. In the process, they made significant contributions to the specification, including original design work. Led by Paul Archer, this team consisted of Peter Burzynski, Rick Feinauer, Eric Jacobsen, Wlodek Nakonieczny, Dragan Tomic, and Brian Tschumper.

Keeping everyone honest was the Test team, who ensured the quality of the software and the specification. They helped identify many ambiguities in the specification and made many suggestions for ways to improve OLE DB. This team was led by Kristi Brandes and consisted of Allan Benson, John Elion, Dina Fleet, Yao Lu, Suryanarayana Putrevu, Xiaohong Su, Ed Triou, and David Zimmerman.

The User Education team wrote the OLE DB specification and the documentation for the software in the OLE DB SDK. Along the way, they fixed inconsistencies in the specification and helped with design work. Led by Mark Bukovec, the team consisted of Ronald Bourret, Lori Dirks, James Gordon, Jim van de Erve, and Emily Spiger. Production support came from Melissa Shaw, Mike McKay, and John Zilly, and the graphic artists were Patricia Hunter, Steven Fulgham, and Andrea Heuston.

Carrying the message of OLE DB to the world were Greg Nelson, Caribe Browne, and Ted Hase. The ActiveX Data Objects (ADO) team and the ITest team (led by Tom Woods) provided feedback on the specification and code shipped in the OLE DB SDK and builds were performed by Debra Dove and the build team. Providing leadership and support to the entire team were Dave Cameron, Bill Baker, Kathleen Carey, and Maya Opavska.

Significant contributions to OLE DB were made by numerous other people inside Microsoft, including Andrei Burago, Jerry Dunietz, Gunnar Mein, Kyle Peltonen, Alan Whitney, and Eugene Zabokritski. Other contributions came from Matthew Bellew, Jeff Bernhardt, Stephen Bremer, Michael Grier, Dax Hawkins, Peter Hussey, Suresh Kannan, Steve Kruy, Steve Proteau, Matthew Senft, Gordon Smith, and Laura Yedwab.

Introduction to OLE DB

CHAPTER 1

Overview

Today, a vast amount of critical information necessary to conduct day-to-day business is found outside of traditional, corporate production databases. Instead, this information is found in file systems, indexed-sequential files such as Btrieve®, personal databases such as Microsoft® Access and Paradox®, and productivity tools such as spreadsheets, project management planners, and electronic mail. To take advantage of the benefits of database technology, such as declarative queries, transactions, and security, businesses must move the data from its original containing system into a DBMS.

This process is expensive and redundant. Furthermore, businesses need applications to exploit the advantages of database technology not just when accessing data within a DBMS, but also when accessing data from any other information container.

OLE DB is a set of OLE interfaces that provide applications with uniform access to data stored in diverse information sources. These interfaces support the amount of DBMS functionality appropriate to the data source, enabling it to share its data.

Access to Diverse Sources

OLE DB enables the development of applications that access diverse data sources. For example, consider a sales representative who wants to find all e-mail messages received within the last two days from Seattle customers, including their addresses, to which no one has yet replied. This query involves searching the mailbox file containing the sales representative's e-mail, as well as a Customers table stored in a Microsoft Access DBMS to identify customers. The query can be formulated in an extended SQL syntax as follows. This syntax is designed for illustration purposes only. It is not implemented in any product of which we are aware.

```
SELECT  m1.*, c.Address FROM
   MakeTable(Mail, d:\mail\smith.mmf) m1,
   MakeTable(Access, d:\access\Enterprise.mdb, Customers) c
   WHERE m1.Date >= date(today(), -2)
      AND m1.From = c.Emailaddr
      AND c.City = "Seattle"
      AND NOT EXISTS
         (SELECT * FROM MakeTable(Mail, d:\mail\smith.mmf) m2
          WHERE m1.MsgId = m2.InReplyTo);
```

Assume that **MakeTable** is a function that makes the mail file D:\MAIL\SMITH.MMF into a table. It also exposes the Customers table from a Microsoft Access database (D:\ACCESS\ENTERPRISE.MDB). The function **date** takes a date and a number of days as arguments and produces a date.

OLE DB makes it easy for applications to access data stored in diverse DBMS and non-DBMS information sources. DBMS sources may include mainframe databases such as IMS™ and DB2®, server databases such as Oracle® and Microsoft SQL Server, and desktop databases such as Microsoft Access, Paradox, and Microsoft FoxPro®. Non-DBMS sources might include information stored in file systems such as Windows NT® and UNIX®, indexed-sequential files, e-mail, spreadsheets, project management tools, and many other sources.

Component Database Management Systems

The benefits of component DBMSs can be discussed from two perspectives: *consumers* and *data providers*. First, consumers have widely varying database management needs. A decision by a consumer to use a particular DBMS implies a decision to use a particular storage manager, file access method, security model, query and scripting language, query processor, and transaction manager. Often, consumers do not require or use all the functionality packaged in a commercial, monolithic DBMS. Yet, they are forced to pay additional resource overhead for functionality they do not need.

Second, there is a large amount of mission-critical data stored in systems that are not classified as DBMSs. Popular data access APIs, such as Open Database Connectivity (ODBC), impose a high entry bar for data providers by requiring them to expose their data through SQL. This requires a non-SQL data provider to implement the equivalent of an SQL engine in the ODBC driver. OLE DB lowers the entry bar for simple tabular data providers by only requiring them to implement the functionality native to their data store. At a minimum, a provider needs to implement the interfaces necessary to expose data as tables. This opens the opportunity for the development of query processor components, such as SQL or geographical query processors, that can consume tabular information from any provider that exposes its data through OLE DB. SQL DBMSs can also expose their functionality in a more layered manner using the OLE DB interfaces.

A component DBMS architecture using OLE DB interfaces

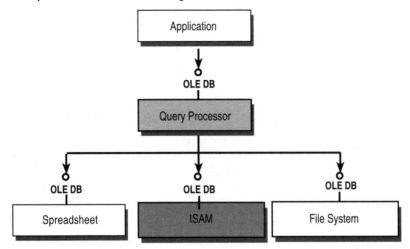

OLE DB defines an open, extensible collection of interfaces that factor and encapsulate orthogonal, reusable portions of DBMS functionality. These interfaces define the boundaries of DBMS components such as row containers, query processors, and transaction coordinators which enable uniform, transactional access to diverse information sources. A DBMS becomes a conglomerate of cooperating components that consume and produce data through a uniform set of interfaces.

The OLE DB functional areas include data access and updates (rowsets), query processing, catalog information, notifications, transactions, security, and remote data access. By defining a uniform set of interfaces to access data, OLE DB components contribute not only to uniform data access among diverse information sources, but also help to reduce the application's footprints by enabling them to use only the DBMS functionality they need. Initially, OLE DB provides uniform access to tabular data. Future versions might provide access to richer models, such as object-oriented and semi-structured data.

OLE DB uses the OLE Component Object Model (COM) infrastructure, which reduces unnecessary duplication of services and provides a higher degree of interoperability not only among diverse information sources, but also among existing programming environments and tools. Indeed, OLE DB is the way to access data in a COM environment. The following section describes the architecture and main interface areas of OLE DB.

Consumers and Providers

A *consumer* is any piece of system or application code that consumes an OLE DB interface; this includes OLE DB components themselves. A *provider* is any software component that exposes an OLE DB interface.

OLE DB providers can be classified broadly into two classes. A *data provider* is any OLE DB provider that owns data and exposes its data in a tabular form as a rowset, which is defined later in this chapter. Examples of data providers include relational DBMSs, storage managers, spreadsheets, ISAMs, and e-mail.

A *service provider* is any OLE DB component that does not own its own data, but encapsulates some service by producing and consuming data through OLE DB interfaces. A service provider is both a consumer and a provider. For example, a heterogeneous query processor is a service provider. Suppose a consumer asks to join data from tables in two different data sources. In its role as a consumer, the query processor retrieves rows from rowsets created over each of the base tables. In its role as a provider, the query processor creates a rowset from these rows and returns it to the consumer.

OLE DB Components

OLE DB defines the following components, each of which is an OLE COM object:

- **Enumerators**—Enumerators search for available data sources and other enumerators. Consumers that are not customized for a particular data source use enumerators to search for a data source to use.

- **Data Source Objects**—Data source objects contain the machinery to connect to a data source, such as a file or a DBMS. They are a factory for sessions.

- **Sessions**—Sessions provide a context for transactions and can be implicitly or explicitly transacted. A single data source object can create multiple sessions. Sessions are a factory for transactions, commands, and rowsets.

- **Transactions**—Transaction objects are used when committing or aborting nested transactions at other than the lowest level.

- **Commands**—Commands execute a text command, such as an SQL statement. If the text command specifies a rowset, such as an SQL **SELECT** statement, the command is a factory for the rowset. A single session can create multiple commands.

- **Rowsets**—Rowsets expose data in tabular format. A special case of a rowset is an index. Rowsets can be created from the session or the command.

- **Errors**—Errors can be created by any interface on any OLE DB object. They contain additional information about an error, including an optional custom error object.

For example, a consumer might use the following objects.

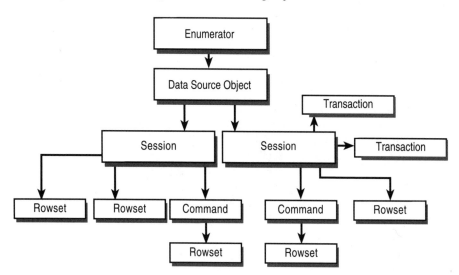

Enumerator Objects

An enumerator exposes the **ISourcesRowset** interface which returns a rowset describing all data sources and enumerators visible to the enumerator. A root enumerator, shipped in the OLE DB Software Development Kit (SDK), traverses the registry looking for data sources and other enumerators. Other enumerators traverse the registry or search in a provider-specific manner. For example, an enumerator over the file system might search for subdirectories.

Data Source Objects and Session Objects

The OLE DB connection model defines how data and service providers are located and activated. Two objects are the basis for the OLE DB connection model: the *data source object* and the *session*. To access an OLE DB provider, a consumer must first instantiate a data source object. Each data provider is identified by a unique class identifier (CLSID) in the registry and is instantiated by calling **CoCreateInstance**, which creates an instance of the object through the object's class factory. The data source object exposes **IDBProperties**, which the consumer uses to provide basic authentication information such as user ID and password (for cases when the data source does not exist in an authenticated environment) as well as the name of the data source (file or database) containing the data to be accessed. It also exposes **IDBInitialize**, which the consumer uses to connect to the data source.

Once a data source object has been successfully initialized, the consumer can call methods in **IDBProperties** to query the capabilities of a provider. These capabilities include the interfaces, rowset properties such as scrollability, transaction properties such as supported isolation levels, and the SQL dialects a provider supports. The consumer can also call methods in **IDBCreateSession** to create a session.

The session acts as a rowset, command, and transaction factory. A data provider that does not support commands exposes the **IOpenRowset** interface, which enables providers to expose their data directly as rowsets without the use of commands.

Rowset Objects

Rowsets are the central object that enable all OLE DB data providers to expose data in tabular form. Conceptually, a rowset is a set of rows in which each row has columns of data. Base table providers present their data in the form of rowsets. Query processors present the result of queries in the form of rowsets. This makes it possible to layer components that consume or produce data through the same object. The most basic rowset object exposes four interfaces: **IRowset**, which contains methods for fetching rows in the rowset sequentially; **IAccessor**, which permits the definition of groups of column bindings describing the way tabular data is bound to consumer program variables; **IColumnsInfo**, which provides information about the columns of the rowset; and **IRowsetInfo**, which provides information about the rowset itself. Using **IRowset**, a consumer can sequentially traverse the rows in the rowset, including traversing backward if the rowset supports it. The following figure illustrates the data structures a generic rowset object might support.

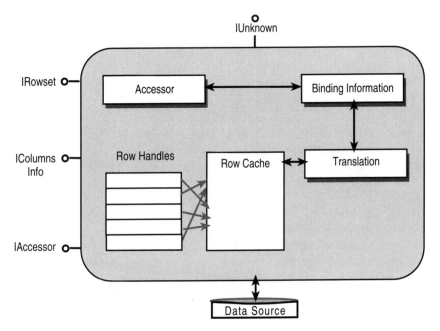

Other rowset interfaces expose additional rowset capabilities. For example, there is an interface to insert, delete, and update rows and interfaces that expose richer row navigation models, such as direct access and scrollability. Rowsets are created in one of two ways. First, they can be created as the result of a query. Second, they can be created directly as the result of calling **IOpenRowset::OpenRowset**. All providers support the latter method, while simple providers, such as those built over a base table, index, file, or in-memory structure, generally do not support the former.

Index rowsets are rowsets whose rows are formed from index entries. Index rowsets have the additional property of allowing efficient access to contiguous rows within a range of keys. They are used primarily by query processor components. Indexes abstract the functionality of B-trees and indexed-sequential files. Indexes are traversed using the **IRowset** interface; information about the index entries is obtained through the **IColumnsInfo** interface; and insertions and deletions are performed through the **IRowsetChange** interface.

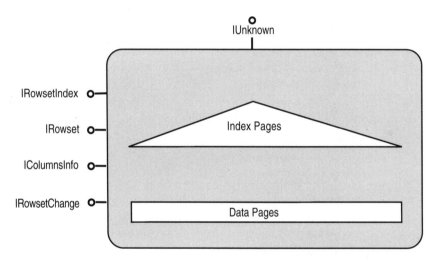

Data Binding and Accessors

Data binding describes the relationship between an element in a consumer structure and a column in a rowset or parameter in a text command. A consumer uses the binding structure to communicate to the provider how it expects the data to be transferred from the provider to the consumer's buffer and vice versa. The binding structure includes information such as the column or parameter being accessed, the data type in the consumer's buffer, the offset to the data in the consumer's data structure, the amount of space available for the data value, and the precision and scale for numeric values. For columns containing OLE objects, the consumer can also request the interface that must be returned to the consumer when the object is fetched.

An accessor is a group of binding structures. It enables consumers to define simultaneous access to multiple columns or parameters and enables providers to optimize access to these multiple columns or parameters.

Command Objects

In OLE DB, Data Definition Language (DDL) and Data Manipulation Language (DML) statements are referred to as text commands. A command object contains a text command and encapsulates the query processing services available in today's DBMSs. Commands expose various interfaces representing different areas of functionality of a query processor including query formulation, preparation, and execution. The following figure illustrates a typical OLE DB query processor.

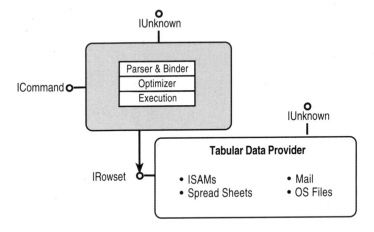

The main purpose of a command object is to execute a text command. Executing a command such as an SQL **SELECT** statement creates a rowset, while executing a command such as an SQL **UPDATE** or **CREATE TABLE** statement does not create a rowset.

Text commands are expressed in a provider-specific language, although this is typically ANSI SQL 92.

An OLE DB consumer that wants to use a command typically performs the following steps:

1. Obtains an interface on the command.

2. Builds a text string representing the command text.

3. Passes the text string to the command.

4. Requests properties to be supported by the resulting rowset, if any, including the interfaces it will expose.

5. Executes the command. If the command text specified the creation of a rowset, the command returns the rowset to the consumer.

Notice that because providers can both consume and produce rowsets, it is possible to compose query processors to process distributed, heterogeneous, or parallel queries. It is also possible to compose specialized query processors, such as SQL query processors, text-search query processors, and geographical or image query processors.

Rowset Properties

During command formulation, OLE DB consumers can request certain properties to be satisfied by the rowsets resulting from a command. Common properties include the set of interfaces to be supported by the resulting rowset. Any rowset returned from a command exposes the mandatory interfaces **IRowset**, **IAccessor**, **IColumnsInfo**, and **IRowsetInfo** described earlier. The basic **IRowset** interface supported by all rowsets enables consumers to, at minimum, navigate the rowset in a forward-only manner. Requesting the rowset property to scroll backwards enables a consumer to navigate the rowset in both directions. Supporting bidirectional rowsets puts additional requirements on the creation of the rowset object to support this functionality efficiently. A forward-only rowset can be fed directly from the query execution plan output. A bidirectional rowset might require materializing the result. In addition to the default interfaces, a consumer may request interfaces to enable direct positioning within a rowset with bookmarks (**IRowsetLocate**), scrollability (**IRowsetScroll**), immediate updatability of rows (**IRowsetChange**), and deferred updatability of rows (**IRowsetUpdate**). It is also possible to request additional properties that specialize the behavior of certain interfaces—for example, to make some columns of the rowset updatable and the rest read-only.

Schema Information

OLE DB consumers obtain catalog information through **IDBSchemaRowset**. This interface enables consumers to request information about types, tables, columns, indexes, views, assertions and constraints, statistics, character sets, collations, and domains. All catalog information is returned to the consumer as rowsets. The schemas of these rowsets are based on the ANSI SQL 92 standard.

Transaction Management

OLE DB defines a basic set of interfaces for transaction management. A transaction enables consumers to define units of work within a provider. These units of work have the atomicity, concurrency, isolation, and durability (ACID) properties. They allow the specification of various isolation levels to enable more flexible access to data among concurrent consumers.

Local Transactions

Local transactions refer to transactions running in the context of a resource manager. A provider that supports transactions exposes **ITransactionLocal** on the session. A call to the **ITransactionLocal::StartTransaction** method begins a transaction on the session. A session can be inside or outside of a transaction at any point in time. When created, a session is outside of a transaction and all the work done under the scope of the session is immediately committed on each OLE DB method call. When a session enters a local or coordinated transaction, all the work done under the session, between the **StartTransaction** and **ITransaction::Commit** or **ITransaction::Abort** method calls, including other objects created underneath it (commands or rowsets), are part of the transaction.

StartTransaction supports various isolation levels that consumers can request when creating a transaction. OLE DB providers do not need to support all possible transaction options defined. A consumer can interrogate the transaction capabilities of a provider through **IDBProperties**.

For providers that support nested transactions, calling **StartTransaction** within an existing transaction begins a new nested transaction below the current transaction. Calling the **Commit** or **Abort** methods commits or aborts the transaction at the lowest level, respectively.

Distributed Transactions

OLE DB supports distributed transactions as defined in the *Microsoft Distributed Transaction Coordinator Resource Manager Implementation Guide*. The interfaces specified a model for coordinating transactions among multiple (possibly distributed) data providers.

Event Notifications

OLE DB uses an OLE controls notification model to implement notifications among OLE DB components and consumers. Notifications are used by groups of cooperating consumers sharing a rowset. All consumers and the rowset-generating actions are assumed to be working within the same transaction. Local notifications enable cooperating consumers sharing a rowset to be informed about actions on the rowset performed by their peers. For example, consider a form containing two data controls, one displaying data in a grid and the other displaying data as a two dimensional histogram. Both controls receive their data from the same rowset and operate individually as consumers of the rowset. An end user can send an update to the rowset through the grid control. Notifications enable the other control to be informed of this change as it occurs, giving it the opportunity to update the histogram as appropriate and ultimately providing a consistent view of the data within the form. Consumers register their interest in receiving local notifications though **IConnectionPointContainer**. Consumers support the **IRowsetNotify** interface, which is called by the rowset as events occur.

Notifications in OLE DB define a basic mechanism on which to implement active data source behavior. **IRowsetNotify** represents one of many possible notification contracts between sources and sinks. Providers can define other notification contracts as needed.

Remote Data Access

Remote data access is not fully supported in OLE DB, Version 1.1. The following description is included to provide direction on how OLE DB plans to address this area in future versions.

OLE DB will enable efficient and transparent access between consumers and providers across threads, process, and machine boundaries. In the following discussion, the term "process boundary" refers to a process or machine boundary. We distinguish two forms of remoting: *data remoting* and *object* (or *interface*) *remoting*. In data remoting, a provider *driver* exposing OLE DB interfaces is present on the client side. All interaction with the provider is through the driver. All details about communication protocol, data transfer format, and the provider's native interface calls are handled internally by the driver. An example of this approach would be an OLE DB provider accessing an SQL DBMS through ODBC. In other words, the process or machine boundary cuts through the provider's driver. The consumer/provider relationship is entirely within a single process.

In interface remoting, an OLE DB provider is running remotely in a different process. Interface remoting provides the infrastructure and mechanisms to allow a method call to return an interface pointer to an object created in a different process. The infrastructure that performs the remoting of interfaces is transparent to both the client and the server object. Neither the client or server object are aware that the other party is in a different process. Distributed COM, another COM technology used by OLE DB available in Windows NT 4.0, provides an open specification and reference implementation of such an infrastructure. The following figure illustrates the various configurations in which consumer and provider code can exist.

Clients always call in-process code; objects are always called by in-process code.

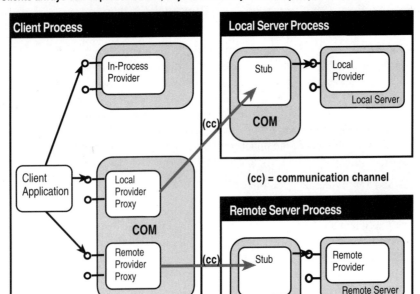

The proxy/stub agents are agents that take care of marshaling arguments across the process boundary and optimize access over the network by trying to hide the latency and bandwidth. The design of proxies and stubs is an open-ended optimization problem. Proxies and stubs may vary in complexity. Simple proxy/stub pairs provide marshaling of arguments to method calls. Sophisticated proxy/stubs may provide client-side caching combined with bulk data transfer over the process boundary to minimize network trips, or may even combine method calls, thereby optimizing network trips across multiple method calls.

Providers may choose to implement their remote data access by either approach. The ODBC Provider shipped in the OLE DB Software Development Kit (SDK) provides an implementation of data remoting through ODBC. In the ODBC Provider, all process and network communications are managed internally by the ODBC driver. Future versions of the OLE DB SDK will provide a reference implementation of interface remoting, packaged as a library of generic proxy/stub pairs for all OLE DB objects. Providers that want to have a tighter control over the performance of their OLE DB implementations across threads, process, and machine boundaries are free to implement their own remoting agents using the network protocol and optimizations of their choice.

Security

Security is not fully supported in OLE DB, Version 1.1. The following description is included to provide direction on how OLE DB plans to address this area in future versions.

OLE DB will define interfaces that support authentication, authorization, and secure administration of access among users, groups, and resources. The role of security in OLE DB is to expose the relevant security functionality encapsulated in the security models of individual data providers or the underlying operating system on which they run, provide a pass-through layer of security interfaces through which the underlying security functionality can be made available to OLE DB consumers, and provide a unified view of security.

For information about the authentication properties defined in OLE DB, see "Initialization Properties" in Appendix C.

Authentication

OLE DB allows authentication through different mechanisms depending on the layer that enforces authentication: operating system, network, or data provider. In *password-based authentication*, the consumer authenticates itself to the data provider by supplying a name and a password. The data provider enforces authentication in this case. When the consumer and provider operate in-process, passwords can be passed directly to the provider. In situations where a network connection is involved, the password must be sent to the provider over the network, which presents additional security problems. *Domain-based authentication* implies the availability of an authentication service provided by the operating system such as Windows NT. In this environment, users authenticate themselves to the domain by providing a password when logging into the system. Once the user is authenticated to the domain, the domain provides identification information on behalf of the user in a trusted manner. *Distributed authentication* assumes the existence of a distributed authentication service such as the one provided by Microsoft's Security Support Provider Interface (SSPI) which is modeled after the General Security Support API from Digital Equipment Corporation®. In OLE DB, Version 1.1, consumers call **IDBProperties** to request the type of authentication mechanism they want to use. They can also request the quality of service they expect when communicating to the provider across a network.

Authorization

Authorization, or access control, is concerned with the enforcement of the privileges defined among users, groups, roles, services, etc. In most cases, authorization is enforced internally by the provider and the consumer only gets return codes from method invocations determining if the call was successful or a permission violation occurred. OLE DB, Version 1.0, defines the return code DB_SEC_E_PERMISSIONDENIED and status codes such as DBSTATUS_E_PERMISSIONDENIED and DBROWSTATUS_E_ PERMISSIONDENIED for this purpose. Future versions of OLE DB will take advantage of a set of security interfaces defined by Distributed COM to control the security of RPC calls between proxies and stubs, the launching of objects, and the impersonation of clients by servers.

Administration

Security administration is concerned with managing the granting and revoking of permissions among users, groups, roles, and any provider-specific object (data or code). OLE DB, Version 1.1, data providers that support commands can process security administration requests formulated by consumers using SQL **GRANT** and **REVOKE** statements. Future versions of OLE DB will define interfaces to enable data providers that don't support commands to expose methods to get and set permissions among users, objects, and groups in a provider-specific manner.

A Rowset Traversal Example

This example illustrates a simple OLE DB program that reads a table through a rowset, printing each row along the way. Familiarity with C++ and OLE is assumed. Code to check status and errors after each OLE call is omitted for clarity.

```
#include<oledb.h>
extern GUID        CLSID_MailProvider
IDBInitialize     *pIDBInit;
IDBProperties     *pIDBProps;
OLECHAR           *szColNames;
HRESULT            hr;
HACCESSOR          hAccessor;
IDBCreateSession  *pIDBCS;
IOpenRowset       *pIOpenRowset;
IRowset           *pIRowset;
IColumnsInfo      *pIColsInfo;
IAccessor         *pIAccessor;
DBCOLUMNINFO      *rgColInfo;
int                irow;
DBID               TableID;
DBBINDSTATUS       rgStatus[10];
HROW              *rghRows;
ULONG              cCol, cBindings, cRowsObtained;
DBBINDING          rgBindings[10];
DBPROPSET          TablePropSet;
void              *rgData;

void PrintData(void*);
void CreateBindingsFromInfo(struct tagDBCOLUMNINFO*, ULONG*,
                    struct tagDBBINDING(*)[10], void**);
```

```
int main() {
   // Initialize OLE
   CoInitialize(NULL);

   // Instantiate a data source object for an email data provider.
   CoCreateInstance(CLSID_MailProvider, 0, CLSCTX_LOCAL_SERVER, IID_IDBInitialize,
                    (void**) &pIDBInit);
   // Initialize the data source object for email data provider.
   DBPROP rgProps[4];

   // Initialize the VARIANTs and the options in rgProps.
   for (ULONG i = 0; i <= 3; i++) {
      VariantInit(&rgProps[i].vValue);
      rgProps[i].dwOptions = DBPROPOPTIONS_REQUIRED;
      rgProps[i].vValue.vt = VT_BSTR;
   };

   rgProps[0].dwPropertyID   = DBPROP_INIT_LOCATION;
   rgProps[0].vValue.bstrVal =
      SysAllocStringLen(OLESTR("email_server "), wcslen(OLESTR("email_server ")));
   rgProps[1].dwPropertyID   = DBPROP_INIT_DATASOURCE;
   rgProps[1].vValue.bstrVal =
      SysAllocStringLen(OLESTR("c:\\mail\\smith.mmf"),
                        wcslen(OLESTR("c:\\mail\\smith.mmf")));
   rgProps[2].dwPropertyID   = DBPROP_AUTH_PASSWORD;
   rgProps[2].vValue.bstrVal =
      SysAllocStringLen(OLESTR("password"), wcslen(OLESTR("password")));
   rgProps[3].dwPropertyID   = DBPROP_AUTH_USERID;
   rgProps[3].vValue.bstrVal =
      SysAllocStringLen(OLESTR("Smith"), wcslen(OLESTR("Smith")));

   // Create the initialization structure.
   DBPROPSET PropSet;
   PropSet.rgProperties    = rgProps;
   PropSet.cProperties     = 4;
   PropSet.guidPropertySet = DBPROPSET_DBINIT;

   // Set the initialization properties.
   pIDBInitialize->QueryInterface(IID_IDBProperties, (void**) &pIDBProps);
   pIDBProps->SetProperties(1, &PropSet);
   pIDBProps->Release();

   // Initialize the data source object.
   hr = pIDBInit->Initialize();

   // Request the IDBCreateSession interface
   pIDBInit->QueryInterface(IID_IDBCreateSession, (void**) &pIDBCS);

   // Create a session returning a pointer to its
   // IOpenRowset interface
   pIDBCS->CreateSession(NULL, IID_IOpenRowset, (LPUNKNOWN*) &pIOpenRowset);
```

```
// Open a rowset corresponding to the email file. First initialize a property set
// "TablePropSet" for the properties that specify the email file, then open the
// rowset.
pIOpenRowset->OpenRowset(NULL,&TableID,NULL, IID_IRowset, 1, &TablePropSet,
                         (LPUNKNOWN*) &pIRowset );

// Get information about column types.
pIRowset->QueryInterface(IID_IColumnsInfo, (void**) &pIColsInfo);
pIColsInfo->GetColumnInfo(&cCol, &rgColInfo, &szColNames);
pIColsInfo->Release();

// Establish bindings using a convenience function.
CreateBindingsFromInfo(rgColInfo,&cBindings, &rgBindings, &rgData);

// Request the IAccessor interface from rowset.
pIRowset->QueryInterface(IID_IAccessor, (void**) &pIAccessor);

// Create an accessor, return an accessor handle.
pIAccessor->CreateAccessor(DBACCESSOR_ROWDATA, cBindings, rgBindings, 0, &hAccessor,
                           rgStatus);

// Read the rows; 100 rows at a time into the rowset.
while(SUCCEEDED(hr = pIRowset->GetNextRows(NULL, 0, 100, &cRowsObtained, &rghRows))
      && cRowsObtained) {
    for(irow = 0; irow < cRowsObtained; irow++) {
        // GetData copies the rows into the local buffers, performing the type
        // conversions specified in the binding structures associated with the
        // accessor.
        pIRowset->GetData(rghRows[irow], hAccessor, (void*) rgData);

        // Convenience function to print the data.
        PrintData(rgData);
    }
    // Release the rows just printed from the rowset.
    pIRowset->ReleaseRows(cRowsObtained, rghRows, NULL, NULL, NULL);
}

// Release the accessor handle and the rowset.
pIAccessor->ReleaseAccessor(hAccessor);
pIAccessor->Release();
pIRowset->Release();

// Release the session and data source object.
pIOpenRowset->Release();
pIDBCS->Release();
pIDBInit->Release();

// Uninitialize OLE.
CoUninitialize();
return;
}
```

CHAPTER 2

Enumerators, Data Source Objects, and Sessions

This chapter discusses enumerators, data source objects, and sessions.

Enumerators

An enumerator is an object that searches for data sources and other enumerators.

```
CoType TEnumerator {
    [mandatory]  IParseDisplayName;
    [mandatory]  ISourcesRowset;
    [optional]   IDBInitialize;
    [optional]   IDBProperties;
    [optional]   ISupportErrorInfo;
}
```

Enumerating Data Sources and Enumerators

Generic consumers should use enumerators to search for data sources and other enumerators, rather than searching the registry directly. In this way, consumers will continue to work if the registry information changes in the future or new root enumerators with additional functionality, such as the ability to enumerate data sources on other machines, are introduced in the future. To create an enumerator, the consumer calls **CoCreateInstance** with the class ID of the enumerator. The consumer generally requests **ISourcesRowset** when creating an enumerator.

To list the data sources and enumerators visible to the current enumerator, the consumer calls **ISourcesRowset::GetSourcesRowset**. This method returns a rowset of information about the currently visible data sources and enumerators. To instantiate a data source or enumerator listed in this rowset, the consumer first calls **IParseDisplayName::ParseDisplayName** for the returned display name. This method returns a moniker, which the consumer can then bind to instantiate the object.

Each row in the rowset returned by **ISourcesRowset** contains a SOURCES_ISPARENT column. For enumerator rows, this column contains VARIANT_TRUE if the enumerator described by the row is the enumerator that can enumerate the current enumerator. For example, if the enumerator lists files and directories in the file system, this is the parent directory. The SOURCES_ISPARENT column thus allows the consumer to traverse backward through a hierarchy of enumerators, such as might be found over a file system. The consumer ignores the SOURCES_ISPARENT column for data source rows.

A root enumerator is shipped in the OLE DB Software Development Kit (SDK). This enumerator traverses the registry searching for providers and enumerators. It has a class ID of CLSID_OLEDB_ENUMERATOR. For more information about it, see the documentation for the OLE DB SDK.

Providers can also support enumerators, although they are not required to do so. These enumerators search for data sources and enumerators known to the provider. For example, suppose a provider exposes data in an SQL DBMS that supports multiple, separate databases in a single installation of the DBMS and treats each database as a separate data source. The enumerator for this provider might search the DBMS for databases. The rowset returned by the enumerator would include one row for each database it finds, marking that database as a data source.

Or suppose a provider exposes data in text files and treats each directory as a data source and each text file in that directory as a table. The enumerator for this provider might traverse the file system. The rowset returned by the enumerator would include two rows for each directory it finds, marking one row as a data source and the other row as an enumerator. To access the files in a directory, the consumer would instantiate a data source object over the directory, using the display name from the row marked as a data source. To search for subdirectories of the directory, the consumer would instantiate an enumerator over the directory, using the display name from the row marked as an enumerator.

For information about the registry entries used by enumerators, see "Enumerator Registry Entries" in Chapter 14.

Enumerator States

If an enumerator does not require initialization, it is created in an *initialized* state and remains in that state. For example, an enumerator that searches the Registry generally does not require initialization.

If an enumerator requires initialization, it is initially created in an *uninitialized* state. For example, if the enumerator enumerates directories, the enumerator does not yet know the starting directory. If the enumerator enumerates databases in an SQL DBMS, the enumerator has not yet connected to the DBMS.

To determine if an enumerator requires initialization, the consumer calls **QueryInterface** for **IDBInitialize**. If this interface is exposed, the enumerator requires initialization and must also expose **IDBProperties**. If it is not exposed, the enumerator does not require initialization. The remainder of this section discusses enumerators that require initialization.

In the uninitialized state, the consumer can only do the following with the enumerator:

- Call **QueryInterface** for **IUnknown**, **IDBInitialize**, **IDBProperties**, or **ISupportErrorInfo**.
- Call **AddRef** or **Release** on any interface obtained from **QueryInterface**.
- Call methods in **IDBProperties** for properties in the Initialization property group.
- Call methods on **IDBInitialize** or **ISupportErrorInfo**.

If the consumer calls any other method, or if the consumer calls **QueryInterface** for an interface other than those listed, the method returns E_UNEXPECTED.

To initialize the enumerator, the consumer first calls **IDBProperties::SetProperties** to set the value of properties in the Initialization property group. For example, if the enumerator enumerates directories, the consumer might specify the server and directory to start with. If the enumerator enumerates databases in an SQL DBMS, the consumer might specify the name of the server on which the DBMS resides along with the user ID and password to use.

Certain properties in the Initialization property group are required by the enumerator for initialization. To determine which properties these are, the consumer calls **IDBProperties::GetPropertyInfo** for properties in the Initialization property group. For required properties, the DBPROPFLAGS_REQUIRED bit is set in the *dwFlags* element of the returned DBPROPINFO structure.

After the consumer has finished setting properties, it calls **IDBInitialize::Initialize**. **Initialize** can prompt for additional information, especially if the consumer has not set values for all required properties. The consumer can control how much **Initialize** prompts, including suppressing prompting altogether. After **Initialize** returns successfully, the enumerator is in an *initialized* state.

If the consumer wants to reinitialize the enumerator after it is initialized, it must first uninitialize it. For example, if the enumerator enumerates directories and the consumer wants to enumerate directories on a different server, the consumer must disconnect from the first server before connecting to the second. If the enumerator enumerates databases in an SQL DBMS and the consumer wants to enumerate databases in a different installation of that DBMS, the consumer must disconnect from the first DBMS before connecting to the second. To uninitialize the enumerator, the consumer calls **IDBInitialize::Uninitialize**.

The following diagram shows the enumerator states and the methods that change them:

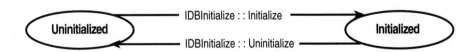

Data Source Objects

Data source objects:

```
CoType TDataSource {
    [mandatory] interface IDBCreateSession;
    [mandatory] interface IDBInitialize;
    [mandatory] interface IDBProperties;
    [mandatory] interface IPersist;
    [optional]  interface IDBDataSourceAdmin;
    [optional]  interface IDBInfo;
    [optional]  interface IPersistFile;
    [optional]  interface ISupportErrorInfo;
}
```

A *data source object* is the initial object that a provider instantiates when the consumer calls **CoCreateInstance** on the class ID for that provider. Consumers generally don't call **CoCreateInstance** directly, but instead bind to the file moniker of a persisted data source object or to a moniker returned by the enumerator object. The code that performs the binding calls **CoCreateInstance** on behalf of the consumer. It is important to distinguish the data source object from the *data source*, which actually contains the data. For example, a data source might be a text file, an SQL database, or an in-memory array in an application.

For information about the registry entries used by providers, which instantiate data source objects, see "Provider Registry Entries" in Chapter 14.

Data Source Object States

When a data source object is initially created, it is in an *uninitialized* state. For example, if the data source is a file, the data source object has not yet opened the file; if the data source is an SQL database, the data source object has not yet connected to the database.

In the uninitialized state, the consumer can only do the following with the data source:

- Call **QueryInterface** for **IUnknown**, **IDBDataSourceAdmin**, **IDBInitialize**, **IDBProperties**, **IPersist**, **IPersistFile**, or **ISupportErrorInfo**.

- Call **AddRef** or **Release** on any interface obtained from **QueryInterface**.

- Call methods in **IDBDataSourceAdmin**, **IDBInitialize**, **IPersist**, **IPersistFile**, **ISupportErrorInfo**.

- Call methods in **IDBProperties** for properties in the Initialization property group.

If the consumer calls any other method, or if the consumer calls **QueryInterface** for an interface other than those listed, the method returns E_UNEXPECTED.

To initialize the data source, the consumer first calls **IDBProperties::SetProperties** to set the value of properties in the Initialization property group. For example, if the data source is a text file, the consumer might specify the name and location of the file. If the data source is a database in an SQL database, the consumer might specify the name of the server on which the database resides along with the user ID and password to use.

Certain properties in the Initialization property group are required by the data source object for initialization. To determine which properties these are, the consumer calls **IDBProperties::GetPropertyInfo** for properties in the Initialization property group. For required properties, the DBPROPFLAGS_REQUIRED bit is set in the *dwFlags* element of the returned DBPROPINFO structure.

After the consumer has finished setting properties, it calls **IDBInitialize::Initialize**. **Initialize** can prompt for additional information, especially if the consumer has not set values for all required properties. The consumer can control how much **Initialize** prompts, including suppressing prompting altogether. After **Initialize** returns successfully, the data source object is in an *initialized* state. The consumer can also initialize a data source by calling **IDBDataSourceAdmin::CreateDataSource** to create and initialize a new data source.

If the consumer wants to reinitialize the data source object after it is initialized, it must first uninitialize it. For example, if the data source is a file and the consumer wants to use a different file, the consumer must close the first file before opening the second. If the data source is an SQL database and the consumer wants to use a different database, the consumer must disconnect from the first database before connecting to the second. To uninitialize the data source object, the consumer calls **IDBInitialize::Uninitialize**.

The following diagram shows the data source object states and the methods that change them:

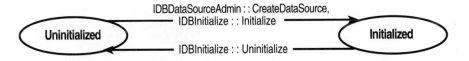

Persisting Data Source Objects

The data source object can be persisted to a file. Any child objects of the data source object, such as sessions, commands, or rowsets, are not persisted with the data source object. The DBPROP_AUTH_PERSIST_SENSITIVE_AUTHINFO property controls whether sensitive authorization information, such as the password, is persisted. If it is persisted, the DBPROP_AUTH_PERSIST_ENCRYPTED property controls whether it is persisted in encrypted form. The provider can make both of these properties read-only to control whether sensitive information can be persisted.

To persist a data source object to a file, the consumer calls **IPersistFile::Save**; the data source object can be in an uninitialized or initialized state. To reload the data source object, the consumer calls **IPersistFile::Load** on an uninitialized data source object; if the data source object is initialized, **Load** returns DB_E_ALREADYINITIALIZED. After loading the persisted file, the consumer must call **IDBInitialize::Initialize** to initialize the data source object.

When the provider persists a data source object, it persists enough information to return all of the properties in the Initialization property group to the state they were in when the data source object was persisted. The provider is not required to save the values of any properties in other property groups that the consumer might have set. Generally, this requires the provider to persist its class ID and the values of any properties set by the consumer. When the consumer loads the persisted file, the provider retrieves the persisted information and overwrites the values of any properties the consumer might have set, returning them to their persisted value, if they were persisted, or default value, if they were not persisted.

If the provider does not support **IPersistFile**, the consumer can save the information necessary to recreate the data source object itself. It calls **IDBProperties::GetProperties** to get the value of all properties in the Initialization property group and calls **IPersist::GetClassID** to get the class ID of the provider. It then saves this information and later uses it to recreate the data source object.

Sessions

Sessions:

```
CoType TSession {
    [mandatory] interface IGetDataSource;
    [mandatory] interface IOpenRowset;
    [mandatory] interface ISessionProperties;
    [optional]  interface IDBCreateCommand;
    [optional]  interface IDBSchemaRowset;
    [optional]  interface IIndexDefinition;
    [optional]  interface ISupportErrorInfo;
    [optional]  interface ITableDefinition;
    [optional]  interface ITransaction;
    [optional]  interface ITransactionJoin;
    [optional]  interface ITransactionLocal;
    [optional]  interface ITransactionObject;
}
```

The primary function of a session is to define a transaction. If the session supports **ITransactionLocal**, the consumer can call **ITransactionLocal::StartTransaction** to start an explicit transaction. The session is then said to be in *manual commit mode* and any work done in the session must be explicitly committed or aborted. If **ITransactionLocal** is not supported or if the consumer does not call

StartTransaction, the session is said to be in *auto-commit mode* and any work done in the session is automatically committed; it cannot be aborted. For more information about transactions, see Chapter 12, "Transactions."

To create a session, a consumer calls **IDBCreateSession::CreateSession** on the data source object. A single data source object can support multiple sessions and, therefore, multiple transactions. From a session, the consumer can do the following:

- Create a command by calling **IDBCreateCommand::CreateCommand**. A single session can support multiple commands. Note that some providers do not support commands.

- Create a rowset by calling **IOpenRowset::OpenRowset**. This is equivalent to creating a rowset over a single table and is supported by all providers.

- Create or modify tables and indexes with **ITableDefinition** and **IIndexDefinition**. Although providers are not required to support these interfaces, any provider built over a data source that supports creating and modifying tables and indexes should support them. For simple providers, such as a provider built over an array of data, **ITableDefinition** might be the only way to create or modify tables.

CHAPTER 3

Commands

Command objects:

```
CoType TCommand {
    [mandatory] interface IAccessor;
    [mandatory] interface IColumnsInfo;
    [mandatory] interface ICommand;
    [mandatory] interface ICommandProperties;
    [mandatory] interface ICommandText;
    [mandatory] interface IConvertType;
    [optional]  interface IColumnsRowset;
    [optional]  interface ICommandPrepare;
    [optional]  interface ICommandWithParameters;
    [optional]  interface ISupportErrorInfo;
}
```

A command is used to execute a provider-specific text command, such as an SQL statement. It is important not to confuse a *command*, which is an OLE COM object, and its *command text*, which is a string. Commands are generally used for *data definition*, such creating a table or granting privileges, and *data manipulation*, such as a updating or deleting rows. A special case of *data manipulation* is creating a rowset, for example, an SQL **SELECT** statement.

Providers are not required to support commands. In general, providers built on top of a DBMS, such as an SQL DBMS, support commands, and providers built on top of a simple data structure, such as a file or an array of data in an application, do not support commands.

Using Commands

Before a consumer can use a command, it must determine if commands are supported. To do this, the consumer calls **QueryInterface** for **IDBCreateCommand** on a session. If this interface is exposed, the provider supports commands. To create a command, the consumer then calls **IDBCreateCommand::CreateCommand** on the session. A single session can be used to create multiple commands.

When the command is first created, it does not contain a command text. The consumer sets the command text with **ICommandText::SetCommandText**. Because the text command syntax is provider-specific, the consumer passes the GUID of the syntax to use. In most cases, this GUID is DBGUID_DBSQL, which signifies that the text command is a superset of ANSI SQL. The level at which the provider supports ANSI SQL is specified by the DBPROP_SQLSUPPORT property.

To execute the command, the consumer calls **ICommand::Execute**. If the command text specifies a rowset, such as an SQL **SELECT** statement, **Execute** instantiates the rowset and returns an interface pointer to it.

Prior to executing a command that creates a rowset, the consumer can specify various properties of the rowset—such as the interfaces to expose and degree of scrollability—by calling **ICommandProperties::SetProperties**; for more information, see "Setting Rowset Properties" in Chapter 4. The consumer can also get information about the columns of the rowset by calling **IColumnsInfo::GetColumnInfo**, which all providers support, or **IColumnsRowset::GetColumnsRowset**, which providers may support on the command. The command text must be set to use these methods and, if the command supports preparation, it must be prepared.

If a command is to be executed multiple times with the same text command or if the consumer wants information about the rowset it will create, the consumer can *prepare* the command by calling **ICommandPrepare::Prepare**. This is equivalent to compiling the command. Providers are not required to support command preparation.

Prepared commands are typically used in conjunction with *parameters*, which are variables in the text command. For example, if the provider supports SQL, the consumer might prepare and repeatedly execute the parameterized SQL statement **UPDATE Employees SET (Salary = ?) WHERE EmployeeID = ?** to update the salaries of a number of employees. Support for parameters is optional, and providers that support them expose **ICommandWithParameters** on the command.

To use parameters, the consumer first describes the parameters to the provider by calling **ICommandWithParameters::SetParameterInfo**. Some providers can describe parameters themselves and do not need consumers to call **SetParameterInfo**. The consumer then creates an accessor that specifies the structure of a buffer and places parameter values in this buffer. Finally, it passes the handle of the accessor and a pointer to the buffer to **Execute**. On later calls to **Execute**, the consumer only needs to place new parameter values in the buffer and call **Execute** with the accessor handle and buffer pointer. For more information, see Chapter 6, "Getting and Setting Data."

Command States

Commands can be in one of four states:

- **Initial**—No command text is set. This is the state a command is in after **IDBCreateCommand::CreateCommand** is called.

- **Unprepared**—The command text is set but the command is not prepared. This is the state a command is in after **ICommandText::SetCommandText** is called.

- **Prepared**—The command text is set and the command is prepared. This is the state a command is in after **ICommandPrepare::Prepare** is called.

- **Executed**—The command text is executed. This is the state a command is in after **ICommand::Execute** is called.

The following table lists each state and shows the code returned by each method in a command interface when it is called in that state. This table uses the following abbreviations:

OK = S_OK
NC = DB_E_NOCOMMAND
NP = DB_E_NOTPREPARED
OO = DB_E_OPENOBJECT

Method	Initial	Unprepared	Prepared	Executed
IColumnsInfo				
GetColumnInfo	NC	OK [1] or NP [2]	OK	OK
MapColumnIDs	NC	OK [1] or NP [2]	OK	OK
IColumnsRowset				
GetAvailableColumns	NC	OK [1] or NP [2]	OK	OK
GetColumnsRowset	NC	OK [1] or NP [2]	OK	OK
ICommand				
Cancel	OK	OK	OK	OK
Execute	NC	OK	OK	OK
GetDBSession	OK	OK	OK	OK
ICommandPrepare				
Prepare	NC	OK	OK	OK [3] or OO [4]
Unprepare	OK	OK	OK	OK [3] or OO [4]
ICommandProperties				
GetProperties	OK	OK	OK	OK
SetProperties	OK	OK	OK	OK [3] or OO [4]

Method	Initial	Unprepared	Prepared	Executed
ICommandText				
GetCommandText	NC	OK	OK	OK
SetCommandText	OK	OK	OK	OK [3] or OO [4]
ICommandWithParameters				
GetParameterInfo	OK [5] or NC [6]	OK [5] or NP [2 and 6]	OK	OK
MapParameterNames	OK [5] or NC [6]	OK [5] or NP [2 and 6]	OK	OK
SetParameterInfo	OK	OK	OK	OK [3] or OO [4]

[1]   **ICommandPrepare** is not supported.

[2]   **ICommandPrepare** is supported.

[3]   **Execute** did not create a rowset.

[4]   **Execute** created a rowset.

[5]   **SetParameterInfo** has been called.

[6]   **SetParameterInfo** has not been called.

The following figures illustrate the state transitions for a command. The first figure shows the case where the command text is set to an empty string. The second figure shows the case where the command text is set to a non-empty string.

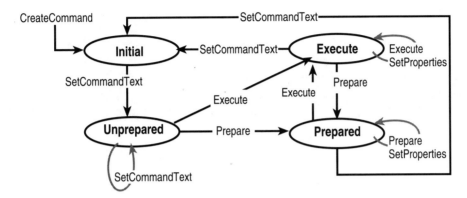

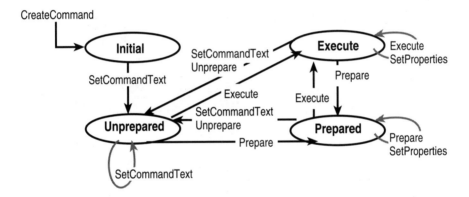

Multiple Results

Multiple results:

```
CoType TMultipleResults {
    [mandatory] interface IMultipleResults;
}
```

A *result* is something returned by a command when it is executed. A result can be either a rowset or a row count, which is the number of rows affected by a command that updates, deletes, or inserts rows. *Multiple results* can be returned if the command text comprises multiple separate text commands, such as a batch of SQL statements, or if more than one set of parameters is passed to a command.

A *multiple results object* is used to retrieve multiple results. Providers are not required to support multiple results objects. Whether a provider supports multiple results objects is specified by the DBPROP_MULTIPLERESULTS property in the Data Source Information property group.

To create a multiple results object, the consumer requests the **IMultipleResults** interface when it calls **ICommand::Execute**. **Execute** returns an interface pointer on the multiple results object to the consumer.

To retrieve each rowset or row count created by the command, the consumer calls **IMultipleResults::GetResult**. **GetResult** returns results in the order they were specified in the command text. If the current result is a rowset, some providers require the consumer to release the rowset before **GetResult** returns the next result; whether the provider requires this is specified by the DBPROP_MULTIPLERESULTS property.

CHAPTER 4

Rowsets

Rowsets:

```
CoType TRowset {
    [mandatory] interface IAccessor;
    [mandatory] interface IColumnsInfo;
    [mandatory] interface IConvertType;
    [mandatory] interface IRowset;
    [mandatory] interface IRowsetInfo;
    [optional]  interface IColumnsRowset;
    [optional]  interface IConnectionPointContainer;
    [optional]  interface IRowsetChange;
    [optional]  interface IRowsetIdentity;
    [optional]  interface IRowsetLocate;
    [optional]  interface IRowsetResynch;
    [optional]  interface IRowsetScroll;
    [optional]  interface IRowsetUpdate;
    [optional]  interface ISupportErrorInfo;
}
```

Rowsets are the central objects that enable all OLE DB data providers to expose data in tabular form. Conceptually, a rowset is a set of rows in which each row has columns of data. Base table providers present their data in the form of rowsets. Query processors present the result of queries in the form of rowsets. This makes it possible to layer components that consume or produce data through the same object.

The most basic rowset exposes the following interfaces: **IRowset**, which contains methods for fetching rows in the rowset sequentially; **IAccessor**, which permits the definition of groups of column bindings describing the way tabular data is bound to consumer program variables; **IColumnsInfo**, which provides information about the columns of the rowset; **IRowsetInfo**, which provides information about the rowset itself; and **IConvertType**, which provides information about the data type conversions supported by the rowset. Using **IRowset**, a consumer can sequentially traverse the rows in the rowset, including traversing backward if the rowset supports it.

Creating and Releasing Rowsets

The consumer typically uses one of two procedures for creating rowsets. The first procedure uses the **IOpenRowset** interface, which deals with the simpler case of retrieving all data from the table. The second procedure involves creating and executing a command to get a rowset that meets specific criteria. All providers must implement the simpler case. Even if the rowset specified by either method has no rows, the rowset is still created. The resulting rowset is fully functional and can be used, for example, to insert new rows or determine column metadata.

Because rowsets are the fundamental objects for getting data, several methods that return information create rowsets, such as **IColumnsRowset::GetColumnsRowset**, **IDBSchemaRowset::GetRowset**, and **ISourcesRowset::GetSourcesRowset**.

Creating a Rowset with IOpenRowset

Some providers need to expose very simple rowsets to their consumers. These rowsets represent the result set of the simple query **SELECT * FROM <table-name>**. To allow providers to interpret this simple query without the overhead of supporting a complete query language, OLE DB provides a simple rowset interface **IOpenRowset**. **IOpenRowset** effectively exposes a rowset in the absence of a command. **IOpenRowset** is implemented on the session as shown in the following illustration.

Getting a rowset directly from a session

Creating a Rowset with a Command

Providers that implement their own query or data definition language can offer their consumers additional functionality by using a command. This process contains three steps:

1. The consumer creates a session. For more information, see "Sessions" in Chapter 2.

2. The consumer calls **IDBCreateCommand::CreateCommand** on the session to get a command. The command is used to hold a text command. The consumer then fills in the text command, thereby stating what data to return in the rowset. The text command can be expressed in SQL, and augmented by properties that request various functional services upon the resulting rowset. For more information about properties, see "Setting Rowset Properties" later in this chapter.

3. The user calls **ICommand::Execute** on the command. **Execute** returns a rowset.

Getting a rowset from a session through a command

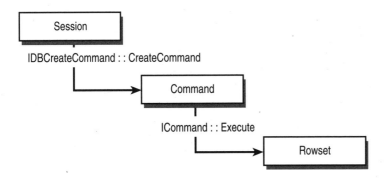

Setting Rowset Properties

ICommandProperties specifies to the command the properties that must be supported by the rowsets returned by **ICommand::Execute**. A special case of these properties, and the ones most commonly requested, are the interfaces the rowset must support. In addition to interfaces, the consumer can request properties that modify the behavior of the rowset or interfaces.

All rowsets must support **IRowset**, **IAccessor**, **IColumnsInfo**, **IRowsetInfo**, and **IConvertType**. Providers can choose to return rowsets exposing other interfaces if doing so is cheaper and exposing the returned interfaces does not affect consumer code that is not expecting them. For example, the rowset can expose **IRowsetLocate** even though the consumer does not request it, because this interface does not change the behavior of the rowset. The rowset cannot expose **IRowsetUpdate** if the consumer does not request, because the existence of this interface changes the behavior of the **IRowsetChange** interface. The *riid* parameter of **Execute** is generally the IID for one of the interfaces listed in the TRowset CoType.

For a complete description of how consumers use properties, see Chapter 11, "Properties."

Releasing Rowsets

Consumers release rowsets with **IRowset::Release**. Releasing a rowset releases any row handles and accessors held by the consumer on that rowset.

Rows

Handles for rows are used with accessors or other functions to manipulate the contents of the rows. Row handles are of type HROW, defined as follows:

```
typedef ULONG HROW;
# define DB_NULL_HROW 0x00 // Always invalid
```

The consumer can use row handles to manage the activity of individual rows, or of sets of rows. Any vector of row handles is allowed, and the consumer can rearrange them into different sets, so long as the consumer keeps track of which rows are actively held and which have been released. Rowsets may have a row capacity (limit on the number of rows which they can keep track of) which is implied by the rowset specification.

When a row is fetched, the data for the row appears to be cached in the provider and left there until the row is released. The columns of the row are reached through the functions **IRowset::GetData** and **IRowsetChange::SetData**, which use *accessors* to define how the data is to be transferred. For more information, see "Accessors" in Chapter 6.

Having a local copy of the row allows multiple consumers to get data from the row without making additional trips to the data source—which might reside on a separate server—and to coordinate changes to the row without transmitting them to the data source until all of the consumers are ready. Whether the row actually exists in the rowset is provider-specific; for example, the row could be a representation of some object running on the provider or it could be a handle to a row in a lower-level service provider.

However, caching rows in the provider means that keeping materialized row handles is costly. Even if a particular provider does not enforce a preset limit on the number of active row handles, it is likely that keeping instantiated row handles even in the order of the hundreds will heavily deteriorate provider performance. Thus, although some providers might be expected to handle rowsets with millions of rows, no provider is expected to materialize many rows simultaneously. Consumers are encouraged to release row handles whenever possible and keep bookmarks to these rows if it is necessary to refetch them. Note that a small number of frequently accessed row handles can be kept in materialized form.

Fetching Rows

Rows are *fetched* by methods such as **IRowset::GetNextRows**, **IRowsetLocate::GetRowsAt**, **IRowsetLocate::GetRowsByBookmarks**, **IRowsetScroll::GetRowsAtRatio**. These methods enable the consumer to get multiple row handles with a single call.

The provider manages its row buffers on behalf of the consumer. When a row is fetched, the provider stores it in a buffer local to the provider. It is probably stored in a native format, although how this is done is provider-specific. The consumer does not have direct access to the provider's row buffer, except through reference accessors. Instead, the consumer uses **IRowset::GetData** to get a copy of the data and **IRowsetChange::SetData** to make changes to the data. For more information, see Chapter 6, "Getting and Setting Data."

Rows are generally processed in parallel. Subject to limitations of the command, or to limits upon resources, the consumer may hold and work with as many rows as it needs. There is no concept of a single current row, although there is a next fetch row for **IRowset::GetNextRows** which is used for sequential read operations.

If the rowset supports **IRowsetLocate**, then any pattern of rows can be held. In a *sequential rowset* (that is, a rowset that does not support **IRowsetLocate**) there may be a rule requiring the release of rows from prior **GetNextRows** calls before a new **GetNextRows** call may be made.

Reference-Counting Row Handles

Individual row handles have associated reference counts. Methods that return row handles increment the reference counts of the returned row handles. Rows are held by the provider until the consumer releases them with **IRowset::ReleaseRows**. The consumer must call **ReleaseRows** for the row once for each time it was fetched or **IRowset::AddRefRows** was called for it.

Rows are implicitly released only when the consumer calls **IRowset::Release**. Deleting a row does not release the row handle; whether the deletion is done by calling **IRowsetChange::DeleteRows**, calling **IRowsetUpdate::Update** on a row with a pending deletion, or calling **IRowsetUpdate::Undo** on a row with a pending insert, the consumer must call **ReleaseRows** to release the row.

Next Fetch Position

GetNextRows keeps track of the next fetch position so that a sequence of calls to this method (with no skips and no changes of direction) reads the entire rowset without skipping or repeating any row. The next fetch position is not connected to or disturbed by the use of any other method that fetches rows. However, it can be set by **IRowsetIndex::Seek**, and, when it is used with **GetNextRows**, it can be reset to its initial position with **IRowset::RestartPosition**.

If the rowset supports reversible fetch direction, and **GetNextRows** is called once in one direction and then in the opposite direction, with no skip, then the last row read in the initial direction will be the first row to be read in the reverse direction.

Fetch Direction

Rowsets can take a negative count of requested rows. This means that the absolute count of rows beginning with the first specified row (for example, the next fetch row in **GetNextRows** or the bookmarked row in **IRowsetLocate::GetRowsAt**) and then moving backward will be returned. Note that this behavior is independent of skip (offset) counts, which can also be negative.

Uniqueness of Rows in the Rowset

If a row is fetched more than once without any intervening calls to release it, it is provider-specific whether the rowset contains one or multiple copies of the row.

However, if the rowset exposes **IRowsetIdentity**, it appears as if there is only a single instance of any given row within the rowset. Thus, if multiple handles point to rows that share the same row in the data source, it does not matter which handle is used to get or set data. How this is implemented is provider-specific. For example, the provider might compare newly fetched rows with existing rows to see if they share the same row in the data source, and then maintain only a single copy of each row in the rowset. Or it might wait until a row is accessed to compare it with all other rows and create a single copy at that time.

If the rowset contains only one copy a row, the DBPROP_LITERALIDENTITY property is set to VARIANT_TRUE. In this case, the consumer can perform a binary comparison of two row handles to determine if they represent the same row. If the rowset can contain multiple copies of the same row, this property is set to VARIANT_FALSE. In this case, the consumer calls **IRowsetIdentity::IsSameRow** to determine whether two row handles represent the same row. Such comparisons are necessary, for example, when the consumer receives a row handle through one of the methods in **IRowsetNotify** and needs to know if it is the handle of a row that the consumer already holds. Whether the handles of newly inserted rows—that is, rows inserted during the lifetime of the rowset—can be compared at all depends on the value of the DBPROP_STRONGIDENTITY property.

If the rowset does not expose **IRowsetIdentity**, there might be multiple, divergent instances of the same row within the rowset. Furthermore, there is no way for consumers to determine whether two different row handles point to the same row. Because of the problems this can cause, providers are strongly encouraged to support **IRowsetIdentity**. If consumers use rowsets that do not expose **IRowsetIdentity**, they should avoid changing rows in those rowsets because of the possibility of updating the same row through two different row handles and losing the changes.

If two different rowsets share the same rows in the data source, their behavior with respect to these rows is undefined. They are not required to recognize that a row in one rowset points to the same row in the data source as a row in the other rowset. Consumers that use such rowsets must be able to tolerate such undefined behavior.

Deferred Columns

For a *deferred* column, the provider is not required to retrieve data from the data source until **IRowset::GetData** is called for that column, or, if the column contains an OLE object, until a method used to access that object is called. It is provider-specific when the data in a deferred column is actually retrieved. For example, it might be retrieved when the command is executed, when the row handle is fetched, lazily in the background, or when **GetData** or a method on another interface is called for the column. If a column is deferred, the DBCOLUMNFLAGS_MAYDEFER flag returned by **IColumnsInfo::GetColumnsInfo** is set for the column.

Whether the data for a deferred column is cached depends on the setting of the DBCOLUMNFLAGS_CACHEDEFERRED flag returned by **GetColumnsInfo**. If this flag is set, the column value is cached when first read. The cached value is returned whenever the column is read. It can be changed by calling **IRowsetChange::SetData** or **IRowsetResynch::ResynchRows** and is released only when the row handle is released. If the DBCOLUMNFLAGS_CACHEDEFERRED flag is not set, then multiple calls to **GetData** (or the method used to read the column, if the column contains OLE objects) can return different values. Note that such calls are not guaranteed to reflect a change to the underlying column unless **ResynchRows** has been called.

To use a deferred column, the consumer sets the DBPROP_DEFERRED property; columns that contain OLE objects are deferred by default.

The consumer should be aware of an increased isolation risk of using deferred columns because deferred data might be read at a different time than non-deferred data. If the consumer is not using Repeatable Read isolation or better, then it may encounter discrepancies between the original and the deferred access to a row. In particular, it may find the column to be missing, because the row has been deleted, or not to match the rest of the row. Under some circumstances, use of a row version column in conjunction with both original and deferred access can be used to warn a consumer about a situation where a concurrent error has occurred; a consumer can determine whether a column contains a row version with the DBCOLUMNFLAGS_ISROWVER flag in **GetColumnInfo**.

Column IDs

Column IDs are used to identify columns, primarily in commands where there are no stable ordinals. Because column IDs are relatively slow to use, column ordinals are used to identify columns in bindings. A consumer calls **IColumnsInfo::MapColumnIDs** to retrieve a column ordinal from a column ID.

```
typedef struct  tagDBID {
    union {
        GUID    guid;
        GUID * pguid;
    } uGuid;
    DBKIND eKind;
    union {
        LPOLESTR pwszName;
        ULONG    ulPropid;
    } uName;
} DBID;
```

The values of DBKIND are described in the following table:

Value	Description
DBKIND_GUID_NAME	Use the *guid* and *pwszName* elements.
DBKIND_GUID_PROPID	Use the *guid* and *ulPropid* elements.
DBKIND_NAME	Use only the *pwszName* element; ignore the *uGuid* element.
DBKIND_PGUID_NAME	Use the *pGuid* and *pwszName* elements.
DBKIND_PGUID_PROPID	Use the *pGuid* and *ulPropid* elements.
DBKIND_PROPID	Use only the *ulPropid* element, ignore the *uGuid* element.
DBKIND_GUID	Use only the *guid* element; ignore the *uName* element.

OLE DB providers never return *pGuid*-style bindings (for example, when the consumer inquires about the bindings for an accessor). They are provided as a convenient shortcut for consumers supplying bindings all covered by the same GUID, which is expected to be common.

The value DB_NULLID is defined as the DBID structure containing all zeroes. Because *pwszName* is a null pointer for DB_NULLID, no attempt should be made to free this string.

When constructing DBIDs to identify tables, indexes, or columns, consumers use the non-NULL columns in the appropriate schema rowset to determine the DBKIND value of the DBID. For example, when specifying a table ID, a consumer would call **IDBSchemaRowset::GetRowset** and examine the TABLES rowset. On discovering that TABLE_NAME has a value and TABLE_GUID is NULL, the consumer would specify DBKIND_NAME for the table ID. In methods that take column DBIDs as parameters, the validation of the DBID should include a check on the validity of the DBID's *eKind*.

Bookmarks

Bookmarks are placeholders designed to allow the consumer to return quickly to a row. Bookmarks should be treated as opaque binary values by consumers using a bookmark to identify a row to a provider. Consumers should not try to interpret these values. Bookmarks are valid only during the lifetime of the rowset to which they refer. For indexes that use bookmarks to reference rows in a base table, the bookmark returned as the pointer column in the index rowset is a valid bookmark in the rowset built over the base table; therefore, the bookmark is valid for the table rowset. Bookmarks are returned in columns in the rowset. An application retrieves them in the same manner as it retrieves data from any other column in the rowset. That is, it creates an accessor that binds to the bookmark column and calls **IRowset::GetData** using this accessor.

Bookmark columns have DBCOLUMNFLAGS_ISBOOKMARK set in their column information. A bookmark may be of a fixed scalar type such as DBTYPE_I4 or it may be a character sequence that appears, for example, as a DBTYPE_STR column. There is no specialized bookmark data type; providers may return any valid type indicator in **IColumnsInfo::GetColumnInfo** for a bookmark column.

Bookmarks can always be read and passed as binary values. When using a bookmark to identify a row to a provider, consumers can always bind bookmark values as DBTYPE_BYTES. Alternatively, if the consumer knows the actual DBTYPE of the bookmark, it can bind to that specific type. For more information about data types, see Appendix A, "Data Types."

Bookmarks are not the same thing as primary keys or row IDs (see "Bookmark Types," later in this chapter). They can be related, and it is possible to use a primary key or row ID to implement a bookmark, but often there are bookmark schemes that are more compact or swifter that work only for the current contents of the rowset. It is important to take advantage of those optimizations in places such as command optimization or result set navigation. Furthermore, bookmarks are not necessarily the same as row handles because they may have ordering semantics or might be used to track non-resident members of very large rowsets.

A rowset implements only one kind of bookmark. The provider may have incompatible solutions for implementing primary key or row ID semantics on bookmarks, so it cannot support both simultaneously.

Bookmarks operate as logical pointers. The encapsulation allows transient, rowset-level bookmarks to be implemented as pointers, although this would be likely only for rowsets small enough to be efficiently instantiated.

When **IRowsetLocate** or one of its direct descendants is present on a rowset, then column zero is the bookmark for the rows. Column zero is present in a rowset if, and only if, the rowset has set the property DBPROP_BOOKMARKS to VARIANT_TRUE. Reading this column will obtain a bookmark value which can be used to reposition to the same row. This is called the *self bookmark*. There may be other bookmark columns referring to the same rowset, for example a Spouse column in a query about people, but those are not the self bookmark.

Bookmark columns can be returned on any rowset, regardless of its source (for example, **ICommand::Execute**, **IOpenRowset::OpenRowset**, **IColumnsRowset::GetColumnsRowset**, or **IDBSchemaRowset::GetRowset**) or whether bookmarks were requested.

The DBIDs of the bookmark columns in a rowset are based on a property set identified by the GUID DBCOL_SPECIALCOL. These DBIDs are constructed as follows:

- The *eKind* element is DBKIND_GUID_PROPID or DBKIND_PGUID_PROPID.
- The *guid* (or *pguid*) element is, or points to, DBCOL_SPECIALCOL.
- The *ulPropid* element is 2 for the self bookmark. It is greater than 2 for bookmarks other than the self bookmark. The *ulPropid* element must not be the same as the *ulPropid* element in the DBID of another bookmark in the same rowset.
- If bookmark column A appears before bookmark column B in the specification of the rowset, the *ulPropid* element in the DBID of bookmark column A is less than the *ulPropid* element in the DBID of bookmark column B.

The DBIDs of bookmark columns can be passed to **IColumnsInfo::MapColumnIDs** to determine the ordinals of those columns. There is no need to pass the DBID of the self bookmark column to **MapColumnIDs** because the ordinal of this column is always zero.

Bookmark Types

OLE DB supports two kinds of bookmarks, numeric and key value. The DBPROP_BOOKMARKTYPE property indicates the bookmarks that a provider supports.

Numeric Bookmarks

Numeric bookmarks are based on a position or index into the rows selected for a rowset. Generally, the rowset builds a set of information about the rows which enables the same row to be retrieved easily. It does not guarantee the existence or consistency of those rows throughout the transaction; that still depends on the transaction isolation level. It returns the same row entity if it can.

The numeric value can be of any size. A small rowset might use a 16-bit index, whereas a rowset against an Oracle table might use Oracle ROWIDs, which are around 6 bytes each. There is no significance to the ordering of numeric values, either logical or physical. The implementation should simply be fast.

If the primary key value of a row is changed while working with a row for which the consumer has a numeric bookmark, the bookmark still points to the same row instance. This is required for a numeric bookmark. Suppose the row also had a non-overlapping candidate key. The primary key may be entirely changed, but the same value would remain in the candidate key column. This is what is meant by same row instance.

Key Value Bookmarks

When a rowset is ordered and there is some combination of columns (not necessarily the primary keys of the base tables) that form a unique key for each row, it becomes useful to use these values as a bookmark. At first it may seem this is redundant, since one could expect an interface such as **IRowsetIndex** to take key values and rapidly return a numeric bookmark. However, the numeric bookmark itself may be costly and unwanted. In some cases the key values enable the provider to access the underlying tables without storing any kind of temporary table.

With a key value bookmark, a consumer could, in theory, cheat and synthesize a set of values which could occur but do not. The result of doing this is undefined; that is, providers are not required to detect forgeries.

If the key value columns of a row are changed while working with a row for which the consumer has a key value bookmark, the bookmark can be left dangling, or fooled into pointing to a new row which usurps the old values.

Comparing Bookmarks

The optimal way to compare bookmarks is by a direct memory comparison. However, some rowsets may include hints within the bookmark that are time- or rowset-generation–dependent and thus might cause binary comparisons between two bookmarks for the same row to fail. If the provider does put hints in the bookmarks, they must expose **IRowsetLocate**, which has methods to compare two bookmarks and to return a stable hash value for a bookmark.

If the DBPROP_LITERALBOOKMARKS property is VARIANT_TRUE, then consumers can do the comparison themselves. The way of doing this depends on the scalar type of the bookmark. For example, if the bookmark was defined as a sequence of DBTYPE_BYTES then the comparison is of unsigned bytes, with the most-significant byte in position zero.

Bookmarks may only be compared if they belong to the same rowset and are used within the lifetime of that rowset. The results of comparing bookmarks from different rowsets, or outside the lifetime of the rowset which they belong to, is undefined.

A consumer does not need an ordered query to have ordered bookmarks. In particular it does not need an SQL **ORDER BY** clause. If a consumer requests **SELECT * FROM <table-name>** and the smart query processor delivers the scan in the least-cost physical seek order (meaningless ordering in terms of content), then the consumer may still be given a rowset with ordered bookmarks. To guarantee ordered bookmarks, the consumer specifies the DBPROP_ORDEREDBOOKMARKS property as VARIANT_TRUE in **ICommandProperties::SetProperties**. For some providers, bookmarks are always ordered.

If DBPROP_ORDEREDBOOKMARKS is VARIANT_TRUE, the order of the bookmarks reflects the order of delivery. That is, if the consumer has bookmark $i < j$, then it calls **IRowsetLocate::GetRowsAt** for bookmark i and keeps scanning, it is guaranteed to find j unless it is deleted, and if it is deleted it can see the gap in order as it passes it by. Conversely if it starts at j and scans forward, it never sees i. It just reaches the end of rowset.

Standard Bookmarks

Several standard bookmark values are provided. If bookmarks are DBTYPE_BYTES then all single-byte (length 1) values are standard bookmarks: ordinary bookmarks must be at least length 2. If bookmarks are other fixed length types such as DBTYPE_I2 or DBTYPE_I4, then all values from 0 through 15 are reserved as special bookmarks.

The values of the following standard bookmarks are guaranteed to be the same for all providers.

Value	Description
DBBMK_INVALID	DBBMK_INVALID has no special meaning in this version of OLE DB. It can be used by applications to initialize and subsequently check bookmark validity, and may be used in future releases to indicate an unused parameter in a method which may take bookmark values.
DBBMK_FIRST	The first row of the rowset.
	A consumer can fetch forwards from this point. For example, if *cRows* is greater than zero and *lRowsOffset* is zero, **IRowsetLocate::GetRowsAt** returns the first *cRows* rows of the rowset.
	A consumer cannot fetch backward before this point. For example, if *cRows* is less than zero and *lRowsOffset* is zero, **GetRowsAt** returns this row; if *cRows* is less than −1, it then returns DB_S_ENDOFROWSET.
DBBMK_LAST	The last row of the rowset.
	A consumer can fetch backwards from this point. For example, if *cRows* is less than zero and *lRowsOffset* is zero, **GetRowsAt** returns the last *cRows* rows of the rowset.
	A consumer cannot fetch forwards past this point. For example, if *cRows* is greater than zero and *lRowsOffset* is zero, **GetRowsAt** returns this row; if *cRows* is greater than one, it then returns DB_S_ENDOFROWSET.

The consumer can begin a sequential scan at either the first or last row.

Invalid Bookmarks

A bookmark can become invalid for any of the following reasons:

- The row it points to is deleted.

- It is based on a primary key and some of those key values were changed.

- The row it points to is no longer in the rowset. This occurs only in rowsets that support DBPROP_OWNUPDATEDELETE when a row is changed in such a way that it no longer meets the search criteria of the rowset, is released, and then is refetched by **IRowset::GetNextRows**. For example, if the rowset contains only those rows with a job title of Assistant Manager, changing the job title in a row to Manager would remove that row from the rowset. From the point of view of that rowset, the row was deleted.

If the consumer tries to use an invalid bookmark, the provider generally returns an error. In some cases, if the DBPROP_BOOKMARKSKIPPED property is VARIANT_TRUE, the provider skips the bookmarked row and proceeds to the next row.

Updating Data in Rowsets

Changing data, also known as *updating* data, consists of updating and deleting existing rows of data and inserting new rows of data. Consumers can change data either through commands, such as the **UPDATE**, **DELETE**, and **INSERT** commands in SQL, or through rowsets. This chapter discusses how consumers change data through rowsets. For information about using commands, see Chapter 3, "Commands."

Changing Data

Consumers change data by calling the methods **SetData**, **DeleteRows**, and **InsertRow** in **IRowsetChange**. These methods change the data for a row in the rowset's copy of the row. Whether the method immediately transmits these changes to the data source depends on whether the rowset exposes **IRowsetUpdate**.

If the rowset does not expose **IRowsetUpdate**, it is said to be in *immediate update mode*. In immediate update mode, the methods in **IRowsetChange** *transmit* changes to the data source, where they become visible to other transactions running at the Read Uncommitted transaction isolation level. Such changes are *transmitted changes*.

If the rowset exposes **IRowsetUpdate**, it is in *delayed update mode*. In delayed update mode, the methods in **IRowsetChange** do not transmit changes to the data source. Instead, they buffer the changes in the rowset; such changes are *pending changes*. While changes are pending, they are wholly local to the rowset and therefore not visible to other transactions, even those running at the Read Uncommitted isolation level.

To transmit pending changes to the data source, the consumer calls **IRowsetUpdate::Update**. As in immediate update mode, such changes then become visible to other transactions running at the Read Uncommitted transaction isolation level and are *transmitted changes*.

If the rowset was created in the context of a transaction, the consumer can commit or abort transmitted changes by calling **ITransaction::Commit** or **ITransaction::Abort** to commit or abort them. Committed changes become visible to other transactions running at the Read Committed transaction isolation level. If the consumer commits or aborts transmitted changes and there are still pending changes, then what happens to those pending changes depends on the DBPROP_COMMITPRESERVE and DBPROP_ABORTPRESERVE properties. For more information, see "Rowset Preservation" in "Commit and Abort Behavior" in Chapter 12.

The following diagram shows how the methods in **IRowsetChange**, **IRowsetUpdate**, and **ITransaction** move data.

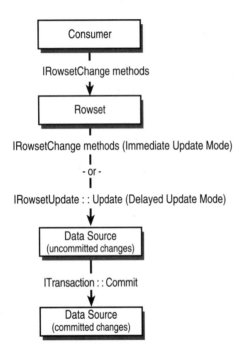

To get a read-only rowset, the consumer does not request **IRowsetChange** or **IRowsetUpdate** as a property of the rowset.

Immediate vs. Delayed Update Mode

Whether the consumer uses immediate or delayed update mode generally depends on how many consumers share the rowset and how they use the rowset. The primary user of immediate update mode is generally a single consumer that wants changes transmitted immediately to the data source. Delayed update mode is used for many reasons, including the following.

- **Shared rowsets**—If multiple consumers share a rowset, they often use notifications to coordinate multiple changes. By using delayed update mode,

consumers can coordinate their changes locally in the rowset before transmitting
them to the data source.

* **Multiple changes to same row**—If a consumer makes multiple changes to the
  same row, such as when multiple accessors are used or changes are input by the
  user at different times, the row might be left in an invalid state. For example, if a
  key consists of several columns and each column is changed in a separate call to
  IRowsetChange::SetData, the intermediate states might be invalid. By using
  delayed update mode, the consumer can buffer these changes in the rowset before
  transmitting them to the data source.

* **Network traffic**—If a rowset resides on one node in a network and the data source
  resides on another node, transmitting changes from the rowset to the data source
  requires a network call. By using delayed update mode, the consumer can bundle
  changes to multiple rows together and send them across the network with a single
  call to **IRowsetUpdate::Update**. This is particularly critical for wide area
  networks such as the Internet, on which network calls are very expensive.

* **Undoing changes**—**IRowsetUpdate::Undo** enables the consumer to undo
  pending changes. By using delayed update mode, consumers can expose an undo
  capability to users without having to implement it.

Row States

A row has a state that depends on whether it has been changed and whether that
change is pending or transmitted. Consumers call **IRowsetUpdate::GetRowStatus** to
determine the state of a row. They call **IRowsetUpdate::GetPendingRows** to get all
rows in a pending change state. The state is indicated by the DBPENDINGSTATUS
enumerated type. The values in this type have the following meaning:

Value	State name	Description
DBPENDINGSTATUS_ NEW	Pending Insert	The row has a pending insert.
DBPENDINGSTATUS_ CHANGED	Pending Update	The row has a pending update.
DBPENDINGSTATUS_ DELETED	Pending Delete	The row has a pending delete.
DBPENDINGSTATUS_ UNCHANGED	Unchanged	No changes have been made to the row or changes have been made to the row and have been transmitted or undone.
DBPENDINGSTATUS_ INVALIDROW	Deleted	The row has been deleted and that deletion has been transmitted to the data source. This status is also used when a row handle passed to **GetRowStatus** was invalid.

The Unchanged and Deleted states are the *non-pending change states*. The Pending Update, Pending Delete, and Pending Insert states are the *pending change states*. The following diagram shows these states, how methods affect them, and the corresponding DBPENDINGSTATUS values.

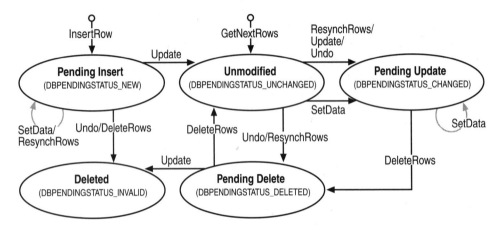

If the consumer calls **IRowset::ReleaseRows** for a row and the reference count for that row falls to zero, release of the row and its resources depends on the row's state. In the non-pending change states, the row and its resources are generally released when the reference count falls to zero, although the actual point of release is provider-specific.

In the pending change states, the row and its resources are not released when the reference count falls to zero, nor are the pending changes lost. The row remains valid until the changes are transmitted or undone (the row moves to a non-pending change state), then the row and its resources are generally released. Rows in a pending change state that have a reference count of zero are still considered active for purposes such as calculating row limits such as those returned by the DBPROP_MAXOPENROWS and DBPROP_MAXPENDINGROWS properties. Although the row handle might remain valid for such rows, consumers should not count on this.

Visibility of Changes

The *visibility* of a change is whether the data returned for a row by **IRowset::GetData** correctly reflects that change. After a consumer changes a row, the change is guaranteed to remain visible as long as the consumer holds the row. This is because the change is made locally in the rowset's copy of the row and any calls to **GetData** return the changed data. However, if the consumer completely releases and subsequently refetches the row, such as with **IRowset::GetNextRows** or **IRowsetLocate::GetRowsAt**, the visibility of any changes made to the row depend on a number of different properties of the rowset.

Visibility of Pending Changes

If the consumer completely releases and then refetches a row with a pending update or delete, the visibility of that pending update or delete depends on whether the rowset exposes **IRowsetIdentity**. If the rowset exposes **IRowsetIdentity**, it appears as if there is only a single instance of any given row within the rowset. Thus, the rowset recognizes that the newly fetched row matches the existing row, which contains the pending update or delete, and returns a handle through which the pending update or delete is visible. If the rowset does not expose **IRowsetIdentity**, the rowset can contain multiple copies of the same row and might return a handle through which the pending update or delete is not visible. For more information, see "Uniqueness of Rows in the Rowset" in Chapter 4.

Whether methods that fetch rows can retrieve pending insert rows depends on the DBPROP_RETURNPENDINGINSERTS property. Consumers should be aware that many providers cannot return pending inserts because they use the row-returning mechanisms of the underlying data source. Because pending inserts have not yet been transmitted to the data source, the mechanisms there cannot return them.

Visibility of Transmitted Changes

If the consumer completely releases and then refetches a row for which changes have been transmitted to the data source, the visibility of those changes depends on the values of the DBPROP_OWNUPDATEDELETE, DBPROP_OWNINSERT, and DBPROP_REMOVEDELETED properties. When multiple consumers share the same rowset, these properties apply to all changes transmitted by any consumer of the rowset. For more information, see "Rowset Properties" in Appendix C.

Position of Inserted Rows

The position of inserted rows, both pending and transmitted, in the rowset is specified by the DBPROP_IMMOBILEROWS property. If this property is VARIANT_TRUE, inserted rows always appear at the end of the rowset. If this property is VARIANT_FALSE, then inserted rows appear in the rowset's proper order, if the rowset is ordered, or in indeterminate order, if the rowset is not ordered.

For information about whether inserted rows are visible, see "Visibility of Pending Changes" and "Visibility of Transmitted Changes" earlier in this chapter.

Visibility of Other Changes

If the consumer completely releases and then refetches a row for which changes have been made by another rowset in the same transaction or by other applications operating outside the transaction, the visibility of these changes depends on the DBPROP_OTHERUPDATEDELETE and DBPROP_OTHERINSERT properties.

The visibility of changes made by other rowsets in the same transaction depends only on these properties. It does not depend on the transaction isolation level because the changes are in the same transaction.

The visibility of changes made by applications outside the current transaction depends on both the values of these properties and the transaction isolation level. The following table shows whether changes made by applications outside the current transaction are visible, depending on the transaction isolation level and the values of these properties.

Property value	Read uncommitted	Read committed	Repeatable read	Serializable
DBPROP_OTHERUPDATE-DELETE:				
VARIANT_TRUE	Yes	Yes	No	No
VARIANT_FALSE	No	No	No	No
DBPROP_OTHERINSERT:				
VARIANT_TRUE	Yes	Yes	Yes	No
VARIANT_FALSE	No	No	No	No

Resynchronizing Rows

The methods in **IRowsetResynch** enable the consumer to retrieve the data in the data source that is visible to the current transaction according to its isolation level. To retrieve a copy of the currently visible data, the consumer calls **IRowsetResynch::GetVisibleData**. To update the copy of a row in the rowset with the currently visible data, the consumer calls **IRowsetResynch::ResynchRows**.

Although this capability is related to the DBPROP_OWNUPDATEDELETE, DBPROP_OWNINSERT, DBPROP_OTHERUPDATEDELETE, and DBPROP_OTHERINSERT properties, it is independent of them. That is, the value of these properties can be VARIANT_FALSE and the rowset can still expose **IRowsetResynch**. However, because of implementation difficulties, many rowsets do not expose **IRowsetResynch** unless the values of the DBPROP_OWNUPDATEDELETE and DBPROP_OTHERUPDATEDELETE properties are VARIANT_TRUE.

Getting and Setting Data

This chapter discusses how data is transferred between the consumer and provider. *Data* refers collectively to parameter data and rowset data. *Parameter data* is the data used for parameters in commands. For example, in the text command **SELECT * FROM MyTable WHERE Name = ?**, the question mark represents a parameter and the consumer sends data for this parameter to the provider when it executes the command. *Rowset data* is the data returned in a rowset, such as the rowset generated by executing the previous command, and key column values passed to an index rowset when setting the index range or seeking for a key value.

Data is stored in both the consumer and the provider. In the consumer, data is stored in a buffer. A *binding* associates, or *binds*, a single column or parameter to the consumer's buffer and a group of bindings is gathered together in an *accessor*. When transferring data, the handle to the accessor and the pointer to the buffer are passed to the provider. In the provider, data is stored in a provider-specific way. For example, it may be placed in a structure, such as the rowset's copy of a row, or passed directly through to the data source.

The provider actually transfers the data from consumer to provider and provider to consumer. *Getting* data is defined as transferring data from the provider to the consumer, as when getting rowset data with **IRowset::GetData** or getting output parameter data with **ICommand::Execute**. *Setting* data is defined as transferring data from the consumer to the provider, as when setting rowset data with **IRowsetChange::SetData**, key values with **IRowsetIndex::SetRange**, or input parameter data with **Execute**.

Data Parts

Data has three parts: the data *value*, the *length* of the data value, and the *status* of the data value. The consumer can bind one, two, or all three of these parts. Except in very rare cases, the consumer always binds the data value and the status, and always binds the length for variable-length data types.

If the consumer is getting data and does not bind a part, the provider does not return that part. Although this is not an error, it is generally of little or no use. For example, if the consumer does not bind the status and the provider returns DB_S_ERRORSOCCURRED, the consumer must assume that the value was not returned correctly.

If the consumer is setting data and does not bind a part, the provider sends the data if it has sufficient information; otherwise it returns an error. For example, if the consumer binds the status but not the value, the provider sends the data if the status is DBSTATUS_S_ISNULL and returns an error if the status is DBSTATUS_S_OK.

The following table explains the behavior of the consumer and provider for each combination of bound parts.

Val	Len	Stat	Use when getting data	Use when setting data
X	X	X	Most commonly used combination when getting variable-length data.	Most commonly used combination when setting variable-length data.
X	X	–	Not generally used. See notes 1 and 2.	Not generally used. See notes 1 and 3.
X	–	X	Most commonly used combination when getting fixed-length data.	Most commonly used combination when setting fixed-length data. See notes 4 and 5.
X	–	–	Not generally used. See notes 1 and 2.	Not generally used. See notes 1, 3, 4, and 6.
–	X	X	Not generally used.	Not generally used. See note 7.
–	X	–	Not generally used. See notes 1 and 2.	If **IColumnsInfo::GetColumnInfo** does not return DBCOLUMNFLAGS_ISLONG for the column, the provider returns DB_S_ERRORSOCCURRED or DB_E_ERRORSOCCURRED.

Val	Len	Stat	Use when getting data	Use when setting data
–	–	X	Not generally used.	Not generally used. Can be used to set the value of a column or parameter to NULL or to specify that the provider is to use the default value for an input or input/output parameter in a procedure. See note 7.
–	–	–	**IAccessor::CreateAccessor** returns DBBINDSTATUS_ BADBINDINFO for the binding.	**IAccessor::CreateAccessor** returns DBBINDSTATUS_ BADBINDINFO for the binding.

1   If the method returns DB_S_ERRORSOCCURRED or DB_E_ERRORSOCCURRED, the consumer must assume that the value for the column was not successfully gotten or set.

2   If the column is nullable, the consumer cannot determine the validity of the returned value or length because it does not know if the column value is NULL.

3   The provider assumes the status is DBSTATUS_S_OK.

4   The provider assumes that string data is null-terminated.

5   If *wType* in the DBBINDING structure is DBTYPE_BYTES and the status is DBSTATUS_S_OK, the provider returns a status of DBSTATUS_E_UNAVAILABLE.

6   If *wType* in the DBBINDING structure is DBTYPE_BYTES, the provider returns a status of DBSTATUS_E_UNAVAILABLE.

7   If the status is DBSTATUS_S_OK, the provider returns a status of DBSTATUS_E_UNAVAILABLE.

Value

The value is the actual value of the data. For example, the value of a column containing last names might be "Smith." Unless the type indicator of the data is DBTYPE_BSTR or is combined with DBTYPE_BYREF, DBTYPE_ARRAY, or DBTYPE_VECTOR, the data is stored directly at the offset specified in the binding. Sufficient space must be allocated for the data.

For example, if the type indicator is DBTYPE_I2, a two byte integer is stored at the specified offset and two bytes must be allocated at that offset. If the type indicator is DBTYPE_STR, an ANSI string is stored at the specified offset. If the length of the string in bytes is longer than the number of bytes specified at the offset in the *cbMaxLen* element of the DBBINDING structure, then the string is truncated.

If the type indicator is DBTYPE_BSTR or is combined with DBTYPE_BYREF, DBTYPE_ARRAY, or DBTYPE_VECTOR, then a pointer to the data is stored at the offset specified in the binding and the data is stored in separately allocated memory. For example, if the type indicator is DBTYPE_BSTR, a pointer to a BSTR is stored at the specified offset and **sizeof(BSTR)** bytes must be allocated at that offset; the BSTR itself is stored in memory allocated with one of the OLE Automation string allocation functions. If the type indicator is DBTYPE_STR | DBTYPE_BYREF, a pointer to an ANSI string is stored at the specified offset and **sizeof(char *)** bytes must be allocated at that offset; the string itself is stored in separately allocated memory. For more information, see "Type Indicators" in Appendix A.

The only exception to these rules is when a reference accessor is used, in which case the value is a pointer to the provider's buffer, for rowset data, or a pointer to the consumer's buffer, for input parameter data. For more information, see "Reference Accessors" later in this chapter.

Length

The length is the length of the data in bytes. It is useful only for variable-length data. For fixed-length data, it is always the size of the data type. For example, the length of the ANSI string "Johnson" is 7, the length of the Unicode string "Lopez" is 10 (five two-byte characters), and the length of any value stored as a two-byte integer is 2.

The length gives the length of the data as it is stored by the consumer. That is, when getting data, it is the length of the data after it is converted from the provider type to the consumer type. When setting data, it is the length of the data before it is converted from the consumer type to the provider type.

Data Length and Buffer Length

It is important not to confuse the length of the data value with the length of the buffer in which the data value is stored. For example, in the following diagram, the length of the buffer is 14 and the length of the data value stored in the buffer is 10.

Data Buffer

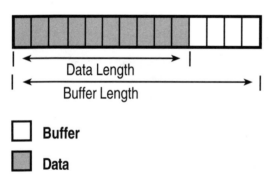

Buffer

Data

The consumer specifies the buffer length with the *cbMaxLen* element of the DBBINDING structure. For information about how the provider uses the buffer length in conjunction with the data length, see *cbMaxLen* in "DBBINDING Structures."

Length Values

The length value itself is a ULONG. The value stored in this ULONG depends on the data type as follows:

- **Variable-length data types**—The length of variable-length data types is the actual length of the untruncated data value in bytes. For string data, the length does not include the length of the null-termination character. If the length is bound, the string can include embedded null characters; that is, the length supercedes the null termination character in determining the end of the string. Embedding null characters is not encouraged. If the length is not bound, the string is assumed to be null terminated.

- **Fixed-length data types**—When getting data, the returned length of fixed-length data types is the size of the data type. Note that for DBTYPE_BSTR, this is **sizeof(void *)**, not the length of the BSTR. For DBTYPE_IUNKNOWN or DBTYPE_IDISPATCH, this is **sizeof(IUnknown *)**, not the length of the object; if there is a way to determine the length of the object, it is through a method on the object itself. When setting data, the provider ignores the length of fixed-length data types.

- **DBTYPE_BYREF**—The length is the same as if DBTYPE_BYREF is not used. That is, it is the length of the data being pointed to. For example, if the type indicator is DBTYPE_STR | DBTYPE_BYREF, the length is the length of the string in bytes, not the length of the pointer.

- **DBTYPE_VECTOR, DBTYPE_ARRAY**—When getting data, the returned length is zero. The reason for this is that there is a single length, while a vector or array can contain multiple values. When setting data, the provider ignores the length.

Status

The status indicates whether the data value or some other value, such as a NULL, is to be used as the value of the column or parameter. If the data value is to be used, the consumer sets the status to DBSTATUS_S_OK on input. On output, the provider returns information about whether the value was successfully gotten or set.

If the data value is not to be used, the status is set to DBSTATUS_S_ISNULL or DBSTATUS_S_DEFAULT. DBSTATUS_S_ISNULL indicates that a NULL value is to be used for the column or parameter; the data value and length are ignored. DBSTATUS_S_DEFAULT indicates that the default value of an input or input/output parameter in a procedure is to be used on input. The data value and length are ignored on input. However, they are used on output for an input/output parameter.

Status Values Used When Getting Data

ICommand::Execute, **IRowset::GetData**, **IRowsetResynch::GetVisibleData**, and **IRowsetUpdate::GetOriginalData** get rowset or output parameter data. As the provider returns the data, its sets the status of each column or output parameter so that the consumer can determine which data values were successfully gotten. It produces the return codes as follows:

- **Success return code (generally S_OK)**—No errors occurred while getting data for any columns or parameters. Warning conditions may have occurred for any columns or parameters.

    Note Truncation is a warning condition when getting data. The corresponding status is set to DBSTATUS_S_TRUNCATED.

- **DB_S_ERRORSOCCURRED**—Errors occurred while getting data for one or more columns or parameters but data was successfully returned for at least one column or parameter. Warning conditions may have occurred for any non-error columns or parameters.

- **DB_E_ERRORSOCCURRED**—Errors occurred while getting data for all columns or parameters. Warning conditions did not occur for any columns or parameters.

If the provider returns a fatal error other than DB_E_ERRORSOCCURRED, such as E_FAIL, the returned status values are undefined. If the consumer did not bind the status for a column or output parameter and the method returns DB_S_ERRORSOCCURRED or DB_E_ERRORSOCCURRED, the consumer must assume that the value for that column or output parameter was not successfully returned.

The following table explains the meaning of each returned status value, whether it is a success, error, or warning condition, and whether data was successfully returned.

Status value	Success, warning, or error	Data returned	Description
DBSTATUS_S_OK	Success	Y	A non-NULL value was returned by the provider.
DBSTATUS_S_ISNULL	Success	Y	A NULL value was returned by the provider.
DBSTATUS_S_TRUNCATED	Warning	Y	Variable-length data or non-significant digits of numeric data were truncated.
DBSTATUS_E_BADACCESSOR	Error	N	Accessor validation was deferred and was performed while the method returned data. The binding was invalid for this column or parameter.
DBSTATUS_E_CANTCONVERTVALUE	Error	N	The data value couldn't be converted for reasons other than sign mismatch or data overflow. For example, the data in the data source was corrupted but the row was still retrievable.
DBSTATUS_E_CANTCREATE	Error	N	One of the following conditions: The provider could not allocate memory in which to return data.

Status value	Success, warning, or error	Data returned	Description
DBSTATUS_E_CANTCREATE (*continued*)	Error	N	The type indicator for the column was DBTYPE_IUNKNOWN and a storage object was already open on the column.
			The type indicator for the column was DBTYPE_IUNKNOWN, the provider supports only one open storage object at a time (DBPROP_MULTIPLESTORAGEOBJECTS was VARIANT_FALSE), and a storage object was already open on the rowset.
DBSTATUS_E_DATAOVERFLOW	Error	N	Conversion failed because the data value overflowed the type specified for the value part in the consumer's buffer.
DBSTATUS_E_SIGNMISMATCH	Error	N	Conversion failed because the data value was signed and the type specified for the value part in the consumer's buffer was unsigned.
DBSTATUS_E_UNAVAILABLE	Error	N	Value could not be determined by the provider. For example, the row was just created, the default for the column was not available, and the consumer had not yet set a new value.

Status Values Used When Setting Data

ICommand::Execute, **IRowsetChange::SetData**, **IRowsetChange::InsertRow**, **IRowsetIndex::Seek**, and **IRowsetIndex::SetRange** set rowset or input parameter data. When using these methods, the consumer must set the status to one of the following values.

Status value	Description
DBSTATUS_S_OK	The value sent to the provider is not NULL and is passed in the consumer's buffer at the offset specified by *obValue* in the binding.
DBSTATUS_S_ISNULL	The value sent to the provider is NULL. The provider ignores the contents of the value and length parts of the consumer's buffer.
DBSTATUS_S_DEFAULT	The provider is to use the default value as the input value for an input or input/output parameter in a procedure. The provider ignores the contents of the value and length parts of the consumer's buffer on input, although it uses them on output for input/output parameters.

As the provider transfers data from the consumer to the provider, it sets the status of each column or input parameter so that the consumer can determine which data values were successfully set. It produces return codes as follows:

- **Success return code (generally S_OK)**—No errors occurred while setting data for any columns or parameters.

- **DB_S_ERRORSOCCURRED**—Errors occurred while setting data for one or more columns or parameters but data was successfully set for at least one column or parameter.

  Note Truncation is an error condition when setting data. The corresponding status is set to DBSTATUS_S_CANTCONVERTVALUE.

- **DB_E_ERRORSOCCURRED**—Errors occurred while setting data for all columns or parameters.

If the provider returns a fatal error other than DB_E_ERRORSOCCURRED, such as E_FAIL, the returned status values are undefined. If the consumer did not bind the status for a column or input parameter and the method returns DB_S_ERRORSOCCURRED or DB_E_ERRORSOCCURRED, the consumer must assume that the value for that column or input parameter was not successfully set.

The following table explains the meaning of each returned status value, whether it is a success or error condition, and whether data was successfully sent.

Status value	Success, warning, or error	Data sent	Description
DBSTATUS_S_OK	Success	Y	A non-NULL value was sent to the provider.
DBSTATUS_S_ISNULL	Success	Y	A NULL value was sent to the provider.
DBSTATUS_S_DEFAULT	Success	Y	The provider used the default value for an input parameter in a procedure. Note that if the provider used the default value on input for an input/output parameter, the status is set to the status of the output value on output.
DBSTATUS_E_BADACCESSOR	Error	N	Accessor validation was deferred and was performed while the method sent data. The binding was invalid for this column or parameter.
DBSTATUS_E_BADSTATUS	Error	N	One of the following conditions: • The status value sent to the provider was not DBSTATUS_S_OK, DBSTATUS_S_ISNULL, or DBSTATUS_S_DEFAULT. • The status value was DBSTATUS_S_DEFAULT and the binding was not for an input or input/output parameter in a procedure.

Status value	Success, warning, or error	Data sent	Description
DBSTATUS_E_ CANTCONVERTVALUE	Error	N	The data value couldn't be converted for reasons other than sign mismatch or data overflow. For example, converting the data would have truncated it, including truncating non-significant digits in numeric data.
DBSTATUS_E_ CANTCREATE	Error	N	One of the following conditions: The type indicator for the column was DBTYPE_IUNKNOWN and a storage object was already open on the column. The type indicator for the column was DBTYPE_IUNKNOWN, the provider supports only one open storage object at a time (DBPROP_ MULTIPLESTORAGEOBJECTS was VARIANT_FALSE), and a storage object was already open on the rowset.
DBSTATUS_E_ DATAOVERFLOW	Error	N	Conversion failed because the data value overflowed the type used by the provider.
DBSTATUS_E_ INTEGRITYVIOLATION	Error	N	The data value violated the integrity constraints for the column.
DBSTATUS_E_ PERMISSIONDENIED	Error	N	The DBPROP_COLUMNRESTRICT property was VARIANT_TRUE and the user did not have permission to write to the column.
DBSTATUS_E_ SCHEMAVIOLATION	Error	N	The data value violated the schema for the column.
DBSTATUS_E_ SIGNMISMATCH	Error	N	Conversion failed because the data value was signed and the type used by the provider was unsigned.
DBSTATUS_E_ UNAVAILABLE	Error	N	The value was not sent for an undetermined reason. For example: • The provider encountered an error while sending a column or parameter value and stopped processing. If the provider backs out changes it made before the error, it also sets the status of the columns from which it backs data out to DBSTATUS_E_UNAVAILABLE.

Status value	Success, warning, or error	Data sent	Description
DBSTATUS_E_ UNAVAILABLE (*continued*)	Error	N	• The consumer did not bind the value part of the data, the status was DBSTATUS_S_OK, and **IColumnsInfo::GetColumnInfo** did not return the DBCOLUMNFLAGS_ISLONG flag for the column.
			• The consumer did not bind the length part of the data, the status was DBSTATUS_S_OK, and *wType* in the DBBINDING structure was DBTYPE_BYTES.

Accessors

An *accessor* is a collection of information that describes how data is stored in the consumer's buffer. For example, it contains the type of each piece of data, the offset in the buffer at which it is stored, the scale and precision used by data stored in a DB_NUMERIC structure, and so on. When the consumer calls a method that transfers data, such as **IRowset::GetData** or **ICommand::Execute**, it passes the handle to an accessor and a pointer to buffer. The provider uses this accessor to determine how to transfer the data contained in the buffer.

Accessors are identified by their handle.

```
typedef ULONG HACCESSOR;
# define DB_NULL_HACCESSOR 0x00
```

DB_NULL_HACCESSOR is an accessor handle value that is always invalid.

Using Accessors

Accessors are created with **IAccessor::CreateAccessor**, reference-counted with **IAccessor::AddRefAccessor**, and released with **IAccessor::ReleaseAccessor**. They can be created and released at any time. An accessor can be a parameter accessor, used for accessing parameter data, a row accessor, used for accessing rowset data, or both. Parameter accessors must be created and used on the command. Row accessors can be created on the command or the rowset and must be used on the rowset. Row accessors created after a row is fetched can still be used against that row.

When **ICommand::Execute** creates a rowset, the rowset inherits all accessors that have been created on that command. To the consumer, it appears as if each accessor has been copied from the command to the rowset: the bindings, flags, and handle of each accessor are the same on both the rowset and the command.

For example, suppose the text command that creates a rowset contains parameters. The consumer might create multiple rowsets by repeatedly executing this text command with different parameters. Because the rowsets are created from the same text command, all can use the same row accessors. It is therefore more efficient to create these accessors once on the command, rather than creating them separately on each rowset. To create a row accessor on a command, the consumer must know the column ordinals. For a text command such as **SELECT * FROM MyTable**, there is no way to know the order of the result columns. In such a case, the consumer must define the row accessor on the rowset or modify the text command to list the columns.

Consumers can create and use more than one accessor on a single row. Thus, the consumer can get or set multiple copies of the same data. For example, suppose a rowset contains employee data including a picture of the employee. The consumer might create two accessors: one for all of the columns except the picture column and another for the picture column. The consumer might then pass the handle of the first accessor to **IRowset::GetData** to get all of the data except the picture. When the user requests the picture, the consumer would then pass the handle to the second accessor to **GetData** to get the picture.

Row accessors can be optimized. How this is done is provider-specific. In general, it is faster to use an optimized accessor than a non-optimized accessor. For example, the provider might structure its internal row buffers to match the types used in the accessor. Optimized row accessors must be created before any rows are fetched.

Reference Accessors

A special type of accessor, called a *reference accessor*, enables consumers to get rowset data directly from the provider's buffer and providers to get input parameter data directly from the consumer's buffer. Such accessors cannot be used when setting row data or with output parameters.

Reference accessors require the consumer to have prior knowledge of the provider's buffer layout; the consumer cannot discover this information at runtime. Because of this, reference accessors are designed for use by tightly coupled consumer/provider pairs. Because they allow direct access to the provider's buffers, providers are not required to support them. Consumers determine whether providers support reference accessors through the DBPROP_BYREFACCESSORS property.

To use reference accessors, the layout of the consumer's buffer must exactly match the layout of the provider's buffer. That is, both buffers must allocate space for the same parts (data value, length, and status), these parts must appear at the same offset in both buffers, the data value parts must have the same type and buffer length in both buffers, and so on. If the provider's buffer does not contain length or status parts, the consumer cannot bind these parts and must determine length and whether the data value is NULL in the same manner as the provider.

To use a reference accessor, the consumer passes the handle of the accessor and a pointer to a buffer to the provider. For rowset data, the provider returns a pointer to its internal buffer in the buffer supplied by the consumer. The consumer then dereferences this pointer and reads directly from the provider's buffer. For input parameter data, the consumer's buffer contains a pointer to the buffer that actually contains the data. The provider dereferences this pointer and reads directly from the consumer's other buffer.

For example, the following code shows how a consumer would read data directly from the provider's buffer using a reference accessor.

```
void *     pv;
ULONG      cRowsObtained;
HACCESSOR  hReferenceAccessor;
HROW       rghRows[1];
DBBINDING  rgBindings[5];

// Assume that the consumer already has a pointer to IAccessor on a rowset (pIAccessor)
// and a pointer to IRowset on the same rowset (pIRowset);

// Fill in the rgBinding array. The bindings must match the layout of the provider's
// buffer. Code not shown.

// Create a reference accessor.
pIAccessor->CreateAccessor(DBACCESSOR_ROWDATA | DBACCESSOR_PASSBYREF, 5, rgBindings, 0,
                           &hReferenceAccessor, NULL);

// Get a row.
pIRowset->GetNextRows(NULL, 0, 1, &cRowsObtained, rghRows);

// Get a pointer to the start of the provider's buffer for the row.
pIRowset->GetData(rghRows[0], hReferenceAccessor, &pv);

// Access the data in the provider's buffer, starting at the address *pv. Code not
// shown.
```

The pointer returned by the provider, for rowset data, or passed by the consumer, for input parameter data, does not need to point to the start of the buffer. The only requirement is that the relative offsets of the elements stored in the buffer match the offsets specified in the accessor. The consumer, for rowset data, or provider, for input parameter data, must not write to this buffer, nor may it free this buffer.

For rowset data, the pointer is guaranteed to remain valid until the consumer calls **IRowsetChange::SetData**, **IRowsetChange::DeleteRows**, **IRowsetResynch::ResynchRows**, **IRowsetUpdate::Undo**, or **IRowsetUpdate::Update** for the row, calls **IRowset::ReleaseRows** for the row and the reference count falls to zero, or releases the rowset. For input parameter data, the pointer is guaranteed to remain valid only until **ICommand::Execute** returns.

Bindings

An accessor is a collection of *bindings*. Each binding associates, or *binds*, a single column or parameter to the consumer's buffer. Columns and output parameters can be bound more than once in a single accessor, but input parameters can be bound only once in a single accessor. It is generally a consumer programming error to bind a column more than once in a single accessor and then use that accessor to set the value of the column, such as with **IRowsetChange::SetData**.

Each binding contains information about the consumer's buffer. The most notable information is the ordinal of the column or parameter to which the binding applies, what is bound (the data value, its length, and its status), the offsets in the buffer to each of these parts, and the length and type of the data value as it exists in the consumer's buffer. For more information, see "Data Parts," earlier in this chapter, and "DBBINDING Structures" later in this chapter.

For example, the following figure shows a consumer's buffer containing ten bytes for a string, two unused bytes to properly align the string's status and length values, four bytes for the string's status, four bytes for the string's length, two unused bytes to properly align the integer's status value, two bytes for a two-byte integer, and four bytes for the integer's status. It also shows the main binding information used to bind the string to column one and the integer to column two.

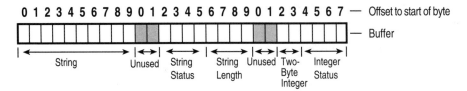

Element	String binding	Integer binding
Ordinal	1	2
Bound parts	DBPART_VALUE | DBPART_LENGTH | DBPART_STATUS	DBPART_VALUE | DBPART_STATUS
Offset to data value	0	22
Offset to status	12	24
Offset to length	16	N/A
Data type	DBTYPE_STR	DBTYPE_I2
Buffer length	10	2

When getting data, the provider uses the information in each binding to determine where and how to retrieve data from the consumer's buffer. When setting data, the provider uses the information in each binding to determine where and how to return data in the consumer's buffer.

DBBINDING Structures

The DBBINDING structure describes a single binding.

```
typedef struct tagDBBINDING {
    ULONG        iOrdinal;
    ULONG        obValue;
    ULONG        obLength;
    ULONG        obStatus;
    ITypeInfo *  pTypeInfo;
    DBOBJECT *   pObject;
    DBBINDEXT *  pBindExt;
    DBPART       dwPart;
    DBMEMOWNER   dwMemOwner;
    DBPARAMIO    eParamIO;
    ULONG        cbMaxLen;
    DWORD        dwFlags;
    DBTYPE       wType;
    BYTE         bPrecision;
    BYTE         bScale;
} DBBINDING;
```

The elements of this structure are used as follows.

Element	Description
iOrdinal	The ordinal of the column or parameter to which the binding applies.
	Column ordinals are fixed for the lifetime of the rowset. The self bookmark column is column zero and other columns start with column one. To retrieve column ordinals, consumers call **IColumnsInfo::GetColumnInfo**, **IColumnsRowset::GetColumnsRowset**, or **IColumnsInfo::MapColumnIDs**. If the rowset is generated from a command, the column ordinals returned by **GetColumnInfo** or **GetColumnsRowset** on the rowset must match the column ordinals returned by the same methods on the command.
	Parameter ordinals are determined from the text command. The first parameter is parameter one. To retrieve parameter ordinals, consumers call **ICommandWithParameters::GetParameterInfo**.
obValue	The offset in bytes in the consumer's buffer to the value part. *obValue* is ignored unless the DBPART_VALUE bit is set in *dwPart*. For more information about the value part, see "Value" earlier in this chapter.

Element	Description
obValue (*continued*)	This offset must be properly aligned for the processor architecture of the consumer's machine. If data is improperly aligned, consumers can expect alignment faults to occur when getting and setting data values. Consumers should use addresses that are multiples of the size of the data type. For example, if *wType* is DBTYPE_I4, the value part should be DWORD aligned.
obLength	The offset in bytes in the consumer's buffer to the length part. *obLength* is ignored unless the DBPART_LENGTH bit is set in *dwPart*. For more information about the length part, see "Length" earlier in this chapter.
	The length itself is a ULONG. This offset must be properly aligned for the processor architecture of the consumer's machine; that is, it should be a multiple of **sizeof(ULONG)**. If improperly aligned, consumers can expect alignment faults to occur when getting and setting length values.
obStatus	The offset in bytes in the consumer's buffer to the status part. *obStatus* is ignored unless the DBPART_STATUS bit is set in *dwPart*. For more information about the status part, see "Status" earlier in this chapter.
	The status part itself is a DBSTATUS value, which is a DWORD. This offset must be properly aligned for the processor architecture of the consumer's machine; that is, it should be a multiple of **sizeof(DWORD)**. If improperly aligned, consumers can expect alignment faults to occur when getting and setting status values.
pTypeInfo	Reserved for future use. Consumers should set *pTypeInfo* to a null pointer.
pObject	Pointer to a DBOBJECT structure. This structure describes how OLE objects in columns or parameters are to be accessed.

For the *pObject* element:

```
typedef struct tagDBOBJECT {
    DWORD dwFlags;
    IID   iid;
} DBOBJECT;
```

The elements of this structure are used as follows:

- *iid*—The interface to be exposed on the OLE object.
- *dwFlags*—The combined storage mode flags to use when instantiating the OLE object.

The storage mode flags are defined by the Structured Storage model in OLE. These are:

- STGM_READ = OF_READ
- STGM_WRITE = OF_WRITE
- STGM_READWRITE = OF_READWRITE
- STGM_SHARE_DENY_NONE = OF_SHARE_DENY_NONE
- STGM_SHARE_DENY_READ = OF_SHARE_DENY_READ
- STGM_SHARE_DENY_WRITE = OF_SHARE_DENY_WRITE
- STGM_SHARE_EXCLUSIVE = OF_SHARE_EXCLUSIVE
- STGM_DIRECT

Element	Description
pObject (*continued*)	<ul><li>STGM_TRANSACTED</li><li>STGM_CREATE = OF_CREATE</li><li>STGM_CONVERT</li><li>STGM_FAILIFTHERE</li><li>STGM_PRIORITY</li><li>STGM_DELETEONRELEASE</li></ul>*pObject* is ignored unless the DBPART_VALUE bit is set in *dwPart* and *wType* is DBTYPE_IUNKNOWN. If neither of these conditions are true, it should be set to a null pointer.
pBindExt	The DBBINDEXT structure may be used for extensions to the binding structure in the future. *pBindExt* is reserved for future use and consumers should set it to a null pointer. ```typedef struct tagDBBINDEXT{\n BYTE * pExtension;\n ULONG ulExtension;\n} DBBINDEXT;```
dwPart	*dwPart* specifies which buffer parts are to be bound to the column or parameter. It is one or more DBPARTENUM values combined; these values have the following meaning:<ul><li>DBPART_VALUE—The binding includes a value part.</li><li>DBPART_LENGTH—The binding includes a length part.</li><li>DBPART_STATUS—The binding includes a status part.</li></ul>
dwMemOwner	For bindings in row accessors, specifies who owns memory allocated by the provider for a column and for which a pointer is returned to the consumer. For example, when *wType* is DBTYPE_BYREF | DBTYPE_STR, the provider allocates memory for the string and returns a pointer to the string to the consumer; *dwMemOwner* specifies whether the consumer or provider owns this memory. The provider ignores this when setting rowset data. The following is a description of each of these values:<ul><li>DBMEMOWNER_CLIENTOWNED—The consumer owns the memory and is responsible for freeing it.</li></ul>

Element	Description
dwMemOwner (*continued*)	• DBMEMOWNER_PROVIDEROWNED—The provider owns the memory and is responsible for freeing it. When getting data, the provider returns a pointer into its copy of the row. When using provider-owned memory, the consumer's type must exactly match the provider's type, except that if *wType* is X I DBTYPE_BYREF, the provider's type can be X or X I DBTYPE_BYREF. If a column is NULL, the provider returns a null pointer for the data value.

The consumer must not write to or free the memory to which the pointer points. The lifetime of the pointer is provider-specific. However, pointers to row data are guaranteed to be valid until **IRowset::ReleaseRows** is called for the row and its reference count falls to zero, a method is called for the row that might invalidate the pointer, or the rowset is released, whichever occurs first. The methods that might invalidate the pointer depend on the method that returned it. These are as follows.

Ptr returned by:	Might be invalidated by:
GetData	**DeleteRows** (immediate update mode)
	ResynchRows
	SetData
	Update
	Undo
GetVisibleData	**GetVisibleData**
GetOriginalData	**ResynchRows**
	SetData
	Update

Although the consumer must not write to provider-owned memory, it can pass pointers to provider-owned memory when setting data. For example, suppose that the consumer wants to copy data efficiently from row A to row B. The consumer creates an accessor to the columns in row A in which *wType* is X I DBTYPE_BYREF and sets *dwMemOwner* to DBMEMOWNER_PROVIDEROWNED. When the consumer calls **IRowset::GetData**, the provider returns pointers to its copy of row A. The consumer then calls **IRowsetChange::SetData** for row B with the same accessor and a pointer to the memory passed to **GetData**. The provider dereferences the pointers and copies the data from the rowset's copy of row A to the rowset's copy of row B.

For bindings in row accessors, consumer-owned memory must be used unless *wType* is DBTYPE_BSTR, X I DBTYPE_BYREF, X I DBTYPE_ARRAY, or X I DBTYPE_VECTOR, in which case either consumer- or provider-owned memory can be used. However, provider-owned memory cannot be used if **IColumnsInfo::GetColumnInfo** returns the DBCOLUMNFLAGS_ISLONG flag the column. Consumers can mix bindings for provider- and consumer-owned memory in the same accessor.

For bindings in parameter accessors, consumer-owned memory must always be used.

dwMemOwner is ignored in reference accessors.

Element	Description
eParamIO	For parameter accesors, *eParamIO* specifies whether the parameter with which the binding is associated is an input, input/output, or output parameter. Providers only support those parameter I/O types that are supported by their underlying data source. *eParamIO* is one or more DBPARAMIOENUM values combined; these values have the following meaning:

- DBPARAMIO_NOTPARAM—The accessor is not used for parameters. *eParamIO* is generally set to this value in row accessors to remind the programmer that it is ignored.
- DBPARAMIO_INPUT—The parameter is an input parameter.
- DBPARAMIO_OUTPUT—The parameter is an output parameter.

For row accessors, *eParamIO* is ignored.

Element	Description
cbMaxLen	The length in bytes of the consumer's data structure allocated for the data value. That is, it is the number of bytes allocated at offset *obValue* for the data value. *cbMaxLen* is ignored unless the DBPART_VALUE bit is set in *dwPart* and the data value stored at that location is of variable length. For information about variable-length data types, see "Fixed- and Variable-Length Data Types" in Chapter 10.

cbMaxLen is used as follows.

- **Variable-length data types**—The provider checks the length in bytes of variable-length data types against *cbMaxLen*. If the length is greater than *cbMaxLen*, the provider truncates the data to *cbMaxLen* bytes.

  When getting data, this is a warning and the provider sets the status to DBSTATUS_S_TRUNCATED and sets the length to the actual number of bytes of data available after conversion and before truncation. Thus, the consumer can determine the actual number of bytes of data available.

  When setting data, this is an error and the provider sets the status to DBSTATUS_E_CANTCONVERTVALUE; generally, this is a consumer programming error.

- **Fixed-length data types**—The provider ignores *cbMaxLen* for fixed-length data types and assumes that the number of bytes available in the consumer's buffer for the data is the size of the data type.

- **DBTYPE_BYREF, DBTYPE_VECTOR, DBTYPE_ARRAY**—The provider ignores *cbMaxLen* and assumes that the number of bytes available in the consumer's buffer is the size dictated by DBTYPE_BYREF, DBTYPE_VECTOR, or DBTYPE_ARRAY. For DBTYPE_BYREF and DBTYPE_ARRAY, this is **sizeof(void *)**. For DBTYPE_VECTOR, this is **sizeof(DBVECTOR)**.

  It is important to note that if DBTYPE_BYREF is combined with the type indicator for a variable-length data type, the data is not truncated to *cbMaxLen* bytes. This is because the data is in separately allocated memory, not the consumer's buffer, and *cbMaxLen* does not apply to this memory. The provider allocates this memory based on the length of the data, as bound at the offset *obLength*, so consumers can guarantee that variable-length data is not truncated if it is retrieved in this manner.

Element	Description
dwFlags	Reserved for future use. Consumers should set this element to zero. Providers ignore this element.
wType	The indicator of the data type of the value part of the buffer. For more information about type indicators, see "Type Indicators" in Appendix A.
	This type forms an implied conversion between the buffer type and the type of the column or parameter. For information about conversions providers are required to support, see "Data Type Conversion" in Chapter 10.
bPrecision	The maximum precision to use when getting data and *wType* is DBTYPE_NUMERIC. This is ignored when setting data, *wType* is not DBTYPE_NUMERIC, or the DBPART_VALUE bit is not set in *dwPart*. For more information, see "Conversions Involving DBTYPE_NUMERIC or DBTYPE_DECIMAL" in Appendix A.
bScale	The scale to use when getting data and *wType* is DBTYPE_NUMERIC or DBTYPE_DECIMAL. This is ignored when setting data, *wType* is not DBTYPE_NUMERIC or DBTYPE_DECIMAL, or the DBPART_VALUE bit is not set in *dwPart*. For more information, see "Conversions Involving DBTYPE_NUMERIC or DBTYPE_DECIMAL" in Appendix A.

Note The offsets specified in *obValue*, *obLength*, and *obStatus* must not point to overlapping areas of memory. The provider is not required to check if this condition occurs and consumers must be careful to avoid this condition when constructing bindings.

Memory Management

When the consumer calls a method that gets or sets data, such as **IRowset::GetData**, **IRowsetChange::SetData**, or **ICommand::Execute**, it passes a pointer to memory containing the data. The consumer allocates and frees this memory by the method it chooses. The provider can only read this memory. It must not free this memory, nor should it assume that this memory exists after the method returns.

If the type indicator is DBTYPE_BSTR or is combined with DBTYPE_BYREF, DBTYPE_ARRAY, or DBTYPE_VECTOR, the consumer's memory contains a pointer to other memory. The other memory actually contains the data value, as distinct from the length and status, for the column or parameter. For example, if the type indicator is DBTYPE_BYREF | DBTYPE_STR, the data value in the consumer's memory is a pointer to a string; if the type indicator is DBTYPE_BSTR, the data value is a pointer to a BSTR. The remainder of this section discusses how this other memory is managed.

Part 1 Introduction to OLE DB

Note Suppose a consumer binds an input/output parameter with a type indicator of DBTYPE_BSTR or with a type indicator that is combined with DBTYPE_BYREF, DBTYPE_ARRAY, or DBTYPE_VECTOR. When the provider returns the output value for the parameter, it overwrites the pointer in the consumer's buffer that points to the input value. To ensure access to the input value after the provider returns the output value—for example, to free it—the consumer should keep a separate copy of the pointer to the input value.

When setting data, the consumer is responsible for allocating and freeing the other memory by whatever method it chooses. The provider can only read this memory. It must not free it, nor should it assume that it exists after the method returns.

When getting data, the provider is responsible for allocating the other memory. The method by which the provider allocates this memory and the responsibility for freeing it is determined by the *dwMemOwner* element of the applicable binding.

If *dwMemOwner* is DBMEMOWNER_PROVIDEROWNED, the provider allocates the memory and frees it by whatever method it chooses. The consumer can only read the memory and must not free it or write to it. The memory is part of the rowset's copy of the row, which saves the provider from separately allocating it and the consumer from freeing it. Consumers generally use provider-owned memory when they need fast, read-only access to the data. For more information about provider-owned memory, see *dwMemOwner* in "DBBINDING Structures" earlier in this chapter.

If *dwMemOwner* is DBMEMOWNER_CLIENTOWNED, the provider allocates and the consumer frees the memory as follows. Although the provider must not access this memory after the method returns, the consumer can access it at any time until it is freed. Consumers use consumer-owned memory when they need their own copy of the data and when they send data to the provider.

- **DBTYPE_BSTR**—BSTRs are allocated and freed with the **Sys*String** functions. For more information, see the *OLE Programmer's Reference, Volume Two*.
- **DBTYPE_BYREF**—Memory is allocated and freed with **IMalloc**.
- **DBTYPE_ARRAY**—SAFEARRAYs are allocated and freed with the **SafeArray*** functions. For more information, see the *OLE Programmer's Reference, Volume Two*.
- **DBTYPE_VECTOR**—Memory is allocated and freed with **IMalloc**.

The consumer can mix bindings in which pointers to the data and the data itself are returned. For example, suppose a rowset has two columns containing ANSI strings, one of which has a maximum length of 10 characters and the other of which has a maximum length of 32,000 characters. The consumer might choose to get the first string directly in its buffer (*wType* is DBTYPE_STR, *cbMaxLen* is 11, and *dwMemOwner* is DBMEMOWNER_CLIENTOWNED) and get a pointer to the provider's data cache for the second string (*wType* is DBTYPE_STR | DBTYPE_BYREF and *dwMemOwner* is DBMEMOWNER_PROVIDEROWNED).

The consumer can also mix bindings in which the consumer and provider own the memory. For example, suppose a rowset contains two columns containing ANSI strings with a maximum length of 32,000 characters, but only one of which is updatable. The consumer might choose to get pointers to both strings (*wType* is DBTYPE_STR | DBTYPE_BYREF) but to use consumer-owned memory (*dwMemOwner* is DBMEMOWNER_CLIENTOWNED) for the updatable string and provider-owned memory (*dwMemOwner* is DBMEMOWNER_PROVIDEROWNED) for the read-only string.

Data Transfer Procedures

The following sections discuss what the consumer and provider do to transfer data.

Getting Data

To get data, such as with **IRowset::GetData** for rowset data or **ICommand::Execute** for output parameter data, the consumer performs the following actions:

1. Creates an accessor to bind the columns or output parameters as desired.

2. Allocates a buffer to hold the data returned by the provider.

3. Calls a method that gets data and passes the handle to the accessor and a pointer to the buffer.

For each column or output parameter specified in the accessor, the provider performs the following actions. This procedure assumes that the consumer has bound the value, length, and status for each column or output parameter. If any of these are not bound, the procedure is the same except that the provider does not return the unbound part.

Note If the accessor is a reference accessor, the provider does not follow this procedure but returns a pointer to the provider's memory that contains the data. For more information, see "Reference Accessors" earlier in this chapter.

1. Validates the accessor against the metadata if it has not already done so. The provider can validate the entire accessor before returning any data or on a binding-by-binding basis while returning data. If validation fails in the former case, the provider produces the appropriate return code and does not return any data. If it fails in the latter case, the provider sets the status of the column or output parameter to DBSTATUS_E_BADACCESSOR and proceeds to the next column or output parameter.

2. Checks if the data is NULL. If it is, the provider sets the status to DBSTATUS_S_ISNULL, sets the length to zero, ignores the value, and proceeds to the next column or output parameter. The address at which the status value is placed is calculated from the buffer address passed to the method and the *obStatus* element of the binding.

3. Converts the data to the type specified by the *wType* element of the binding. If an error occurs while converting the data, the provider sets the status accordingly and proceeds to the next column or output parameter. For a list of status values that describe conversion errors, see "Status Values Used When Getting Data" in "Status," earlier in this chapter. For more information about converting data, see "Data Type Conversion Rules" in Appendix A.

4. Sets the length as follows. The address at which the length value is placed is calculated from the buffer address passed to the method and the *obLength* element of the binding.

   - **Variable-length data types**—The length of variable-length data types is the length of the untruncated data in bytes, not counting the null-termination character for strings.

   - **Fixed-length data types**—The length of fixed-length data types is the size of the data type. Note that if *wType* is DBTYPE_IUNKNOWN or DBTYPE_IDISPATCH, the length is **sizeof(IUnknown*)**, not the size of the object to which the interface pointer points, and if *wType* is DBTYPE_BSTR, the length is **sizeof(BSTR)**, not the length of the string itself.

   - **DBTYPE_BYREF**—DBTYPE_BYREF does not affect the length value. For example, if *wType* is DBTYPE_BYREF | DBTYPE_STR, the length is the length in bytes of the string, not the length of the pointer.

   - **DBTYPE_VECTOR, DBTYPE_ARRAY**—If the type indicator is OR'd with DBTYPE_ARRAY or DBTYPE_VECTOR, the length is zero.

5. Sets the data value to the converted data as follows. The address at which the data value is placed is calculated from the buffer address passed to the method and the *obValue* element of the binding.

   - **Variable-length data types**—If the length in bytes of the converted, variable-length data is greater than *cbMaxLen* bytes, the provider truncates the data to *cbMaxLen* bytes before placing it in the consumer buffer and sets the status to DBSTATUS_S_TRUNCATED. Otherwise, the provider places the data in the consumer buffer without truncating it.

   - **Fixed-length data types**—The provider places the converted, fixed-length data in the consumer's buffer. The provider ignores *cbMaxLen*; it does not truncate the data before placing it in the consumer's buffer.

     If the type indicator is DBTYPE_IUNKNOWN or DBTYPE_IDISPATCH, the data value is a pointer to an interface on the OLE object, not the object itself. For more information, see Chapter 7, "BLOBs and OLE Objects."

     If the type indicator is DBTYPE_BSTR, the provider places the converted data in a BSTR and places a pointer to the BSTR in the consumer's buffer. The provider ignores *cbMaxLen*; it does not truncate the data before placing it in the consumer's buffer. For information on how the BSTR is allocated and freed, see "Memory Management" earlier in this chapter.

- **DBTYPE_BYREF, DBTYPE_VECTOR, DBTYPE_ARRAY**—For DBTYPE_BYREF, the provider places the converted data in separately allocated memory and places a pointer to this memory in the consumer's buffer. For DBTYPE_VECTOR, the provider places the converted data in an array and places the count of array elements and a pointer to the array in a DBVECTOR structure in the consumer's buffer. For DBTYPE_ARRAY, the provider places the converted data in a SAFEARRAY and places a pointer to the SAFEARRAY in the consumer's buffer. In each case, the provider ignores *cbMaxLen*; that is, it does not truncate the data before placing it in the separate memory, array, or SAFEARRAY. For information on how the separate memory, array, or SAFEARRAY is allocated and freed, see "Memory Management" earlier in this chapter.

6. Sets the status to DBSTATUS_S_OK if it hasn't already been set to another value.

If the provider encounters an error while returning a column or output parameter value, it sets the status value of that column or output parameter. The provider then continues to process the remaining columns or output parameters. After it has processed all columns or output parameters, it produces one of the following return codes.

- **DB_S_ERRORSOCCURRED**—The method successfully returned data for at least one column or output parameter.

- **DB_E_ERRORSOCCURRED**—The method did not successfully return data for any columns or output parameters.

The consumer checks the status values to determine the columns or output parameters for which data was successfully returned. If the consumer did not bind a status value for column or output parameter and a method returns DB_S_ERRORSOCCURRED or DB_E_ERRORSOCCURRED, the consumer must assume that the column or output parameter value was not successfully returned.

The provider frees any memory it allocated for return to the consumer but did not return to the consumer due to an error. If the method fails completely, the contents of the consumer's buffer are undefined.

Setting Data

To set data, such as with **IRowsetChange::SetData**, for rowset data, or
ICommand::Execute, for input parameter data, the consumer performs the following
actions:

1. Creates an accessor to bind the columns or input parameters.

2. Allocates a buffer to hold the data to pass to the provider.

3. Places data in this buffer. For more information, see the next procedure.

4. Calls a method that sets data and passes the handle to the accessor and a pointer to
   the buffer.

For each column, except as noted later, or input parameter specified in the accessor,
the consumer performs the following actions. When passing key values to an index
rowset, the consumer performs this procedure only for the number of key columns
specified in the *cKeyValues* argument in **IRowsetIndex::Seek**, or the *cStartKeyValues*
or *cEndKeyValues* arguments in **IRowsetIndex::SetRange**. This procedure assumes
that the consumer has bound the value, length, and status for each column or input
parameter. If any of these are not bound, the procedure is the same except that the
consumer does not set the unbound part.

1. If the data is NULL, sets the status to DBSTATUS_S_ISNULL and proceeds to the
   next column or input parameter. If the provider is to use the default as the input
   value for an input or input/output parameter in a procedure, sets the status to
   DBSTATUS_S_DEFAULT and proceeds to the next column or input parameter.
   Otherwise, sets the status to DBSTATUS_S_OK. The address at which the status
   value is placed is calculated from the buffer address passed to the method and the
   obStatus element of the binding.

2. If *wType* is DBTYPE_STR, DBTYPE_WSTR, and DBTYPE_BYTES, or any of
   these values combined with DBTYPE_BYREF, sets the length to the length of the
   data in bytes, not counting the null-termination character for strings. For all other
   data types, the provider ignores the length, so the consumer does not need to set it.

3. Sets the data value. The address at which the data value is placed is calculated from
   the buffer address passed to the method and the *obValue* element of the binding. If
   wType is DBTYPE_BSTR or is combined with DBTYPE_BYREF,
   DBTYPE_VECTOR, or DBTYPE_ARRAY, the consumer places the data in
   separately allocated memory and places a pointer to the data in its buffer. For
   information on how this memory is allocated and freed, see "Memory
   Management" earlier in this chapter.

For each column, except as noted later, or input parameter specified in the accessor,
the provider performs the following actions. When passing key values to an index
rowset, the provider performs this procedure only for the number of key columns
specified in the *cKeyValues* argument in **Seek**, or the *cStartKeyValues* or

cEndKeyValues arguments in **SetRange**. This procedure assumes that the consumer has bound the value, length, and status for each column or input parameter. If any of these are not bound, the procedure is the same except that the provider does not attempt to retrieve the unbound part from the consumer's buffer; for more information, see "Data Parts" earlier in this chapter.

1. Validates the accessor against the metadata if it has not already done so. The provider can validate the entire accessor before setting any data or on a binding-by-binding basis while setting data. If validation fails in the former case, the provider produces the appropriate return code and does not set any data. If it fails in the latter case, the provider sets the status to DBSTATUS_E_BADACCESSOR and proceeds to the next column or output parameter.

2. Retrieves the status value from the consumer's buffer. If the status is DBSTATUS_S_ISNULL, the provider uses a NULL value and proceeds to the next column or input parameter. If the status is DBSTATUS_S_DEFAULT, the provider uses the default value for the procedure parameter and proceeds to the next input parameter. If the status is DBSTATUS_S_OK, the provider proceeds to the next step. If the status is any other value, the provider sets the status to DBSTATUS_E_BADSTATUS and proceeds to the next column or input parameter. The address from which the status value is retrieved is calculated from the buffer address passed to the method and the *obStatus* element of the binding.

3. If *wType* is DBTYPE_STR, DBTYPE_WSTR, DBTYPE_BYTES, or one of these indicators combined with DBTYPE_BYREF, the provider retrieves the length from the consumer's buffer. For all other data types, the provider ignores the length. The address from which the length value is retrieved is calculated from the buffer address passed to the method and the *obLength* element of the binding.

4. Retrieves the data value from the consumer's buffer as follows. The address from which the data value is retrieved is calculated from the buffer address passed to the method and the *obValue* element of the binding.

   - **Variable-length data types**—The provider retrieves the number of bytes of variable-length data as specified by the length, up to *cbMaxLen* bytes. It is generally a consumer programming error if the length is greater than *cbMaxLen*. If no length is bound, the provider retrieves strings up to the first null termination character; this is an error for DBTYPE_BYTES.

   - **Fixed-length data types**—The provider retrieves the number of bytes of fixed-length data from the consumer's buffer based on the size of the data type; it ignores *cbMaxLen*.

     If the type indicator is DBTYPE_IUNKNOWN or DBTYPE_IDISPATCH, the provider retrieves a pointer to an interface on the object from the consumer's buffer. For information about how the provider retrieves the object itself, see Chapter 7, "BLOBs and OLE Objects."

If the type indicator is DBTYPE_BSTR, the provider retrieves the pointer to the BSTR from the consumer's buffer and the BSTR from the memory to which this pointer points. Note that the provider ignores *cbMaxLen*; that is, it does not truncate the BSTR to *cbMaxLen* bytes.

- **DBTYPE_BYREF**—The provider retrieves a pointer to the data from the consumer's buffer and the data from the memory to which this pointer points. The provider retrieves the data from this memory as if it were retrieving it directly from the consumer's buffer, except that it always ignores *cbMaxLen*, even when DBTYPE_BYREF is combined with DBTYPE_STR, DBTYPE_WSTR, or DBTYPE_BYTES.

- **DBTYPE_VECTOR**—The provider retrieves a pointer to an array of data and a count of the number of elements in the array from a DBVECTOR structure in the consumer's buffer. It retrieves the data itself from the array to which this pointer points. The provider retrieves the data from this memory as if it were retrieving it directly from the consumer's buffer.

- **DBTYPE_ARRAY**—The provider retrieves a pointer to a SAFEARRAY from the consumer's buffer. It retrieves the data from the SAFEARRAY to which this pointer points.

5. Converts the data from the type it is stored in the consumer's buffer, as specified by the *wType* element of the binding, to the type of the column or input parameter. If an error occurs while converting the data, the provider sets the status accordingly and proceeds to the next column or output parameter. For a list of status values that describe conversion errors, see "Status Values Used When Setting Data" in "Status," earlier in this chapter. For more information about converting data, see "Data Type Conversion Rules" in Appendix A.

If the provider encounters an error while retrieving a column or input parameter value, it sets the status value of that column or input parameter. It is provider-specific whether the provider stops processing and backs out any changes already made, stops processing and leaves any changes already made, or continues processing some or all of the remaining columns or input parameters. If the provider stops processing, it must set the status value of any column or input parameter that was not in error and was not successfully set to DBSTATUS_E_UNAVAILABLE. This way, the consumer can determine which column or input parameter values were valid, which were invalid, and which were not validated.

When setting column data, except when seeking for a key value or setting the index range, the provider then produces one of the following return codes:

- **DB_S_ERRORSOCCURRED**—The method successfully set data for at least one column.

- **DB_E_ERRORSOCCURRED**—The method did not successfully set data for any columns.

When setting input parameter data, seeking for a key value, or setting the index range, the provider then returns DB_E_ERRORSOCCURRED.

The consumer checks the status values to determine the columns or input parameters for which data was successfully set. If the consumer did not bind a status value for column or input parameter and a method returns DB_S_ERRORSOCCURRED or DB_E_ERRORSOCCURRED, the consumer must assume that the column or input parameter value was not successfully set.

BLOBs and OLE Objects

Rowsets must support the efficient storage and retrieval of binary large objects (BLOBs) and OLE objects. To a rowset, a BLOB or OLE object is a large sequence of uninterpreted bytes that a consumer stores in a column. The consumer is entirely responsible for interpreting the contents of the BLOB or OLE object; the provider is responsible only for providing the mechanism or mechanisms with which the consumer stores and retrieves BLOBs and OLE objects.

In the future, abstract data types will be definable by the consumer on top of the types identified by the DBTYPE enumeration. They will relate to the types identified by this enumeration in much the same way that C++ types relate to C types.

BLOBs and OLE objects fall into the following categories:

- **BLOB**—An uninterpreted sequence of bytes or characters. There is no behavior encapsulated in a BLOB. All the logic for interpreting a BLOB is in the consumer. The type indicator of a BLOB column is DBTYPE_BYTES, DBTYPE_STR, or DBTYPE_WSTR.

- **IPersist* object**—An OLE object supporting either **IPersistStream**, **IPersistStreamInit**, or **IPersistStorage**. The type indicator of an IPersist* column is DBTYPE_IUNKNOWN.

- **Non-IPersist* object**—A COM object supporting some persistence model other than **IPersistStream**, **IPersistStreamInit**, or **IPersistStorage**. These are not supported in OLE DB, Version 1.1.

- **Abstract Data Type (ADT)**—An encapsulated object supporting a behavior not in the form of a COM interface. These are not supported in OLE DB, Version 1.1.

A consumer determines what types of BLOBs and OLE objects a provider supports by calling **IDBProperties::GetProperties** with the DBPROP_OLEOBJECTS property.

Accessing BLOB Data

BLOBs can be accessed as in-memory data, that is, a sequence of bytes sent or retrieved in one piece, or as a storage object, that is, through **ISequentialStream**, **IStream**, **IStorage**, or **ILockBytes**. The method a consumer uses depends on the setting of the DBCOLUMNFLAGS_ISLONG flag returned by **IColumnsInfo::GetColumnInfo** and the length of the BLOB data.

The DBCOLUMNFLAGS_ISLONG flag is set by the provider to inform the consumer that the BLOB data is very long and is best accessed as a storage object. Although the consumer can still choose to access the BLOB as in-memory data, there may be provider-specific problems in doing so. For example, the BLOB might be truncated due to machine limits on memory or **IRowset::GetData** might fail if called more than once for the BLOB.

If the DBCOLUMNFLAGS_ISLONG flag is not set, the consumer can safely access the BLOB as in-memory data. Whether it chooses to do so or to access the BLOB as a storage object generally depends on the length of the BLOB, which the consumer might already know or which it determines from the *ulColumnSize* element of the DBCOLUMNINFO structure returned by **GetColumnInfo**. If the BLOB is small enough that the consumer can allocate sufficient memory to hold it in its entirety, the consumer generally treats it as in-memory data. Otherwise, the consumer accesses it as a storage object.

Creating BLOB Columns

To create a BLOB column in a table, the consumer either uses a text command or calls **CreateTable** or **AddColumn** in **ITableDefinition**. In either case, it passes the maximum length in bytes (for binary data) or characters (for character data) of the BLOB column to the provider. Whether the column will best be accessed as in-memory data or as a storage object depends on the value of the IS_LONG column in the PROVIDER_TYPES schema rowset for the data type. The value in this column determines the setting of the DBCOLUMNFLAGS_ISLONG flag returned by **IColumnsInfo::GetColumnInfo**. For more information, see "Accessing BLOB Data" earlier in this chapter.

BLOBs as In-Memory Data

When a BLOB is treated as in-memory data, it is sent or retrieved in a single piece of memory. If the consumer allocates the memory for the BLOB, it generally binds the column with a type indicator of DBTYPE_BYTES, DBTYPE_STR, or DBTYPE_WSTR, depending on the data contained in the BLOB. When getting data, if the consumer wants the provider to allocate the memory for the BLOB, it generally binds the column with one of the preceding type indicators combined with DBTYPE_BYREF.

To get the BLOB data, the consumer calls a method such as **IRowset::GetData** with an accessor containing this binding and the provider returns the entire contents of the BLOB to the consumer. To set the BLOB data, the consumer calls a method such as **IRowsetChange::SetData** with an accessor containing this binding and sends the entire contents of the BLOB to the provider. This is no different from binding and getting or setting data in other columns, such as getting or setting data in an integer column. Note that character-data gotten or set in this manner is null terminated.

For example, the following code retrieves a 5,000 byte BLOB and stores it in consumer memory:

```
#include<oledb.h>

IMalloc*    pIMalloc;
IAccessor*  pIAccessor;
IRowset*    pIRowset;

int main() {
   HACCESSOR    hAccessor;
   DBBINDSTATUS rgStatus[1];
   DBBINDING    rgBinding[1] = {
      1,                                        // Column 1
      0,                                        // Offset to data,
      5000,                                     // Offset to length
      5004,                                     // Offset to status
      NULL,                                     // No type info
      NULL,                                     // Not an object
      NULL,                                     // No binding extensions
      DBPART_VALUE|DBPART_LENGTH|DBPART_STATUS, // Bind value, length, status
      DBMEMOWNER_CLIENTOWNED,                   // Memory ownered by consumer
      DBPARAMIO_NOTPARAM,                       // Not a parameter
      5000,                                     // Max length
      0 ,                                       // Reserved
      DBTYPE_BYTES,                             // Type DBTYPE_BYTES
      0,                                        // Precision not applicable
      0                                         // Scale not applicable
   };
```

```
pIRowset->QueryInterface(IID_IAccessor, (void**) &pIAccessor);
pIAccessor->CreateAccessor(DBACCESSOR_ROWDATA, 1, rgBinding,
                    (5000 + sizeof(ULONG) + sizeof(DBSTATUS)), &hAccessor, rgStatus);
pIAccessor->Release();

// Allocate memory for the in-memory data.  The first 5000 bytes are for the data,
// the next sizeof(ULONG) bytes are for the length, and the final sizeof(DBSTATUS)
// bytes are for the status.

void * pData = pIMalloc->Alloc(5000 + sizeof(ULONG) + sizeof(DBSTATUS));

// Get the next row, get the data in that row, and process the data. Assume the
// length of the data is known to be <=5000 bytes, so no need to check truncation.
HROW* rghRows;
ULONG cRows;

pIRowset->GetNextRows(NULL, 0, 1, &cRows, &rghRows);
pIRowset->GetData(rghRows[0], hAccessor, pData);


if ((DBSTATUS)(((BYTE*) pData)[rgBinding[0].obStatus]) == DBSTATUS_S_ISNULL) {
    // Process NULL data
} else if ((DBSTATUS)((BYTE*)pData)[rgBinding[0].obStatus] == DBSTATUS_S_OK) {
    // Process data.  Length is (ULONG)pData[rgBinding[0].obLength].
}
};
```

BLOBs as Storage Objects

When a BLOB is treated as a storage object, it can be gotten or set in pieces through **ISequentialStream**, **IStream**, **IStorage**, or **ILockBytes**, collectively known as the *storage interfaces*. The rowset acts as a *factory* for the objects that expose these interfaces, which are collectively known as *storage objects*.

The rows in the rowset act as *containers* of the storage objects. The relationship between a storage object and the row that contains it is the same as the relationship between an **IStream** or **IStorage** object and its parent **IStorage** object in Chapter 8, "Persistent Storage for Objects," of the *OLE 2.0 Design Specification* in the *Microsoft Development Library*.

This relationship dictates the behavior of the storage object with respect to its containing row in many circumstances. For example, the Structured Storage specification states that, when a parent **IStorage** is released, all child **IStorage** and **IStream** objects are invalidated. Similarly, if a row handle is released with **IRowset::ReleaseRows**, any storage objects open in that row become zombies. Any questions not specifically answered in this specification about the relationship between rows and storage objects can be answered by looking at the Structured Storage specification.

The following table shows the rowset methods and interfaces that are analogous to **IStorage** methods and modes:

IStorage method or mode	Rowset method or interface
Transacted mode	Delayed update mode
Direct mode	Immediate update mode
IStorage::Commit	**IRowsetUpdate::Update**
IStorage::Revert	**IRowsetUpdate::Undo**
IStorage::CreateStream, **IStorage::OpenStream**, **IStorage::CreateStorage**, **IStorage::OpenStorage**	**IRowset::GetData**. By default, BLOB columns are deferred. Their data is generally not fetched and storage objects are generally not created until **GetData** is called. Methods that fetch rows, such as **IRowset::GetNextRows**, do not generally return data for BLOB columns in the rowset's copy of the row.

For more information, see "Getting and Setting BLOB Data with Storage Objects" later in this chapter and "Deferred Columns" in Chapter 4. |
| **IStorage::DestroyElement** | **IRowsetChange::SetData**. For more information, see "Getting and Setting BLOB Data with Storage Objects," later in this chapter. |

The only significant difference between a parent **IStorage** object in the Structured Storage model and a row in a rowset is that a row can contain a storage object that exposes **ISequentialStream**, **IStream**, **IStorage**, or **ILockBytes**, whereas a parent **IStorage** object can only expose a child that exposes **IStorage** or **IStream**. For purposes of the analogy between Structured Storage and rows, **ISequentialStream** and **ILockBytes** storage objects are generally treated as **IStream** storage objects.

Limitations of Storage Objects

Storage objects are subject to the following limitations. Whether these limitations always exist is provider-specific.

- **Number of storage objects**—Some providers can support only one open storage object at a time, while others can support multiple open storage objects. If the provider supports only one open storage object at a time, any method that attempts to open a second storage object returns a status of DBSTATUS_E_CANTCREATE for the column or parameter, regardless of whether the objects are constructed over the same column, different columns in the same row, or different rows. A consumer determines whether a provider supports one or many storage objects by calling **IDBProperties::GetProperties** for the DBPROP_MULTIPLESTORAGEOBJECTS property.

- **Exclusionary behavior of storage objects**—Because of the way storage objects are implemented by some providers, using a storage object might prevent the use of other methods on the rowset. That is, after a storage object is created and before it is released, methods other than those on the storage object might return E_UNEXPECTED. A consumer determines whether storage objects might prevent other methods by calling **IDBProperties::GetProperties** for the DBPROP_BLOCKINGSTORAGEOBJECTS property.

- **Length of storage object must be known**—Some providers need to know the number of bytes of BLOB data that will be sent before any of the data is sent. This is generally due to a similar requirement in the underlying DBMS. For more information, see "Getting and Setting BLOB Data with Storage Objects," later in this chapter.

Lifetime of Storage Objects

A storage object created by the provider remains valid until one of the following events occur:

- The consumer calls **IRowset::ReleaseRows** to release the row containing the storage object or **Release** to release the rowset containing the row.

- The consumer calls **ITransaction::Commit** or **ITransaction::Abort** and the retaining flag is set such that the rowset becomes a zombie.

- The consumer deletes the row containing the storage object and transmits the deletion to the data source.

- The consumer calls **Release** on the storage object.

In the first three cases, the storage object is zombied. When a storage object enters a zombie state, it is not automatically released. Instead, if the consumer calls any method on the storage object except **Release**, that method returns E_UNEXPECTED. It is the consumer's responsibility to release the storage object, even if it is in a zombie state.

Getting and Setting BLOB Data with Storage Objects

The following sections discuss how to bind, get, and set BLOB data using storage objects.

Binding BLOB Data as a Storage Object

To bind to BLOB data as a storage object, a consumer creates an accessor that includes a binding to the BLOB column. The consumer performs the following actions:

1. Sets the *wType* element of the DBBINDING structure for the BLOB column to DBTYPE_IUNKNOWN.

2. Sets the *iid* element of the DBOBJECT structure in the binding to IID_ISequentialStream, IID_IStream, IID_IStorage, or IID_ILockBytes. If the consumer specifies an interface that is not supported by the provider, the provider returns E_NOINTERFACE when it validates the accessor; this can occur in **IAccessor::CreateAccessor** or a method that uses the accessor, such as **IRowset::GetData**. To determine which interfaces are supported by the provider, the consumer calls **IDBProperties::GetProperties** with the DBPROP_STRUCTUREDSTORAGE property.

3. Sets the *dwFlags* element of the DBOBJECT structure in the binding. If the consumer specifies any invalid or unsupported flags, the provider returns DB_E_BADSTORAGEFLAG when it validates the accessor; this can occur in **CreateAccessor** or a method that uses the accessor, such as **GetData**.

Getting BLOB Data with Storage Objects

To get BLOB data using a storage object, a consumer performs the following actions:

1. Creates an accessor that includes a binding for the column. For more information, see "Binding BLOB Data as a Storage Object" earlier in this section.

2. Calls **IRowset::GetData**, **IRowsetResynch::GetVisibleData**, or **IRowsetUpdate::GetOriginalData** with this accessor. The provider creates a storage object over the BLOB's data and returns a pointer to the requested storage interface (**ISequentialStream**, **IStream**, **IStorage**, or **ILockBytes**) on this object. If the provider supports only a single open storage object at a time and another storage object is open, the method returns a status of DBSTATUS_E_CANTCREATE for the column.

3. Calls methods on the storage interface to get the BLOB's data, such as, **ISequentialStream::Read**, **IStream::Read**, **ILockBytes::ReadAt**, or **IStorage::OpenStream**. Character-data gotten with these methods is not null terminated.

If the consumer calls **GetData**, **GetVisibleData**, or **GetOriginalData** multiple times for the BLOB column, the provider returns distinct pointers to storage interfaces on each call. This is similar to opening a file multiple times and returning a different file handle each time. It is the consumer's responsibility to call **Release** on each of these storage interfaces separately.

For example, the following code binds to a BLOB column and uses **ISequentialStream::Read** to get the data.

```
#include<oledb.h>

IRowset*   pIRowset;
IAccessor* pIAccessor;
IMalloc*   pIMalloc;

int main() {
    // Assume the consumer has a pointer (pIRowset) that points to the rowset. Create an
    // accessor for the BLOB column. Assume it is column 1.

    HACCESSOR     hAccessor;
    DBBINDSTATUS  rgStatus[1];
    DBOBJECT      ObjectStruct;
    DBBINDING     rgBinding[1] = {
        1,                                      // Column 1
        0,                                      // Offset to data
        0,                                      // Ignore length field
        sizeof(IUnknown *),                     // Offset to status field
        NULL,                                   // No type info
        &ObjectStruct,                          // Object structure
        NULL,                                   // Ignore  binding extensions
        DBPART_VALUE|DBPART_STATUS,             // Bind value and status
        DBMEMOWNER_CLIENTOWNED,                 // Consumer owned memory
        DBPARAMIO_NOTPARAM,                     // Not a parameter
        0,                                      // Ignore size of data
        0,                                      // Reserved
        DBTYPE_IUNKNOWN,                        // Type DBTYPE_IUNKNOWN
        0,                                      // Precision not applicable
        0                                       // Scale not applicable
    } ;

    // Set the elements in the object structure so that the provider creates a readable
    // ISequentialStream object over the column.  The consumer will read data from this
    // object.
    ObjectStruct.dwFlags = STGM_READ;
    ObjectStruct.iid     = IID_ISequentialStream;

    pIRowset->QueryInterface(IID_IAccessor, (void**) &pIAccessor);
    pIAccessor->CreateAccessor(DBACCESSOR_ROWDATA, 1, rgBinding,
                        sizeof(IUnknown *) + sizeof(ULONG), &hAccessor, rgStatus);
    pIAccessor->Release();
```

```
// Allocate memory for the returned pointer and the status field. The first
// sizeof(IUnknown*) bytes are for the pointer to the object and the next
// sizeof(ULONG) bytes are for the status.

void * pData = pIMalloc->Alloc(sizeof(IUnknown *) + sizeof(ULONG));

// Get the next row, get the pointer to ISequentialStream.
HROW * rghRows;
ULONG cRows;

pIRowset->GetNextRows(NULL, 0, 1, &cRows, &rghRows);
pIRowset->GetData(rghRows[0], hAccessor, pData);

// Read and process 5000 bytes at a time.
BYTE  rgBuffer[5000];
ULONG cb;

if ((ULONG)((BYTE*)pData)[rgBinding[0].obStatus] == DBSTATUS_S_ISNULL) {
    // Process NULL data
} else if ((ULONG)((BYTE *)pData)[rgBinding[0].obStatus] == DBSTATUS_S_OK) {
    do {
        (*((ISequentialStream **)pData))->Read(rgBuffer, sizeof(rgBuffer), &cb);
        if (cb > 0) {
            ; // Process data
        }
    } while (cb >= sizeof(rgBuffer));
};
};
```

Setting BLOB Data with Storage Objects

There are two ways a consumer can set BLOB data using a storage object:

- **Writing data directly to the provider's storage object**—The provider creates a storage object over the BLOB column and returns a pointer to this storage object to the consumer. The consumer writes data directly to this storage object.

- **Passing a pointer to a consumer storage object**—The consumer creates a storage object containing the data and passes a pointer to this storage object to the provider. The provider then reads data from the consumer storage object and writes it to the BLOB column.

Writing Data Directly to the Provider's Storage Object

To write data directly to the provider's storage object, the consumer:

1. Creates an accessor that binds the value of the BLOB column; for more information, see "Binding BLOB Data as a Storage Object" earlier in this section.

2. Calls **IRowset::GetData** with the accessor that binds the value of the BLOB column. The provider creates a storage object over the BLOB's data and returns a pointer to the requested storage interface (**ISequentialStream**, **IStream**, **IStorage**, or **ILockBytes**) on this object. If the provider supports only a single open storage object at a time and another storage object is open, the method returns a status of DBSTATUS_E_CANTCREATE for the column.

3. Calls a method on the storage interface to set data, such as **ISequentialStream::Write**, **IStream::Write**, or **ILockBytes::WriteAt**. Character-data set with these methods is not null terminated.

   If the storage object is transacted (that is, the STGM_TRANSACTED flag is set in the *dwFlags* element of the DBOBJECT structure in the binding), the storage object does not publish the changes to the containing rowset until the consumer calls **Commit** on the storage interface. If the storage object is not transacted (that is, the STGM_DIRECT flag is set), the storage object publishes the changes to the containing rowset when the consumer calls a method on the storage interface to set the changes. **ILockBytes** is never transacted.

For a similar code example, see "Getting BLOB Data with Storage Objects" earlier in this section. The code for setting BLOB data is essentially the same, except that the consumer must set the *dwFlags* element of the *ObjectStruct* structure so that it can write to the storage object. Also, the consumer calls **ISequentialStream::Write** instead of **ISequentialStream::Read**.

Passing a Pointer to a Consumer Storage Object

To pass a pointer to its own storage object, the consumer:

1. Creates an accessor that binds the value of the BLOB column; for more information, see "Binding BLOB Data as a Storage Object," earlier in this section. If the consumer's storage object exposes **ISequentialStream** and the provider needs to know the number of bytes of BLOB data that will be sent before any of the data is sent, this accessor must also bind the length of the BLOB column; for more information, see "Limitations of Storage Objects," earlier in this chapter.

2. Calls **IRowsetChange::SetData** or **IRowsetChange::InsertRow** with the accessor that binds the BLOB column. It passes a pointer to a storage interface on the consumer's storage object. If the provider already has a storage object open over the BLOB's data, the method returns a status of DBSTATUS_E_CANTCREATE for the column.

   Otherwise, the provider copies the data from the consumer's storage object to the BLOB column. This is equivalent to the provider destroying the existing data, creating a new (empty) storage object over the BLOB column, repeatedly calling methods to read data from the consumer's storage object and write data to the storage object over the BLOB column, and, if the storage mode is transacted, committing the changes on the storage object over the BLOB column. Character data set in this manner is not null terminated.

If the provider needs to know the number of bytes of BLOB data that will be sent before any of the data is sent, it retrieves this number with the **IStream::Stat**, **IStorage::Stat**, or **ILockBytes::Stat** method on the consumer's storage object (if the consumer's storage object exposes **IStream**, **IStorage**, or **ILockBytes**) or from the length part of the binding (if the consumer's storage object exposes **ISequentialStream**). If the consumer binds the length and the provider does not need to know this information or the consumer's storage object exposes **IStream**, **IStorage**, or **ILockBytes**, the provider ignores the bound length value.

When the provider has finished using the consumer's storage object, it calls **IUnknown::Release** to release the pointer. After **SetData** or **InsertRow** returns, the provider must not hold any pointers or reference counts on the consumer's storage object. If the consumer wants to ensure access to its storage object after **SetData** returns, it must call **IUnknown::AddRef** on the pointer before calling **SetData**.

To delete the data in the column, the consumer sets the status flag to DBSTATUS_S_OK. It then either passes a null pointer (instead of a pointer to its own storage object) or passes a pointer to a storage object that contains no data. The provider deletes the BLOB data in the column. This is different from setting the status value for the column to DBSTATUS_S_ISNULL. If the consumer sets the column value to NULL and then calls **GetData**, **GetData** returns a status value of DBSTATUS_S_ISNULL; if the consumer deletes the data in the column and then calls **GetData**, **GetData** returns a pointer to a storage object that contains no data.

For example, the following code passes a pointer to a different **ISequentialStream** object to **SetData** to overwrite the existing value.

```
#include<oledb.h>

IRowsetChange *      pIRowsetChange;
IAccessor *          pIAccessor;
ISequentialStream *  pISeqStr;
HROW                 hrow;

int main() {

    // Assume the consumer has a pointer (pIRowsetChange) that points to the rowset and
    // a pointer (pISeqStr) that points to an ISequentialStream object not in the
    // rowset. Create an accessor for the BLOB column. Assume it is column 1.
```

```
HACCESSOR     hAccessor;
DBBINDSTATUS  rgStatus[1];
DBOBJECT      ObjectStruct;
DBBINDING     rgBinding[1] = {
  1,                                    // Column 1
  0,                                    // Offset to data
  0,                                    // Ignore length field
  0,                                    // Ignore status field
  NULL,                                 // No type info
  &ObjectStruct,                        // Object structure
  NULL,                                 // Ignore binding extension
  DBPART_VALUE,                         // Bind value
  DBMEMOWNER_CLIENTOWNED,               // Consumer owned memory
  DBPARAMIO_NOTPARAM,                   // Not a parameter binding
  0,                                    // Ignore maxlength
  0,                                    // Reserved
  DBTYPE_IUNKNOWN,                      // Type DBTYPE_IUNKNOWN
  0,                                    // Precision not applicable
  0,                                    // Scale not applicable
};

// Set the elements in the object structure so that the provider creates a writable
// ISequentialStream object over the column.  The provider will read data from the
// ISequentialStream object passed to SetData and write it to this object.
ObjectStruct.dwFlags = STGM_WRITE | STGM_SHARE_EXCLUSIVE ;
ObjectStruct.iid     = IID_ISequentialStream;

pIRowsetChange->QueryInterface(IID_IAccessor, (LPVOID FAR*) &pIAccessor);
pIAccessor->CreateAccessor(DBACCESSOR_ROWDATA, 1, rgBinding, sizeof(IUnknown *),
                           &hAccessor, rgStatus);
pIAccessor->Release();

// Assume you already have an HROW (hrow).  Call SetData and pass it the address of
// the pointer to the ISequentialStream object not in the rowset.  The rowset will
// copy the data from the ISequentialStream object to the rowset.

pIRowsetChange->SetData(hrow, hAccessor, &pISeqStr);
} ;
```

Storage Objects and Rowset Update Semantics

When does the data set in a storage object become visible to other transactions operating at the Read Uncommitted isolation level? For providers built over database servers, this question can also be phrased as, "When does data set in a storage object become visible at the data source?"

The rules for storage objects are generally the same as the rules for data in other columns. That is, if the rowset is in immediate update mode, data made available to the rowset is immediately made available to Read Uncommitted transactions. If the rowset is in delayed update mode, data made available to the rowset is not made available to Read Uncommitted transactions until the consumer calls **IRowsetUpdate::Update**.

However, storage objects differ from other, non-storage columns in the rowset in two ways:

- **Storage mode**—Storage objects can have another layer of buffering based on the storage mode in which they operate. If the storage object operates in transacted mode, data is not available to the rowset until the consumer calls **Commit** on the storage interface. If the storage object operates in direct mode, data is immediately available to the rowset when the consumer sets it in the storage object.

- **Ignore delayed update mode**—Because storage objects can be large, using them in delayed update mode can be expensive as the provider must locally cache any changes to them until **Update** is called. So that consumers can control this expense, the DBPROP_DELAYSTORAGEOBJECTS property controls whether storage objects are always in immediate update mode, regardless of whether the rowset is in immediate or delayed update mode. For some providers this is a read-only property.

This is best shown in the following illustration:

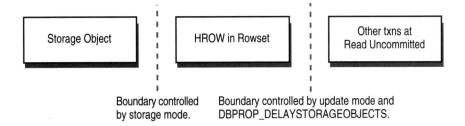

The following table shows the sequence of calls needed to make data set in a storage object visible to other transactions operating at the Read Uncommitted isolation level. In this table, **Write** refers collectively to any method on a storage interface that set data, such as **ISequentialStream::Write**, **IStream::Write,** or **ILockBytes::WriteAt**, and **SetData** refers collectively to **IRowsetChange::SetData** and **IRowsetChange::InsertRow**. Note that **ILockBytes** storage objects are always in Direct mode.

Storage mode	Update mode	DBPROP_DELAY STORAGEOBJECTS	Calls needed to expose data to other transactions running at Read Uncommitted
Direct	Immediate	Not applicable	**Write** −OR− **SetData**
Direct	Delayed	VARIANT_FALSE	**Write** −OR− **SetData**

Storage mode	Update mode	DBPROP_DELAY STORAGEOBJECTS	Calls needed to expose data to other transactions running at Read Uncommitted
Direct	Delayed	VARIANT_TRUE	**Write** **Update** –OR– **SetData** **Update**
Transacted	Immediate	Not applicable	**Write** **Commit** on storage interface –OR– **SetData**
Transacted	Delayed	VARIANT_FALSE	**Write** **Commit** on storage interface –OR– **SetData**
Transacted	Delayed	VARIANT_TRUE	**Write** **Commit** on storage interface **Update** –OR– **SetData** **Update**

When the rowset is in delayed update mode, the consumer cannot undo any pending changes made through a storage object if that object is still open. That is, if the provider creates a storage object over the BLOB and returns a pointer to it through **IRowset::GetData**, the consumer must release this storage object before calling **IRowsetUpdate::Undo**. If the consumer fails to release the storage object, **Undo** returns a status of DBROWSTATUS_E_OBJECTOPEN for the row.

Storage Objects and Transactions

Whether storage objects are transacted on the data source depends on the DBPROP_TRANSACTEDOBJECT property, which can be set on a per column basis. If the value of this property is VARIANT_TRUE, then any storage object created on the column is transacted. That is, when a consumer calls **ITransaction::Commit** and the provider commits all data visible to the rowset, this includes data made visible to the rowset through storage objects. When a consumer calls **ITransaction::Abort** and the provider rolls back all data visible to the rowset, this includes data made visible to the rowset through storage objects. For information about what data in storage objects is visible to the rowset, see "Storage Objects and Rowset Update Semantics" earlier in this chapter.

Whether uncommitted data in transacted storage objects remains valid and whether the storage objects themselves remain valid when the transaction is committed or aborted depends on the retaining flag used in the call to **Commit** or **Abort**. If a commit is retaining, then the storage objects and any uncommitted data in them remain valid. If an abort is retaining, then the storage objects remain valid, but any uncommitted data in them is lost; furthermore, the provider must synchronize the object with its state in the data source after the transaction was aborted there. If the rowset is not preserved after a commit or abort, then the storage objects become zombies and any uncommitted data in them is lost; the consumer can only call **Release** on such objects—all other methods return E_UNEXPECTED. Whether the rowset is preserved depends on the DBPROP_COMMITPRESERVE and DBPROP_ABORTPRESERVE properties.

If the value of DBPROP_TRANSACTEDOBJECT is VARIANT_FALSE, then any storage object created on the column is not transacted. That is, all changes to the storage object are permanent once they are made visible to the data source. Whether a nontransacted storage object remains valid after **Commit** or **Abort** is called depends on the implementation of the rowset and the object itself.

IPersist* Objects

OLE objects can be stored in columns in a rowset. Such objects are required to expose either **IPersistStream**, **IPersistStreamInit**, or **IPersistStorage**. So that the rowset knows how to instantiate these objects, it must store the class ID for the objects. How this is done is provider-specific. For example, the provider might store a separate class ID in the data source with each object, as might be the case for a column that can store objects that use arbitrary class IDs, it might store a single class ID for an entire column in the metadata for that column, as might be the case when a column can only store a single type of object—see DBCOLUMN_CLSID in **IColumnsRowset::GetColumnsRowset**, or it might not store a class ID at all and always use a default class ID, as might be the case when the provider can support only a single type of object.

Getting and Setting IPersist* Objects

The following sections explain how to get and set IPersist* objects.

Getting IPersist* Objects

To get an IPersist* object from a column, a consumer performs the following actions:

1. Creates an accessor that includes a binding to the column. It sets the *wType* element of the DBBINDING structure to DBTYPE_IUNKNOWN and sets the *iid* element of the DBOBJECT structure in the binding to the needed interface.

2. Calls **IRowset::GetData**, **IRowsetResynch::GetVisibleData**, or **IRowsetUpdate::GetOriginalData**.

If the object is not currently loaded, the provider, in turn:

1. Creates an instance of the IPersist* object and obtains an **IPersistStorage**, **IPersistStreamInit**, or **IPersistStream** pointer on it. For example, it might call **CoCreateInstance** with *rclsid* set to the class ID of the object and *riid* set to IID_IPersistStorage. How the provider determines the class ID of the object is provider-specific. For more information, see "IPersist* Objects," earlier in this chapter.

2. Creates an **IStream** or **IStorage** instance over the data in the column. If there is no data in the column, as is the case for a newly created row, the provider then calls **InitNew** on either **IPersistStorage** or **IPersistStreamInit**. If the provider supports only a single open storage object at a time and another storage object is open, the method returns a status of DBSTATUS_E_CANTCREATE for the column.

3. Loads the IPersist* object by calling **Load** on the **IPersist*** interface on the object and passing the interface pointer obtained in step 2.

4. Performs the operations required to enable future calls to the method to detect that the object has already been loaded (for example, using a moniker to the object) and to return a pointer on the loaded object.

5. Returns a pointer to the requested interface to the consumer. If the object does not support the requested interface, the method returns E_NOINTERFACE. After the method returns, the rowset does not hold any reference counts on the object.

If the object is currently loaded—which the provider can determine by virtue of the operations performed in step 4 in the preceding procedure—the provider performs the following action, in turn:

- Returns a pointer to the requested interface to the consumer. If the object does not support this interface, the method returns E_NOINTERFACE.

If any errors occur during these procedures, the provider ensures that no objects remain instantiated when **GetData**, **GetVisibleData**, or **GetOriginalData** returns.

Setting IPersist* Objects

To set an IPersist* object in a column, a consumer uses one of two procedures. In the first procedure, the consumer performs the following actions:

1. Calls **IRowset::GetData** to retrieve an **IStorage** or **IStream** pointer over the object's data. It does this in the same way it retrieves an **IStorage** or **IStream** pointer over BLOB data. The provider does not load the object, as is the case when the consumer calls **GetData** and requests a different interface, such as **IPersistStorage**. If the provider supports only one open storage object at a time and another storage object is open, the method returns a status of DBSTATUS_E_CANTCREATE for the column.

2. Calls **Save** on the **IPersist*** interface of the IPersist* object and passes it the storage interface pointer retrieved in step 1.

3. Calls **IPersistStorage::SaveCompleted** on the IPersist* object if **IPersistStorage** is used. The consumer should be careful if it sets the *pStgNew* parameter to a non-null pointer, as the provider does not dissociate the column's storage object from the IPersist* object.

This procedure should be used only by consumers that know what kind of IPersist* objects should be stored in a column. Because the storage object, which is implemented by the rowset, does not have a pointer to the IPersist* object, the rowset cannot determine whether the IPersist* object uses a class ID that matches the class ID used by the objects in the column. The possibility therefore arises that the consumer could store an object in the column of a type that the rowset will not be able to instantiate later.

In the second procedure, the consumer performs the following action:

- Calls **IRowsetChange::SetData** or **IRowsetChange::InsertRow** and passes a pointer to an interface on the IPersist* object.

The provider performs the following actions, in turn:

1. Creates a new storage object for the column and retrieves a storage interface pointer on that object. If there is an existing storage object on the column that the provider cannot release, **SetData** or **InsertRow** returns a status of DBSTATUS_E_CANTCREATE for the column. For example, this occurs if there is an IPersist* object loaded on the column. If the provider only supports one open storage object at a time and a storage object is open over another column or row, the method returns a status of DBSTATUS_E_CANTCREATE for the column.

2. May call **IPersist::GetClassID** on the IPersist* object to check that the specified IPersist* object is of a type that can be stored in the column.

3. Calls **Save** on the **IPersist*** interface of the IPersist* object and passes it the storage interface pointer retrieved in step 1. If the provider calls **IPersistStorage::Save**, it sets the *fSameAsLoad* argument to FALSE; if the provider calls **IPersistStream::Save** or **IPersistStreamInit::Save**, it sets the *fClearDirty* flag to TRUE.

4. Calls **IPersistStorage::SaveCompleted** on the IPersist* object if **IPersistStorage** is used. The provider sets the *pStgNew* argument to a null pointer.

5. Performs the operations required to enable future calls to **GetData**, **GetVisibleData**, or **GetOriginalData** to detect whether the object is loaded and to return a pointer on the loaded object. After **SetData** or **InsertRow** returns, the rowset does not hold any reference counts on the IPersist* object.

This second procedure can be used by any consumer. It should be used by consumers that do not know what kind of IPersist* objects can be stored in the column because the provider can check the class ID of the object before storing it.

Lifetime of IPersist* Objects

An IPersist* object instantiated by the provider remains valid until it is released. However, if the row associated with the IPersist* object is released, the storage object associated with the IPersist* object becomes a zombie and the IPersist* object will no longer be able to use it.

IPersist* Objects, Rowset Update Semantics, and ITransaction

IPersist* objects provide yet another layer between the object and the data on the data source. Data stored in an IPersist* object is not exposed to its underlying storage object, and hence, to other transactions until it is persisted with **IPersist***. After the data is persisted, the storage object to which it was persisted controls when it is available to the rowset and to other transactions. For more information, see "Storage Objects and Rowset Update Semantics" and "Storage Objects and Transactions" earlier in this chapter.

Note that the methods on **ITransaction** can indirectly affect IPersist* objects; for example, committing or aborting a transaction might zombie the storage object associated with the IPersist* object. For more information, see "Storage Objects and Transactions" earlier in this chapter.

OLE Object Storage Systems

Providers can be built on top of OLE object storage system. In this case, the columns of the rowset generally correspond to the properties of the objects, rather than to the objects themselves. One of these properties is the *self* property. The value stored in the column corresponding to the self property is the OLE object itself. That is, when the consumer gets the value of this column, it gets the OLE object to which the other properties in the rowset apply. For information about how the consumer gets or sets this object, see "Getting and Setting IPersist* Objects," earlier in this chapter.

In the column ID for this column, the *guid* element is DBCOL_SELFCOLUMNS and the *pwszName* or *ulPropid* element is assigned by the object (command or session) that created the rowset. The *pwszName* or *ulPropid* elements will be needed, for example, when joining two rows, each of which contains an OLE object and each of which therefore has a column corresponding to the self property.

Indexes

Indexes:

```
CoType TIndex {
    [mandatory] interface IAccessor;
    [mandatory] interface IColumnsInfo;
    [mandatory] interface IConvertType;
    [mandatory] interface IRowset;
    [mandatory] interface IRowsetIndex;
    [mandatory] interface IRowsetInfo;
    [optional]  interface IRowsetChange;
    [optional]  interface ISupportErrorInfo;
};
```

An OLE DB index, also known as an *index rowset*, is a rowset built over an index in a data source. It is generally used in conjunction with a rowset built over a base table in the same data source. Each row of the index rowset contains a bookmark that points to a row in the base table rowset. Thus, the consumer can traverse the index rowset and use it to access rows in the base table rowset.

The primary consumer for the **IRowsetIndex** interface is a query processor component using it during query execution. Although an SQL provider can expose **IRowsetIndex** by translating **IRowsetIndex** methods into SQL statements, this is not efficient. Instead, general consumers of SQL providers should use the **ICommand** interface as the primary data access mechanism and rely on the query processor in the SQL provider to optimize access to data.

The primary index interface, **IRowsetIndex**, exposes the functionality required by file access methods based on ISAM and B+-trees. It does not support functionality such as hashing, required by unordered indexes, R+-trees, required by access methods for spatial data, or signature files, required by access methods for text.

Index rowsets can be used in the following situations:

- Reading records efficiently by means of a key. The following are example SQL queries whose execution plan can exploit the capabilities of the **IRowsetIndex** interface:

  - Retrieving rows ordered by some column. For example, **SELECT * FROM Table ORDER BY Table.x**, where x is indexed.

  - Scanning records having a column value within a continuous range. For example, **SELECT * FROM Table WHERE Table.x BETWEEN 4 AND 20**.

  - Computing joins. For example, **SELECT * FROM R INNER JOIN S ON R.x = S.x**.

  - Retrieving distinct rows. For example, **SELECT DISTINCT R.x FROM R**, where R.x is indexed.

  - Positioning at a particular index entry, such as skipping over key entries within a range.

- Supporting indexes with multi-column keys. The values in each column can be in ascending or descending order.

- Traversing indexes in ascending or descending order to support **ORDER BY** clauses.

Structure of Index Rowsets

A row in an index rowset consists of at least two entries: one or more columns that form a key value used to search in the index rowset and a column containing a bookmark (primary key or row identifier). The bookmark points to the row in the corresponding base table rowset that contains the key value. The provider must guarantee that these bookmarks consistently identify a row in the base table rowset.

The key columns must occur in the order of most significant key column to least significant key column. The consumer can determine this order from the order in which column metadata is returned by **IColumnsInfo::GetColumnInfo**. The consumer can determine which columns are key columns from the DBINDEXCOLUMNDESC structure returned by **IRowsetIndex::GetIndexInfo**.

The bookmark that points to the base table rowset is not the self bookmark. That is, it is not the bookmark in column zero that points to the row in the index rowset. Instead, it is a column with an ordinal greater than zero for which the DBCOLUMNFLAGS_ISBOOKMARK flag returned by **GetColumnInfo** is set.

The index rowset can contain other columns in addition to the key value columns and bookmark column. For example, it might contain a timestamp column. Such columns should be discussed in the documentation that describes the index provider. Although such columns are not barred from containing bookmarks, additional bookmark columns preclude the ability of generic query processors to use the index rowset. That is, such query processors are unable to determine which column contains the bookmark pointing to the base table rowset and which column contains a bookmark pointing elsewhere.

Using Index Rowsets

Index implementations vary in their support of certain capabilities. Before an index rowset is created, consumers can determine the capabilities of the underlying index by calling **IDBSchemaRowset::GetRowset** for the INDEXES schema rowset. They can determine the capabilities of an index rowset to which they already have an interface pointer by calling **IRowsetIndex::GetIndexInfo**.

To use an index rowset, a consumer generally performs the following actions.

1. Instantiates a rowset over a base table and a rowset over an index designed for use with that base table.

2. Calls **IColumnsInfo::GetColumnInfo** on the index rowset to determine which column contains the bookmarks that point to rows in the base table column. The ordinal of this column is greater than zero and the DBCOLUMNFLAGS_ISBOOKMARK flag is set on it. **GetColumnInfo** also returns the key columns in the order of most significant column to least significant column. The consumer can determine which columns are the key columns by inspecting the DBINDEXCOLUMNDESC structure returned by **GetIndexInfo**.

3. May call **IRowsetIndex::SetRange** on the index rowset to set the range in which to search for key values in the index. If the consumer does not call **SetRange**, the index rowset will search the entire index.

4. Calls **IRowsetIndex::Seek** on the index rowset to set the next fetch position to a specified key value. This key value must be in the range set in step 3.

5. Calls **IRowset::GetNextRows** on the index rowset to get the row or rows from the index starting with the key value specified in step 4. **GetNextRows** is limited to the range set in step 3.

6. Calls **IRowset::GetData** on the index rowset for each fetched row to get the bookmarks pointing to the base table rowset.

7. Calls **IRowsetLocate::GetRowsByBookmark** on the base table rowset to retrieve the rows in that rowset that correspond to the index rows fetched in step 5.

Because an index is a rowset, the consumer can treat it like any other rowset. For example, the consumer can call methods in **IRowsetChange** to add, delete, and update rows in the index.

Index Example

The following code accesses the Employees table through the Emp_LastName_Index index, using **IRowsetIndex** for the index and **IRowsetLocate** for the table.

The index has two columns. The first column, Emp_LastName, is of type DBTYPE_WSTR with a length of 30 characters and is the key column. The second column is of type DBTYPE_BYTES with a length of 4 and contains the bookmark for the Employees table. In the information returned by **IColumnsInfo::GetColumnInfo** for this column, the DBCOLUMNFLAGS_ISBOOKMARK is set.

The code sample performs the following actions:

1. Initializes the database and creates a session (not shown).

2. Obtains interfaces for the table and index. Only the latter is shown.

3. Gets information about the column types of the index rowset (not shown).

4. Establishes bindings for the table and index columns. Only the latter is shown.

5. Creates accessors for the table and index rowsets. Only the latter is shown.

6. Reads the index rowset and retrieves the corresponding row from the table rowset.

```
#include<oledb.h>
#include<stddef.h>

GetTableRowsetLocate(IOpenRowset* , BSTR, IRowsetLocate**);
PrintData(OLECHAR*, ULONG, HROW*);
IMalloc * pMalloc;  // pMalloc is the default memory allocator
HRESULT    hr;

int main() {
    IOpenRowset     *pIOpenRowset = NULL;
    DBID             IndxId;
    IRowsetIndex    *pIndex = NULL;
    IRowset         *pIndexRows = NULL;
    IRowsetLocate   *pIRSLocate =NULL;
    ULONG           *pColumns = NULL;
    DBCOLUMNINFO    **prgInfo;
    OLECHAR         **ppStringsBuffer;
    IColumnsInfo    *pIndxColsInfo = NULL;
    IAccessor       *pIndxAccsr = NULL;
    HACCESSOR        hIndexAccBmk = DB_NULL_HACCESSOR;

    // Initialize the database, create a session, and obtain, from the session object, a
    // pointer pIOpenRowset to an IOpenRowset interface.  Code not shown.

    // Use IOpenRowset::OpenRowset to obtain a pointer to IRowsetIndex.
    // Set the Index's DBID
    IndxId.eKind = DBKIND_GUID_NAME;
    IndxId.uName.pwszName = OLESTR("Emp_LastName_Index");
```

```
// Open the Index with default properties and default interfaces (IRowsetIndex,
// IAccessor, IRowset, IColumnsInfo, IRowsetInfo).
pIOpenRowset->OpenRowset(NULL, NULL, &IndxId, IID_IRowsetIndex, 0, NULL,
                         (IUnknown**) &pIndex);

// Get a rowset for the table using a helper function.
GetTableRowsetLocate(pIOpenRowset, OLESTR("Employees"), &pIRSLocate);

// Get an accessor for the index.
pIndex->QueryInterface(IID_IAccessor, (LPVOID FAR*) &pIndxAccsr);

// Get a rowset for index traversal.
pIndex->QueryInterface(IID_IRowset, (LPVOID FAR*) &pIndexRows);

// Get a pointer to IColumnsInfo on the index and get information about the columns
// of the index.
pIndex->QueryInterface(IID_IColumnsInfo, (LPVOID FAR*) &pIndxColsInfo);
pIndxColsInfo->GetColumnInfo(pColumns, prgInfo, ppStringsBuffer);

// Explore the DBCOLUMNINFO structures. The structure not corresponding to column
// zero and with a flag DBCOLUMNFLAGS_ISBOOKMARK set is the bookmark to the base
// table. Let's suppose that the IColumnsInfo says that there are two columns, that
// column 1 (which corresponds to the key), contains a string, and that the base
// table bookmark is in Column 2 and that it needs 4 bytes. Code not shown.

// Create index and table bindings and corresponding accessors.
typedef struct tagBmk{
    OLECHAR * Name;
    ULONG     cBookmark;
    BYTE      vBookmark[4];
} Bmk;

DBBINDSTATUS rgStatus[2];
static DBBINDING IndxBinds[2]= {
    {
        1,                        // Ordinal of key column
        0,                        // obValue
        0,                        // No length
        0,                        // No status
        NULL,                     // No TypeInfo
        NULL,                     // No Object
        NULL,                     // No binding extensions
        DBPART_VALUE,             // Bind value
        DBMEMOWNER_CLIENTOWNED,   // Client-owned memory
        DBPARAMIO_NOTPARAM,
        0,                        // cbMaxLen ignored
        0,
        DBTYPE_STR | DBTYPE_BYREF, // DBTYPE
        0,                        // No Scale
        0                         // No Precision
    },
    {
        2,                        // Ordinal of base table bookmark
        offsetof(Bmk, vBookmark), // Offset to value
```

```
            offsetof(Bmk,cBookmark),          // Offset to length
            0,                                 // No status
            NULL,                              // No Type Info
            NULL,                              // No object
            NULL,                              // No binding extensions
            DBPART_VALUE | DBPART_LENGTH,      // Bind value and length
            DBMEMOWNER_CLIENTOWNED,            // Client-owned memory
            DBPARAMIO_NOTPARAM,
            4,                                 // max length
            0,
            DBTYPE_BYTES,                      // DBTYPE
            0,                                 // No Scale
            0                                  // No Precision
        }
    };

    pIndxAccsr->CreateAccessor(DBACCESSOR_ROWDATA, 2, IndxBinds, 0, &hIndexAccBmk,
                               rgStatus);
    //...

    // Set a range Emp_LastName LIKE "Smith*". Notice that only the Name element of the
    // Bmk structure is used.
    Bmk Bookmark;
    Bookmark.Name = OLESTR("Smith");
    pIndex->SetRange(hIndexAccBmk, 1, &Bmk, 0, NULL, DBRANGE_PREFIX);
    pIndex->Seek(hIndexAccBmk, 1, &Bmk, DBSEEK_GE);

    // Traverse index within the range. For each matching index entry, retrieve the
    // corresponding record in Employees table.
    ULONG        cIdxRows = 0, cTabRows = 0;
    HROW         *phIdxRows = NULL, *phTabRows = NULL;
    DBROWSTATUS  rgRowStatus[1];

    while(SUCCEEDED(hr = pIndexRows->GetNextRows(0, 0, 1, &cIdxRows, &phIdxRows)) &&
          cIdxRows > 0) {
       // Extract the bookmark from the index and read the table directly.
       pIndexRows->GetData(*phIdxRows, hIndexAccBmk, &Bookmark);
       pIRSLocate->GetRowsAt(0, NULL, Bookmark.cBookmark, &(Bookmark.vBookmark[0]), 0,
                             1, &cTabRows, &phTabRows);
       PrintData(Bookmark.Name, cTabRows, phTabRows);

       // Release memory
       pMalloc->Free(Bookmark.Name);

       // Release the index and table rows
       pIndexRows->ReleaseRows(cIdxRows, phIdxRows, NULL, rgRowStatus);
       pIRSLocate->ReleaseRows(cTabRows, phTabRows, NULL, rgRowStatus);
    };

    //Release the accessor
    pIndxAccsr->ReleaseAccessor(hIndexAccBmk);

    //...
};
```

Notifications

Consumers may need to be aware of changes other consumers make to a shared rowset. For example, suppose multiple consumers share a rowset and some of these consumers update the rowset directly using **IRowsetChange** or **IRowsetUpdate**. The non-updating consumers may want to be notified of changes made by updating consumers to be able to refresh their local state.

To be notified of such changes, which are called *endogenous changes*, consumers implement **IRowsetNotify** and register it on a connection point with the provider. Providers call the methods in this interface to notify the consumers of changes made by other consumers of the same rowset.

When Notifications Are Sent

Notifications occur on significant changes to row or rowset state. Many of the events have multiple phases, which occur because multiple consumers may need to cooperate to validate and safely perform the transitions. These phases correspond to initial validation, preparation, commit, and operation completion.

Providers do not send notifications when no work will be done. For example, providers might not send notifications in the following cases:

- The method returns a trivial error, such as E_INVALIDARG.

- The method accepts an array of values to operate on and the array size is zero.

- The provider is in a state where the method will always fail.

It is possible for notifications to be nested. That is, sending one notification can cause a consumer to take actions that cause another notification to be sent.

Notifications can also be grouped, although this is relevant only to the provider and cannot be detected by the consumer. If an action causes the provider to send multiple notifications, all of those notifications must be approved by the consumer before the provider performs the action. If a consumer cancels a single notification, the provider does not perform the action and returns DB_E_CANCELED. For example, if a call to **IRowsetChange::SetData** changes multiple columns, the consumer must approve the changes to all of the columns before the provider changes any of the columns; if the consumer disallows a change to any of the columns, no columns are updated.

Consumers can screen out unwanted events or phases of an event by returning DB_S_UNWANTEDREASON or DB_S_UNWANTEDPHASE from the methods on **IRowsetNotify**. There is no guaranteed effect, but an optimized provider may cease sending the unwanted event or phase of an event. Screening out a phase only applies to that particular event; other events will still send out notifications for all phases unless they are also screened.

States and State Transitions in Providers

The following finite-state machine describes the events that take place within a rowset method, such as **IRowsetChange::SetData** implementing notifications.

States

- Enter Method and Exit Method (light gray) are conceptual states representing the initial and final states of a method issuing notifications.

- OK To Do, About To Do, Synch After, Did Event, and Failed To Do (white) are states representing notifications sent by the method to consumers.

- Preliminary Work, Permanent Work, and Undo Work (dark gray) are internal states representing work done by the provider between notification phases.

Transitions

- Arrows with a heavy continuous line represent transitions within states when all consumers return S_OK as a result of the notification sent by the state at the start of the arrow. In general, a transition through a heavy continuous line represents an acceptance path by the consumer on the notification.

- Arrows with a light continuous line represent transitions within states when at least one consumer returns S_FALSE as a result of the notification sent by the state at the start of the arrow. In general, a transition through a light continuous line represents an cancellation path by the consumer on the notification.

- Arrows with a dashed line represent internal transitions within the method. The transitions from Preliminary Work or Permanent Work to Failed to Do are transitions that result from some error in the execution of the method. A transition from Enter Method to Exit Method represents a path where the method detects some error condition which implies no notification work.

Provider State Machine Diagram

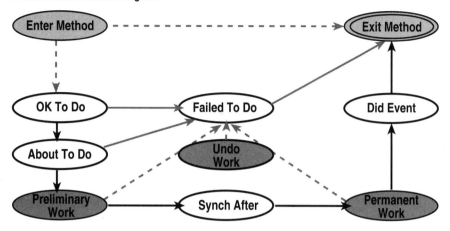

States and State Transitions in Consumers

The following finite-state machine describes the actions that may take place within a consumer inside each of the methods of the **IRowsetNotify** interface.

States

- Initial (white) is a conceptual state denoting the initial state of any **IRowsetNotify** method before any phase starts. Full phased events such as DBREASON_COLUMN_SET can at this point receive an OK To Do or Failed To Do phase. Any other phase at this point is unexpected, causing the method to transition to the Undo Work2 state that returns S_FALSE.

- OK To Do, About To Do, Synch After, and Did Event (dark gray) are states to which the method transitions upon receiving the phase of the same name. All these states may involve some internal work by the consumer. All states, except Did Event, may receive a Failed To Do notification which causes the method to transition to the Undo Work1 state.

- Undo Work1 (dark gray) is an internal state to which the listener transitions from any state (except Did Event) upon reception of a Failed To Do phase. In this state, any work done by the consumer is undone. After the work is undone, the method transitions back to the Initial State and returns S_OK.

- Undo Work2 (light gray) is an internal state that captures any unexpected phase. In this state, any work done by the consumer is undone. Once the work is undone, the method transitions back to the Initial state and returns S_FALSE.

Transitions

- Arrows with a continuous heavy line represent transitions within states upon reception of some expected phase.

- Arrows with a continuous light line represent transitions resulting from receiving an unexpected phase.

- Arrows with a dashed line represent internal transition by the consumer.

Consumer State Machine Diagram

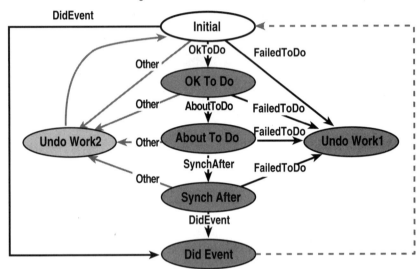

Data Types in OLE DB

OLE DB uses standard OLE and Windows data types. To describe a data type, a *type indicator* is used. This is a variable of the enumerated type DBTYPE that is passed as metadata. Although it is easy to confuse the two, type indicators are not data types. For example, DBTYPE_GUID is an integer with a value of 72, not a GUID. It is used to indicate that a piece of memory contains a GUID. Type indicators are used in many places, including the following:

- **Metadata**—Type indicators are used to specify the data type of a column or parameter.

- **DBBINDING Structures**—The *wType* element of the DBBINDING structure describes the type of the bound data value. When getting data, this is the type to which the provider converts the data before returning it to the consumer. When setting data, this is the type from which the provider converts the data after retrieving it from the consumer.

- **VARIANT Structures**—The *vt* element, a short integer, of the VARIANT structure indicates the type of the data that is stored in the structure. The remainder of the structure is 14 bytes which are structured according to the *vt* tag. The DBTYPE enumerated type is a superset of the VARENUM enumerated type, so some DBTYPE values cannot be used in VARIANT structures.

For a complete list of type indicators, see "Type Indicators" in Appendix A.

Using Type Indicators in Providers

A provider begins by selecting a subset of types—as represented by type indicators—it wants to support. The provider maps its underlying data types to these types and advertises them through the PROVIDER_TYPES schema rowset. The underlying data types are unimportant to the consumer. What is important is that the provider guarantees that it can always safely transfer data in the type represented by the indicator it advertises for a column or parameter. For examples of how various providers might map underlying data types to OLE DB data types, see the following sections.

Providers are not required to support all OLE DB data types, nor are they required to support all possible conversions among them. For information about what conversions a provider is required to support, see "Data Type Conversion" later in this chapter.

Although one goal of OLE DB is to provide a unified type system, there are two exceptions to this goal:

- It does not standardize type names as used in text commands. The TYPE_NAME column in the PROVIDER_TYPES schema rowset contains the type name consumers should use when executing Data Definition Language (DDL) commands. This saves providers from having to parse such commands before passing them to the data source.

- It exposes data source–specific type names for parameters in text commands. For more information, see **ICommandWithParameters::SetParameterInfo**.

In future versions of OLE DB, consumers and providers will be able to define their own data types through the DBTYPE_UDT (user-defined data type) type indicator.

Type Indicators in an ANSI SQL Provider

The following table shows how an ANSI SQL provider might map its data types to OLE DB data types.

SQL data type	OLE DB type indicator
CHAR (n) $1 \leq n \leq 255$	DBTYPE_STR
VARCHAR (n) $1 \leq n \leq 255$	DBTYPE_STR
CLOB	DBTYPE_STR
DECIMAL(p,s)	DBTYPE_NUMERIC
NUMERIC(p,s)	DBTYPE_NUMERIC
BIT	DBTYPE_BOOL
TINYINT (signed)	DBTYPE_I1
TINYINT (unsigned)	DBTYPE_UI1
SMALLINT (signed)	DBTYPE_I2
SMALLINT (unsigned)	DBTYPE_UI2
INTEGER (signed)	DBTYPE_I4
INTEGER (unsigned)	DBTYPE_UI4
BIGINT (signed)	DBTYPE_I8
BIGINT (unsigned)	DBTYPE_UI8
REAL	DBTYPE_R4
FLOAT	DBTYPE_R8
DOUBLE PRECISION	DBTYPE_R8

SQL data type	OLE DB type indicator
BINARY (n)	DBTYPE_BYTES
VARBINARY(n)	DBTYPE_BYTES
BLOB	DBTYPE_BYTES
DATE	DBTYPE_DBDATE
TIME	DBTYPE_DBTIME
TIMESTAMP	DBTYPE_DBTIMESTAMP

Type Indicators in a Microsoft Access Provider

The following table shows how a Microsoft Access provider might map its data types to OLE DB data types.

Microsoft Access data type	OLE DB type indicator
BINARY (< 255 bytes)	DBTYPE_BYTES
BIT	DBTYPE_BOOL
BYTE	DBTYPE_UI1
COUNTER	DBTYPE_I4
CURRENCY	DBTYPE_CY
DATETIME	DBTYPE_DATE
DOUBLE	DBTYPE_R8
GUID	DBTYPE_GUID
LONG	DBTYPE_I4
LONGBINARY	DBTYPE_BYTES
LONGTEXT	DBTYPE_STR
SHORT	DBTYPE_I2
SINGLE	DBTYPE_R4
TEXT (< 255 bytes)	DBTYPE_STR

Type Indicators in a Microsoft SQL Server Provider

The following table shows how a Microsoft SQL Server provider might map its data types to OLE DB data types.

Microsoft SQL Server data type	OLE DB type indicator
char [(n)] ($1 \leq n \leq 255$)	DBTYPE_STR
varchar [(n)] ($1 \leq n \leq 255$)	DBTYPE_STR
binary [(n)] ($1 \leq n \leq 255$)	DBTYPE_BYTES
varbinary [(n)] ($1 \leq n \leq 255$)	DBTYPE_BYTES
numeric [(p[,s])]	DBTYPE_NUMERIC

Microsoft SQL Server data type	OLE DB type indicator
decimal [(p[,s])]	DBTYPE_NUMERIC
tinyint	DBTYPE_UI1
smallint	DBTYPE_I2
int	DBTYPE_I4
real	DBTYPE_R4
float [(n)]	DBTYPE_R8
smalldatetime	DBTYPE_DATE, DBTYPE_DBTIMESTAMP
datetime	DBTYPE_DATE, DBTYPE_DBTIMESTAMP
timestamp	DBTYPE_UI8
text (≤ 2**31 bytes)	DBTYPE_STR
image (≤ 2**31 bytes)	DBTYPE_BYTES
smallmoney	DBTYPE_CY
money	DBTYPE_CY
user-defined-type	DBTYPE_UDT

Using Type Indicators in Consumers

Consumers use type indicators to create and alter tables and when getting and setting data.

Using Type Indicators When Creating Tables

A consumer can create a table through **ICommandText** or **ITableDefinition**. If a provider supports **ICommandText**, then a consumer builds a text command to create a table, such as an SQL **CREATE TABLE** statement, using the value of the TYPE_NAME column in the PROVIDER_TYPES schema rowset. OLE DB does not define standard type names, which saves providers from having to parse such text commands and replace standardized names with provider-specific names. No type indicators are involved in this process.

If the provider supports **ITableDefinition**, then columns are described using the DBCOLUMNDESC structure. The *wType* and *pwszTypeName* elements of this structure correspond to the DATA_TYPE and TYPE_NAME column values from the PROVIDER_TYPES schema rowset. In most cases, there is no reason for a consumer to specify values for *wType* and *pwszTypeName* that are different than the values listed in the PROVIDER_TYPES schema rowset. A consumer is guaranteed to always get a safe conversion when getting or setting values of the column using the type indicator specified in *wType*.

For example, a provider built on top of a ANSI SQL 92 compliant DBMS might contain the following rows in the PROVIDER_TYPES schema rowset.

TYPE_NAME	DATA_TYPE	COLUMN_ SIZE	MINIMUM_ SCALE	MAXIMUM_ SCALE
"CHAR"	DBTYPE_STR	32000	NULL	NULL
"VARCHAR"	DBTYPE_STR	32000	NULL	NULL

For the CHAR type, COLUMN_SIZE indicates the maximum length in characters of a value of that type supported by this provider. When defining a column of this type, the consumer is free to assign any value between 1 and 32000 to the *ulColumnSize* element of the DBCOLUMNDESC structure associated with the column. Internally, the provider may choose any representation for values of the type, provided that it always returns data to the consumer as a null-terminated string.

Using Type Indicators When Getting and Setting Data

When consumers allocate memory in which to get or set data, they generally use the type corresponding to the indicator returned by **IColumnsInfo::GetColumnInfo** for the column. When data is gotten or set as this type, the provider guarantees it can always transfer the data safely. The consumer specifies this indicator in the *wType* element of the DBBINDING structure used to bind the memory.

The consumer can allocate and bind memory of a different type only if the provider supports a conversion from that type to the type returned by **GetColumnsInfo**. Such conversions are not guaranteed to be safe. For more information, see "Data Type Conversion" later in this chapter.

String Data

The term *string* is used collectively to refer to ANSI strings, Unicode strings, and BSTRs. Where a specific type is intended, that type can be determined from looking at the data type of the programming construct that contains the string. When used as metadata, such as in a schema rowset, a metadata interface such as **IColumnsInfo**, or a data definition interface such as **ITableDefinition**, string lengths are always measured in characters. When passing data, such as with **IRowset::GetData**, string lengths are always measured in bytes.

When a consumer gets string data from a provider, the provider always returns a null-terminated string to the consumer. If the consumer's buffer is smaller than the length in bytes of the character data plus the null termination character (that is, *cbMaxLen* in the DBBINDING structure is less than the length in bytes), the provider truncates the data and adds a null termination character to the truncated data.

To ensure that strings returned by the provider are not truncated, consumers should allocate an additional byte, for ANSI strings, or two bytes, for Unicode strings, in their buffer to allow for the null termination character. The following examples illustrate three cases where the buffer size determines whether all significant data is copied into the consumer's buffer.

- When the size of the buffer is less than the size in bytes of the string (that is, *cbMaxLen* is less than the length in bytes), the string is truncated and a null termination character is added. For example, the ANSI string ABCDEF\0 is stored in a five byte buffer as ABCD\0.

- When the size of the buffer is equal to the size in bytes of the character data but no allowance has been made for the null termination character (that is, *cbMaxLen* equals the length in bytes), the string is truncated and a null termination character is added. Note that one character of data is lost, even though the size of the buffer is equal to the size in bytes of the character data. For example, the ANSI string ABCDEF\0 is stored in a six byte buffer as ABCDE\0.

- When the size of the buffer is greater than or equal to the size in bytes of the character data plus the null termination character (that is, *cbMaxLen* is greater than or equal to the length in bytes plus one, for ANSI strings, or two, for Unicode strings), the complete string is copied into the consumer's buffer. For example, the ANSI string ABCDEF\0 is stored in a seven byte buffer as ABCDEF\0.

Whether character data is stored in the provider with a null-termination character is specific to each provider. If the consumer binds the character as another type, such as binary, the character data is returned without a null termination character.

For ANSI strings and Unicode strings, the length returned in the length part of the binding is the actual length of the data in bytes; the null-termination character is not counted. For BSTRs, the length returned in the length part of the binding is **sizeof(BSTR)**, not the length of the actual string. The length of the actual string is stored in a DWORD preceding the string; for more information, see "Type Indicators" in Appendix A.

Fixed- and Variable-Length Data Types

Data types are either *fixed-* or *variable-length*. This refers to whether the provider can predict how much memory is allocated for the data based on its type indicator. If the provider can predict this (fixed-length data types), it ignores the *cbMaxLen* element of the DBBINDING structure. If the provider cannot predict this (variable-length data types), the consumer must specify how much memory was allocated for the data in *cbMaxLen*.

When the length part of a binding is applied to a column the length includes all bytes of the value. It should be the length passed to **IMalloc** to allocate a buffer big enough to hold the data value. If the value is converted, the length should be the length in bytes that the value has after conversion, in the type specified by the consumer.

If a value is truncated when it is copied into the consumer's structure then it fills the buffer up to the limit of the specified width and is truncated abruptly. No attempt is made to trailing-align or trim the value, although strings are null-terminated. The returned length is the length in bytes of the untruncated value, which the consumer can compare to *cbMaxLen* to determine how many bytes were truncated.

Note that DBTYPE_BYREF, DBTYPE_ARRAY, and DBTYPE_VECTOR are modifiers of data types and do not affect whether a data type is fixed- or variable-length. However, these do affect how data is stored and the meaning of *cbMaxLen* in the DBBINDING structure.

For a complete list of fixed- and variable-length data types, see "Fixed-Length Data Types" and "Variable-Length Data Types" in Appendix A.

Data Type Conversion

Providers are required to support the following data type conversions:

- In the type used by the provider for the column or parameter, as returned by **IColumnsInfo::GetColumnInfo** or **ICommandWithParameters::GetParameterInfo**. Such transfers must be performed without loss of data.

- To and from DBTYPE_WSTR if such a conversion is defined by OLE DB. For more information, see "Conversion Tables" in Appendix A. Note that conversions to and from DBTYPE_WSTR are defined for virtually all types.

Support for additional conversions is optional and might result in truncation of data or a conversion error. The consumer can determine what conversions a provider supports by calling **IConvertType::CanConvert** with the indicators for the to and from types. If a provider offers additional functions that the consumer can call to convert data types, these functions are described in a type library pointed to by the PROVIDER_TYPES schema rowset.

For more information about how data is converted, see "Data Type Conversion Rules" in Appendix A.

Properties

Properties are attributes of an object. For example, a rowset has properties which describe the maximum number of rows that can be open at one time, whether the rowset exposes bookmarks, and the rowset's threading model. Consumers set property values to request specific object behavior. For example, consumers use properties to specify which interfaces they want a rowset to expose. Consumers get property values to determine the capabilities of an object. For example, consumers use properties to determine what transaction isolation levels a data source can support.

Each property has a value, a type, a description, a read/write attribute, and, for rowset properties, whether it can be applied on a column-by-column basis.

Property Sets and Property Groups

A property is identified by a GUID and an integer representing the property ID. A *property set* is the set of all properties that share the same GUID. Generally, a property set is a way of determining which provider defined the property. OLE DB predefines a number of property sets and the properties in them. Providers can also define provider-specific property sets containing their own properties.

Each property belongs to one or more *property groups*. A property group is the set of all properties that apply to a particular object, such as a rowset or a data source object. Property groups are identified by a DBPROPFLAGS value that is returned in the DBPROPINFO structure. OLE DB defines property groups; providers cannot define provider-specific property groups.

Property sets and property groups overlap. That is, a property group can contain properties from more than one property set and a property set can contain properties from more than one property group. For example, a provider could define properties A and B in the property set identified by a GUID generated by the provider, where property A is in the Data Source property group and property B is in the Rowset property group.

Property Sets

The following property sets are defined by OLE DB. Providers can also define their own property sets.

Property set GUID	Description
DBPROPSET_COLUMN	All OLE DB–defined properties in the Column property group.
DBPROPSET_DATASOURCE	All OLE DB–defined properties in the Data Source property group.
DBPROPSET_ DATASOURCEINFO	All OLE DB–defined properties in the Data Source Information property group.
DBPROPSET_DBINIT	All OLE DB–defined properties in the Initialization property group.
DBPROPSET_INDEX	All OLE DB–defined properties in the Index property group.
DBPROPSET_ PROPERTIESINERROR	If **ICommand::Execute**, **ICommandPrepare::Prepare**, or **IDBInitialize::Initialize** returns DB_S_ERRORSOCCURRED or DB_E_ERRORSOCCURRED, the consumer can immediately call **ICommandProperties::GetProperties** or **IDBProperties::GetProperties** with a single DBPROPIDSET structure to return all the properties that were in error. This property set is not returned from **GetProperties**.
	In the DBPROPIDSET structure, the consumer sets *guidPropertySet* to DBPROPSET_PROPERTIESINERROR, *cPropertyIDs* to 0, and *rgPropertyIDs* to a null pointer. If the consumer fails to set any of these correctly, **GetProperties** returns E_INVALIDARG.
	It is an error to pass this property set to any method that sets properties—the method returns the same error it would for any other unsupported property set—and methods that return information about properties do not return information about this property set. If any other property sets are passed to **GetProperties** with this property set, **GetProperties** returns E_INVALIDARG. Calling **GetProperties** with DBPROPSET_PROPERTIESINERROR at a time other than immediately after the call that returns DB_S_ERRORSOCCURRED or DB_E_ERRORSOCCURRED might yield inconsistent results, because the consumer's actions might have caused the provider to clear or alter the list of properties in error.
DBPROPSET_ROWSET	All OLE DB–defined properties in the Rowset property group.
DBPROPSET_SESSION	All OLE DB–defined properties in the Session property group.
DBPROPSET_TABLE	All OLE DB–defined properties in the Table property group.

Property Groups

The following property groups are defined by OLE DB. Providers cannot define their own property groups.

Property group	Description
Column	Properties used to create columns.
Data Source	Properties that apply to data sources. These properties can be set for some providers.
Data Source Creation	Properties used to create data sources.
Data Source Information	Properties that describe data sources. These properties are read-only for all providers and constitute a set of static information about the provider and data source.
Initialization	Properties used to initialize the data source object or enumerator.
Index	Properties used to create and describe indexes.
Rowset	Properties that apply to rowsets.
Session	Properties that apply to sessions.
Table	Properties used to create tables.

For information about how a consumer determines which group a property is in, see "Getting Information about Properties" later in this chapter.

Setting Property Values

To set property values, a consumer performs the following actions:

1. Determines the properties for which to set values. To set the value of a property to a different value, the property must be writeable. However, consumers can set the value of a read-only property to its current value. For information about how to determine if a property is writeable, see "Getting Information about Properties," later in this chapter.

2. Determines the property sets that contain the identified properties.

3. Allocates an array of DBPROPSET structures, one for each identified property set.

4. Allocates an array of DBPROP structures for each property set. The number of elements in each array is the number of properties, identified in step 1, that belong to that property set.

5. Places the property's value and a flag showing whether it is required or optional in the DBPROP structure for each property. If the provider cannot set the value of a required property, it will fail to create the object to which the property applies and the method will return DB_E_ERRORSOCCURRED. If the provider cannot easily set the value of an optional property, it will create the object to which the property applies and the method will return DB_S_ERRORSOCCURRED.

   If the property belongs to the Rowset property group and applies to a single column, the consumer sets the *colid* element of the DBPROP structure to the ID of the column.

6. For each property set, places the property set GUID in the DBPROPSET structure. It then places the count of elements in and the pointer to the corresponding DBPROP array in the DBPROPSET structure.

7. Calls a method that sets properties and passes it the count and array of DBPROPSET structures. The provider returns the status of each property in the *dwStatus* element of the DBPROP structure for that property; that is, whether the property was set and, if not, why it wasn't set.

For example, assume that the consumer wants to set values for five properties, where properties 1, 2, and 3 are in property set A and properties 4 and 5 are in property set B. The consumer would use the following structures.

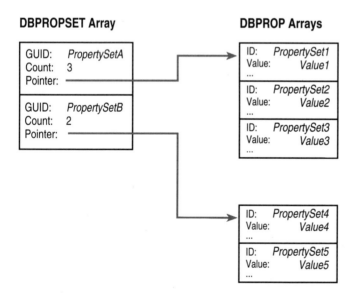

The following table lists the methods that consumers use to set property values.

Property group	Methods used to set property values
Column	**ITableDefinition::CreateTable**
Data Source	**IDBProperties::SetProperties**

Property group	Methods used to set property values
Data Source Creation	**IDBDataSourceAdmin::CreateDataSource**
Initialization	**IDBProperties::SetProperties**
Index	**IIndexDefinition::CreateIndex**
Rowset	**IColumnsRowset::GetColumnsRowset** **ICommandProperties::SetProperties** **IDBSchemaRowset::GetRowset** **IOpenRowset::OpenRowset** **ISourcesRowset::GetSourcesRowset** **ITableDefinition::CreateTable**
Session	**ISessionProperties::SetProperties**
Table	**ITableDefinition::CreateTable**

Getting Property Values

To get property values, a consumer performs the following actions:

1. Determines the properties for which to get values.

2. Determines the property sets that contain the identified properties.

3. Allocates an array of DBPROPIDSET structures, one for each identified property set.

4. Allocates an array of DBPROPIDs for each property set. The number of elements in each array is the number of properties identified in step 1 that belong to that property set.

5. Places the ID of each property in the DBPROPID array.

6. Places the property set GUID in the DBPROPIDSET structure for each property set. It then places the count of elements in and the pointer to the corresponding DBPROPID array in the DBPROPIDSET structure.

7. Calls a method that gets properties and passes it the count and array of DBPROPIDSET structures.

To return property values, the provider performs the following actions:

1. Allocates an array of DBPROPSET structures. The elements of this array correspond to the elements of the DBPROPIDSET array.

2. For each element of the DBPROPIDSET array, allocates an array of DBPROP structures. The elements of the DBPROP array correspond to the elements of the DBPROPID array.

3. Places the value, column ID, whether the property is required or optional, and status of each property in the DBPROP structure that corresponds to the DBPROPID value for the property.

4. Places the property set GUID in the DBPROPSET structure for each property set. It then places the count of elements in and the pointer to the corresponding DBPROP array in the DBPROPSET structure.

5. Returns the count and array of DBPROPSET structures to the consumer.

For example, assume that the consumer wants to get values for five properties, where properties 1, 2, and 3 are in property set A and properties 4 and 5 are in property set B. The consumer would use the following structures.

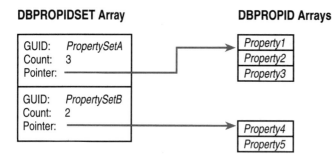

The provider returns the following structures.

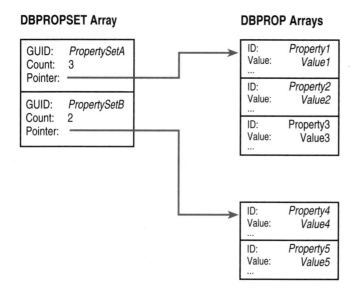

The following table lists the methods that consumers use to get property values.

Property group	Methods used to get property values
Data Source	**IDBProperties::GetProperties**
Data Source Information	**IDBProperties::GetProperties**
Index	**IRowsetIndex::GetIndexInfo**
Initialization	**IDBProperties::GetProperties**
Rowset	**ICommandProperties::GetProperties** **IRowsetInfo::GetProperties**
Session	**ISessionProperties::GetProperties**

Getting Information about Properties

To get information about properties, a consumer performs the following actions:

1. Determines the properties for which to get information.

2. Determines the property sets that contain the identified properties.

3. Allocates an array of DBPROPIDSET structures, one for each identified property set.

4. Allocates an array of DBPROPIDs for each property set. The number of elements in each array is the number of properties identified in step 1 that belong to that property set.

5. Places the ID of each property in the DBPROPID array.

6. Places the property set GUID in the DBPROPIDSET structure for each property set. It then places the count of elements in and the pointer to the corresponding DBPROPID array in the DBPROPIDSET structure.

7. Calls a method that gets properties and passes it the count and array of DBPROPIDSET structures.

To return property values, the provider performs the following actions:

1. Allocates an array of DBPROPINFOSET structures. The elements of this array correspond to the elements of the DBPROPIDSET array.

2. For each element of the DBPROPIDSET array, allocates an array of DBPROPINFO structures. The elements of the DBPROPINFO array correspond to the elements of the DBPROPID array.

3. Places the ID, description, type, property group, whether the property can be read from or written to, and list of valid values of each property in the DBPROPINFO structure that corresponds to the DBPROPID value for the property.

4. Places the property set GUID in the DBPROPINFOSET structure for each property set. It then places the count of elements in and the pointer to the corresponding DBPROPINFO array in the DBPROPINFOSET structure.

5. Returns the count and array of DBPROPINFOSET structures to the consumer.

For example, assume that the consumer wants to get information about five properties, where properties 1, 2, and 3 are in property set A and properties 4 and 5 are in property set B. The consumer would use the following structures.

DBPROPIDSET Array   **DBPROPID Arrays**

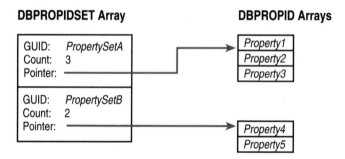

The provider returns the following structures.

DBPROPINFOSET Array   **DBPROPINFO Arrays**

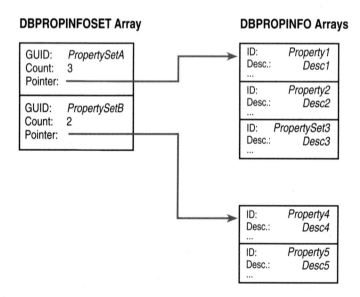

The following table lists the methods consumers use to get information about properties.

Property group	Methods used to get information about properties
All property groups	**IDBProperties::GetPropertyInfo**
Data Source Creation	**IDBDataSourceAdmin::GetCreationProperties**
Initialization	**IDBDataSourceAdmin::GetCreationProperties**
Session	**IDBDataSourceAdmin::GetCreationProperties**

Property Structures and Enumerated Types

The following structures and types are used to pass property values and information about properties. They are described in later sections.

Structure or enumerated type	Description
DBPROP	A structure used by the consumer or provider to pass a value for a single property.
DBPROPFLAGS	A value used by the provider in a DBPROPINFO structure to describe a single property.
DBPROPID	A value used by the consumer or provider to identify a property. This value is used in conjunction with a property set GUID.
DBPROPIDSET	A structure used by the consumer to pass an array of DBPROPID values that identify properties for which the consumer wants to get values or information.
DBPROPINFO	A structure used by the provider to return information about a single property.
DBPROPINFOSET	A structure used by the provider to return an array of DBPROPINFO structures.
DBPROPOPTIONS	A value used in a DBPROP structure by the consumer or provider to specify whether a property value is required or optional.
DBPROPSET	A structure used by the consumer or provider to pass an array of DBPROP structures.
DBPROPSTATUS	A value used in a DBPROP structure by the provider to specify whether it was able to set a property value.

DBPROP Structure

Consumers and providers use DBPROP structures to pass property values. An array of DBPROP structures is passed in a DBPROPSET structure.

The DBPROP structure is defined as:

```
typedef struct tagDBPROP {
    DBPROPID      dwPropertyID;
    DBPROPOPTIONS dwOptions;
    DBPROPSTATUS  dwStatus;
    DBID          colid;
    VARIANT       vValue;
} DBPROP;
```

The elements of this structure are used as follows.

Element	Description
dwPropertyID	The ID of the property.
dwOptions	The options that further describe the property. For example, when setting properties, the consumer can request that providers set the value of that property only if it is cheap; alternatively, consumers can request that providers set the value of the property regardless of the cost.
dwStatus	The status returned by the provider to indicate the success or failure in setting or getting the property value. This value is ignored on input.
	When getting property values, and the provider returns DBPROPSTATUS_NOTSUPPORTED in this element, the values of *dwOptions*, *colid*, and *vValue* are undefined.
colid	An optional ID for a column to which the property applies. To specify that a particular property applies to all columns, the consumer sets *colid* to DB_NULLID.
	This is ignored unless the property can be applied to a column; that is, the DBPROPFLAGS_COLUMNOK flag is returned for the property in the *dwFlags* element of the DBPROPINFO structure.
vValue	The value of the property.
	When getting property values, if the consumer requests the value of a property that has not been set and has no default, VT_EMPTY is returned.
	When setting property values, specifying VT_EMPTY returns the property to its default value.

DBPROPFLAGS Enumerated Type

Providers use DBPROPFLAGS values to describe the property, such as the group to which a property belongs and whether the property can be read from or written to. DBPROPFLAGS is used in the DBPROPINFO structure.

The DBPROPFLAGS enumerated type is defined as follows. These flags can be combined except as noted.

Value	Description
DBPROPFLAGS_NOTSUPPORTED	The property is not supported or the consumer has requested information about properties not in the Initialization property group and the data source object is uninitialized.
	If this value is returned, it cannot be combined with any of the other DBPROPFLAGS values.
DBPROPFLAGS_COLUMN	The property belongs to the Column property group.
	The flags DBPROPFLAGS_COLUMN, DBPROPFLAGS_DATASOURCE, DBPROPFLAGS_DATASOURCECREATE, DBPROPFLAGS_DATASOURCEINFO, DBPROPFLAGS_DBINIT, DBPROPFLAGS_INDEX, DBPROPFLAGS_ROWSET, DBPROPFLAGS_SESSION, DBPROPFLAGS_TABLE are mutually exclusive.
	For a description of property groups, see "Property Groups" earlier in this chapter.
DBPROPFLAGS_DATASOURCE	The property belongs to the Data Source property group.
DBPROPFLAGS_DATASOURCECREATE	The property belongs to the Data Source Creation property group.
DBPROPFLAGS_DATASOURCEINFO	The property belongs to the Data Source Information property group.
DBPROPFLAGS_DBINIT	The property belongs to the Initialization property group.
DBPROPFLAGS_INDEX	The property belongs to the Index property group.
DBPROPFLAGS_ROWSET	The property belongs to the Rowset property group.
DBPROPFLAGS_SESSION	The property belongs to the Session property group.
DBPROPFLAGS_TABLE	The property belongs to the Table property group.

Value	Description
DBPROPFLAGS_COLUMNOK	This flag applies only to properties in the Rowset property group and can be set only when DBPROPFLAGS_ROWSET is set.
	If it is set, the property can be applied to all columns in the rowset or to a specific column in the rowset. Whether the property applies to a specific column or all columns depends on the value of *colid* in the DBPROP structures used to set or get the property value.
	If it is not set, the property applies to all columns in the rowset.
DBPROPFLAGS_READ	The property's value can be gotten. For a list of methods that get properties, see "Getting Property Values" earlier in this chapter.
DBPROPFLAGS_WRITE	The property's value can be set. For a list of methods that set properties, see "Setting Property Values" earlier in this chapter.
DBPROPFLAGS_REQUIRED	When returned by **IDBProperties::GetPropertyInfo**, this flag applies only to properties in the Initialization property group and can be set only when DBPROPFLAGS_DBINIT is set. If it is set, the consumer must specify a value for the property before calling **IDBInitialize::Initialize** to initialize the data source or enumerator. If it is not set, the data source or enumerator can be initialized even if the consumer does not specify a value for the property before calling **IDBInitialize::Initialize**.
	When returned by **IDBDataSourceAdmin:: GetCreationProperties**, this flag applies to properties in the Data Source Creation and Session property groups and properties in the Initialization property group that can be used in data source creation. If it is set, the consumer must specify a value for the property when calling **IDBDataSourceAdmin:: CreateDataSource**. If it is not set, the data source can be created even if the consumer does not specify a value for the property.

DBPROPID Type

Consumers and providers use DBPROPID values, in conjunction with property set GUIDs, to identify properties. An array of DBPROPID values is passed in a DBPROPIDSET structure.

Within a property set, each property has a unique ID. The property IDs within a property set begin with the number 2.

```
typedef DWORD DBPROPID;
```

DBPROPIDSET Structure

Consumers use DBPROPIDSET structures to pass an array of property IDs for which the consumer wants to get values or information. The properties identified in a single DBPROPIDSET structure all belong to the same property set.

The DBPROPIDSET structure is defined as:

```
typedef struct tagDBPROPIDSET {
    DBPROPID * rgPropertyIDs;
    ULONG      cPropertyIDs
    GUID       guidPropertySet;
} DBPROPIDSET;
```

The elements of this structure are used as follows.

Element	Description
rgPropertyIDs	A pointer to an array of property IDs for which to return values or information. If cPropertyIDs is zero, this is ignored.
cPropertyIDs	The number of properties from the property set for which to return values or information. If cPropertyIDs is zero, the method ignores rgPropertyIDs and returns values for or information about all of the properties in the property set.
guidPropertySet	A GUID that identifies the property set to which the properties belong.
	If the provider does not support this property set, the method to which this is passed returns DB_S_ERRORSOCCURRED or DB_E_ERRORSOCCURRED. If cPropertyIDs is zero, the method sets cProperties and rgProperties in the corresponding DBPROPSET structure or cPropertyInfos and rgPropertyInfos in the corresponding DBPROPINFOSET structure to zero and a null pointer respectively. If cPropertyIDs is not zero, then, for each property specified in rgPropertyIDs the method sets dwStatus in the corresponding DBPROP structure to DBPROPSTATUS_NOTSUPPORTED or dwFlags in the corresponding DBPROPINFO structure to DBPROPFLAGS_NOTSUPPORTED.

DBPROPINFO Structure

Providers use DBPROPINFO structures to return information about properties. An array of DBPROPINFO values is passed in a DBPROPINFOSET structure.

The DBPROPINFO structure is defined as:

```
typedef struct tagDBPROPINFO {
    LPOLESTR       pwszDescription;
    DBPROPID       dwPropertyID;
    DBPROPFLAGS    dwFlags;
    VARTYPE        vtType;
    VARIANT        vValues;
} DBPROPINFO;
```

The elements of this structure are used as follows.

Element	Description
pwszDescription	A localized text description of the property. For properties defined by OLE DB, this should be a localized version of the description listed for the property in Appendix C, "OLE DB Properties." Generally, the description is used when displaying property sheets.
dwPropertyID	The ID of the property.
dwFlags	A bitmask that describes the property, such as the group it belongs to and whether it can be read from or written to. For more information, see "DBPROPFLAGS Enumerated Type" earlier in this chapter.
	If the property is not supported, this is DBPROPFLAGS_NOTSUPPORTED and the values of *pwszDescription*, *vtType*, and *vValues* are undefined.
vtType	The type indicator of the property. This is used in the *vt* element of the VARIANT structure passed in the DBPROP structure.
vValues	A list of the supported values for the property. This list is returned only if the property can be set and either:
	• The property type is an integer and the possible values of the property are an enumerated type.
	• The property type is a string and the possible values form a small, well-defined set. The definition of a small, well-defined set is provider-specific. For example, the provider might return the list of possible authentication services (DBINIT_OPT_AUTH_INTEGRATED property), but not the list of possible user IDs (DBINIT_OPT_AUTH_USERID property).
	If this list is returned, the *vt* element in *vValues* is VT_ARRAY combined with the type indicator returned in *vtType*. If this list is not returned, the *vt* element is VT_EMPTY. The consumer must free any memory pointed to by elements of *vValues* by calling **VariantClear**.

DBPROPINFOSET Structure

Providers use DBPROPINFOSET structures to return an array of DBPROPINFO structures. The properties identified in a single DBPROPINFOSET structure all belong to the same property set.

The DBPROPINFOSET structure is defined as follows:

```
typedef struct tagDBPROPINFOSET {
    DBPROPINFO * rgPropertyInfos;
    ULONG        cPropertyInfos;
    GUID         guidPropertySet;
} DBPROPINFOSET;
```

The elements of this structure are used as follows.

Element	Description
rgPropertyInfos	A pointer to an array of DBPROPINFO structures in which information is being returned.
cPropertyInfos	The number of properties from the property set for which information is being returned.
guidPropertySet	A GUID that identifies the property set to which the properties belong.

DBPROPOPTIONS Enumerated Type

Consumers use DBPROPOPTIONS values to specify whether a property value is required or optional. The values of DBPROPOPTIONS are mutually exclusive. DBPROPOPTIONS is used in the DBPROP structure.

The values of DBPROPOPTIONS have the following meanings.

Value	Description
DBPROPOPTIONS_ REQUIRED	The specified property value is required.
	If the provider does not support the specified property, it sets the *dwStatus* element of the DBPROP structure to DBPROPSTATUS_NOTSUPPORTED and returns DB_E_ERRORSOCCURRED. Whatever action the method was to take, such as initializing a data source or creating a rowset, fails.
	If the provider supports the specified property, then all methods except **ICommandProperties::SetProperties** can determine whether the specified value is supported. If the provider does not support the specified value, it sets *dwStatus* to DBPROPSTATUS_NOTSUPPORTED and returns DB_E_ERRORSOCCURRED. Whatever action the method was to take, such as initializing a data source or creating a rowset, fails.

Value	Description
DBPROPOPTIONS_ REQUIRED (*continued*)	If **SetProperties** can determine that the provider cannot support the specified value, it sets *dwStatus* to DBPROPSTATUS_NOTSUPPORTED and returns DB_S_ERRORSOCCURRED. If **SetProperties** cannot determine whether the provider can support the specified value, it sets *dwStatus* to DBPROPSTATUS_OK. When **ICommand::Execute** is called, the provider determines whether it can support the specified value. If the provider cannot support the specified value, **Execute** returns DB_E_ERRORSOCCURRED.
DBPROPOPTIONS_ SETIFCHEAP	The provider should set the property to the requested value only if doing so is cheap; that is, it does not require extensive resources.
	If the provider does not support the specified property, it sets the *dwStatus* element of the DBPROP structure to DBPROPSTATUS_NOTSUPPORTED and returns DB_S_ERRORSOCCURRED. Whatever action the method was to take, such as initializing a data source or creating a rowset, succeeds.
	If the provider supports the specified property, then all methods except **SetProperties** can determine whether the specified value can be cheaply supported. If the provider cannot cheaply support the specified value, it sets *dwStatus* to DBPROPSTATUS_NOTSET and returns DB_S_ERRORSOCCURRED. Whatever action the method was to take, such as initializing a data source or creating a rowset, succeeds.
	If **SetProperties** can determine that the provider can cheaply support the specified value, it sets *dwStatus* to DBPROPSTATUS_OK; **ICommandProperties::GetProperties** returns the specified value in the *vValue* element of the DBPROP structure and DBPROPOPTIONS_REQUIRED in the *dwOptions* element of the DBPROP structure. If **SetProperties** can determine that the provider cannot cheaply support the specified value, it sets *dwStatus* to DBPROPSTATUS_NOTSET and returns DB_S_ERRORSOCCURRED; **GetProperties** returns the specified value *vValue* and DBPROPOPTIONS_REQUIRED in the *dwOptions*.
	If **SetProperties** cannot determine whether the provider can cheaply support the specified value, it sets *dwStatus* to DBPROPSTATUS_OK; **GetProperties** returns the specified value in *vValue* and DBPROPOPTIONS_SETIFCHEAP in *dwOptions*. When **Execute** is called, the provider determines whether it can cheaply support the specified value. If the provider cannot cheaply support the specified value, **Execute** returns DB_S_ERRORSOCCURRED, but successfully executes the command.

DBPROPSET Structure

Consumers and providers use DBPROPSET structures to pass an array of DBPROP structures. The properties identified in a single DBPROPSET structure all belong to the same property set.

The DBPROPSET structure is defined as:

```
typedef struct tagDBPROPSET {
    DBPROP * rgProperties;
    ULONG    cProperties;
    GUID     guidPropertySet;
} DBPROPSET;
```

The elements of this structure are used as follows.

Element	Description
rgProperties	A pointer to an array of DBPROP structures. These structures contain property values. If *cProperties* is zero, this is ignored.
cProperties	The number of properties from the property set for which to set or get values. If *cProperties* is zero, the provider ignores *rgProperties* and does not set or get values for any properties in the set.
guidPropertySet	A GUID that identifies the property set to which the properties belong.

DBPROPSTATUS Enumerated Type

Providers use DBPROPSTATUS values to return information about whether property values could be set. DBPROPSTATUS is used in the DBPROP structure.

The values of DBPROPSTATUS have the following meanings.

Value	Description
DBPROPSTATUS_OK	The property's value was successfully set. This includes the case where the value of a read-only property was set to its current value.
DBPROPSTATUS_BADCOLUMN	The *colid* element of the DBPROP structure was invalid.
DBPROPSTATUS_BADOPTION	The value of *dwOptions* was invalid.

Value	Description
DBPROPSTATUS_BADVALUE	The data type in *vValue* was not the data type of the property or was not VT_EMPTY. For example, the property was DBPROP_MEMORYUSAGE, which has a data type of VT_I4, and the data type was VT_I8.
	The value in *vValue* was not a valid value. For example, the property was DBPROP_MEMORYUSAGE and the value was negative.
DBPROPSTATUS_CONFLICTING	The property's value was not set because doing so would have conflicted with an existing property.
DBPROPSTATUS_NOTALLSETTABLE	A property was specified to be applied to all columns, but could not be applied to one or more of them.
DBPROPSTATUS_NOTSET	The property's value was not set to the specified value because *dwOptions* was DBPROPOPTIONS_SETIFCHEAP and setting the property to the specified value would not have been cheap.
DBPROPSTATUS_NOTSETTABLE	The property was read only or the consumer attempted to set values of properties in the Initialization property group after the data source object was initialized. Note that consumers can set the value of a read-only property to its current value.
DBPROPSTATUS_NOTSUPPORTED	The property's value was not set because the provider did not support the property, the provider did not support the property set, or the consumer attempted to get or set values of properties not in the Initialization property group and the data source object is uninitialized.

Transactions

Transactions:

```
CoType TTransaction {
    [mandatory] interface IConnectionPointContainer;
    [mandatory] interface ITransaction;
    [optional]  interface ISupportErrorInfo;
};
```

Transaction Options:

```
CoType TTransactionOptions {
    [mandatory] interface ITransactionOptions;
    [optional]  interface ISupportErrorInfo;
};
```

Transactions are the mechanism used to define persistent units of work within an application, and to define how the different units relate to each other in a system with parallel activities.

Simple Transactions

If the provider supports transactions, the session supports **ITransactionLocal**, which inherits from **ITransaction**. Calling **ITransactionLocal::StartTransaction** begins a transaction on the session.

A session may be inside or outside of a transaction at any point in time. When created, a session is outside of a transaction, and all work done within the scope of that session is immediately committed on each method call. When a session enters a local or coordinated transaction, all work done by the session, or the commands and rowsets associated with that session, are part of that transaction.

There may be multiple sessions associated with a single data source object. Each of these sessions may be inside or outside of a transaction at any point in time, and each session that is in a transaction defines the scope of objects affected by that transaction.

Commit and Abort Behavior

On completion of a transaction, two behaviors are of interest:

- Retention, whether another work unit is implicitly started.
- Preservation, with respect to the capabilities of rowsets.

Transaction Retention

Committing or aborting the transaction with the *fRetaining* flag in
ITransaction::Commit or **ITransaction::Abort** set to TRUE commits or aborts and
implicitly starts a new unit of work. If the *fRetaining* flag is set to FALSE, the
transaction is committed or aborted with no new unit of work created—any new work
done on the session is outside the scope of a transaction. This is sometimes referred to
as auto-commit or implicit mode. Attempting to explicitly commit or abort a
transaction when there is no outstanding transaction returns an error.

Commands are always fully functional after a retaining commit or abort. The
command also remains active in the case of a non-retaining commit or abort, but the
prepared state may be lost.

Rowset Preservation

After a rowset's transaction commits or aborts, there are two possibilities: the full
functionality of the rowset is preserved or the rowset becomes a zombie. A preserved
rowset is an object with all its capabilities intact. A zombie rowset is an object whose
functionality is virtually lost. Specifically, zombie rowsets only support **IUnknown**
operations and the release of the outstanding row and accessor handles. All other
operations on the rowset produce the error E_UNEXPECTED.

The behavior of a rowset after a commit is determined by the property
DBPROP_COMMITPRESERVE. If this property is VARIANT_FALSE, then the
rowset becomes a zombie. However, if the property is VARIANT_TRUE, then the
rowset remains fully functional after the commit, with all of its rows, bookmarks,
pending changes, and so on still valid.

Similarly, the behavior of a rowset on an abort is determined by the property
DBPROP_ABORTPRESERVE. If the property is VARIANT_FALSE, then, rowsets
created with the aborting transaction become zombies after an abort. If the property is
VARIANT_TRUE, then the rowset remains fully functional, with all of its rows,
bookmarks, pending changes, and so on still valid after an abort. However, all changes
made visible to the data source within the aborted transaction are undone.

Preserved rowsets never automatically synchronize with the data source. For example,
if the transaction is aborted and DBPROP_ABORTPRESERVE is VARIANT_TRUE,
then changes undone in the data source are not undone in the rowset. In delayed
update mode, any pending changes are not undone in the rowset. The consumer must
call **IRowsetResynch::ResynchRows** to synchronize the rowset with the data source.

Even if a rowset is created with preserving properties, it may become a zombie if other objects on which it depends are destroyed as the result of an abort. For example, a rowset may become a zombie if a table on which it was built was created as part of the same transaction that was aborted.

Nested Transactions

A nested transaction occurs when a database-transaction object (the parent transaction) sets up a transaction. Changes made within the inner transaction are completely invisible to the outer transaction until the inner transaction is committed. Even then, the changes are not visible outside the outer transaction until that transaction is committed. The inner transaction object must be released before the parent can be released.

For providers that support nested transactions, calling **ITransactionLocal::StartTransaction** with an existing transaction begins a new transaction nested below the current transaction. **StartTransaction** returns the level of the new transaction, starting with *pulTransactionLevel* = 1 for the root transaction. Calling **ITransactionLocal::Commit** or **ITransactionLocal::Abort** commits or aborts the transaction at the current (lowest) level. If the *fRetaining* flag is set to TRUE, a new unit of work for the nested transaction is begun; if the *fRetaining* flag is set to FALSE, no new nested transaction is begun and additional work is done within the scope of the parent transaction.

Transaction Objects

Providers that support extended transaction functionality support **ITransactionObject** on the session. The consumer can call **ITransactionObject::GetTransactionObject** to get the transaction object associated with a particular transaction level.

Committing or Aborting a Transaction Object

The transaction object supports **ITransaction** for committing or aborting a transaction directly. This enables the consumer to commit or abort at other than the current (lowest) level of a nested transaction. Calling **ITransactionLocal::Commit** or **ITransactionLocal::Abort** on the session is equivalent to calling **ITransaction::Commit** or **ITransaction::Abort** on a transaction object associated with the current transaction.

Calling **Commit** or **Abort** on the transaction object with the *fRetaining* flag set to TRUE implicitly begins a new unit of work and the transaction object remains valid. Calling **Commit** or **Abort** with *fRetaining* set to FALSE terminates the transaction and the transaction object becomes a zombie. At this point, the only valid action which can be performed on the transaction object is to release it.

Notification Events

The transaction object may also support **ITransactionOutcomeEvents** as a notification sink. Using this notification sink, the consumer can be notified when a transaction is committed or aborted.

ITransactionOutcomeEvents is an interface implemented by the consumer in order to discover the outcome of transaction events. The consumer can call **QueryInterface** for the **IConnectionPointContainer** interface on the session, obtain the **IConnectionPoint** interface for IID_ITransactionOutcomeEvent, and pass its **ITransactionOutcomeEvents** interface to that connection point. When a commit or abort is processed, the session notifies each registered **ITransactionOutcomeEvents** interface of the outcome of the transaction.

Coordinated Transactions

If the provider can participate in coordinated transactions, it supports **ITransactionJoin** on the session. The consumer calls **QueryInterface** for **ITransactionJoin** to determine whether the provider supports coordinated transactions. The consumer uses this interface to enlist the session in a coordinated transaction. Once the consumer has joined a coordinated transaction, it calls the **ITransaction** interface of the transaction coordinator to commit or abort the transaction. If the consumer calls **ITransaction::Commit** or **ITransaction::Abort** on the transaction coordinator with the *fRetaining* flag set to TRUE, the transaction commits or aborts, **ITransaction** remains valid, and the session remains enlisted in the transaction. Calling **ITransaction::Commit** or **ITransaction::Abort** with the *fRetaining* flag set to FALSE commits or aborts the transaction, **ITransaction** becomes invalid, and the session is no longer part of a coordinated transaction.

It is an error to call **ITransactionJoin::JoinTransaction** if the session is already participating in either a local or coordinated transaction.

If the consumer calls **ITransactionLocal::StartTransaction** to begin a local transaction while in a coordinated transaction, that new transaction acts as a nested transaction within the coordinated transaction.

Isolation Levels

The following phenomena are commonly used to characterize isolation levels:

- **Dirty Read**—Transaction A changes a row. Transaction B reads the changed row before transaction A commits the change. If transaction A aborts the change, transaction B will have read a row that is considered to have never existed.

- **Nonrepeatable read** —Transaction A reads a row. Transaction B updates or deletes that row and commits this change. If transaction A attempts to reread the row, it will receive different row values or discover that the row has been deleted.

- **Phantom** —Transaction A reads a set of rows that satisfy some search criteria. Transaction B inserts a row that matches the search criteria. If transaction A re-executes the statement that read the rows, it receives a different set of rows.

According to these phenomena, the isolation levels defined by OLE DB are as follows:

- **Read Uncommitted (Browse)**—A transaction operating at the Read Uncommitted level can see uncommitted changes made by other transactions. At this level of isolation, dirty reads, nonrepeatable reads, and phantoms are all possible.

- **Read Committed (Cursor Stability)**—A transaction operating at the Read Committed level cannot see changes made by other transactions until those transactions are committed. At this level of isolation, dirty reads are not possible, but nonrepeatable reads and phantoms are possible.

- **Repeatable Read**—A transaction operating at the Repeatable Read level is guaranteed not to see any changes made by other transactions in values it has already read. At this level of isolation, dirty reads and nonrepeatable reads are not possible, but phantoms are possible.

- **Serializable (Isolated)**—A transaction operating at the Serializable level guarantees that all concurrent transactions will interact only in ways that produce the same effect as if each transaction were entirely executed one after the other. At this isolation level, dirty reads, nonrepeatable reads, and phantoms are not possible.

Locking

Transactions lock resources to regulate their sharing and isolation.

Locking may occur with any of the methods that interact with rows on the data source: these include **IRowsetLocate::GetRowsAt**, **IRowsetLocate::GetRowsByBookmark**, **IRowsetUpdate::Update**, and others. These operations take locks and may wait for locks to be released by other transactions. A lock held by another transaction generally does not invalidate an operation, but the lock delays the transaction until the other transaction has finished and releases the lock. Therefore, the default behavior on encountering a lock is to queue until it is released. There is time limit on how long to queue before returning with a timeout failure, and the timeout may be set to zero for infinite timeout. These are set as a transaction option.

Locking is implemented by the provider using a strategy which corresponds to the isolation level. These strategies vary by provider.

Errors

Errors:

```
CoType TErrorObject {
   [mandatory] interface IErrorInfo;
   [mandatory] interface IErrorRecords;
}
```

Custom Errors:

```
CoType TCustomErrorObject {
   [optional]  interface ISQLErrorInfo;
}
```

Methods return error information in two ways. The code returned by a method indicates the overall success or failure of the method, and error objects provide detailed information about the error, such as text describing the error, the Help file containing information about the error, a text description of the program that was the source of the error, and any provider-specific error information. Error objects in OLE DB are an extension of the error objects in OLE Automation, they use many of the same mechanisms, and can be used as OLE Automation error objects.

Return Codes

Each method returns a code, known as the *return code*, that indicates the overall success or failure of the method. These return codes are of type HRESULT. Program logic is generally based on return codes. There are two general classes of return codes: success and warning codes, and error codes.

Success and warning codes begin with S_ or DB_S_ and indicate that the method successfully completed. If the return code is other than S_OK or S_FALSE, it is likely that an error occurred from which the method was able to recover. For example, **IRowset::GetNextRows** returns DB_S_ENDOFROWSET when it is unable to return the requested number of rows due to reaching the end of the rowset. If a single warning condition occurs, the method returns the code for that condition;

if multiple warning conditions occur, the method describes the hierarchy of warning return codes—that is, which warning code should be returned when given a choice between multiple warning return codes.

Error codes begin with E_ or DB_E_ and indicate that the method failed completely and was unable to do any useful work. For example, **GetNextRows** returns E_INVALIDARG when the pointer in which it is to return a pointer to an array of row handles (*prghRows*) is null. An exception to this is that some of the methods that return DB_E_ERRORSOCCURRED allocate memory in which to return additional information about these errors. Consumers must free this memory. For information about which methods allocate memory in this case, see the methods that return DB_E_ERRORSOCCURRED. Although error codes can indicate runtime errors such as running out of memory, they generally indicate programming errors. If multiple errors occur, which code is returned is provider-specific. If both errors and warnings occur, the method fails and returns an error code.

All methods can return S_OK, E_FAIL, and E_OUTOFMEMORY. The reference sections list S_OK and E_FAIL for all methods. Generally E_OUTOFMEMORY is listed only for those methods which allocate memory that is returned to the consumer. The reason for listing E_OUTOFMEMORY in these sections is to remind the consumer programmer that they can generally call the method successfully by requesting fewer returned values, such as fewer rows from **GetNextRows**.

Note   Methods that return DB_S_ERRORSOCCURRED return this error only when one or more errors occur. Consumers should be aware that some providers incorrectly return DB_S_ERRORSOCCURRED when no errors but one or more warnings occur.

Arrays of Errors

A number of methods operate on multiple items or arrays of items. For example, **IRowsetLocate::GetRowsByBookmark** accepts an array of bookmarks and retrieves the rows associated with those bookmarks. When methods that operate on multiple items encounter an item-level error, such as when the row associated with bookmark has been deleted, they flag that error and continue processing. They then return the code DB_S_ERRORSOCCURRED, if at least one item was processed successfully, or the code DB_E_ERRORSOCCURRED, if no items were processed successfully.

If the consumer requests it, these methods also return an array of DBROWSTATUS values which detail the specific errors and warnings that occurred. The array is returned if the method returns a success code (such as S_OK), a warning code (such as DB_S_ERRORSOCCURRED), or the error code DB_E_ERRORSOCCURRED; it is not returned if the method returns any other error (E_ or DB_E_) code. DB_S_ERRORSOCCURRED is returned only if an error occurred; if only successes or warnings occurred, the method returns a success code or a warning code other than DB_S_ERRORSOCCURRED.

If the DBROWSTATUS value includes the characters "_ S_", it indicates that the operation on the row was successful. Except for DBROWSTATUS_S_OK, the status is a warning that something else occurred. If the DBROWSTATUS value includes the characters "_E_", it indicates that the operation on the row failed.

DBROWSTATUS values are defined as follows. For information about the conditions under which each is returned, see the methods that return them.

- DBROWSTATUS_S_OK
- DBROWSTATUS_S_MULTIPLECHANGES
- DBROWSTATUS_S_PENDINGCHANGES
- DBROWSTATUS_E_CANCELED
- DBROWSTATUS_E_CANTRELEASE
- DBROWSTATUS_E_CONCURRENCYVIOLATION
- DBROWSTATUS_E_DELETED
- DBROWSTATUS_E_INTEGRITYVIOLATION
- DBROWSTATUS_E_INVALID
- DBROWSTATUS_E_LIMITREACHED
- DBROWSTATUS_E_MAXPENDCHANGESEXCEEDED
- DBROWSTATUS_E_NEWLYINSERTED
- DBROWSTATUS_E_OBJECTOPEN
- DBROWSTATUS_E_OUTOFMEMORY
- DBROWSTATUS_E_PENDINGINSERT
- DBROWSTATUS_E_PERMISSIONDENIED
- DBROWSTATUS_E_SCHEMAVIOLATION

OLE Automation Error Objects

The following is a brief description of OLE Automation error objects; OLE DB error objects use many of the same mechanisms. For more information about error handling in OLE Automation, see the OLE Automation documentation.

How an OLE Automation Component Returns an Error Object

When a component using OLE Automation causes an error, it can return an object to describe that error. To do this, it makes the following calls:

1. Calls **CreateErrorInfo** in the OLE Automation DLL. This function creates an OLE Automation error object that exposes **ICreateErrorInfo** and **IErrorInfo**.

2. Calls the methods in **ICreateErrorInfo** to store information in the error object, such as the string describing the error and the GUID of the interface that caused the error.

3. Calls **QueryInterface** to retrieve the **IErrorInfo** interface pointer on the error object. This interface pointer will identify the error object to all OLE Automation components.

4. Calls **SetErrorInfo** in the OLE Automation DLL and passes it the **IErrorInfo** interface pointer. **SetErrorInfo** replaces its current error object, if any, with the new error object and adds a reference count to the new error object.

5. Calls **Release** to release its reference count on the error object. This effectively transfers ownership of the error object from the component that caused the error to the OLE Automation DLL.

The following code shows an example of how an OLE Automation component might create an OLE Automation error object and transfer ownership of the object to the OLE Automation DLL.

```
#include <oledb.h>
int main() {
    ICreateErrorInfo *pcerrinfo;
    IErrorInfo       *perrinfo;

    // Error occurs in a method in the provider. (Not shown.) Create an OLE Automation
    // error object.
    CreateErrorInfo(&pcerrinfo);

    // Use the returned ICreateErrorInfo interface pointer to add error information to
    // the object. (Not shown.)

    // Retrieve an IErrorInfo interface pointer on the object and call SetErrorInfo to
    // pass the error object to the OLE Automation DLL.
    pcerrinfo->QueryInterface(IID_IErrorInfo, (LPVOID FAR*)&perrinfo);

    SetErrorInfo(0, perrinfo);

    // Release the interface pointers on the object to finish transferring ownership of
    // the object to the OLE Automation DLL.
    perrinfo->Release();
    pcerrinfo->Release();
} ;
```

How an OLE Automation Consumer Retrieves an Error Object

When an OLE Automation consumer retrieves an error object in response to a return code it received, it makes the following calls:

1. Calls **QueryInterface** on the component that returned the code to retrieve an **ISupportErrorInfo** interface pointer on that component. This interface must be supported by all components that create error objects.

2. Calls the **InterfaceSupportsErrorInfo** method in this interface and passes it the IID of the interface containing the method that returned the code. The **InterfaceSupportsErrorInfo** method returns S_OK if the interface supports error objects (meaning the consumer should retrieve the current error object) and S_FALSE if the interface does not support error objects (meaning the consumer should not retrieve the current error object because it applies to another interface and method).

3. Calls the **GetErrorInfo** function in the OLE Automation DLL. This function returns an **IErrorInfo** interface pointer on the current error object and releases its reference count on the error object, thus transferring ownership of the error object to the consumer.

4. Calls the methods in the **IErrorInfo** interface to retrieve information from the error object.

5. Calls **Release** on the error object to release it.

The following code shows an example of how an OLE Automation consumer might retrieve and use an OLE Automation error object.

```
#include <oledb.h>
IUnknown *pMyObject;
extern GUID IID_IMyInterface;

int main() {
   IErrorInfo        *perrinfo;
   ISupportErrorInfo *pserrinfo;
   HRESULT           hr;

   // Error occurs when calling method. (Not shown.) Check that the current interface
   // supports error objects.
   hr = pMyObject->QueryInterface(IID_ISupportErrorInfo, (LPVOID FAR*) &pserrinfo);
   if (SUCCEEDED(hr)) {
      hr = pserrinfo->InterfaceSupportsErrorInfo(IID_IMyInterface);
      if (hr == S_OK) {
         // Get the current error object.
         GetErrorInfo(0, &perrinfo);
```

```
            // Use the returned IErrorInfo interface to retrieve error information.
            // (Not shown).

            // Release the error object.
            perrinfo->Release();
        }
    }
} ;
```

OLE Automation Error Objects and Threads

The OLE Automation DLL maintains one error object per thread. Because the consumer is not required to retrieve the error object, the OLE Automation DLL might be holding the error object generated by a previous method when a new method is called. Thus, components that return error objects must call the **SetErrorInfo** function with a null pointer at the start of each method in an interface that can generate error objects. This clears the current error object on the thread and ensures that any error object available after the method returns applies to the current method.

OLE DB Error Objects

OLE Automation error objects do not support two capabilities required by OLE DB:

- The ability to return multiple error records from a single call.

- The ability to return provider-specific error information.

For example, each service provider in the chain of service providers that constitutes a provider might want to add its own error information and a provider might want to expose error information that is unique to it.

To solve this problem, OLE DB extends OLE Automation error objects. In particular, it adds the ability for an error object to contain multiple *error records*. That is, an OLE Automation error object effectively contains a single error record and looks like this:

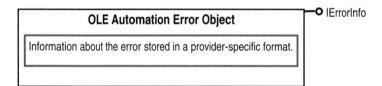

An OLE DB error object contains multiple error records and looks like this:

	OLE DB Error Object				
Rec 0	ERRORINFO Structure	Error Params	Ptr to Custom Error Object	Dynamic ErrorID	Lookup ID
Rec 1	ERRORINFO Structure	Error Params	Ptr to Custom Error Object	Dynamic ErrorID	Lookup ID
Rec 2	ERRORINFO Structure	Error Params	Ptr to Custom Error Object	Dynamic ErrorID	Lookup ID

—O IErrorInfo
—O IErrorRecords

Support for OLE DB error objects is optional. Providers can choose to generate them from all of their interfaces, from some of their interfaces, or from none of their interfaces. OLE DB error objects can be created by any method call. Although they are most commonly created when the method returns an error or warning, such as the DB_E_ERRORSINCOMMAND code returned by **ICommand::Execute** or the DB_S_ERRORSOCCURRED code returned by **IRowsetUpdate::Update**, they can also be returned when the method succeeds completely and returns S_OK or S_FALSE.

Error Records

Records in OLE DB error objects are numbered starting from zero. The methods in **IErrorRecords** allow consumers to specify the record from which to retrieve error information. As error records are added, they are added to the top of the list (that is, the number of the existing error records is increased by one and a new record zero is added), so consumers can start with the highest level of error information and then retrieve increasingly more detailed information.

Each error record is composed of five parts: an ERRORINFO structure, error parameters, a pointer to a custom error object, a dynamic error ID, and a lookup ID.

ERRORINFO Structure

The ERRORINFO structure returns most of the basic information associated with an error:

```
typedef struct tagERRORINFO {
   HRESULT hrError;
   DWORD   dwMinor;
   CLSID   clsid;
   IID     iid;
   DISPID  dispid;
} ERRORINFO;
```

The elements of this structure are used as follows.

Element	Description
hrError	The code returned by the method. This might be different in different records in the error object. For example, suppose a query processor service provider opens rowsets provided by base table providers. If **ICommand::Execute** in the query processor calls **IOpenRowset::OpenRowset** in a base table provider and **OpenRowset** fails with DB_E_NOTABLE, **Execute** might return DB_E_ERRORSINCOMMAND.
dwMinor	A provider-specific error code.
clsid	The class ID of the object that returned the error.
iid	The interface ID of the interface that generated the error. *iid* can be different than the ID of the interface that defines the method the consumer called. For example, if a consumer calls **Execute** in a query processor, the query processor calls **OpenRowset** in a base table provider, and **OpenRowset** fails, *iid* is IID_IOpenRowset, not IID_ICommand.
	If the method that generates an error belongs to more than one interface due to inheritance, this is the ID of the first interface in which the method is defined. For example, suppose **IRowsetLocate::GetRowsAt** is called through a pointer to **IRowsetScroll**, which inherits from **IRowsetLocate**. If **GetRowsAt** fails, *iid* is IID_IRowsetLocate, not IID_IRowsetScroll.
dispid	If defined, this might indicate the method that returned the error.

Error Parameters

The error parameters are provider-specific values that are incorporated into error messages. For example, the provider might associate the error message:

```
Cannot open table <param1>.
```

with a *dwMinor* value of 10; the error parameters would be used to supply the name of the table that could not be opened. Error parameters are substituted into error messages by a provider-specific *error lookup service*. Thus, the format of error parameters and how they are substituted into error messages is completely provider specific. The error lookup service is called by the code in **IErrorInfo**. For more information, see "Error Lookup Services" later in this chapter.

Custom Error Objects

Associated with each error record is a custom error object; an interface pointer to the object is stored in the record. If no custom error object exists, this pointer is null. The custom error object is the mechanism by which OLE DB error objects are extensible.

When an error record is added, the error object calls **AddRef** to add a reference to the custom error object. The provider that created the custom error object calls **Release** to release its hold on the custom error object. Thus, ownership of the custom error object is effectively transferred from the provider to the error object. The error object releases all custom error objects when it is released.

For example, ODBC-related providers can expose **ISQLErrorInfo** on a custom error object to return the SQLSTATE. For more information, see **ISQLErrorInfo**.

Dynamic Error ID

The dynamic error ID is the ID of an error message created at run time by the error lookup service, as opposed to an error message hard-coded in the lookup service. The dynamic error ID is used by the error object to release the dynamic error message when the error object is released. Generally, all error messages associated with a single error object have the same dynamic error ID. For more information, see "Error Lookup Services" later in this chapter.

Lookup ID

The lookup ID is used by the error lookup service in conjunction with the return code to identify the error description, Help file, and context ID for a specific error. It can also be a special value, IDENTIFIER_SDK_ERROR, that tells the implementation of **IErrorInfo** that is shipped with the OLE DB SDK to ignore the provider's lookup service and use the description supplied in the error resource DLL shipped with the OLE DB SDK. For more information, see "Error Lookup Services" later in this chapter.

Interfaces Used by OLE DB Error Objects

The following table describes which interfaces providers must implement to support OLE DB error objects, which interfaces are implemented by code in the OLE DB SDK, and which functions are implemented by the OLE Automation DLL.

Interface or function	Comments
ISupportErrorInfo	**Defined by:** OLE Automation **Implemented by:** Provider **Implemented on:** OLE DB object (for example, rowset or command) This interface is used by the consumer to determine whether an object can return OLE DB error objects and, if so, which interfaces on that object can return OLE DB error objects.
IErrorLookup	**Defined by:** OLE DB **Implemented by:** Provider **Implemented on:** Error lookup service The error lookup service is required by the error object code in the OLE DB SDK and is used by that code to implement **IErrorRecords** and **IErrorInfo**. For more information, see "Error Lookup Services" later in this chapter.

Interface or function	Comments
IErrorRecords	**Defined by:** OLE DB **Implemented by:** OLE DB SDK **Implemented on:** OLE DB error object This is the main interface through which OLE DB error objects are accessed.
IErrorInfo	**Defined by:** OLE Automation **Implemented by:** OLE DB SDK **Implemented on:** OLE DB error object OLE DB error objects expose **IErrorInfo** at the top level (that is, on the object itself) only so they can be treated by the OLE Automation DLL and by OLE Automation consumers as OLE Automation error objects. If the methods on this interface are called, they will retrieve the information from record zero using the default locale ID. To retrieve error information from other records, the consumer calls **IErrorRecords::GetErrorInfo** and passes a record number and locale ID. The OLE DB error object returns a pointer to an **IErrorInfo** interface which will return error information from the specified error record using the specified locale ID. Note that the **IErrorInfo** pointer returned on a particular record is not the same as the **IErrorInfo** interface pointer exposed by the OLE DB error object through **QueryInterface**. For more information about how these interface pointers are used, see "How a Consumer Retrieves an OLE DB Error Object" and "Error Lookup Services" later in this chapter.
IClassFactory	**Defined by:** OLE Automation **Implemented by:** OLE DB SDK **Implemented on:** OLE DB error object class factory OLE DB error objects are created by a class factory exposed by the error object code in the OLE DB SDK. They can be created by calling **CoCreateInstance** with the CLSID_EXTENDEDERRORINFO class ID or by calling **IClassFactory::CreateInstance** on a class factory object retrieved with **DllGetClassObject**. If the provider frequently creates error objects, the latter method is faster and therefore preferred. OLE DB error objects cannot be created by the **CreateErrorInfo** function in the OLE Automation DLL because the function can only create OLE Automation error objects.
GetErrorInfo	**Defined by:** OLE Automation **Implemented by:** OLE Automation DLL **Implemented on:** N/A **GetErrorInfo** transfers ownership of the OLE DB error object on the current thread from the OLE Automation DLL to the consumer. It identifies error objects by their **IErrorInfo** interface pointer, which is one reason OLE DB error objects directly expose **IErrorInfo**.
SetErrorInfo	**Defined by:** OLE Automation **Implemented by:** OLE Automation DLL **Implemented on:** N/A **SetErrorInfo** transfers ownership of the OLE DB error object on the current thread from the provider to the OLE Automation DLL. It identifies error objects by their **IErrorInfo** interface pointer, which is one reason OLE DB error objects directly expose **IErrorInfo**.

How a Provider Returns an OLE DB Error Object

When an error occurs in a provider, the provider can return an OLE DB error object to describe that error. To do this, it makes the following calls:

1. Calls **GetErrorInfo** in the OLE Automation DLL to obtain ownership of the error object on the current thread and to retrieve an **IErrorInfo** interface pointer on it. Such an error object will exist only if added by a lower level provider. Thus, a provider at the bottom of a chain of providers will not find an error object, while a provider in the middle (a service provider) might find such an object. Note that in the latter case, the service provider is merely gaining temporary ownership of the error object before returning it to the OLE Automation DLL.

2. Creates an OLE DB error object if none was retrieved in step 1. To do this, the provider calls **CoCreateInstance** with the CLSID_EXTENDEDERRORINFO class ID or **IClassFactory::CreateInstance** on a class factory object created earlier for this class. The latter method is faster and therefore preferred if the provider frequently creates error objects.

3. Calls **IErrorRecords::AddErrorRecord** to add one or more error records to the error object. To **AddErrorRecord** it passes an ERRORINFO structure, the lookup ID, the error parameters, if any, an interface pointer on the custom error object that further describes the error, and a dynamic error ID.

4. Calls **QueryInterface** to retrieve an **IErrorInfo** interface pointer on the error object. This interface pointer identifies the error object to all OLE Automation components.

5. Calls the function **SetErrorInfo** in the OLE Automation DLL and passes it the **IErrorInfo** interface pointer. **SetErrorInfo** replaces the current error object on the thread, if any, with the new error object and adds a reference count to hold the new error object.

6. Calls **Release** to release its reference count on the error object. This transfers ownership of the error object from the provider to the OLE Automation DLL.

The following code shows an example of how a provider might create an OLE DB error object in response to being unable to open a table and transfer ownership of the object to the OLE Automation DLL.

```
#include <oledb.h>

IClassFactory       *m_pErrorObjectFactory ;
IParseDisplayName   *pppwow;
DWORD                errCantOpenTable;
IOpenRowset         *pSimpleProvider;
DBPROPSET            rgPropertySets[1];
IRowset             *pRowset;
DBID                 TableID;
extern GUID          CLSID_THISISAM;
extern DISPID        DISPID_OpenRowset;
BSTR                 bstrTableName;

int main() {
    ERRORINFO       ErrorInfo;
    HRESULT         hr, hrErr;
    IErrorInfo     *pErrorInfo;
    IErrorRecords  *pErrorRecords;

    // Clear the current error object.
    SetErrorInfo(0, NULL);

    // Try to open the table or call another provider to do it.
    hrErr = pSimpleProvider->OpenRowset(NULL, &TableID, NULL, IID_IRowset, 1,
                                        rgPropertySets, (IUnknown**) &pRowset);

    if (!FAILED(hrErr))
        return hrErr;

    // An error or warning occurred while opening the table. Get the current error
    // object. If one does not exist, create a new one.
    GetErrorInfo(0, &pErrorInfo);

    if (!pErrorInfo)
        hr = m_pErrorObjectFactory->CreateInstance(NULL, CLSID_EXTENDEDERRORINFO,
                                          (LPVOID *) &pErrorInfo);

    // Get an IErrorRecords interface pointer on the error object.
    hr = pErrorInfo->QueryInterface(IID_IErrorRecords, (LPVOID *) &pErrorRecords);

    // Set up a parameter to pass to the object.
    VARIANTARG  varg;
    VariantInit (&varg);
    DISPPARAMS  dispparams = {&varg, NULL, 1, 0};

    varg.vt = VT_BSTR;
    varg.bstrVal = SysAllocString(bstrTableName);
```

```
    // Fill in the ERRORINFO structure and add the error record.

    ErrorInfo.hrError = hrErr;
    ErrorInfo.dwMinor = errCantOpenTable;
    ErrorInfo.clsid   = CLSID_THISISAM;
    ErrorInfo.iid     = IID_IOpenRowset;
    ErrorInfo.dispid  = DISPID_OpenRowset;
    hr = pErrorRecords->AddErrorRecord(&ErrorInfo,ErrorInfo.dwMinor,&dispparams,NULL,0);

    VariantClear(&varg);

    // Call SetErrorInfo to pass the error object to the OLE Automation DLL.
    hr = SetErrorInfo(0, pErrorInfo);

    // Release the interface pointers on the object to finish transferring ownership of
    // the object to the OLE Automation DLL.

    pErrorRecords->Release();
    pErrorInfo->Release();
    return hr;
};
```

The following code example shows how a provider adds a record to an OLE DB error
object that includes a pointer to a custom error object.

```
#include <oledb.h>

class CSQLStateObject:public ISQLErrorInfo {
    public:
        CSQLStateObject(OLECHAR );
        CSQLStateObject();
        HRESULT __stdcall QueryInterface(REFIID, void** );
        ULONG __stdcall   AddRef(void);
        ULONG __stdcall   Release(void);
        HRESULT __stdcall GetSQLInfo(
            /* [out] */ BSTR __RPC_FAR *pbstrSQLState,
            /* [out] */ LONG __RPC_FAR *plNativeError);
};

IClassFactory *g_pErrorObjectFactory ;
extern DISPID  DISPID_GetData;
extern GUID    CLSID_THISISAM;
DWORD          errGeneralError;

int main() {
    ERRORINFO       ErrorInfo;
    HRESULT         hr, hrErr;
    IErrorInfo      *pErrorInfo;
    IErrorRecords   *pErrorRecords;

    // Clear the current error object.
    SetErrorInfo(0, NULL);
```

```
// Do something that causes an error to occur. (Not shown.)

if (!FAILED(hrErr))
    return hrErr;

// An error or warning occurred. Get the current error object. If one does not
// exist, create one.
GetErrorInfo(0, &pErrorInfo);
if (!pErrorInfo)
    hr = g_pErrorObjectFactory->CreateInstance(NULL, CLSID_EXTENDEDERRORINFO,
                                               (LPVOID *) &pErrorInfo);

// Get an IErrorRecords interface pointer on the error object.
hr = pErrorInfo->QueryInterface(IID_IErrorRecords, (LPVOID *) &pErrorRecords);

// Create a custom error object.
CSQLStateObject* pMyErrObj = new CSQLStateObject(OLESTR("HY000"));

// Fill in the ERRORINFO structure and add the error record.
ErrorInfo.hrError = hrErr;
ErrorInfo.dwMinor = errGeneralError;
ErrorInfo.clsid   = CLSID_THISISAM;
ErrorInfo.iid     = IID_IRowset;
ErrorInfo.dispid  = DISPID_GetData;
hr = pErrorRecords->AddErrorRecord(&ErrorInfo, ErrorInfo.dwMinor, NULL,
                                   (LPVOID) pMyErrObj, 0);

// Release the interface pointer on the custom error object to finish transferring
// ownership of it to the error object.
pMyErrObj->Release();

// Call SetErrorInfo to pass the error object to the OLE Automation DLL.
hr = SetErrorInfo(0, pErrorInfo);

// Release the interface pointers on the object to finish transferring ownership of
// the object to the OLE Automation DLL.
pErrorRecords->Release();
pErrorInfo->Release();
return hr;
};
```

How a Consumer Retrieves an OLE DB Error Object

When a consumer wants to retrieve an error object in response to a return code it
received, it:

1. Calls **QueryInterface** on the component that returned the code to retrieve an
   ISupportErrorInfo interface pointer on that component. This interface must be
   supported by all components that create error objects.

2. Calls the **InterfaceSupportsErrorInfo** method in this interface and passes it the
   IID of the interface containing the method that returned the code. The
   InterfaceSupportsErrorInfo method returns S_OK if the interface supports error

objects (meaning the consumer should retrieve the current error object) and S_FALSE if the interface does not support error objects (meaning the consumer should not retrieve the current error object because it applies to another interface and method).

3. Calls the **GetErrorInfo** function in the OLE Automation DLL. This function returns an **IErrorInfo** interface pointer on the current error object and releases its reference count on the error object, thus transferring ownership of the error object to the consumer.

4. Calls **QueryInterface** to return an **IErrorRecords** interface pointer on the error object.

5. Calls the methods in **IErrorRecords** to retrieve information from the error object. To retrieve the error message, source, Help file, or Help context ID from a particular record, it first calls **IErrorRecords::GetErrorInfo** to retrieve an **IErrorInfo** interface pointer for that record; note that this interface pointer is different from the one retrieved in step 3 as it applies to a specific record. The consumer then calls methods using this pointer.

6. Calls **Release** on the error object to release it.

For example, the following code shows how a consumer might retrieve and use an OLE DB error object.

```
#include <oledb.h>
#include <stdio.h>
IUnknown    *pMyObject;
extern GUID IID_IMyInterface;
DWORD       MYLOCALEID;
BSTR        bstrSourceOfError, bstrDescriptionOfError;

int main() {
    IErrorInfo         *pErrorInfo;
    IErrorInfo         *pErrorInfoRec;
    IErrorRecords      *pErrorRecords;
    ISupportErrorInfo  *pSupportErrorInfo;
    HRESULT            hr, hrErr;
    ULONG              i, ulNumErrorRecs;
    ERRORINFO          ErrorInfo;

    // Error or warning occurs when calling method.  (Not shown.)
    if (!FAILED(hrErr))
       return (hrErr);

    // Check that the current interface supports error objects.
    hr = pMyObject->QueryInterface(IID_ISupportErrorInfo,
                        (LPVOID FAR*) &pSupportErrorInfo);
```

```
if (SUCCEEDED(hr)) {
    hr = pSupportErrorInfo->InterfaceSupportsErrorInfo(IID_IMyInterface);
    if (hr == S_OK) {
        // Get the current error object. Return if no error object exists.
        GetErrorInfo(0,&pErrorInfo);
        if (!pErrorInfo) return (hrErr);

        // Get the IErrorRecord interface and get the count of error recs.
        pErrorInfo->QueryInterface(IID_IErrorRecords, (LPVOID FAR*) &pErrorRecords);
        pErrorRecords->GetRecordCount(&ulNumErrorRecs);

        // Read through error records and display them.
        for (i = 0; i < ulNumErrorRecs; i++) {
            // Get basic error information.
            pErrorRecords->GetBasicErrorInfo(i, &ErrorInfo);

            // Get error description and source through the IErrorInfo interface
            // pointer on a particular record.
            pErrorRecords->GetErrorInfo(i, MYLOCALEID, &pErrorInfoRec);
            BSTR bstrDescriptionOfError = NULL;
            BSTR bstrSourceOfError = NULL;

            pErrorInfoRec->GetDescription(&bstrDescriptionOfError);
            pErrorInfoRec->GetSource(&bstrSourceOfError);

            // At this point, we could call GetCustomErrorObject and query for
            // additional interfaces to determine what else happened.

            wprintf(
                OLESTR("HRESULT: %lx, Minor Code: %lu, Source: %s, Description: %s"),
                ErrorInfo.hrError,
                ErrorInfo.dwMinor,
                bstrSourceOfError,
                bstrDescriptionOfError);

            // Free the resources
            SysFreeString(bstrDescriptionOfError);
            SysFreeString(bstrSourceOfError);
            pErrorInfoRec->Release();
        }

        // Release the error object.
        pErrorInfo->Release();
        pErrorRecords->Release();
    }
}
return (hrErr);
};
```

OLE DB Error Objects and Threads

Like OLE Automation error objects, OLE DB error objects use the OLE Automation DLL to maintain one error object per thread. Because the consumer is not required to retrieve the error object, the OLE Automation DLL might be holding the error object generated by the previous method when a new method is called. Thus, providers that return error objects must call the **SetErrorInfo** function with a null pointer at the start of each method in an interface that can generate error objects. This clears the current error object on the thread and ensures that any error object available after the method returns applies to the current method.

Because providers at each level must clear the current error object, providers should be careful not to transfer ownership of an error object to the OLE Automation DLL and then call a method in a lower-level provider. Doing so might result in the lower-level provider clearing the just-created error object from the thread and losing the information it contains.

Error Lookup Services

The ERRORINFO structure does not contain the error messages and help file information that can be returned by **IErrorInfo**. Instead, this information is stored in a provider-specific lookup service. There are several reasons for this. First, it allows the information to be easily localized. Second, it means that the information is not created and passed around until it is requested. Third, it provides an easy mechanism by which the provider can parameterize error messages.

The information in this lookup service can be created when the lookup service is written or it can be created at run time. The former case, known as *static errors*, is common when the lookup service is tied to a single database and the programmer knows ahead of time what the error messages are. For example, a provider built directly over an Oracle database might use static errors.

The latter case, known as *dynamic errors*, is common when the lookup service is not tied to any particular database and the programmer cannot predict what the error messages will be. For example, a provider built on top of any ODBC driver might use dynamic errors. The lookup service creates dynamic errors at run time and releases them when the error object with which they are associated calls **IErrorLookup::ReleaseErrors** as part of its release code. Dynamic errors are identified by a *dynamic error ID*; generally, all dynamic errors associated with a single error object have the same ID. This is not required, but it is more efficient when releasing error objects.

An error lookup service must be created by each provider that supports OLE DB error objects. The lookup service exposes the **IErrorLookup** interface. For information about the registry entries used by error lookup services, see "Error Lookup Service Registry Entries" in Chapter 14.

When a consumer calls **IErrorInfo::GetDescription** or **IErrorInfo::GetSource** for a particular record in an OLE DB error object, the error object creates an instance of the error lookup service. It then calls **IErrorLookup::GetErrorDescription** and passes the *hrError* element of the ERRORINFO structure in the record, along with the lookup ID, the locale ID, and the parameters. **GetErrorDescription** uses the information provided to retrieve the error description and inserts the parameters into this description. However, if the lookup ID is set to IDENTIFIER_SDK_ERROR, the error object bypasses the error lookup service and retrieves the error description from the error resource DLL shipped with the OLE DB SDK. Finally, the error object returns the completed, localized error message and source to the error object, which returns them to the consumer.

A similar process occurs when the consumer calls **IErrorInfo::GetHelpFile** or **IErrorInfo::GetHelpContext**, although no parameters are passed. If the lookup ID is set to IDENTIFIER_SDK_ERROR, then the error object uses the error lookup service to get the Help file and Help context ID.

Programming Considerations

This chapter discusses various OLE DB programming considerations.

Aggregation

OLE DB objects, like other COM objects, can support aggregation. To facilitate this, all methods that create a new object accept an **IUnknown** interface pointer to the controlling unknown. If a method, such as **IRowsetInfo::GetSpecification**, returns an interface pointer to an existing object, it should use the controlling unknown of the object to return the interface pointer, as opposed to using the object itself.

Registry Entries

OLE DB defines registry entries for providers, enumerators, and error lookup services. These entries contain the class ID of the component and its associated DLL, description, display name, and so on. There are several reasons for registering these OLE DB components.

- Registration is required as part of being an OLE COM component, and provides a way to instantiate an OLE object.

- Registration provides the mechanism for the root enumerator shipped in the OLE DB SDK to obtain a list of providers on the machine.

- Registration provides the mechanism for the root enumerator to obtain a list of other enumerators. An enumerator is an OLE COM server that implements **ISourcesRowset**.

- Registration provides the mechanism for the standard OLE DB error object to invoke the provider's custom error lookup service.

- Data may be available in different formats. Registration provides a way to obtain a list of data formats, and the providers which support those data formats. Data formats are created by providers, and could be provider-specific. Each provider may consider itself capable of supporting many data formats. A usage example is to group providers together and help consumers interactively decide which provider might work for them.

For more information about registry entries, see the *OLE Programmer's Reference, Volume 1*.

Enumerator Registry Entries

Enumerators are identified in the registry by the OLE DB Enumerator subkey under the class ID of the enumerator. Under the HKEY_CLASSES_ROOT key, enumerators must have the following subkeys and values for the programmatic identifier (ProgID):

EnumeratorProgID = *FriendlyDisplayName*
*EnumeratorProgID***CLSID** = *EnumeratorCLSID*

Under the HKEY_CLASSES_ROOT\CLSID subkey, enumerators must have the following subkeys and values:

EnumeratorCLSID = *FriendlyDisplayName*
*EnumeratorCLSID***ProgID** = *EnumeratorProgID*
*EnumeratorCLSID***VersionIndependentProgID** = *VersionIndependentProgID*
*EnumeratorCLSID***InprocServer32** = *EnumeratorDLLFilename*
*EnumeratorCLSID***InprocServer32\ThreadingModel** = **Apartment** | **Free** | **Both**
*EnumeratorCLSID***OLE DB Enumerator** = *Description*

For more information about enumerators, see "Enumerators" in Chapter 2.

Provider Registry Entries

Providers are identified in the registry by the OLE DB Provider subkey under the class ID of the provider. Under the HKEY_CLASSES_ROOT key, providers must have the following subkeys and values for the extension of persisted data source object files:

.PersistedFilenameExtension = *ProviderProgID*

Under the HKEY_CLASSES_ROOT key, providers must have the following subkeys and values for the programmatic identifier (ProgID):

ProviderProgID = *FriendlyDisplayName*
*ProviderProgID***CLSID** = *ProviderCLSID*

Under the HKEY_CLASSES_ROOT\CLSID subkey, providers must have the following subkeys and values:

ProviderCLSID = *FriendlyDisplayName*
*ProviderCLSID***ProgID** = *ProviderProgID*
*ProviderCLSID***VersionIndependentProgID** = *VersionIndependentProgID*

ProviderCLSID**InprocServer32** = *ProviderDLLFilename*
ProviderCLSID**InprocServer32\ThreadingModel** = **Apartment** I **Free** I **Both**
ProviderCLSID**OLE DB Provider** = *Description*

When first instantiated, providers return an interface pointer on a data source object. For more information about data source objects, see "Data Source Objects" in Chapter 2.

Error Lookup Service Registry Entries

Error lookup services are identified in the registry by the ExtendedErrors subkey under the class ID of the error lookup service. Under the HKEY_CLASSES_ROOT key, error lookup services must have the following subkeys and values for programmatic identifier (ProgID):

*ProviderProgID***Errors** = *FriendlyDisplayName*
*ProviderProgID***Errors\CLSID** = *LookupCLSID*

Under the HKEY_CLASSES_ROOT\CLSID subkey, error lookup services must have the following subkeys and values:

ProviderCLSID**ExtendedErrors** = *FriendlyDisplayName*
ProviderCLSID**ExtendedErrors***LookupCLSID*= *Description*

LookupCLSID = *DisplayName*
LookupCLSID**ProgID** = *LookupProgID*
LookupCLSID**VersionIndependentProgID** = *VersionIndependentProgID*
LookupCLSID**InprocServer32** = *ErrorLookupServiceDLLFilename*
LookupCLSID**InprocServer32\ThreadingModel** = **Apartment** I **Free** I **Both**

Note that the first two class ID entries are entered under the class ID of the provider to identify the error lookup service for that provider. For more information about error lookup services, see "Error Lookup Services" in Chapter 13.

Provider Threading Models

Providers can support single, apartment, or free-threaded OLE DB objects as long as they advertise which models are supported. OLE DB recommends that providers build free-threaded implementations, which provide the best combination of speed and safety.

The threading model of a data source object is described in its class ID's registry and by the property DBPROP_DSOTHREADMODEL. The threading model for all non-rowset objects is the same as that of the data source object. The threading model for rowsets is described by the property DBPROP_ROWTHREADMODEL. For more information, see "Rowset Properties" in Appendix C.

Single-Threaded Providers and Consumers

Single-threaded providers only work reliably with single-threaded consumers. Single-threaded consumers can work with all types of objects.

Provider Threading Responsibilities

Free-threaded in-process OLE DB objects have the following threading responsibilities:

- To implement the guarding mechanisms necessary to guarantee safe operation of the OLE DB objects, when objects are called from different threads. The choice of these mechanisms is provider-specific.

- To guarantee an operation free of deadlocks and of starvation.

- In the case of rowset objects, to shield other threads executing concurrently from the effects of methods like **IRowsetUpdate::Update** or **IRowsetResynch::ResynchRows** that may change the state of the rowset's copies of the rows. **Update** should be an atomic operation. While working in immediate update mode, all methods that modify the rowset's copies of the rows (**IRowsetChange::SetData**, **IRowsetChange::DeleteRows**, and so on) should also be atomic operations.

- In the case of rowset objects, to guarantee that all other provider-implemented objects for which the rowset is a factory (such as other rowsets or OLE storage objects) are also free-threaded.

- To guarantee a minimum of marshaling support for their use by apartment-model consumers; for instance, by aggregating to them an **IMarshal** object obtained from **CoCreateFreeThreadedMarshaler**. For more information, see the Microsoft Win32® SDK, *OLE Programmer's Reference*. The provider can perform this aggregation lazily, that is, defer it until **QueryInterface** requests for **IMarshal**.

Apartment model in-process OLE DB objects have the following threading responsibilities:

- The provider must assume that the OLE DB object will always receive direct calls on the same thread (apartment) on which it was created. Objects, however, can be created on different threads. Apartment objects belong to the same thread for all their existence.

- Apartment objects must use a proxy-stub mechanism to accept calls from other apartments. For this, OLE's **CoMarshalInterface** accepts a flag

(MSHCTX_INPROC) to describe an inter-apartment communication. In the apartment model, calls using these proxy-stubs are synchronized by OLE in the same manner as Windows messages synchronize calls.

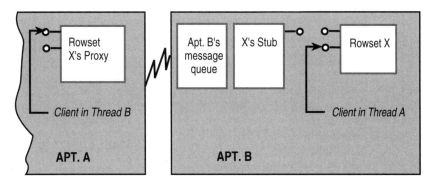

- In the case of rowset objects, the provider should guarantee that all other objects created by the rowset and returned by it, like other rowsets or OLE storage objects, are also apartment-model and belong to the same thread as their ancestor rowset.

- Apartment OLE DB objects should not share state with other OLE DB objects, because these objects may reside in different threads. The exception to this rule is OLE DB objects that have an ancestor/descendant relationship, like those created by **IColumnsRowset::GetColumnsRowset**. Because these objects belong to the same apartment, they are guaranteed to execute serially and may share state safely, if needed.

- Strictly speaking, the provider should furnish marshaling support (proxy/stub) for all the object's interfaces.

Consumer Threading Responsibilities

Free-threaded consumers have the following threading responsibilities:

- To call **CoInitializeEx** on each thread, with a null pointer as the first parameter and COINIT_MULTITHREADED as the second parameter, to initialize it as free-threaded.

- When passing interfaces to other threads, to transfer pointers directly only when a) the other thread is free-threaded, and b) the pointers correspond to free-threaded objects. The set of threads initialized as free-threaded acts similarly to single big apartment, so pointers can be freely passed between these threads. To transfer a free-threaded object to a real apartment, or to transfer an apartment-threaded object to any free-threaded thread, it is necessary to marshal the pointer at the source and unmarshal it at the destination.

Apartment-threaded consumers have the following threading responsibilities:

- To implement a message queue.

- To call **CoInitialize** or **OLEInitialize** on the thread.

- To always marshal pointers of OLE DB (and other OLE) objects to other apartments using **CoMarshalInterface** and **CoUnmarshalInterface** calls. Calls to these methods trigger the deployment of proxies and stubs by the COM infrastructure. Well behaved apartment-model consumers may interact efficiently with free-threaded servers if the free-threaded server aggregates with a generic free-threaded marshaler supplied by COM using **CoCreateFreeThreadedMarshaler**.

Threading and Notifications

In the case of a free-threaded rowset objects, **IConnectionPoint** should be enabled to handle apartment-model or single-thread listeners. Single-threaded listeners should always be called on their thread so the listeners are not unduly interrupted from the wrong thread.

The creator of a rowset must use **CoMarshalInterface** when making the object's interfaces available to other threads—because these are free-threaded rowsets, COM will stay out of the way. If **IConnectionPoint** receives an interface from **IRowsetNotify** and it wants to use that interface on another thread, it must also use **CoMarshalInterface** to move the interface to another thread. Whatever moves the interface to another thread must call **CoMarshalInterface**. The receiving thread doesn't just get the pointer, but becomes involved by extracting the pointer through **CoUnmarshalInterface**.

This entails that a rowset is written internally to use multiple threads, not just to run on multiple threads. As a consequence of this, a rowset should keep track of the threads on which a listener is connected to it.

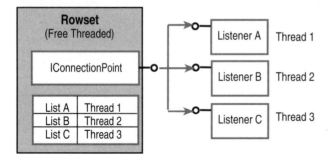

Threading and Error Objects

Free-threaded OLE DB objects should produce free-threaded error objects. Apartment-threaded OLE DB objects should produce apartment-model error objects, which will be associated to the same thread.

Since OLE Automation maintains an error object for each thread, a provider that implements free-threaded rowsets must take care of calling **SetErrorInfo** using the same thread that invoked the offending method.

Threading and Transactions

All consumers accessing a shared object such as a rowset through different threads are assumed to be within the same transaction.

Threading and OLE Objects

OLE DB supports two kinds of OLE objects in columns and parameters: storage objects and IPersist* objects.

Rowsets are factories of storage objects and determine the threading model of these objects. While accessing a storage object through **IRowset::GetData**, free-threaded rowsets return free-threaded objects, and apartment rowsets return apartment objects that will belong to the same thread.

IPersist* objects are implemented by the other parties. Their threading model is dictated by threading marking of their class factory. This marking may be absent and, if present, it can be either "Apartment" or "Both." Consumers need mechanisms to obtain information about the IPersist* object's threading marking when **GetData** returns the object. This will not be addressed until a later version of OLE DB.

For more information about storage objects and IPersist* objects, see Chapter 7, "BLOBs and OLE Objects."

OLE DB Reference

IAccessor

IAccessor provides methods for accessor management. For information about accessors, see "Accessors" in Chapter 6.

When to Implement

All rowsets and commands must implement **IAccessor**.

Accessors can be used for rowset data, parameter data, or both. Row and parameter accessors can be created on a command. The consumer must verify that row accessors created on the command are still valid following a change to the command. Accessors created on a command are not persisted with that command. Accessors created on a command are inherited by the rowsets it creates. To the consumer, it appears as if each accessor has been copied from the command to the rowset: the bindings, flags, and handle of each accessor are the same on both the rowset and the command.

Accessors created on a rowset are only available to that rowset. They are not available to the command that created the rowset or other rowsets created by the command.

When an accessor is created on a rowset or command, it has a reference count of one. If a rowset inherits an accessor from a command, the accessor has a reference count of one on the rowset, regardless of the reference count of the same accessor on the command. Calls to **AddRefAccessor** increment the reference count of the accessor and calls to **ReleaseAccessor** decrement the reference count of the accessor. When the reference count of an accessor reaches zero, the accessor and all resources used by that accessor are released. If the accessor is created on a command and inherited by the rowset, releasing the accessor on the command does not affect the "copy" of the accessor on the rowset and vice versa.

When the reference count of a rowset reaches zero, all accessors created on that rowset or inherited from the command that created it are released completely. If any accessors were inherited from the command, the "copies" of these parent accessors on the command are not affected.

When the reference count of a command reaches zero, all accessors created on the command are released completely. If any rowsets inherited accessors from the command, the "copies" of these accessors on the rowsets are not affected.

When to Call

To create an accessor, a consumer calls **CreateAccessor**. The consumer may create and release accessors at any time while the rowset or command remains in existence. When one thread of a consumer shares an accessor with another thread, it calls **AddRefAccessor** to increment the reference count of that accessor.

When the consumer is done with a rowset, it calls **ReleaseAccessor** to release any accessors on the rowset, including accessors inherited from the command. When the consumer is done with a command, it calls **ReleaseAccessor** to release any accessors created on the command. In both cases, the consumer must call **ReleaseAccessor** once for each reference count on the accessor.

Method	Description
AddRefAccessor	Adds a reference count to an existing accessor.
CreateAccessor	Creates an accessor from a set of bindings.
GetBindings	Returns the bindings in an accessor.
ReleaseAccessor	Releases an accessor.

IAccessor::AddRefAccessor

Adds a reference count to an existing accessor.

HRESULT AddRefAccessor (
    HACCESSOR   *hAccessor,*
    ULONG *   *pcRefCount*);

Parameters

hAccessor [in]
    The handle of the accessor for which to increment the reference count.

pcRefCount [out]
    A pointer to memory in which to return the reference count of the accessor handle. If *pcRefCount* is a null pointer, no reference count is returned.

Return Code

S_OK
    The method succeeded.

E_FAIL
    A provider-specific error occurred.

E_UNEXPECTED
    ITransaction::Commit or **ITransaction::Abort** was called and the object is in a zombie state. This error can be returned only when the method is called on a rowset.

DB_E_BADACCESSORHANDLE
    hAccessor was invalid.

Comments

The consumer must increment the reference count on an accessor by calling **AddRefAccessor** before passing it to another thread.

See Also

IAccessor::CreateAccessor, **IAccessor::ReleaseAccessor**

IAccessor::CreateAccessor

CreateAccessor creates an accessor from a set of bindings.

HRESULT CreateAccessor (
    DBACCESSORFLAGS   *dwAccessorFlags,*
    ULONG   *cBindings,*
    const DBBINDING   *rgBindings[],*
    ULONG   *cbRowSize,*
    HACCESSOR *   *phAccessor,*
    DBBINDSTATUS   *rgStatus[]);*

Parameters

dwAccessorFlags [in]

A bitmask that describes the properties of the accessor and how it is to be used. These flags have the following meaning:

Value	Description
DBACCESSOR_ INVALID	This flag is used by **GetBindings** to indicate that the method failed.
DBACCESSOR_ PASSBYREF	The accessor is a reference accessor.
	The value passed in the consumer buffer is a pointer to the passer's internal buffer. This pointer need not point to the start of the internal buffer, as long as the relative offsets of all elements of the buffer align with the offsets specified in the accessor. The passee must know the internal structure of the passer's buffer in order to read information from it. The passee must not free the buffer at the pointer, nor may it write to this buffer.
	For row accessors, this buffer is the rowset's copy of the row. The consumer reads information directly from this copy of the row at a later point in time, so the provider must guarantee that the pointer remains valid.
	For parameter accessors, this buffer is the consumer's buffer. The provider reads data from this buffer only when **ICommand::Execute** is called, so the pointer is not required to remain valid after **Execute** returns.
	Support for this flag is optional. A consumer determines whether a provider supports this bit by calling **IDBProperties::GetProperties** for the DBPROP_BYREFACCESSORS property.

Value	Description
DBACCESSOR_ PASSBYREF (*continued*)	When this flag is used, the *dwMemOwner* in the DBBINDING structure is ignored. If the accessor is used for row data, the accessor refers to the provider's memory; the consumer must not write to or free this memory. If the accessor is used for input parameters, the provider copies the row of data without assuming ownership.
	It is an error to specify an output or input/output parameter in a reference accessor.
	For more information, see "Reference Accessors" in Chapter 6.
DBACCESSOR_ PARAMETERDATA	The accessor is a parameter accessor and describes bindings to parameters in the command text. In a parameter accessor, it is an error to bind an input or an input/output parameter more than once.
DBACCESSOR_ OPTIMIZED	The row accessor is to be optimized. This hint may affect how a provider structures its internal buffers. A particular column can only be bound by one optimized accessor. The column can also be bound by other, non-optimized accessors, but the types specified in the non-optimized accessors must be convertable from the type in the optimized accessor. All optimized accessors must be created before the first row is fetched with **IRowset::GetNextRows**, **IRowsetLocate::GetRowsAt**, **IRowsetLocate::GetRowsByBookmark**, or **IRowsetScroll::GetRowsAtRatio**.
	This flag is ignored for parameter accessors.

cBindings [in]
The number of bindings in the accessor.

If *cBindings* is zero, **CreateAccessor** creates a null accessor. Null accessors are used only by **IRowsetChange::InsertRow** to create a new row in which each column is set to its default value, NULL, or a status of DBSTATUS_E_UNAVAILABLE. Providers that support **InsertRow** must support the creation of null accessors. For more information, see **InsertRow**.

rgBindings [in]
An array of DBBINDING structures. For more information, see "DBBINDING Structures" in Chapter 6.

cbRowSize [in]
The number of bytes allocated for a single set of parameters in the consumer's buffer. It is not used by row accessors.

cbRowSize is used by **ICommand::Execute** to process multiple sets of parameters, each of which is described by the same accessor. *cbRowSize* is generally the size of the structure that contains a single set of parameter values and is used as the offset to the start of the next set of parameter values within the array of structures. For example, if *cParamSets* is greater than one in the DBPARAMS structure passed to

Execute, the provider assumes that the *pData* element of this structure points to an array of structures containing parameter values, each one *cbRowSize* bytes in size.

cbRowSize must be large enough to contain the structure defined by the bindings in *rgBindings*. The provider is not required to check that this is the case, although it may.

phAccessor [out]

A pointer to memory in which to return the handle of the created accessor. If **CreateAccessor** fails, it must attempt to set **phAccessor* to a null handle.

rgStatus [out]

An array of *cBindings* DBBINDSTATUS values in which **CreateAccessor** returns the status of each binding; that is, whether it was successfully validated or not. If *rgStatus* is a null pointer, no bind status values are returned. The consumer allocates and owns the memory for this array. The bind status values are returned for the following reasons.

Value	Description
DBBINDSTATUS_OK	No errors were found in the binding. Because accessor validation can be deferred, a status of DBBINDSTATUS_OK does not necessarily mean that the binding was successfully validated.
DBBINDSTATUS_ BADORDINAL	A parameter ordinal was zero in a parameter accessor. If the accessor is validated against the metadata when **CreateAccessor** is called, DBBINDSTATUS_BADORDINAL can be returned for the following reasons: • In a row accessor, a column ordinal in a binding was outside the range of available columns on the rowset. • In a parameter accessor, a parameter ordinal was greater than the number of parameters in the command text. Note that some providers may support binding more parameters than the number of parameters in the command text, and such providers do not return DBBINDSTATUS_BADORDINAL in this case.
DBBINDSTATUS_ UNSUPPORTED CONVERSION	If the accessor is validated against the metadata when **CreateAccessor** is called, DBBINDSTATUS_UNSUPPORTEDCONVERSION can be returned for the following reason: • The specified conversion was not supported by the provider. For a list of conversions the accessor must support, see "Data Type Conversion" in Chapter 10.

Value	Description

DBBINDSTATUS_
BADBINDINFO
	dwPart in a binding was not one of the following:
	
	    DBPART_VALUE
	    DBPART_LENGTH
	    DBPART_STATUS
	
	eParamIO in a binding in a parameter accessor was not one of the following:
	
	    DBPARAMIO_INPUT
	    DBPARAMIO_OUTPUT
	    DBPARAMIO_INPUT I DBPARAMIO_OUTPUT
	
	A row accessor was optimized and a column ordinal in a binding was already used in another optimized accessor.
	
	In a parameter accessor, two or more bindings contained the same ordinal for an input or input/output parameter.
	
	wType in a binding was DBTYPE_EMPTY or DBTYPE_NULL.
	
	wType in a binding was one of the following:
	
	    DBTYPE_BYREF I DBTYPE _EMPTY,
	    DBTYPE_BYREF I DBTYPE_NULL, or
	    DBTYPE_BYREF I DBTYPE_RESERVED.
	
	wType in a binding was used with more than one of the following mutually exclusive type indicators: DBTYPE_BYREF, DBTYPE_ARRAY, or DBTYPE_VECTOR.
	
	wType in a binding was DBTYPE_IUNKNOWN and *pObject* in the same binding was a null pointer.
	
	Provider-owned memory was specified for a non-pointer type in a non-reference row accessor.
	
	Provider-owned memory was specified for a column for which **IColumnsInfo::GetColumnInfo** returned DBCOLUMNFLAGS_ISLONG.
	
	In a non-reference parameter accessor, a binding specified provider-owned memory.
	
	An output or input/output parameter was specified in a parameter reference accessor.
	
	If the accessor is validated against the metadata when **CreateAccessor** is called, DBBINDSTATUS_BADBINDINFO can be returned for the following reasons:
	
	• A row accessor was not optimized, a column number in a binding specified a column that was already used in an optimized accessor, and the provider did not support a conversion from the type specified in the optimized accessor for the column to the type specified in *wType*.

Value	Description
DBBINDSTATUS_ BADBINDINFO (*continued*)	• In a parameter accessor, *eParamIO* in a binding specified the incorrect I/O type for the parameter. Some providers cannot determine parameter I/O types and never return DBBINDSTATUS_BADBINDINFO in this case.
	• In a reference accessor, the value specified for *dwPart*, *obValue*, *cbMaxLen*, or *wType* in a binding did not match the format of the corresponding element in the rowset's copy of the row.
	• In a non-reference accessor, a binding specified provider-owned memory, *wType* was X I DBTYPE_BYREF and the data type of the corresponding element of the rowset's copy of the row was not X or X I DBTYPE_BYREF.
	• In a non-reference accessor, a binding specified provider-owned memory, *wType* was DBTYPE_BSTR and the data type of the corresponding element of the rowset's copy of the row was not DBTYPE_BSTR.
	• The accessor was used for passing key column values in **IRowsetIndex::Seek** or **IRowsetIndex::SetRange** and the order in which the key columns were bound did not match the order in which they were returned in **IColumnsInfo::GetColumnInfo**.
	• The accessor was used for passing key column values in **Seek** or **SetRange** and a less significant key column was bound without binding all more significant key columns.
	• The accessor was used for passing key column values in **Seek** or **SetRange** and a non-key column was bound before the last bound key column.
DBBINDSTATUS_ BADSTORAGE FLAGS	*dwFlags*, in the DBOBJECT structure pointed to by a binding, specified invalid storage flags.
	If the accessor is validated against the metadata when **CreateAccessor** is called, DBBINDSTATUS_BADSTORAGEFLAGS can be returned for the following reason:
	• *dwFlags*, in the DBOBJECT structure pointed to by a binding, specified a valid storage flag that was not supported by the object.

Value	Description
DBBINDSTATUS_ NOINTERFACE	If the accessor is validated against the metadata when **CreateAccessor** is called, DBBINDSTATUS_NOINTERFACE can be returned for the following reasons:

- The provider did not support the storage interface specified in *iid* in the DBOBJECT structure pointed to by a binding in the accessor.

- The OLE object in a column or parameter did not support the interface specified in *iid* in the DBOBJECT structure pointed to by the corresponding binding in the accessor.

- The provider supports only one open storage object at a time —that is, DBPROP_MULTIPLESTORAGEOBJECTS is VARIANT_FALSE—and *wType* in more than one binding was DBTYPE_IUNKNOWN.

Return Code

S_OK

The method succeeded. If *rgStatus* is not a null pointer, each element is set to DBBINDSTATUS_OK.

E_FAIL

A provider-specific error occurred.

E_INVALIDARG

phAccessor was a null pointer.

cBindings was not zero and *rgBindings* was a null pointer.

E_UNEXPECTED

ITransaction::Commit or **ITransaction::Abort** was called and the object is in a zombie state. This error can be returned only when the method is called on a rowset.

DB_E_BADACCESSORFLAGS

dwAccessorFlags was invalid.

Neither the DBACCESSOR_PARAMETERDATA bit nor the DBACCESSOR_ROWDATA bit was set in *dwAccessorFlags*.

A method that fetches rows (**IRowset::GetNextRows**, **IRowsetLocate::GetRowsAt**, **IRowsetLocate::GetRowsByBookmark**, or **IRowsetScroll::GetRowsAtRatio**) had already been called and the DBACCESSOR_OPTIMIZED bit in *dwAccessorFlags* was set.

The DBACCESSOR_ PARAMETERDATA bit was set and **CreateAccessor** was called on a rowset.

DB_E_BYREFACCESSORNOTSUPPORTED

dwAccessorFlags was DBACCESSOR_PASSBYREF and the value of the DBPROP_BYREFACCESSORS property is VARIANT_FALSE.

DB_E_ERRORSOCCURRED
Accessor validation failed. To determine which bindings failed, the consumer checks the values returned in *rgStatus*, at least one of which is not DBBINDSTATUS_OK.

DB_E_NOTREENTRANT
The provider called a method from **IRowsetNotify** in the consumer and the method has not yet returned.

DB_E_NULLACCESSORNOTSUPPORTED
cBindings was zero and the rowset does not support **IRowsetChange::InsertRow** or **CreateAccessor** was called on a command.

Comments

For general information about accessors, see "Accessors" in Chapter 6.

CreateAccessor always checks all error conditions that do not require it to validate the accessor against the metadata. As a general rule, this means it checks the error conditions for all of the return codes except those that return DB_E_ERRORSOCCURRED. **CreateAccessor** may validate the accessor against the metadata for row accessors created on the rowset; it never validates the accessor against the metadata for row or parameter accessors created on the command. When **CreateAccessor** validates the accessor against the metadata, it validates each binding in the accessor, setting the appropriate DBBINDSTATUS values as it goes. If **CreateAccessor** fails in any way, it does not create the accessor and sets **phAccessor* to a null handle.

If **CreateAccessor** does not validate the accessor against the metadata, then the validation is said to be *delayed*. **CreateAccessor** simply creates the accessor and validation is done by the first method that uses the accessor. If the accessor is found to be invalid, it remains in existence and can be used again.

If accessor validation is delayed, the provider determines whether the method validating the accessor validates it against the metadata before or during data transfer. If the method validates the accessor before transferring any data, it can return any of the return codes listed below for this purpose. If the method validates the accessor while transferring the data, it sets the status value of any column or parameter for which the accessor is invalid (within the context of the method) to DBSTATUS_E_BADACCESSOR and returns DB_S_ERRORSOCCURRED or DB_E_ERRORSOCCURRED. Whether the method continues processing other columns or parameters depends on both the method and the provider.

The following return codes are returned by methods that perform delayed accessor validation before transferring any data. The DBBINDSTATUS value to which each corresponds is also listed.

Return Code	DBBINDSTATUS Value
E_NOINTERFACE	DBBINDSTATUS_NOINTERFACE
DB_E_BADBINDINFO	DBBINDSTATUS_BADBINDINFO
DB_E_BADORDINAL	DBBINDSTATUS_BADORDINAL
DB_E_BADSTORAGEFLAGS	DBBINDSTATUS_BADSTORAGEFLAGS
DB_E_UNSUPPORTEDCONVERSION	DBBINDSTATUS_UNSUPPORTEDCONVERSION

See Also

IAccessor::GetBindings, **IAccessor::ReleaseAccessor**,
IConvertType::CanConvert, **IRowset::GetData**, **IRowsetChange::SetData**

IAccessor::GetBindings

Returns the bindings in an accessor.

HRESULT GetBindings (
      HACCESSOR   *hAccessor,*
      DBACCESSORFLAGS *   *pdwAccessorFlags,*
      ULONG *   *pcBindings,*
      DBBINDING **   *prgBindings);*

Parameters

hAccessor [in]

The handle of the accessor for which to return the bindings.

pdwAccessorFlags [out]

A pointer to memory in which to return a bitmask that describes the properties of the accessor and how it is intended to be used. For more information, see *dwAccessorFlags* in **CreateAccessor**. If this method fails, **pdwAccessorFlags* is set to DBACCESSOR_INVALID.

pcBindings [out]

A pointer to memory in which to return the number of bindings in the accessor. If this method fails, **pcBindings* is set to zero.

prgBindings [out]

A pointer to memory in which to return an array of DBBINDING structures. One DBBINDING structure is returned for each binding in the accessor. The provider allocates memory for these structures and any structures pointed to by elements of these structures; for example, if *pObject* in a binding structure is not a null pointer, the provider allocates a DBOBJECT structure for return to the consumer. The provider returns the address to the memory for these structures; the consumer releases the memory for these structures with **IMalloc::Free** when it no longer needs the bindings. If **pcBindings* is zero on output or the method fails, the provider does not allocate any memory and ensures that **prgBindings* is a null pointer on output. For information about bindings, see "DBBINDING Structures" in chapter 6.

Return Code

S_OK

The method succeeded.

E_FAIL

A provider-specific error occurred.

E_INVALIDARG

pdwAccessorFlags, *pcBindings*, or *prgBindings* was a null pointer.

E_OUTOFMEMORY
> The provider was unable to allocate sufficient memory in which to return the binding structures.

E_UNEXPECTED
> **ITransaction::Commit** or **ITransaction::Abort** was called and the object is in a zombie state. This error can be returned only when the method is called on a rowset.

DB_E_BADACCESSORHANDLE
> *hAccessor* was invalid.

DB_E_NOTREENTRANT
> The provider called a method from **IRowsetNotify** in the consumer and the method has not yet returned.

Comments

This method makes no logical change to the state of the object.

If the accessor is a null accessor, then the method sets *pcBindings* to zero and *prgBindings* to a null pointer.

See Also

IAccessor::CreateAccessor

IAccessor::ReleaseAccessor

Releases an accessor.

HRESULT ReleaseAccessor (
    HACCESSOR   *hAccessor,*
    ULONG *   *pcRefCount*);

Parameters

hAccessor [in]
    The handle of the accessor to release.

pcRefCount [out]
    A pointer to memory in which to return the remaining reference count of the
    accessor handle. If *pcRefCount* is a null pointer, no reference count is returned.

Return Code

S_OK
    The method succeeded.

E_FAIL
    A provider-specific error occurred.

DB_E_BADACCESSORHANDLE
    hAccessor was invalid.

DB_E_NOTREENTRANT
    The provider called a method from **IRowsetNotify** in the consumer and the method
    has not yet returned.

Comments

ReleaseAccessor decrements the reference count of the accessor. If the reference
count reaches zero, it releases the accessor and all resources used by the accessor.
After an accessor is released, methods called with the handle to that accessor return
DB_E_BADACCESSORHANDLE.

On rowsets, accessors are read-only and can be shared among threads in a free-
threaded style without synchronization. The consumer must call **ReleaseAccessor** to
decrement the reference count on an accessor that has been passed to a thread and is
no longer needed by that thread.

This method can be called while the rowset is in a zombie state to enable the
consumer to clean up after a transaction has been committed or aborted.

See Also

IAccessor::AddRefAccessor, IAccessor::CreateAccessor

IColumnsInfo

IColumnsInfo is the simpler of two interfaces which can be used to expose information about columns of a rowset or prepared command. It provides a limited set of information in an array.

When to Implement

All rowsets and commands implement **IColumnsInfo**. Service providers can synthesize **IColumnsRowset** from this so that consumers and providers have independent choice of whether they want to code for simple limited information, or to work with flexible and open-ended column descriptions.

IColumnsInfo is required on both commands and rowsets.

When to Call

GetColumnInfo returns the most commonly used metadata: column IDs, data types, updatability, and so on. **GetColumnInfo** returns the metadata in an array of structures, which can be created and accessed quickly. The metadata returned, however, is limited.

Consumers that require more complete metadata can obtain it by calling **IColumnsRowset::GetColumnsRowset**.

Note For commands that expose **ICommandPrepare**, the methods on this interface can be called only after the command is prepared or the rowset is instantiated. If a command text is set but not prepared, any calls to methods on **IColumnsInfo** return DB_E_NOTPREPARED. For commands that do not expose **ICommandPrepare**, the methods on this interface can be called only after the command text has been set.

Method	Description
GetColumnInfo	Returns the column metadata needed by most consumers.
MapColumnIDs	Returns an array of ordinals of the columns in a rowset that are identified by the specified column IDs.

IColumnsInfo::GetColumnInfo

Returns the column metadata needed by most consumers.

HRESULT GetColumnInfo (
    ULONG *   *pcColumns,*
    DBCOLUMNINFO ** *prgInfo,*
    OLECHAR **   *ppStringsBuffer*);

Parameters

pcColumns [out]

A pointer to memory in which to return the number of columns in the rowset; this number includes the bookmark column, if there is one. If **GetColumnInfo** is called on a command that does not return rows, **pcColumns* is set to zero. If this method terminates due to an error, **pcColumns* is set to zero.

prgInfo [out]

A pointer to memory in which to return an array of DBCOLUMNINFO structures. One structure is returned for each column in the rowset. The provider allocates memory for the structures and returns the address to this memory; the consumer releases this memory with **IMalloc::Free** when it no longer needs the column information. If **pcColumns* is zero on output or terminates due to an error, the provider does not allocate any memory and ensures that **prgInfo* is a null pointer on output. For more information, see "DBCOLUMNINFO Structures" in the Comments section.

ppStringsBuffer [out]

A pointer to memory in which to return a pointer to storage for all string values (names used either within *columnid* or for **pwszName*) within a single allocation block. If no returned columns have either form of string name, or if this method terminates due to error, this parameter returns a null pointer. If there are any string names then this will be a buffer containing all the values of those names. The consumer should free the buffer with **IMalloc::Free** when finished working with the names. If **pcColumns* is zero on output, the provider does not allocate any memory and ensures that **ppStringsBuffer* is a null pointer on output. Each of the individual string values stored in this buffer is terminated by a null termination character. Therefore, the buffer may contain one or more strings, each with its own null termination character, and may contain embedded null termination characters.

Return Code

S_OK

The method succeeded.

E_FAIL

A provider-specific error occurred.

E_INVALIDARG

pcColumns, *prgInfo*, or *ppStringsBuffer* was a null pointer.

E_OUTOFMEMORY

The provider was unable to allocate sufficient memory in which to return the column information structures.

E_UNEXPECTED

ITransaction::Commit or **ITransaction::Abort** was called and the object is in a zombie state. This error can be returned only when the method is called on a rowset.

DB_E_NOCOMMAND

No command text was set. This error can be returned only when this method is called from the command object.

DB_E_NOTPREPARED

The command exposed **ICommandPrepare** and the command text was set, but the command was not prepared. This error can be returned only when this method is called from the command object.

DB_E_NOTREENTRANT

The provider called a method from **IRowsetNotify** in the consumer and the method has not yet returned.

DB_SEC_E_PERMISSIONDENIED

The consumer did not have sufficient permission to retrieve the column information.

Comments

This function makes no logical change to the state of the object.

GetColumnInfo returns a fixed set of column metadata in an array of DBCOLUMNINFO structures, one per column. The returned metadata is that most commonly used by consumers, such as the data type and column ID.

The order of the structures is the order in which the columns appear in the rowset (column ordinal order). This is the same order as they appear in **IColumnsRowset**, and is predictable from the ordering of requested columns in the command text.

Bookmark columns may be returned on any rowset, regardless of its source (for example, **ICommand::Execute**, **IOpenRowset::OpenRowset**, **IColumnsRowset::GetColumnsRowset**, or **IDBSchemaRowset::GetRowset**) or whether bookmarks were requested. When bookmarks are returned, they will always appear as the first element of *prgInfo* with *iOrdinal* equal to zero. When processing the columns returned by **GetColumnInfo**, generic consumers should be prepared to receive and handle bookmark columns appropriately (that is, not display them to the user if not appropriate for the application).

GetColumnInfo provides a quick alternative to **GetColumnsRowset**. While **GetColumnsRowset** returns all available column metadata, it does so in a rowset. To get the metadata, the consumer must therefore create the column metadata rowset, create one or more accessors, fetch each row in the rowset, and get the data from rowset.

Calling **GetColumnInfo** on a command before the command is executed may be an expensive operation.

DBCOLUMNINFO Structures

GetColumnInfo returns column metadata in DBCOLUMNINFO structures.

```
typedef struct tagDBCOLUMNINFO {
    LPOLESTR        pwszName;
    ITypeInfo *     pTypeInfo;
    ULONG           iOrdinal;
    DBCOLUMNFLAGS   dwFlags;
    ULONG           ulColumnSize;
    DBTYPE          wType;
    BYTE            bPrecision;
    BYTE            bScale;
    DBID            columnid;
} DBCOLUMNINFO;
```

The elements of this structure are used as follows.

Element	Description
pwszName	Pointer to the name of the column; this might not be unique. If this cannot be determined, a null pointer is returned.
	The name can be different from the string part of the column ID if the column has been renamed by the command text. This name always reflects the most recent renaming of the column in the current view or command text.
pTypeInfo	Reserved for future use. Providers should return a null pointer in *pTypeInfo*.
iOrdinal	The ordinal of the column. This is zero for the bookmark column of the row, if any. Other columns are numbered starting from one.
dwFlags	A bitmask that describes column characteristics. The DBCOLUMNFLAGS enumerated type specifies the bits in the bitmask. For more information, see the following section.
ulColumnSize	The maximum possible length of a value in the column. For columns that use a fixed-length data type, this is the size of the data type. For columns that use a variable-length data type, this is one of the following:
	• The maximum length of the column in characters, for DBTYPE_STR and DBTYPE_WSTR, or bytes, for DBTYPE_BYTES, if one is defined. For example, a CHAR(5) column in an SQL table has a maximum length of 5.

Element	Description
ulColumnSize (*continued*)	• The maximum length of the data type in characters, for DBTYPE_STR and DBTYPE_WSTR, or bytes, for DBTYPE_BYTES, if the column does not have a defined length.
	• ~0 (bitwise, the value is not 0; that is, all bits are set to 1) if neither the column nor the data type has a defined maximum length.
	For data types that do not have a length, this is set to ~0 (bitwise, the value is not 0; that is, all bits are set to 1).
wType	The indicator of the column's data type. If the data type of the column varies from row to row, this must be DBTYPE_VARIANT. For a list of valid type indicators, see "Type Indicators" in Appendix A.
bPrecision	If *wType* is a numeric data type, this is the maximum precision of the column. The precision of columns with a data type of DBTYPE_DECIMAL or DBTYPE_NUMERIC depends on the definition of the column. For the precision of all other numeric data types, see "Precision of Numeric Data Types" in Appendix A.
	If the column's data type is not numeric, this is ~0 (bitwise, the value is not 0; that is, all bits are set to 1).
bScale	If *wType* is DBTYPE_DECIMAL or DBTYPE_NUMERIC, this is the number of digits to the right of the decimal point. Otherwise, this is ~0 (bitwise, the value is not 0; that is, all bits are set to 1).
columnid	The column ID of the column.
	The column ID of a base table should be invariant under views.

DBCOLUMNFLAGS Enumerated Type

The *dwFlags* element of the DBCOLUMNINFO structure is a bitmask that describes column characteristics. The DBCOLUMNFLAGS enumerated type specifies the bits in the bitmask; the meaning of these values is as follows.

Value	Description
DBCOLUMNFLAGS_ CACHEDEFERRED	Set if, when a deferred column is first read, its value is cached by the provider. Later reads of the column are done from this cache. The contents of the cache can be overwritten by **IRowsetChange::SetData** or **IRowsetResynch::ResynchRows**. The cached value is released when the row handle is released. Otherwise, not set.
	This flag can be set through the DBPROP_CACHEDEFERRED property in the Rowset property group.
DBCOLUMNFLAGS_ ISBOOKMARK	Set if the column contains a bookmark. Otherwise, not set.

Value	Description
DBCOLUMNFLAGS_ISFIXEDLENGTH	Set if all data in the column has the same length. Otherwise, not set.
DBCOLUMNFLAGS_ISLONG	Set if the column contains a BLOB that contains very long data. The definition of very long data is provider-specific. The setting of this flag corresponds to the value of the IS_LONG column in the PROVIDER_TYPES schema rowset for the data type.
	When this flag is set, the BLOB is best manipulated through one of the storage interfaces. Although such BLOBs can be retrieved in a single piece with **IRowset::GetData**, there may be provider-specific problems in doing so. For example, the BLOB might be truncated due to machine limits on memory or **GetData** might fail if called more than once for the BLOB. Furthermore, when this flag is set, the provider might not be able to accurately return the maximum length of the BLOB data in *ulColumnSize* in the DBCOLUMNINFO structure.
	When this flag is not set, the BLOB can be accessed either through **GetData** or through a storage interface.
	For more information, see "Accessing BLOB Data" in Chapter 7.
DBCOLUMNFLAGS_ISNULLABLE	Set if the column can be set to NULL. Otherwise, not set. This reflects only declarative rules.
DBCOLUMNFLAGS_ISROWID	Set if the column contains a persistent row identifier which cannot be written to and has no meaningful value except to identify the row.
DBCOLUMNFLAGS_ISROWVER	Set if the column contains a timestamp or other versioning mechanism which cannot be written to directly and which is automatically updated to a new, increasing value when the row is updated and committed. The data type of a version column is provider-specific. How a version column is used—for example, how two version values are compared—is also provider-specific.
DBCOLUMNFLAGS_MAYBENULL	Set if NULL can be gotten from the column, or if the provider cannot guarantee that NULLs cannot be gotten from the column. Otherwise, not set.
	DBCOLUMFLAGS_MAYBENULL can be set even if DBCOLUMNFLAGS_ISNULLABLE is not set. For example, in a left outer join, if there is no row on the right side that matches a row on the left side, the columns from the right side in the joined row contain NULLs, even if the underlying columns are non-nullable; that is, if DBCOLUMNFLAGS_ISNULLABLE is not set.

Value	Description
DBCOLUMNFLAGS_ MAYDEFER	Set if the column is deferred. Otherwise, not set.
	A deferred column is one for which the data is not fetched from the data source until the consumer attempts to get it. That is, the data is not fetched when the row is fetched, but when **IRowset::GetData** is called. This flag can be set through the DBPROP_DEFERRED property in the Rowset property group.
	For more information, see "Deferred Columns" in Chapter 4.
DBCOLUMNFLAGS_ WRITE	Set if **IRowsetChange::SetData** can be called for the column. Otherwise, not set.
	This flag can be set through the DBPROP_MAYWRITECOLUMN property in the Rowset property group.
	Providers never set both DBCOLUMNFLAGS_WRITE and DBCOLUMNFLAGS_WRITEUNKNOWN; they are mutually exclusive. Absence of these flags means the column is read-only.
DBCOLUMNFLAGS_ WRITEUNKNOWN	Set if it is not known whether **IRowsetChange::SetData** can be called for the column.
	Providers never set both DBCOLUMNFLAGS_WRITE and DBCOLUMNFLAGS_WRITEUNKNOWN; they are mutually exclusive. Absence of these flags means the column is read-only.

See Also

IColumnsRowset::GetColumnsRowset, **IColumnsInfo::MapColumnIDs**, **IRowsetInfo::GetProperties**

IColumnsInfo::MapColumnIDs

Returns an array of ordinals of the columns in a rowset that are identified by the specified column IDs.

HRESULT MapColumnIDs (
    ULONG   *cColumnIDs*,
    const DBID *rgColumnIDs[]*,
    ULONG   *rgColumns[]*);

Parameters

cColumnIDs [in]

The number of column IDs to map. If *cColumnIDs* is zero, **MapColumnIDs** does nothing and returns S_OK.

rgColumnIDs [in]

An array of IDs of the columns of which to determine the column ordinals. If *rgColumnIDs* contains a duplicate column ID, a column ordinal is returned once for each occurrence of the column ID. If the column ID is invalid, the corresponding element of *rgColumns* is set to DB_INVALIDCOLUMN.

rgColumns [out]

An array of *cColumnIDs* ordinals of the columns identified by the elements of *rgColumnIDs*. The consumer allocates, but is not required to initialize, memory for this array and passes the address of this memory to the provider. The provider returns the column IDs in the array.

Return Code

S_OK

The method succeeded. All elements of *rgColumns* are set to values other than DB_INVALIDCOLUMN.

DB_S_ERRORSOCCURRED

An element of *rgColumnIDs* was invalid. If the column ID is invalid, the corresponding element of *rgColumns* is set to DB_INVALIDCOLUMN.

E_FAIL

A provider-specific error occurred.

E_INVALIDARG

cColumnIDs was not zero and *rgColumnIDs* was a null pointer.

rgColumns was a null pointer.

E_UNEXPECTED

ITransaction::Commit or **ITransaction::Abort** was called and the object is in a zombie state. This error can be returned only when the method is called on a rowset.

DB_E_ERRORSOCCURRED

All elements of *rgColumnIDs* were invalid. All elements of *rgColumns* are set to DB_INVALIDCOLUMN.

DB_E_NOCOMMAND

No command text was set. This error can be returned only when this method is called from the command object.

DB_E_NOTPREPARED

The command exposed **ICommandPrepare** and the command text was set, but the command was not prepared. This error can be returned only when this method is called from the command object.

DB_E_NOTREENTRANT

The provider called a method from **IRowsetNotify** in the consumer and the method has not yet returned.

Comments

This method makes no logical change to the state of the object.

MapColumnIDs returns the ordinals of the columns in the rowset that are identified by the elements of *rgColumnIDs*. These column ordinals do not change during the life of the rowset. Column ordinals may change between different instantiations of a rowset if the command text does not define an order, such as a **SELECT * FROM MyTable**.

Two column IDs that are the same except that one contains a GUID and the other contains a pointer to a GUID are equivalent if both use the same GUID. Both are mapped to the same column ordinal.

See Also

IColumnsInfo::GetColumnInfo, IColumnsRowset::GetColumnsRowset

IColumnsRowset

This interface supplies complete information about columns in a rowset. The methods in it can be called from a rowset or a command.

When to Implement

Advanced providers implement this interface.

A service provider can be used to synthesize **IColumnsRowset** from the simpler **IColumnsInfo** (with defaults and NULL values to round out the information).

IColumnsRowset is optional on both commands and rowsets.

When to Call

Consumers use the methods in **IColumnsRowset** for detailed and flexible information about the columns of a rowset.

Note For commands that expose **ICommandPrepare**, the methods on this interface can be called only after the command is prepared or the rowset is instantiated. If a command text is set but not prepared, any calls to methods on **IColumnsInfo** return DB_E_NOTPREPARED. For commands that do not expose **ICommandPrepare**, the methods on this interface can be called only after the command text has been set.

Method	Description
GetAvailableColumns	Returns a list of optional metadata columns that can be supplied in a column's rowset.
GetColumnsRowset	Returns a rowset containing metadata about each column in the current rowset. The rowset is known as the *column metadata rowset* and is read-only.

IColumnsRowset::GetAvailableColumns

Returns a list of optional metadata columns that can be supplied in a column metadata rowset.

HRESULT GetAvailableColumns (
    ULONG *   *pcOptColumns*,
    DBID **   *prgOptColumns*);

Parameters

pcOptColumns [out]

A pointer to memory in which to return the count of the elements in **prgOptColumns*. If an error occurs, **pcOptColumns* is set to zero.

prgOptColumns [out]

A pointer to memory in which to return an array of the optional columns this provider can supply. In addition to the optional columns listed in **GetColumnsRowset**, the provider can return provider-specific columns. The rowset or command allocates memory for the structures and returns the address to this memory; the consumer releases this memory with **IMalloc::Free** when it no longer needs the list of columns. If **pcOptColumns* is zero on output or an error occurs, the provider does not allocate any memory and ensures that **prgOptColumns* is a null pointer on output.

Return Code

S_OK

The method succeeded.

E_FAIL

A provider-specific error occurred.

E_INVALIDARG

pcOptColumns or *prgOptColumns* was a null pointer.

E_OUTOFMEMORY

The provider was unable to allocate sufficient memory in which to return the column IDs.

E_UNEXPECTED

ITransaction::Commit or **ITransaction::Abort** was called and the object is in a zombie state. This error can be returned only when the method is called on a rowset.

DB_E_NOCOMMAND

No command text was set. This error can be returned only when this method is called from the command object.

DB_E_NOTPREPARED

The command exposed **ICommandPrepare** and the command text was set, but the command was not prepared. This error can be returned only when this method is called from the command object.

DB_E_NOTREENTRANT

The provider called a method from **IRowsetNotify** in the consumer and the method has not yet returned.

DB_SEC_E_PERMISSIONDENIED

The consumer did not have sufficient permission to retrieve the available optional metadata columns.

Comments

This method makes no logical change to the state of the object.

Calling **GetAvailableColumns** on a command before the command is executed may be an expensive operation.

See Also

IColumnsRowset::GetColumnsRowset

IColumnsRowset::GetColumnsRowset

Returns a rowset containing metadata about each column in the current rowset. This rowset is known as the *column metadata rowset* and is read-only.

HRESULT GetColumnsRowset (
IUnknown *	*pUnkOuter*,
ULONG	*cOptColumns*,
const DBID	*rgOptColumns*[],
REFIID	*riid*,
ULONG	*cPropertySets*,
DBPROPSET	*rgPropertySets*[],
IUnknown **	*ppColRowset*);

Parameters

pUnkOuter [in]

A pointer to the controlling **IUnknown** interface if the column metadata rowset is being created as part of an aggregate. It is a null pointer if the rowset is not part of an aggregate.

cOptColumns [in]

The number of the elements in *rgOptColumns*. If *cOptColumns* is zero, then *rgOptColumns* is ignored, and the provider returns all available columns in the columns rowset.

rgOptColumns [in]

An array that specifies the optional columns to return. In addition to the optional columns listed below, the consumer can request provider-specific columns.

riid [in]

The IID of the requested rowset interface.

cPropertySets [in]

The number of DBPROPSET structures in *rgPropertySets*. If this is zero, the provider ignores *rgPropertySets*.

rgPropertySets [in/out]

An array of DBPROPSET structures containing properties and values to be set. The properties specified in these structures must belong to the Rowset property group. If the same property is specified more than once in *rgPropertySets*, then it is provider-specific which value is used. If *cPropertySets* is zero, this argument is ignored.

For information about the properties in the Rowset property group that are defined by OLE DB, see "Rowset Properties" in Appendix C. For information about the DBPROPSET and DBPROP structures, see "DBPROPSET Structure" and "DBPROP Structure" in Chapter 11.

ppColRowset [out]

A pointer to memory in which to return the requested interface pointer on the column metadata rowset. If an error occurs, the returned pointer is null. If **GetColumnsRowset** is called on a command that does not return rows, then the column metadata rowset will be empty.

Return Code

S_OK

The method succeeded. In all DBPROP structures passed to the method, *dwStatus* is set to DBPROPSTATUS_OK.

DB_S_ERRORSOCCURRED

The rowset was opened but one or more properties—for which the *dwOptions* element of the DBPROP structure was DBPROPOPTIONS_SETIFCHEAP—were not set. The consumer checks *dwStatus* in the DBPROP structures to determine which properties were not set. The method can fail to set properties for a number of reasons, including:

- The property was not supported by the provider.
- The property was not in the Rowset property group.
- The property set was not supported by the provider.
- It was not cheap to set the property.
- *colid* in the DBPROP structure was invalid.
- The data type in *vValue* in the DBPROP structure was not the data type of the property or was not VT_EMPTY.
- The value in *vValue* in the DBPROP structure was invalid.
- The property's value conflicted with an existing property.
- A property was specified to be applied to all columns, but could not be applied to one or more columns.

E_FAIL

A provider-specific error occurred.

E_INVALIDARG

ppColRowset was a null pointer.

cPropertySets was greater than 0 and *rgPropertySets* was a null pointer.

In an element of *rgPropertySets*, *cProperties* was not zero and *rgProperties* was a null pointer.

E_NOINTERFACE

The column metadata rowset did not support the interface specified in *riid*.

E_UNEXPECTED

ITransaction::Commit or **ITransaction::Abort** was called and the object is in a zombie state. This error can be returned only when the method is called on a rowset.

DB_E_ABORTLIMITREACHED

The method failed because a resource limit has been reached. For example, a query used to implement the method timed out. No rowset is returned.

DB_E_BADCOLUMNID

An element of *rgOptColumns* was an invalid DBID.

DB_E_ERRORSOCCURRED

No rowset was returned because one or more properties—for which the *dwOptions* element of the DBPROP structure was DBPROPOPTIONS_REQUIRED or an invalid value—were not set. The consumer checks *dwStatus* in the DBPROP structures to determine which properties were not set. None of the satisfiable properties are remembered. The method can fail to set properties for any of the reasons specified in DB_S_ERRORSOCCURRED except the reason that states that it was not cheap to set the property.

DB_E_NOAGGREGATION

pUnkOuter was not a null pointer and the columns' rowset does not support aggregation.

DB_E_NOCOMMAND

No command text was set. This error can be returned only when this method is called from the command object.

DB_E_NOTPREPARED

The command exposed **ICommandPrepare** and the command text was set, but the command was not prepared. This error can be returned only when this method is called from the command object.

DB_E_NOTREENTRANT

The provider called a method from **IRowsetNotify** in the consumer and the method has not yet returned.

DB_SEC_E_PERMISSIONDENIED

The consumer did not have sufficient permission to create the column metadata rowset.

Comments

This method makes no logical change to the state of the object.

GetColumnsRowset creates a rowset containing metadata about a rowset. Unlike **IColumnsInfo::GetColumnInfo**, it provides all of the metadata, but it is more complex to implement and use.

The rows in the column metadata rowset describe the columns in the underlying rowset. The column metadata rowset contains one row for each column in the rowset. This includes the columns of the base table and any pseudo-columns generated by the provider or data source, such as bookmarks and row IDs.

The order of the rows is the order in which the columns appear in the rowset (column ordinal order). This is the same order as they appear in **IColumnsInfo**. The order is usually predictable from the ordering of requested columns in the command text; if the command text does not specify an order, such as **SELECT * FROM MyTable**, then the order is determined by the provider, such as when the command is prepared.

Each column in the column metadata rowset describes a single attribute, such as the name or data type, of a column in the original rowset. The order of the required columns is the same as the order in which they are listed below. The order of the optional columns is arbitrary, although they must be after the required columns. That is, the optional columns in the column metadata rowset can occur in any order after the required columns.

The column metadata rowset always includes the required columns. It contains only those optional columns which are requested.

GetColumnsRowset can be called for rowsets created by **GetColumnsRowset**.

Calling **GetColumnsRowset** on a command before the command is executed may be an expensive operation.

Required Metadata Columns

The column metadata rowset always contains the following columns; these columns return the same information as **GetColumnInfo**.

Column ID	Type Indicator	Description
DBCOLUMN_IDNAME	DBTYPE_WSTR	Column name. This column, together with the DBCOLUMN_GUID and DBCOLUMN_PROPID columns, form the ID of the column. One or more of these columns will be NULL depending on which elements of the DBID structure the provider uses. The column ID of a base table should be invariant under views.
DBCOLUMN_GUID	DBTYPE_GUID	Column GUID.
DBCOLUMN_PROPID	DBTYPE_UI4	Column property ID.
DBCOLUMN_NAME	DBTYPE_WSTR	The name of the column; this might not be unique. If this cannot be determined, a NULL is returned. The name can be different from the value returned in DBCOLUMN_IDNAME if the column has been renamed by the command text. This name always reflects the most recent renaming of the column in the current view or command text. If **GetColumnsRowset** is called for a column metadata rowset (the rowset returned by **GetColumnsRowset**), the name of each column is the name of the column ID constant. For example, the name of the DBCOLUMN_SCALE column is "DBCOLUMN_SCALE".

Column ID	Type Indicator	Description
DBCOLUMN_NUMBER	DBTYPE_UI4	The ordinal of the column. This is zero for the bookmark column of the row, if any. Other columns are numbered starting with one. This column cannot contain a NULL value.
DBCOLUMN_TYPE	DBTYPE_UI2	The indicator of the column's data type. If the data type of the column varies from row to row, this must be DBTYPE_VARIANT. This column cannot contain a NULL value. For a list of valid type indicators, see "Type Indicators" in Appendix A.
DBCOLUMN_TYPEINFO	DBTYPE_ IUNKNOWN	Reserved for future use. Providers should return a null pointer in *pTypeInfo*.
DBCOLUMN_ COLUMNSIZE	DBTYPE_UI4	The maximum possible length of a value in the column. For columns that use a fixed-length data type, this is the size of the data type. For columns that use a variable-length data type, this is one of the following: <ul><li>The maximum length of the column in characters, for DBTYPE_STR and DBTYPE_WSTR, or bytes, for DBTYPE_BYTES, if one is defined. For example, a CHAR(5) column in an SQL table has a maximum length of 5.</li><li>The maximum length of the data type in characters, for DBTYPE_STR and DBTYPE_WSTR, or bytes, for DBTYPE_BYTES, if the column does not have a defined length.</li><li>~0 (bitwise, the value is not 0; that is, all bits are set to 1) if neither the column nor the data type has a defined maximum length.</li></ul>For data types that do not have a length, this is set to ~0 (bitwise, the value is not 0; that is, all bits are set to 1).
DBCOLUMN_ PRECISION	DBTYPE_UI2	If DBCOLUMN_TYPE is a numeric data type, this is the maximum precision of the column. The precision of columns with a data type of DBTYPE_DECIMAL or DBTYPE_NUMERIC depends on the definition of the column. For the precision of all other numeric data types, see "Precision of Numeric Data Types" in Appendix A. If DBCOLUMN_TYPE is not a numeric data type, this is NULL.

Column ID	Type Indicator	Description
DBCOLUMN_SCALE	DBTYPE_I2	If DBCOLUMN_TYPE is DBTYPE_DECIMAL or DBTYPE_NUMERIC, this is the number of digits to the right of the decimal point. Otherwise, this is NULL.
DBCOLUMN_FLAGS	DBTYPE_UI4	A bitmask that describes column characteristics. The DBCOLUMNFLAGS enumerated type specifies the bits in the bitmask. For more information, see **IColumnsInfo::GetColumnInfo**. This column cannot contain a NULL value.

Optional Metadata Columns

The following columns are optional; if the column metadata rowset does not contain one of them, the consumer can safely use the default value. The default value is the value the consumer should assume if the provider does not support that information. It is also the value the column metadata rowset returns when the provider does have support, but does not specify that information for a particular column. The provider can also have optional, provider-specific columns.

Column ID	Type Indicator	Description
DBCOLUMN_ BASECATALOGNAME	DBTYPE_WSTR	The name of the catalog in the data source that contains the column. NULL if the base catalog name cannot be determined. The default of this column is NULL.
DBCOLUMN_ BASECOLUMNNAME	DBTYPE_WSTR	The name of the column in the data source. This might be different than the column name returned in the DBCOLUMN_NAME column if an alias was used. NULL if the base column name cannot be determined. The default of this column is NULL.
DBCOLUMN_ BASESCHEMANAME	DBTYPE_WSTR	The name of the schema in the data source that contains the column. NULL if the base schema name cannot be determined. The default of this column is NULL.
DBCOLUMN_ BASETABLENAME	DBTYPE_WSTR	The name of the table in the data source that contains the column. NULL if the base table name cannot be determined. The default of this column is NULL.
DBCOLUMN_CLSID	DBTYPE_GUID	If all objects in the column all have the same class ID, this is that class ID. If the column may contain objects with different class IDs, or if the column is not of DBTYPE_IUNKNOWN, this is set to NULL. The default of this column is NULL.

Column ID	Type Indicator	Description
DBCOLUMN_ COLLATINGSEQUENCE	DBTYPE_I4	The locale ID (LCID) that defines the collating sequence for the column. For more information, see the OLE documentation. The default of this column is the code page installed on the local machine.
DBCOLUMN_ COMPUTEMODE	DBTYPE_I4	Whether a column is computed. One of the following: DBCOMPUTEMODE_COMPUTED: The column is computed, such as Salary/12. DBCOMPUTEMODE_DYNAMIC: The column is computed and **IRowset::GetData** returns the value of the column based on the current values of its component columns, which might have been changed with **IRowsetChange::SetData** or **IRowsetChange::InsertRow**. DBCOMPUTEDMODE_NOTCOMPUTED: The column is not computed. This is the default.
DBCOLUMN_ DATETIMEPRECISION	DBTYPE_UI4	The datetime precision—number of digits in the fractional seconds portion—if the column is a datetime or interval type. The default of this column is derived from the value in column DATETIME_PRECISION in the COLUMNS schema rowset.
DBCOLUMN_ DEFAULTVALUE	DBTYPE_ VARIANT	The column default value if declared statically. Dynamic initialization is handled by notifications. NULL if the default value cannot be determined. For a list of possible values, see the COLUMN_DEFAULT in "COLUMNS Rowset" in Appendix B. The default of this column is NULL.
DBCOLUMN_ DOMAINCATALOG	DBTYPE_WSTR	The name of the catalog containing the column's domain. NULL if the domain catalog name cannot be determined. The default of this column is NULL.
DBCOLUMN_ DOMAINSCHEMA	DBTYPE_WSTR	The name of the schema containing the column's domain. NULL if the domain schema name cannot be determined. The default of this column is NULL.

Column ID	Type Indicator	Description
DBCOLUMN_DOMAINNAME	DBTYPE_WSTR	The name of the domain of which the column is a member. NULL if the domain name cannot be determined. The default of this column is NULL.
DBCOLUMN_HASDEFAULT	DBTYPE_BOOL	VARIANT_TRUE: The column has a default value. VARIANT_FALSE: The column does not have a default value. NULL: The provider could not determine if the column has a default value or if a default value does not make sense for the column. For example, it is a computed, derived, or non-updatable column. The default of this column is VARIANT_FALSE.
DBCOLUMN_ISAUTOINCREMENT	DBTYPE_BOOL	VARIANT_TRUE: The column assigns values to new rows in fixed increments. VARIANT_FALSE: The column does not assign values to new rows in fixed increments. The default of this column is VARIANT_FALSE.
DBCOLUMN_ISCASESENSITIVE	DBTYPE_BOOL	VARIANT_TRUE if the order of the column is case sensitive and if searches on the column are case sensitive. Otherwise, VARIANT_FALSE. The default of this column is VARIANT_TRUE.
DBCOLUMN_ISSEARCHABLE	DBTYPE_UI4	An integer indicating the searchability of a column. For more information, see the SEARCHABLE column in "PROVIDER_TYPES Rowset" in Appendix B. The default of this column is derived from the value of the SEARCHABLE column in the PROVIDER_TYPES schema rowset.
DBCOLUMN_ISUNIQUE	DBTYPE_BOOL	VARIANT_TRUE: No two rows in the base table—the table returned in DBCOLUMN_BASETABLENAME—can have the same value in this column. DBCOLUMN_ISUNIQUE is guaranteed to be VARIANT_TRUE if the column constitutes a key by itself, or if there is a constraint of type UNIQUE that applies only to this column. VARIANT_FALSE: The column can contain duplicate values in the base table. The default of this column is VARIANT_FALSE.

Column ID	Type Indicator	Description
DBCOLUMN_OCTETLENGTH	DBTYPE_UI4	The maximum length in octets (bytes) of the column, if column is a character or binary type. A value of zero means the column has no maximum length. NULL for all other types of columns.
		The default of this column is derived from the value of the CHARACTER_OCTET_LENGTH column in the COLUMNS schema rowset.

See Also

IColumnsInfo::GetColumnInfo, **IColumnsRowset::GetAvailableColumns**, **IRowsetInfo::GetProperties**

ICommand

ICommand contains methods to execute commands. A command can be executed many times and the parameter values can vary. This interface is mandatory on commands.

A command object contains a single text command, which is specified through **ICommandText**.

Method	Description
Cancel	Cancels the current command execution.
Execute	Executes the command.
GetDBSession	Returns an interface pointer to the session that created the command.

ICommand::Cancel

Cancels the current command execution.

HRESULT Cancel();

Parameters

None.

Return Code

S_OK

The method succeeded.

The command was not executing.

E_FAIL

A provider-specific error occurred.

DB_E_CANTCANCEL

The executing command cannot be canceled.

Comments

Cancel may be called on a separate thread while **Execute** is executing any type of command. If the executing command can be canceled, the method returns S_OK, and **Execute** returns DB_E_CANCELED. If the executing command cannot be canceled, **Cancel** returns DB_E_CANTCANCEL and **Execute** continues. If the command is not executing, the method returns S_OK.

See Also

ICommand::Execute

ICommand::Execute

Executes the command.

HRESULT Execute (
      IUnknown *   *pUnkOuter,*
      REFIID   *riid,*
      DBPARAMS * *pParams,*
      LONG *   *pcRowsAffected,*
      IUnknown ** *ppRowset***);**

Parameters

pUnkOuter [in]

A pointer to the controlling **IUnknown** interface if the rowset is being created as part of an aggregate; otherwise, it is null.

riid [in]

The requested IID for the rowset returned in **ppRowset*.

If this is IID_NULL, then *ppRowset* is ignored and no rowset is returned, even if the command would otherwise generate a rowset. Specifying IID_NULL is useful in the case of text commands that do not generate rowset, such as data definition commands, as a hint to the provider that no rowset properties need to be verified.

If *riid* is IID_IMultipleResults, the provider creates a multiple results object and returns a pointer to it in **ppRowset*; it does this even if the command generates a single result. If the provider supports multiple results and the command generates multiple results but *riid* is not IID_IMultipleResults, the provider returns the first result and discards any remaining results. If *riid* is IID_IMultipleResults and the provider does not support multiple results, **Execute** returns E_NOINTERFACE.

pParams [in/out]

A pointer to a DBPARAMS structure that specifies the values for one or more parameters. In text commands that use parameters, if no value is specified for a parameter through *pParams*, an error occurs.

```
struct DBPARAMS {
    void *    pData;
    ULONG     cParamSets;
    HACCESSOR hAccessor;
};
```

The elements of this structure are used as follows.

Element	Description
pData	Pointer to a buffer from which the provider retrieves input parameter data and to which the provider returns output parameter data, according to the bindings specified by *hAccessor*. For more information, see "Setting Data" and "Getting Data" in Chapter 6.
	When output parameter data is available to the consumer depends on the DBPROP_OUTPUTPARAMETERAVAILABILITY property.
cParamSets	The number of sets of parameters in **pData*. If *cParamSets* is greater than one, then the bindings described by *hAccessor* define the offsets within **pData* for each set of parameters, and *cbRowSize* (as specified in **IAccessor::CreateAccessor**) defines a single fixed offset between each of those values and the corresponding values for the next set of parameters. Sets of multiple parameters (*cParamSets* is greater than one) can be specified only if DBPROP_MULTIPLEPARAMSETS is VARIANT_TRUE and the command does not return any rowsets.
hAccessor	Handle of the accessor to use. If *hAccessor* is the handle of a null accessor (*cBindings* in **CreateAccessor** was 0), then **Execute** does not retrieve or return any parameter values.

If the command text does not include parameters, the provider ignores this argument.

pcRowsAffected [out]

A pointer to memory in which to return the count of rows affected by a command that updates, deletes, or inserts rows. If *cParamSets* is greater than 1, **pcRowsAffected* is the total number of rows affected by all of the sets of parameters specified in the execution. If the number of affected rows is not available, **pcRowsAffected* is set to −1 on output. If *riid* is IID_IMultipleResults, the value returned in **pcRowsAffected* is either −1 or the total number of rows affected by the entire command; to retrieve individual row counts, the consumer calls **IMultipleResults::GetResult**. If the command does not update, delete, or insert rows, **pcRowsAffected* is undefined on output. If *pcRowsAffected* is a null pointer, no count of rows is returned.

ppRowset [in/out]

A pointer to the memory in which to return the rowset's pointer. If *ppRowset* is a null pointer, no rowset is created.

Return Code

S_OK

The method succeeded. In all DBPROP structures returned by the method, *dwStatus* is set to DBPROPSTATUS_OK, the status of all input parameters bound by the accessor is set to DBSTATUS_S_OK or DBSTATUS_S_ISNULL, and the status of all output parameters bound by the accessor is set to DBSTATUS_S_OK, DBSTATUS_S_ISNULL, or DBSTATUS_S_TRUNCATED or is unknown because the parameter value has not been returned yet.

DB_S_ERRORSOCCURRED

This can be returned for any of the following reasons.

- The command was executed but an error occurred while returning one or more output parameter values. To determine which output parameters were not returned, the consumer checks the status values. For a list of status values that can be returned by this method, see "Status Values Used When Getting Data" in "Status" in Chapter 6.

- The rowset was opened but one or more properties—for which the *dwOptions* element of the DBPROP structure was DBPROPOPTIONS_SETIFCHEAP— were not set. The consumer calls **IRowsetInfo::GetProperties** to determine which properties were set.

DB_S_STOPLIMITREACHED

Execution has been stopped because a resource limit has been reached. The results obtained so far have been returned. Execution cannot be resumed.

This return code takes precedence over DB_S_ERRORSOCCURRED. That is, if the conditions described here and in those described in DB_S_ERRORSOCCURRED both occur, the provider returns this code. When the consumer receives this return code, it should also check for the conditions described in DB_S_ERRORSOCCURRED.

E_FAIL

A provider-specific error occurred.

E_INVALIDARG

pParams was not ignored, *cParamSets* in the DBPARAMS structure pointed to by *pParams* was greater than 1, *ppRowset* was not a null pointer, and the provider does not support multiple results.

pParams was not ignored and, in the DBPARAMS structure pointed to by *pParams*, *pData* was a null pointer.

pParams was not ignored, was not a null pointer, and in the DBPARAMS structure pointed to by *pParams*, *cParamSets* was zero.

riid was not IID_NULL and *ppRowset* was a null pointer.

E_NOINTERFACE

The rowset did not support the interface specified in *riid*.

riid was IID_IMultipleResults and the provider did not support multiple results objects.

DB_E_ABORTLIMITREACHED

Execution has been aborted because a resource limit has been reached. For example, a query timed out. No results have been returned.

DB_E_BADACCESSORHANDLE

pParams was not ignored and *hAccessor* in the DBPARAMS structure pointed to by *pParams* was invalid.

DB_E_BADACCESSORTYPE

hAccessor in the DBPARAMS structure pointed to by *pParams* was not the handle of a parameter accessor.

DB_E_CANCELED

The command was canceled by a call to **Cancel** on another thread.

DB_E_CANTCONVERTVALUE

A literal value in the command text could not be converted to the type of the associated column for reasons other than data overflow.

DB_E_DATAOVERFLOW

A literal value in the command text overflowed the type specified by the associated column.

DB_E_ERRORSINCOMMAND

The command text contained one or more errors. Providers should use OLE DB error objects to return details about the errors.

DB_E_ERRORSOCCURRED

The method failed due to one or more invalid input parameter values. To determine which input parameter values were invalid, the consumer checks the status values. For a list of status values that can be returned by this method, see "Status Values Used When Setting Data" in "Status" in Chapter 6.

The command was not executed and no rowset was returned because one or more properties—for which the *dwOptions* element of the DBPROP structure was DBPROPOPTIONS_REQUIRED—were not set.

DB_E_MULTIPLESTATEMENTS

The command text contained more than one command statement or SQL statement and the provider does not support multi-statement commands.

DB_E_NOAGGREGATION

pUnkOuter was not a null pointer and the rowset being created does not support aggregation.

DB_E_NOCOMMAND

No command text was currently set on the command object.

DB_E_PARAMNOTOPTIONAL

A value was not supplied for a required parameter.

The command text used parameters and *pParams* was a null pointer.

DB_SEC_E_PERMISSIONDENIED

The consumer did not have sufficient permission to execute the command. For example, a rowset-returning command specified a column for which the consumer does not have read permission, or an update command specified a column for which the consumer does not have write permission.

If this method performs deferred accessor validation and that validation takes place before any data is transferred, it can also return any of the following HRESULTs for the reasons listed in the corresponding DBBINDSTATUS values in **IAccessor::CreateAccessor**:

E_NOINTERFACE
DB_E_BADBINDINFO
DB_E_BADORDINAL
DB_E_BADSTORAGEFLAGS
DB_E_UNSUPPORTEDCONVERSION

Comments

If the command returns rows, such as an SQL **SELECT** statement, the result of this method is a rowset over the result rows. If no rows match the command, the rowset is still created. The resulting rowset is fully functional and can be used, for example, to insert new rows or determine column metadata.

If the command returns multiple results (rowsets or row counts), the consumer requests a multiple results object by setting *riid* to IID_IMultipleResults. **Execute** creates the multiple results object and returns an **IMultipleResults** interface pointer to it in *ppRowset. The consumer repeatedly calls **IMultipleResults::GetResult** to retrieve the results in order. For more information, see "Multiple Results" in Chapter 3.

If **Execute** is called multiple times for a single command, with or without changes to the command text, the outcome may reflect changes in the underlying stored data, depending on the isolation level specified for the surrounding transaction.

Execute can be called when a rowset is already open on the command only if the only change between the calls is a change in the value of existing parameters (calls to **ICommandWithParameters::SetParameterInfo** will fail). Methods that modify the command (**ICommandPrepare::Prepare**, **ICommandPrepare::Unprepare**, **ICommandProperties::SetProperties**, and **ICommandText::SetCommandText**) while a rowset is open will fail and return DB_E_OBJECTOPEN. Each call to **Execute** creates a new rowset, which must be explicitly released by **IRowset::Release**.

Execute does not affect the prepared state of a command.

The consumer determines whether the command supports parameters by calling **QueryInterface** for **ICommandWithParameters**. If this interface is exposed, the command supports parameters; if it is not exposed, the command does not support parameters. If the command does not support parameters, **Execute** ignores *pParams*. However, if the command text includes parameters, **Execute** returns DB_E_ERRORSINCOMMAND.

If an input parameter value is not specified, **Execute** returns DB_E_PARAMNOTOPTIONAL. If the provider cannot describe parameters and the consumer has not called **SetParameterInfo** for all parameters, the behavior of **Execute** is undefined. For example, **Execute** might guess at the parameter information or it might fail completely. For more information, see **SetParameterInfo**.

If **Execute** returns DB_S_ERRORSOCCURRED or DB_E_ERRORSOCCURRED, the consumer can immediately call **ICommandProperties::GetProperties** with the DBPROPSET_PROPERTIESINERROR property set to return the properties that could not be set. For more information, see "Property Sets" in Chapter 11.

Execute does not alter the value of any properties. That is, **ICommandProperties::GetProperties** returns the same value for a property regardless of whether it is called before or after **Execute** and whether **Execute** succeeded or failed. However, if a property value is not required, **IRowsetInfo::GetProperties** can return a different value for that property than **ICommandProperties::GetProperties**. For more information, see **IRowsetInfo::GetProperties**.

If several threads concurrently request execution of a given command, the corresponding executions are serialized, and each thread will block until its corresponding execution concludes.

Execute can fail even if **ICommandPrepare::Prepare** has succeeded; this may be the case if, for example, the underlying schema has changed between the **Prepare** and **Execute** calls and the command text had therefore become illegal.

See Also

ICommand::Cancel, **ICommandPrepare::Prepare**, **ICommandText::SetCommandText**, **ICommandWithParameters::SetParameterInfo**

ICommand::GetDBSession

Returns an interface pointer to the session that created the command.

HRESULT GetDBSession (
    REFIID   *riid*,
    IUnknown ** *ppSession*);

Parameters

riid [in]

The IID of the interface on which to return a pointer.

ppSession [out]

A pointer to memory in which to return the interface pointer. If the provider does not have an object that created the command, it sets **ppSession* to a null pointer. If **GetDBSession** fails, it must attempt to set **ppSession* to a null pointer.

Return Code

S_OK

The method succeeded.

S_FALSE

The provider did not have an object that created the command. Therefore, it set **ppSession* to a null pointer.

E_FAIL

A provider-specific error occurred.

E_INVALIDARG

ppSession was a null pointer.

E_NOINTERFACE

The session did not support the interface specified in *riid*.

ICommandPrepare

This optional interface encapsulates command optimization, a separation of compile-time and run-time, as found in traditional relational database systems. The result of this optimization is a *command execution plan*.

If the provider supports command preparation, by supporting this interface, commands must be in a prepared state prior to calling the following methods.

- **IColumnsInfo::GetColumnInfo**,
- **IColumnsInfo::MapColumnIDs**,
- **IColumnsRowset::GetAvailableColumns**, and
- **IColumnsRowset::GetColumnsRowset**.

Method	Description
Prepare	Validates and optimizes the current command.
Unprepare	Discards the current command execution plan.

ICommandPrepare::Prepare

Validates and optimizes the current command.

HRESULT Prepare (
    ULONG   *cExpectedRuns*);

Parameters

cExpectedRuns [in]

Using this parameter, the consumer can indicate how often the command execution plan, which is produced by **Prepare**, will be used; that is, how often the command is likely to be executed without renewed optimization. This guides the optimizer in determining tradeoffs between search effort and run-time processing effort. A value of zero indicates that the consumer is unable to provide an estimate, and leaves it to the optimizer to choose a default value.

Return Code

S_OK

The method succeeded.

DB_S_ERRORSOCCURRED

The command was prepared but one or more properties—for which the *dwOptions* element of the DBPROP structure was DBPROPOPTIONS_SETIFCHEAP—were not set. The consumer calls **ICommandProperties::GetProperties** to determine which properties were set.

E_FAIL

A provider-specific error occurred.

E_OUTOFMEMORY

The provider ran out of memory while preparing the command.

DB_E_ABORTLIMITREACHED

Preparation has been aborted because a resource limit has been reached. For example, the preparation timed out.

DB_E_ERRORSINCOMMAND

The command text contained one or more errors. Providers should use OLE DB error objects to return details about the errors.

DB_E_ERRORSOCCURRED

The command was not prepared because one or more properties—for which the *dwOptions* element of the DBPROP structure was DBPROPOPTIONS_REQUIRED—were not set. The consumer calls **ICommandProperties::GetProperties** to determine which properties were not set.

DB_E_NOCOMMAND

No command text was currently set on the command object.

DB_E_OBJECTOPEN

A rowset was open on the command.

DB_SEC_E_PERMISSIONDENIED

The consumer did not have sufficient permission to prepare the command.

Comments

Although they are not required to do so, consumers should set any properties before calling **Prepare**, as these properties might be relevant to preparing the command.

If **Prepare** is called redundantly, the provider determines whether command optimization is re-invoked; the provider returns S_OK.

If **Prepare** returns DB_S_ERRORSOCCURRED or DB_E_ERRORSOCCURRED, the consumer can immediately call **ICommandProperties::GetProperties** with the DBPROPSET_PROPERTIESINERROR property set to return the properties that could not be set. For more information, see "Property Sets" in Chapter 11.

See Also

ICommand::Execute, ICommandPrepare::Unprepare, ICommandWithParameters::SetParameterInfo

ICommandPrepare::Unprepare

Discards the current command execution plan.

HRESULT Unprepare();

Parameters

None.

Return Code

S_OK

The method succeeded.

E_FAIL

A provider-specific error occurred.

DB_E_OBJECTOPEN

A rowset was open on the command.

Comments

This method has no effect if the command was not prepared; the provider returns S_OK.

See Also

ICommandPrepare::Prepare

ICommandProperties

ICommandProperties specifies to the command the properties from the Rowset property group that must be supported by the rowsets returned by **ICommand::Execute**. A special case of these properties, and the ones most commonly requested, are the interfaces the rowset must support. In addition to interfaces, the consumer can request properties that modify the behavior of the rowset or interfaces.

All rowsets must support **IRowset**, **IAccessor**, **IColumnsInfo**, **IRowsetInfo**, and **IConvertType**. Providers may choose to return rowsets supporting other interfaces if doing so is cheaper and the support for the returned interfaces does not affect consumer code that is not expecting them. The *riid* parameter of **ICommand::Execute** should be one of the interfaces returned by **IRowsetInfo::GetProperties**.

This interface is mandatory on commands.

Method	Description
GetProperties	Returns the list of properties in the Rowset property group that are currently requested for the rowset.
SetProperties	Sets properties in the Rowset property group.

ICommandProperties::GetProperties

Returns the list of properties in the Rowset property group that are currently requested for the rowset.

HRESULT GetProperties (
    const ULONG   *cPropertyIDSets,*
    const DBPROPIDSET   *rgPropertyIDSets[],*
    ULONG *   *pcPropertySets,*
    DBPROPSET **   *prgPropertySets);*

Parameters

cPropertyIDSets[in]

The number of DBPROPIDSET structures in *rgPropertyIDSets*.

If *cPropertySets* is zero, the provider ignores *rgPropertyIDSets* and returns the values of all properties in the Rowset property group for which values have been set or defaults exist. It does not return the values of properties in the Rowset property group for which values have not been set and no defaults exist, nor does it return the values of properties for which no value has been set, nor default exists, and for which a value will be set automatically because a value for another property in the Rowset property group has been set.

If *cPropertyIDSets* is not zero, the provider returns the values of the requested properties. If a property is not supported, the returned value of *dwStatus* in the returned DBPROP structure for that property is DBPROPSTATUS_NOTSUPPORTED and the value of *dwOptions* is undefined.

rgPropertyIDSets [in]

An array of *cPropertyIDSets* DBPROPIDSET structures. The properties specified in these structures must belong to the Rowset property group. The provider returns the values of the properties specified in these structures. If *cPropertyIDSets* is zero, then this parameter is ignored.

For information about the properties in the Rowset property group that are defined by OLE DB, see "Rowset Properties" in Appendix C. For information about the DBPROPIDSET structure, see "DBPROPIDSET Structure" in Chapter 11.

pcPropertySets [out]

A pointer to memory in which to return the number of DBPROPSET structures returned in **prgPropertySets*. If *cPropertyIDSets* is zero, **pcPropertySets* is the total number of property sets for which the provider supports at least one property in the Rowset property group. If *cPropertyIDSets* is greater than zero, **pcPropertySets* is set to *cPropertyIDSets*. If an error other than DB_E_ERRORSOCCURRED occurs, **pcPropertySets* is set to zero.

prgPropertySets [out]

A pointer to memory in which to return an array of DBPROPSET structures. If *cPropertyIDSets* is zero, then one structure is returned for each property set that contains at least one property belonging to the Rowset property group. If *cPropertyIDSets* is not zero, then one structure is returned for each property set specified in *rgPropertyIDSets*.

If *cPropertyIDSets* is not zero, the DBPROPSET structures in **prgPropertySets* are returned in the same order as the DBPROPIDSET structures in *rgPropertyIDSets*; that is, for corresponding elements of each array, the *guidPropertySet* elements are the same. If *cPropertyIDs*, in an element of *rgPropertyIDSets*, is not zero, the DBPROP structures in the corresponding element of **prgPropertySets* are returned in the same order as the DBPROPID values in *rgPropertyIDs*; that is, for corresponding elements of each array, the property IDs are the same.

The provider allocates memory for the structures and returns the address to this memory; the consumer releases this memory with **IMalloc::Free** when it no longer needs the structures. Before calling **IMalloc::Free** for **prgPropertySets*, the consumer should call **IMalloc::Free** for the *rgProperties* element within each element of **prgPropertySets*. If **pcPropertySets* is zero on output or an error other than DB_E_ERRORSOCCURRED occurs, the provider does not allocate any memory and ensures that **prgPropertySets* is a null pointer on output.

For information about the DBPROPSET and DBPROP structures, see "DBPROPSET Structure" and "DBPROP Structure" in Chapter 11.

Return Code

S_OK

The method succeeded. In all DBPROP structures returned by the method, *dwStatus* is set to DBPROPSTATUS_OK.

DB_S_ERRORSOCCURRED

No value was returned for one or more properties. The consumer checks *dwStatus* in the DBPROP structure to determine the properties for which values were not returned. **GetProperties** can fail to return properties for a number of reasons, including:

- The property was not supported by the provider.

- The property was not in the Rowset property group.

- The property set was not supported by the provider. If *cPropertyIDs* in the DBPROPIDSET structure for the property set was zero, the provider cannot set *dwStatus* in the DBPROP structure because it does not know the IDs of any properties in the property set. Instead, it sets *cProperties* to zero in the DBPROPSET structure returned for the property set.

E_FAIL

A provider-specific error occurred.

E_INVALIDARG

cPropertyIDSets was not equal to zero and *rgPropertyIDSets* was a null pointer.

pcPropertySets or *prgPropertySets* was a null pointer.

In an element of *rgPropertyIDSets*, *cPropertyIDs* was not zero and *rgPropertyIDs* was a null pointer.

In an element of *rgPropertyIDSets*, *guidPropertySet* was DBPROPSET_PROPERTIESINERROR and *cPropertyIDs* was not 0 or *rgPropertyIDs* was not a null pointer.

cPropertyIDSets was greater than 1 and, in an element of *rgPropertyIDSets*, *guidPropertySet* was DBPROPSET_PROPERTIESINERROR.

E_OUTOFMEMORY

The provider was unable to allocate sufficient memory in which to return the DBPROPSET or DBPROP structures.

DB_E_ERRORSOCCURRED

No values were returned for any properties. The provider allocates memory for *prgPropertySets* and the consumer checks *dwStatus* in the DBPROP structures to determine why properties were not returned. The consumer frees this memory when it no longer needs the information.

Comments

GetProperties returns the current values of properties that have been set by the consumer with **ICommandProperties::SetProperties**. For all values not set by the consumer, **GetProperties** returns the initial property value.

Even though **IDBProperties::GetPropertyInfo** lists a property as being supported by the provider, **GetProperties** will not return a value for it if it does not apply to the current circumstances. For example, the provider's ability to support the property might be affected by the current transaction or the current command text.

The property values returned by **ICommandProperties::GetProperties** are not affected by executing the command. However, **IRowsetInfo::GetProperties** might return a different value for a property than does **ICommandProperties::GetProperties**. For example, if a consumer requests ordered bookmarks if they are cheap, it calls **SetProperties** to set the value of DBPROP_ORDEREDBOOKMARKS to VARIANT_TRUE and specifies a *dwOptions* value of DBPROPOPTIONS_SETIFCHEAP. If the provider cannot determine at this point in the definition of the command whether this is cheap, **ICommandProperties::GetProperties** returns a value of VARIANT_TRUE and a *dwOptions* of DBPROPOPTIONS_SETIFCHEAP for this property. If the provider determines during optimization or execution that ordered bookmarks are not cheap, **IRowsetInfo::GetProperties** returns a value of VARIANT_FALSE and a *dwOptions* of zero.

If **ICommand::Execute** returns DB_E_ERRORSOCCURRED, the consumer can immediately call **GetProperties** with the DBPROPSET_PROPERTIESINERROR property set to return all the properties that were in error. For more information, see "Property Sets" in Chapter 11.

See Also

ICommandProperties::SetProperties, **IDBProperties::GetPropertyInfo**, **IRowsetInfo::GetProperties**

ICommandProperties::SetProperties

Sets properties in the Rowset property group.

HRESULT SetProperties (
    ULONG   *cPropertySets,*
    DBPROPSET   *rgPropertySets*[]);

Parameters

cPropertySets [in]

The number of DBPROPSET structures in *rgPropertySets*. If this is zero, the provider ignores *rgPropertySets* and the method does not do anything.

rgPropertySets [in/out]

An array of DBPROPSET structures containing properties and values to be set. The properties specified in these structures must belong to the Rowset property group. If the same property is specified more than once in *rgPropertySets*, then which value is used is provider-specific. If *cPropertySets* is zero, this parameter is ignored.

For information about the properties in the Rowset property group that are defined by OLE DB, see "Rowset Properties" in Appendix C. For information about the DBPROPSET and DBPROP structures, see "DBPROPSET Structure" and "DBPROP Structure" in Chapter 11.

Return Code

S_OK

The method succeeded. In all DBPROP structures passed to the method, *dwStatus* is set to DBPROPSTATUS_OK.

DB_S_ERRORSOCCURRED

One or more properties were not set. Properties not in error remain set. The consumer checks *dwStatus* in the DBPROP structures to determine which properties were not set. **SetProperties** can fail to set properties for a number of reasons, including:

- The property was not supported by the provider.

- The property was not in the Rowset property group.

- The property set was not supported by the provider.

- It was not cheap to set the property.

- The value of *dwOptions* in a DBPROP structure was invalid.

- The property was not supported by the provider.

- *colid* in the DBPROP structure was not DB_NULLID and the property cannot be set on a column.

- The data type in *vValue* in the DBPROP structure was not the data type of the property or was not VT_EMPTY.

- The value in *vValue* in the DBPROP structure was invalid.
- The property's value conflicted with an existing property.

E_FAIL
  A provider-specific error occurred.

E_INVALIDARG
  cPropertySets was not equal to zero and *rgPropertySets* was a null pointer.

  In an element of *rgPropertySets*, *cProperties* was not zero and *rgProperties* was a null pointer.

DB_E_ERRORSOCCURRED
  All property values were invalid and no properties were set. The consumer checks *dwStatus* in the DBPROP structures to determine why properties were not set. The method can fail to set properties for any of the reasons specified in DB_S_ERRORSOCCURRED except the reason that states that it was not cheap to set the property.

DB_E_OBJECTOPEN
  Properties cannot be set while there is an open rowset.

Comments

Consumers should first set properties for interfaces and then set other properties that modify those interfaces. The combination of the values of an interface property and a non-interface property might result in another interface being requested. However, the value of a non-interface property, by itself, never results in another interface being requested.

Setting property values is a cumulative operation. That is, each call to **SetProperties** attempts to change the values of the specified properties. If a new value is illegal or conflicts with the value of another property, the value of the property is not changed and **SetProperties** returns DBPROPSTATUS_BADVALUE or DBPROPSTATUS_CONFLICTING in the *dwStatus* element of the DBPROP structure for the property. Properties are processed from the beginning of the array to the end of the array. As they are processed, properties that conflict with previously set properties, including those set previously on the same call, are marked with DBPROPSTATUS_CONFLICTING, and processing continues through the array of properties.

SetProperties cannot always determine whether a property can be set to its requested value. For example, the provider often cannot determine whether the rowset is updatable until it creates the rowset. In this case, **SetProperties** appears to successfully set the property value and the provider delays the determination until **ICommand::Execute** is called.

If the value of *dwOptions* for a property is DBPROPOPTIONS_SETIFCHEAP, the provider attempts to determine whether it can cheaply set the property to the requested value. If it can make this determination, it sets the property and returns DBPROPSTATUS_OK or does not set the property and returns

DBPROPSTATUS_NOTSET. If it cannot make this determination, it can delay setting the property until the command is executed; in this case, the value of *dwOptions* returned for the property by **GetProperties** is DBPROPOPTIONS_SETIFCHEAP.

Consumers should not attempt to unset mandatory rowset interfaces such as **IRowset**, **IAccessor**, **IColumnsInfo**, and **IRowsetInfo**. These interfaces are always supported and **SetProperties** returns DBPROPSTATUS_NOTSETTABLE for them.

Even if **IDBProperties::GetPropertyInfo** lists a property as being supported by the provider, **SetProperties** can return DBPROPSTATUS_NOTSUPPORTED when the consumer attempts to set the property value if the property does not apply to the current circumstances. For example, the provider's ability to support the property might be affected by the current transaction or the current command text.

If an error occurs when setting a particular property, **SetProperties** flags the error in *dwStatus* in the DBPROP structure and continues processing.

Although providers allow changing properties at any time before command execution, consumers are encouraged to set all properties prior to preparing the command to avoid forcing the provider to re-prepare the command at execution.

See Also

ICommandProperties::GetProperties, **IDBProperties::GetPropertyInfo**, **IRowsetInfo::GetProperties**

ICommandText : ICommand

This interface is mandatory on commands.

A command object can have only one text command. When the command text is specified through **SetCommandText**, it replaces the existing command text.

Method	Description
GetCommandText	Returns the text command set by the last call to **SetCommandText**.
SetCommandText	Sets the command text, replacing the existing command text.

ICommandText::GetCommandText

Returns the text command set by the last call to **SetCommandText**.

HRESULT GetCommandText (
    GUID *   *pguidDialect*,
    LPOLESTR * *ppwszCommand*);

Parameters

pguidDialect [in/out]

A pointer to memory containing a GUID that specifies the syntax and general rules for parsing the command text. If *pguidDialect* is a null pointer on input, it returns the command in **ppwszCommand* in a dialect that makes the most sense to the provider. Providers can define GUIDs for their own dialects.

OLE DB defines a common dialect denoted by the GUID DBGUID_DBSQL. This GUID specifies that the command text is to be interpreted according to a superset of ANSI SQL syntax rules. To determine the level of ANSI SQL syntax supported by a provider, a consumer calls **IDBProperties::GetProperties** for the DBPROP_SQLSUPPORT property. Providers reporting this syntax are free to use extensions to ANSI SQL, or any subset of ANSI SQL according to their reported level of support, but must comply with the rules defined in ANSI SQL for any syntax defined in that specification. If **GetCommandText** returns an error, **pguidDialect* is set to DB_NULLGUID.

ppwszCommand [out]

A pointer to memory in which to return the command text. The command object allocates memory for the command text and returns the address to this memory. The consumer releases this memory with **IMalloc::Free** when it no longer needs the text. If **GetCommandText** returns an error, **ppwszCommand* is set to a null pointer.

Return Code

S_OK

The method succeeded.

DB_S_DIALECTIGNORED

The method succeeded, but the input value of *pguidDialect* was ignored. The text is returned in the dialect specified in **SetCommandText** or the dialect that makes the most sense to the provider. The value returned in **pguidDialect* represents that dialect.

E_FAIL

A provider-specific error occurred.

E_INVALIDARG

ppwszCommand was a null pointer.

E_OUTOFMEMORY

The provider was unable to allocate sufficient memory in which to return the command text.

DB_E_NOCOMMAND

No command text was currently set on the command object.

See Also

ICommandText::SetCommandText

ICommandText::SetCommandText

Sets the command text, replacing the existing command text.

HRESULT SetCommandText (
     REFGUID   *rguidDialect*,
     LPCOLESTR   *pwszCommand*);

Parameters

rguidDialect [in]

A GUID that specifies the syntax and general rules for the provider to use in parsing the command text. For a complete description of dialects, see **GetCommandText**.

pwszCommand [in]

A pointer to the text of the command.

If **pwszCommand* is an empty string ("") or *pwszCommand* is a null pointer, the current command text is cleared and the command is put in an unprepared state. Any properties that have been set on the command are unaffected; that is, they retain their current values. Methods that require a command, such as **ICommand::Execute** and **ICommandPrepare::Prepare**, will return DB_E_NOCOMMAND until a new command text is set.

Return Code

S_OK

The method succeeded.

E_FAIL

A provider-specific error occurred.

DB_E_DIALECTNOTSUPPORTED

The provider did not support the dialect specified in *rguidDialect*.

DB_E_OBJECTOPEN

A rowset was open on the command.

Comments

A command object contains a single text command, usually an SQL statement. The new command text is copied into the command object; thus, the consumer can delete the original text without affecting the command object. All meaningful error checking, such as syntax checking and parsing, is deferred until **ICommandPrepare::Prepare** or **ICommand::Execute** is called. **SetCommandText** only verifies that the command text can be copied into the command object's space.

If the text of a prepared or unprepared command is overwritten with new command text, by calling **SetCommandText**, the command object is left in an unprepared state.

SetCommandText does not alter the value of any properties. That is, **ICommandProperties::GetProperties** returns the same value for a property regardless of whether it is called before or after **SetCommandText** and whether **SetCommandText** succeeded or failed.

See Also

ICommand::Execute, **ICommandPrepare::Prepare**, **ICommandText::GetCommandText**, **ICommandWithParameters::SetParameterInfo**

ICommandWithParameters

Providers that support parameters must support **ICommandWithParameters**. Note that any provider that returns DBPROPVAL_SQL_ANSI92_INTERMEDIATE or DBPROPVAL_SQL_ANSI92_FULL for the DBPROP_SQLSUPPORT property can support parameters.

This optional interface encapsulates parameters. Parameters are scalar values, or a vector of scalar values, typically expressed in predicates but possibly supported by many providers in any scalar expression.

For scalar parameters of prepared commands, there is a presumption that different parameter values do not require different plans. In other words, a single preparation and its resulting plan are satisfactory for all possible values of scalar parameters.

Parameter values are set when a command is executed. Methods are included here to offer a means for setting and obtaining a list of parameters and their types.

Method	Description
GetParameterInfo	Gets a list of the command's parameters, their names, and their types.
MapParameterNames	Returns an array of column ordinals when given named parameters.
SetParameterInfo	Specifies the native data type of each parameter.

ICommandWithParameters:: GetParameterInfo

Gets a list of the command's parameters, their names, and their types.

HRESULT GetParameterInfo (
      ULONG *   *pcParams***,**
      DBPARAMINFO ** *prgParamInfo***,**
      OLECHAR **   *ppNamesBuffer***);**

Parameters

pcParams [out]

A pointer to memory in which to return the number of parameters in the command. If an error occurs, **pcParams* is set to zero.

prgParamInfo [out]

A pointer to memory in which to return an array of parameter information structures. The command allocates memory for the array, as well the strings, and returns the address to this memory. The consumer releases the array memory with **IMalloc::Free** when it no longer needs the parameter information. If **pcParams* is zero on output or an error occurs, the provider does not allocate any memory and ensures that **prgParamInfo* is a null pointer on output.

The DBPARAMINFO structure is

```
typedef struct tagDBPARAMINFO {
    DBPARAMFLAGS    dwFlags;
    ULONG           iOrdinal;
    LPOLESTR        pwszName;
    ITypeInfo *     pTypeInfo;
    ULONG           ulParamSize;
    DBTYPE          wType;
    BYTE            bPrecision;
    BYTE            bScale;
} DBPARAMINFO;
```

The elements of this structure are used as follows.

Element	Description
dwFlags	A bitmask describing parameter characteristics; these values have the following meaning:
	• DBPARAMFLAGS_ISINPUT—Whether a parameter accepts values on input. Not set if this is unknown.
	• DBPARAMFLAGS_ISOUTPUT—Whether a parameter returns values on output. Not set if this is unknown. Providers only support those parameter types that make sense for their data source.

Element	Description
dwFlags (*continued*)	• DBPARAMFLAGS_ISSIGNED—Whether a parameter is signed. This is ignored if the type is inherently signed, such as DBTYPE_I2, or if sign does not apply to the type, such as DBTYPE_BSTR. It is generally used in **SetParameterInfo** so the consumer can tell the provider if a provider-specific type name refers to a signed or unsigned type.
	• DBPARAMFLAGS_ISNULLABLE—Whether parameter accepts NULLs. If nullability is unknown, this flag is set.
	• DBPARAMFLAGS_ISLONG—Whether a parameter contains a BLOB that contains very data. The definition of very long data is provider-specific. Note that the flag setting corresponds to the value of the IS_LONG column in the PROVIDER_TYPES schema rowset for the data type.
	When this flag is set, the BLOB is best manipulated through one of the storage interfaces. Although such BLOBs can be sent in a single piece with **ICommand::Execute**, there may be provider-specific problems in doing so. For example, the BLOB might be truncated due to machine limits on memory. Furthermore, when this flag is set, the provider might not be able to accurately return the maximum length of the BLOB data in *ulParamSize* in **GetParameterInfo**.
	When this flag is not set, the BLOB can be accessed either through **ICommand::Execute** or through a storage interface.
	For more information, see "Accessing BLOB Data" in Chapter 7.
iOrdinal	The ordinal of the parameter, starting with one.
pwszName	The name of the parameter; it is a null pointer if there is no name. Names are normal names. The colon prefix (where used within SQL text) is stripped.
pTypeInfo	**ITypeInfo** describes the type, if *pTypeInfo* is not a null pointer.
ulParamSize	The maximum possible length of a value in the parameter. For parameters that use a fixed-length data type, this is the size of the data type. For parameters that use a variable-length data type, this is one of the following:
	• The maximum length of the parameters in characters, for DBTYPE_STR and DBTYPE_WSTR, or bytes, for DBTYPE_BYTES, if one is defined. For example, a parameter for a CHAR(5) column in an SQL table has a maximum length of 5.
	• The maximum length of the data type in characters, for DBTYPE_STR and DBTYPE_WSTR, or bytes, for DBTYPE_BYTES, if the parameter does not have a defined length.
	• ~0 (bitwise, the value is not 0; that is, all bits are set to 1) if neither the parameter nor the data type has a defined maximum length.
	For data types that do not have a length, this is set to ~0 (bitwise, the value is not 0; that is, all bits are set to 1).

Element	Description
wType	The indicator of the parameter's data type.
bPrecision	If *wType* is a numeric type, *bPrecision* is the maximum number of digits, expressed in base 10. Otherwise, this is ~0 (bitwise, the value is not 0; that is, all bits are set to 1).
bScale	If *wType* is a numeric type with a fixed scale, *bScale* is the number of digits to the right, if *bScale* is positive, or left, if *bScale* is negative, of the decimal point. Otherwise, this is ~0 (bitwise, the value is not 0; that is, all bits are set to 1).

ppNamesBuffer [out]

A pointer to memory in which to store all string values (names used within the *pwszName* element of the DBPARAMINFO structures) with a single, globally-allocated buffer. Specifying a null pointer for *ppNamesBuffer* suspends the return of parameter names. The command allocates memory for the buffer and returns the address to this memory. The consumer releases the memory with **IMalloc::Free** when it no longer needs the parameter information. If **pcParams* is zero on output or an error occurs, the provider does not allocate any memory and ensures that **ppNamesBuffer* is a null pointer on output.

Each of the individual string values stored in this buffer is terminated by a null termination character. Therefore, the buffer may contain one or more strings, each with its own null termination character, and may contain embedded null termination characters.

Return Code

S_OK

The method succeeded.

E_FAIL

A provider-specific error occurred.

E_INVALIDARG

pcParams or *prgParamInfo* was a null pointer.

E_OUTOFMEMORY

The provider was unable to allocate sufficient memory in which to return the parameter data array or parameter names.

DB_E_NOCOMMAND

The provider can derive parameter information, but it does not support command preparation. However, no command text was currently set on the command object and no parameter information had been specified with **SetParameterInfo**.

DB_E_NOTPREPARED

The provider can derive parameter information, and it supports command preparation. However, the command was in an unprepared state and no parameter information was specified with **SetParameterInfo**.

DB_E_PARAMUNAVAILABLE

The provider cannot derive parameter information from the command and **SetParameterInfo** has not been called.

Comments

This method makes no logical change to the state of the object.

If **SetParameterInfo** has not been called for any parameters or **SetParameterInfo** has been called with *cParams* equal to zero, **GetParameterInfo** returns information about the parameters only if the provider can derive parameter information. If the provider cannot derive parameter information, **GetParameterInfo** returns DB_E_PARAMUNAVAILABLE.

If **SetParameterInfo** has been called for at least one parameter, **GetParameterInfo** returns the parameter information only for those parameters for which **SetParameterInfo** has been called. It does this even if the provider can derive information about the parameters for which **SetParameterInfo** was not called. The provider does not return a warning in this case because it often cannot determine the number of parameters and therefore cannot determine whether it has returned information for all parameters.

See Also

ICommandWithParameters::MapParameterNames,
ICommandWithParameters::SetParameterInfo

ICommandWithParameters:: MapParameterNames

Returns an array of column ordinals when given named parameters.

HRESULT MapParameterNames (
    ULONG   *cParamNames,*
    const OLECHAR *   *rgParamNames[],*
    LONG   *rgParamOrdinals[]);*

Parameters

cParamNames [in]

The number of parameter names to map. If *cParamNames* is zero, **MapParameterNames** does nothing and returns S_OK.

rgParamNames [in]

An array of parameter names of which to determine the column ordinals. If a parameter name is not found, the corresponding element of *rgParamOrdinals* is set to zero and the method returns DB_S_ERRORSOCCURRED.

rgParamOrdinals [out]

An array of *cParamNames* ordinals of the parameters identified by the elements of *rgParamNames*. The consumer allocates (but is not required to initialize) memory for this array and passes the address of this memory to the provider. The provider returns the parameter ordinals in the array.

Return Code

S_OK

The method succeeded. Each element of *rgParamOrdinals* is set to a nonzero value.

DB_S_ERRORSOCCURRED

An element of *rgParamNames* was invalid. The corresponding element of *rgParamOrdinals* is set to zero.

E_FAIL

A provider-specific error occurred.

E_INVALIDARG

cParamNames was not zero and *rgParamNames* or *rgParamOrdinals* was a null pointer.

DB_E_ERRORSOCCURRED

All elements of *rgParamNames* were invalid. All elements of *rgParamOrdinals* are set to zero.

DB_E_NOCOMMAND

No command text was currently set on the command object and no parameter information had been specified with **SetParameterInfo**.

DB_E_NOTPREPARED

The provider can derive parameter information and supports command preparation. However, the command was in an unprepared state and no parameter information had been specified with **SetParameterInfo**.

DB_E_NOTREENTRANT

The provider called a method from **IRowsetNotify** in the consumer and the method had not yet returned.

See Also

ICommandWithParameters::GetParameterInfo

ICommandWithParameters:: SetParameterInfo

Specifies the native data type of each parameter.

HRESULT SetParameterInfo (
> **ULONG**   *cParams,*
> **const ULONG**   *rgParamOrdinals[],*
> **const DBPARAMBINDINFO** *rgParamBindInfo[]);*

Parameters

cParams [in]
> The number of parameters for which to set type information. If *cParams* is zero, the type information for all parameters is discarded, and *rgParamOrdinals* and *rgParamBindInfo* are ignored.

rgParamOrdinals [in]
> An array of *cParams* ordinals. These are the ordinals of the parameters for which to set type information. Type information for parameters whose ordinals are not specified is not affected.

rgParamBindInfo [in]
> An array of *cParams* DBPARAMBINDINFO structures. If *rgParamBindInfo* is a null pointer, then the type information for the parameters specified by the ordinals in *rgParamOrdinals* is discarded.
>
> The DBPARAMBINDINFO structure is:

```
typedef struct tagDBPARAMBINDINFO {
    LPOLESTR      pwszDataSourceType;
    LPOLESTR      pwszName;
    ULONG         ulParamSize;
    DBPARAMFLAGS  dwFlags;
    BYTE          bPrecision;
    BYTE          bScale;
} DBPARAMBINDINFO;
```

> The elements of this structure are used as follows.

Element	Description
pwszDataSourceType	A pointer to the provider-specific name of the parameter's data type or a standard data type name. This name is not returned by **GetParameterInfo**; instead, the provider maps the data type specified by this name to an OLE DB type indicator and returns that type indicator. For a list of standard data type names, see "Comments."
pwszName	The name of the parameter. This is a null pointer if the parameter does not have a name.

Element	Description
ulParamSize	The maximum possible length of a value in the parameter. For parameters that use a fixed-length data type, this is the size of the data type. For parameters that use a variable-length data type, this is one of the following:
	• The maximum length of the parameters in characters, for DBTYPE_STR and DBTYPE_WSTR, or bytes, for DBTYPE_BYTES, if one is defined. For example, a parameter for a CHAR(5) column in an SQL table has a maximum length of 5.
	• The maximum length of the data type in characters, for DBTYPE_STR and DBTYPE_WSTR, or bytes, for DBTYPE_BYTES, if the parameter does not have a defined length.
	• ~0 (bitwise, the value is not 0; that is, all bits are set to 1) if neither the parameter nor the data type has a defined maximum length.
	For data types that do not have a length, this is set to ~0 (bitwise, the value is not 0; that is, all bits are set to 1).
dwFlags	See the *dwFlags* element of the DBPARAMINFO structure in **GetParameterInfo**.
bPrecision	If *pwszDataSourceType* is a numeric type, *bPrecision* is the maximum number of digits, expressed in base 10. Otherwise, it is ignored.
bScale	If *pwszDataSourceType* is a numeric type with a fixed scale, *bScale* is the number of digits to the right, if *bScale* is positive, or left, if *bScale* is negative, of the decimal point. Otherwise, it is ignored.

Return Code

S_OK

The method succeeded.

DB_S_TYPEINFOOVERRIDDEN

The provider was capable of deriving the parameter type information and **SetParameterInfo** was called. The parameter type information specified in **SetParameterInfo** was used.

SetParameterInfo replaced parameter type information specified in a previous call to **SetParameterInfo**.

E_FAIL

A provider-specific error occurred.

E_INVALIDARG

cParams was not zero and *rgParamOrdinals* was a null pointer.

An element of *rgParamOrdinals* was zero.

In an element of *rgParamBindInfo*, the *pwszDataSourceType* element was a null pointer.

In an element of *rgParamBindInfo*, the *dwFlags* element was invalid.

DB_E_BADPARAMETERNAME

In an element of *rgParamBindInfo*, the *pwszName* element specified an invalid parameter name. The provider does not check whether the name was correct for the specified parameter, just whether it was a valid parameter name.

DB_E_BADTYPENAME

In an element of *rgParamBindInfo*, the *pwszDataSourceType* element specified an invalid data type name. The provider does not check whether the data type was correct for the specified parameter, just whether it was a data type name supported by the provider.

DB_E_OBJECTOPEN

A rowset was open on the command.

Comments

Providers generally derive parameter type information from the data source and return it to the consumer through **GetParameterInfo**. Consumers then use this information to build parameter accessors for use with **ICommand::Execute**.

Some providers—notably many SQL database providers—cannot derive parameter type information from the data source. For these providers, the consumer must supply the native parameter type information through **SetParameterInfo**. The provider uses the type information specified by **SetParameterInfo** to determine how to convert parameter data from the type supplied by the consumer (as indicated by the *wType* value in the binding structure) to the native type used by the data source. When the consumer specifies a data type with known precision, scale, and size values, any information supplied by the consumer for precision, scale, or size should be ignored by the provider.

The information that the consumer supplies must be correct and must be supplied for all parameters. Providers that cannot derive parameter type information cannot verify the supplied information against the parameter metadata, although they can determine that the specified values are legal values for the provider. Such providers sometimes cannot even determine the number of parameters in the command. The result of executing a command using incorrect parameter information or passing parameter information for the wrong number of parameters is undefined. For example, if the parameter type is LONG and the consumer specifies a type indicator of DBTYPE_STR in **SetParameterInfo**, the provider converts the data to a string before sending it to the data source. Because the data source is expecting a LONG, this will likely result in an error.

When the consumer calls **SetParameterInfo**, it specifies a provider-specific data type name (as derived from the PROVIDER_TYPES schema rowset) or a standard type name. If the consumer passes a standard type name, the provider maps it to a provider-specific type name. For example, a provider for an SQL DBMS might map "DBTYPE_I2" to "SMALLINT".

The following is a list of standard type names and their associated type indicators. This list contains many commonly-known types. Individual providers may allow other, provider-specific names as well.

Standard Type Name	Type Indicator
"DBTYPE_I1"	DBTYPE_I1
"DBTYPE_I2"	DBTYPE_I2
"DBTYPE_I4"	DBTYPE_I4
"DBTYPE_I8"	DBTYPE_I8
"DBTYPE_UI1"	DBTYPE_UI1
"DBTYPE_UI2"	DBTYPE_UI2
"DBTYPE_UI4"	DBTYPE_UI4
"DBTYPE_UI8"	DBTYPE_UI8
"DBTYPE_R4"	DBTYPE_R4
"DBTYPE_R8"	DBTYPE_R8
"DBTYPE_CY"	DBTYPE_CY
"DBTYPE_DECIMAL"	DBTYPE_DECIMAL
"DBTYPE_NUMERIC"	DBTYPE_NUMERIC
"DBTYPE_BOOL"	DBTYPE_BOOL
"DBTYPE_ERROR"	DBTYPE_ERROR
"DBTYPE_UDT"	DBTYPE_UDT
"DBTYPE_VARIANT"	DBTYPE_VARIANT
"DBTYPE_IDISPATCH"	DBTYPE_IDISPATCH
"DBTYPE_IUNKNOWN"	DBTYPE_IUNKNOWN
"DBTYPE_GUID"	DBTYPE_GUID
"DBTYPE_DATE"	DBTYPE_DATE
"DBTYPE_DBDATE"	DBTYPE_DBDATE
"DBTYPE_DBTIME"	DBTYPE_DBTIME
"DBTYPE_DBTIMESTAMP"	DBTYPE_DBTIMESTAMP
"DBTYPE_BSTR"	DBTYPE_BSTR
"DBTYPE_CHAR"	DBTYPE_STR
"DBTYPE_VARCHAR"	DBTYPE_STR
"DBTYPE_LONGVARCHAR"	DBTYPE_STR
"DBTYPE_WCHAR"	DBTYPE_WSTR

Standard Type Name	Type Indicator
"DBTYPE_WVARCHAR"	DBTYPE_WSTR
"DBTYPE_WLONGVARCHAR"	DBTYPE_WSTR
"DBTYPE_BINARY"	DBTYPE_BYTES
"DBTYPE_VARBINARY"	DBTYPE_BYTES
"DBTYPE_LONGVARBINARY"	DBTYPE_BYTES

After the consumer calls **SetParameterInfo** to specify the parameter type information, it can call **GetParameterInfo** to retrieve the type indicator for each parameter. These values—which are based on the information specified in **SetParameterInfo**—represent the best fit of OLE DB types to the native parameter types. The provider guarantees that, if the consumer uses these types in a parameter accessor, it will be able to convert the data from the OLE DB type to the native parameter type.

If the provider can derive parameter type information and the consumer calls **SetParameterInfo**, **SetParameterInfo** uses the specified type information and returns DB_S_TYPEINFOOVERRIDDEN. Because deriving type information can be an expensive operation, this may result in more efficient code.

See Also

ICommandWithParameters::GetParameterInfo

IConvertType

This interface is mandatory on commands, rowsets, and index rowsets.

This interface contains a single method that gives information on the availability of type conversions on a command or on a rowset.

Method	Description
CanConvert	Gives information on the availability of type conversions on a command or on a rowset.

IConvertType::CanConvert

Gives information on the availability of type conversions on a command or on a rowset.

HRESULT CanConvert (
DBTYPE	*wFromType,*
DBTYPE	*wToType,*
DBCONVERTFLAGS	*dwConvertFlags*)**;**

Parameters

wFromType [in]

The source type of the conversion.

wToType [in]

The target type of the conversion.

dwConvertFlags [in]

Whether **CanConvert** is to determine if the conversion is supported on the rowset or on the command. These flags have the following meaning:

Conversion Flag	Description
DBCONVERTFLAGS_ COLUMN	**CanConvert** is to determine if the conversion is supported on the columns of the rowset. This flag is mutually exclusive with DBCONVERTFLAGS_PARAMETER.
DBCONVERTFLAGS_ PARAMETER	**CanConvert** is to determine if the conversion is supported on the parameters of the command.

Return Code

S_OK

The requested conversion is available.

S_FALSE

The requested conversion is not available.

E_FAIL

A provider-specific error occurred.

E_INVALIDARG

wFromType or *wToType* was not a valid type indicator.

DB_E_BADCONVERTFLAG

dwConvert flags was invalid.

The method was called on a command and its flags inquired about a conversion on a rowset, but the property DBPROP_ROWSETCONVERSIONSONCOMMAND was VARIANT_FALSE.

The DBCONVERTFLAG_PARAMETER bit was set and **CanConvert** was called on a rowset.

Comments

CanConvert can be called from a command or a rowset. The consumer can call it on a command to inquire about conversions supported by that command and on a rowset to inquire about conversions supported by that rowset. The consumer might be able to call it on a command to inquire about conversions supported on rowsets generated from that command; whether this is supported is specified by the DBPROP_ROWSETCONVERSIONSONCOMMAND property.

See Also

IAccessor::CreateAccessor

IDBCreateCommand

Consumers call **IDBCreateCommand::CreateCommand** on a session to obtain a new command.

Method	Description
CreateCommand	Creates a new command.

IDBCreateCommand::CreateCommand

Creates a new command.

HRESULT CreateCommand(
    IUnknown * *pUnkOuter,*
    REFIID *riid,*
    IUnknown ** *ppCommand*);

Parameters

pUnkOuter [in]

A pointer to the controlling **IUnknown** interface if the new command is being created as part of an aggregate. It is a null pointer if the command is not part of an aggregate.

riid [in]

The IID of the interface requested on the command.

ppCommand [out]

A pointer to memory in which to return the interface pointer on the newly created command.

Return Code

S_OK

The method succeeded.

E_FAIL

A provider-specific error occurred.

E_INVALIDARG

ppCommand was a null pointer.

E_NOINTERFACE

The command did not support the interface specified in *riid*.

E_OUTOFMEMORY

The provider did not have enough memory to create the command.

DB_E_NOAGGREGATION

pUnkOuter was not a null pointer and the command being created does not support aggregation.

Comments

If the session is transacted, the command and any actions performed as a result of executing that command are within the scope of the transaction.

See Also

ICommand

IDBCreateSession

Consumers call **IDBCreateSession::CreateSession** on a data source object to obtain a new session.

Method	Description
CreateSession	Creates a new session from the data source object and returns the requested interface on the newly created session.

IDBCreateSession::CreateSession

Creates a new session from the data source object and returns the requested interface on the newly created session.

HRESULT CreateSession (
    IUnknown * *pUnkOuter,*
    REFIID *riid,*
    IUnknown ** *ppDBSession*);

Parameters

pUnkOuter [in]

A pointer to the controlling **IUnknown** interface if the new session is being created as part of an aggregate. It is a null pointer if the session is not part of an aggregate.

riid [in]

The IID of the interface.

ppDBSession [out]

A pointer to memory in which to return the interface pointer.

Return Code

S_OK

The method succeeded.

E_FAIL

A provider-specific error occurred.

E_INVALIDARG

ppDBSession was a null pointer.

E_NOINTERFACE

The session did not support the interface specified in *riid*.

E_OUTOFMEMORY

The provider did not have enough memory to create the session.

E_UNEXPECTED

The data source object was in an uninitialized state.

DB_E_NOAGGREGATION

pUnkOuter was not a null pointer and the session being created does not support aggregation.

See Also

IDBProperties::GetPropertyInfo, ISessionProperties::SetProperties

IDBDataSourceAdmin

IDBDataSourceAdmin is an optional interface for creating, destroying, and modifying data sources.

It is important to distinguish between the data source object and the data source. The data source object is the object used by the consumer code. The data source is the actual source of data, such as a server database.

Method	Description
CreateDataSource	Creates a new data source and data source object, and initializes the data source object to the data source.
DestroyDataSource	Destroys the current data source and leaves the data source object in an uninitialized state.
GetCreationProperties	Returns information about the data source creation properties supported by the provider.
ModifyDataSource	Modifies the current data source.

IDBDataSourceAdmin::CreateDataSource

Creates a new data source and data source object, and initializes the data source object to the data source.

HRESULT CreateDataSource(
ULONG	*cPropertySets*,
DBPROPSET	*rgPropertySets*[],
IUnknown*	*pUnkOuter*,
REFIID	*riid*,
IUnknown**	*ppSession*);

Parameters

cPropertySets [in]

The number of DBPROPSET structures in *rgPropertySets*. If this is zero, the provider ignores *rgPropertySets* and the method does not do anything.

rgPropertySets [in/out]

An array of DBPROPSET structures containing properties and values to be set. The properties specified in these structures must belong to the Data Source Creation or Initialization property groups; Initialization properties must be supported by the provider for use in data source creation. If *ppSession* is not a null pointer, the properties can also belong to the Session property group. If the same property is specified more than once in *rgPropertySets*, then which value is used is provider-specific. If a provider cannot support a property, then the property is ignored. If *cPropertySets* is zero, this argument is ignored.

For information about the properties in the Data Source Creation, Initialization, and Session property groups that are defined by OLE DB, see "Data Source Creation Properties," "Initialization Properties," and "Session Properties" in Appendix C. For information about the DBPROPSET and DBPROP structures, see "DBPROPSET Structure" and "DBPROP Structure" in Chapter 11.

pUnkOuter [in]

A pointer to the controlling **IUnknown** interface if a session is desired and is to be created as part of an aggregate. Otherwise, it is a null pointer.

riid [in]

The requested interface for the session returned in *ppSession. Ignored if *ppSession* is a null pointer.

ppSession [in/out]

A pointer to memory in which to return the pointer to the session. If *ppSession* is a null pointer, no session is created.

Return Code

S_OK

The method succeeded. In all DBPROP structures passed to the method, *dwStatus* is set to DBPROPSTATUS_OK.

DB_S_ERRORSOCCURRED

The new data source was created but one or more properties—for which the *dwOptions* element of the DBPROP structure was DBPROPOPTIONS_SETIFCHEAP—were not set. The consumer checks *dwStatus* in the DBPROP structures to determine which properties were not set. The method can fail to set properties for a number of reasons, including:

- The property was not in the Data Source Creation, Initialization, or Session property group.

- The property was in the Initialization property group but was not supported for use in data source creation.

- The property set was not supported by the provider.

- It was not cheap to set the property.

E_FAIL

A provider-specific error occurred.

E_INVALIDARG

cPropertySets was not zero and *rgPropertySets* was a null pointer.

In an element of *rgPropertySets*, *cProperties* was not zero and *rgProperties* was a null pointer.

E_NOINTERFACE

The session did not support the interface specified in *riid*.

E_OUTOFMEMORY

The provider was unable to allocate sufficient memory to create the new data source.

DB_E_ALREADYINITIALIZED

Initialize had already been called for the data source object and an intervening call to **Uninitialize** had not been made.

DB_E_DUPLICATEDATASOURCE

A data source with the same name already exists.

DB_E_ERRORSOCCURRED

The data source was not created because one or more properties—for which the *dwOptions* element of the DBPROP structure was DBPROPOPTIONS_REQUIRED or an invalid value—were not set. The consumer checks *dwStatus* in the DBPROP structures to determine which properties were not set. None of the satisfiable properties are remembered. The method can fail to set properties for a number of reasons, including:

- The property was not in the Data Source Creation, Initialization, or Session property group.

- The property was in the Initialization property group but was not supported for use in data source creation.

- The property set was not supported by the provider.

DB_E_NOAGGREGATION
pUnkOuter was not a null pointer and the data source being created does not support aggregation.

DB_SEC_E_AUTH_FAILED
The provider required initialization but an authentication failed. The data source was not created and the data source object remains in an uninitialized state.

DB_SEC_E_PERMISSIONDENIED
The consumer did not have permission to create a new data source.

Comments

CreateDataSource creates a data source and a data source object and initializes the data source object in one atomic operation.

The properties DBPROP_INIT_DATASOURCE and DBPROP_INIT_LOCATION are always required by **CreateDataSource**. If DBPROP_INIT_LOCATION is set to VT_EMPTY, the data source is created in the default location.

See Also

IDBDataSourceAdmin::DestroyDataSource,
IDBDataSourceAdmin::ModifyDataSource

IDBDataSourceAdmin::DestroyDataSource

Destroys the current data source and leaves the data source object in an uninitialized state.

HRESULT DestroyDataSource ();

Parameters

None.

Return Code

S_OK

The method succeeded.

E_FAIL

A provider-specific error occurred.

DB_E_UNINITIALIZED

Initialize had not been called for the data source object.

DB_E_NOTSUPPORTED

The provider does not support this method.

DB_SEC_E_PERMISSIONDENIED

The consumer did not have permission to destroy the current data source.

Comments

DestroyDataSource destroys the current data source and leaves the data source object in an uninitialized state. It is an error to call **DestroyDataSource** when there are open sessions, commands, or rowsets on the data source object. The consumer must release all interface pointers on all sessions, commands, and rowsets on the data source object before calling **DestroyDataSource**.

See Also

IDBDataSourceAdmin::CreateDataSource

IDBDataSourceAdmin:: GetCreationProperties

Returns information about the data source creation properties supported by the data provider.

HRESULT GetCreationProperties (
ULONG	*cPropertyIDSets,*
const DBPROPIDSET	*rgPropertyIDSets*[],
ULONG *	*pcPropertyInfoSets,*
DBPROPINFOSET **	*prgPropertyInfoSets,*
OLECHAR **	*ppDescBuffer*);

Parameters

cPropertyIDSets [in]

The number of DBPROPIDSET structures in *rgPropertyIDSets*.

If *cPropertySets* is zero, the provider ignores *rgPropertyIDSets* and returns information about all of the properties in the Data Source Creation and Session property groups it supports and all of the properties in the Initialization property group it supports for use in creating data sources.

If *cPropertyIDSets* is not zero, the provider returns information about the requested properties. If a property is not supported, or if a property in the Initialization property group cannot be used to create data sources, the returned value of *dwStatus* in the returned DBPROPINFO structure for that property is DBPROPFLAGS_NOTSUPPORTED and the values of the *pwszDescription*, *vtType*, and *vValues* elements are undefined.

rgPropertyIDSets [in]

An array of *cPropertyIDSets* DBPROPIDSET structures. The properties specified in these structures must belong to the Data Source Creation or Session property group or belong to the Initialization property group and be supported for use in creating data sources. The provider returns information about the properties specified in these structures. If *cPropertyIDSets* is zero, then this parameter is ignored.

For information about the properties in the Data Source Creation, Initialization, and Session property groups that are defined by OLE DB, see "Data Source Creation Properties," "Initialization Properties," and "Session Properties" in Appendix C. For information about the DBPROPIDSET structure, see "DBPROPIDSET Structure" in Chapter 11.

pcPropertyInfoSets [out]

A pointer to memory in which to return the number of DBPROPINFOSET structures returned in **prgPropertyInfoSets*. If *cPropertyIDSets* is zero, **pcPropertyInfoSets* is the total number of property sets for which the provider supports at least one property in the Data Source Creation, Initialization, or Session property groups. If *cPropertyIDSets* is greater than zero, **pcPropertyInfoSets* is set to *cPropertyIDSets*. If an error occurs, **pcPropertyInfoSets* is set to zero.

prgPropertyInfoSets [out]

A pointer to memory in which to return an array of DBPROPINFOSET structures. If *cPropertyIDSets* is zero, then one structure is returned for each property set that contains at least one property belonging to the Data Source Creation, Initialization or Session property group. If *cPropertyIDSets* is not zero, then one structure is returned for each property set specified in *rgPropertyIDSets*.

If *cPropertyIDSets* is not zero, the DBPROPINFOSET structures in **prgPropertyInfoSets* are returned in the same order as the DBPROPIDSET structures in *rgPropertyIDSets*; that is, for corresponding elements of each array, the *guidPropertySet* elements are the same. If *cPropertyIDs*, in an element of *rgPropertyIDSets*, is not zero, the DBPROPINFO structures in the corresponding element of **prgPropertyInfoSets* are returned in the same order as the DBPROPID values in *rgPropertyIDs*; that is for corresponding elements of each array, the property IDs are the same.

The provider allocates memory for the structures and returns the address to this memory; the consumer releases this memory with **IMalloc::Free** when it no longer needs the structures. Before calling **IMalloc::Free** for **prgPropertyInfoSets*, the consumer should call **IMalloc::Free** for the *rgPropertyInfos* element in each element of **prgPropertyInfoSets*. If **pcPropertyInfoSets* is zero on output or an error occurs, then **prgPropertyInfoSets* must be a null pointer on output.

For information about the DBPROPINFOSET and DBPROPINFO structures, see "DBPROPINFOSET Structure" and "DBPROPINFO Structure" in Chapter 11.

ppDescBuffer [out]

A pointer to memory in which to return a pointer to storage for all string values returned in the **pwszDescription* element of the DBPROPINFO structure. The provider allocates this memory with **IMalloc** and the consumer frees it with **IMalloc::Free** when it no longer needs the property descriptions. If *ppDescBuffer* is a null pointer on input, **GetCreationProperties** does not return the property descriptions. If **pcPropertyInfoSets* is zero on output or an error occurs, the provider does not allocate any memory and ensures that **ppDescBuffer* is a null pointer on output.

Return Code

S_OK

The method succeeded. In all DBPROPINFO structures returned by the method, *dwFlags* is set to a value other than DBPROPFLAGS_NOTSUPPORTED.

DB_S_ERRORSOCCURRED

One or more properties specified in *rgPropertyIDSets* were not supported by the provider. The *dwFlags* element of the DBPROPINFO structure for such properties is set to DBPROPFLAGS_NOTSUPPORTED.

One or more properties specified in *rgPropertyIDSets* were not in the Data Source Creation, Initialization, or Session property groups. The *dwFlags* element of the DBPROPINFO structure for such properties is set to DBPROPFLAGS_NOTSUPPORTED.

One or more properties specified in *rgPropertyIDSets* were in the Initialization property group but could not be used to create data sources. The *dwFlags* element of the DBPROPINFO structure for such properties is set to DBPROPFLAGS_NOTSUPPORTED.

One or more property sets specified in *rgPropertyIDSets* were not supported by the provider. The *dwFlags* element of the DBPROPINFO structure for all specified properties in these sets is set to DBPROPFLAGS_NOTSUPPORTED. If *cPropertyIDs* in the DBPROPIDSET structure for the property set was zero, the provider cannot set *dwStatus* in the DBPROP structure because it does not know the IDs of any properties in the property set. Instead, it sets *cProperties* to zero in the DBPROPSET structure returned for the property set.

E_FAIL

A provider-specific error occurred.

E_INVALIDARG

pcPropertyInfoSets or *prgPropertyInfoSets* was a null pointer.

cPropertyIDSets was not equal to zero and *rgPropertyIDSets* was a null pointer.

In an element of *rgPropertyIDSets*, *cPropertyIDs* was not zero and *rgPropertyIDs* was a null pointer.

E_OUTOFMEMORY

The provider was unable to allocate sufficient memory in which to return the DBPROPINFOSET or DBPROPINFO structures or the property descriptions.

Comments

GetCreationProperties returns properties in the Data Source Creation and Session property groups and properties in the Initialization property group that can be used in data source creation. It is possible that there are properties in the Initialization property group that cannot be used in data source creation. The properties for which values must be set to create a data source are indicated in the *dwFlags* element of the DBPROPINFO structure as DBPROPFLAGS_REQUIRED.

This method can be called before the data source object has been initialized.

See Also

IDBDataSourceAdmin::CreateDataSource

IDBDataSourceAdmin::ModifyDataSource

Modifies the current data source.

HRESULT ModifyDataSource (
  ULONG   *cPropertySets,*
  DBPROPSET   *rgPropertySets*[]**);**

Parameters

cPropertySets [in]

The number of DBPROPSET structures in *rgPropertySets*. If this is zero, the provider ignores *rgPropertySets* and the method does not do anything.

rgPropertySets [in/out]

An array of DBPROPSET structures containing properties and values to be set. The properties specified in these structures must belong to the Data Source Creation or Initialization property groups; Initialization properties must be supported by the provider for use in data source creation. If the same property is specified more than once in *rgPropertySets*, then which value is used is provider-specific. If a provider cannot support a property, then the property is ignored. If *cPropertySets* is zero, this argument is ignored.

For information about the properties in the Data Source Creation and Initialization property groups that are defined by OLE DB, see "Data Source Creation Properties" and "Initialization Properties" in Appendix C. For information about the DBPROPSET and DBPROP structures, see "DBPROPSET Structure" and "DBPROP Structure" in Chapter 11.

Return Code

S_OK

The method succeeded. In all DBPROP structures passed to the method, *dwStatus* is set to DBPROPSTATUS_OK.

DB_S_ERRORSOCCURRED

The data source was modified but one or more properties—for which the *dwOptions* element of the DBPROP structure was DBPROPOPTIONS_SETIFCHEAP—were not set. The consumer checks *dwStatus* in the DBPROP structures to determine which properties were not set. The method can fail to set properties for a number of reasons, including:

- The property was not in the Data Source Creation or Initialization property group.

- The property was in the Initialization property group but was not supported for use in data source creation.

- The property set was not supported by the provider.

- It was not cheap to set the property.

E_FAIL

A provider-specific error occurred.

E_INVALIDARG

cPropertySets was not zero and *rgPropertySets* was a null pointer.

In an element of *rgPropertySets*, *cProperties* was not zero and *rgProperties* was a null pointer.

DB_E_UNINITIALIZED

Initialize had not been called for the data source object.

DB_E_ERRORSOCCURRED

The data source was not modified because one or more properties—for which the *dwOptions* element of the DBPROP structure was DBPROPOPTIONS_REQUIRED—were not set. The consumer checks *dwStatus* in the DBPROP structures to determine which properties were not set. None of the satisfiable properties are remembered. The method can fail to set properties for a number of reasons, including:

- The property was not in the Data Source Creation or Initialization property group.

- The property was in the Initialization property group but was not supported for use in data source creation.

- The property set was not supported by the provider.

- The value of *dwOptions* in a DBPROP structure was invalid.

DB_E_NOTSUPPORTED

The provider does not support this method.

DB_SEC_E_PERMISSIONDENIED

The consumer did not have permission to modify the current data source.

Comments

ModifyDataSource modifies the current data source and leaves the data source object in an initialized state. It is an error to call **ModifyDataSource** when there are open sessions, commands, or rowsets on the data source object; that is, the consumer must release all interface pointers on all sessions, commands, and rowsets on the data source object before calling **ModifyDataSource**.

See Also

IDBDataSourceAdmin::CreateDataSource,
IDBDataSourceAdmin::DestroyDataSource

IDBInfo

IDBInfo returns information about the keywords and literals a provider supports. It is an optional interface on the data source objects.

Method	Description
GetKeywords	Returns a list of provider-specific keywords.
GetLiteralInfo	Returns information about literals used in text commands and in **ITableDefinition** and **IIndexDefinition**.

IDBInfo::GetKeywords

Returns a list of provider-specific keywords.

HRESULT GetKeywords(
    LPOLESTR *   *ppwszKeywords*);

Parameters

ppwszKeywords [out]

A pointer to memory in which to return the address of a string. The string contains a comma-separated list of all keywords unique to this provider; that is, a comma-separated list of keywords that are not in the list in the Comments section. If there are no keywords unique to this provider or an error occurs, the provider sets **ppwszKeywords* to a null pointer.

The provider allocates memory for the string and returns the address to this memory; the consumer releases this memory with **IMalloc::Free** when it no longer needs the string.

Return Code

S_OK

The method succeeded.

E_FAIL

A provider-specific error occurred.

E_INVALIDARG

ppwszKeywords was a null pointer.

E_OUTOFMEMORY

The provider was unable to allocate sufficient memory in which to return the keywords.

E_UNEXPECTED

The data source object was in an uninitialized state.

Comments

The following lists the keywords from OLE DB.

ABSOLUTE	ARE
ACTION	AS
ADD	ASC
ALL	ASSERTION
ALLOCATE	AT
ALTER	AUTHORIZATION
AND	AVG
ANY	BEGIN

BETWEEN

BIT

BIT_LENGTH

BOTH

BY

CASCADE

CASCADED

CASE

CAST

CATALOG

CHAR

CHARACTER

CHAR_LENGTH

CHARACTER_LENGTH

CHECK

CLOSE

COALESCE

COLLATE

COLLATION

COLUMN

COMMIT

CONNECT

CONNECTION

CONSTRAINT

CONSTRAINTS

CONTINUE

CONVERT

CORRESPONDING

COUNT

CREATE

CROSS

CURRENT

CURRENT_DATE

CURRENT_TIME

CURRENT_TIMESTAMP

CURRENT_USER

CURSOR

DATE

DAY

DEALLOCATE

DEC

DECIMAL

DECLARE

DEFAULT

DEFERRABLE

DEFERRED

DELETE

DESC

DESCRIBE

DESCRIPTOR

DIAGNOSTICS

DISCONNECT

DISTINCT

DISTINCTROW

DOMAIN

DOUBLE

DROP

ELSE

END

END-EXEC

ESCAPE

EXCEPT

EXCEPTION

EXEC

EXECUTE

EXISTS

EXTERNAL

EXTRACT

FALSE

FETCH

FIRST

FLOAT

FOR	LIKE
FOREIGN	LOCAL
FOUND	LOWER
FROM	MATCH
FULL	MAX
GET	MIN
GLOBAL	MINUTE
GO	MODULE
GOTO	MONTH
GRANT	NAMES
GROUP	NATIONAL
HAVING	NATURAL
HOUR	NCHAR
IDENTITY	NEXT
IMMEDIATE	NO
IN	NOT
INDICATOR	NULL
INITIALLY	NULLIF
INNER	NUMERIC
INPUT	OCTET_LENGTH
INSENSITIVE	OF
INSERT	ON
INT	ONLY
INTEGER	OPEN
INTERSECT	OPTION
INTERVAL	OR
INTO	ORDER
IS	OUTER
ISOLATION	OUTPUT
JOIN	OVERLAPS
KEY	PARTIAL
LANGUAGE	POSITION
LAST	PRECISION
LEADING	PREPARE
LEFT	PRESERVE
LEVEL	PRIMARY

PRIOR	TIME
PRIVILEGES	TIMESTAMP
PROCEDURE	TIMEZONE_HOUR
PUBLIC	TIMEZONE_MINUTE
READ	TO
REAL	TRAILING
REFERENCES	TRANSACTION
RELATIVE	TRANSLATE
RESTRICT	TRANSLATION
REVOKE	TRIGGER
RIGHT	TRIM
ROLLBACK	TRUE
ROWS	UNION
SCHEMA	UNIQUE
SCROLL	UNKNOWN
SECOND	UPDATE
SECTION	UPPER
SELECT	USAGE
SESSION	USER
SESSION_USER	USING
SET	VALUE
SIZE	VALUES
SMALLINT	VARCHAR
SOME	VARYING
SQL	VIEW
SQLCODE	WHEN
SQLERROR	WHENEVER
SQLSTATE	WHERE
SUBSTRING	WITH
SUM	WORK
SYSTEM_USER	WRITE
TABLE	YEAR
TEMPORARY	ZONE
THEN	

See Also

IDBInfo::GetLiteralInfo, **IDBProperties::GetProperties**

IDBInfo::GetLiteralInfo

Returns information about literals used in text commands and in **ITableDefinition** and **IIndexDefinition**.

HRESULT GetLiteralInfo(
    ULONG   *cLiterals,*
    const DBLITERAL   *rgLiterals*[],
    ULONG *   *pcLiteralInfo,*
    DBLITERALINFO ** *prgLiteralInfo,*
    OLECHAR **   *ppCharBuffer*);

Parameters

cLiterals [in]

The number of literals being asked about. If this is 0, the provider ignores *rgLiterals* and returns information about all of the literals it supports.

rgLiterals [in]

An array of *cLiterals* literals about which to return information. If the consumer specifies an invalid DBLITERAL value in this array, **GetLiteralInfo** returns FALSE in *fSupported* in the corresponding element of the **prgLiteralInfo* array.

If *cLiterals* is 0, this parameter is ignored.

pcLiteralInfo [out]

A pointer to memory in which to return the number of literals for which information was returned. If *cLiterals* is 0, this is the total number of literals supported by the provider. If an error other than DB_E_ERRORSOCCURRED occurs, **pcLiteralInfo* is set to 0.

prgLiteralInfo [out]

A pointer to memory in which to return a pointer to an array of DBLITERALINFO structures. One structure is returned for each literal. The provider allocates memory for the structures and returns the address to this memory; the consumer releases this memory with **IMalloc::Free** when it no longer needs the structures. If **pcLiteralInfo* is 0 on output or an error other than DB_E_ERRORSOCCURRED occurs, the provider does not allocate any memory and ensures that **prgLiteralInfo* is a null pointer on output. For information about DBLITERALINFO structures, see the Comments section.

ppCharBuffer [out]

A pointer to memory in which to return a pointer for all string values (*pwszLiteralValue*, *pwszInvalidChars*, and *pwszInvalidStartingChars*) within a single allocation block. The provider allocates this memory and the consumer releases it with **IMalloc::Free** when it no longer needs it. If **pcLiteralInfo* is 0 on output or an error occurs, the provider does not allocate any memory and ensures that **ppCharBuffer* is a null pointer on output. Each of the individual string values stored in this buffer is terminated by a null termination character. Therefore, the buffer may contain one or more strings, each with its own null termination character, and may contain embedded null termination characters.

Return Code

S_OK

The method succeeded. In each structure returned in *prgLiteralInfo*, the *fSupported* element is set to TRUE.

DB_S_ERRORSOCCURRED

rgLiterals contained at least one unsupported or invalid literal. In the structures returned in *prgLiteralInfo* for unsupported or invalid literals, the *fSupported* element is set to FALSE.

E_FAIL

A provider-specific error occurred.

E_INVALIDARG

cLiterals was not equal to zero and *rgLiterals* was a null pointer.

pcLiteralInfo, *prgLiteralInfo*, or *ppCharBuffer* was a null pointer.

E_OUTOFMEMORY

The provider was unable to allocate sufficient memory in which to return the DBLITERALINFO structures or the strings containing the valid and starting characters.

E_UNEXPECTED

The data source object was in an uninitialized state.

DB_E_ERRORSOCCURRED

All literals were either invalid or unsupported. The provider allocates memory for *prgLiteralInfo* and sets the value of the *fSupported* element in all of the structures to FALSE. The consumer frees this memory when it no longer needs the information.

Comments

In the context of **GetLiteralInfo**, a literal is one of several things:

- A special character or characters used by text commands, such as the character used to quote identifiers. **GetLiteralInfo** returns the character or characters.

- A literal data value, such as a character literal in an SQL statement. For such literal data values, **GetLiteralInfo** returns the maximum length of the literal in characters, a list of the characters that cannot be used in the literal, and a list of the characters that cannot be used as the first character of the literal.

- The name of a database object such as a column or table. For such names, **GetLiteralInfo** returns the maximum length of the name in characters, a list of the characters that cannot be used in the name, and a list of the characters that cannot be used as the first character of the name.

Information about literals is returned in the DBLITERALINFO structure:

```
typedef struct tagDBLITERALINFO {
    LPOLESTR    pwszLiteralValue;
    LPOLESTR    pwszInvalidChars;
    LPOLESTR    pwszInvalidStartingChars;
    DBLITERAL   lt;
    BOOL        fSupported;
    ULONG       cchMaxLen;
} DBLITERALINFO;
```

The elements of this structure are used as follows.

Element	Description
pwszLiteralValue	A pointer to a string in the **ppCharBuffer* buffer containing the actual literal value.
	For example, if *lt* is DBLITERAL_LIKE_PERCENT, and the percent character (%) is used to match 0 or more characters in a LIKE clause, this would be "%". This is used for DBLITERAL_CATALOG_SEPARATOR, DBLITERAL_ESCAPE_PERCENT, DBLITERAL_ESCAPE_UNDERSCORE, DBLITERAL_LIKE_PERCENT, DBLITERAL_LIKE_UNDERSCORE, and DBLITERAL_QUOTE. For all other DBLITERAL values *pwszLiteralValue* is not used and is set to a null pointer.
pwszInvalidChars	A pointer to a string in the **ppCharBuffer* buffer containing the characters that are not valid in the literal.
	For example, if table names can contain anything other than a numeric character, this would be "0123456789" when *lt* is DBLITERAL_TABLE_NAME. If the literal can contain any valid character, this is a null pointer. This is not used for DBLITERAL_BINARY_LITERAL, DBLITERAL_CATALOG_SEPARATOR, DBLITERAL_ESCAPE_PERCENT, DBLITERAL_ESCAPE_UNDERSCORE, DBLITERAL_LIKE_PERCENT, DBLITERAL_LIKE_UNDERSCORE, and DBLITERAL_QUOTE; *pwszInvalidChars* is set to a null pointer for these DBLITERAL values.
pwszInvalidStartingChars	A pointer to a string in the **ppCharBuffer* buffer containing the characters that are not valid as the first character of the literal. If the literal can start with any valid character, this is a null pointer.
	For example, if table names can begin with anything other than a numeric character, this would be "0123456789" when *lt* is DBLITERAL_TABLE_NAME. This is not used for DBLITERAL_CATALOG_SEPARATOR, DBLITERAL_ESCAPE_PERCENT, DBLITERAL_ESCAPE_UNDERSCORE, DBLITERAL_LIKE_PERCENT, DBLITERAL_LIKE_UNDERSCORE, and DBLITERAL_QUOTE; *pwszInvalidStartingChars* is set to a null pointer for these DBLITERAL values.
lt	The literal described in the structure. For more information, see the following section.

Element	Description
fSupported	TRUE if the provider supports the literal specified by *lt*. Note that if *cLiterals* is 0, this is always TRUE, as **GetLiteralInfo** only returns information about literals it supports in this case.
	FALSE if the provider does not support the literal or the value of the corresponding element of the *rgLiterals* array was not a valid value in the DBLITERAL enumerated type.
cchMaxLen	The maximum number of characters in the literal. If there is no maximum or the maximum is unknown, *cchMaxLen* is set to ~0 (bitwise, the value is not 0; that is, all bits are set to 1). For DBLITERAL_CATALOG_SEPARATOR, DBLITERAL_ESCAPE_PERCENT, DBLITERAL_ESCAPE_UNDERSCORE, DBLITERAL_LIKE_PERCENT, DBLITERAL_LIKE_UNDERSCORE, and DBLITERAL_QUOTE, this is the actual number of characters in the literal.

The following values of DBLITERAL are supported:

Value	Description
DBLITERAL_INVALID	An invalid value.
DBLITERAL_ BINARY_LITERAL	A binary literal in a text command.
DBLITERAL_ CATALOG_NAME	A catalog name in a text command.
DBLITERAL_ CATALOG_SEPARATOR	The character that separates the catalog name from the rest of the identifier in a text command.
DBLITERAL_ CHAR_LITERAL	A character literal in a text command.
DBLITERAL_ COLUMN_ALIAS	A column alias in a text command.
DBLITERAL_ COLUMN_NAME	A column name used in a text command or in a data-definition interface.
DBLITERAL_ CORRELATION_NAME	A correlation name (table alias) in a text command.
DBLITERAL_ CURSOR_NAME	A cursor name in a text command.
DBLITERAL_ ESCAPE_PERCENT	The character used in a **LIKE** clause to escape the character returned for the DBLITERAL_LIKE_PERCENT literal. For example, if a percent sign (%) is used to match zero or more characters and this is a backslash (\), the characters "abc\%%" matches all character values that start with "abc%".

Value	Description
DBLITERAL_ESCAPE_PERCENT (*continued*)	Note that some SQL dialects support a clause (the **ESCAPE** clause) that can be used to override this value.
DBLITERAL_ESCAPE_UNDERSCORE	The character used in a **LIKE** clause to escape the character returned for the DBLITERAL_LIKE_UNDERSCORE literal. For example, if an underscore (_) is used to match exactly one character and this is a backslash (\\), the characters "abc\\ _" matches all character values that are five characters long and start with "abc_".
	Note that some SQL dialects support a clause (the **ESCAPE** clause) that can be used to override this value.
DBLITERAL_INDEX_NAME	An index name used in a text command or in a data-definition interface.
DBLITERAL_LIKE_PERCENT	The character used in a **LIKE** clause to match zero or more characters. For example, if this is a percent sign (%), the characters "abc%" matches all character values that start with "abc".
DBLITERAL_LIKE_UNDERSCORE	The character used in a **LIKE** clause to match exactly one character. For example, if this is an underscore (%), the characters "abc_" matches all character values that are four characters long and start with "abc".
DBLITERAL_PROCEDURE_NAME	A procedure name in a text command.
DBLITERAL_SCHEMA_NAME	A schema name in a text command.
DBLITERAL_TABLE_NAME	A table name used in a text command or in a data-definition interface.
DBLITERAL_TEXT_COMMAND	A text command, such as an SQL statement.
DBLITERAL_USER_NAME	A user name in a text command.
DBLITERAL_VIEW_NAME	A view name in a text command.
DBLITERAL_QUOTE	The character used in a text command to quote identifiers that contain special characters.

See Also

IDBInfo::GetKeywords, **IDBProperties::GetProperties**

IDBInitialize

IDBInitialize is used to initialize and uninitialize data source objects and enumerators. It is a mandatory interface on data source objects and an optional interface on enumerators.

Method	Description
Initialize	Initializes a data source object or enumerator.
Uninitialize	Returns the data source object or enumerator to an uninitialized state.

IDBInitialize::Initialize

Initializes a data source object or enumerator.

HRESULT Initialize();

Parameters

None.

Return Code

S_OK

The method succeeded.

DB_S_ERRORSOCCURRED

The data source object or enumerator was initialized but one or more properties—
for which the *dwOptions* element of the DBPROP structure was
DBPROPOPTIONS_SETIFCHEAP—were not set. To determine which properties
were in error, the consumer calls **IDBProperties::GetProperties** with the
DBPROP_INIT_PROPERTIESINERROR property in the Initialization property
set as the only property. **GetProperties** returns the properties that could not be set.
The method can fail to set properties for a number of reasons, including:

- It was not cheap to set the property.

- The value in *vValue* in the DBPROP structure was invalid.

- The property's value conflicted with an existing property.

E_FAIL

A provider-specific error occurred.

E_OUTOFMEMORY

The provider was unable to allocate sufficient memory in order to initialize the data
source object or enumerator.

DB_E_ALREADYINITIALIZED

Initialize had already been called for the data source object or enumerator and an
intervening call to **Uninitialize** had not been made.

DB_E_ERRORSOCCURRED

The data source object or enumerator was not initialized because one or more
properties—for which the *dwOptions* element of the DBPROP structure was
DBPROPOPTIONS_REQUIRED—were not set. The consumer checks *dwStatus*
in the DBPROP structures to determine which properties were in error. The method
can fail to set properties for any of the reasons specified in
DB_S_ERRORSOCCURRED except the reason that states that it was not cheap to
set the property.

DB_SEC_E_AUTH_FAILED

Authentication of the consumer to the data source or enumerator failed. The data
source object or enumerator remains in the uninitialized state.

Comments

Initialize initializes the data source object or enumerator. It uses the values of properties in the Initialization property group that have been set with **IDBProperties::SetProperties**. If the consumer has not set values for all required properties, **Initialize** can prompt for values.

If **Initialize** returns DB_S_ERRORSOCCURRED or DB_E_ERRORSOCCURRED, the consumer can immediately call **IDBProperties::GetProperties** with the DBPPROPSET_PROPERTIESINERROR property set to return the properties that could not be set. For more information, see "Property Sets" in Chapter 11.

For information about what the consumer can and cannot do with a data source object or enumerator before it is initialized, see "Data Source Object States" and "Enumerator States" in Chapter 2.

Initializing a Data Source Object Through a Network Connection

The following shows how to instantiate a data source object as an in-process object using **CoCreateInstance**.

```
#include <oledb.h>
extern CLSID CLSID_DSO;
int main() {
    HRESULT          hr;
    IDBInitialize *pIDBInitialize;

    // Create the data source object.
    hr = CoCreateInstance(CLSID_DSO, NULL, CLSCTX_INPROC_SERVER,
                        IID_IDBInitialize, (void**) &pIDBInitialize);

    // Set the initialization properties.
    DBPROP rgProps[8];
    for (ULONG i = 0; i <= 7; i++) {
        VariantInit(&rgProps[i].vValue);
        rgProps[i].dwOptions = DBPROPOPTIONS_REQUIRED;
    };

    rgProps[0].dwPropertyID   = DBPROP_INIT_LOCATION;
    V_VT(rgProps[0].vValue)   = VT_BSTR;
    V_BSTR(rgProps[0].vValue) = SysAllocStringLen(OLESTR("server"),
                                                  wcslen(OLESTR("server")));

    rgProps[1].dwPropertyID   = DBPROP_INIT_DATASOURCE;
    V_VT(rgProps[1].vValue)   = VT_BSTR;
    V_BSTR(rgProps[1].vValue) = SysAllocStringLen(OLESTR("database"),
                                                  wcslen(OLESTR("database")));

    rgProps[2].dwPropertyID   = DBPROP_AUTH_PASSWORD;
    V_VT(rgProps[2].vValue)   = VT_BSTR;
    V_BSTR(rgProps[2].vValue) = SysAllocStringLen(OLESTR("password"),
                                                  wcslen(OLESTR("password")));
```

```
            rgProps[3].dwPropertyID    = DBPROP_AUTH_USERID;
            V_VT(rgProps[3].vValue)    = VT_BSTR;
            V_BSTR(rgProps[3].vValue)  = SysAllocStringLen(OLESTR("username"),
                                                    wcslen(OLESTR("username"))));

            rgProps[4].dwPropertyID    = DBPROP_AUTH_ENCRYPT_PASSWORD;
            V_VT(rgProps[4].vValue)    = VT_BOOL;
            V_BOOL(rgProps[4].vValue)  = VARIANT_TRUE;

            rgProps[5].dwPropertyID    = DBPROP_AUTH_CACHE_AUTHINFO;
            V_VT(rgProps[5].vValue)    = VT_BOOL;
            V_BOOL(rgProps[5].vValue)  = VARIANT_TRUE;

            rgProps[6].dwPropertyID    = DBPROP_AUTH_PERSIST_SENSITIVE_AUTHINFO;
            V_VT(rgProps[6].vValue)    = VT_BOOL;
            V_BOOL(rgProps[6].vValue)  = VARIANT_TRUE;

            rgProps[7].dwPropertyID    = DBPROP_AUTH_PERSIST_ENCRYPTED;
            V_VT(rgProps[7].vValue)    = VT_BOOL;
            V_BOOL(rgProps[7].vValue)  = VARIANT_TRUE;

            // Create the structure containing the properties.
            DBPROPSET PropSet;
            PropSet.rgProperties    = rgProps;
            PropSet.cProperties     = 8;
            PropSet.guidPropertySet = DBPROPSET_DBINIT;

            // Get an IDBProperties pointer and set the initialization properties.
            IDBProperties *pIDBProperties;
            pIDBInitialize->QueryInterface(IID_IDBProperties, pIDBProperties);
            pIDBProperties->SetProperties(1, &PropSet);
            pIDBProperties->Release();

            // Initialize the data source object.
            hr = pIDBInitialize->Initialize();
            return hr;
        };
```

See Also

IDBInitialize::Uninitialize, IDBProperties::SetProperties

IDBInitialize::Uninitialize

Returns the data source object or enumerator to an uninitialized state.

HRESULT Uninitialize();

Parameters

None.

Return Code

S_OK

The method succeeded.

E_FAIL

A provider-specific error occurred.

DB_E_OBJECTOPEN

There were open sessions, commands, or rowsets on the data source object.

Comments

The consumer is not required to uninitialize a data source object or enumerator before releasing it, but may use this method to release state associated with the data source object or enumerator so that it can be reinitialized with **Initialize** or a new state loaded on a data source object, such as with **IPersistFile::Load**.

It is an error to call **Uninitialize** when there are open sessions, commands, or rowsets on the data source object; that is, the consumer must release all interface pointers on all sessions, commands, and rowsets on the data source object before calling **Uninitialize**. It is not an error to call **Uninitialize** if **Initialize** has not been called.

For information about what the consumer can and cannot do with a data source object or enumerator that is uninitialized, see "Data Source Object States" and "Enumerator States" in Chapter 2.

See Also

IDBInitialize::Initialize

IDBProperties

IDBProperties is used to set and get the values of properties on the data source object or enumerator and to get information about all properties supported by the provider.

Before the data source object or enumerator is initialized, the consumer can work only with properties in the Initialization property group. After the data source object or enumerator is initialized, the consumer can work with properties in the Initialization, Data Source, and Data Source Information property groups, although it cannot set the value of properties in the Initialization property group.

Only properties in the Initialization property group are guaranteed to survive uninitialization. That is, if the consumer uninitializes and reinitializes a data source object or enumerator, it might need to reset the values of properties in groups other than Initialization.

IDBProperties is a mandatory interface for data source objects and an optional interface for enumerators. However, if an enumerator exposes **IDBInitialize**, it must expose **IDBProperties**.

Method	Description
GetProperties	Returns the values of properties in the Data Source, Data Source Information, and Initialization property groups that are currently set on the data source object or the values of properties in the Initialization property group that are currently set on the enumerator.
GetPropertyInfo	Returns information about all properties supported by the provider.
SetProperties	Sets properties in the Data Source and Initialization property groups, for data source objects, or the Initialization property group, for enumerators.

IDBProperties::GetProperties

Returns the values of properties in the Data Source, Data Source Information, and Initialization property groups that are currently set on the data source object or the values of properties in the Initialization property group that are currently set on the enumerator.

HRESULT GetProperties (
ULONG	*cPropertyIDSets*,
const DBPROPIDSET	*rgPropertyIDSets*[],
ULONG *	*pcPropertySets*,
DBPROPSET **	*prgPropertySets*);

Parameters

cPropertyIDSets [in]

The number of DBPROPIDSET structures in *rgPropertyIDSets*.

If *cPropertySets* is zero, the provider ignores *rgPropertyIDSets*. If the data source object or enumerator has not been initialized, the provider returns the values of all properties in the Initialization property group for which values have been set or defaults exist. If the data source object or enumerator has been initialized, the provider returns the values of all properties in the Data Source, Data Source Information, and Initialization property groups, for data source objects, or the Initialization property group, for enumerators, for which values have been set or defaults exist. The provider does not return the values of properties in any of these property groups for which values have not been set and no defaults exist.

If *cPropertyIDSets* is not zero, the provider returns the values of the requested properties. If a property is not supported, or if the data source object or enumerator is not initialized and the value of a property in a group other than the Initialization property group is requested, the returned value of *dwStatus* in the returned DBPROP structure for that property is DBPROPSTATUS_NOTSUPPORTED and the value of *dwOptions* is undefined.

rgPropertyIDSets [in]

An array of *cPropertyIDSets* DBPROPIDSET structures. If the data source object or enumerator has not been initialized, the properties specified in these structures must belong to the Initialization property group. If the data source object or enumerator has been initialized, the properties specified in these structures must belong to the Data Source, Data Source Information, or Initialization property group, for data source objects, or the Initialization property group, for enumerators. The provider returns the values of the properties specified in these structures. If *cPropertyIDSets* is zero, then this argument is ignored.

For information about the properties in the Data Source, Data Source Information, and Initialization property groups that are defined by OLE DB, see "Data Source Properties," "Data Source Information Properties," and "Initialization Properties" in Appendix C. For information about the DBPROPIDSET structure, see "DBPROPIDSET Structure" in Chapter 11.

pcPropertySets [out]

A pointer to memory in which to return the number of DBPROPSET structures returned in **prgPropertySets*. If *cPropertyIDSets* is 0, **pcPropertySets* is the total number of property sets for which the providers supports at least one property in the Data Source, Data Source Information, or Initialization property group, for data source objects, or the Initialization property group, for enumerators. If *cPropertyIDSets* is greater than 0, **pcPropertySets* is set to *cPropertyIDSets*. If an error other than DB_E_ERRORSOCCURRED occurs, **pcPropertySets* is set to 0.

prgPropertySets [out]

A pointer to memory in which to return an array of DBPROPSET structures. If *cPropertyIDSets* is zero, then one structure is returned for each property set that contains at least one property belonging to Initialization property group (if the data source object or enumerator is not initialized), the Data Source, Data Source Information, or Initialization property group (if the data source object is initialized), or the Initialization property group (if the enumerator is initialized). If *cPropertyIDSets* is not zero, then one structure is returned for each property set specified in *rgPropertyIDSets*.

In the case of properties in the Initialization property group and for a previously persisted data source object, those properties related to sensitive authentication information such as password will be returned in an encrypted form if DBPROP_AUTH_PERSIST_ENCRYPTED is VARIANT_TRUE.

If *cPropertyIDSets* is not zero, the DBPROPSET structures in **prgPropertySets* are returned in the same order as the DBPROPIDSET structures in *rgPropertyIDSets*; that is, for corresponding elements of each array, the *guidPropertySet* elements are the same. If *cPropertyIDs*, in an element of *rgPropertyIDSets*, is not zero, the DBPROP structures in the corresponding element of **prgPropertySets* are returned in the same order as the DBPROPID values in *rgPropertyIDs*; that is, for corresponding elements of each array, the property IDs are the same.

The provider allocates memory for the structures and returns the address to this memory; the consumer releases this memory with **IMalloc::Free** when it no longer needs the structures. Before calling **IMalloc::Free** for **prgPropertySets*, the consumer should call **IMalloc::Free** for the *rgProperties* element within each element of **prgPropertySets*. If **pcPropertySets* is zero on output or an error other than DB_E_ERRORSOCCURRED occurs, the provider does not allocate any memory and ensures that **prgPropertySets* is a null pointer on output.

For information about the DBPROPSET and DBPROP structures, see "DBPROPSET Structure" and "DBPROP Structure" in Chapter 11.

Return Code

S_OK

The method succeeded. In all DBPROP structures returned by the method, *dwStatus* is set to DBPROPSTATUS_OK.

DB_S_ERRORSOCCURRED

No value was returned for one or more properties. The consumer checks *dwStatus* in the DBPROP structure to determine the properties for which values were not returned. **GetProperties** can fail to return properties for a number of reasons, including:

- The property was not supported by the provider.

- The data source object or enumerator was not initialized and the property was not in the Initialization property group.

- The method was called on the data source object, the data source object was initialized, and the property was not in the Data Source, Data Source Information, or Initialization property groups.

- The method was called on the enumerator, the enumerator was initialized, and the property was not in the Initialization property group.

- The property set was not supported by the provider. If *cPropertyIDs* in the DBPROPIDSET structure for the property set was zero, the provider cannot set *dwStatus* in the DBPROP structure because it does not know the IDs of any properties in the property set. Instead, it sets *cProperties* to zero in the DBPROPSET structure returned for the property set.

E_FAIL

A provider-specific error occurred.

E_INVALIDARG

cPropertyIDSets was not equal to zero and *rgPropertyIDSets* was a null pointer.

pcPropertySets or *prgPropertySets* was a null pointer.

In an element of *rgPropertyIDSets*, *cPropertyIDs* was not zero and *rgPropertyIDs* was a null pointer.

In an element of *rgPropertyIDSets*, *guidPropertySet* was DBPROPSET_PROPERTIESINERROR and *cPropertyIDs* was not 0 or *rgPropertyIDs* was not a null pointer.

cPropertyIDSets was greater than 1 and, in an element of *rgPropertyIDSets*, *guidPropertySet* was DBPROPSET_PROPERTIESINERROR.

E_OUTOFMEMORY

The provider was unable to allocate sufficient memory in which to return the DBPROPSET or DBPROP structures.

DB_E_ERRORSOCCURRED

Values were not returned for any properties. The provider allocates memory for *prgPropertySets* and the consumer checks *dwStatus* in the DBPROP structures to determine why properties were not returned. The consumer frees this memory when it no longer needs the information.

Comments

If **IDBInitialize::Initialize** returns DB_E_ERRORSOCCURRED, the consumer can immediately call **GetProperties** with the DBPROPSET_PROPERTIESINERROR property set to return all the properties that were in error. For more information, see "Property Sets" in Chapter 11.

See Also

IDBProperties::GetPropertyInfo, **IDBProperties::SetProperties**

IDBProperties::GetPropertyInfo

GetPropertyInfo returns information about all properties supported by the provider.

HRESULT GetPropertyInfo(
ULONG	*cPropertyIDSets*,
const DBPROPIDSET	*rgPropertyIDSets*[],
ULONG *	*pcPropertyInfoSets*,
DBPROPINFOSET **	*prgPropertyInfoSets*,
OLECHAR **	*ppDescBuffer*);

Parameters

cPropertyIDSets [in]

The number of DBPROPIDSET structures in *rgPropertyIDSets*.

If *cPropertySets* is zero, the provider ignores *rgPropertyIDSets*. When called on the enumerator, the provider returns information about all properties in the Initialization property group. When called on the data source object, if the data source object has not been initialized, the provider returns information about all properties in the Initialization property group. If the data source object has been initialized, the provider returns information about all of the properties in all of the property sets it supports.

If *cPropertyIDSets* is not zero, the provider returns information about the requested properties. If a property is not supported, or if the method is called on an enumerator or an uninitialized data source object and the value of a property in a group other than the Initialization property group is requested, the returned value of *dwStatus* in the returned DBPROPINFO structure for that property is DBPROPFLAGS_NOTSUPPORTED and the value of the *pwszDescription*, *vtType*, and *vValues* elements are undefined.

rgPropertyIDSets [in]

An array of *cPropertyIDSets* DBPROPIDSET structures. When called on the enumerator, the properties specified in these structures must belong to the Initialization property group. When called on the data source object, if the data source object has not been initialized, the properties must belong to the Initialization property group. If the data source object has been initialized, the properties can belong to any property group. The provider returns information about the properties specified in these structures. If *cPropertyIDSets* is zero, then this parameter is ignored. For information about the DBPROPIDSET structure, see "DBPROPIDSET Structure" in Chapter 11.

The following special GUIDs are defined for use with **GetPropertyInfo**. All of these GUIDs can be used on data source objects; only the DBPROPSET_DBINITALL GUID can be used on enumerators. If any of these GUIDs are specified in the *guidPropertySet* element of a DBPROPIDSET

structure, the *cPropertyIDs* and *rgPropertyIDs* elements of that structure are
ignored. However, the consumer should set these to zero and a null pointer,
respectively, as the provider might attempt to check that they are valid values.
Consumers cannot pass special GUIDs and the GUIDs of other property sets in the
same call to **GetPropertyInfo**. That is, if one element of *rgPropertyIDSets*
contains a special GUID, all elements of *rgPropertyIDSets* must contain special
GUIDs. These GUIDs are not returned in the *guidPropertySet* element of the
DBPROPINFOSET structures returned in *rgPropertyInfoSets*. Instead, the GUID
of the property set to which the property belongs is returned.

Property Set GUID	Description
DBPROPSET_DATASOURCEALL	Returns all properties in the Data Source property group, including provider-specific properties.
DBPROPSET_DATASOURCEINFOALL	Returns all properties in the Data Source Information property group, including provider-specific properties.
DBPROPSET_DBINITALL	Returns all properties in the Initialization property group, including provider-specific properties.
DBPROPSET_ROWSETALL	Returns all properties in the Rowset property group, including provider-specific properties.
DBPROPSET_SESSIONALL	Returns all properties in the Session property group, including provider-specific properties.

pcPropertyInfoSets [out]
A pointer to memory in which to return the number of DBPROPINFOSET
structures returned in **prgPropertyInfoSets*. If *cPropertyIDSets* is zero,
*pcPropertyInfoSets is the total number of property sets for which the provider
supports at least one property. If *cPropertyInfoSets* is not zero and one of the
special GUIDs listed in *rgPropertyIDSets* was used, **pcPropertyInfoSets* may
differ from *cPropertyInfoSets*. If an error other than DB_E_ERRORSOCCURRED
occurs, **pcPropertyInfoSets* is set to zero.

prgPropertyInfoSets [out]
A pointer to memory in which to return an array of DBPROPINFOSET structures.
If *cPropertyIDSets* is zero, then one structure is returned for each property set that
contains at least one property supported by the provider. If *cPropertyIDSets* is not
zero, then one structure is returned for each property set specified in
rgPropertyIDSets.

If *cPropertyIDSets* is not zero, the DBPROPINFOSET structures in
*prgPropertyInfoSets are returned in the same order as the DBPROPIDSET
structures in *rgPropertyIDSets*; that is, for corresponding elements of each array,
the *guidPropertySet* elements are the same. If *cPropertyIDs*, in an element of
rgPropertyIDSets, is not zero, the DBPROPINFO structures in the corresponding
element of **prgPropertyInfoSets* are returned in the same order as the DBPROPID
values in *rgPropertyIDs*; that is for corresponding elements of each array, the
property IDs are the same. The only exception to these rules is when one of the
special GUIDs listed in *rgPropertyIDSets* was used. In this case, the order of the
property information returned may differ from the order specified in
rgPropertyIDSets.

The provider allocates memory for the structures and returns the address to this
memory; the consumer releases this memory with **IMalloc::Free** when it no longer
needs the structures. Before calling **IMalloc::Free** for **prgPropertyInfoSets*, the
consumer should call **IMalloc::Free** for the *rgPropertyInfos* element within each
element of **prgPropertyInfoSets*. If **pcPropertyInfoSets* is zero on output or if an
error other than DB_E_ERRORSOCCURRED occurs, then **prgPropertyInfoSets*
must be a null pointer on output.

For information about the DBPROPINFOSET and DBPROPINFO structures, see
"DBPROPINFOSET Structure" and "DBPROPINFO Structure" in Chapter 11.

ppDescBuffer [out]
A pointer to memory in which to return a pointer to storage for all string values
returned in the **pwszDescription* element of the DBPROPINFO structure. The
provider allocates this memory with **IMalloc** and the consumer frees it with
IMalloc::Free when it no longer needs the property descriptions. If *ppDescBuffer*
is a null pointer on input, **GetPropertyInfo** does not return the property
descriptions. If **pcPropertyInfoSets* is zero on output or if an error occurs, the
provider does not allocate any memory and ensures that **ppDescBuffer* is a null
pointer on output. Each of the individual string values stored in this buffer is
terminated by a null termination character. Therefore, the buffer may contain one
or more strings, each with its own null termination character, and may contain
embedded null termination characters.

Return Code

S_OK
The method succeeded. In all DBPROPINFO structures returned by the method,
dwFlags is set to a value other than DBPROPFLAGS_NOTSUPPORTED.

DB_S_ERRORSOCCURRED
In an element of *rgPropertyIDSets*, a property specified in *rgPropertyIDs* was not
supported by the provider; this includes the case in which the property set to which
the property belongs is not supported by the provider. In the DBPROPINFO
structures returned for the property, *dwFlags* is set to
DBPROPFLAGS_NOTSUPPORTED.

In an element of *rgPropertyIDSets*, the property set specified in *guidPropertySet* was not supported by the provider. In the DBPROPINFOSET structure returned for the property set, *cPropertyInfos* is set to zero, and *rgPropertyInfos* is set to a null pointer.

The method was called on the enumerator and, in an element of *rgPropertyIDSets*, a property belonged to a group other than the Initialization property group.

The method was called on an uninitialized data source object and, in an element of *rgPropertyIDSets*, a property belonged to a group other than the Initialization property group.

E_FAIL

A provider-specific error occurred.

E_INVALIDARG

pcPropertyInfoSets or *prgPropertyInfoSets* was a null pointer.

cPropertyIDSets was not equal to zero and *rgPropertyIDSets* was a null pointer.

In an element of *rgPropertyIDSets*, *cPropertyIDs* was not zero and *rgPropertyIDs* was a null pointer.

In one element of *rgPropertyIDSets*, *guidPropertySet* specified one of the special GUIDs listed in the description of *rgPropertyIDSets*. In a different element of *rgPropertyIDSets*, *guidPropertySet* specified the GUID of a normal property set.

E_OUTOFMEMORY

The provider was unable to allocate sufficient memory in which to return the DBPROPINFOSET or DBPROPINFO structures or the property descriptions.

E_UNEXPECTED

ITransaction::Commit or **ITransaction::Abort** was called and the object is in a zombie state.

DB_E_ERRORSOCCURRED

Errors occurred while attempting to return information about all properties. The provider allocates memory for **prgPropertyInfoSets* and the consumer checks *dwFlags* in the DBPROPINFO structures to determine why information about each property was not returned. The consumer frees this memory when it no longer needs the information. The method can fail to return information about properties for any of the reasons specified in DB_S_ERRORSOCCURRED.

Comments

GetPropertyInfo returns information about supported properties, including the property set to which they belong, their ID, their data type, the object to which they apply, and whether they can be read or written. Properties in the Initialization and Data Source Creation property groups for which the consumer must supply a value before calling **Initialize** are marked with the DBPROPFLAGS_REQUIRED bit in the *dwFlags* element of the DBPROPINFO structure.

Whether a property is supported is different from its value. For example, if a provider supports **IRowsetLocate**, it supports the DBPROP_IRowsetLocate property. Whether a rowset actually exposes **IRowsetLocate** depends on whether the consumer sets the value of the corresponding property to VARIANT_TRUE or VARIANT_FALSE.

See Also

IDBProperties::GetProperties, **IDBProperties::SetProperties**

IDBProperties::SetProperties

Sets properties in the Data Source and Initialization property groups, for data source objects, or the Initialization property group, for enumerators.

HRESULT SetProperties (
    ULONG   *cPropertySets,*
    DBPROPSET   *rgPropertySets[]);*

Parameters

cPropertySets [in]

The number of DBPROPSET structures in *rgPropertySets*. If this is zero, the provider ignores *rgPropertySets* and the method does not do anything.

rgPropertySets [in/out]

An array of DBPROPSET structures containing properties and values to be set. If the data source object or enumerator is uninitialized, the properties specified in these structures must belong to the Initialization property group. If the data source object is initialized, the properties must belong to the Data Source property group. If the enumerator is initialized, it is an error to call this method. If the same property is specified more than once in *rgPropertySets*, then which value is used is provider-specific. If *cPropertySets* is zero, this parameter is ignored.

For information about the properties in the Data Source and Initialization property groups that are defined by OLE DB, see "Data Source Properties" and "Initialization Properties" in Appendix C. For information about the DBPROPSET and DBPROP structures, see "DBPROPSET Structure" and "DBPROP Structure" in Chapter 11.

Return Code

S_OK

The method succeeded. In all DBPROP structures passed to the method, *dwStatus* is set to DBPROPSTATUS_OK.

DB_S_ERRORSOCCURRED

One or more properties were not set. Properties not in error remain set. The consumer checks *dwStatus* in the DBPROP structures to determine which properties were not set. **SetProperties** can fail to set properties for a number of reasons, including:

- The property was not supported by the provider.

- The data source object or enumerator was not initialized and the property was not in the Initialization property group.

- The data source object was initialized and the property was not in the Data Source property group.

- The property set was not supported by the provider.

- It was not cheap to set the property.

- *colid* in the DBPROP structure was not DB_NULLID.
- The value of *dwOptions* in the DBPROP structure was invalid.
- The data type in *vValue* in the DBPROP structure was not the data type of the property or was not VT_EMPTY.
- The value in *vValue* in the DBPROP structure was invalid.
- The property's value conflicted with an existing property.

E_FAIL
A provider-specific error occurred.

E_INVALIDARG
cPropertySets was not equal to zero and *rgPropertySets* was a null pointer.

In an element of *rgPropertySets*, *cProperties* was not zero and *rgProperties* was a null pointer.

DB_E_ALREADYINITIALIZED
The method was called on the enumerator and the enumerator was already initialized.

DB_E_ERRORSOCCURRED
All property values were invalid and no properties were set. The consumer checks *dwStatus* in the DBPROP structures to determine why properties were not set. The method can fail to set properties for any of the reasons specified in DB_S_ERRORSOCCURRED except the reason that states that it was not cheap to set the property.

See Also

IDBProperties::GetProperties, **IDBProperties::GetPropertyInfo**

IDBSchemaRowset

This is an optional interface on sessions. It is used to provide advanced schema information.

Consumers can get information about a data source without knowing its structure by using the **IDBSchemaRowset** methods. For example, the data source might be a Microsoft SQL Server database that organizes each database into a set of schemas which contain the tables and queries for each schema; the data source might be a Microsoft Access 2.0 database that has a container of tables and a container of queries; or the data source might be a Microsoft Access for Windows® 95 database that enables users to define folders to group tables into an arbitrary hierarchy.

For the following schema rowsets, it is suggested that providers pay particular attention to rowset construction and data retrieval performance, because these methods will be used frequently by consumers.

This schema defines a minimum content of the system schema. It is assumed that consumers will precompile and store the specialized queries used for things like command planning and execution-time plan validation, and storage engines may have specialized optimizations associated with those plans. Consumers can also look at the schema tables in the schema, and thus discover other schema tables and attributes beyond the minimum set.

For information about the schema rowsets, see Appendix B, "Schema Rowsets." Providers must return all of the columns in the rowsets they return. If they cannot return the information in a column, they must return an appropriate value. Generally, this is NULL. Providers can return provider-specific columns after the last column defined by OLE DB.

Schema rowsets are identified by GUIDs. The following table lists these GUIDs and the columns for which restrictions can be specified on the schema rowset. The number of restriction columns for each schema rowset are defined as constants prefixed with CRESTRICTIONS_ in the header files. Restriction values are treated as literals rather than as search patterns. For example, the restriction value "A_C" matches "A_C" but not "ABC".

GUID	Number of restrictions	Restriction columns
DBSCHEMA_ASSERTIONS	3	CONSTRAINT_CATALOG CONSTRAINT_SCHEMA CONSTRAINT_NAME
DBSCHEMA_CATALOGS	1	CATALOG_NAME
DBSCHEMA_CHARACTER_SETS	3	CHARACTER_SET_CATALOG CHARACTER_SET_SCHEMA CHARACTER_SET_NAME

GUID	Number of restrictions	Restriction columns
DBSCHEMA_CHECK_CONSTRAINTS	3	CONSTRAINT_CATALOG CONSTRAINT_SCHEMA CONSTRAINT_NAME
DBSCHEMA_COLLATIONS	3	COLLATION_CATALOG COLLATION_SCHEMA COLLATION_NAME
DBSCHEMA_COLUMN_DOMAIN_ USAGE	4	DOMAIN_CATALOG DOMAIN_SCHEMA DOMAIN_NAME COLUMN_NAME
DBSCHEMA_COLUMN_PRIVILEGES	6	TABLE_CATALOG TABLE_SCHEMA TABLE_NAME COLUMN_NAME GRANTOR GRANTEE
DBSCHEMA_COLUMNS	4	TABLE_CATALOG TABLE_SCHEMA TABLE_NAME COLUMN_NAME
DBSCHEMA_CONSTRAINT_ COLUMN_USAGE	4	TABLE_CATALOG TABLE_SCHEMA TABLE_NAME COLUMN_NAME
DBSCHEMA_CONSTRAINT_ TABLE_USAGE	3	TABLE_CATALOG TABLE_SCHEMA TABLE_NAME
DBSCHEMA_FOREIGN_KEYS	6	PK_TABLE_CATALOG PK_TABLE_SCHEMA PK_TABLE_NAME FK_TABLE_CATALOG FK_TABLE_SCHEMA FK_TABLE_NAME
DBSCHEMA_INDEXES	5	TABLE_CATALOG TABLE_SCHEMA INDEX_NAME TYPE TABLE_NAME

GUID	Number of restrictions	Restriction columns
DBSCHEMA_KEY_COLUMN_ USAGE	7	CONSTRAINT_CATALOG CONSTRAINT_SCHEMA CONSTRAINT_NAME TABLE_CATALOG TABLE_SCHEMA TABLE_NAME COLUMN_NAME
DBSCHEMA_PRIMARY_KEYS	3	TABLE_CATALOG TABLE_SCHEMA TABLE_NAME
DBSCHEMA_PROCEDURE_COLUMNS	4	PROCEDURE_CATALOG PROCEDURE_SCHEMA PROCEDURE_NAME COLUMN_NAME
DBSCHEMA_PROCEDURE_ PARAMETERS	4	PROCEDURE_CATALOG PROCEDURE_SCHEMA PROCEDURE_NAME PARAMETER_NAME
DBSCHEMA_PROCEDURES	4	PROCEDURE_CATALOG PROCEDURE_SCHEMA PROCEDURE_NAME PROCEDURE_TYPE
DBSCHEMA_PROVIDER_TYPES	2	DATA_TYPE BEST_MATCH
DBSCHEMA_REFERENTIAL_ CONSTRAINTS	3	CONSTRAINT_CATALOG CONSTRAINT_SCHEMA CONSTRAINT_NAME
DBSCHEMA_SCHEMATA	3	CATALOG_NAME SCHEMA_NAME SCHEMA_OWNER
DBSCHEMA_SQL_LANGUAGES	0	none
DBSCHEMA_STATISTICS	3	TABLE_CATALOG TABLE_SCHEMA TABLE_NAME

GUID	Number of restrictions	Restriction columns
DBSCHEMA_TABLE_CONSTRAINTS	7	CONSTRAINT_CATALOG CONSTRAINT_SCHEMA CONSTRAINT_NAME TABLE_CATALOG TABLE_SCHEMA TABLE_NAME CONSTRAINT_TYPE
DBSCHEMA_TABLE_PRIVILEGES	5	TABLE_CATALOG TABLE_SCHEMA TABLE_NAME GRANTOR GRANTEE
DBSCHEMA_TABLES	4	TABLE_CATALOG TABLE_SCHEMA TABLE_NAME TABLE_TYPE
DBSCHEMA_TRANSLATIONS	3	TRANSLATION_CATALOG TRANSLATION_SCHEMA TRANSLATION_NAME
DBSCHEMA_USAGE_PRIVILEGES	6	OBJECT_CATALOG OBJECT_SCHEMA OBJECT_NAME OBJECT_TYPE GRANTOR GRANTEE
DBSCHEMA_VIEW_COLUMN_USAGE	3	VIEW_CATALOG VIEW_SCHEMA VIEW_NAME
DBSCHEMA_VIEW_TABLE_USAGE	3	VIEW_CATALOG VIEW_SCHEMA VIEW_NAME
DBSCHEMA_VIEWS	3	TABLE_CATALOG TABLE_SCHEMA TABLE_NAME

For **IDBSchemaRowset**, providers must support the following GUIDs:

- DBSCHEMA_TABLES
- DBSCHEMA_COLUMNS
- DBSCHEMA_PROVIDER_TYPES

Method	Description
GetRowset	Returns a schema rowset.
GetSchemas	Returns a list of schema rowsets accessible by **IDBSchemaRowset::GetRowset**.

IDBSchemaRowset::GetRowset

Returns a schema rowset.

HRESULT GetRowset (
    IUnknown *   *punkOuter,*
    REFGUID   *rguidSchema,*
    ULONG   *cRestrictions,*
    const VARIANT   *rgRestrictions[],*
    REFIID   *riid,*
    ULONG   *cPropertySets,*
    DBPROPSET   *rgPropertySets[],*
    IUnknown **   *ppRowset);*

Parameters

pUnkOuter [in]

A pointer to the controlling **IUnknown** interface if the rowset is being created as part of an aggregate. If the **IDBSchemaRowset** interface is not being aggregated, it is a null pointer.

rguidSchema [in]

A GUID identifying the schema rowset. For more information, see the "Comments" section and **IDBSchemaRowset**.

cRestrictions [in]

The count of restriction values.

rgRestrictions [in]

An array of restriction values. These are applied in order to the restriction columns. That is, the first restriction value applies to the first restriction column, the second restriction value applies to the second restriction column, and so on. For more information, see the Comments section.

riid [in]

The IID of the requested rowset interface.

cPropertySets [in]

The number of DBPROPSET structures in *rgPropertySets*. If this is 0, the provider ignores *rgPropertySets*.

rgPropertySets [in/out]

An array of DBPROPSET structures containing properties and values to be set. The properties specified in these structures must belong to the Rowset property group. If the same property is specified more than once in *rgPropertySets*, then it is provider-specific which value is used. If *cPropertySets* is 0, this argument is ignored.

For information about the properties in the Rowset property group that are defined by OLE DB, see "Rowset Properties" in Appendix C. For information about the DBPROPSET and DBPROP structures, see "DBPROPSET Structure" and "DBPROP Structure" in Chapter 11.

ppRowset [out]

A pointer to memory in which to return the requested interface pointer on the schema rowset. This rowset is read-only. If no applicable schema information exists, an empty rowset is returned.

Return Code

S_OK

The method succeeded. In all DBPROP structures passed to the method, *dwStatus* is set to DBPROPSTATUS_OK.

DB_S_ERRORSOCCURRED

The rowset was opened but one or more properties—for which the *dwOptions* element of the DBPROP structure was DBPROPOPTIONS_SETIFCHEAP—were not set. The consumer checks *dwStatus* in the DBPROP structures to determine which properties were not set. The method can fail to set properties for a number of reasons, including:

- The property was not supported by the provider.

- The property was not in the Rowset property group.

- The property set was not supported by the provider.

- It was not cheap to set the property.

- The *colid* in the DBPROP structure was invalid.

- The data type in *vValue* in the DBPROP structure was not the data type of the property or was not VT_EMPTY.

- The value in *vValue* in the DBPROP structure was invalid.

- The property's value conflicted with an existing property.

- A property was specified to be applied to all columns, but could not be applied to one or more columns.

E_FAIL

A provider-specific error occurred.

E_INVALIDARG

rguidSchema was invalid.

rguidSchema specified a schema rowset that was not supported by the provider.

cRestrictions was greater than the number of restriction columns for the schema rowset specified in *rguidSchema*.

In one or more restriction values specified in *rgRestrictions*, the *vt* element of the VARIANT was the incorrect type.

cRestrictions was greater than zero and *rgRestrictions* was a null pointer.

In an element of *rgRestrictions*, the *vt* element of the VARIANT was not VT_EMPTY and the provider did not support the corresponding restriction.

ppRowset was a null pointer.

In an element of *rgPropertySets*, *cProperties* was not 0 and *rgProperties* was a null pointer.

cPropertySets was greater than zero and *rgPropertySets* was a null pointer.

E_NOINTERFACE

The schema rowset did not support the interface specified in *riid*.

E_OUTOFMEMORY

The provider was unable to allocate sufficient memory in which to create the rowset.

DB_E_ABORTLIMITREACHED

The method failed because a resource limit has been reached. For example, a query used to implement the method timed out. No rowset is returned.

DB_E_ERRORSOCCURRED

No rowset was returned because one or more properties—for which the *dwOptions* element of the DBPROP structure was DBPROPOPTIONS_REQUIRED or an invalid value—were not set. The consumer checks *dwStatus* in the DBPROP structures to determine which properties were not set. None of the satisfiable properties are remembered. The method can fail to set properties for any of the reasons specified in DB_S_ERRORSOCCURRED except the reason that states that it was not cheap to set the property.

DB_E_NOAGGREGATION

pUnkOuter was not a null pointer and the rowset being created does not support aggregation.

DB_E_NOTSUPPORTED

The provider does not support restrictions on one or more of the columns in the corresponding schema.

DB_SEC_E_PERMISSIONDENIED

The consumer did not have sufficient permission to create the schema rowset.

Comments

When preparing an array of restriction values, consumers are not required to specify values for all of the restriction columns on a rowset. Any columns for which no restriction values are specified are not restricted.

There are two ways for a consumer to explicitly specify that there is no restriction value for a column. First, the consumer can not specify a restriction value for the column. For example, if there are three restriction columns, the consumer passes only two restriction values; these apply to the first two restriction columns and no value is specified for the third restriction column.

Second, the consumer can set the *vt* element of the VARIANT specified for the column to VT_EMPTY, even if the provider does not support restrictions on the column. For example, suppose there are three restriction columns, the provider supports restrictions on the first and third columns, and the consumer wants to restrict values on these two columns. The consumer passes three restriction values. The first and third values are the desired restrictions and the second value is a VARIANT with a *vt* element of VT_EMPTY.

If the *vt* element of the VARIANT specified for a restriction column is VT_NULL, this means that the column must be NULL to satisfy the restriction. This is equivalent to the **IS NULL** predicate in SQL. If the *vt* element of the VARIANT specified for a restriction column is VT_BSTR and the *bstrVal* element is set to a null pointer, this means that the column must contain an empty string to satisfy the restriction.

See Also

IDBSchemaRowset::GetSchemas

IDBSchemaRowset::GetSchemas

Returns a list of schema rowsets accessible by **IDBSchemaRowset::GetRowset**.

HRESULT GetSchemas (
    ULONG *   *pcSchemas*,
    GUID **   *prgSchemas*,
    ULONG**   *prgRestrictionSupport*);

Parameters

pcSchemas [out]

A pointer to memory in which to return the number of GUIDs in **prgSchemas*. The returned count of schema GUIDs is always at least 3, because all providers must support the TABLES, COLUMNS, and PROVIDER_TYPES schema rowsets. If an error occurs, **pcSchemas* is set to 0.

prgSchemas [out]

A pointer to memory in which to return an array of GUIDs identifying supported schema rowsets. For more information, see **IDBSchemaRowset**. The rowset allocates memory for the GUIDs and returns the address to this memory. The consumer releases this memory with **IMalloc::Free** when it no longer needs the list of GUIDs. If an error occurs, **prgSchemas* is set to a null pointer.

prgRestrictionSupport [out]

A pointer to memory in which to return an array of ULONGs, one element for each supported schema rowset, describing the restriction columns supported for that schema rowset. For a given schema rowset, the array element corresponding to the schema rowset will have the appropriate bit set if the provider implements a restriction on that column. Bits that do not correspond to currently-defined restriction columns should not be set.

For example, the specification lists three restriction columns for the schema DBSCHEMA_ASSERTIONS. The array element corresponding to this schema will represent the CONSTRAINT_CATALOG column in bit 0, the CONSTRAINT_SCHEMA column in bit 1, and the CONSTRAINT_NAME column in bit 2. The following code shows how the consumer might determine whether a restriction on the CONSTRAINT_CATALOG column is supported on the ASSERTIONS schema rowset.

```
ULONG   cSchemas;
GUID  *rgSchemas;
ULONG *rgRestSupport;

pIDBSchemaRowset->GetSchemas(&cSchemas, &rgSchemas, &rgRestSupport);
```

```
// Assume rgSchemas[0] is the GUID DBSCHEMA_ASSERTIONS. The following
// code checks whether the restriction on the CONSTRAINT_CATALOG
// column is supported.
if (rgRestSupport[0] & 0x1) {
    // Restriction is supported.
} else {
    // Restriction is not supported.
}
```

The rowset allocates memory for the restrictions and returns the address to this memory. The consumer releases this memory with **IMalloc::Free** when it no longer needs the list of restrictions. If an error occurs, *prgRestrictionSupport* is set to a null pointer.

If *prgRestrictionSupport* is a null pointer, the rowset does not allocate any memory or return any restrictions.

Return Code

S_OK

The method succeeded.

E_FAIL

A provider-specific error occurred.

E_INVALIDARG

pcSchemas, *prgSchemas*, or *prgRestrictionSupport* was a null pointer.

E_OUTOFMEMORY

The provider was unable to allocate sufficient memory in which to return the array of schema GUIDs or restriction support information.

See Also

IDBSchemaRowset::GetRowset

IErrorInfo

IErrorInfo is defined by OLE Automation; the following describes how the interface is used in OLE DB. **IErrorInfo** returns information about an error in addition to the return code. It returns the error message, name of the component, and GUID of the interface in which the error occurred, and the name and topic of the Help file that applies to the error.

When to Implement

IErrorInfo is implemented by code in the OLE DB Software Development Kit (SDK). This code calls provider-specific code in **IErrorLookup** to retrieve error messages, sources, and Help file information.

OLE DB error objects expose **IErrorInfo** at two levels. First, it is exposed on the OLE DB error object itself, which enables OLE Automation consumers to use OLE DB error objects. The interface pointer is returned by **GetErrorInfo** in the OLE Automation DLL; it can also be returned by **QueryInterface**. **IErrorInfo** returns the information stored in record 0 of the OLE DB error object and uses the default locale ID.

IErrorInfo is also exposed on individual records in the OLE DB error object. These **IErrorInfo** interface pointers, returned by **IErrorRecords::GetErrorInfo**, are different from the **IErrorInfo** interface pointer exposed on the OLE DB error object itself, and cannot be returned by **QueryInterface**. The record to which the interface pointer applies and the locale ID it uses is specified by the consumer in **IErrorRecords::GetErrorInfo**.

When to Call

OLE Automation consumers call **GetErrorInfo** in the OLE Automation DLL to get an **IErrorInfo** interface pointer on the OLE DB error object.

OLE DB consumers also call **GetErrorInfo** in the OLE Automation DLL. However, they do not generally use the returned **IErrorInfo** interface pointer. Instead, they call **QueryInterface** to get an **IErrorRecords** interface pointer and then call **IErrorRecords::GetErrorInfo** to get an **IErrorInfo** interface pointer on a particular record in the OLE DB error object. Then the OLE DB consumers use this interface pointer to retrieve the error information.

Method	Description
GetDescription	Returns a text description of the error.
GetGUID	Returns the GUID of the interface that defined the error.
GetHelpContext	Returns the Help context ID for the error.
GetHelpFile	Returns the path of the Help file that describes the error.
GetSource	Returns the name of the component that generated the error, such as "ODBC *driver-name*".

IErrorInfo::GetDescription

Returns a text description of the error.

HRESULT GetDescription (
    BSTR * *pbstrDescription*);

Parameters

pbstrDescription [out]

A pointer to memory in which to return a pointer to a string that describes the error. If there is no error description or an error occurs, the returned value (*pbstrDescription) is set to a null pointer. The memory for this string is allocated by the provider and must be freed by the consumer with a call to **SysFreeString**.

Return Code

S_OK

The method succeeded.

E_INVALIDARG

pbstrDescription was a null pointer.

E_OUTOFMEMORY

The provider was unable to allocate sufficient memory in which to return the error description.

DB_E_NOLOCALE

The locale ID specified by the *lcid* parameter in **IErrorRecords::GetErrorInfo** was not supported by the provider.

Comments

If the lookup ID is IDENTIFIER_SDK_ERROR, the implementation of this method retrieves the error description from the error resource DLL shipped with the OLE DB SDK. Otherwise, **GetDescription** calls **IErrorLookup::GetErrorDescription** to retrieve the string. If the description is parameterized, such as "Cannot open table <param1>," the lookup service incorporates the parameter values before returning the string.

See Also

IErrorLookup::GetErrorDescription

IErrorInfo::GetGUID

Returns the GUID of interface that defined the error.

HRESULT GetGUID (
    GUID * *pguid*);

Parameters

pguid [out]

A pointer to memory in which to return the GUID of the interface that defined the error. If the error was defined by the operating system, the returned GUID is DB_NULLGUID. Note that this is the same value as is returned in the *iid* element of the ERRORINFO structure returned by **IErrorRecords::GetBasicErrorInfo**.

Return Code

S_OK

The method succeeded.

E_INVALIDARG

pguid was a null pointer.

Comments

This GUID does not necessarily represent the source of the error; the source is the class or application that raised the error. Using the GUID, an application can handle errors in an interface independent of the class that implements the interface.

IErrorInfo::GetHelpContext

Returns the Help context ID for the error.

HRESULT GetHelpContext (
    DWORD **pdwHelpContext***);**

Parameters

pdwHelpContext [out]

A pointer to memory in which to return the Help context ID for the error. If there is no Help file (**pbstrHelpFile* returned by **GetHelpFile** is a null pointer), then the returned value has no meaning.

Return Code

S_OK

The method succeeded.

E_INVALIDARG

pdwHelpContext was a null pointer.

DB_E_NOLOCALE

The locale ID specified by the *lcid* parameter in **IErrorRecords::GetErrorInfo** was not supported by the provider.

Comments

The implementation of this method shipped with the OLE DB SDK calls **IErrorLookup::GetHelpInfo** to retrieve the Help context ID.

See Also

IErrorInfo::GetHelpFile, IErrorLookup::GetHelpInfo

IErrorInfo::GetHelpFile

Returns the path of the Help file that describes the error.

HRESULT GetHelpFile (
    BSTR * *pbstrHelpFile*);

Parameters

pbstrHelpFile [out]

A pointer to memory in which to return a pointer to a string containing the fully qualified path of the Help file. If there is no Help file or an error occurs, the returned value (**pbstrHelpFile*) is set to a null pointer. The memory for this string is allocated by the provider and must be freed by the consumer with a call to **SysFreeString**.

Return Code

S_OK

The method succeeded.

E_INVALIDARG

pbstrHelpFile was a null pointer.

E_OUTOFMEMORY

The provider was unable to allocate sufficient memory in which to return the Help file path.

DB_E_NOLOCALE

The locale ID specified by the *lcid* parameter in **IErrorRecords::GetErrorInfo** was not supported by the provider.

Comments

The implementation of this method shipped with the OLE DB SDK calls **IErrorLookup::GetHelpInfo** to retrieve the path of the Help file.

See Also

IErrorInfo::GetHelpContext, IErrorLookup::GetHelpInfo

IErrorInfo::GetSource

Returns the name of the component that generated the error, such as "ODBC *driver-name*."

HRESULT GetSource (
    BSTR * *pbstrSource*);

Parameters

pbstrSource [out]

A pointer to memory in which to return a pointer to the name of the component the generated the error. If an error occurs, **pbstrSource* is set to a null pointer. The memory for this string is allocated by the provider and must be freed by the consumer with a call to **SysFreeString**.

Return Code

S_OK

The method succeeded.

E_INVALIDARG

pbstrSource was a null pointer.

E_OUTOFMEMORY

The provider was unable to allocate sufficient memory in which to return the component name.

DB_E_NOLOCALE

The locale ID specified by the *lcid* parameter in **IErrorRecords::GetErrorInfo** was not supported by the provider.

Comments

The implementation of this method shipped with the OLE DB SDK calls **IErrorLookup::GetErrorDescription** to retrieve the error source.

See Also

IErrorLookup::GetErrorDescription

IErrorLookup

IErrorLookup is used by OLE DB error objects to determine the values of the error message, source, Help file path, and context ID based on the return code and a provider-specific error number.

IErrorLookup is exposed by a provider-specific error lookup service that is mandatory for all providers that return OLE DB error objects.

When to Implement

All providers that return OLE DB error objects must implement **IErrorLookup** in a separate lookup service. For information about the registry entries used by error lookup services, see "Error Lookup Service Registry Entries" in Chapter 14.

When to Call

IErrorLookup is called by the code shipped in the OLE DB SDK that implements OLE DB error objects. It should not be called by general consumers.

When an error occurs, the following sequence of events takes place:

1. The provider creates an OLE DB error object and adds a record to that object.

2. The consumer retrieves the error object and gets an **IErrorInfo** interface on a particular record in that object. It then calls a method in **IErrorInfo**.

3. Except for the **IErrorInfo::GetGUID** method, the OLE DB error object code, which is shipped with the OLE DB SDK, loads the error lookup service based on the class ID stored in the error record.

4. The OLE DB error object code returns the *hrError* element of the ERRORINFO structure, the lookup ID, and the error parameters from the error record. It also returns the locale ID requested in **IErrorRecords::GetErrorInfo**. It passes all of this information to the appropriate **IErrorLookup** method.

5. The **IErrorLookup** method returns the requested information, based on the *hrError*, *dwLookupID*, and *lcid* arguments, integrates the parameters, and returns this to the error object code.

6. The OLE DB error object code returns the requested information to the consumer.

7. The consumer releases the OLE DB error object.

8. The OLE DB error object code calls **IErrorLookup::ReleaseErrors** for all error records with a non-zero dynamic error ID to release the error information associated with that record.

Method	Description
GetErrorDescription	Returns the error message and source, based on the return code and the provider-specific error number.
GetHelpInfo	Returns the path of the Help file and the context ID of the topic that explains the error.
ReleaseErrors	Releases any dynamic error information associated with a dynamic error ID.

IErrorLookup::GetErrorDescription

Returns the error message and source, based on the return code and the provider-specific error number.

HRESULT GetErrorDescription (
HRESULT	*hrError,*
DWORD	*dwLookupID,*
DISPPARAMS *	*pdispparams,*
LCID	*lcid,*
BSTR *	*pbstrSource,*
BSTR *	*pbstrDescription***);**

Parameters

hrError [in]

The code returned by the method that caused the error.

dwLookupID [in]

The provider-specific number of the error.

pdispparams [in]

The parameters of the error. If there are no error parameters, this is a null pointer.

lcid [in]

The locale ID for which to return the description and source.

pbstrSource [out]

A pointer to memory in which to return a pointer to the name of the component that generated the error. If an error occurs, *pbstrSource is set to a null pointer. The memory for this string is allocated by the provider and must be freed by the consumer with a call to **SysFreeString**.

pbstrDescription [out]

A pointer to memory in which to return a pointer to a string that describes the error. If *pdispparams* was not a null pointer, then the error parameters are integrated into this description. If there is no error description or an error occurs, the returned value (*pbstrDescription) is a null pointer. The memory for this string is allocated by the provider and must be freed by the consumer with a call to **SysFreeString**.

Return Code

S_OK

The method succeeded.

E_FAIL

A provider-specific error occurred.

E_INVALIDARG

pbstrSource or *pbstrDescription* was a null pointer.

E_OUTOFMEMORY
The provider was unable to allocate sufficient memory in which to return the error source or description.

DB_E_BADHRESULT
hrError was invalid.

DB_E_BADLOOKUPID
dwLookupID was invalid.

DB_E_NOLOCALE
The locale ID specified in *lcid* was not supported by the provider.

See Also

IErrorInfo::GetDescription, IErrorLookup::GetHelpInfo

IErrorLookup::GetHelpInfo

Returns the path of the Help file and the context ID of the topic that explains the error.

HRESULT GetHelpInfo (
    HRESULT   *hrError*,
    DWORD   *dwLookupID*,
    LCID   *lcid*,
    BSTR *   *pbstrHelpFile*,
    DWORD * *pdwHelpContext***);**

Parameters

hrError [in]
    The code returned by the method that caused the error.

dwLookupID [in]
    The provider-specific number of the error.

lcid [in]
    The locale ID for which to return the Help file path and context ID.

pbstrHelpFile [out]
    A pointer to memory in which to return a pointer to a string containing the fully qualified path of the Help file. If there is no Help file or an error occurs, the returned value (**pbstrHelpFile*) is a null pointer. The memory for this string is allocated by the provider and must be freed by the consumer with a call to **SysFreeString**.

pdwHelpContext [out]
    A pointer to memory in which to return the Help context ID for the error. If there is no Help file (**pbstrHelpFile* is a null pointer), then the returned value has no meaning.

Return Code

S_OK
    The method succeeded.

E_FAIL
    A provider-specific error occurred.

E_INVALIDARG
    pbstrHelpFile or *pdwHelpContext* was a null pointer.

E_OUTOFMEMORY
    The provider was unable to allocate sufficient memory in which to return the Help file path.

DB_E_BADHRESULT
    hrError was invalid.

DB_E_BADLOOKUPID
dwLookupID was invalid.

DB_E_NOLOCALE
The locale ID specified in *lcid* was not supported by the provider.

See Also

IErrorInfo::GetHelpContext, **IErrorInfo::GetHelpFile**,
IErrorLookup::GetErrorDescription

IErrorLookup::ReleaseErrors

Releases any dynamic error information associated with a dynamic error ID.

HRESULT ReleaseErrors (
    const DWORD   *dwDynamicErrorID***);**

Parameters

dwDynamicErrorID [in]
    The ID of the dynamic error information to release.

Return Code

S_OK
    The method succeeded.

E_FAIL
    A provider-specific error occurred.

DB_E_BADDYNAMICERRORID
    dwDynamicErrorID was invalid.

Comments

Dynamic error information is created at run time. It is released when the OLE DB error object calls **ReleaseErrors** with the ID of the error information to release.

Although it is not required, it is more efficient for providers to use the same error ID for all records in a single error object. This allows **ReleaseErrors** to release all of this information in a single call.

For more information, see "Error Lookup Services" in Chapter 13.

IErrorRecords

IErrorRecords is defined by OLE DB. It is used to add and retrieve records in an OLE DB error object. Information is passed to and from OLE DB error objects in an ERRORINFO structure. For information about this structure, see "Error Records" in Chapter 13.

When to Implement

IErrorRecords is implemented by code in the OLE DB SDK.

When to Call

Consumers use this interface to retrieve information stored in the records of an OLE DB error object. They call **QueryInterface** to get a pointer to this interface after retrieving an OLE DB error object with **GetErrorInfo** in the OLE Automation DLL.

Providers use this interface to add records to an OLE DB error object. If they get an existing OLE DB error object with **GetErrorInfo** in the OLE Automation DLL, they call **QueryInterface** on that object to get a pointer to this interface. If they create a new OLE DB error object through a class factory or with **CoCreateInstance**, they request that a pointer to this interface be returned.

Method	Description
AddErrorRecord	Adds a record to an OLE DB error object.
GetBasicErrorInfo	Returns basic information about the error, such as the return code and provider-specific error number.
GetCustomErrorObject	Returns a pointer to an interface on the custom error object.
GetErrorInfo	Returns an **IErrorInfo** interface pointer on the specified record.
GetErrorParameters	Returns the error parameters.
GetRecordCount	Returns the count of records in the OLE DB error object.

IErrorRecords::AddErrorRecord

Adds a record to an OLE DB error object.

HRESULT AddErrorRecord (
    ERRORINFO *   *pErrorInfo*,
    DWORD   *dwLookupID*,
    DISPPARAMS *   *pdispparams*,
    IUnknown *   *punkCustomError*,
    DWORD   *dwDynamicErrorID*);

Parameters

pErrorInfo [in]

A pointer to an ERRORINFO structure containing information about the error. This structure is allocated and freed by the consumer. For more information, see "Error Records" in Chapter 13.

dwLookupID [in]

The value used by the provider's error lookup service in conjunction with the return code to identify the error description, Help file, and context ID for an error. This can be a provider-specific value, such as the *dwMinor* element of **pErrorInfo*. It can also be a special value, IDENTIFIER_SDK_ERROR, that tells the implementation of **IErrorInfo** that is shipped with the OLE DB SDK to ignore the provider's lookup service and use the description supplied in the OLE DB SDK error resource DLL.

```
const DWORD IDENTIFIER_SDK_MASK  = 0xF000000;
const DWORD IDENTIFIER_SDK_ERROR = 0x1000000;
```

pdispparams [in]

A pointer to the parameters for the error. This is a null pointer if there are no error parameters. The error parameters are inserted into the error text by the error lookup service. This structure is allocated and freed by the consumer. For more information, see "Error Parameters" in "Error Records" in Chapter 13.

punkCustomError [in]

An interface pointer to the custom error object. This is a null pointer if there is no custom object for the error. For more information, see "OLE DB Error Objects" in Chapter 13.

dwDynamicErrorID [in]

If the error lookup service uses static errors—that is, error information that is hard coded in the lookup service—*dwDynamicErrorID* is zero.

If the error lookup service uses dynamic errors—that is, error information that is created at run-time—*dwDynamicErrorID* is the ID of the error record. This ID is used to release the error information when the OLE DB error object is released. Although it is not required, it is more efficient for all error records in a single OLE DB error object to have the same dynamic error ID.

For more information, see "Error Lookup Services" in Chapter 13.

Return Code

S_OK

The method succeeded.

E_INVALIDARG

pErrorInfo was a null pointer.

E_OUTOFMEMORY

The OLE DB error object was unable to allocate sufficient memory with which to add a new record.

Comments

This method should be used only by providers; there are no reasons for consumers to use it.

Records are added to the top of the list. That is, the number of the newly added record is record 0 and the number of all other records is increased by 1.

AddErrorRecord adds a reference count on the custom error object. After adding a custom error object to a record in an OLE DB error object, the provider must call **Release** on all interface pointers it holds on that custom error object. This transfers ownership of the custom error object to the OLE DB error object. When it is released, the OLE DB error object will release all custom error objects.

See Also

IErrorRecords::GetBasicErrorInfo, IErrorRecords::GetCustomErrorObject, IErrorRecords::GetErrorParameters

IErrorRecords::GetBasicErrorInfo

Returns basic information about the error, such as the return code and provider-specific error number.

HRESULT GetBasicErrorInfo (
    ULONG   *ulRecordNum*,
    ERRORINFO * *pErrorInfo*);

Parameters

ulRecordNum [in]
The zero-based number of the record for which to return information.

pErrorInfo [out]
A pointer to an ERRORINFO structure in which to return basic error information. This structure is allocated and freed by the consumer. For more information, see "Error Records" in Chapter 13.

Return Code

S_OK
The method succeeded.

E_INVALIDARG
pErrorInfo was a null pointer.

DB_E_BADRECORDNUM
ulRecordNum, which is zero-based, was greater than or equal to the count, which is one-based, of records returned by **GetRecordCount**.

Comments

This method should be used only by consumers; there are no reasons for providers to use it.

See Also

IErrorRecords::GetCustomErrorObject, IErrorRecords::GetErrorInfo, IErrorRecords::GetErrorParameters

IErrorRecords::GetCustomErrorObject

Returns a pointer to an interface on the custom error object.

HRESULT GetCustomErrorObject (
    ULONG   *ulRecordNum,*
    REFIID   *riid,*
    IUnknown ** *ppObject);*

Parameters

ulRecordNum [in]
    The zero-based number of the record for which to return a custom error object.

riid [in]
    The IID of the interface to return.

ppObject [out]
    A pointer to memory in which to return an interface pointer on the custom error object. If there is no custom error object, a null pointer is returned; that is, **ppObject* is a null pointer.

Return Code

S_OK
    The method succeeded.

E_INVALIDARG
    ppObject was a null pointer.

E_NOINTERFACE
    The custom error object did not support the interface specified in *riid*.

DB_E_BADRECORDNUM
    ulRecordNum, which is zero-based, was greater than or equal to the count, which is one-based, of records returned by **GetRecordCount**.

Comments

This method should be used only by consumers; there are no reasons for providers to use it.

See Also

IErrorRecords::GetBasicErrorInfo, IErrorRecords::GetErrorParameters

IErrorRecords::GetErrorInfo

Returns an **IErrorInfo** interface pointer on the specified record.

HRESULT GetErrorInfo (
    ULONG   *ulRecordNum,*
    LCID   *lcid,*
    IErrorInfo **   *ppErrorInfo*);

Parameters

ulRecordNum [in]

The zero-based number of the record for which to return an **IErrorInfo** interface pointer.

lcid [in]

The locale ID for which to return error information. This parameter is checked when it is passed to methods in **IErrorInfo**.

ppErrorInfo [out]

A pointer to memory in which to return a pointer to an **IErrorInfo** interface on the specified record. This **IErrorInfo** interface pointer is different than the **IErrorInfo** interface pointer exposed on the OLE DB error object with **QueryInterface**. For more information, see "OLE DB Error Objects" in Chapter 13.

Return Code

S_OK

The method succeeded.

E_INVALIDARG

ppErrorInfo was a null pointer.

DB_E_BADRECORDNUM

ulRecordNum, which is zero-based, was greater than or equal to the count, which is one-based, of records returned by **GetRecordCount**.

Comments

This method should be used only by consumers; there are no reasons for providers to use it.

See Also

IErrorRecords::GetBasicErrorInfo, IErrorRecords::GetCustomErrorObject, IErrorRecords::GetErrorParameters

IErrorRecords::GetErrorParameters

Returns the error parameters.

HRESULT GetErrorParameters (
      ULONG   *ulRecordNum,*
      DISPPARAMS *   *pdispparams***);**

Parameters

ulRecordNum [in]
> The zero-based number of the record for which to return parameters.

pdispparams [out]
> A pointer to a DISPPARAMS structure in which to return the error parameters. The consumer allocates the memory for the DISPPARAMS structure itself, but the provider allocates the memory for any arrays pointed to by elements of the DISPPARAMS structure.

Return Code

S_OK
> The method succeeded.

E_INVALIDARG
> *pdispparams* was a null pointer.

E_OUTOFMEMORY
> The provider was unable to allocate sufficient memory in which to return the data pointed to by elements of **pdispparams*.

DB_E_BADRECORDNUM
> *ulRecordNum*, which is zero-based, was greater than or equal to the count, which is one-based, of records returned by **GetRecordCount**.

Comments

This method is used by consumers only when the meaning of the error parameters is known to the consumer; error parameters are generally passed to the error lookup service and incorporated into error messages by the provider through that lookup service. There is no reason for providers to use this method.

See Also

IErrorRecords::GetBasicErrorInfo, **IErrorRecords::GetCustomErrorObject**

IErrorRecords::GetRecordCount

Returns the count of records in the OLE DB error object.

HRESULT GetRecordCount (
    ULONG * *pcRecords*);

Parameters

pcRecords [out]
> A pointer to memory in which to return the count of error records. Note that this is a one-based count while error records are zero-based. If **pcRecords* is zero, there are no records in the OLE DB error object and calls to **GetBasicErrorInfo**, **GetErrorInfo**, **GetErrorParameters**, and **GetCustomErrorObject** will return DB_E_BADRECORDNUM.

Return Code

S_OK
> The method succeeded.

E_INVALIDARG
> *pcRecords* was a null pointer.

Comments

This method should be used only by consumers; there are no reasons for providers to use it.

See Also

IErrorRecords::GetBasicErrorInfo, IErrorRecords::GetCustomErrorObject, IErrorRecords::GetErrorInfo, IErrorRecords::GetErrorParameters

IGetDataSource

This is a mandatory interface on the session for obtaining an interface pointer to the data source object.

Method	Description
GetDataSource	Returns an interface pointer on the data source object that created this session.

IGetDataSource::GetDataSource

Returns an interface pointer on the data source object that created the session.

HRESULT GetDataSource (
    REFIID   *riid*,
    IUnknown ** *ppDataSource*);

Parameters

riid [in]

    The IID of the interface on which to return a pointer.

ppDataSource [out]

    A pointer to memory in which to return the interface pointer. If **GetDataSource**
    fails, it must attempt to set **ppDataSource* to a null pointer.

Return Code

S_OK

    The method succeeded.

E_FAIL

    A provider-specific error occurred.

E_INVALIDARG

    ppDataSource was a null pointer.

E_NOINTERFACE

    The object that created this session did not support the interface specified in *riid*.

See Also

ICommand::GetDBSession, IRowsetInfo::GetSpecification

IIndexDefinition

IIndexDefinition exposes simple methods to create and drop indexes from the data source object.

When to Implement

IIndexDefinition is optional for providers that do not otherwise support index creation; it is mandatory for providers that support creating and dropping indexes through commands.

Method	Description
CreateIndex	Adds a new index to a base table.
DropIndex	Drops an index from a base table.

IIndexDefinition::CreateIndex

Adds a new index to a base table.

HRESULT CreateIndex(
DBID *	*pTableID,*
DBID *	*pIndexID,*
ULONG	*cIndexColumnDescs,*
const DBINDEXCOLUMNDESC	*rgIndexColumnDescs*[],
ULONG	*cPropertySets,*
DBPROPSET	*rgPropertySets*[],
DBID **	*ppIndexID*);

Parameters

pTableID [in]

A pointer to the DBID of the table for which to create an index.

pIndexID [in]

A pointer to the ID of the new index to create. If this is a null pointer, the provider assigns an ID to the index. The ID must be unique.

cIndexColumnDescs [in]

The count of DBINDEXCOLUMNSDESC structures in *rgIndexColumnDescs*.

rgIndexColumnDescs [in]

An array of DBINDEXCOLUMNDESC structures that describe how to construct the index. The order of the DBINDEXCOLUMNDESC structures in *rgIndexColumnDescs* determines the order of the columns in the index key. That is, the column identified by the first element of this array is the most significant column in the index key and the column identified by the last element is the least significant column. When the index is opened as a rowset, the key columns occur in order of most significant column to least significant column.

```
typedef struct {
   DBID *         pColumnID;
   DBINDEXCOLORDER eIndexColOrder;
} DBINDEXCOLUMNDESC;
```

The elements of this structure are used as follows.

Element	Description
pColumnID	A pointer to the ID of the base table column.
eIndexColOrder	Whether the index is ascending or descending in this column.
	• DBINDEXCOLORDER_ASC—Ascending
	• DBINDEXCOLORDER_DESC—Descending

cPropertySets [in]

> The number of DBPROPSET structures in *rgPropertySets*. If this is zero, the provider ignores *rgPropertySets*.

rgPropertySets [in/out]

> An array of DBPROPSET structures containing properties and values to be set. The properties specified in these structures must belong to the Index property group. If the same property is specified more than once in *rgPropertySets*, then it is provider-specific which value is used. If *cPropertySets* is zero, this argument is ignored.
>
> For information about the properties in the Index property group that are defined by OLE DB, see "Index Properties" in Appendix C. For information about the DBPROPSET and DBPROP structures, see "DBPROPSET Structure" and "DBPROP Structure" in Chapter 11.

ppIndexID [out]

> A pointer to memory in which to return a pointer to the DBID of newly created index. If *ppIndexID* is a null pointer, no DBID is returned.

Return Code

S_OK

> The method succeeded and the new index has been created. In all DBPROP structures passed to the method, *dwStatus* is set to DBPROPSTATUS_OK.

DB_S_ERRORSOCCURRED

> The index was created but one or more properties—for which the *dwOptions* element of the DBPROP structure was DBPROPOPTIONS_SETIFCHEAP—were not set. The consumer checks *dwStatus* in the DBPROP structures to determine which properties were not set. The method can fail to set properties for a number of reasons, including:
>
> - The property was not supported by the provider.
>
> - The property was not in the Index property group.
>
> - The property set was not supported by the provider.
>
> - It was not cheap to set the property.
>
> - The *colid* in the DBPROP structure was not DB_NULLID.
>
> - The data type in *vValue* in the DBPROP structure was not the data type of the property or was not VT_EMPTY.
>
> - The value in *vValue* in the DBPROP structure was invalid.
>
> - The property's value conflicted with an existing property.

E_FAIL

> A provider-specific error occurred.

E_INVALIDARG

pTableID was a null pointer.

pIndexID and *ppIndexID* were both null pointers.

cIndexColumnDescs was zero.

rgIndexColumnDescs was a null pointer.

eIndexColOrder in an element of *rgIndexColumnDescs* was not a valid value.

cPropertySets was not zero and *rgPropertySets* was a null pointer.

In an element of *rgPropertySets*, *cProperties* was not zero and *rgProperties* was a null pointer.

DB_E_BADCOLUMNID

A column specified in an element of *rgIndexColumnDescs* did not exist.

DB_E_DUPLICATEINDEXID

The specified index already exists in the current data source object.

DB_E_ERRORSOCCURRED

No index was created because one or more properties—for which the *dwOptions* element of the DBPROP structure was DBPROPOPTIONS_REQUIRED or an invalid value—were not set. The consumer checks *dwStatus* in the DBPROP structures to determine which properties were not set. None of the satisfiable properties are remembered. The method can fail to set properties for any of the reasons specified in DB_S_ERRORSOCCURRED except the reason that states that it was not cheap to set the property.

DB_E_NOTABLE

The specified table does not exist in the current data source object.

DB_SEC_E_PERMISSIONDENIED

The consumer did not have sufficient permission to create the index.

Comments

If **CreateIndex** returns any errors, the index is not created.

See Also

IIndexDefinition::DropIndex, IRowsetIndex, ITableDefinition

IIndexDefinition::DropIndex

Drops an index from the base table.

HRESULT DropIndex(
    DBID * *pTableID*,
    DBID * *pIndexID*);

Parameters

pTableID [in]
    A pointer to the DBID of the base table.

pIndexID [in]
    A pointer to the DBID of the index to drop. This must be an index on the table
    specified with *pTableID*. If *pIndexId* is a null pointer, all indexes for the table
    specified with *pTableID* are dropped.

Return Code

S_OK
    The method succeeded and the index has been dropped from the base table.

E_FAIL
    A provider-specific error occurred.

E_INVALIDARG
    pTableID was a null pointer.

DB_E_INDEXINUSE
    The specified index was in use.

DB_E_NOINDEX
    The specified index does not exist in the current data source or did not apply to the
    specified table.

DB_E_NOTABLE
    The specified table does not exist in the current data source .

DB_SEC_E_PERMISSIONDENIED
    The consumer did not have sufficient permission to drop the index.

Comments

For partitioned indexes, a call to this method drops all partitions.

If **DropIndex** returns any errors, the index is not dropped.

See Also

IIndexDefinition::CreateIndex

IMultipleResults

IMultipleResults is used to retrieve multiple results (rowsets or row counts) created by a command. For more information, see "Multiple Results" in Chapter 3.

When to Implement

IMultipleResults is a mandatory interface on multiple results objects. Providers specify whether they support multiple results objects and what restrictions they have on these objects through the DBPROP_MULTIPLERESULTS property in the Data Source Information property group.

When to Call

To create a multiple results object, a consumer creates a command, sets the command text, and calls **ICommand::Execute** with *riid* set to IID_IMultipleResults. The command text generally specifies multiple results, although this is not required. To retrieve each result in succession, the consumer repeatedly calls **IMultipleResults::GetResult**.

Method	Description
GetResult	Returns the next in a series of multiple results from the provider.

IMultipleResults::GetResult

Returns the next in a series of multiple results from the provider.

HRESULT GetResult(
      IUnknown * *pUnkOuter,*
      LONG   *lReserved,*
      REFIID   *riid,*
      LONG *   *pcRowsAffected,*
      IUnknown ** *ppRowset);*

Parameters

pUnkOuter [in]

A pointer to the controlling **IUnknown** interface if the object is being created as part of an aggregate; otherwise, it is a null pointer.

lReserved [in]

Reserved. Must be set to zero.

riid [in]

The requested interface to return in **ppRowset*. If this is IID_NULL, then *ppRowset* is ignored and no rowset is returned, even if one exists.

pcRowsAffected [out]

A pointer to memory in which to return the count of rows affected by an update, delete, or insert. If the value of *cParamSets* passed into **ICommand::Execute** was greater than 1, then **pcRowsAffected* is the total number of rows affected by all of the sets of parameters represented by the current result. If the count of affected rows is not available, **pcRowsAffected* is set to −1 on output. If the result is not a count of rows affected by an update, delete, or insert, **pcRowsAffected* is undefined on output. If an error occurs, **pcRowsAffected* is set to −1. If *pcRowsAffected* is a null pointer, no count of affected rows is returned.

Some providers do not support returning individual counts of rows, but instead return an overall count of the total rows affected by the call to **Execute**, or do not return row counts at all. Such providers set **pcRowsAffected* to −1 when the count of affected rows is not available.

ppRowset [out]

A pointer to memory in which to return the interface for the next result. If the next result is not a rowset (for instance, if it is the count of the rows affected by an update, delete, or insert), this is set to a null pointer. If an error occurs, **ppRowset* is set to a null pointer.

If *ppRowset* is a null pointer, no rowset is created.

Return Value

S_OK

The method succeeded.

DB_S_ERRORSOCCURRED

This can be returned for any of the following reasons.

- An error occurred returning one or more output parameter values associated with the next result. To determine which output parameters were not returned, the consumer checks the status values. For a list of status values that can be returned by this method, see "Status Values Used When Getting Data" in "Status" in Chapter 6.

- The rowset was opened but one or more properties—for which the *dwOptions* element of the DBPROP structure was DBPROPOPTIONS_SETIFCHEAP— were not set. The consumer calls **IRowsetInfo::GetProperties** to determine which properties were set.

DB_S_NORESULT

There are no more results. **ppRowset* is set to a null pointer and **pcRowsAffected* is set to –1.

DB_S_STOPLIMITREACHED

Execution has been stopped because a resource limit has been reached. The results obtained so far have been returned. Calling **GetResult** again returns information for the next result, or DB_S_NORESULT if no more results can be obtained, either because they do not exist or because the resource limit applies across multiple results.

This return code takes precedence over DB_S_ERRORSOCCURRED. That is, if the conditions described here and those described in DB_S_ERRORSOCCURRED both occur, the provider returns this code. When the consumer receives this return code, it should also check for the conditions described in DB_S_ERRORSOCCURRED.

E_FAIL

A provider-specific error occurred.

E_INVALIDARG

lReserved was not zero.

E_NOINTERFACE

The interface specified in *riid* was not supported on the rowset.

E_OUTOFMEMORY

The provider was unable to allocate sufficient memory in which to create the rowset.

E_UNEXPECTED

ITransaction::Commit or **ITransaction::Abort** was called and the object is in a zombie state.

DB_E_ABORTLIMITREACHED
Execution has been aborted because a resource limit has been reached. No results have been returned. Calling **GetResult** again returns information for the next result, or DB_S_NORESULT if no more results can be obtained, either because they do not exist or because the resource limit applies across multiple results.

DB_E_CANTCONVERTVALUE
A literal value in the command text associated with the next result could not be converted to the type of the associated column for reasons other than data overflow.

DB_E_DATAOVERFLOW
A literal value in the command text associated with the next result overflowed the type specified by the associated column.

DB_E_ERRORSINCOMMAND
The command text associated with the next result contained one or more errors. Providers should use OLE DB error objects to return details about the errors.

DB_E_ERRORSOCCURRED
The method failed due to one or more invalid input parameter values associated with the next result. To determine which input parameter values were invalid, the consumer checks the status values. For a list of status values that can be returned by this method, see "Status Values Used When Setting Data" in "Status" in Chapter 6.

The rowset was not returned because one or more properties—for which the *dwOptions* element of the DBPROP structure was DBPROPOPTIONS_REQUIRED—could not be satisfied.

DB_E_NOAGGREGATION
pUnkOuter was not a null pointer and the object being created does not support aggregation.

DB_E_OBJECTOPEN
The previous rowset is still open, and the provider does not support multiple open results simultaneously (DBPROP_MULTIPLERESULTS is DBPROPVAL_MR_SUPPORTED).

DB_SEC_E_PERMISSIONDENIED
The consumer did not have sufficient permission to get the next result.

Comments
GetResult returns the next in a series of multiple results from the provider. If the requested result is a rowset, **GetResult** returns the requested interface on that rowset. If the requested result is a row count, **GetResult** returns the count of rows affected in **pcRowsAffected*.

Providers will generally only be able to process one result at a time. For maximum interoperability, consumers should free any rowset obtained by a previous call to **GetResult** before requesting the next result.

Providers may check the entire command text for errors at execute time, or may check the command text associated with each result when that result is retrieved. Therefore, the syntax errors returned by **ICommand::Execute** can also be returned by **GetResult**. In this case, the next call to **GetResult** moves on to the next result, or returns DB_S_NORESULT if no more results are available.

When **GetResult** returns an error, its behavior depends on the error that occurred:

- If **GetResult** returns E_INVALIDARG, DB_E_NOAGGREGATION, or DB_E_OBJECTOPEN, the current result is still available. Assuming there are no other errors, the next call to **GetResult** returns the current result.

- If **GetResult** returns any other error, the current result is lost. The next call to **GetResult** returns either the next result or DB_S_NORESULT if the error caused the provider to lose all remaining results. Providers that can recover the current result in this situation must discard it and return the next result.

The following example shows how a consumer might process multiple results:

```
hr = pICommandText->Execute(pUnkOuter, IID_IMultipleResults, pParams, &cRowsAffected,
                            &pIMultipleResults);

if (pIMultipleResults) {
   while(hr != DB_S_NORESULT) {
      if(SUCCEEDED(hr = pIMultipleResults->GetResult(pUnkOuter, 0, IID_IRowset,
                                                     &cRowsAffected, &pIRowset))) {
         if(pIRowset) {
            // The next result is a rowset. Process the rowset.
            pIRowset->Release();
         } else {
            // The next result is not a rowset. Process the non-rowset result.
         }
      } else {
         // Process error from GetResult.
         break;
      }
   }
   pIMultipleResults->Release();
}
```

See Also

ICommand::Execute

IOpenRowset

IOpenRowset is a required interface on the session. It can be supported by providers that do not support creating rowsets through commands.

The **IOpenRowset** model enables consumers to open and work directly with individual tables or indexes in a data source by using **IOpenRowset::OpenRowset**, which generates a rowset of all rows in the table or index.

Method	Description
OpenRowset	Opens and returns a rowset that includes all rows from a single base table or index.

IOpenRowset::OpenRowset

Opens and returns a rowset that includes all rows from a single base table or index.

HRESULT OpenRowset(
    IUnknown *   *pUnkOuter,*
    DBID *   *pTableID,*
    DBID *   *pIndexID,*
    REFIID   *riid,*
    ULONG   *cPropertySets,*
    DBPROPSET   *rgPropertySets[],*
    IUnknown **   *ppRowset);*

Parameters

pUnkOuter[in]

The controlling **IUnknown** if the rowset is to be aggregated, otherwise a null pointer.

pTableID [in]

The DBID of the table to open. For more information, see the "Comments" section.

pIndexID [in]

The DBID of the index to open. For more information, see the "Comments" section.

riid [in]

The IID of the interface to return in **ppRowset*. This must be an interface that the rowset supports, even when *ppRowset* is set to a null pointer and no rowset is created.

cPropertySets [in]

The number of DBPROPSET structures in *rgPropertySets*. If this is zero, the provider ignores *rgPropertySets*.

rgPropertySets [in/out]

An array of DBPROPSET structures containing properties and values to be set. The properties specified in these structures must belong to the Rowset property group. If the same property is specified more than once in *rgPropertySets*, then it is provider-specific which value is used. If *cPropertySets* is zero, this argument is ignored.

For information about the properties in the Rowset property group that are defined by OLE DB, see "Rowset Properties" in Appendix C. For information about the DBPROPSET and DBPROP structures, see "DBPROPSET Structure" and "DBPROP Structure" in Chapter 11.

ppRowset [in/out]

A pointer to memory in which to return the interface pointer to the created rowset. If *ppRowset* is a null pointer, no rowset is created; properties are verified and if a required property cannot be set, DB_E_ERRORSOCCURRED is returned. If **OpenRowset** fails, **ppRowset* is set to a null pointer.

Return Code

S_OK

The method succeeded and the rowset is opened. In all DBPROP structures passed to the method, *dwStatus* is set to DBPROPSTATUS_OK.

DB_S_ERRORSOCCURRED

The rowset was opened but one or more properties—for which the *dwOptions* element of the DBPROP structure was DBPROPOPTIONS_SETIFCHEAP—were not set. The consumer checks *dwStatus* in the DBPROP structures to determine which properties were not set. The method can fail to set properties for a number of reasons, including:

- *colid* in the DBPROP structure was invalid.

- The data type in *vValue* in the DBPROP structure was not the data type of the property or was not VT_EMPTY.

- The value in *vValue* in the DBPROP structure was invalid.

- The property's value conflicted with an existing property.

- A property was specified to be applied to all columns, but could not be applied to one or more columns.

- The property was not supported by the provider.

- It was not cheap to set the property.

E_FAIL

A provider-specific error occurred.

E_INVALIDARG

pTableID and *pIndexID* were both null pointers.

cPropertySets was not zero and *prgPropertySets* was a null pointer.

In an element of *rgPropertySets*, *cProperties* was not zero and *rgProperties* was a null pointer.

E_NOINTERFACE

The rowset did not support the interface specified in *riid* or *riid* was IID_NULL.

DB_E_ERRORSOCCURRED

No rowset was returned because one or more properties—for which the *dwOptions* element of the DBPROP structure was DBPROPOPTIONS_REQUIRED or an invalid value—were not set. The consumer checks *dwStatus* in the DBPROP structures to determine which properties were not set. None of the satisfiable properties are remembered. The method can fail to set properties for any of the reasons specified in DB_S_ERRORSOCCURRED except the reason that states that it was not cheap to set the property.

DB_E_ABORTLIMITREACHED
The method failed because a resource limit has been reached. For example, a query used to implement the method timed out. No rowset is returned.

DB_E_NOAGGREGATION
pUnkOuter was not a null pointer and the rowset being created does not support aggregation.

DB_E_NOINDEX
The specified index does not exist in the current data source or did not apply to the specified table.

DB_E_NOTABLE
The specified table does not exist in the current data source.

DB_SEC_E_PERMISSIONDENIED
The consumer did not have sufficient permission to open the rowset. For example, a rowset included a column for which the consumer does not have read permission.

Comments

If the table or index has no rows, the rowset is still created. The resulting rowset is fully functional and can be used, for example, to insert new rows or determine column metadata.

pTableID and *pIndexID* are used in the following combinations:

- If *pTableID* is not a null pointer and *pIndexID* is a null pointer, the table identified by **pTableID* is opened.

- If *pTableID* is a null pointer and *pIndexID* is not a null pointer, **pIndexID* must uniquely and fully identify an index; this index is opened. If **pIndexID* does not uniquely and fully identify an index, DB_E_NOINDEX is returned.

- If neither *pTableID* nor *pIndexID* is a null pointer, **pIndexID* must identify an index for the table identified by **pTableID*; this index is opened. If **pIndexID* does not identify an index for the table identified by **pTableID*, DB_E_NOINDEX is returned.

- If both *pTableID* and *pIndexID* are null pointers, E_INVALIDARG is returned.

The threading model of the returned rowset is determined by the property DBPROP_ROWTHREADMODEL.

See Also

IDBCreateCommand::CreateCommand

IRowset

IRowset is the base rowset interface. It provides methods for fetching rows sequentially, getting the data from those rows, and managing rows.

IRowset requires **IAccessor** and **IRowsetInfo**.

When to Implement

IRowset is required for all providers that support general consumers.

When to Call

Consumers use the methods in **IRowset** for all basic rowset operations, including fetching and releasing rows and getting column values.

When a consumer first gets an interface pointer on a rowset, usually its first step is to determine the rowset's capabilities using **IRowsetInfo::GetProperties**. This returns information about the interfaces exposed by the rowset as well as those capabilities of the rowset which do not show up as distinct interfaces, such as the maximum number of active rows and how many rows can have pending updates at the same time.

For most consumers, the next step is to determine the characteristics, or metadata, of the columns in the rowset. For this they use either **IColumnsInfo** or **IColumnsRowset**, for simple or extended column information respectively. These interfaces are also available on prepared commands prior to execution, allowing advance planning.

The consumer determines which columns it needs, either from the metadata or on the basis of knowing the text command that generated the rowset. It determines the ordinals of the needed columns from the ordering of the column information returned by **IColumnsInfo** or from ordinals in the column metadata rowset returned by **IColumnsRowset**.

Some consumers do not use a command or do not want to browse the column information: they may know the name or property identifier for the columns they want to use. They call **IColumnsInfo::MapColumnIDs** to retrieve the column ordinals.

The ordinals are used to specify a binding to a column. A binding is a structure that associates an element of the consumer's structure with a column. The binding can bind the column's data value, length, and status value. For more information about bindings, see "Bindings" in Chapter 6.

A set of bindings is gathered together in an *accessor*, which is created with **IAccessor::CreateAccessor**. An accessor can contain multiple bindings so that the data for multiple columns can be retrieved or set in a single call. The consumer can create several accessors to match different usage patterns in different parts of the application. It can create and release accessors at any time while the rowset remains in existence. For more information about accessors, see "Accessors" in Chapter 6.

To fetch rows from the database, the consumer calls a method such as **GetNextRows** or **IRowsetLocate::GetRowsAt**. To create and initialize a new row to be inserted into the data source, the consumer calls **IRowsetChange::InsertRow**.

The methods that fetch rows do not actually return data to the consumer. Instead, they return the handles to these rows a local copy of the rows is stored in the rowset.

After the rows are returned, the consumer can access the data in the rows. The consumer calls **GetData** and passes it the handle to a row, the handle to an accessor, and a pointer to a consumer-allocated buffer. **GetData** converts the data (if it does not match the native provider storage) and returns the columns as specified in the bindings used to create the accessor. The consumer can call **GetData** more than once for a row, using different accessors and buffers; thus, the consumer can have multiple copies of the same data. For example, if a column contains a text document, the consumer might call **GetData** with an accessor that binds the first 50 bytes of the document. When the user double-clicks on the displayed heading text, the consumer could then call **GetData** with a different accessor to retrieve the entire document.

Data from variable-length columns may be treated several ways. First, such columns can be bound to a finite section of the consumer's structure, which causes truncation when the length of the data exceeds the length of the buffer. The consumer can determine that truncation has occurred by checking if the status is DBSTATUS_S_TRUNCATED. The returned length is always the true length in bytes, so the consumer also determine how much data was truncated. Another way to obtain data from such columns is by reference. For example, if a binary column is bound with a type indicator of DBTYPE_BYTES | DBTYPE_BYREF, the provider allocates memory for the all of the data in the column and returns this memory to the consumer.

In both cases, it is likely that such large values may be best optimized as deferred columns and accessed only when necessary. Performance varies with different servers, but in general BLOB columns are stored separately from other records and may be more costly to access than ordinary columns, so they would not routinely be pulled in for browsing or scanning. For more information, see "Deferred Columns" in Chapter 4.

Another way to handle BLOB columns may be implemented on some providers, and that is to request they be delivered as OLE **ILockBytes**, **IStorage**, **ISequentialStream**, or **IStream** objects. For more information, see "BLOBs as Storage Objects" in Chapter 7.

For a description of how to update and delete rows, see Chapter 5, "Updating Data in Rowsets."

When the consumer is finished fetching or updating rows, it releases them with **ReleaseRows**. This releases resources from the rowset's copy of the rows and makes room for new rows. The consumer can then repeat its cycle of fetching or creating rows and accessing the data in them.

When the consumer is done with the rowset, it calls **IAccessor::ReleaseAccessor** to release any accessors. It calls **IUnknown::Release** on all interfaces exposed by the rowset to release the rowset. When the rowset is released, it forces the release of any remaining rows or accessors the consumer may hold. Such handle objects are subordinate to the rowset. That is, they do not take reference counts upon the rowset and cannot cause the rowset to linger beyond the point where all the interfaces for the rowset have been released. The rowset must clean up all such subordinate objects.

Method	Description
AddRefRows	Adds a reference count to an existing row handle.
GetData	Retrieves data from the rowset's copy of the row.
GetNextRows	Fetches rows sequentially, remembering the previous position.
ReleaseRows	Releases rows.
RestartPosition	Repositions the next fetch position to its initial position; that is, its position when the rowset was first created.

IRowset::AddRefRows

Adds a reference count to an existing row handle.

HRESULT AddRefRows(
    ULONG   *cRows*,
    const HROW   *rghRows*[],
    ULONG   *rgRefCounts*[],
    DBROWSTATUS *rgRowStatus*[]);

Parameters

cRows [in]

The number of rows for which to increment the reference count.

rghRows [in]

An array of row handles for which to increment the reference count. The reference count of row handles is incremented by one for each time they appear in the array.

rgRefCounts [out]

An array with *cRows* elements in which to return the new reference count for each row handle. The consumer allocates memory for this array. If *rgRefCounts* is a null pointer, no reference counts are returned.

rgRowStatus [out]

An array with *cRows* elements in which to return values indicating the status of each row specified in *rghRows*. If no errors occur while incrementing the reference count of a row, the corresponding element of *rgRowStatus* is set to DBROWSTATUS_S_OK. If an error occurs while incrementing the reference count of a row, the corresponding element is set as specified in DB_S_ERRORSOCCURRED. The consumer allocates memory for this array. If *rgRowStatus* is a null pointer, no row statuses are returned. For information about the DBROWSTATUS enumerated type, see "Arrays of Errors" in Chapter 13.

Return Code

S_OK

The method succeeded. The reference count of all rows was successfully incremented. The following value can be returned in *prgRowStatus:

- The reference count of the row was successfully incremented. The corresponding element of *prgRowStatus contains DBROWSTATUS_S_OK.

DB_S_ERRORSOCCURRED

An error occurred while incrementing the reference count of a row, but the reference count of at least one row was incremented. Successes can occur for the reason listed under S_OK. The following errors can occur:

- A row handle was invalid. The reference count of the row was not incremented and the corresponding element of *rgRowStatus* contains DBROWSTATUS_E_INVALID.

- A row handle referred to a row that had a reference count of zero. The reference count of the row was not incremented and the corresponding element of *rgRowStatus* contains DBROWSTATUS_E_INVALID.

- A row handle referred to a row for which a deletion had been transmitted to the data source. The reference count of the row was not incremented and the corresponding element of *rgRowStatus* contains DBROWSTATUS_E_DELETED.

E_FAIL

A provider-specific error occurred.

E_INVALIDARG

rghRows was a null pointer and *cRows* was not zero.

E_UNEXPECTED

ITransaction::Commit or **ITransaction::Abort** was called and the object is in a zombie state.

DB_E_ERRORSOCCURRED

Errors occurred while incrementing the reference count of all of the rows. Errors can occur for the reasons listed under DB_S_ERRORSOCCURRED.

Comments

AddRefRows must be supported for implementing multiple references to the same row even if the rowset does not support **IRowsetIdentity**.

It is always possible for a consumer to call **AddRefRows** while it is processing a method in **IRowsetNotify**. That is, the rowset must be re-entrant through **AddRefRows** during notification.

If **AddRefRows** encounters an error while incrementing the reference count of a row, it sets the corresponding element in *rgRowStatus* to the appropriate DBROWSTATUS value and continues processing.

If a row handle is duplicated in *rghRows*, the corresponding row will have its reference counted incremented by one for each time it appears in the array.

See Also

IRowset::ReleaseRows

IRowset::GetData

Retrieves data from the rowset's copy of the row.

HRESULT GetData (
    HROW   *hRow,*
    HACCESSOR *hAccessor,*
    void *   *pData***);**

Parameters

hRow [in]

The handle of the row from which to get the data.

Caution The consumer must ensure that *hRow* contains a valid row handle; the provider might not validate *hRow* before using it. The result of passing the handle of a deleted row is provider-specific, although the provider cannot terminate abnormally. For example, the provider might return DB_E_BADROWHANDLE, DB_E_DELETEDROW, or it might get data from a different row. The result of passing an invalid row handle in *hRow* is undefined.

---

hAccessor [in]

The handle of the accessor to use. If *hAccessor* is the handle of a null accessor (*cBindings* in **IAccessor::CreateAccessor** was zero), then **GetData** does not get any data values.

Caution The consumer must ensure that *hAccessor* contains a valid accessor handle; the provider might not validate *hAccessor* before using it. The result of passing an invalid accessor handle in *hAccessor* is undefined.

---

pData [out]

A pointer to a buffer in which to return the data. The consumer allocates memory for this buffer.

Return Code

S_OK

The method succeeded. The status of all columns bound by the accessor is set to DBSTATUS_S_OK, DBSTATUS_S_ISNULL, or DBSTATUS_S_TRUNCATED.

DB_S_ERRORSOCCURRED

An error occurred while returning data for one or more columns, but data was successfully returned for at least one column. To determine the columns for which data was returned, the consumer checks the status values. For a list of status values that can be returned by this method, see "Status Values Used When Getting Data" in "Status" in Chapter 6.

E_FAIL

A provider-specific error occurred.

E_INVALIDARG

pData was a null pointer and the accessor was not a null accessor.

E_UNEXPECTED

ITransaction::Commit or **ITransaction::Abort** was called and the object is in a zombie state.

DB_E_BADACCESSORHANDLE

hAccessor was invalid. Providers are not required to check for this condition, because doing so might slow the method significantly.

DB_E_BADACCESSORTYPE

The specified accessor was not a row accessor.

DB_E_BADROWHANDLE

hRow was invalid. Providers are not required to check for this condition, because doing so might slow the method significantly.

DB_E_DELETEDROW

hRow referred to a pending delete row or a row for which a deletion had been transmitted to the data source. Providers are not required to check for this condition, because doing so might slow the method significantly.

DB_E_ERRORSOCCURRED

Errors occurred while returning data for all columns. To determine what errors occurred, the consumer checks the status values. For a list of status values that can be returned by this method, see "Status Values Used When Getting Data" in "Status" in Chapter 6.

If this method performs deferred accessor validation and that validation takes places before any data is transferred, it can also return any of the following return codes for the reasons listed in the corresponding DBBINDSTATUS values in **IAccessor::CreateAccessor**:

E_NOINTERFACE
DB_E_BADBINDINFO
DB_E_BADORDINAL
DB_E_BADSTORAGEFLAGS
DB_E_UNSUPPORTEDCONVERSION

Comments

This method makes no logical change to the state of the object.

A consumer calls **GetData** to retrieve data from rows which have been fetched by prior calls to methods such as **GetNextRows**. For a complete description of how **GetData** retrieves data, see "Getting Data" in Chapter 6.

A consumer can call **GetData** any number of times. In each call, it can pass a different accessor and the address of a different buffer. This means that the consumer can get as many copies of the data as it wants and it can get data in different types if alternate conversions are available.

GetData does not enforce any security restrictions. The provider must not create a rowset that includes columns for which the consumer does not have read privileges, so **GetData** never encounters problems accessing the data for a column. Note that the rowset can contain columns to which the consumer does not have write permission if DBPROP_COLUMNRESTRICT is VARIANT_TRUE. The methods that fetch rows must not return the handles of rows for which the consumer does not have read privileges, so **GetData** never encounters problems accessing a row. Note that such rows might exist if the DBPROP_ROWRESTRICT property is VARIANT_TRUE.

If **GetData** fails, the memory to which *pData* points is not freed but its contents are undefined. If, before **GetData** failed, the provider allocated any memory for return to the consumer, the provider frees this memory and does not return it to the consumer.

GetData must be reentrant during notifications. If the provider calls a method from **IRowsetNotify** in the consumer, the consumer must be able to call **GetData** while processing the notification method.

The following example shows how a reference accessor is used.

```
#include <oledb.h>
#include <stddef.h>

IRowset    *TheRowset;
IAccessor *TheRowsetAccessor;
HROW        hRow;

int main() {
   struct ExactlyTheSame {
      long   l;
      double d;
      short  i;
   };
   HACCESSOR hRawAccess;

   static DBBINDING ExactBindings [3] = {
      {
         1,                           // iOrdinal
         offsetof (ExactlyTheSame,l), // obValue
         0,                           // No length binding
         0,                           // No Status binding
         NULL,                        // No TypeInfo
         NULL,                        // No Object
         NULL,                        // No Extensions
         DBPART_VALUE,
         DBMEMOWNER_PROVIDEROWNED,    // Ignored
         DBPARAMIO_NOTPARAM,
         sizeof (long),
         0,
         DBTYPE_I4,
         0,                           // No Precision
         0                            // No Scale
      },
```

```
    {
        2,                              // iOrdinal
        offsetof (ExactlyTheSame, d), // obValue
        0,                              // No length binding
        0,                              // No Status binding
        NULL,                           // No TypeInfo
        NULL,                           // No Object
        NULL,                           // No Extensions
        DBPART_VALUE,
        DBMEMOWNER_PROVIDEROWNED,       // Ignored
        DBPARAMIO_NOTPARAM,
        sizeof (double),
        0,
        DBTYPE_R8,
        0,                              // No Precision
        0                               // No Scale
    },
    {
        3,                              // iOrdinal
        offsetof (ExactlyTheSame,i),   // obValue
        0,                              // No length binding
        0,                              // No Status binding
        NULL,                           // No TypeInfo
        NULL,                           // No Object
        NULL,                           // No Extensions
        DBPART_VALUE,
        DBMEMOWNER_PROVIDEROWNED,       // Ignored
        DBPARAMIO_NOTPARAM,
        sizeof (short),
        0,
        DBTYPE_I2,
        0,                              // No Precision
        0                               // No Scale
    }
};

TheRowsetAccessor->CreateAccessor (DBACCESSOR_PASSBYREF, 3, ExactBindings, 0,
                                   &hRawAccess, NULL);
```

To read the column *i* of some row, the consumer should do the following:

```
short           value;
ExactlyTheSame *pRow;

TheRowset->GetData(hRow, hRawAccess, &pRow);

value = pRow->i;
```

The following example shows how provider-owned memory is used.

```c
#include <oledb.h>
#include <stddef.h>

IRowset   *TheRowset;
IAccessor *TheRowsetAccessor;
HROW       hRow;

int main() {
   struct IndirectlySimilar {
      long   * pl;
      double * pd;
      short * pi;
   };
   HACCESSOR hFastAccess;

   static DBBINDING IndirectBindings [3] = {
      {
         1,                               // iOrdinal
         offsetof (IndirectlySimilar, pl), // obValue
         0,                               // No length binding
         0,                               // No Status binding
         NULL,                            // No TypeInfo
         NULL,                            // No Object
         NULL,                            // No Extensions
         DBPART_VALUE,
         DBMEMOWNER_PROVIDEROWNED,
         DBPARAMIO_NOTPARAM,
         sizeof (long*),
         0,
         DBTYPE_BYREF|DBTYPE_I4,
         0,                               // No Precision
         0                                // No Scale
      },
      {
         2,                               // iOrdinal
         offsetof (IndirectlySimilar, pd), // obValue
         0,                               // No length binding
         0,                               // No Status binding
         NULL,                            // No TypeInfo
         NULL,                            // No Object
         NULL,                            // No Extensions
         DBPART_VALUE,
         DBMEMOWNER_PROVIDEROWNED,
         DBPARAMIO_NOTPARAM,
         sizeof (double*),
         0,
         DBTYPE_BYREF|DBTYPE_R8,
         0,                               // No Precision
         0                                // No Scale
      },
```

```
    {
        3,                              // iOrdinal
        offsetof (IndirectlySimilar,pi), // obValue
        0,                              // No length binding
        0.                              // No Status binding
        NULL,                           // No TypeInfo
        NULL,                           // No Object
        NULL,                           // No Extensions
        DBPART_VALUE,
        DBMEMOWNER_PROVIDEROWNED,
        DBPARAMIO_NOTPARAM,
        sizeof(short*),
        0,
        DBTYPE_BYREF|DBTYPE_I2,
        0,                              // No Precision
        0                               // No Scale
    }
};

TheRowsetAccessor->CreateAccessor (DBACCESSOR_ROWDATA, 3, IndirectBindings, 0,
                                   &hFastAccess, NULL );
```

To read the column *i* of some row, the consumer should do the following:

```
short              value;
IndirectlySimilar rowPs;

TheRowset->GetData (hRow, hFastAccess, &rowPs);

if (rowPs.pi)              // Avoid null pointers
    value = *(rowPs.pi);
```

See Also

IRowset::GetNextRows, IRowsetChange::SetData

IRowset::GetNextRows

Fetches rows sequentially, remembering the previous position.

HRESULT GetNextRows (
    HCHAPTER *hReserved*,
    LONG   *lRowsOffset*,
    LONG   *cRows*,
    ULONG * *pcRowsObtained*,
    HROW ** *prghRows*);

Parameters

hReserved [in]

Reserved for future use. Providers ignore this parameter.

lRowsOffset [in]

The signed count of rows to skip before fetching rows. If this value is zero and *cRows* continues in the same direction as the previous **GetNextRows** call, then the first row fetched will be the next row after the last one fetched in the previous call. If this value is zero and *cRows* reverses direction then the first row fetched will be the last one fetched in the previous call.

lRowsOffset can be a negative number only if the value of the DBPROP_CANSCROLLBACKWARDS property is VARIANT_TRUE.

There is no guarantee that skipping rows is done efficiently on a sequential rowset. If the data source resides on a remote server, there may be remote support for skipping without transferring the intervening records across the network, but this is not guaranteed. For information about how the provider implements skipping, see the documentation for the provider.

cRows [in]

The number of rows to fetch. A negative number means to fetch backwards. *cRows* can be a negative number only if the value of the DBPROP_CANFETCHBACKWARDS property is VARIANT_TRUE.

If *cRows* is zero, no rows are fetched and the next fetch position is unchanged. If the provider does not discover any other errors, the method returns S_OK; whether the provider checks for any other errors is provider-specific.

pcRowsObtained [out]

A pointer to memory in which to return the actual number of fetched rows. If a warning condition occurs, this number may be less than the number of rows available or requested, and is the number of rows actually fetched before the warning condition occurred. If the consumer has insufficient permission to fetch all rows, **GetNextRows** fetches all rows for which the consumer has sufficient permission and skips all other rows. If the method fails, **pcRowsObtained* is set to zero.

prghRows [out]

A pointer to memory in which to return an array of handles of the fetched rows. If **prghRows* is not a null pointer on input, it must be a pointer to memory large enough to return the handles of the requested number of rows. If **prghRows* is a null pointer on input, the rowset allocates memory for the row handles and returns the address to this memory; the consumer releases this memory with **IMalloc::Free** after it releases the row handles. If **prghRows* is a null pointer on input and **pcRowsObtained* is zero on output or if the method fails, the provider does not allocate any memory and ensures that **prghRows* is a null pointer on output.

Return Code

S_OK

The method succeeded.

DB_S_ENDOFROWSET

GetNextRows reached the start or the end of the rowset or the start or end of the range on an index rowset and could not fetch all requested rows because the count extended beyond the end. The next fetch position is before the start or after the end of the rowset. The number of rows actually fetched is returned in **pcRowsObtained*; this will be less than *cRows*.

DB_S_ROWLIMITEXCEEDED

Fetching the number of rows specified in *cRows* would have exceeded the total number of active rows supported by the rowset. The number of rows that were actually fetched is returned in **pcRowsObtained*. Note that this condition can occur only when there are more rows available than can be handled by the rowset. Thus, this condition never conflicts with those described in DB_S_ENDOFROWSET and DB_S_STOPLIMITREACHED, both of which imply that no more rows were available.

DB_S_STOPLIMITREACHED

Fetching rows required further execution of the command, such as when the rowset uses a server-side cursor. Execution has been stopped because a resource limit has been reached. The number of rows that were actually fetched is returned in **pcRowsObtained*.

E_FAIL

A provider-specific error occurred.

E_INVALIDARG

pcRowsObtained or *prghRows* was a null pointer.

E_OUTOFMEMORY

The provider was unable to allocate sufficient memory in which to instantiate the rows or return the row handles.

E_UNEXPECTED

ITransaction::Commit or **ITransaction::Abort** was called and the object is in a zombie state.

DB_E_BADSTARTPOSITION

lRowsOffset would have positioned the first row fetched past either end of the rowset, regardless of the *cRows* value specified.

DB_E_CANCELED

Fetching rows was canceled during notification. No rows were fetched.

DB_E_CANTFETCHBACKWARDS

cRows was negative and the rowset cannot fetch backward.

DB_E_CANTSCROLLBACKWARDS

lRowsOffset was negative and the rowset cannot scroll backward.

DB_E_NOTREENTRANT

The consumer called this method while it was processing a notification, and it is an error to call this method while processing the specified DBREASON value.

DB_E_ROWSNOTRELEASED

The provider requires release of existing rows before new ones can be fetched. For more information, see DBPROP_CANHOLDROWS in "Rowset Properties" in Appendix C.

DB_SEC_E_PERMISSIONDENIED

The consumer did not have sufficient permission to fetch any of the rows; no rows were fetched.

Comments

GetNextRows fetches a sequence of rows. It maintains a *next fetch position* to remember the last time it was called and resume with the next row not yet fetched. If direction is reversed after **GetNextRows** has been called, then the first row to be fetched in the new direction is the last row that was fetched in the previous direction, assuming no rows are skipped.

For a newly created rowset, the next fetch position is computed as follows, where N is the number of rows in the rowset. Note that *lRowsOffset* can be less than zero only if DBPROP_CANSCROLLBACKWARDS is VARIANT_TRUE.

Value of *lRowsOffset*	Next fetch position
lRowsOffset > 0	After *lRowsOffset*
lRowsOffset < 0	After N−abs(*lRowsOffset*)
lRowsOffset = 0	Before first row if *cRows* > 0, after last row if *cRows* < 0

For example:

GetNextRows call	Row fetched	New next fetch position
GetNextRows(hReserved, 2, 1, pcRowsObtained, prghRows);	3rd row	After 3rd row
GetNextRows(hReserved, 2, -1, pcRowsObtained, prghRows);	2nd row	After 1st row
GetNextRows(hReserved, -2, 1, pcRowsObtained, prghRows);	N−1st row	After N−1st row
GetNextRows(hReserved, -2, -1, pcRowsObtained, prghRows);	N−2nd row	After N−3rd row

None of the other methods that fetch rows, such as **IRowsetLocate::GetRowsAt**, have any affect upon the next fetch position. However, **IRowsetIndex::Seek** sets the next fetch position to the row specified in the seek criteria and **RestartPosition** resets the next fetch position to the same position as when the rowset is first created.

GetNextRows increments the reference count of each row for which it returns a handle by one. Thus, if a handle is returned for a row that has already been fetched, the reference count of that row will be greater than one. **ReleaseRows** must be called once for each time the handle to a row has been returned.

If the provider encounters a problem fetching a row—for example, data stored in a text file contains a letter in a numeric column—**GetNextRows** fetches the row normally, returns the row handle, and returns S_OK. However, when the consumer calls **GetData** for the row, the provider returns DBSTATUS_E_CANTCONVERTVALUE as the status for the offending column.

GetNextRows must always check for the conditions that cause E_INVALIDARG, E_UNEXPECTED, DB_E_CANTFETCHBACKWARDS, DB_E_CANTSCROLLBACKWARDS, DB_E_NOTREENTRANT, and DB_E_ROWSNOTRELEASED before changing the next fetch position. If it returns any other error besides these, the next fetch position is unknown. For example, the provider might have to perform actions that change the next fetch position in order to determine that the error DB_E_BADSTARTPOSITION occurred. When the next fetch position is unknown, the consumer generally calls **RestartPosition** to return it to a known position.

For information about what **GetNextRows** does when it fetches a row that it already has in its internal buffers, see "Uniqueness of Rows in the Rowset" in Chapter 4. For information about whether **GetNextRows** can detect changes made to rows in the rowset, see "Visibility of Changes" in Chapter 5.

See Also

> **IRowset::GetData**, **IRowsetLocate::GetRowsAt**,
> **IRowsetLocate::GetRowsByBookmark**, **IRowsetScroll::GetRowsAtRatio**

IRowset::ReleaseRows

Releases rows.

HRESULT ReleaseRows (
ULONG	*cRows*,
const HROW	*rghRows*[],
DBROWOPTIONS	*rgRowOptions*[]
ULONG	*rgRefCounts*[],
DBROWSTATUS	*rgRowStatus*[]);

Parameters

cRows [in]

The number of rows to release. If *cRows* is zero, **ReleaseRows** does not do anything.

rghRows [in]

An array of handles of the rows to be released. The row handles need not form a logical cluster, they may have been obtained at separate times and need not be for contiguous underlying rows. They must belong to the current thread. Row handles are decremented by one reference count for each time they appear in the array.

rgRowOptions [in]

An array of *cRows* elements containing bitmasks indicating additional options to be specified when releasing a row. This parameter is reserved for future use and should be set to a null pointer.

```
typedef DWORD DBROWOPTIONS;
```

rgRefCounts [out]

An array with *cRows* elements in which to return the new reference count of each row. If *rgRefCounts* is a null pointer, no counts are returned. The consumer allocates, but is not required to initialize, memory for this array and passes the address of this memory to the provider. The provider returns the reference counts in the array.

rgRowStatus [out]

An array with *cRows* elements in which to return values indicating the status of each row specified in *rghRows*. If no errors or warnings occur while releasing a row, the corresponding element of *rgRowStatus* is set to DBROWSTATUS_S_OK. If an error or warning occurs while releasing a row, the corresponding element is set as specified in DB_S_ERRORSOCCURRED. The consumer allocates memory for this array. If *rgRowStatus* is a null pointer, no row statuses are returned. For information about the DBROWSTATUS enumerated type, see "Arrays of Errors" in Chapter 13.

Return Code

S_OK

The method succeeded. All rows were successfully released. The following values can be returned in **prgRowStatus*:

- The row was successfully released. The corresponding element of **prgRowStatus* contains DBROWSTATUS_S_OK.

- A row had a pending change. The row was released and the corresponding element of *rgRowStatus* contains DBROWSTATUS_S_PENDINGCHANGES.

DB_S_ERRORSOCCURRED

An error occurred while releasing a row, but at least one row was successfully released. Successes and warnings can occur for the reasons listed under S_OK. The following errors can occur:

- A row handle was invalid. The row was not released and the corresponding element of *rgRowStatus* contains DBROWSTATUS_E_INVALID.

E_FAIL

A provider-specific error occurred.

E_INVALIDARG

rghRows was a null pointer and *cRows* was not equal to zero.

DB_E_ERRORSOCCURRED

Errors occurred while releasing all of the rows. Errors can occur for the reasons listed under DB_S_ERRORSOCCURRED.

DB_E_NOTREENTRANT

The consumer called this method while it was processing a notification, and it is an error to call this method while processing the specified DBREASON value.

Comments

ReleaseRows decreases the reference count on the specified rows. It must be called once for each time that a row was fetched. For example, if the row was fetched three times, **ReleaseRows** must be called three times. Furthermore, if a row handle is duplicated in *rghRows*, the corresponding row will have its reference count decremented by one for each time it appears in the array.

If a provider doesn't support exact reference counts on rows, it should return a reference count of one while the row is active. Consumers should be aware of this behavior and should use the returned reference count for debugging purposes only; consumers should not rely on the returned reference count to indicate whether the row would survive another release.

If a consumer releases a row with pending changes, the row remains valid and **ReleaseRows** returns DBROWSTATUS_S_PENDINGCHANGES in *rgRowStatus*.

When the reference count for a row decreases to zero, the row is released:

- Subject to the rules of the current transaction, the rowset is free to discard any resources used by a row that has a reference count of zero. For example, these might include memory, locks, and original values. When the rowset actually discards these resources is provider-specific.

- If the row has pending changes, the row still remains valid even though its reference count is zero. Consumers should not use the handle of a row that has a reference count of zero, even though the handle might still be valid. If **IRowsetUpdate::Update** is called to transmit pending changes for a row with a reference count of zero to the data source, it transmits the changes of the row and releases the row and its resources if the update succeeds. If **IRowsetUpdate::Undo** is called to undo the pending changes for a row with a reference count of zero, it releases the row and its resources.

After a row is released, methods called with the handle to that row return DB_E_BADROWHANDLE if the row has pending changes. After the pending changes are transmitted to the data source, methods might continue to return this error. However, the provider might have an implementation that recycles row handles and thereafter cannot detect the misuse. Because provider behavior varies, consumers should not use the handles of released rows.

If **ReleaseRows** encounters an error while decrementing the reference count of a row or releasing the row, it sets the corresponding element in *rgRowStatus* to the appropriate DBROWSTATUS value and continues processing.

This method can be called while the rowset is in a zombie state to allow the consumer to clean up after a transaction has been committed or aborted.

See Also

IRowset::AddRefRows

IRowset::RestartPosition

Repositions the next fetch position to its initial position; that is, its position when the rowset was first created.

HRESULT RestartPosition (
    HCHAPTER *hReserved*);

Parameters

hReserved [in]
    Reserved for future use. Providers ignore this parameter.

Return Code

S_OK
    The method succeeded.

DB_S_COLUMNSCHANGED
    The order of the columns was not specified in the object that created the rowset. The provider had to re-execute the command to reposition the next fetch position to its initial position, and the order of the columns changed.

    The provider had to re-execute the command to reposition the next fetch position to its initial position, and columns were added or removed from the rowset. This is generally due to a change in the underlying schema and is extremely uncommon.

    This return code takes precedence over DB_S_COMMANDREEXECUTED. That is, if the conditions described here and in those described in DB_S_COMMANDREEXECUTED both occur, the provider returns this code. Note that a change to the columns generally implies that the command was re-executed.

DB_S_COMMANDREEXECUTED
    The command associated with this rowset was re-executed. If the properties DBPROP_OWNINSERT and DBPROP_OWNUPDATEDELETE are VARIANT_TRUE, then the consumer will see its own changes. If the properties DBPROP_OWNINSERT or DBPROP_OWNUPDATEDELETE are VARIANT_FALSE, then the rowset may see its changes. The order of the columns remains unchanged.

E_FAIL
    A provider-specific error occurred.

E_UNEXPECTED
    ITransaction::Commit or **ITransaction::Abort** was called and the object is in a zombie state.

DB_E_CANCELED
    RestartPosition was canceled during notification. The next fetch position remains unmodified.

DB_E_CANNOTRESTART
The rowset was built over a live data stream (for example, a stock feed) and the position cannot be restarted.

DB_E_NOTREENTRANT
The provider called a method from **IRowsetNotify** in the consumer and the method has not yet returned.

DB_E_ROWSNOTRELEASED
The provider requires release of existing rows before the next fetch position can be positioned to its initial position. For more information, see DBPROP_CANHOLDROWS in "Rowset Properties" in Appendix C.

DB_SEC_E_PERMISSIONDENIED
The consumer did not have sufficient permission to reposition the next fetch position.

Comments

For information about the next fetch position when the rowset is first created, see **GetNextRows**.

If the underlying command contains output parameters, **RestartPosition** should not reset those parameters.

If the rowset was generated as a result of a procedure call, and the rowset is forward-only, the procedure may be re-executed in order to satisfy the call to **RestartPosition**. This may cause other side-affects to occur. Additionally, if the stored procedure has been changed, the rowset may have a different schema. If the rowset is able to restart the next fetch position without re-executing the procedure, **RestartPosition** should not re-execute it.

How expensive **RestartPosition** is depends on the provider, the rowset characteristics, and the tables underlying the rowset. If the rowset supports **IRowsetLocate**, then **RestartPosition** is always an inexpensive operation.

If the rowset is sequential, then **RestartPosition** might require re-execution of the underlying command. For some providers, this is always the case. For other providers, a rule of thumb is that rowsets built from a single table are not expensive to restart, but rowsets built by joining two or more tables are expensive to restart. If the provider re-executes the command to restart the next fetch position, then the new rowset might return a different set of rows, differently ordered columns, and, in extreme cases, a different set of columns.

A consumer can determine whether a provider can quickly restart the next fetch position by attempting to set DBPROP_QUICKRESTART to VARIANT_TRUE. Setting this property to VARIANT_TRUE does not guarantee that the rowset can be quickly restarted because the provider is not required to honor the property. This behavior is necessary because the provider cannot evaluate the command at the time the property is set. For example, the consumer can set DBPROP_QUICKRESTART to VARIANT_TRUE and then change the command text.

In implementations that require re-execution of a command to reposition the next fetch position to its initial position, the provider is responsible for caching all parameters required by the command.

If **RestartPosition** returns DB_S_COLUMNSCHANGED and the consumer subsequently calls methods in **IColumnsInfo** or **IColumnsRowset**, these methods must reflect the new metadata. Existing rowset accessors are not updated to reflect the new metadata. That is, **IAccessor::GetBindings** returns exactly the same information it would have returned before **RestartPosition** was called. If such accessors are subsequently used, such as in a call to **GetData**, the provider must revalidate them. If none of the columns bound by the accessor have changed, the accessor can be used successfully. If any of the columns have changed, the appropriate error or warning is returned.

See Also

    IRowset::GetNextRows

IRowsetChange

The methods in **IRowsetChange** are used to update the values of columns in existing rows, delete existing rows, and insert new rows.

IRowsetChange requires **IAccessor** and **IRowset**.

When to Implement

Rowsets implement **IRowsetChange** if they support updating, deleting, or inserting rows. They are not required to support all three, but must support at least one of these operations to support **IRowsetChange**. The rowset reports which operations it supports through the DBPROP_UPDATABILITY property.

When to Call

The consumer calls methods in **IRowsetChange** to modify rows as follows.

- **SetData** sets column data in an existing row.

- **DeleteRows** deletes existing rows.

- **InsertRow** creates a new row and sets initial values.

SetData and **InsertRow** require the use of an accessor. For more information about accessors, see "Accessors" in Chapter 6.

SetData and **InsertRow** can fail for a number of reasons. The most common of these is that new data values do not meet the schema or integrity constraints of the column. Furthermore, rowsets can have row-by-row and column-by-column access permissions that override the general permissions of the table or column. For more information, see the DBPROP_COLUMNRESTRICT and DBPROP_ROWRESTRICT properties "Rowset Properties" in Appendix C.

If **IRowsetUpdate** is exposed on the rowset, then changes made through **IRowsetChange** are buffered in the rowset and not transmitted to the data source until **IRowsetUpdate::Update** is called; this is known as *delayed update mode*. If **IRowsetUpdate** is not exposed on the rowset, then changes made through **IRowsetChange** are immediately transmitted to the data source; this is known as *immediate update mode*. For more information, see "Changing Data" in Chapter 5.

Method	Description
DeleteRows	Deletes rows.
InsertRow	Creates and initializes a new row.
SetData	Sets data in one or more columns in a row.

IRowsetChange::DeleteRows

Deletes rows.

HRESULT DeleteRows (
    HCHAPTER   *hReserved,*
    ULONG   *cRows,*
    const HROW   *rghRows[],*
    DBROWSTATUS *rgRowStatus[]);*

Parameters

hReserved [in]

    Reserved for future use. Providers ignore this parameter.

cRows [in]

    The number of rows to be deleted. If *cRows* is zero, **DeleteRows** does not do anything.

rghRows [in]

    An array of handles of the rows to be deleted.

    If *rghRows* includes a duplicate row handle, **DeleteRows** behaves as follows. If the row handle is valid, it is provider-specific whether the returned row status information for each row or a single instance of the row is set to DBROWSTATUS_S_OK. If the row handle is invalid, the row status information for each occurrence of the row contains the appropriate error.

rgRowStatus [out]

    An array with *cRows* elements in which to return values indicating the status of each row specified in *rghRows*. If no errors or warnings occur while deleting a row, the corresponding element of *rgRowStatus* is set to DBROWSTATUS_S_OK. If warning occurs while deleting a row, the corresponding element is set as specified in S_OK. If an error occurs while deleting a row, the corresponding element is set as specified in DB_S_ERRORSOCCURRED. The consumer allocates memory for this array. If *rgRowStatus* is a null pointer, no row statuses are returned. For information about the DBROWSTATUS enumerated type, see "Arrays of Errors" in Chapter 13.

Return Code

S_OK

    The method succeeded. All rows were successfully deleted. The following values can be returned in *rgRowStatus*:

    • The row was successfully deleted and no warning conditions occurred. The corresponding element of *rgRowStatus* contains DBROWSTATUS_S_OK.

- The rowset was in immediate update mode and deleting a single row caused more than one row to be deleted in the data source. For more information, see the DBPROP_REPORTMULTIPLECHANGES property. The corresponding element of *rgRowStatus* contains DBROWSTATUS_S_MULTIPLECHANGES.

DB_S_ERRORSOCCURRED

An error occurred while deleting a row, but at least one row was successfully deleted. Successes and warnings can occur for the reasons listed under S_OK. The following errors can occur:

- An element of *rghRows* was invalid or was a row handle to which the current thread does not have access rights. The corresponding element of *rgRowStatus* contains DBROWSTATUS_E_INVALID.

- Deletion of a row was canceled during notification. The row was not deleted and the corresponding element of *rgRowStatus* contains DBROWSTATUS_E_CANCELED.

- An element of *rghRows* referred to a row with a pending delete or for which a deletion had been transmitted to the data source. The corresponding element of *rgRowStatus* contains DBROWSTATUS_E_DELETED.

- Deleting a row referred to by an element of *rghRows* violated the integrity constraints for the column or table. The corresponding element of *rgRowStatus* contains DBROWSTATUS_E_INTEGRITYVIOLATION.

- The rowset was in immediate update mode and the row was not deleted due to reaching a limit on the server, such as a query execution timing out. The error in the corresponding element of *rgRowStatus* contains DBROWSTATUS_E_LIMITREACHED.

- Deleting a row would exceed the limit for pending changes specified by the rowset property DBPROP_MAXPENDINGROWS. The corresponding element of *rgRowStatus* contains DBROWSTATUS_E_MAXPENDCHANGESEXCEEDED.

- DBPROP_CHANGEINSERTEDROWS was VARIANT_FALSE and an element of *rghRows* referred to a row for which the insertion has been transmitted to the data source. The corresponding element of *rgRowStatus* contains DBROWSTATUS_E_NEWLYINSERTED.

- The consumer did not have sufficient permission to delete a row. This error can be returned only if the value of the DBPROP_ROWRESTRICT property is VARIANT_TRUE. The corresponding element of *rgRowStatus* contains DBROWSTATUS_E_PERMISSIONDENIED. If the rowset is in delayed update mode, this error might not be returned until **IRowsetUpdate::Update** is called.

E_FAIL

A provider-specific error occurred.

E_INVALIDARG

rghRows was a null pointer and *cRows* was greater than or equal to one.

E_UNEXPECTED

ITransaction::Commit or **ITransaction::Abort** was called and the object is in a zombie state.

DB_E_ERRORSOCCURRED

Errors occurred while deleting all of the rows. Errors can occur for the reasons listed under DB_S_ERRORSOCCURRED.

DB_E_NOTREENTRANT

The consumer called this method while it was processing a notification, and it is an error to call this method while processing the specified DBREASON value.

DB_E_NOTSUPPORTED

The provider does not support this method.

Comments

In delayed update mode, **DeleteRows** marks rows for deletion, rather than actually deleting them. Rows with pending deletes cannot be used in any methods except **IRowsetResynch::GetVisibleData**, **IRowsetUpdate::Undo,** **IRowsetUpdate::Update**, **IRowsetUpdate::GetOriginalData**, and **IRowset::ReleaseRows**. The deletion is not transmitted to the data source until **Update** is called. In immediate update mode, **DeleteRows** transmits deletions to the data source immediately. For more information, see "Changing Data" in Chapter 5.

After a deletion has been transmitted to the data source, it cannot be undone. The row cannot be used with any method except **ReleaseRows**. Note that neither **DeleteRows** nor **Update** releases rows after transmitting deletions to the data source. The consumer must release the row with **ReleaseRows**.

If **DeleteRows** is called for a row with a pending insert, the row is placed in the same state as a row for which a deletion has been transmitted to the data source. That is, if a row is inserted and then deleted in delayed update mode, the deletion cannot be undone. The row cannot be used with any method except **ReleaseRows**, which must be called to release it.

If an error occurs while deleting a row, **DeleteRows** continues deleting the other rows in *rghRows* and returns DB_S_ERRORSOCCURRED or DB_E_ERRORSOCCURRED. It returns status information about each row in *rgRowStatus*.

If the DBPROP_ROWRESTRICT property is VARIANT_TRUE, the consumer may have permission to delete some rows but not other rows.

See Also

IRowsetUpdate::Undo, **IRowsetUpdate::Update**

IRowsetChange::InsertRow

Creates and initializes a new row.

HRESULT InsertRow (
    HCHAPTER   *hReserved,*
    HACCESSOR *hAccessor,*
    void *   *pData,*
    HROW *   *phRow);*

Parameters

hReserved [in]
> Reserved for future use. Providers ignore this parameter.

hAccessor [in]
> The handle of the accessor to use.

> If *hAccessor* is a null accessor (that is, an accessor for which *cBindings* in **IAccessor::CreateAccessor** was zero), then *pData* is ignored and the rows are initialized as specified in the Comments. Thus, the role of a null accessor is to construct a default row; it is a convenient way for a consumer to obtain a handle for a new row without having to set any values in that row initially.

pData [in]
> A pointer to memory containing the new data values, at offsets that correspond to the bindings in the accessor.

phRow [out]
> A pointer to memory in which to return the handle of the new row. If this is a null pointer, then no reference count is held on the row. This is useful for consumers that are inserting rows that they do not want to immediately get data from and for which the rowset therefore does not need to keep local copies.

Return Code

S_OK
> The method succeeded. The status of all columns bound by the accessor is set to DBSTATUS_S_OK or DBSTATUS_S_ISNULL.

DB_S_ERRORSOCCURRED
> An error occurred while setting data for one or more columns, but data was successfully set for at least one column. To determine the columns for which values were invalid, the consumer checks the status values. For a list of status values that can be returned by this method, see "Status Values Used When Setting Data" in "Status" in Chapter 6.

E_FAIL
> A provider-specific error occurred.

E_INVALIDARG
> *pData* was a null pointer and *hAccessor* was not a null accessor.

E_OUTOFMEMORY

The provider was unable to allocate sufficient memory in which to instantiate the row.

E_UNEXPECTED

ITransaction::Commit or **ITransaction::Abort** was called and the object is in a zombie state.

DB_E_ABORTLIMITREACHED

The rowset was in immediate update mode and the row was not inserted due to reaching a limit on the server, such as a query execution timing out.

DB_E_BADACCESSORHANDLE

hAccessor was invalid.

DB_E_BADACCESSORTYPE

The specified accessor was not a row accessor or was a reference accessor.

DB_E_CANCELED

The insertion was canceled during notification. The row was not inserted.

DB_E_ERRORSOCCURRED

An error occurred while setting data for one or more columns and data was not successfully set for any columns. To determine the columns for which values were invalid, the consumer checks the status values. For a list of status values that can be returned by this method, see "Status Values Used When Setting Data" in "Status" in Chapter 6.

DB_E_MAXPENDCHANGESEXCEEDED

The number of rows that have pending changes has exceeded the limit specified by the DBPROP_MAXPENDINGROWS property.

DB_E_NOTREENTRANT

The provider called a method from **IRowsetNotify** in the consumer and the method has not yet returned.

DB_E_NOTSUPPORTED

The provider does not support this method.

DB_E_ROWLIMITEXCEEDED

Creating another row would have exceeded the total number of active rows supported by the rowset.

DB_E_ROWSNOTRELEASED

The consumer attempted to insert a new row before releasing previously-retrieved row handles and DBPROP_CANHOLDROWS is VARIANT_FALSE.

DB_SEC_E_PERMISSIONDENIED

The consumer did not have sufficient permission to insert a new row. This error can be returned only if the value of the DBPROP_ROWRESTRICT property is VARIANT_TRUE. If the rowset is in delayed update mode, this error might not be returned until **IRowsetUpdate::Update** is called.

If this method performs deferred accessor validation and that validation takes place before any data is transferred, it can also return any of the following return codes for the applicable reasons listed in the corresponding DBBINDSTATUS values in **IAccessor::CreateAccessor**:

E_NOINTERFACE
DB_E_BADBINDINFO
DB_E_BADORDINAL
DB_E_BADSTORAGEFLAGS
DB_E_UNSUPPORTEDCONVERSION

Comments

InsertRow creates a new row and initializes its columns. If *phRow* is not a null pointer, it then returns the handle of this row to the consumer and sets its reference count to one. In delayed update mode, the row is created locally to the rowset and is transmitted to the data source only when **IRowsetUpdate::Update** is called. In immediate update mode, the row is immediately transmitted to the data source. For more information, see "Changing Data" in Chapter 5.

To the consumer, newly inserted rows are almost indistinguishable from other rows. For example, they can be deleted with **DeleteRows** and updated with **SetData**. However, methods that fetch rows might not be able to return them—for more information, see "Visibility of Pending Changes" and "Visibility of Transmitted Changes" in Chapter 5. Furthermore, they might not contain the correct values for computed columns, including bookmark columns on some providers.

For information about where rows are inserted in the rowset, see "Position of Inserted Rows" in Chapter 5.

The DBPROP_COLUMNRESTRICT and DBPROP_ROWRESTRICT properties affect how security is enforced and how security errors are returned. If DBPROP_COLUMNRESTRICT is VARIANT_TRUE, the consumer might not have write permission on some columns. If the consumer attempts to write to these columns, **InsertRows** returns a column status of DBSTATUS_E_PERMISSIONDENIED and a return code of DB_S_ERRORSOCCURRED. If the DBPROP_ROWRESTRICT property is VARIANT_TRUE, the consumer might not have permission to insert some rows. If the consumer attempts to insert one of these rows, **InsertRows** returns a code of DB_SEC_E_PERMISSIONDENIED and no new row is created.

When a row is created, initialization proceeds in an orderly fashion.

1. The provider sets all columns to their default value. If there is no default value and the column is nullable, it sets the column to NULL. If the column is non-nullable, it sets the column status to DBSTATUS_E_UNAVAILABLE. If the provider is unable or unwilling to determine the default value of a column or whether that column is nullable, it sets the column status to DBSTATUS_E_UNAVAILABLE;

the provider might be unwilling to determine default values and nullability if doing so requires a call to the data source.

If the column status is DBSTATUS_E_UNAVAILABLE, the consumer can still send this value to the data source to use the default. In this case, the default is available after the insertion is transmitted to the data source. To see the default, the consumer must call **GetVisibleData** or **ResynchRows**. However, if there is no default for the column and it is non-nullable, this will cause a schema violation.

2. The provider calls **IRowsetNotify::OnRowChange** with DBREASON_ROW_INSERT if any consumer of the rowset is using notifications. This serves as a hook allowing, among other things, more complex non-declarative default values to be set in the row. For more information about notifications, see **IRowsetNotify**.

3. **InsertRow** does not further modify the column values if the accessor is a null accessor; it returns the handle to the newly created row.

4. The provider uses the accessor, if it is not a null accessor, to set columns with the values provided by the consumer in *pData*. During this process, the provider does not generate notifications like it does when setting data in **SetData**. This prevents, for example, DBREASON_COLUMN_SET notifications from being generated for a row that is not yet properly constructed. For a complete description of how **InsertRow** sets data, see "Setting Data" in Chapter 6.

The provider is not required to compute the value of computed columns. If the provider does not compute the value of these columns, but lets the data source do so, then the computed value is not available until after the change is transmitted to the data source—that is, after **InsertRow** is called in immediate update mode or after **IRowsetUpdate::Update** if **InsertRow** is called in delayed update mode. To retrieve the computed value, the consumer calls **ResynchRows** or **GetVisibleData** in **IRowsetResynch**. Note that bookmark columns are often computed, such as when the bookmark is the primary key or is a ROWID assigned by the data source.

Domain and schema validation is enforced as it is with **SetData**.

If **InsertRow** returns an error, it does not create a new row.

Here is an example of how one might write a projection-join to a temporary file.

```
#include <oledb.h>
#include <stddef.h>
int main() {
    IRowset        *pLeftRowset;
    IRowset        *pRightRowset;
    IAccessor      *pLeftRowsetAcc;
    IAccessor      *pRightRowsetAcc;
    IAccessor      *pJoinRowsetAcc;
    IRowsetChange  *pJoinRowsetNew;
    ULONG          cSortedRows;
    HROW           rghLeftRows [500];
    HROW           rghRightRows [500];
```

```
//...
//< sort and prepare the rows >
//..

struct join {
    long   *pl;
    double *pd;
    short  *pi;
};

static DBBINDING LeftBindings [1] = {
    {
        1,
        offsetof (join, pl),
        0,                          // No length binding
        0,                          // No status binding
        NULL,                       // No TypeInfo
        NULL,                       // No object
        NULL,                       // No extensions
        DBPART_VALUE,
        DBMEMOWNER_PROVIDEROWNED,
        DBPARAMIO_NOTPARAM,
        sizeof (void*),
        0,
        DBTYPE_I4 | DBTYPE_BYREF,
        0,                          // No precision
        0                           // No scale
    }
};
static DBBINDING RightBindings [2]=   {
    {
        1,
        offsetof (join, pd),
        0,                          // No length binding
        0,                          // No status binding
        NULL,                       // No TypeInfo
        NULL,                       // No object
        NULL,                       // No extensions
        DBPART_VALUE,
        DBMEMOWNER_PROVIDEROWNED,
        DBPARAMIO_NOTPARAM,
        sizeof (void*),
        0,
        DBTYPE_R8 | DBTYPE_BYREF,
        0,                          // No precision
        0                           // No scale
    },
    {
        2,
        offsetof (join, pi),
        0,                          // No length binding
        0,                          // No status binding
        NULL,                       // No TypeInfo
        NULL,                       // No object
```

```
            NULL,                       // No extensions
            DBPART_VALUE,
            DBMEMOWNER_PROVIDEROWNED,
            DBPARAMIO_NOTPARAM,
            sizeof (void*),
            0,
            DBTYPE_I2 | DBTYPE_BYREF,
            0,                          // No precision
            0                           // No scale
        }
    };


    static DBBINDING JoinBindings [3] = {
        {
            1,
            offsetof (join, pl),
            0,                          // No length binding
            0,                          // No status binding
            NULL,                       // No TypeInfo
            NULL,                       // No object
            NULL,                       // No extensions
            DBPART_VALUE,
            DBMEMOWNER_PROVIDEROWNED,
            DBPARAMIO_NOTPARAM,
            sizeof (void*),
            0,
            DBTYPE_I4 | DBTYPE_BYREF,
            0,                          // No precision
            0                           // No scale
        },
        {
            2,
            offsetof (join, pd),
            0,                          // No length binding
            0,                          // No status binding
            NULL,                       // No TypeInfo
            NULL,                       // No object
            NULL,                       // No extensions
            DBPART_VALUE,
            DBMEMOWNER_PROVIDEROWNED,
            DBPARAMIO_NOTPARAM,
            sizeof (void*),
            0,
            DBTYPE_R8 | DBTYPE_BYREF,
            0,                          // No precision
            0                           // No scale
        },
```

```
            {
                3,
                offsetof (join, pi),
                0,                      // No length binding
                0,                      // No status binding
                NULL,                   // No TypeInfo
                NULL,                   // No object
                NULL,                   // No extensions
                DBPART_VALUE,
                DBMEMOWNER_PROVIDEROWNED,
                DBPARAMIO_NOTPARAM,
                sizeof (void*),
                0,
                DBTYPE_I2 | DBTYPE_BYREF,
                0,                      // No precision
                0                       // No scale
            }
        };

        HACCESSOR hLeft;
        HACCESSOR hRight;
        HACCESSOR hJoin;
        join      theJoin;

        pLeftRowsetAcc->CreateAccessor(DBACCESSOR_ROWDATA, 1, LeftBindings, 0, &hLeft,
                                    NULL);

        pRightRowsetAcc->CreateAccessor(DBACCESSOR_ROWDATA, 2, RightBindings, 0, &hRight,
                                    NULL);

        pJoinRowsetAcc->CreateAccessor(DBACCESSOR_ROWDATA, 3, JoinBindings, 0, &hJoin,
                                    NULL);

        for (ULONG j = 0; j < cSortedRows;  j++) {
            pLeftRowset->GetData(rghLeftRows[j], hLeft, &theJoin);
            pRightRowset->GetData(rghRightRows[j], hRight, &theJoin);
            pJoinRowsetNew->InsertRow(NULL, hJoin, &theJoin, NULL);
        } ;
    };
```

See Also

IRowset::GetData, IRowsetChange::SetData, IRowsetUpdate::Undo, IRowsetUpdate::Update

IRowsetChange::SetData

Sets data values in one or more columns in a row.

HRESULT SetData (
    HROW   *hRow*,
    HACCESSOR *hAccessor*,
    void *   *pData*);

Parameters

hRow [in]
    The handle of the row in which to set data.

hAccessor [in]
    The handle of the accessor to use. If *hAccessor* is the handle of a null accessor
    (*cBindings* in **IAccessor::CreateAccessor** was zero), then **SetData** does not set
    any data values.

pData [in]
    A pointer to memory containing the new data values, at offsets that correspond to
    the bindings in the accessor.

Return Code

S_OK
    The method succeeded. The status of all columns bound by the accessor is set to
    DBSTATUS_S_OK or DBSTATUS_S_ISNULL

DB_S_ERRORSOCCURRED
    An error occurred while setting data for one or more columns, but data was
    successfully set for at least one column. To determine the columns for which data
    was returned, the consumer checks the status values. For a list of status values that
    can be returned by this method, see "Status Values Used When Setting Data" in
    "Status" in Chapter 6.

DB_S_MULTIPLECHANGES
    The rowset was in immediate update mode and updating the row caused more than
    one row to be updated in the data source. For more information, see
    DBPROP_REPORTMULTIPLECHANGES in "Rowset Properties" in Appendix
    C.

    This return code takes precedence over DB_S_ERRORSOCCURRED. That is, if
    the conditions described here and in those described in
    DB_S_ERRORSOCCURRED both occur, the provider returns this code. When the
    consumer receives this return code, it should also check for the conditions
    described in DB_S_ERRORSOCCURRED.

E_FAIL
    A provider-specific error occurred.

E_INVALIDARG

pData was a null pointer and the accessor was not a null accessor.

E_UNEXPECTED

ITransaction::Commit or **ITransaction::Abort** was called and the object is in a zombie state.

DB_E_ABORTLIMITREACHED

The rowset was in immediate update mode and the row was not updated due to reaching a limit on the server, such as a query execution timing out.

DB_E_BADACCESSORHANDLE

hAccessor was invalid.

DB_E_BADACCESSORTYPE

The specified accessor was not a row accessor or was a reference accessor.

DB_E_BADROWHANDLE

hRow was invalid or was the handle to a row to which the current thread does not have access rights.

DB_E_CANCELED

The change was canceled during notification. No columns are changed.

DB_E_CONCURRENCYVIOLATION

The rowset was using optimistic concurrency and the value of a column has been changed since the containing row was last fetched or resynchronized. **SetData** returns this error only when the rowset is in immediate update mode.

DB_E_DELETEDROW

hRow referred to a row with a pending delete or for which a deletion had been transmitted to the data source.

DB_E_ERRORSOCCURRED

An error occurred while setting data for one or more columns and data was not successfully set for any columns. To determine the columns for which values were invalid, the consumer checks the status values. For a list of status values that can be returned by this method, see "Status Values Used When Setting Data" in "Status" in Chapter 6.

DB_E_MAXPENDCHANGESEXCEEDED

The number of rows that have pending changes has exceeded the limit specified by the DBPROP_MAXPENDINGROWS property.

DB_E_NEWLYINSERTED

DBPROP_CHANGEINSERTEDROWS was VARIANT_FALSE and *hRow* referred to a row for which the insertion has been transmitted to the data source.

DB_E_NOTREENTRANT

The consumer called this method while it was processing a notification, and it is an error to call this method while processing the specified DBREASON value.

DB_E_NOTSUPPORTED

The provider does not support this method.

DB_SEC_E_PERMISSIONDENIED

The consumer did not have sufficient permission to update the row. This error can be returned only if the value of the DBPROP_ROWRESTRICT property is VARIANT_TRUE. If the rowset is in delayed update mode, this error might not be returned until **IRowsetUpdate::Update** is called.

If this method performs deferred accessor validation and that validation takes places before any data is transferred, it can also return any of the following return codes for the applicable reasons listed in the corresponding DBBINDSTATUS values in **IAccessor::CreateAccessor**:

E_NOINTERFACE
DB_E_BADBINDINFO
DB_E_BADORDINAL
DB_E_BADSTORAGEFLAGS
DB_E_UNSUPPORTEDCONVERSION

Comments

SetData sets data values in one or more columns in a row. For a complete description of how **SetData** sets data, see "Setting Data" in Chapter 6.

In delayed update mode, these changes are buffered locally in the rowset and are transmitted to the data source only when **IRowsetUpdate::Update** is called. In immediate update mode, the changes are immediately transmitted to the data source. For more information, see "Changing Data" in Chapter 5.

If a computed column depends on a column that is changed with **SetData**, the provider is not required to compute the new value of the computed column. If the provider computes the new value, it sends a notification to the consumer. If the provider does not compute the new value, but lets the data source do so, then the computed value is not available until after the change is transmitted to the data source—that is, after **SetData** is called in immediate update mode or after **IRowsetUpdate::Update** if **SetData** is called in delayed update mode. To retrieve the computed value in this case, the consumer calls **ResynchRows** or **GetVisibleData** in **IRowsetResynch**. Note that bookmark columns are often computed, such as when the bookmark is the primary key or is a ROWID assigned by the data source.

If **SetData** changes a column that is used to order the rowset, the DBPROP_IMMOBILEROWS property describes whether the row is moved based on its new value. If this property is VARIANT_TRUE, the row is not moved. If this property is VARIANT_FALSE, the row is moved. If the rowset is not ordered, then the position of updated rows is not changed.

When the consumer passes a pointer to a storage object to **SetData**, **SetData** replaces the data in the column with the data in the new storage object. If the consumer wants only to delete the data in the column, it sets the column status to DBSTATUS_S_OK and passes a null pointer instead of a pointer to a storage object. For more information, see "Getting and Setting BLOB Data with Storage Objects" in Chapter 7.

If the rowset is in immediate updatc mode, storage object data is always transmitted immediately to the data source. If it is in delayed update mode, whether it is transmitted immediately or delayed depends on the DBPROP_DELAYSTORAGEOBJECTS property.

Although **SetData** can detect domain constraint and some table constraint schema violations, it is not required to do so. Such validation can be delayed until the changes are transmitted to the data source with **Update** or the transaction is committed with **ITransaction::Commit**. This delay is often necessary because of dependencies on values in other columns or tables.

SetData cannot be called for rows with pending or transmitted deletes.

The DBPROP_COLUMNRESTRICT and DBPROP_ROWRESTRICT properties affect how security is enforced and how security errors are returned. If DBPROP_COLUMNRESTRICT is VARIANT_TRUE, the consumer might not have write permission on some columns. If the consumer attempts to write to these columns, **SetData** returns a column status of DBSTATUS_E_PERMISSIONDENIED and a return code of DB_S_ERRORSOCCURRED. If the DBPROP_ROWRESTRICT property is VARIANT_TRUE, the consumer might not have permission to update some rows. If the consumer attempts to update one of these rows, **SetData** returns a code of DB_SEC_E_PERMISSIONDENIED and no data is set.

If any consumer of the rowset is using notifications, the provider sends notifications. These notifications can be vetoed, in which case the provider sends the DBEVENTPHASE_FAILEDTODO phase of the notification. When the consumer then calls **Update**, if the update is in delayed mode, the provider does not send additional DBREASON_COLUMN_SET notifications for the rows. However, if **Update** computes the value of computed columns, it sends DBREASON_COLUMN_RECALCULATED notifications. In this case, the provider must either be prepared to undo all pending changes for the row, and return DBREASON_ROW_UNDOCHANGE, or set the *fCantDeny* flag to TRUE.

The following sequence of notifications occurs for a rowset operating in delayed update mode:

1. If the row is being changed for the first time since it was created or changes were transmitted, the provider sends the DBEVENTPHASE_OKTODO and DBEVENTPHASE_ABOUTTODO phases of the DBREASON_ROW_FIRSTCHANGE notification.

2. The provider sends the DBEVENTPHASE_OKTODO, DBEVENTPHASE_ABOUTTODO, and DBEVENTPHASE_SYNCHAFTER phases of the DBREASON_COLUMN_SET notification, in that order, provided none of the listeners veto any of the phases. The notification covers all the columns defined by the accessor used in the call to **SetData**.

3. The provider sends the DBEVENTPHASE_SYNCHAFTER phase of the DBREASON_ROW_FIRSTCHANGE notification, assuming the provider sent the earlier phases of this notification.

4. The provider sends the DBEVENTPHASE_DIDEVENT phase of the DBREASON_COLUMN_SET notification.

5. The provider sends the DBEVENTPHASE_DIDEVENT phase of the ROW_FIRSTCHANGE notification.

See Also

IRowset::GetData, IRowsetChange::InsertRow, IRowsetUpdate::Undo, IRowsetUpdate::Update

IRowsetIdentity

IRowsetIdentity is the interface that indicates row instance identity is implemented on the rowset and enables testing for row identity. If a rowset supports this interface, any two row handles representing the same underlying row will always reflect the same data and state.

IRowsetIdentity depends on **IRowset**.

When to Implement

IRowsetIdentity is required for all providers which intend to support general consumers.

If the provider inherently supports row identity, this interface will be supported even if the command does not require it. For such providers, row identity is not disabled if the consumer does not request **IRowsetIdentity**.

If the DBPROP_LITERALIDENTITY property is set to VARIANT_TRUE, then the provider supports binary comparison of row handles.

This interface can be implemented even when row identity cannot be perfectly implemented, the rowset may reasonably take steps to be partially correct; for more information see "Uniqueness of Rows in the Rowset" in Chapter 4.

When to Call

Consumers call **IsSameRow** whenever they need to determine if two row handles represent the same underlying row. For example, if a row handle is returned to the consumer during notification, the consumer can compare it to its own list of row handles to see if it is the handle of a row that is of interest.

Method	Description
IsSameRow	Compares two row handles to see if they refer to the same row instance.

IRowsetIdentity::IsSameRow

Compares two row handles to see if they refer to the same row instance.

HRESULT IsSameRow (
    HROW *hThisRow*,
    HROW *hThatRow*);

Parameters

hThisRow [in]
    The handle of an active row.

hThatRow [in]
    The handle of an active row.

Return Code

S_FALSE
    The method succeeded and the row handles do not refer to the same row instance.

S_OK
    The method succeeded and the row handles do refer to the same row instance.

E_FAIL
    A provider-specific error occurred.

E_UNEXPECTED
    ITransaction::Commit or **ITransaction::Abort** was called and the object is in a zombie state.

DB_E_BADROWHANDLE
    hRowThis or *hRowThat* was invalid.

DB_E_DELETEDROW
    hRowThis or *hRowThat* referred to a row for which a deletion had been transmitted to the data source.

DB_E_NEWLYINSERTED
    The provider is unable to determine identity for a row for which an insertion had been transmitted to the data source. This condition can occur when DBPROP_STRONGIDENTITY is set to VARIANT_FALSE.

Comments

This method makes no logical change to the state of the object.

The row handles refer to the same row instance if the value set in any column in the row by means of one row handle will be the value returned for that column when gotten through the other row handle.

Rowsets that support this interface must also implement the detection of row identity within their rowset. That is, if they fetch rows at different times, they can detect when the row handles are referring to the same logical row and arrange for both row handles to reflect the same data and state.

The value of the row handles, their bit patterns as handles, is not necessarily the same if the underlying row is the same. This depends on the value of the DBPROP_LITERALIDENTITY property.

The outcome of **IsSameRow** is not changed when one or both of its parameters correspond to a row with a pending delete.

IRowsetIndex

IRowsetIndex is the primary interface for exposing index functionality in OLE DB.
For a complete description of indexes, see Chapter 8, "Indexes."

When to Implement

The **IRowsetIndex** interface is implemented by providers to expose the functionality
of a file access method such as a B+-tree, or linear hash.

A provider may also support other rowset interfaces on indexes, such as
IRowsetScroll.

When to Call

The methods in **IRowsetIndex** are used to define a range of index entries to be read,
to position at an index entry within the range, to fetch the index entry, and to access
the contents of the index entry.

The following table shows how to perform various index operations.

Operation	Comments
Open an index	To get a handle to an **IRowsetIndex** object, the consumer calls **IOpenRowset::OpenRowset**, passing it the DBID of the index. The method returns a pointer to an index rowset.
Close an index	An index is closed by releasing all references to the index rowset.
Insert an index entry	New key entries are inserted into an index by using **IRowsetChange**.
Delete an index entry	Key entries are deleted from an index by using **IRowsetChange**.
Update an index entry	Key entries are updated in an index by first deleting the old index entry and then inserting a new index entry.
Traverse the index	To traverse an index a user calls methods on **IRowset**. For more information, see "Using Index Rowsets" in Chapter 8.

Method	Description
GetIndexInfo	Returns information about the index rowset capabilities.
Seek	Allows direct positioning at a key value within the current range.
SetRange	Restricts the set of row entries visible through calls to **IRowset::GetNextRows** and **IRowsetIndex::Seek**.

IRowsetIndex::GetIndexInfo

Returns information about the index rowset capabilities.

HRESULT GetIndexInfo (
    ULONG *   *pcKeyColumns***,**
    DBINDEXCOLUMNDESC ***prgIndexColumnDesc***,**
    ULONG *   *pcIndexProperties***,**
    DBPROPSET **   *prgIndexProperties***);**

Parameters

pcKeyColumns [out]
    A pointer to memory in which to return the number of key columns in the index.

prgIndexColumnDesc [out]
    A pointer to memory in which to return an array of DBINDEXCOLUMNDESC structures. For more information, see **IIndexDefinition::CreateIndex**. The size of the array is equal to **pcKeyColumns*. If an error occurs, **prgIndexColumnDesc* is set to a null pointer.

pcIndexProperties [out]
    A pointer to memory in which to return the number of DBPROPSET structures returned in **prgIndexProperties*. **pcIndexProperties* is the total number of property sets for which the providers supports at least one property in the Index property group. If an error occurs, **pcIndexProperties* is set to zero.

prgIndexProperties [out]
    A pointer to memory in which to return an array of DBPROPSET structures. One structure is returned for each property set that contains at least one property belonging to the Index property group. For information about the properties in the Index property group that are defined by OLE DB, see "Index Properties" in Appendix C.

    The provider allocates memory for the structures and returns the address to this memory; the consumer releases this memory with **IMalloc::Free** when it no longer needs the structures. Before calling **IMalloc::Free** for **prgPropertySets*, the consumer should call **IMalloc::Free** for the *rgProperties* element within each element of **prgPropertySets*. If **pcIndexProperties* is zero on output, or if an error occurs, the provider does not allocate any memory and ensures that **prgIndexProperties* is a null pointer on output.

    For information about the DBPROPSET and DBPROP structures, see "DBPROPSET Structure" and "DBPROP Structure" in Chapter 11.

Return Code

S_OK

The method succeeded.

E_FAIL

A provider-specific error occurred.

E_INAVLIDARG

pcKeyColumns, *prgIndexColumnDesc*, *pcIndexProperties*, or *prgIndexProperties* was a null pointer.

E_OUTOFMEMORY

The provider was unable to allocate sufficient memory in which to return the column description structures or properties of the index.

See Also

IDBProperties::GetPropertyInfo, IIndexDefinition::CreateIndex

IRowsetIndex::Seek

Allows direct positioning at a key value within the current range established by the **IRowsetIndex::SetRange** method.

HRESULT Seek (
    HACCESSOR   *hAccessor*,
    ULONG   *cKeyValues*,
    void *   *pData*,
    DBSEEK   *dwSeekOptions*);

Parameters

hAccessor [in]

The handle of the accessor to use. This accessor must meet the following criteria, which are illustrated with a key that consists of columns A, B, and C, where A is the most significant column and C is the least significant column:

- For each key column this accessor binds, it must also bind all more significant key columns. For example, the accessor can bind column A, columns A and B, or columns A, B, and C.

- Key columns must be bound in order from most significant key column to least significant key column. For example, if the accessor binds columns A and B, then the first binding must bind column A and the second binding must bind column B.

- If the accessor binds any non-key columns, key columns must be bound first. For example, if the accessor binds columns A, B, and the bookmark column, then the first binding must bind column A, the second binding must bind column B, and the third binding must bind the bookmark column.

If the accessor does not meet these criteria, the method returns DB_E_BADBINDINFO or a status of DBSTATUS_E_BADACCESSOR for the offending column.

If *hAccessor* is the handle of a null accessor, (*cBindings* in **IAccessor::CreateAccessor** was zero), then **Seek** does not change the next fetch position.

cKeyValues [in]

The number of bindings in *hAccessor* for which **pData* contains valid data. **SetRange** retrieves data from the first *cKeyValues* key columns from **pData*. For example, suppose the accessor binds columns A, B, and C of the key in the previous example and *cKeyValues* is 2. **SetRange** retrieves data for columns A and B.

pData [in]

A pointer to a buffer containing the key values to which to seek, at offsets that correspond to the bindings in the accessor.

dwSeekOptions [in]

A bitmask describing the options for the **Seek** method. The values in DBSEEKENUM have the following meanings:

Value	Description
DBSEEK_FIRSTEQ	First key with values equal to the values in *pData.
DBSEEK_LASTEQ	Last key with values equal to the values in *pData.
DBSEEK_GE	First key with values greater than or equal to the values in *pData.
DBSEEK_GT	First key with values greater than the values in *pData.
DBSEEK_LE	First key with values less than or equal to the values in *pData.
DBSEEK_LT	First key with values less than the values in *pData.

Return Code

S_OK

The method succeeded.

E_FAIL

A provider-specific error occurred.

E_INVALIDARG

dwSeekOptions was invalid.

hAccessor was the handle of a null accessor.

cKeyValues was zero.

pData was a null pointer.

DB_E_BADACCESSORHANDLE

hAccessor was invalid.

DB_E_BADACCESSORTYPE

The specified accessor was not a row accessor.

DB_E_ERRORSOCCURRED

An error occurred while transferring data for one or more key columns. To determine the columns for which values were invalid, the consumer checks the status values. For a list of status values that can be returned by this method, see "Status Values Used When Setting Data" in "Status" in Chapter 6.

DB_E_NOTFOUND

No key value matching the described characteristics could be found within the current range.

If this method performs deferred accessor validation and that validation takes place before any data is transferred, it can also return any of the following return codes for the reasons listed in the corresponding DBBINDSTATUS values in **IAccessor::CreateAccessor**.

E_NOINTERFACE
DB_E_BADBINDINFO
DB_E_BADORDINAL
DB_E_BADSTORAGEFLAGS
DB_E_UNSUPPORTEDCONVERSION

Comments

The **Seek** method provides the caller more control over the traversal of an index. Consider a relational query processor component implementing a merge join over inputs R1 and R2. R1, the outer input, is a rowset ordered by the joining column R1.X. R2, the inner input, is an indexed rowset on column R2.X. Suppose that R1.X has values {10, 20, 100, 110} and that R2.X has values {10, 20, ..., 30, ..., 40, ..., 50, ..., 100, ...}, then when searching R2.X, one could seek directly from 20 to 100 knowing the values of the input R1.X. In some cases, this strategy could be cost effective.

For information about how **Seek** transfers data from *pData*, see "Setting Data" in Chapter 6.

See Also

IRowset::GetNextRows, **IRowsetIndex::SetRange**

IRowsetIndex::SetRange

Restricts the set of row entries visible through calls to **IRowset::GetNextRows** and **IRowsetIndex::Seek**.

HRESULT SetRange (
    HACCESSOR   *hAccessor*,
    ULONG   *cStartKeyColumns*,
    void *   *pStartData*,
    ULONG   *cEndKeyColumns*,
    void *   *pEndData*,
    DBRANGE   *dwRangeOptions***);**

Parameters

hAccessor [in]

The handle of the accessor to use for both **pStartData* and **pEndData*. This accessor must meet the following criteria, which are illustrated with a key that consists of columns A, B, and C, where A is the most significant column and C is the least significant column:

- For each key column this accessor binds, it must also bind all more significant key columns. For example, the accessor can bind column A, columns A and B, or columns A, B, and C.

- Key columns must be bound in order from most significant key column to least significant key column. For example, if the accessor binds columns A and B; then the first binding must bind column A and the second binding must bind column B.

- If the accessor binds any non-key columns, key columns must be bound first. For example, if the accessor binds columns A, B, and the bookmark column; then the first binding must bind column A, the second binding must bind column B, and the third binding must bind the bookmark column.

If the accessor does not meet these criteria, the method returns DB_E_BADBINDINFO or a status of DBSTATUS_E_BADACCESSOR for the offending column.

If *hAccessor* is the handle of a null accessor, (*cBindings* in **IAccessor::CreateAccessor** was zero), then **SetRange** does not set a range.

cStartKeyColumns [in]

The number of bindings in *hAccessor* for which **pStartData* contains valid data. **SetRange** retrieves data from the first *cStartKeyValues* key columns from **pStartData*. For example, suppose the accessor binds columns A, B, and C of the key in the previous example and *cStartKeyValues* is 2. **SetRange** retrieves data for columns A and B.

pStartData [in]

A pointer to a buffer containing the starting key values of the range, at offsets that correspond to the bindings in the accessor.

cEndKeyColumns [in]

The number of bindings in *hAccessor* for which **pEndData* contains valid data. **SetRange** retrieves data from the first *cEndKeyValues* key columns from **pEndData*. For example, suppose the accessor binds columns A, B, and C of the key in the previous example and *cEndKeyValues* is 2. **SetRange** retrieves data for columns A and B.

pEndData [in]

A pointer to a buffer containing the ending key values of the range, at offsets that correspond to the bindings in the accessor.

dwRangeOptions [in]

A bit mask describing the options of the range. The values in DBRANGEENUM have the following meanings:

Value	Description
DBRANGE_ INCLUSIVESTART	The start boundary is inclusive (the default).
DBRANGE_ EXCLUSIVESTART	The start boundary is exclusive.
DBRANGE_ INCLUSIVEEND	The end boundary is inclusive (the default).
DBRANGE_ EXCLUSIVEEND	The end boundary is exclusive.
DBRANGE_ EXCLUDENULLS	Exclude NULLs from the range.
DBRANGE_PREFIX	Use **pStartData* as a prefix. **pEndData* must be a null pointer. Prefix matching can be specified entirely using the inclusive and exclusive flags. However, since prefix matching is an important common case, this flag enables the consumer specify only the **pStartData* values, and enables the provider to interpret this request quickly.
DBRANGE_MATCH	Set the range to all keys that match **pStartData*. **pStartData* must specify a full key. **pEndData* must be a null pointer. Used for fast equality match.

Return Code

S_OK

The method succeeded.

E_FAIL

A provider-specific error occurred.

E_INVALIDARG

dwRangeOptions was invalid.

cStartKeyValues was not zero and *pStartData* was a null pointer.

cEndKeyValues was not zero and *pEndData* was a null pointer.

hAccessor was the handle of a null accessor.

DB_E_BADACCESSORHANDLE

hAccessor was invalid.

DB_E_BADACCESSORTYPE

The specified accessor was not a row accessor.

DB_E_ERRORSOCCURRED

An error occurred while transferring data for one or more key columns. To determine the columns for which values were invalid, the consumer checks the status values. For a list of status values that can be returned by this method, see "Status Values Used When Setting Data" in "Status" in Chapter 6.

If this method performs deferred accessor validation and that validation takes place before any data is transferred, it can also return any of the following return codes for the reasons listed in the corresponding DBBINDSTATUS values in **IAccessor::CreateAccessor**.

E_NOINTERFACE
DB_E_BADBINDINFO
DB_E_BADORDINAL
DB_E_BADSTORAGEFLAGS
DB_E_UNSUPPORTEDCONVERSION

Comments

A range defines a view in the index containing a contiguous set of key values. The **pStartData* and **pEndData* values always specify the starting and ending positions in the range, respectively. Thus, for an ascending index, **pStartData* contains the smaller value and **pEndData* contains the larger value; for a descending index, **pStartData* contains the larger value and **pEndData* contains the smaller value.

A range on the entire index is defined by calling **SetRange** (*hAcc*, 0, NULL, 0, NULL, 0). When a range is set, **Seek** can only position to rows in the current range.

For information about how **SetRange** transfers data from **pDataStart* and **pDataEnd*, see "Setting Data" in Chapter 6.

Inclusive and Exclusive Ranges with Ascending Indexes

The DBRANGE_INCLUSIVE* and DBRANGE_EXCLUSIVE* flags apply only to the last value in the *pStartData* and *pEndData* buffers. The other values are always inclusive.

Examples with full keys

a) open ranges (single column key)

Desired range	SetRange call
X > 5	SetRange(hAcc, 1, {5}, 0, NULL, DBRANGE_EXCLUSIVESTART);
X ≥ 5	SetRange(hAcc, 1, {5}, 0, NULL, DBRANGE_INCLUSIVESTART);
X < 5	SetRange(hAcc, 0, NULL, 1, {5}, DBRANGE_EXCLUSIVEEND);
X ≤ 5	SetRange(hAcc, 0, NULL, 1, {5}, DBRANGE_INCLUSIVEEND);

b) closed ranges (single column key)

Desired range	SetRange call
X ≥ 5 and X ≤ 10	SetRange(hAcc, 1, {5}, 1, {10}, DBRANGE_INCLUSIVESTART | DBRANGE_INCLUSIVEEND);
X ≥ 5 and X < 10	SetRange(hAcc, 1, {5}, 1, {10}, DBRANGE_INCLUSIVESTART | DBRANGE_EXCLUSIVEEND);
X > 5 and X ≤ 10	SetRange(hAcc, 1, {5}, 1, {10}, DBRANGE_EXCLUSIVESTART | DBRANGE_INCLUSIVEEND);
X > 5 and X < 10	SetRange(hAcc, 1, {5}, 1, {10}, DBRANGE_EXCLUSIVESTART | DBRANGE_EXCLUSIVEEND);

c) open ranges (multicolumn key [A, B])

The only way to specify open ranges with multi-column indexes is by using partial keys. See the examples with partial keys below.

Notice that the range A > 5 and B = 1 cannot be specified since it does not correspond to a contiguous range.

d) closed ranges (multi-column key [A, B])

Desired range	SetRange call

A = 1 and
B ≥ 5 and
B ≤ 10
	`SetRange(hAcc, 2, {1, 5}, 2, {1, 10},`
	`DBRANGE_INCLUSIVESTART |`
	`DBRANGE_INCLUSIVEEND);`

A = 1 and B > 5	`SetRange(hAcc, 2, {1, 5}, 1, {1},`
	`DBRANGE_EXCLUSIVESTART |`
	`DBRANGE_INCLUSIVEEND);`

A = 1 and B < 5	`SetRange(hAcc, 1, {1}, 2, {1, 5},`
	`DBRANGE_INCLUSIVESTART |`
	`DBRANGE_EXCLUSIVEEND);`

Examples with partial keys

e) open ranges (multi-column key [A, B])

Desired range	SetRange call
A > 5	`SetRange(hAcc, 1, {5}, 0, NULL,` `DBRANGE_EXCLUSIVESTART);`
A ≥ 5	`SetRange(hAcc, 1, {5}, 0, NULL,` `DBRANGE_INCLUSIVESTART);`

A = 5	`SetRange(hAcc, 1, {5}, 1,{5},`
	`DBRANGE_INCLUSIVESTART |`
	`DBRANGE_INCLUSIVEEND);`

A < 5	`SetRange(hAcc, 0, NULL, 1, {5},` `DBRANGE_EXCLUSIVEEND);`
A ≤ 5	`SetRange(hAcc, 0, NULL, 1, {5},` `DBRANGE_INCLUSIVEEND);`

f) closed ranges (multi-column key [A,B])

Desired range	SetRange call

A > 5 and A ≤ 10	`SetRange(hAcc, 1, {5}, 1, {10},`
	`DBRANGE_EXCLUSIVESTART |`
	`DBRANGE_INCLUSIVEEND);`

Prefix Matching

SetRange provides the DBRANGE_PREFIX flag to make it easier for a consumer to formulate ranges involving keys whose value represents a prefix. Consider the text command **SELECT * FROM T WHERE T.A LIKE "abc*"**. This range can be formulated using only the inclusive and exclusive flags as follows for an ascending index:

```
SetRange (hAcc, 1, {"abc"}, 1, {"abd"}, DBRANGE_INCLUSIVESTART | DBRANGE_EXCLUSIVEEND);
```

This requires the consumer to know the collation order. The DBRANGE_PREFIX flag is provided to make it easier for the consumer to formulate this very common case as follows:

```
SetRange(hAcc, 1, {"abc"}, 0, NULL, DBRANGE_PREFIX);
```

Examples

Desired range	SetRange call
A = 1 and B like "abc*"	`SetRange(hAcc, 2, {1, "abc"}, 0, NULL,` `DBRANGE_PREFIX);`

Note that this call is the same regardless of whether DBRANGE_PREFIX is used with an ascending or descending index.

Equality Matching

To facilitate the formulation of ranges involving equality, the **SetRange** method offers the DBRANGE_MATCH option flag. Consider the example **SELECT * FROM T WHERE T.X = 5**. The corresponding range can be formulated in terms of the inclusive and exclusive flags as follows:

```
SetRange(hAcc, 1, {5}, 1, {5}, DBRANGE_INCLUSIVESTART | DBRANGE_INCLUSIVEEND);
```

The same range can be formulated using the match flags as follows:

```
SetRange(hAcc, 1, {5}, 0, NULL, DBRANGE_MATCH);
```

Example

Desired range	SetRange call

A = 5 and B= 6	`SetRange(hAcc, 2, {5, 6}, 2, {5, 6},`
	`DBRANGE_INCLUSIVESTART |`
	`DBRANGE_INCLUSIVEEND);`

A = 5 and B= 6	`SetRange(hAcc, 2, {5, 6}, 0, NULL,` `DBRANGE_MATCH);`

Note that these calls are the same regardless of whether DBRANGE_MATCH is used with an ascending or descending index.

Ranges that Include NULLs

To save consumers from having to determine whether NULL values sort at the start or the end of an index, DBRANGE_EXCLUDENULLS excludes NULL values from the final column specified in *pStartData* or *pEndData*. This value of *dwRangeOptions* can only be used with partial keys. It is equivalent to one of the following:

- If NULL values sort at the start of the index, it is equivalent to specifying an additional column in *pStartData*, setting the value of the status of that column to DBSTATUS_S_ISNULL, and setting the DBRANGE_EXCLUSIVESTART value in *dwRangeOptions*. Thus, the range will start after the last NULL value in the column.

- If NULL values sort at the end of the index, it is equivalent to specifying an additional column in *pEndData*, setting the value of the status of that column to DBSTATUS_S_ISNULL, and setting the DBRANGE_EXCLUSIVEEND value in *dwRangeOptions*. Thus, the range will end before the first NULL value in the column.

Thus, the consumer does not need to know if NULL values sort at the start or end of the index. This is equivalent to the predicate **<column> NOT NULL**. Note that DBRANGE_EXCLUDENULLS does not affect whether individual index columns contain NULL values. For example, suppose an index contains two columns, X and Y, as search keys. If *pStartData* and *pEndData* are non-null pointers, and DBRANGE_EXCLUDENULLS is set in *dwRangeOptions*, then the returned rows might contain NULL values in either X or Y, but not in both columns. Similarly, if *pStartData* and *pEndData* are null pointers (denoting a range over the entire index), and DBRANGE_EXCLUDENULLS is set in *dwRangeOptions*, then the returned rows might contain NULL values in either X or Y, but not in both columns.

The DBRANGE_EXCLUDENULLS flag is defined to allow consumers to easily obtain contiguous key values excluding NULLs at the start or end of the range. For multi-column indexes (for example, [X, Y]), this means that key values for the prefix or suffix of the key must be an equality match. For example, it makes sense to set a range on **X = 5** and DBRANGE_EXCLUDENULLS, or on **Y = 3** and DBRANGE_EXCLUDENULLS, but not on **X BETWEEN 4 AND 6** and DBRANGE_EXCLUDENULLS because the range **X BETWEEN 4 AND 6** and **Y IS NOT NULL** is not contiguous. Therefore, to use DBRANGE_EXCLUDENULLS a consumer must use either an equality comparison or MATCH on the prefix or suffix of a multi-column key.

To determine how an index treats NULLs, a consumer checks the information returned by **GetIndexInfo** method or the INDEXES schema rowset of **IDBSchemaRowset**.

Examples

Desired range	SetRange call
X is NULL	`SetRange(hAcc, 1, {NULL}, 1, {NULL}, DBRANGE_INCLUSIVESTART | DBRANGE_INCLUSIVEEND);`
X is not NULL	`SetRange(hAcc, 0, NULL, 0, NULL, DBRANGE_EXCLUDENULLS);`
A = 4 and B is not NULL	`SetRange(hAcc, 1,{4}, 1, {4}, DBRANGE_INCLUSIVESTART | DBRANGE_INCLUSIVEEND | DBRANGE_EXCLUDENULLS);`
A = 4 and B is not NULL	`SetRange(hAcc, 1, {4}, 0, NULL, DBRANGE_MATCH | DBRANGE_EXCLUDENULLS );`

Duplicate Keys

A **SetRange** request with the exclusive flag on an ascending index allowing duplicate keys, sets the index position at the first index entry greater than the *pStartData* value. If the index is descending, then **SetRange** sets the position at the first entry less than the *pStartData* value.

End of Range

An index is traversed using **IRowset::GetNextRows**. This method returns DB_S_ENDOFROWSET when it reaches the end of the currently set range, or when it tries to read before the beginning or after the end of the index.

Inclusive and Exclusive Ranges with Descending Indexes

As mentioned earlier, with descending indexes the user specifies the values that determine the start of the range using *pStartData* and the values that determine the end of the range using *pEndData*. The following are some examples.

Examples with full keys

a) open ranges (single column key)

Desired range	SetRange call
X > 5	SetRange(hAcc, 0, NULL, 1, {5}, DBRANGE_EXCLUSIVEEND);
X ≥ 5	SetRange(hAcc, 0, NULL, 1, {5}, DBRANGE_INCLUSIVEEND);
X < 5	SetRange(hAcc, 1, {5}, 0, NULL, DBRANGE_EXCLUSIVESTART);
X ≤ 5	SetRange(hAcc, 1, {5}, 0, NULL, DBRANGE_INCLUSIVESTART);

b) closed ranges (single column key)

Desired range	SetRange call
X ≥ 5 and X ≤ 10	SetRange(hAcc, 1, {10}, 1, {5}, DBRANGE_INCLUSIVESTART | DBRANGE_INCLUSIVEEND);
X ≥ 5 and X < 10	SetRange(hAcc, 1, {10}, 1, {5}, DBRANGE_EXCLUSIVESTART | DBRANGE_INCLUSIVEEND);
X > 5 and X ≤ 10	SetRange(hAcc, 1, {10}, 1, {5}, DBRANGE_INCLUSIVESTART | DBRANGE_EXCLUSIVEEND);
X > 5 and X < 10	SetRange(hAcc, 1, {10}, 1, {5}, DBRANGE_EXCLUSIVESTART | DBRANGE_EXCLUSIVEEND);

c) open ranges (multicolumn key [A, B])

The only way to specify open ranges with multicolumn indexes is by using partial keys. See examples with partial keys below.

Notice that the range A > 5 and B = 1 cannot be specified since it does not correspond to a contiguous range.

d) closed ranges (multicolumn key [A, B])

Desired range	SetRange call
A = 1 and B ≥ 5 and B ≤ 10	SetRange(hAcc, 2, {1, 10}, 2, {1, 5}, DBRANGE_INCLUSIVESTART | DBRANGE_INCLUSIVEEND);
A = 1 and B > 5	SetRange(hAcc, 1, {1}, 2, {1, 5}, DBRANGE_INCLUSIVESTART | DBRANGE_EXCLUSIVEEND);
A = 1 and B < 5	SetRange(hAcc, 2, {1, 5}, 1, {1}, DBRANGE_EXCLUSIVESTART | DBRANGE_INCLUSIVEEND);

Examples with partial keys

e) open ranges (multicolumn key [A, B])

Desired range	SetRange call
A > 5	SetRange(hAcc, 0, NULL, 1, {5}, DBRANGE_EXCLUSIVEEND);
A ≥ 5	SetRange(hAcc, 0, NULL, 1, {5}, DBRANGE_INCLUSIVEEND);
A = 5	SetRange(hAcc, 1, {5}, 1, {5}, DBRANGE_INCLUSIVESTART | DBRANGE_INCLUSIVEEND);
A < 5	SetRange(hAcc, 1, {5}, 0, NULL, DBRANGE_EXCLUSIVESTART);
A ≤ 5	SetRange(hAcc, 1, {5}, 0, NULL, DBRANGE_INCLUSIVESTART);

f) closed ranges (multicolumn key [A,B])

Desired range	SetRange call
A > 5 and A ≤ 10	SetRange(hAcc, 1, {10}, 1, {5}, DBRANGE_INCLUSIVESTART | DBRANGE_EXCLUSIVEEND);

See Also

IRowset::GetNextRows, IRowsetIndex::Seek

IRowsetInfo

IRowsetInfo provides information about a rowset.

When to Implement

All rowsets must implement **IRowsetInfo**.

When to Call

When a consumer gets an interface pointer on a rowset, its first step usually is to determine the rowset's capabilities using **IUnknown::QueryInterface**. It may call **GetProperties** to learn the properties of the rowset which do not show up as distinct interfaces, such as the maximum number of active rows and how many rows can have pending updates at the same time.

IRowsetInfo also provides methods for retrieving objects associated with the rowset. **GetSpecification** gets the object (command or session) that created the rowset. **GetReferencedRowset** gets the rowset that is referenced by a bookmark-valued column.

Method	Description
GetProperties	Returns the current setting of all properties supported by the rowset.
GetReferencedRowset	Returns an interface pointer to the rowset to which a bookmark applies.
GetSpecification	Returns an interface pointer on the object (command or session) that created the rowset.

IRowsetInfo::GetProperties

Returns the current settings of all properties supported by the rowset.

HRESULT GetProperties (
    const ULONG   *cPropertyIDSets*,
    const DBPROPIDSET *rgPropertyIDSets*[],
    ULONG *   *pcPropertySets*,
    DBPROPSET **   *prgPropertySets*);

Parameters

cPropertyIDSets [in]

The number of DBPROPIDSET structures in *rgPropertyIDSets*.

If *cPropertySets* is zero, the provider ignores *rgPropertyIDSets* and returns the values of all properties in the Rowset property group for which values exist, including properties for which values were not set but for which defaults exist and also including properties for which values were set automatically because values were set for other properties.

If *cPropertyIDSets* is not zero, the provider returns the values of the requested properties. If a property is not supported, the returned value of *dwStatus* in the returned DBPROP structure for that property is DBPROPSTATUS_NOTSUPPORTED and the value of *dwOptions* is undefined.

rgPropertyIDSets [in]

An array of *cPropertyIDSets* DBPROPIDSET structures. The properties specified in these structures must belong to the Rowset property group. The provider returns the values of the properties specified in these structures. If *cPropertyIDSets* is zero, then this parameter is ignored.

For information about the properties in the Rowset property group that are defined by OLE DB, see "Rowset Properties" in Appendix C. For information about the DBPROPIDSET structure, see "DBPROPIDSET Structure" in Chapter 11.

pcPropertySets [out]

A pointer to memory in which to return the number of DBPROPSET structures returned in *prgPropertySets. If *cPropertyIDSets* is zero, *pcPropertySets is the total number of property sets for which the provider supports at least one property in the Rowset property group. If *cPropertyIDSets* is greater than zero, *pcPropertySets is set to *cPropertyIDSets*. If an error other than DB_E_ERRORSOCCURRED occurs, *pcPropertySets is set to zero.

prgPropertySets [out]

A pointer to memory in which to return an array of DBPROPSET structures. If *cPropertyIDSets* is zero, then one structure is returned for each property set that contains at least one property belonging to the Rowset property group. If *cPropertyIDSets* is not zero, then one structure is returned for each property set specified in *rgPropertyIDSets*.

If *cPropertyIDSets* is not zero, the DBPROPSET structures in **prgPropertySets* are returned in the same order as the DBPROPIDSET structures in *rgPropertyIDSets*; that is, for corresponding elements of each array, the *guidPropertySet* elements are the same. If *cPropertyIDs*, in an element of *rgPropertyIDSets*, is not zero, the DBPROP structures in the corresponding element of **prgPropertySets* are returned in the same order as the DBPROPID values in *rgPropertyIDs*; that is for corresponding elements of each array, the property IDs are the same.

The provider allocates memory for the structures and returns the address to this memory; the consumer releases this memory with **IMalloc::Free** when it no longer needs the structures. Before calling **IMalloc::Free** for **prgPropertySets*, the consumer should call **IMalloc::Free** for the *rgProperties* element within each element of **prgPropertySets*. If **pcPropertySets* is zero on output or an if error other than DB_E_ERRORSOCCURRED occurs, the provider does not allocate any memory and ensures that **prgPropertySets* is a null pointer on output.

For information about the DBPROPSET and DBPROP structures, see "DBPROPSET Structure" and "DBPROP Structure" in Chapter 11.

Return Code

S_OK
> The method succeeded. In all DBPROP structures returned by the method, *dwStatus* is set to DBPROPSTATUS_OK.

DB_S_ERRORSOCCURRED
> No value was returned for one or more properties. The consumer checks *dwStatus* in the DBPROP structure to determine the properties for which values were not returned. **GetProperties** can fail to return properties for a number of reasons, including:
>
> * The property was not supported by the provider.
>
> * The property was not in the Rowset property group.
>
> * The property set was not supported by the provider. If *cPropertyIDs* in the DBPROPIDSET structure for the property set was zero, the provider cannot set *dwStatus* in the DBPROP structure because it does not know the IDs of any properties in the property set. Instead, it sets *cProperties* to zero in the DBPROPSET structure returned for the property set.

E_FAIL
> A provider-specific error occurred.

E_INVALIDARG
> *cPropertyIDSets* was not equal to zero and *rgPropertyIDSets* was a null pointer.
>
> *pcPropertySets* or *prgPropertySets* was a null pointer.
>
> In an element of *rgPropertyIDSets*, *cPropertyIDs* was not zero and *rgPropertyIDs* was a null pointer.

E_OUTOFMEMORY

The provider was unable to allocate sufficient memory in which to return the DBPROPSET or DBPROP structures.

E_UNEXPECTED

ITransaction::Commit or **ITransaction::Abort** was called and the object is in a zombie state.

DB_E_ERRORSOCCURRED

Values were not returned for any properties. The provider allocates memory for *prgPropertySets* and the consumer checks *dwStatus* in the DBPROP structures to determine why properties were not returned. The consumer frees this memory when it no longer needs the information.

Comments

This method makes no logical change to the state of the object.

Even though **IDBProperties::GetPropertyInfo** lists a property as being supported by the provider, **GetProperties** will not return a value for it if it does not apply to the current circumstances. For example, the provider's ability to support the property might be affected by the current transaction or the current command text.

IRowsetInfo::GetProperties might return a different value for a property than does **ICommandProperties::GetProperties**. For example, if a consumer requests ordered bookmarks if they are cheap, it calls **ICommandProperties::SetProperties** to set the value of DBPROP_ORDEREDBOOKMARKS to VARIANT_TRUE and specifies a *dwOptions* value of DBPROPOPTIONS_SETIFCHEAP. If the provider cannot determine whether this is cheap, **ICommandProperties::GetProperties** returns a value of VARIANT_TRUE and a *dwOptions* of DBPROPOPTIONS_SETIFCHEAP for this property. If the provider determines during execution that ordered bookmarks are not cheap, **IRowsetInfo::GetProperties** returns a value of VARIANT_FALSE and a *dwOptions* of zero.

See Also

ICommandProperties::SetProperties, **IDBProperties::GetPropertyInfo**

IRowsetInfo::GetReferencedRowset

Returns an interface pointer to the rowset to which a bookmark applies.

HRESULT GetReferencedRowset (
    ULONG   *iOrdinal,*
    REFIID   *riid,*
    IUnknown ** *ppReferencedRowset*);

Parameters

iOrdinal [in]

The bookmark column for which to get the related rowset.

riid [in]

The IID of the interface pointer to return in **ppReferencedRowset*.

ppReferencedRowset [out]

A pointer to memory in which to return an **IUnknown** interface pointer on the
rowset that interprets values from this column. If this is not a reference column,
**ppReferencedRowset* is set to a null pointer.

Return Code

S_OK

The method succeeded.

E_FAIL

A provider-specific error occurred.

E_INVALIDARG

ppReferencedRowset was a null pointer.

E_NOINTERFACE

The interface specified in *riid* was not implicitly or explicitly specified as a rowset
property of the rowset. The current rowset remains valid.

E_UNEXPECTED

ITransaction::Commit or **ITransaction::Abort** was called and the object is in a
zombie state.

DB_E_BADORDINAL

The column specified by *iOrdinal* did not exist.

DB_E_NOTAREFERENCECOLUMN

The column specified by *iOrdinal* did not contain bookmarks.

DB_E_NOTREENTRANT

The provider called a method from **IRowsetNotify** in the consumer and the method
has not yet returned.

DB_E_NOTSUPPORTED

The interface was exposed on an index rowset.

Comments

This method makes no logical change to the state of the current rowset.

All of the bookmarks in a column make reference to a single rowset. The references can apply to the current rowset (an example would be genealogy relations on a People table), or they can apply to a different rowset (an example of which would be Customer Orders).

For more information, see "Bookmarks" in Chapter 4.

See Also

IColumnsInfo, IColumnsRowset

IRowsetInfo::GetSpecification

Returns an interface pointer on the object (command or session) that created this rowset.

HRESULT GetSpecification (
    REFIID   *riid*,
    IUnknown ** *ppSpecification*);

Parameters

riid [in]
    The IID of the interface on which to return a pointer.

ppSpecification [out]
    A pointer to memory in which to return the interface pointer. If the provider does not have an object that created the rowset, it sets **ppSpecification* to a null pointer and returns S_FALSE. If **GetSpecification** fails, it must attempt to set **ppSpecification* to a null pointer.

Return Code

S_OK
    The method succeeded.

S_FALSE
    The provider does not have an object that created the rowset.

E_FAIL
    A provider-specific error occurred.

E_INVALIDARG
    ppSpecification was a null pointer.

E_NOINTERFACE
    The object that created this rowset did not support the interface specified in *riid*.

E_UNEXPECTED
    ITransaction::Commit or **ITransaction::Abort** was called and the object is in a zombie state.

DB_E_NOTREENTRANT
    The provider called a method from **IRowsetNotify** in the consumer and the method has not yet returned.

Comments

This method makes no logical change to the state of the current rowset.

GetSpecification returns an interface pointer on the object that created the rowset. If the rowset was created by **ICommand::Execute**, this object is a command. If the rowset was created by **IOpenRowset::OpenRowset**, this object is a session.

If the object is not a command, then it must specify the contents of the rowset. That is, it must expose interfaces that can be used to modify the contents of the rowset before the rowset is created, or be used to gain additional information about the rowset. If the object cannot expose such interfaces, **GetSpecification** should return a null pointer in **ppSpecification*. In a simple provider, such as a provider that creates a rowset over a fixed set of data, there might not be an object that created the rowset; in this case, **GetSpecification** returns a null pointer in **ppSpecification.*

See Also

ICommand::GetDBSession, IGetDataSource::GetDataSource

IRowsetLocate : IRowset

IRowsetLocate is the interface for fetching arbitrary rows of a rowset. A rowset that does not implement this interface is a *sequential* rowset. **IRowsetLocate** is a prerequisite for **IRowsetScroll**.

When **IRowsetLocate** or one of its direct descendants is present on a rowset, then column zero is the bookmark for the rows. Reading this column will obtain a bookmark value which can be used to reposition to the same row.

When to Implement

IRowsetLocate is required for all providers that intend to support general consumers.

Method	Description
Compare	Compares two bookmarks.
GetRowsAt	Fetches rows, starting with the row specified by an offset from a bookmark.
GetRowsByBookmark	Fetches the rows that match the specified bookmarks.
Hash	Returns hash values for the specified bookmarks.

IRowsetLocate::Compare

Compares two bookmarks.

HRESULT Compare (
    HCHAPTER   *hReserved*,
    ULONG   *cbBookmark1*,
    const BYTE *   *pBookmark1*,
    ULONG   *cbBookmark2*,
    const BYTE *   *pBookmark2*,
    DBCOMPARE *   *pComparison*);

Parameters

hReserved [in]
Reserved for future use. Providers ignore this parameter.

cbBookmark1 [in]
The length in bytes of the first bookmark.

pBookmark1 [in]
A pointer to the first bookmark. This can be a pointer to DBBMK_FIRST or DBBMK_LAST.

cbBookmark2 [in]
The length in bytes of the second bookmark.

pBookmark2 [in]
A pointer to the second bookmark. This can be a pointer to DBBMK_FIRST or DBBMK_LAST.

pComparison [out]
A pointer to memory in which to return a flag that specifies the result of the comparison. The returned flag will be one of the following values.

Value	Description
DBCOMPARE_LT	The first bookmark is before the second.
DBCOMPARE_EQ	The two bookmarks are equal.
DBCOMPARE_GT	The first bookmark is after the second.
DBCOMPARE_NE	The bookmarks are not equal and not ordered.
DBCOMPARE_NOTCOMPARABLE	The two bookmarks cannot be compared.

Return Code

S_OK
The method succeeded.

E_FAIL
A provider-specific error occurred.

E_INVALIDARG

cbBookmark1 or *cbBookmark2* was zero.

pBookmark1, *pBookmark2*, or *pComparison* was a null pointer.

E_UNEXPECTED

ITransaction::Commit or **ITransaction::Abort** was called and the object is in a zombie state.

DB_E_BADBOOKMARK

*pBookmark1 or **pBookmark2* was invalid, incorrectly formed, or DBBMK_INVALID.

DB_E_NOTREENTRANT

The provider called a method from **IRowsetNotify** in the consumer and the method has not yet returned.

Comments

This method makes no logical change to the state of the object.

If bookmarks are ordered, they can be compared to determine the relative position of their associated rows in the rowset. The DBPROP_ORDEREDBOOKMARKS property indicates whether bookmarks are ordered. If bookmarks are not ordered, then the returned comparison value, will be DBCOMPARE_EQ or DBCOMPARE_NE. If bookmarks are ordered, then the returned comparison value will be DBCOMPARE_LT, DBCOMPARE_EQ, or DBCOMPARE_GT. The command that creates the rowset does not have to have an ordered text command, such as an SQL statement containing an **ORDER BY** clause, to have ordered bookmarks.

Compare can compare any valid bookmarks. The consumer is not required to have permission to read the corresponding rows, nor are the rows even required to exist— for example, they might have been deleted.

If the DBPROP_LITERALBOOKMARKS property is VARIANT_TRUE then consumers can directly compare values.

Specifying the bookmark DBBMK_FIRST or DBBMK_LAST returns DBCOMPARE_EQ when compared with itself and DBCOMPARE_NE when compared with any other bookmark.

See Also

IRowsetLocate::Hash, IRowsetIdentity::IsSameRow

IRowsetLocate::GetRowsAt

Fetches rows starting with the row specified by an offset from a bookmark.

HRESULT GetRowsAt (
HWATCHREGION	*hReserved1,*
HCHAPTER	*hReserved2*
ULONG	*cbBookmark,*
const BYTE *	*pBookmark,*
LONG	*lRowsOffset,*
LONG	*cRows,*
ULONG *	*pcRowsObtained,*
HROW **	*prghRows);*

Parameters

hReserved1 [in]
Reserved for future use. Providers ignore this parameter.

hReserved2 [in]
Reserved for future use. Providers ignore this parameter.

cbBookmark [in]
The length in bytes of the bookmark. This must not be zero.

pBookmark [in]
A pointer to a bookmark which identifies the base row to be used. This can be a pointer to DBBMK_FIRST or DBBMK_LAST. If *lRowsOffset* is zero then the provider fetches this row first, otherwise the provider skips this and subsequent rows up to the count specified in the offset, then fetches the following rows.

lRowsOffset [in]
The signed count of rows from the origin bookmark to the target row. The first row fetched is determined by the bookmark and this offset. For example, if *lRowsOffset* is zero, the first row fetched is the bookmarked row; if *lRowsOffset* is 1, the first row fetched is the row after the bookmarked row; if *lRowsOffset* is −1, the first row fetched is the row before the bookmarked row.

lRowsOffset can be a negative number only if the value of the DBPROP_CANSCROLLBACKWARDS property is VARIANT_TRUE.

cRows [in]
The number of rows to fetch. A negative number means to fetch backwards. *cRows* can be a negative number only if the value of the DBPROP_CANFETCHBACKWARDS property is VARIANT_TRUE.

If *cRows* is zero, no rows are fetched. If the provider does not discover any other errors, the method returns S_OK; whether the provider checks for any other errors is provider-specific.

See the Comments section for a full description of the semantics of *lRowsOffset* and *cRows* parameters.

pcRowsObtained [out]

A pointer to memory in which to return the actual number of fetched rows. If the consumer has insufficient permission to fetch all rows, **GetRowsAt** fetches all rows for which the consumer has sufficient permission and skips all other rows. If the method fails, **pcRowsObtained* is set to zero.

prghRows [in/out]

A pointer to memory in which to return an array of handles of the fetched rows. If **prghRows* is not a null pointer on input, it must be a pointer to memory large enough to return the handles of the requested number of rows. If **prghRows* is a null pointer on input, the rowset allocates memory for the row handles and returns the address to this memory. The consumer releases this memory with **IMalloc::Free** after it releases the row handles. If **prghRows* was a null pointer on input and **pcRowsObtained* is zero on output or if the method fails, the provider does not allocate any memory and ensures that **prghRows* is a null pointer on output.

Return Code

S_OK

The method succeeded.

DB_S_BOOKMARKSKIPPED

The following behavior is only supported on rowsets that set the DBPROP_BOOKMARKSKIPPED property to VARIANT_TRUE. If this property is VARIANT_FALSE, this return code is never returned.

lRowsOffset was zero and the row specified by **pBookmark* was deleted or is no longer a member of the rowset, or the row specified by the combination of **pBookmark* and *lRowsOffset* is a row to which the consumer does not have access rights. **GetRowsAt** skipped that row. The full count of actual rows (*cRows*) will be met if there are enough rows available. The array of returned row handles does not have gaps for missing rows; the returned count is the number of rows actually fetched.

If a row is skipped, it is counted as one of the rows to be skipped for *lRowsOffset*. For example, if an offset of one is requested and the bookmark points to a row which is now missing, the offset is decremented by one and the provider begins by fetching the next row.

If this condition occurs along with another warning condition, the method returns the code for the other warning condition. Thus, whenever a consumer receives the return code for another warning condition, it should check to see if this condition occurred.

DB_S_ENDOFROWSET

GetRowsAt reached the start or the end of the rowset and could not fetch all of the requested rows because the count extended beyond the end. The number of rows actually fetched is returned in **pcRowsObtained*; this will be less than *cRows*.

DB_S_ROWLIMITEXCEEDED

Fetching the number of rows specified in *cRows* would have exceeded the total number of active rows supported by the rowset. The number of rows that were actually fetched is returned in **pcRowsObtained*. Note that this condition can occur only when there are more rows available than can be handled by the rowset. Thus, this condition never conflicts with those described in DB_S_ENDOFROWSET and DB_S_STOPLIMITREACHED, both of which imply that no more rows were available.

DB_S_STOPLIMITREACHED

Fetching rows required further execution of the command, such as when the rowset uses a server-side cursor. Execution has been stopped because a resource limit has been reached. The number of rows that were actually fetched is returned in **pcRowsObtained*.

E_FAIL

A provider-specific error occurred.

E_INVALIDARG

cbBookmark was zero or *pBookmark* was a null pointer.

pcRowsObtained or *prghRows* was a null pointer.

E_OUTOFMEMORY

The provider was unable to allocate sufficient memory in which to instantiate the rows or return the row handles.

E_UNEXPECTED

ITransaction::Commit or **ITransaction::Abort** was called and the object is in a zombie state.

DB_E_BADBOOKMARK

*pBookmark was invalid, incorrectly formed, or DBBMK_INVALID.

*pBookmark did not match any rows in the rowset and DBPROP_BOOKMARKSKIPPED was VARIANT_FALSE. This includes the case when the row corresponding to the bookmark has been deleted.

DB_E_BADSTARTPOSITION

lRowsOffset would have positioned the first row fetched past either end of the rowset, regardless of the *cRows* value specified.

DB_E_CANTFETCHBACKWARDS

cRows was negative and the rowset cannot fetch backward.

DB_E_CANTSCROLLBACKWARDS

lRowsOffset was negative and the rowset cannot scroll backward.

DB_E_NOTREENTRANT

The consumer called this method while it was processing a notification, and it is an error to call this method while processing the specified DBREASON value.

DB_E_ROWSNOTRELEASED

The provider requires release of existing rows before new ones can be fetched. For more information, see DBPROP_CANHOLDROWS in "Rowset Properties" in Appendix C.

DB_SEC_E_PERMISSIONDENIED

The consumer did not have sufficient permission to fetch any of the rows; no rows were fetched.

Comments

Given values for a bookmark, offset, and number of rows to fetch:

- The provider determines a starting position for the fetch as the bookmark plus the offset.

- If the starting position is off either end of the rowset, the method returns DB_E_BADSTARTPOSITION.

- If the starting position is in the rowset, the provider fetches rows in the specified direction until it has fetched the requested number of rows or hits the end of the rowset.

- If it fetches the requested number of rows, it returns S_OK. If it hits the end of the rowset, it stops fetching, returns DB_S_ENDOFROWSET, and returns the rows it has fetched.

- The rows are returned in rowset traversal order, that is, the direction in which they were fetched. For example, if the consumer passes the bookmark for row 10 to **GetRowsAt** and specifies *cRows* equal to −5 and *lRowsOffset* equal to 0, **GetRowsAt** returns rows 10 through 6. That is, *$*prghRows$*[0] is the handle for row 10 and *$*prghRows$*[4] is the handle for row 6.

The following table defines the behavior of **GetRowsAt** for all combinations of these parameters:

Variable	Description
N	Total rows in rowset
B	Row in the rowset specified by the bookmark parameters *cbBookmark* and *pBookmark*. Assume $1 \le B \le N$, DBBMK_FIRST is equivalent to B = 1, and DBBMK_LAST is equivalent to B = N.
F	*lRowsOffset*
r	*cRows*

B + F	r	cRowsObtained	Return code
B + F < 1 or B + F > N	N/A	0	DB_E_BADSTARTPOSITION
$1 \leq B + F \leq N$	0	0	S_OK
$1 \leq B + F \leq N$	$1 \leq r \leq N - B - F + 1$	r	S_OK
$1 \leq B + F \leq N$	$r > N - B - F + 1$	N−B−F+1	DB_S_ENDOFROWSET
$1 \leq B + F \leq N$	r < 0 and abs(r) ≤ B + F	abs(r)	S_OK
$1 \leq B + F \leq N$	r < 0 and abs(r) > B + F	B + F	DB_S_ENDOFROWSET

Consumers that want to fetch forward, for example, 20 rows at a time, can use the call **GetRowsAt**(..., B, 1, 20, ...) which allows for an easy check when reaching the end of the rowset. Similarly, consumers that want to fetch backward can use the call **GetRowsAt**(..., B, −1, −20, ...) to facilitate the detection of the beginning of the rowset. In the latter case DBPROP_CANFETCHBACKWARDS must be set to VARIANT_TRUE.

The DBPROP_BOOKMARKSKIPPED property defines the behavior for cases in which there is no exact match for the bookmark pointed to by *pBookmark*. If this property is set to VARIANT_FALSE, then DB_E_BADBOOKMARK will be returned because the corresponding position is not well-defined. The behavior when this property is set to VARIANT_TRUE is as follows:

- If *lRowsOffset* is zero, then the row is skipped, the requested number of rows are fetched from subsequent rows, and a DB_S_BOOKMARKSKIPPED warning is returned.

- If *lRowsOffset* and *cRows* are any value except zero, the fetch succeeds, based on the position of the row before it became invalid. For example, suppose row 20 is deleted. If a consumer calls **GetRowsAt** with *lRowsOffset* set to 5 and a bookmark that points to row 20, then **GetRowsAt** moves to row 25.

If the provider encounters a problem fetching a row—for example, data stored in a text file contains a letter in a numeric column—**GetRowsAt** fetches the row normally, returns the row handle, and returns S_OK. However, when the consumer calls **IRowset::GetData** for the row, the provider returns DBSTATUS_E_CANTCONVERTVALUE as the status for the offending column.

For information about what **GetRowsAt** does when it fetches a row that it already has in its internal buffers, see "Uniqueness of Rows in the Rowset" in Chapter 4. For information about whether **GetRowsAt** can detect changes made to rows in the rowset, see "Visibility of Changes" in Chapter 5.

GetRowsAt increments the reference count of each row for which it returns a handle by one. Thus, if a handle is returned for a row that has already been fetched, the reference count of that row will be greater than one. **ReleaseRows** must be called once for each time the handle to a row has been returned.

In order to use **GetRowsAt** several times in sequence to obtain successive rows, the consumer should obtain the bookmark of the last row of the previous set and use that, with a skip of one, to position for fetching the next rows.

See Also

IRowset::GetData, IRowset::GetNextRows, IRowsetLocate::GetRowsByBookmark, IRowsetScroll::GetRowsAtRatio

IRowsetLocate::GetRowsByBookmark

Fetches the rows that match the specified bookmarks.

HRESULT GetRowsByBookmark (
HCHAPTER	*hReserved*,
ULONG	*cRows*,
const ULONG	*rgcbBookmarks*[],
const BYTE *	*rgpBookmarks*[],
HROW	*rghRows*[],
DBROWSTATUS	*rgRowStatus*[]);

Parameters

hReserved [in]

Reserved for future use. Providers ignore this parameter.

cRows [in]

The number of rows to fetch. If *cRows* is zero, no rows are fetched. If the provider does not discover any other errors, the method returns S_OK; whether the provider checks for any other errors is provider-specific.

rgcbBookmarks [in]

An array containing the length in bytes of each bookmark.

rgpBookmarks [in]

An array containing a pointer to the bookmark of each row sought. These cannot be pointers to a standard bookmark (DBBMK_FIRST, DBBMK_LAST, DBBMK_INVALID). If *rgpBookmarks* contains a duplicate bookmark, the corresponding row is fetched and the reference count incremented once for each occurrence of the bookmark.

rghRows [out]

An array with *cRows* elements in which to return the handles of the fetched rows. The consumer allocates this array but is not required to initialize the elements of it. In each element of this array, if the row was fetched, the provider returns the handle of the row identified by the bookmark in the corresponding element of *rgpBookmarks*. If the row was not fetched, the provider returns DB_NULL_HROW.

rgRowStatus [out]

An array with *cRows* elements in which to return values indicating the status of each row specified in *rgpBookmarks*. If no errors or warnings occur while fetching a row, the corresponding element of *rgRowStatus* is set to DBROWSTATUS_S_OK. If an error occurs while fetching a row, the corresponding element is set as specified in DB_S_ERRORSOCCURRED. The consumer allocates memory for this array but is not required to initialize it. If *rgRowStatus* is a null pointer, no row statuses are returned. For information about the DBROWSTATUS enumerated type, see "Arrays of Errors" in Chapter 13.

Return Code

S_OK

The method succeeded. All rows were successfully fetched. The following value can be returned in *rgRowStatus*:

- The row was successfully fetched. The corresponding element of *rgRowStatus* contains DBROWSTATUS_S_OK.

DB_S_ERRORSOCCURRED

An error occurred while fetching a row, but at least one row was successfully fetched. Successes can occur for the reasons listed under S_OK. The following errors can occur:

- An element of *rgpBookmarks* pointed to an invalid or incorrectly formed bookmark. The corresponding element of *rgRowStatus* contains DBROWSTATUS_E_INVALID.

- An element of *rgpBookmarks* pointed to a bookmark that did not match any rows in the rowset. This includes the case when the row corresponding to the bookmark has been deleted. The corresponding element of *rgRowStatus* contains DBROWSTATUS_E_INVALID.

- An element of *rgcbBookmarks* was zero. The corresponding element of *rgRowStatus* contains DBROWSTATUS_E_INVALID.

- An element of *rgpBookmarks* was a null pointer. The corresponding element of *rgRowStatus* contains DBROWSTATUS_E_INVALID.

- An element of *rgpBookmarks* pointed to a standard bookmark (DBBMK_FIRST, DBBMK_LAST, DBBMK_INVALID). The corresponding element of *rgRowStatus* contains DBROWSTATUS_E_INVALID.

- The row corresponding to the bookmark was not fetched because fetching it would have exceeded the total number of active rows supported by the rowset. The corresponding element of *rgRowStatus* contains DBROWSTATUS_E_LIMITREACHED.

- The row corresponding to the bookmark was not fetched for the following reason. Fetching rows required further execution of the command, such as when the rowset uses a server-side cursor. Execution has been stopped because a resource limit has been reached. Execution cannot be resumed. The corresponding element of *rgRowStatus* contains DBROWSTATUS_E_LIMITREACHED.

- The rowset ran out of memory and was unable to fetch the row. The corresponding element of *rgRowStatus* contains DBROWSTATUS_E_OUTOFMEMORY.

- The consumer did not have sufficient permission to fetch a row. The corresponding element of *rgRowStatus* contains DBROWSTATUS_E_PERMISSIONDENIED.

E_FAIL

A provider-specific error occurred.

E_INVALIDARG

rghRows was a null pointer.

rgcbBookmarks or *rgpBookmarks* was a null pointer.

E_OUTOFMEMORY

The provider was unable to allocate sufficient memory in which to return the row handles.

E_UNEXPECTED

ITransaction::Commit or **ITransaction::Abort** was called and the object is in a zombie state.

DB_E_ERRORSOCCURRED

Errors occurred while fetching all of the rows. Errors can occur for the reasons listed under DB_S_ERRORSOCCURRED.

DB_E_NOTREENTRANT

The consumer called this method while it was processing a notification, and it is an error to call this method while processing the specified DBREASON value.

DB_E_ROWSNOTRELEASED

The provider requires release of existing rows before new ones can be fetched. For more information, see DBPROP_CANHOLDROWS in "Rowset Properties" in Appendix C.

Comments

GetRowsByBookmark increments the reference count of each row for which it returns a handle by one. Thus, if a handle is returned for a row that has already been fetched, the reference count of that row will be greater than one. **ReleaseRows** must be called once for each time the handle to a row has been returned.

If the provider encounters a problem fetching a row—for example, data stored in a text file contains a letter in a numeric column—**GetRowsByBookmark** fetches the row normally, returns the row handle, and returns S_OK. However, when the consumer calls **IRowset::GetData** for the row, the provider returns DBSTATUS_E_CANTCONVERTVALUE as the status for the offending column.

If **GetRowsByBookmark** encounters an error while attempting to fetch a row, such as a bad bookmark or the row has been deleted, it notes the error in the *rgRowStatus* array, continues processing, and returns DB_S_ERRORSOCCURRED or DB_E_ERRORSOCCURRED. Although the rows are fetched in undefined order, the ordering of the error array must match the order of the bookmark array, so the consumer can perform a side-by-side scan of each array to determine which rows were not fetched.

For information about what **GetRowsByBookmark** does when it fetches a row that it already has in its internal buffers, see "Uniqueness of Rows in the Rowset" in Chapter 4. For information about whether **GetRowsByBookmark** can detect changes made to rows in the rowset, see "Visibility of Changes" in Chapter 5.

See Also

IRowset::GetData, **IRowset::GetNextRows**, **IRowsetLocate::GetRowsAt**, **IRowsetScroll::GetRowsAtRatio**

IRowsetLocate::Hash

Returns hash values for the specified bookmarks.

HRESULT Hash (
HCHAPTER	*hReserved*,
ULONG	*cBookmarks*,
const ULONG	*rgcbBookmarks*[],
const BYTE *	*rgpBookmarks*[],
DWORD	*rgHashedValues*[],
DBROWSTATUS	*rgBookmarkStatus*[]);

Parameters

hReserved [in]

Reserved for future use. Providers ignore this parameter.

cBookmarks

The number of bookmarks to hash. If *cBookmarks* is zero, **Hash** does not do anything.

rgcbBookmarks [in]

An array containing the length in bytes for each bookmark.

rgpBookmarks [in]

An array of pointers to bookmarks. The bookmarks cannot be standard bookmarks (DBBMK_FIRST, DBBMK_LAST, DBBMK_INVALID). If *rgpBookmarks* contains a duplicate bookmark, a hash value is returned once for each occurrence of the bookmark.

Caution The consumer must ensure that all bookmarks in *rgpBookmarks* are valid. The provider is not required to validate bookmarks before hashing them. Thus, hash values might be returned for invalid bookmarks.

---

rgHashedValues [out]

An array of *cBookmarks* hash values corresponding to the elements of *rgpBookmarks*. The consumer allocates, but is not required to initialize, memory for this array and passes the address of this memory to the provider. The provider returns the hash values in the array.

rgBookmarkStatus [out]

An array with *cBookmarks* elements in which to return values indicating the status of each bookmark specified in *rgpBookmarks*. If no errors occur while hashing a bookmark, the corresponding element of *rgBookmarkStatus* is set to DBROWSTATUS_S_OK. If an error occurs while hashing a bookmark, the corresponding element is set as specified in DB_S_ERRORSOCCURRED. The consumer allocates memory for this array but is not required to initialize it. If *rgBookmarkStatus* is a null pointer, no bookmark statuses are returned. For information about the DBROWSTATUS enumerated type, see "Arrays of Errors" in Chapter 13.

Return Code

S_OK

The method succeeded. All bookmarks were successfully hashed. The following value can be returned in *rgRowStatus*:

- The bookmark was successfully hashed. The corresponding element of *rgRowStatus* contains DBROWSTATUS_S_OK.

DB_S_ERRORSOCCURRED

An error occurred while hashing a bookmark, but at least one bookmark was successfully hashed. Successes can occur for the reason listed under S_OK. The following errors can occur:

- An element of *rgpBookmarks* pointed to an invalid or incorrectly formed bookmark. The corresponding element of *rgBookmarkStatus* contains DBROWSTATUS_E_INVALID. Providers are not required to check for this condition, because doing so might slow the method significantly.

- An element of *rgcbBookmarks* was zero. The corresponding element of *rgBookmarkStatus* contains DBROWSTATUS_E_INVALID.

- An element of *rgpBookmarks* was a null pointer. The corresponding element of *rgBookmarkStatus* contains DBROWSTATUS_E_INVALID.

- An element of *rgpBookmarks* pointed to a standard bookmark (DBBMK_FIRST, DBBMK_LAST, DBBMK_INVALID). The corresponding element of *rgBookmarkStatus* contains DBROWSTATUS_E_INVALID.

E_FAIL

A provider-specific error occurred.

E_INVALIDARG

cBookmarks was not zero and *rgcbBookmarks* or *rgpBookmarks* was a null pointer.

rgHashedValues was a null pointer.

E_UNEXPECTED

ITransaction::Commit or **ITransaction::Abort** was called and the object is in a zombie state.

DB_E_ERRORSOCCURRED

Errors occurred while hashing all of the bookmarks. Errors can occur for the reasons listed under DB_S_ERRORSOCCURRED.

DB_E_NOTREENTRANT

The provider called a method from **IRowsetNotify** in the consumer and the method has not yet returned.

Comments

This method makes no logical change to the state of the object.

If two bookmarks point to the same underlying row, the same hash value is returned for both bookmarks. That is, if **Compare** returns DBCOMPARE_EQ for two bookmarks, **Hash** must return the same value for these two bookmarks.

If **Hash** encounters an error while attempting to hash a bookmark, such as a bad bookmark, it notes the error in the error array, continues processing, and returns DB_S_ERRORSOCCURRED or DB_E_ERRORSOCCURRED. Although the rows are hashed in undefined order, the ordering of the error array must match the order of the bookmark array, so the consumer can perform a side-by-side scan of each array to determine which rows were not hashed.

Hash can hash any valid bookmarks. The consumer is not required to have permission to read the corresponding row, nor is the row even required to exist—for example, it might have been deleted.

Standard bookmarks cannot be hashed.

See Also

IRowsetLocate::Compare

IRowsetNotify

IRowsetNotify is the *callback* interface that a *consumer* must support to connect to local notifications provided by a rowset. The notifications are intended to synchronize objects which are attached to the same rowset instance. The notifications do not reflect changes in underlying shared tables that occur through other programs or users.

The notifications use the standard OLE connection point scheme for events. A rowset supports **IConnectionPointContainer** and the consumer calls **FindConnectionPoint** for IID_IRowsetNotify to obtain the correct **IConnectionPoint** interface. The consumer then advises that connection point to connect and supplies a pointer to the consumer's **IRowsetNotify** interface.

For more information about notifications, see Chapter 9, "Notifications."

When to Implement

IRowsetNotify is implemented by consumers that require notification. If the command requests support for **IConnectionPointContainer**, then the rowset is required to support a connection point for **IRowsetNotify**. Providers should implement this connection point if they expect to work directly with general purpose consumers.

Notification about transactions is not handled through rowsets. There may be multiple rowsets for each transaction, leading to a flood of events. Consumers that need to be notified of transaction activity should connect to the transaction coordinator. For more information, see "Notification Events" in Chapter 12.

IRowset is a prerequisite for notification.

DBEVENTPHASE

Events may have phases. A phased event is a notification method which is called multiple times, each time with a different phase in the sequence. Some events do not have phases. The phases are similar to phases in two-phase commit protocol, because ensuring that all controls authorize and succeed in handling an event is a problem very similar to ensuring resource managers all agree to, and succeed in, committing a transaction.

In the following descriptions, all consumer objects that connect their **IRowsetNotify** interface to the rowset are the *listeners*.

Value	Description
DBEVENTPHASE_ OKTODO	Informs a listener of an impending event. All listeners must return S_OK from DBEVENTPHASE_OKTODO for the event to proceed. Any listener can cancel the event by returning S_FALSE. The listener can prepare for the event, but should do nothing irreversible or time consuming.

Value	Description
DBEVENTPHASE_ OKTODO (*continued*)	If a listener cancels the event, all listeners that have already been called will be called again with DBEVENTPHASE_FAILEDTODO.
DBEVENTPHASE_ ABOUTTODO	Informs a listener that DBEVENTPHASE_OKTODO has been approved and all listeners can proceed to final preparations which must be reversible, but which may be lengthy. The listener should cancel this phase only if it is stopped by an error; it should have cleared all logical objections at the earlier DBEVENTPHASE_OKTODO phase.
	If a listener cancels the event by returning S_FALSE, all listeners that have already been called will be called again with DBEVENTPHASE_FAILEDTODO.
DBEVENTPHASE_ SYNCHAFTER	Informs a listener that the event has occurred after the rowset's copy of the row has been modified, but before the data source has received the change. The listener can synchronize itself with the rowset and ensure that it has no physical reason not to agree to commit the event's changes.
	If a listener cancels the event by returning S_FALSE, all listeners that have already been called will be called again with DBEVENTPHASE_FAILEDTODO.
DBEVENTPHASE_ FAILEDTODO	The event occurs. If the event fails, the connection point calls DBEVENTPHASE_FAILEDTODO in all connected listeners, including the listener that canceled the event. The listener should reverse all changes and synchronize with the state of the rowset.
DBEVENTPHASE_ DIDEVENT	Informs a listener that all consumers have synchronized themselves and agreed to commit the event's changes. The listener should now commit its changes. It must comply.

The final phase of an event is always either DBEVENTPHASE_FAILEDTODO or DBEVENTPHASE_DIDEVENT. If the event has no phases, it is equivalent to DBEVENTPHASE_DIDEVENT.

All providers must support the DBEVENTPHASE_FAILEDTODO and DBEVENTPHASE_DIDEVENT phases. Whether providers support DBEVENTPHASE_OKTODO, DBEVENTPHASE_ABOUTTODO, and DBEVENTPHASE_SYNCHAFTER is provider specific, although all but the most simple providers support these phases. To determine which phases a provider supports, a consumer calls **IDBProperties::GetProperties** for the DBPROP_NOTIFICATIONPHASES property.

If a method changes multiple rows and generates a single-phased event, such as DBREASON_ROW_ACTIVATE or DBREASON_ROW_RELEASE, the provider makes a single call to **IRowsetNotify::OnRowChange** and passes an array containing the handles of all of the affected rows.

If a method changes multiple rows and generates a multi-phased event, such as DBREASON_ROW_UPDATE or DBREASON_ROW_UNDOCHANGE, the number of calls to **OnRowChange** for each phase depends on the DBPROP_NOTIFICATIONGRANULARITY property.

DBREASON

Reasons are fine tunings of events. The receiver of events is expected to care only about the general effect of the event, but there may be other effects which more specialized consumers need to know about. The DBEVENT is the basic event, and the DBREASON is a single level of derived subevent.

Important The DBREASON types may be expanded in later versions of OLE DB. **IRowsetNotify** methods must return S_OK or DB_S_UNWANTEDREASON when they receive a DBREASON value they do not recognize.

Providers are not expected to add new DBREASONs to the defined set. Providers defining new DBREASONs should do so through an entirely new notification interface with its own IID.

The following **#define** values are valid for DBREASON:

Value	Description
DBREASON_ ROWSET_ FETCHPOSITIONCHANGE	The next fetch position changed as a result of a call to **IRowset::GetNextRows** or **IRowset::RestartPosition**. All phases can occur.
DBREASON_ ROWSET_RELEASE	The rowset is being released; that is, its reference count is zero. Only the DBEVENTPHASE_DIDEVENT phase occurs. The rowset no longer exists when this event is sent out, so recipients must not make any calls upon it. Due to OLE rules, there is no way to deny permission to **IUnknown::Release**.
DBREASON_ ROWSET_CHANGED	The rowset metadata has changed.
	Pointers to interfaces on the rowset remain valid.
	Providers must revalidate accessors against the metadata and this might fail due to the changes in the metadata. For example, the accessor might now specify an unsupported conversion.
	Handles to rows might no longer be valid. For example, **IRowset::GetData** might return DB_E_BADROWHANDLE or **IRowsetUpdate::Update** might return DBROWSTATUS_E_INVALID. The result of passing such a row handle is provider-specific, although the provider cannot terminate abnormally.
DBREASON_ COLUMN_SET	A column value is set. All phases can occur.

Value	Description
DBREASON_ COLUMN_RECALCULATED	A calculated column takes a new value because its input columns change. Only the DBEVENTPHASE_DIDEVENT phase occurs.
DBREASON_ ROW_ACTIVATE	A function, such as **IRowset::GetNextRows** or **IRowsetLocate::GetRowsAt**, caused a new set of rows to be fetched. Only the DBEVENTPHASE_DIDEVENT phase occurs.
DBREASON_ ROW_RELEASE	**IRowset::ReleaseRows** was called and the row's reference count is zero. The array of row handles the provider passed to the listeners is the subset of the original array of row handles passed to **ReleaseRows**; that is, those row handles for which the reference count is zero. Only the DBEVENTPHASE_DIDEVENT phase occurs. The returned row handles might be invalid and, therefore, should not be used with any methods.
DBREASON_ ROW_DELETE	**IRowsetChange::DeleteRows** has been called. All phases can occur.
DBREASON_ ROW_FIRSTCHANGE	The first time any column in the row is set, this notification occurs. It precedes DBREASON_COLUMN_SET. All phases can occur. This event occurs only when the rowset is in delayed update mode. It occurs the first time a column in a row is modified after the row was fetched or after the last call to **IRowsetUpdate::Update**, whichever is more recent. A call to **IRowsetUpdate::Undo** does not clear the DBREASON_ROW_FIRSTCHANGE status.
DBREASON_ ROW_INSERT	**IRowsetChange::InsertRow** has been called. All phases can occur.
DBREASON_ ROW_RESYNCH	**IRowsetResynch::ResynchRows** has been called. All phases can occur.
DBREASON_ ROW_UNDOCHANGE	**IRowsetUpdate::Undo** has been called on a pending change row. All phases can occur.
DBREASON_ ROW_UNDOINSERT	**IRowsetUpdate::Undo** has been called on an pending insert row. All phases can occur.
DBREASON_ ROW_UNDODELETE	**IRowsetUpdate::Undo** has been called on a pending delete row. All phases can occur.
DBREASON_ ROW_UPDATE	**IRowsetUpdate::Update** has been called. All phases can occur.

The following table lists all rowset methods, the DBREASON values they generate, and the phases for each reason. Nested notifications occur when the consumer calls another rowset method while processing a notification.

Method	DBREASON Generated [1]	Phases
IUnknown::AddRef	None	N/A
IUnknown::QueryInterface	None	N/A
IUnknown::Release	_ROWSET_RELEASE	DIDEVENT
IRowset::AddRefRows	None	N/A
IRowset::GetData	None	N/A
IRowset::GetNextRows	_ROW_ACTIVATE	DIDEVENT
	_ROWSET_FETCHPOSITION CHANGE	All Phases
IRowset::ReleaseRows	_ROW_RELEASE	DIDEVENT
IRowset::RestartPosition	_ROWSET_FETCHPOSITION CHANGE	All Phases
	_ROWSET_CHANGED [2]	All Phases
IRowsetChange::DeleteRows	_ROW_DELETE	All Phases
IRowsetChange::InsertRow	_ROW_INSERT	All Phases
IRowsetChange::SetData	_ROW_FIRSTCHANGE [3]	All Phases
	_COLUMN_SET	All Phases
	COLUMN RECALCULATED	DIDEVENT
IRowsetIndex::Seek	_ROWSET_FETCHPOSITION CHANGE	All Phases
IRowsetLocate::Compare	None	--
IRowsetLocate::GetRowsAt	_ROW_ACTIVATE	DIDEVENT
IRowsetLocate:: GetRowsByBookmark	_ROW_ACTIVATE	DIDEVENT
IRowsetLocate::Hash	None	N/A
IRowsetResynch::GetVisibleData	None	N/A
IRowsetResynch::ResynchRows	_ROW_RESYNCH	All Phases

Method	DBREASON Generated [1]	Phases
IRowsetScroll:: GetApproximatePosition	None	N/A
IRowsetScroll::GetRowsAtRatio	_ROW_ACTIVATE	DIDEVENT
IRowsetUpdate::GetOriginalData	None	N/A
IRowsetUpdate::GetPendingRows	None	N/A
IRowsetUpdate::Undo	_ROW_UNDOCHANGE	All Phases
	_ROW_UNDOINSERT	All Phases
	_ROW_UNDODELETE	All Phases
IRowsetUpdate::Update	_ROW_UPDATE	All Phases
All other rowset methods	None	N/A

[1] Methods only generate the listed DBREASON values, even though other reasons might seem appropriate. For example, **InsertRow** only generates DBREASON_ROW_INSERT even though DBREASON_COLUMN_SET, DBREASON_ROW_FIRSTCHANGE, and DBREASON_ROW_ACTIVATE might appear to be applicable.

[2] **IRowset::RestartPosition** generates this DBREASON only when the metadata for the columns has changed.

[3] DBREASON_ROW_FIRSTCHANGE is only generated the first time a column in the row is changed. For more information, see the table earlier in this section.

Method	Description
OnFieldChange	Notifies the consumer on any change to the value of a column.
OnRowChange	Notifies the consumer on the first change to a row, or any change that affects the entire row.
OnRowsetChange	Notifies the consumer on any change affecting the entire rowset.

IRowsetNotify::OnFieldChange

Notifies the consumer on any change to the value of a column.

HRESULT OnFieldChange (
    IRowset*   *pRowset,*
    HROW   *hRow,*
    ULONG   *cColumns,*
    ULONG   *rgColumns[],*
    DBREASON   *eReason,*
    DBEVENTPHASE *ePhase,*
    BOOL   *fCantDeny)*;

Parameters

pRowset [in]

A pointer to the rowset, because the consumer may be receiving notifications from multiple rowsets and this identifies which one is calling.

hRow [in]

The handle of the row in which the column value was changed. After this method returns, the reference count of this row will be unchanged unless the consumer explicitly changes it. This is different from other methods that return rows to the consumer, in which the provider explicitly increments the reference count. Therefore, if the consumer wants to guarantee that this row handle is valid after this method returns, it must call **IRowset::AddRefRows** for the row while it is processing this method.

cColumns [in]

The count of columns in *rgColumns*.

rgColumns [in]

An array of columns in the row for which the value was changed.

eReason [in]

The reason of the event that caused this change. If this value is not recognized by the method, the method returns S_OK or DB_S_UNWANTEDREASON.

ePhase [in]

The phase of this notification.

fCantDeny [in]

When this flag is set to TRUE, the consumer cannot veto the event by returning S_FALSE because the provider cannot undo the event.

Return Code

S_OK

The method succeeded.

S_FALSE

The event/phase is vetoed by reason of logical objection or a failure to be able to implement.

DB_S_UNWANTEDPHASE

The consumer is not interested in receiving this phase for this reason. The provider can optimize by making no further calls with this reason and phase. The phases for other reasons are unaffected.

DB_S_UNWANTEDREASON

The consumer is not interested in receiving any phases for this reason. The provider can optimize by making no further calls with this reason.

E_FAIL

A provider-specific error occurred.

Comments

Possible reasons are DBREASON_COLUMN_SET and DBREASON_COLUMN_RECALCULATED.

All phases can occur for a DBREASON_COLUMN_SET event. The new value is visible beginning with the DBEVENTPHASE_SYNCHAFTER phase. For a DBREASON_COLUMN_RECALCULATED event, only the DBEVENTPHASE_DIDEVENT phase occurs.

Setting a column to its current value may, but is not required to, generate a notification for that column.

See Also

IRowsetNotify::OnRowChange, IRowsetNotify::OnRowsetChange

IRowsetNotify::OnRowChange

Notifies the consumer on the first change to a row, or any change that affects the entire row.

HRESULT OnRowChange (
    IRowset*   *pRowset,*
    ULONG   *cRows,*
    const HROW   *rghRows[],*
    DBREASON   *eReason,*
    DBEVENTPHASE *ePhase,*
    BOOL   *fCantDeny*);

Parameters

pRowset [in]

A pointer to the rowset, because the consumer may be receiving notifications from multiple rowsets and this identifies which one is calling.

cRows [in]

The count of row handles in *rghRows*.

rghRows [in]

An array of handles of rows that are changing. This array belongs to the caller (rowset) and must not be freed or used beyond the duration of the method call.

After this method returns, the reference count of these rows will be unchanged unless the consumer explicitly changes them. This is different from other methods that return rows to the consumer, in which the provider explicitly increments the reference counts. Therefore, if the consumer wants to guarantee that these row handles are valid after this method returns, it must call **IRowset::AddRefRows** for these rows while it is processing this method.

eReason [in]

The reason of the event which caused this change. If this value is not recognized by the method, the method returns S_OK or DB_S_UNWANTEDREASON.

ePhase [in]

The phase of this notification.

fCantDeny [in]

When this flag is set to TRUE, the consumer cannot veto the event by returning S_FALSE because the provider cannot undo the event.

Return Code

S_OK

The method succeeded.

S_FALSE

The event/phase is vetoed by reason of logical objection or a failure to be able to implement, as permitted for the phase.

DB_S_UNWANTEDPHASE

The consumer is not interested in receiving this phase for this reason. The provider can optimize by making no further calls with this reason and phase. The phases for other reasons are unaffected.

DB_S_UNWANTEDREASON

The consumer is not interested in receiving any phases for this reason. The provider can optimize by making no further calls with this reason.

E_FAIL

A provider-specific error occurred.

Comments

Possible reasons are any of the DBREASON_ROW_* reasons.

Phases occur as documented for the DBREASON enumeration. Prior values remain in the row up to and including the DBEVENTPHASE_ABOUTTODO phase. The new value is visible with the DBEVENTPHASE_SYNCHAFTER or later phases.

When a DBREASON_ROW_ACTIVATE notification is triggered, the array of row handles passed to **OnRowChange** is exactly the order in which the rows were fetched.

See Also

IRowsetNotify::OnFieldChange, **IRowsetNotify::OnRowsetChange**

IRowsetNotify::OnRowsetChange

Notifies the consumer on any change affecting the entire rowset.

HRESULT OnRowsetChange (
    IRowset*   *pRowset*,
    DBREASON   *eReason*,
    DBEVENTPHASE *ePhase*,
    BOOL   *fCantDeny*);

Parameters

pRowset [in]

A pointer to the rowset, because the consumer may be receiving notifications from multiple rowsets and this identifies which one is calling.

eReason [in]

The reason for the event that caused this change. If this value is not recognized by the method, the method returns S_OK or DB_S_UNWANTEDREASON.

ePhase [in]

The phase of this notification.

fCantDeny [in]

When this flag is set to TRUE, the consumer cannot veto the event by returning S_FALSE because the provider cannot undo the event.

Return Code

S_OK

The method succeeded.

S_FALSE

The event/phase is vetoed by reason of logical objection or a failure to be able to implement.

DB_S_UNWANTEDPHASE

The consumer is not interested in receiving this phase for this reason. The provider can optimize by making no further calls with this reason and phase. The phases for other reasons are unaffected.

DB_S_UNWANTEDREASON

The consumer is not interested in receiving any phases for this reason. The provider can optimize by making no further calls with this reason.

Comments

Possible reasons are DBREASON_ROWSET_RELEASED.

No phases occur; this method is equivalent to DBEVENTPHASE_DIDEVENT.

See Also

IRowsetNotify::OnFieldChange, **IRowsetNotify::OnRowChange**

IRowsetResynch

IRowsetResynch is used to retrieve the values for rows that are currently visible to the transaction.

When to Implement

IRowsetResynch is optional. If it is exposed, the rowset must also expose **IRowsetIdentity**.

To support **IRowsetResynch**, the provider must be able to get the latest value of the data that is visible to the transaction. If the value of the DBPROP_OTHERUPDATEDELETE property is VARIANT_TRUE, such as when the rowset is implemented on top of a dynamic or keyset-driven cursor in ODBC, the rowset can do this by the mechanism it uses to fetch rows from the server. However, if the value of DBPROP_OTHERUPDATEDELETE is VARIANT_FALSE, such as when the rowset is implemented on top of a static cursor in ODBC, the rowset must have another mechanism for retrieving data from the data source, such as executing a separate command to retrieve the currently visible values. If the rowset does not have such a mechanism, it cannot support this interface.

When to Call

IRowsetResynch is used to synchronize rows in the rowset with those in the data source. The primary uses of **IRowsetResynch** are:

- To implement optimistic concurrency.
- To perform row fix-up in a disconnected environment.

IRowsetResynch is useful only at isolation levels lower than Repeatable Read. For isolation levels Repeatable Read and higher, the data that is currently visible for a row that has already been read does not change.

If the consumer requests **IRowsetResynch**, it is exposed regardless of the isolation level, even though it is not useful at isolation levels Repeatable Read and higher. This allows consumers to develop common code independent of their isolation level.

Method	Description
GetVisibleData	Gets the data in the data source that is visible to the transaction for the specified row.
ResynchRows	Gets the data in the data source that is visible to the transaction for the specified rows and updates the rowset's copies of those rows.

IRowsetResynch::GetVisibleData

Gets the data in the data source that is visible to the transaction for the specified row.

HRESULT GetVisibleData (
    HROW   *hRow,*
    HACCESSOR *hAccessor,*
    void *   *pData);*

Parameters

hRow [in]

    The handle of the row for which to get the visible data. This can be the handle of a row with a pending delete.

hAccessor [in]

    The handle of the accessor to use. If *hAccessor* is the handle of a null accessor (*cBindings* in **IAccessor::CreateAccessor** was zero), then **GetVisibleData** does not get any data values.

pData [out]

    A pointer to a buffer in which to return the data. The consumer allocates memory for this buffer.

Return Code

S_OK

    The method succeeded. The status of all columns bound by the accessor is set to DBSTATUS_S_OK, DBSTATUS_S_ISNULL, or DBSTATUS_S_TRUNCATED.

DB_S_ERRORSOCCURRED

    An error occurred while returning data for one or more columns, but data was successfully returned for at least one column. To determine the columns for which data was returned, the consumer checks the status values. For a list of status values that can be returned by this method, see "Status Values Used When Getting Data" in "Status" in Chapter 6.

E_FAIL

    A provider-specific error occurred.

E_INVALIDARG

    pData was a null pointer and *hAccessor* was not a null accessor.

E_UNEXPECTED

    ITransaction::Commit or **ITransaction::Abort** was called and the object is in a zombie state.

DB_E_BADACCESSORHANDLE

    hAccessor was invalid. It is possible for a reference accessor or an accessor that has a binding that uses provider-owned memory to be invalid for use with this method, even if the accessor is valid for use with **IRowset::GetData** or **IRowsetChange::SetData**.

DB_E_BADACCESSORTYPE
The specified accessor was not a row accessor.

DB_E_BADROWHANDLE
hRow was invalid.

DB_E_DELETEDROW
hRow referred to a row for which a deletion had been transmitted to the data source.

DB_E_ERRORSOCCURRED
Errors occurred while returning data for all columns. To determine what errors occurred, the consumer checks the status values. For a list of status values that can be returned by this method, see "Status Values Used When Getting Data" in "Status" in Chapter 6.

DB_E_ABORTLIMITREACHED
The provider was unable to retrieve the visible data due to reaching a limit on the server, such as a query execution timing out.

DB_E_NEWLYINSERTED
DBPROP_STRONGIDENTITY was VARIANT_FALSE and *hRow* referred to a row for which an insertion had been transmitted to the data source.

DB_E_NOTREENTRANT
The provider called a method from **IRowsetNotify** in the consumer and the method has not yet returned.

DB_E_PENDINGINSERT
The rowset was in delayed update mode and *hRow* referred to a pending insert row.

If this method performs deferred accessor validation and that validation takes places before any data is transferred, it can also return any of the following return codes for the applicable reasons listed in the corresponding DBBINDSTATUS values in **IAccessor::CreateAccessor**:

E_NOINTERFACE
DB_E_BADBINDINFO
DB_E_BADORDINAL
DB_E_BADSTORAGEFLAGS
DB_E_UNSUPPORTEDCONVERSION

Comments

This method makes no logical change to the state of the object.

A consumer calls **GetVisibleData** to retrieve the data in the data source that is visible to the transaction for the specified row. However, **GetVisibleData** does not affect the values in the rowset's copy of the row. For a complete description of how **GetVisibleData** retrieves data, see "Getting Data" in Chapter 6. For a description of what values will be retrieved, see **ResynchRows**.

OLE objects and storage objects over BLOBs are limited to the versioning facilities built into the storage interfaces.

The purpose of this optional service, generally combined with **IRowsetUpdate::GetOriginalData**, is to allow consumers to repair or display collisions occuring with optimistic updates. It is not necessarily recommended as the best or only way to recover; the best strategy depends on the kind of transaction.

If **GetVisibleData** fails, the memory to which *pData* points is not freed but its contents are undefined. If, before **GetVisibleData** failed, the provider allocated any memory for return to the consumer, the provider frees this memory and does not return it to the consumer.

GetVisibleData does not enforce any security restrictions. The provider must not create a rowset that includes columns for which the consumer does not have read privileges, so **GetVisibleData** never encounters problems accessing the data for a column. Note that the rowset can contain columns to which the consumer does not have write permission if DBPROP_COLUMNRESTRICT is VARIANT_TRUE. The methods that fetch rows must not return the handles of rows for which the consumer does not have read privileges, so **GetVisibleData** never encounters problems accessing a row. Note that such rows might exist if the DBPROP_ROWRESTRICT property is VARIANT_TRUE.

See Also

IRowset::GetData, **IRowsetUpdate::GetOriginalData**, **IRowsetResynch::ResynchRows**

IRowsetResynch::ResynchRows

Gets the data in the data source that is visible to the transaction for the specified rows and updates the rowset's copies of those rows.

HRESULT ResynchRows (
    ULONG   *cRows,*
    const HROW   *rghRows[],*
    ULONG*   *pcRowsResynched,*
    HROW**   *prghRowsResynched,*
    DBROWSTATUS** *prgRowStatus);*

Parameters

cRows [in]

The count of rows to resynchronize. If *cRows* is zero, **ResynchRows** ignores *rghRows* and reads the current value of all active rows.

rghRows [in]

An array of *cRows* row handles to be resynchronized. If *cRows* is zero, this argument is ignored.

pcRowsResynched [out]

A pointer to memory in which to return the number of rows the method attempted to resynchronize. The caller may supply a null pointer if no list is desired. If an error occurs, the provider sets **pcRowsResynched* to zero.

prghRowsResynched [out]

A pointer to memory in which to return the array of row handles the method attempted to resynchronize. If *cRows* is not zero, then the elements of this array are in one-to-one correspondence with those of *rghRows*. If *cRows* is zero, the elements of this array are the handles of all active rows in the rowset. When *cRows* is zero, **ResynchRows** will add to the reference count of the rows whose handles are returned in *prghRowsResynched*.

The rowset allocates memory for the handles and the client should release this memory with **IMalloc::Free** when no longer needed. This argument is ignored if *pcRowsResynched* is a null pointer and must not be a null pointer otherwise. If **pcRowsResynched* is 0 on output or the method fails, the provider does not allocate any memory and ensures that **prghRowsResynched* is a null pointer on output.

prgRowStatus [out]

A pointer to memory in which to return an array of row status values. The elements of this array correspond one-to-one with the elements of **prghRowsResynched*. If no errors occur while resynchronizing a row, the corresponding element of **prgRowStatus* is set to DBROWSTATUS_S_OK. If an error occurs while resynchronizing a row, the corresponding element is set as specified in DB_S_ERRORSOCCURRED. If *prgRowStatus* is a null pointer, no row status values are returned.

The rowset allocates memory for the row status values and returns the address to this memory; the client releases this memory with **IMalloc::Free** when it is no longer needed. This argument is ignored if *pcRowsResynched* is a null pointer. If *pcRowsResynched* is zero on output or the method fails, the provider does not allocate any memory and ensures that *prgRowStatus* is a null pointer on output.

Return Code

S_OK

The method succeeded. All rows were successfully resynchronized. The following value can be returned in *prgRowStatus*:

- The row was successfully resynchronized. The corresponding element of *prgRowStatus* contains DBROWSTATUS_S_OK.

DB_S_ERRORSOCCURRED

An error occurred while resynchronizing a row, but at least one row was successfully resynchronized. Successes can occur for the reason listed under S_OK. The following errors can occur:

- An element of *rghRows* was invalid or referred to a row that this thread does not have access to. The corresponding element of *prgRowStatus* contains DBROWSTATUS_E_INVALID.

- Resynchronizing a row was canceled during notification. The row was not resynchronized and the corresponding element of *prgRowStatus* contains DBROWSTATUS_E_CANCELED.

- An element of *rghRows* referred to a row for which a deletion had been transmitted to the data source. The corresponding element of *prgRowStatus* contains DBROWSTATUS_E_DELETED.

- The row was not resynchronized due to reaching a limit on the server, such as a query execution timing out. The error in the corresponding element of *prgRowStatus* contains DBROWSTATUS_E_LIMITREACHED.

- An element of *rghRows* referred to a row on which a storage object was open. The corresponding element of *prgRowStatus* contains DBROWSTATUS_E_OBJECTOPEN.

- An element of *rghRows* referred to a pending insert row. The corresponding element of *prgRowStatus* contains DBROWSTATUS_E_PENDINGINSERT.

- DBPROP_STRONGIDENTITY was VARIANT_FALSE and an element of *rghRows* referred to a row for which an insertion had been transmitted to the data source. The row was not resynchronized and the corresponding element of *prgRowStatus* contains DBROWSTATUS_E_NEWLYINSERTED.

E_FAIL

A provider-specific error occurred.

E_INVALIDARG

cRows was not zero and *rghRows* was a null pointer.

pcRowsResynched was not a null pointer and *prghRowsResynched* was a null pointer.

E_UNEXPECTED

ITransaction::Commit or **ITransaction::Abort** was called and the object is in a zombie state.

DB_E_ERRORSOCCURRED

Errors occurred while resynchronizing all of the rows. Errors can occur for the reasons listed under DB_S_ERRORSOCCURRED.

DB_E_NOTREENTRANT

The provider called a method from **IRowsetNotify** in the consumer and the method has not yet returned.

DB_SEC_E_PERMISSIONDENIED

The consumer did not have sufficient permission to resynchronize the rows.

Comments

ResynchRows refreshes the values in the rowset's copy of each of the specified rows with the currently visible contents of the underlying row. Changes made to the row by the current transaction are always visible to **ResynchRows,** including changes made by other rowsets in the same transaction. Whether changes made by other transactions are visible to **ResynchRows** depends on the isolation level of the current transaction. Thus, **ResynchRows** uses values as follows:

- **Read Uncommitted**. The changes most recently made, committed or uncommitted, by any transaction are used. If no changes have been made by any transaction, the original row is used.

- **Read Committed**. The changes most recently made by the current transaction or committed by other transactions are used. If no changes have been made by the current transaction or committed by other transactions, the original row is used.

- **Repeatable Read and higher**. The changes most recently made by the current transaction are used. If no changes have been made by the current transaction, the original row is used.

If a specified row has been deleted from the data source and this deletion is visible, **ResynchRows** returns DBROWSTATUS_E_DELETED in the error status array for the row and the row is treated as a deleted row.

Any changes transmitted to the data source are not lost; they will be committed or aborted when the transaction is committed or aborted. All pending changes are lost because they they exist only in the rowset's copy of the row and **ResynchRows** overwrites the contents of this copy. The pending change status is removed from the row.

If **ResynchRows** encounters an error while attempting to resynchronize a row, such as a bad row handle, it notes the error in *prgRowStatus*, continues processing, and returns DB_S_ERRORSOCCURRED or DB_E_ERRORSOCCURRED. Although the rows are resynchronized in undefined order, the ordering of *prgRowStatus* must match the order of the row handle array, so the consumer can perform a side-by-side scan of each array to determine which rows were not resynchronized.

If *cRows* is zero and *pcRowsResynched* and *prghRowsResynched* are not null pointers, **ResynchRows** adds to the reference count of the rows it returns in *prghRowsResynched* to ensure that the consumer has these row handles.

See Also

IRowsetResynch::GetVisibleData

IRowsetScroll : IRowsetLocate

IRowsetScroll enables consumers to fetch rows at approximate positions in the rowset.

When to Implement

IRowsetScroll is required for all providers that intend to support general consumers. It is implemented for rowsets intended to work smoothly with long lists browsed directly by the user interface.

IRowsetScroll implies **IRowsetLocate**.

When to Call

IRowsetScroll enables consumers to fetch rows located at approximate positions within a rowset. This method can be used for cases where precise positioning is not critical.

Method	Description
GetApproximatePosition	Gets the approximate position of a row corresponding to a specified bookmark.
GetRowsAtRatio	Fetches rows starting from a fractional position in the rowset.

IRowsetScroll::GetApproximatePosition

Gets the approximate position of a row corresponding to a specified bookmark.

HRESULT GetApproximatePosition (
HCHAPTER	*hReserved*,
ULONG	*cbBookmark*,
const BYTE *	*pBookmark*,
ULONG *	*pulPosition*,
ULONG *	*pcRows*);

Parameters

hReserved [in]

Reserved for future use. Providers ignore this parameter.

cbBookmark [in]

The length in bytes of the bookmark. If this is zero, then *pBookmark* is ignored, **pcRows* is set to the count of rows, and no position is returned in **pulPosition*.

pBookmark [in]

A pointer to a bookmark that identifies the row of which to find the position. This can be a pointer to DBBMK_FIRST or DBBMK_LAST. The consumer is not required to have permission to read the row.

pulPosition [out]

A pointer to memory in which to return the position of the row identified by the bookmark. The returned number is one-based; that is, the first row in the rowset is one and the last row is equal to **pcRows*. If **pcRows* is zero, the provider sets **pulPosition* to zero also, regardless of the bookmark that was passed. If *pulPosition* is a null pointer, no position is returned. In case of error, **pulPosition* is not changed.

pcRows [out]

A pointer to memory in which to return the total number of rows. This number is zero if there are no rows. If *pcRows* is a null pointer, no count of rows is returned. In case of error, **pcRows* is not changed.

Return Code

S_OK

The method succeeded.

E_FAIL

A provider-specific error occurred.

E_INVALIDARG

cbBookmark was not zero and *pBookmark* was a null pointer.

E_UNEXPECTED

ITransaction::Commit or **ITransaction::Abort** was called and the object is in a zombie state.

DB_E_BADBOOKMARK
> *pBookmark* was invalid, incorrectly formed, or DBBMK_INVALID.

> *pBookmark* did not match any of the rows in the rowset. This includes the case when the row corresponding to the bookmark has been deleted.

DB_E_NOTREENTRANT
> The provider called a method from **IRowsetNotify** in the consumer and the method has not yet returned.

Comments

This method makes no logical change to the state of the object.

There is no guarantee the row position will be accurate. The provider is expected to choose the fastest possible estimation technique that is not completely in error. *pcRows* must be greater than or equal to *pulPosition*. The ratio is intended to be useful for scrolling and similar noncritical uses.

See Also

IRowsetScroll::GetRowsAtRatio

IRowsetScroll::GetRowsAtRatio

Fetches rows starting from a fractional position in the rowset.

HRESULT GetRowsAtRatio (

HWATCHREGION	*hReserved1,*
HCHAPTER	*hReserved2,*
ULONG	*ulNumerator,*
ULONG	*ulDenominator,*
LONG	*cRows,*
ULONG *	*pcRowsObtained,*
HROW **	*prghRows);*

Parameters

hReserved1 [in]

Reserved for future use. Providers ignore this parameter.

hReserved2 [in]

Reserved for future use. Providers ignore this parameter.

ulNumerator [in]

See *ulDenominator* below.

ulDenominator [in]

The provider determines the first row to fetch from the ratio of *ulNumerator* to *ulDenominator*, roughly using the formula:

```
(ulNumerator x Number of Rows in Rowset) / ulDenominator
```

How accurately the provider applies this ratio is provider-specific. For example, if *ulNumerator* is 1 and *ulDenominator* is 2, some providers will fetch rows starting exactly halfway through the rowset while other providers will fetch rows starting forty percent of the way through the rowset.

However, all providers must handle the following conditions correctly.

Condition	GetRowsAtRatio action
(*ulNumerator* = 0) AND (*cRows* > 0)	Fetches rows starting with first row in rowset
(*ulNumerator* = 0) AND (*cRows* < 0)	Returns DB_S_ENDOFROWSET
(*ulNumerator* = *ulDenominator*) AND (*cRows* > 0)	Returns DB_S_ENDOFROWSET
(*ulNumerator* = *ulDenominator*) AND (*cRows* < 0)	Fetches rows starting with last row in rowset

cRows [in]

    The number of rows to fetch. A negative number means to fetch backward. *cRows* can be a negative number only if the value of the DBPROP_CANFETCHBACKWARDS property is VARIANT_TRUE. The rows are returned in rowset traversal order, that is, the direction in which they were fetched.

    If *cRows* is zero, no rows are fetched. If the provider does not discover any other errors, the method returns S_OK; whether the provider checks for any other errors is provider-specific.

pcRowsObtained [out]

    A pointer to memory in which to return the number of rows fetched. If the consumer has insufficient permissions to return all rows, **GetRowsAtRatio** fetches all rows for which the consumer has sufficient permission and skips all other rows. If the method fails, **pcRowsObtained* is set to 0.

prghRows [in/out]

    A pointer to memory in which to return an array of handles of the fetched rows. If **prghRows* is not a null pointer on input, it must be a pointer to memory large enough to return the handles of the requested number of rows. If **prghRows* is a null pointer on input, the rowset allocates memory for the row handles and returns the address to this memory; the consumer releases this memory with **IMalloc::Free** after it releases the row handles. If **prghRows* was a null pointer on input and **pcRowsObtained* is zero on output or the method fails, the provider does not allocate any memory and ensures that **prghRows* is a null pointer on output.

Return Code

S_OK

    The method succeeded.

DB_S_ENDOFROWSET

    GetRowsAtRatio reached the start or the end of the rowset and could not fetch all requested rows because the count extended beyond the end. The number of rows actually fetched is returned in **pcRowsObtained*; this will be less than *cRows*.

DB_S_ROWLIMITEXCEEDED

    Fetching the number of rows specified in *cRows* would have exceeded the total number of active rows supported by the rowset. The number of rows that were actually fetched is returned in **pcRowsObtained*. Note that this condition can occur only when there are more rows available than can be handled by the rowset. Thus, this condition never conflicts with those described in DB_S_ENDOFROWSET and DB_S_STOPLIMITREACHED, both of which imply that no more rows were available.

DB_S_STOPLIMITREACHED

Fetching rows required further execution of the command, such as when the rowset uses a server-side cursor. Execution was stopped because a resource limit was reached. The number of rows that were actually fetched is returned in *pcRowsObtained*.

E_FAIL

A provider-specific error occurred.

E_INVALIDARG

pcRowsObtained or *prghRows* was a null pointer.

E_OUTOFMEMORY

The provider was unable to allocate sufficient memory in which to instantiate the rows or return the row handles.

E_UNEXPECTED

ITransaction::Commit or **ITransaction::Abort** was called and the object is in a zombie state.

DB_E_BADRATIO

ulNumerator was greater than *ulDenominator*.

ulDenominator was zero.

DB_E_CANTFETCHBACKWARDS

cRows was negative and the rowset cannot fetch backward.

DB_E_NOTREENTRANT

The consumer called this method while it was processing a notification, and it is an error to call this method while processing the specified DBREASON value.

DB_E_ROWSNOTRELEASED

The provider requires release of existing rows before new ones can be fetched. For more information, see DBPROP_CANHOLDROWS in "Rowset Properties" in Appendix C.

DB_SEC_E_PERMISSIONDENIED

The consumer did not have sufficient permission to fetch any of the rows; no rows were fetched.

Comments

GetRowsAtRatio increments the reference count of each row for which it returns a handle by one. Thus, if a handle is returned for a row that has already been fetched, the reference count of that row will be greater than one. **ReleaseRows** must be called once for each time the handle to a row has been returned.

If the provider encounters a problem fetching a row—for example, data stored in a text file contains a letter in what is supposed to be a numeric column—**GetRowsAtRatio** fetches the row normally, returns the row handle, and returns

S_OK. However, when the consumer calls **IRowset::GetData** for the row, the provider returns DBSTATUS_E_CANTCONVERTVALUE as the status for the offending column.

For information about what **GetRowsAtRatio** does when it fetches a row that it already has in its internal buffers, see "Uniqueness of Rows in the Rowset" in Chapter 4. For information about whether **GetRowsAtRatio** can detect changes made to rows in the rowset, see "Visibility of Changes" in Chapter 5.

See Also

IRowset::GetData, **IRowset::GetNextRows**, **IRowsetLocate::GetRowsAt**, **IRowsetLocate::GetRowsByBookmark**, **IRowsetScroll::GetApproximatePosition**

IRowsetUpdate : IRowsetChange

IRowsetUpdate enables consumers to delay the transmission of changes made with **IRowsetChange** to the data source. This interface also enables consumers to undo changes before transmission.

IRowsetUpdate is optional.

When to Implement

Rowsets that want to allow delayed transmission of changes and to support undo capabilities implement **IRowsetUpdate**. Generally, this requires the rowset to locally cache a copy of each row as it is changed with **IRowsetChange::SetData**.

If **IRowsetUpdate** is not requested as a property of the rowset, it must not be exposed by the rowset.

When to Call

If **IRowsetUpdate** is exposed on the rowset, then changes made through **IRowsetChange** are buffered in the rowset and not transmitted to the data source until **IRowsetUpdate::Update** is called; this is known as *delayed update mode*. If **IRowsetUpdate** is not exposed on the rowset, then changes made through **IRowsetChange** are immediately transmitted to the data source; this is known as *immediate update mode*. For more information, see "Changing Data" in Chapter 5.

The consumer calls the methods in **IRowsetChange** to update, delete, and insert rows. The rowset buffers these changes. When the consumer is ready to transmit these changes to the data source, it calls **Update**. Before calling **Update**, the consumer can back out any changes with **Undo**.

Method	Description
GetOriginalData	Gets the data most recently fetched from or transmitted to the data source; does not get values based on pending changes.
GetPendingRows	Returns a list of rows with pending changes.
GetRowStatus	Returns the status of rows.
Undo	Undoes any changes made to a row since it was last fetched or since **Update** was called for it.
Update	Transmits any changes made to a row since it was last fetched or since **Update** was called for it.

IRowsetUpdate::GetOriginalData

Gets the data most recently fetched from or transmitted to the data source; does not get values based on pending changes.

HRESULT GetOriginalData (
    HROW   *hRow*,
    HACCESSOR *hAccessor*,
    void *   *pData*);

Parameters

hRow [in]

The handle of the row for which to get the original data. This can be the handle of a row with a pending insert or delete.

hAccessor [in]

The handle of the accessor to use. If *hAccessor* is the handle of a null accessor (*cBindings* in **IAccessor::CreateAccessor** was zero), then **GetOriginalData** does not get any data values.

pData [out]

A pointer to a buffer in which to return the data. The consumer allocates memory for this buffer.

Return Code

S_OK

The method succeeded. The status of all columns bound by the accessor is set to DBSTATUS_S_OK, DBSTATUS_S_ISNULL, or DBSTATUS_S_TRUNCATED.

DB_S_ERRORSOCCURRED

An error occurred while returning data for one or more columns, but data was successfully returned for at least one column. To determine the columns for which data was returned, the consumer checks the status values. For a list of status values that can be returned by this method, see "Status Values Used When Getting Data" in "Status" in Chapter 6.

E_FAIL

A provider-specific error occurred.

E_INVALIDARG

pData was a null pointer and *hAccessor* was not a null accessor.

E_UNEXPECTED

ITransaction::Commit or **ITransaction::Abort** was called and the object is in a zombie state.

DB_E_BADACCESSORHANDLE

hAccessor was invalid. It is possible for a reference accessor or an accessor that has a binding that uses provider-owned memory to be invalid for use with this method, even if the accessor is valid for use with **IRowset::GetData** or **IRowsetChange::SetData**.

DB_E_BADACCESSORTYPE
The specified accessor was not a row accessor.

DB_E_BADROWHANDLE
hRow was invalid.

DB_E_DELETEDROW
hRow referred to a row for which a deletion had been transmitted to the data source.

DB_E_ERRORSOCCURRED
Errors occurred while returning data for all columns. To determine what errors occurred, the consumer checks the status values. For a list of status values that can be returned by this method, see "Status Values Used When Getting Data" in "Status" in Chapter 6.

DB_E_NOTREENTRANT
The provider called a method from **IRowsetNotify** in the consumer and the method has not yet returned.

If this method performs deferred accessor validation and that validation takes places before any data is transferred, it can also return any of the following return codes for the applicable reasons listed in the corresponding DBBINDSTATUS values in **IAccessor::CreateAccessor**:

E_NOINTERFACE
DB_E_BADBINDINFO
DB_E_BADORDINAL
DB_E_BADSTORAGEFLAGS
DB_E_UNSUPPORTEDCONVERSION

Comments

This method makes no logical change to the state of the object.

GetOriginalData retrieves the values the row contained when it was last fetched or had changes transmitted to the data source. It does not retrieve any pending changes or changes made by other rowsets in the same transaction or other applications in other transactions. It also does not affect the current values for the row. For a complete description of how **GetOriginalData** retrieves data, see "Getting Data" in Chapter 6.

How **GetOriginalData** works is best illustrated in the following examples. In the first example, **GetOriginalData** fetches the values last fetched from the data source:

1. The consumer fetches a row.

2. The consumer calls **IRowsetChange::SetData** to update values in the row.

3. The consumer calls **GetOriginalData**. The consumer retrieves the values it would have retrieved had it called **IRowset::GetData** after step 1 and before step 2.

In the second example, **GetOriginalData** fetches the values last transmitted to the data source:

1. The consumer fetches a row.

2. The consumer calls **SetData** to update values in the row.

3. The consumer calls **Update**.

4. The consumer calls **SetData** to update values in the row.

5. The consumer calls **GetOriginalData**. The consumer retrieves the values it would have retrieved had it called **GetData** after step 3 and before step 4.

To implement **GetOriginalData**, the provider generally caches the original values just before making a change to a row and discards the cached values when **Undo** or **Update** is called for the row.

If *hRow* refers to a pending insert row, **GetOriginalData** returns the column defaults and, for columns without defaults or for which the provider was unable to determine the defaults, NULLs.

Whether **GetOriginalData** can retrieve the original value of an OLE object that is stored in a column, or a storage object that is created over a BLOB after changes have been made to that OLE object or BLOB, depends on the value of the DBPROP_DELAYSTORAGEOBJECTS rowset property.

GetOriginalData does not enforce any security restrictions. The provider must not create a rowset that includes columns for which the consumer does not have read privileges, so **GetOriginalData** never encounters problems accessing the data for a column. Note that the rowset can contain columns to which the consumer does not have write permission if DBPROP_COLUMNRESTRICT is VARIANT_TRUE. The methods that fetch rows must not return the handles of rows for which the consumer does not have read privileges, so **GetOriginalData** never encounters problems accessing a row. Note that such rows might exist if the DBPROP_ROWRESTRICT property is VARIANT_TRUE.

If **GetOriginalData** fails, the memory to which *pData* points is not freed but its contents are undefined. If, before **GetOriginalData** failed, the provider allocated any memory for return to the consumer, the provider frees this memory and does not return it to the consumer.

See Also

IRowset::GetData, **IRowsetResynch::GetVisibleData**, **IRowsetUpdate::Undo**, **IRowsetUpdate::Update**

IRowsetUpdate::GetPendingRows

Returns a list of rows with pending changes.

HRESULT GetPendingRows (
HCHAPTER	*hReserved*,
DBPENDINGSTATUS	*dwRowStatus*,
ULONG *	*pcPendingRows*,
HROW **	*prgPendingRows*,
DBPENDINGSTATUS **	*prgPendingStatus*);

Parameters

hReserved [in]

Reserved for future use. Providers ignore this parameter.

dwRowStatus [in]

Indicates whether consumers want rows with pending updates, deletes, or inserts. The following DBPENDINGSTATUS values are valid and can be combined:

DBPENDINGSTATUS_NEW
DBPENDINGSTATUS_CHANGED
DBPENDINGSTATUS_DELETED

For information about the DBPENDINGSTATUS type, see "Row States" in Chapter 5.

pcPendingRows [out]

A pointer to memory in which to return the number of rows with pending changes. If this is a null pointer, *prgPendingRows* and *prgPendingStatus* are ignored. This is useful when the consumer wants to check the returned return code to determine if there are any pending changes. If an error occurs, **pcPendingRows* is set to zero.

prgPendingRows [out]

A pointer to memory in which to return an array of handles of rows with pending changes. If this is a null pointer, no row handles are returned. The rowset allocates memory for the row handles and returns the address to this memory; the consumer releases this memory with **IMalloc::Free** when it no longer needs the row handles. This argument is ignored if *pcPendingRows* is a null pointer. If **pcPendingRows* is zero on output or an error occurs, the provider does not allocate any memory and ensures that **prgPendingRows* is a null pointer on output.

prgPendingStatus [out]

A pointer to memory in which to return an array of DBPENDINGSTATUS values. These values are in one-to-one correspondence with the row handles returned in **prgPendingRows* and indicate the type of pending change. For information about the DBPENDINGSTATUS type, see "Row States" in Chapter 5. If this is a null pointer, no status information is returned.

The rowset allocates memory for the row statuses and returns the address to this memory; the consumer releases this memory with **IMalloc::Free** when it no longer needs the row statuses. This argument is ignored if *pcPendingRows* is a null pointer. If **pcPendingRows* is zero on output or an error occurs, the provider does not allocate any memory and ensures that **prgPendingStatus* is a null pointer on output.

Return Code

S_OK

The method succeeded and changes were pending.

S_FALSE

The method succeeded and no changes were pending.

E_FAIL

A provider-specific error occurred.

E_INVALIDARG

dwRowStatus was DBPENDINGSTATUS_INVALIDROW, DBPENDINGSTATUS_UNCHANGED, or any other invalid value.

E_OUTOFMEMORY

The provider was unable to allocate sufficient memory in which to return the handles of rows with pending changes or the array of DBPENDINGSTATUS values.

E_UNEXPECTED

ITransaction::Commit or **ITransaction::Abort** was called and the object is in a zombie state.

Comments

GetPendingRows increments the reference of each row handle it returns in **prgPendingRows*. The consumer must call **ReleaseRows** for these rows. If multiple changes are made to a single row, **GetPendingRows** returns the status as follows.

- If **IRowsetChange::SetData** is called for a pending insert row, the row is still considered a pending insert row.

- If **IRowsetChange::DeleteRows** is called for a pending update row, the row is considered a pending delete row.

- If **IRowsetChange::DeleteRows** is called for a pending insert row, the row is considered a transmitted delete row; such rows are not returned by **GetPendingRows**.

- If **IRowsetResynch::ResynchRows** is called for a pending insert row, the row is still considered a pending insert row.

For a complete description of pending change states, see "Row States" in Chapter 5.

See Also

IRowsetUpdate::GetRowStatus

IRowsetUpdate::GetRowStatus

Returns the status of rows.

HRESULT GetRowStatus(
    HCHAPTER   *hReserved,*
    ULONG   *cRows,*
    const HROW   *rghRows[],*
    DBPENDINGSTATUS *rgPendingStatus[]);*

Parameters

hReserved [in]

Reserved for future use. Providers ignore this parameter.

cRows [in]

The count of elements in *rghRows* and *rgPendingStatus*. If this value is zero , **GetRowStatus** ignores *rghRows* and *rgPendingStatus* and does not return any status.

rghRows [in]

An array of handles of rows for which to return the status. This array is allocated by the consumer and must not be freed by the provider.

rgPendingStatus [out]

An array of DBPENDINGSTATUS values. **GetRowStatus** returns the DBPENDINGSTATUS values for all rows specified in the *rghRows* array. The DBPENDINGSTATUS_INVALIDROW value is used to indicate an invalid row handle. For information about the DBPENDINGSTATUS type, see "Row States" in Chapter 5.

The *rgPendingStatus* array is allocated, but not necessarily initialized, by the caller and must not be freed by the provider.

Return Code

S_OK

The method succeeded. Status values were successfully retrieved for all rows and each element of *rgPendingStatus* is set to DBPENDINGSTATUS_NEW, DBPENDINGSTATUS_CHANGED, DBPENDINGSTATUS_DELETED, or DBPENDINGSTATUS_UNCHANGED.

DB_S_ERRORSOCCURRED

An error occurred while getting the status of a row, but the status of at least one row was successfully retrieved. Successes can occur for the reasons listed under S_OK. The following error can occur:

- A row handle in *rghRows* was invalid. The corresponding element of *rgRowStatus* contains DBPENDINGSTATUS_INVALIDROW.

E_FAIL

A provider-specific error occurred.

E_INVALIDARG

cRows was greater than zero and *rghRows* was a null pointer.

rgPendingStatus was a null pointer.

E_UNEXPECTED

ITransaction::Commit or **ITransaction::Abort** was called and the object is in a zombie state.

DB_E_ERRORSOCCURRED

Errors occurred getting the status of all of the rows. Errors can occur for the reason listed under DB_S_ERRORSOCCURRED.

Comments

If multiple changes are made to a single row, **GetRowStatus** returns the status as described in **GetPendingRows**. Note that if **IRowsetChange::DeleteRows** is called for a pending insert row, a status of DBPENDINGSTATUS_INVALIDROW is returned for the row.

For a complete description of row states, see "Row States" in Chapter 5.

See Also

IRowsetUpdate::GetPendingRows

IRowsetUpdate::Undo

Undoes any changes made to a row since it was last fetched or **Update** was called for it.

HRESULT Undo (
    HCHAPTER   *hReserved,*
    ULONG   *cRows,*
    const HROW   *rghRows[],*
    ULONG *   *pcRows,*
    HROW **   *prgRows,*
    DBROWSTATUS ** *prgRowStatus***);**

Parameters

hReserved [in]

    Reserved for future use. Providers ignore this parameter.

cRows [in]

    The count of rows to undo. If *cRows* is nonzero, **Undo** undoes all pending changes in the rows specified in *rghRows*. If *cRows* is zero, **Undo** ignores *rghRows* and undoes all pending changes to all rows in the rowset.

rghRows [in]

    An array of handles of the rows to undo. Elements of this array can refer to rows with pending deletes.

    If *rghRows* includes a row that does not have any pending changes, **Undo** does not return an error. Instead, the row remains unchanged from its original state—which is the intention of **Undo**—and its row status is set to DBROWSTATUS_S_OK.

    If *rghRows* includes a duplicate row, **Undo** treats the occurrences as if the row was passed to the method two times sequentially. Thus, on the first occurrence, **Undo** undoes any pending changes. On the second occurrence, **Undo** treats the row as a row with no pending changes and leaves it in its current (now original) state.

pcRows [out]

    A pointer to memory in which to return the number of rows **Undo** attempted to undo. If this is a null pointer, no count of rows is returned. If the method fails with an error other than DB_E_ERRORSOCCURRED, **pcRows* is set to zero.

prgRows [out]

    A pointer to memory in which to return an array containing the handles of all the rows **Undo** attempted to undo. If *rghRows* is not a null pointer, then the elements of this array are in one-to-one correspondence with those in *rghRows*. For example, if a row appears twice in *rghRows*, it appears twice in **prgRows*. When *rghRows* is not a null pointer, **Undo** does not add to the reference count of the rows it returns in **prgRows*; the reason is that the consumer already has these row handles.

    If *rghRows* is a null pointer, the elements of this array are the handles of all the rows that had pending changes, regardless of whether **Undo** was successful at undoing those changes. The consumer checks *prgRowStatus* to determine which rows were undone. When *rghRows* is a null pointer, **Undo** adds to the reference count of the rows it returns in *prgRows*; the reason is that the consumer is not guaranteed to already have these row handles. A side effect of this is that rows with a reference count of zero but with pending changes at the time **Undo** is called are brought back into existence; that is, their reference count is increased to one and they must be rereleased.

The rowset allocates memory for the array of handles and returns the address to this memory; the consumer releases this memory with **IMalloc::Free** when it no longer needs the handles. This argument is ignored if *pcRows* is a null pointer, and must not be a null pointer otherwise. If **pcRows* is zero on output or the method fails with an error other than DB_E_ERRORSOCCURRED, the provider does not allocate any memory and ensures that **prgRows* is a null pointer on output.

prgRowStatus [out]

A pointer to memory in which to return an array of row status values. The elements of this array correspond one-to-one with the elements of *rghRows* (if *rghRows* is not a null pointer) or **prgRows* (if *rghRows* is a null pointer). If no errors occur while undoing a row, the corresponding element of **prgRowStatus* is set to DBROWSTATUS_S_OK. If an error occurs while undoing a row, the corresponding element is set as specified in DB_S_ERRORSOCCURRED. If *prgRowStatus* is a null pointer, no row status values are returned. For information about the DBROWSTATUS enumerated type, see "Arrays of Errors" in Chapter 13.

The rowset allocates memory for the row status values and returns the address to this memory; the consumer releases this memory with **IMalloc::Free** when it no longer needs the row status values. This argument is ignored if *cRows* is zero and *pcRows* is a null pointer. If **Undo** does not attempt to undo any rows or the method fails with an error other than DB_E_ERRORSOCCURRED, the provider does not allocate any memory and ensures that **prgRowStatus* is a null pointer on output.

Return Code

S_OK

The method succeeded. The changes in all rows were successfully undone. The following value can be returned in **prgRowStatus*:

- The changes in the row were successfully undone. The corresponding element of **prgRowStatus* contains DBROWSTATUS_S_OK.

DB_S_ERRORSOCCURRED

An error occurred while undoing the changes in a row, but the changes in at least one row were successfully undone. Successes can occur for the reasons listed under S_OK. The following errors can occur:

- Undoing the changes in a row was canceled during notification. Changes made to the row were not undone and the corresponding element of *rgRowStatus* contains DBROWSTATUS_E_CANCELED.

- A row handle in *rghRows* referred to a row for which a delete had been transmitted to the data source. The corresponding element of **prgRowStatus* contains DBROWSTATUS_E_DELETED.

- A row handle in *rghRows* was invalid. The corresponding element of **prgRowStatus* contains DBROWSTATUS_E_INVALID.

- A row handle in *rghRows* referred to a row on which a storage object or OLE object was open. The corresponding element of **prgRowStatus* contains DBROWSTATUS_E_OBJECTOPEN.

E_FAIL

A provider-specific error occurred.

E_INVALIDARG

cRows was not 0 and *rghRows* was a null pointer.

pcRows was not a null pointer and *prgRows* was a null pointer.

E_OUTOFMEMORY

The provider was unable to allocate sufficient memory in which to return either the handles of the rows **Undo** attempted to undo or the array of row status values.

E_UNEXPECTED

ITransaction::Commit or **ITransaction::Abort** was called and the object is in a zombie state.

DB_E_ERRORSOCCURRED

Errors occurred while undoing all of the rows. The provider allocates memory for **prgRows* and **prgRowStatus* and the consumer checks the values in **prgRowStatus* to determine why the pending changes were not undone. The consumer frees this memory when it no longer needs the information. Errors can occur for the reasons listed under DB_S_ERRORSOCCURRED.

DB_E_NOTREENTRANT

The consumer called this method while it was processing a notification, and it is an error to call this method while processing the specified DBREASON value.

Comments

Undo backs any pending changes out of the specified rows and clears their pending change status. That is, it undoes any changes made to the row since it was last fetched or **Update** was called for the row. If multiple changes were made to a row, **Undo** undoes all of these changes; the provider does not remember intermediate steps. If **Update** is called for a row immediately after **Undo** is called for the row, **Update** does not transmit any changes to the data source for the row. For more information about pending changes, see "Changing Data" in Chapter 5.

How **Undo** works is best illustrated in the following examples. In the first example, **Undo** backs out any changes made since the row was last fetched from the data source.

1. The consumer fetches a row.

2. The consumer deletes the row with **IRowsetChange::DeleteRows** or updates value in it with **IRowsetChange::SetData**.

3. The consumer repeats step 2 as often as it likes for the row, except that after it calls **DeleteRows** for the row it cannot call either **SetData** or **DeleteRows** for the row.

4. The consumer calls **Undo** for the row. The values in the row are changed to those it had after completing step 1.

In the second example, **Undo** backs out any changes made since values were last transmitted to the data source:

1. The consumer fetches a row.

2. The consumer updates the value in a row with **SetData**.

3. The consumer repeats step 2 as often as it likes for the row.

4. The consumer calls **Update** for the row.

5. The consumer deletes the row with **DeleteRows** or updates the value in it with **SetData**.

6. The consumer repeats step 5 as often as it likes for the row, except that after it calls **DeleteRows** for the row it cannot call either **SetData** or **DeleteRows** for the row.

7. The consumer calls **Undo** for the row. The values in the row are changed to those it had after completing step 4.

To implement **Undo**, the provider generally caches the original values just before making a change to a row and discards the cached values when **Undo** or **Update** is called for the row. This same cache can be used by **GetOriginalData** to retrieve the original data for the row.

If **Undo** is called for a row with a pending insert, the row is deleted from the rowset. That is, calls to **IRowset::GetData** or **SetData** for the row fail with DB_E_DELETEDROW. The consumer must still call **IRowset::ReleaseRows** to release the row.

Whether **Undo** can undo changes made to an OLE object stored in a column or to a storage object created over a BLOB depends on the value of the DBPROP_DELAYSTORAGEOBJECTS rowset property.

If **Undo** is called for a row that has a reference count of zero and exists only because the row has a pending change, **Undo** releases the row and all its resources. The only exception to this is when the handle to the row is returned in *prgRows*, in which case the reference count is set to one.

The order in which **Undo** processes rows is provider-specific. If **Undo** encounters an error, it continues processing rows until it has attempted to undo all specified rows, then returns the appropriate warning. Because **Undo** is generally implemented by copying data from a cache of original data, such errors should be extremely rare and generally represent a consumer programming error, such as passing an invalid row handle.

If any consumer of the rowset is using notifications, the provider sends notifications that pending changes for the specified rows are being undone.

See Also

IRowsetChange, IRowsetUpdate::GetOriginalData, IRowsetUpdate::Update

IRowsetUpdate::Update

Transmits any changes made to a row since it was last fetched or **Update** was called for it.

HRESULT Update (
    HCHAPTER   *hReserved,*
    ULONG   *cRows,*
    const HROW   *rghRows[],*
    ULONG *   *pcRows,*
    HROW **   *prgRows,*
    DBROWSTATUS**   *prgRowStatus*);

Parameters

hReserved [in]

Reserved for future use. Providers ignore this parameter.

cRows [in]

The count of rows to update. If *cRows* is nonzero, **Update** updates all pending changes in the rows specified in *rghRows*. If *cRows* is zero, **Update** ignores *rghRows* and updates all pending changes to all rows in the rowset.

rghRows [in]

An array of handles of the rows to update.

If *rghRows* includes a row that does not have any pending changes, **Update** does not return an error. Instead, the row remains unchanged and hence has no pending changes after **Update** returns—which is the intention of **Update**—and the row status value associated with that row is DBROWSTATUS_OK. Furthermore, **Update** guarantees not to transmit any value for the row to the data source.

If *rghRows* includes a duplicate row, **Update** behaves as follows. If the row handle is valid, no errors occur and **prgRowStatus* contains DBROWSTATUS_S_OK for each occurrence. If the row handle is invalid, **prgRowStatus* contains the appropriate error for each occurrence.

pcRows [out]

A pointer to memory in which to return the number of rows **Update** attempted to update. If this is a null pointer, no count of rows is returned. If the method fails with an error other than DB_E_ERRORSOCCURRED, **pcRows* is set to zero.

prgRows [out]

A pointer to memory in which to return an array containing the handles of all the rows **Update** attempted to update. If *rghRows* is not a null pointer, then the elements of this array are in one-to-one correspondence with those in *rghRows*. For example, if a row appears twice in *rghRows*, it appears twice in **prgRows*. When *rghRows* is not a null pointer, **Update** does not add to the reference count of the rows it returns in **prgRows*; the reason is that the consumer already has these row handles.

If *rghRows* is a null pointer, the elements of this array are handles of all the rows that had pending changes, regardless of whether **Update** was successful at transmitting those changes to the data source. The consumer checks **prgRowStatus* to determine which rows were updated. When *rghRows* is a null pointer, **Update** adds to the reference count of the rows it returns in **prgRows*; the reason is that the consumer is not guaranteed to already have these row handles. A side effect of this is that rows with a reference count of zero, but with pending changes at the time **Update** is called, are brought back into existence; that is, their reference count is increased to one and they must be rereleased.

The rowset allocates memory for the array of handles and returns the address to this memory; the consumer releases this memory with **IMalloc::Free** when it no longer needs the handles. This argument is ignored if *pcRows* is a null pointer, and must not be a null pointer otherwise. If **pcRows* is zero on output or the method fails with an error other than DB_E_ERRORSOCCURRED, the provider does not allocate any memory and ensures that **prgRows* is a null pointer on output.

prgRowStatus [out]

A pointer to memory in which to return an array of row status values. The elements of this array correspond one-to-one with the elements of *rghRows* (if *rghRows* is not a null pointer) or **prgRows* (if *rghRows* is a null pointer). If no errors or warnings occur while updating a row, the corresponding element of **prgRowStatus* is set to DBROWSTATUS_S_OK. If an error or warning occurs while updating a row, the corresponding element is set as specified in DB_S_ERRORSOCCURRED. If *prgRowStatus* is a null pointer, no row status values are returned. For information about the DBROWSTATUS enumerated type, see "Arrays of Errors" in Chapter 13.

The rowset allocates memory for the row status values and returns the address to this memory; the consumer releases this memory with **IMalloc::Free** when it no longer needs the row status values. This argument is ignored if *cRows* is zero and *pcRows* is a null pointer. If **Update** does not attempt to update any rows or the method fails with an error other than DB_E_ERRORSOCCURRED, the provider does not allocate any memory and ensures that **prgRowStatus* is a null pointer on output.

Return Code

S_OK

The method succeeded. The changes in all rows were successfully updated. The following values can be returned in **prgRowStatus*:

- The changes in the row were successfully undone. The corresponding element of **prgRowStatus* contains DBROWSTATUS_S_OK.

- Updating or deleting a single row caused more than one row to be updated or deleted in the data source. For more information, see DBPROP_REPORTMULTIPLECHANGES in "Rowset Properties" in Appendix C. The corresponding element of **prgRowStatus* contains DBROWSTATUS_S_MULTIPLECHANGES.

DB_S_ERRORSOCCURRED

An error occurred while updating a row, but at least one row was successfully updated. Successes can occur for the reasons listed under S_OK. The following errors can occur:

- Updating a row was canceled during notification. The row was not updated and the corresponding element of *rgRowStatus* contains DBROWSTATUS_E_CANCELED.

- The rowset was using optimistic concurrency, a row was being updated or deleted, and the value of a column in that row has been changed since it was last fetched. The error in the corresponding element of **prgRowStatus* contains DBROWSTATUS_E_CONCURRENCYVIOLATION.

- An element of *rghRows* referred to a row for which a deletion had been transmitted to the data source. The error in the corresponding element of **prgRowStatus* contains DBROWSTATUS_E_DELETED.

- A row was being inserted or updated and a value specified for that row violated the integrity constraints for the column or table. The error in the corresponding element of **prgRowStatus* contains DBROWSTATUS_E_INTEGRITYVIOLATION.

- A row was being deleted and doing so violated the integrity constraints for the column or table. The error in the corresponding element of **prgRowStatus* contains DBROWSTATUS_E_INTEGRITYVIOLATION.

- An element of *rghRows* was invalid. The error in the corresponding element of **prgRowStatus* contains DBROWSTATUS_E_INVALID.

- The consumer did not have sufficient permission to update, delete, or insert a row. This error can be returned only if the value of the DBPROP_ROWRESTRICT property is VARIANT_TRUE. The error in the corresponding element of **prgRowStatus* contains DBROWSTATUS_E_PERMISSIONDENIED.

- The update, delete, or insert failed due to reaching a limit on the server, such as a query execution timing out. The error in the corresponding element of **prgRowStatus* contains DBROWSTATUS_E_LIMITREACHED.

- A column value did not meet the schema requirements for the column. The error in the corresponding element of **prgRowStatus* contains DBROWSTATUS_E_SCHEMAVIOLATION.

- The values for two or more columns did not meet the multiple-column schema requirements for those columns. The error in the corresponding element of **prgRowStatus* contains DBROWSTATUS_E_SCHEMAVIOLATION.

- A row was being inserted, no value was specified for a column, the column does not have a default, and the column is non-nullable. The error in the corresponding element of **prgRowStatus* contains DBROWSTATUS_E_SCHEMAVIOLATION.

E_FAIL
A provider-specific error occurred.

E_INVALIDARG
cRows was not zero and *rghRows* was a null pointer.

pcRows was not a null pointer and *prgRows* was a null pointer on input.

E_OUTOFMEMORY
The provider was unable to allocate sufficient memory in which to return either the handles of the rows **Update** attempted to update or the array of row status values.

E_UNEXPECTED
ITransaction::Commit or **ITransaction::Abort** was called and the object is in a zombie state.

DB_E_ERRORSOCCURRED
Errors occurred while updating all of the rows. The provider allocates memory for **prgRows* and **prgRowStatus* and the consumer checks the values in **prgRowStatus* to determine why the pending changes were not updated. The consumer frees this memory when it no longer needs the information. Errors can occur for the reasons listed under DB_S_ERRORSOCCURRED.

DB_E_NOTREENTRANT
The provider called a method from **IRowsetNotify** in the consumer and the method has not yet returned.

Comments

Update transmits pending changes for the specified rows to the data source and clears their pending change status. That is, it transmits any changes made to the row since it was last fetched or **Update** was called for the row. For more information about pending changes, see "Changing Data" in Chapter 5.

The order in which **Update** processes rows is provider-specific. If **Update** encounters an error, it continues processing rows until it has attempted to update all specified rows, then it returns the appropriate warning. This might leave the rowset in a state where changes have been transmitted for some rows but not others. When the consumer repairs the cause of the error, it can call **Update** again and the provider guarantees it will not transmit data to the data source for those rows for which data was already successfully transmitted.

If any consumer of the rowset is using notifications, the provider sends notifications that pending changes for the specified rows are being transmitted to the data source.

If **Update** is called for a row that has a reference count of zero and exists only because the row has a pending change, **Update** releases the row and all its resources. The only exception to this is when the handle to the row is returned in **prgRows*, in which case the reference count is set to one.

If the provider cached original values to implement **GetOriginalData** and **Undo**, it discards them as part of **Update**.

If the rowset is released with **IUnknown::Release** before **Update** is called, all pending changes are lost.

See Also

IRowsetChange, **IRowsetUpdate::Undo**

ISessionProperties

ISessionProperties returns information about the properties a session supports and the current settings of those properties. It is a mandatory interface on sessions.

Method	Description
GetProperties	Returns the list of properties in the Session property group that are currently set on the session.
SetProperties	Sets properties in the Session property group.

ISessionProperties::GetProperties

Returns the list of properties in the Session property group that are currently set on the session.

HRESULT GetProperties (
    ULONG   *cPropertyIDSets*,
    const DBPROPIDSET   *rgPropertyIDSets*[],
    ULONG *   *pcPropertySets*,
    DBPROPSET **   *prgPropertySets*);

Parameters

cPropertyIDSets [in]
    The number of DBPROPIDSET structures in *rgPropertyIDSets*.

    If *cPropertySets* is zero, the provider ignores *rgPropertyIDSets* and returns the values of all properties in the Session property group for which values have been set or defaults exist. It does not return the values of properties in the Session property group for which values have not been set and no defaults exist.

    If *cPropertyIDSets* is not zero, the provider returns the values of the requested properties. If a property is not supported, the returned value of *dwStatus* in the returned DBPROP structure for that property is DBPROPSTATUS_NOTSUPPORTED and the value of *dwOptions* is undefined.

rgPropertyIDSets [in]
    An array of *cPropertyIDSets* DBPROPIDSET structures. The properties specified in these structures must belong to the Session property group. The provider returns the values of information about the properties specified in these structures. If *cPropertyIDSets* is zero, then this parameter is ignored.

    For information about the properties in the Session property group that are defined by OLE DB, see "Session Properties" in Appendix C. For information about the DBPROPIDSET structure, see "DBPROPIDSET Structure" in Chapter 11.

pcPropertySets [out]
    A pointer to memory in which to return the number of DBPROPSET structures returned in **prgPropertySets*. If *cPropertyIDSets* is zero, **pcPropertySets* is the total number of property sets for which the provider supports at least one property in the Session property group. If *cPropertyIDSets* is greater than zero, **pcPropertySets* is set to *cPropertyIDSets*. If an error other than DB_E_ERRORSOCCURRED occurs, **pcPropertySets* is set to zero.

prgPropertySets [out]
    A pointer to memory in which to return an array of DBPROPSET structures. If *cPropertyIDSets* is zero, then one structure is returned for each property set that contains at least one property belonging to the Session property group. If *cPropertyIDSets* is not zero, then one structure is returned for each property set specified in *rgPropertyIDSets*.

If *cPropertyIDSets* is not zero, the DBPROPSET structures in **prgPropertySets* are returned in the same order as the DBPROPIDSET structures in *rgPropertyIDSets*; that is, for corresponding elements of each array, the *guidPropertySet* elements are the same. If *cPropertyIDs*, in an element of *rgPropertyIDSets*, is not zero, the DBPROP structures in the corresponding element of **prgPropertySets* are returned in the same order as the DBPROPID values in *rgPropertyIDs*; that is for corresponding elements of each array, the property IDs are the same.

The provider allocates memory for the structures and returns the address to this memory; the consumer releases this memory with **IMalloc::Free** when it no longer needs the structures. Before calling **IMalloc::Free** for **prgPropertySets*, the consumer should call **IMalloc::Free** for the *rgProperties* element within each element of **prgPropertySets*. If **pcPropertySets* is zero on output or if an error other than DB_E_ERRORSOCCURRED occurs, the provider does not allocate any memory and ensures that **prgPropertySets* is a null pointer on output.

For information about the DBPROPSET and DBPROP structures, see "DBPROPSET Structure" and "DBPROP Structure" in Chapter 11.

Return Code

S_OK

The method succeeded. In all DBPROP structures returned by the method, *dwStatus* is set to DBPROPSTATUS_OK.

DB_S_ERRORSOCCURRED

No value was returned for one or more properties. The consumer checks *dwStatus* in the DBPROP structure to determine the properties for which values were not returned. **GetProperties** can fail to return properties for a number of reasons, including:

- The property was not supported by the provider.

- The property was not in the Session property group.

- The property set was not supported by the provider. If *cPropertyIDs* in the DBPROPIDSET structure for the property set was zero, the provider cannot set *dwStatus* in the DBPROP structure because it does not know the IDs of any properties in the property set. Instead, it sets *cProperties* to zero in the DBPROPSET structure returned for the property set.

E_FAIL

A provider-specific error occurred.

E_INVALIDARG

cPropertyIDSets was not equal to zero and *rgPropertyIDSets* was a null pointer.

pcPropertySets or *prgPropertySets* was a null pointer.

In an element of *rgPropertyIDSets*, *cPropertyIDs* was not zero and *rgPropertyIDs* was a null pointer.

E_OUTOFMEMORY

The provider was unable to allocate sufficient memory in which to return the DBPROPSET or DBPROP structures.

DB_E_ERRORSOCCURRED

Values were not returned for any properties. The provider allocates memory for *prgPropertySets* and the consumer checks *dwStatus* in the DBPROP structures to determine why properties were not returned. The consumer frees this memory when it no longer needs the information.

See Also

IDBProperties::GetPropertyInfo, ISessionProperties::SetProperties

ISessionProperties::SetProperties

Sets properties in the Session property group.

HRESULT SetProperties (
    ULONG   *cPropertySets*,
    DBPROPSET   *rgPropertySets*[]);

Parameters

cPropertySets [in]
> The number of DBPROPSET structures in *rgPropertySets*. If this is zero, the provider ignores *rgPropertySets* and the method does not do anything.

rgPropertySets [in/out]
> An array of DBPROPSET structures containing properties and values to be set. The properties specified in these structures must belong to the Session property group. If the same property is specified more than once in *rgPropertySets*, then which value is used is provider-specific. If *cPropertySets* is zero, this parameter is ignored.

> For information about the properties in the Session property group that are defined by OLE DB, see "Session Properties" in Appendix C. For information about the DBPROPSET and DBPROP structures, see "DBPROPSET Structure" and "DBPROP Structure" in Chapter 11.

Return Code

S_OK
> The method succeeded. In all DBPROP structures passed to the method, *dwStatus* is set to DBPROPSTATUS_OK.

DB_S_ERRORSOCCURRED
> One or more properties were not set. Properties not in error remain set. The consumer checks *dwStatus* in the DBPROP structures to determine which properties were not set. **SetProperties** can fail to set properties for a number of reasons, including:

> - The property was not supported by the provider.
> - The property was not in the Session property group.
> - The property set was not supported by the provider.
> - It was not cheap to set the property.
> - *colid* in the DBPROP structure was not DB_NULLID.
> - The value of *dwOptions* in the DBPROP structure was invalid.
> - The data type in *vValue* in the DBPROP structure was not the data type of the property or was notVT_EMPTY.

- The value in *vValue* in the DBPROP structure was invalid.

- The property's value conflicted with an existing property.

E_FAIL

A provider-specific error occurred.

E_INVALIDARG

cPropertySets was not equal to zero and *rgPropertySets* was a null pointer.

In an element of *rgPropertySets*, *cProperties* was not zero and *rgProperties* was a null pointer.

DB_E_ERRORSOCCURRED

All property values were invalid and no properties were set. The consumer checks *dwStatus* in the DBPROP structures to determine why properties were not set.

See Also

IDBProperties::GetPropertyInfo, **ISessionProperties::GetProperties**

ISourcesRowset

ISourcesRowset returns a rowset of data sources and enumerators visible from the current enumerator. For more information about enumerators, see "Enumerators" in Chapter 2.

Method	Description
GetSourcesRowset	Returns a rowset of the data sources and enumerators visible from the current enumerator.

ISourcesRowset::GetSourcesRowset

Returns a rowset of the data sources and enumerators visible from the current enumerator.

HRESULT GetSourcesRowset(

IUnknown	*pUnkOuter*,
REFIID	*riid*,
ULONG	*cPropertySets*,
DBPROPSET	*rgPropertySets*[],
IUnknown **	*ppSourcesRowset*);

Parameters

pUnkOuter

A pointer to the controlling **IUnknown** interface if the sources rowset is being created as part of an aggregate. If the rowset is not part of an aggregate, this must be set to a null pointer.

riid

The IID of the interface on which to return a pointer.

cPropertySets [in]

The number of DBPROPSET structures in *rgPropertySets*. If this is zero, the provider ignores *rgPropertySets*.

rgPropertySets [in/out]

An array of DBPROPSET structures containing properties and values to be set. The properties specified in these structures must belong to the Rowset property group. If the same property is specified more than once in *rgPropertySets*, then it is provider-specific which value is used. If *cPropertySets* is 0, this argument is ignored.

For information about the properties in the Rowset property group that are defined by OLE DB, see "Rowset Properties" in Appendix C. For information about the DBPROPSET and DBPROP structures, see "DBPROPSET Structure" and "DBPROP Structure" in Chapter 11.

ppSourcesRowset

A pointer to memory in which to return the requested interface pointer on the rowset. If an error occurs, the returned pointer is null.

Return Code

S_OK

The method succeeded. In all DBPROP structures passed to the method, *dwStatus* is set to DBPROPSTATUS_OK.

DB_S_ERRORSOCCURRED

The rowset was opened but one or more properties—for which the *dwOptions* element of the DBPROP structure was DBPROPOPTIONS_SETIFCHEAP—were not set. The consumer checks *dwStatus* in the DBPROP structures to determine which properties were not set. The method can fail to set properties for a number of reasons, including:

- The property was not supported by the provider.
- The property was not in the Rowset property group.
- The property set was not supported by the provider.
- It was not cheap to set the property.
- The *colid* in the DBPROP structure was invalid.
- The data type in *vValue* in the DBPROP structure was not the data type of the property or was not VT_EMPTY.
- The value in *vValue* in the DBPROP structure was invalid.
- The property's value conflicted with an existing property.
- A property was specified to be applied to all columns, but could not be applied to one or more columns.

E_FAIL

A provider-specific error occurred.

E_INVALIDARG

ppSourcesRowset was a null pointer.

cPropertySets was not 0 and *rgPropertySets* was a null pointer.

In an element of *rgPropertySets*, *cProperties* was not 0 and *rgProperties* was a null pointer.

E_NOINTERFACE

The rowset did not support the interface specified in *riid*.

E_OUTOFMEMORY

The provider did not have enough memory to create the rowset object.

E_UNEXPECTED

The enumerator object was in an uninitialized state.

DB_E_ABORTLIMITREACHED

The method failed because a resource limit has been reached. For example, a query used to implement the method timed out. No rowset is returned.

DB_E_ERRORSOCCURRED

No rowset was returned because one or more properties—for which the *dwOptions* element of the DBPROP structure was DBPROPOPTIONS_REQUIRED or an invalid value—were not set. The consumer checks *dwStatus* in the DBPROP structures to determine which properties were not set. None of the satisfiable properties are remembered. The method can fail to set properties for any of the reasons specified in DB_S_ERRORSOCCURRED except the reason that states that it was not cheap to set the property.

DB_E_NOAGGREGATION
pUnkOuter was not a null pointer and the rowset did not support aggregation.

Comments

GetSourcesRowset returns the following rowset. The rowset is read-only. The columns are returned in the order shown.

Column Name	Type Indicator	Description
SOURCES_NAME	DBTYPE_WSTR	The name of the data source or enumerator.
SOURCES_PARSENAME	DBTYPE_WSTR	String to pass to **IParseDisplayName** to obtain a moniker for the data source or enumerator.
SOURCES_DESCRIPTION	DBTYPE_WSTR	The description of the data source or enumerator.
SOURCES_TYPE	DBTYPE_UI2	Whether the row describes a data source or an enumerator: • DBSOURCETYPE_DATASOURCE • DBSOURCETYPE_ENUMERATOR If a single piece of code is capable of being used both as a data source and as an enumerator, it is listed in the rowset twice, once in each role.
SOURCES_ISPARENT	DBTYPE_BOOL	If the row describes an enumerator, SOURCES_ISPARENT is VARIANT_TRUE if the enumerator is the parent enumerator; that is, the enumerator whose enumeration contains the enumerator on which **ISourcesRowset::GetSourcesRowset** was just called. This allows the consumer to go backwards through the enumeration. Whether an enumerator is able to enumerate its parent is provider-specific. Otherwise, SOURCES_ISPARENT is VARIANT_FALSE. If the row describes a data source, SOURCES_ISPARENT is ignored by the consumer.

See Also

IDBProperties::GetPropertyInfo

ISQLErrorInfo

ISQLErrorInfo is used to return the SQLSTATE and native error code.

When to Implement

Providers for SQL databases can implement **ISQLErrorInfo** on custom error objects returned with the OLE DB error object.

When to Call

Consumers call the methods on **ISQLErrorInfo** to retrieve the SQLSTATE and native error code. To retrieve a custom error object, a consumer calls **IErrorRecords::GetCustomErrorObject**.

Method	Description
GetSQLInfo	Returns the SQLSTATE and native error code associated with an error.

ISQLErrorInfo::GetSQLInfo

Returns the SQLSTATE and native error code associated with an error.

HRESULT GetSQLInfo (
      BSTR *   *pbstrSQLState*,
      LONG *   *plNativeError*);

Parameters

pbstrSQLState [out]

A pointer to memory in which to return a pointer to a string that contains the
SQLSTATE. An SQLSTATE is a five-character string defined by the ANSI SQL
standard. The memory for this string is allocated by the provider and must be freed
by the consumer with a call to **SysFreeString**. If an error occurs, **pbstrSQLState*
is set to a null pointer.

plNativeError [out]

A pointer to memory in which to return a provider-specific, native error code. Note
that **plNativeError* is not necessarily the same as the *dwMinor* element in the
ERRORINFO structure returned by **IErrorRecords::GetErrorInfo**. The
combination of the *hrError* and *dwMinor* elements of the ERRORINFO structure is
used to identify an error to the error lookup service, whereas **plNativeError* has no
such restrictions.

Return Code

S_OK

The method succeeded.

E_FAIL

A provider-specific error occurred.

E_INVALIDARG

pbstrSQLState or *plNativeError* was a null pointer.

E_OUTOFMEMORY

The provider was unable to allocate sufficient memory in which to return the
SQLSTATE.

ISupportErrorInfo

ISupportErrorInfo is defined by OLE Automation; the following describes how the interface is used in OLE DB. **ISupportErrorInfo** indicates whether a specific interface can return OLE Automation error objects. Because OLE DB error objects are returned through the same mechanism as OLE Automation error objects, support for them is also indicated through this interface.

When to Implement

ISupportErrorInfo must be implemented by the provider on any object that exposes an interface that can return OLE DB error objects.

When to Call

A consumer uses this interface to determine whether a particular OLE DB interface can return an OLE DB error object.

Method	Description
InterfaceSupportsErrorInfo	Indicates whether a specific OLE DB interface can return OLE DB error objects.

ISupportErrorInfo:: InterfaceSupportsErrorInfo

Indicates whether a specific OLE DB interface can return OLE DB error objects.

HRESULT InterfaceSupportsErrorInfo (
   REFIID *riid*);

Parameters

riid [in]
   The IID of the interface in question.

Return Code

S_OK
   The interface can return OLE Automation error objects; therefore, it can return OLE DB error objects.

S_FALSE
   The interface cannot return OLE Automation error objects; therefore, it cannot return OLE DB error objects.

Comments

To retrieve an OLE DB error object, the consumer takes the following steps:

1. The consumer calls **QueryInterface** to retrieve a pointer to **ISupportErrorInfo**.

2. The consumer calls **ISupportErrorInfo::InterfaceSupportsErrorInfo** and passes it the IID of the OLE DB interface that returned the error.

3. The consumer calls **GetErrorInfo** in the OLE Automation DLL if **InterfaceSupportsErrorInfo** returns S_OK. **GetErrorInfo** returns an **IErrorInfo** interface pointer on the OLE DB error object. If **InterfaceSupportsErrorInfo** returns S_FALSE, the consumer should discard any error object returned by **GetErrorInfo** because it applies to a different method and interface.

ITableDefinition

The **ITableDefinition** interface exposes simple methods to create, drop, and alter tables on the data source.

When to Implement

ITableDefinition is optional for providers that do not otherwise support table creation; it is mandatory for providers that support table creation through commands.

Method	Description
AddColumn	Adds a new column to a base table.
CreateTable	Creates a new base table in the data source.
DropColumn	Drops a column from a base table.
DropTable	Drops a base table in the data source.

ITableDefinition::AddColumn

Adds a new column to a base table.

HRESULT AddColumn(
  DBID *   *pTableID,*
  DBCOLUMNDESC * *pColumnDesc,*
  DBID **   *ppColumnID***);**

Parameters

pTableID [in]
  A pointer to the DBID of the table to which the column is to be added.

pColumnDesc [in]
  A pointer to the DBCOLUMNDESC structure that describes the new column.

ppColumnID [out]
  A pointer to memory in which to return the returned DBID of newly created
  column. If this is a null pointer, no DBID is returned.

Return Code

S_OK
  The method succeeded.

E_FAIL
  A provider-specific error occurred.

E_INVALIDARG
  pTableID or *pColumnDesc* was a null pointer.

DB_E_BADCOLUMNID
  dbcid in **pColumnDesc* was an invalid column ID.

DB_E_BADPRECISION
  The precision in **pColumnDesc* was invalid.

DB_E_BADPROPERTYVALUE
  The value of a property was invalid.

DB_E_BADSCALE
  The scale in **pColumnDesc* was invalid.

DB_E_BADTYPE
  The *wType* in **pColumnDesc* was invalid.

DB_E_DUPLICATECOLUMNID
  dbcid in **pColumnDesc* was the same as an existing column ID.

DB_E_NOTABLE
  The specified table does not exist in the current data source.

DB_E_TABLEINUSE
The specified table was in use.

DB_SEC_E_PERMISSIONDENIED
The consumer did not have sufficient permission to add a column.

Comments

If **AddColumn** returns any errors, the column is not created.

See Also

IDBProperties::GetPropertyInfo, ITableDefinition::CreateTable, ITableDefinition::DropColumn

ITableDefinition::CreateTable

Creates a new base table in the data source.

HRESULT CreateTable(
IUnknown *	*pUnkOuter,*
DBID *	*pTableID,*
ULONG	*cColumnDescs,*
DBCOLUMNDESC	*rgColumnDescs[],*
REFIID	*riid,*
ULONG	*cPropertySets,*
DBPROPSET	*rgPropertySets[],*
DBID **	*ppTableID,*
IUnknown **	*ppRowset);*

Parameters

pUnkOuter [in]

The controlling unknown if the rowset is to be aggregated, otherwise a null pointer.

pTableID [in]

A pointer to the ID of the table to create. If this is a null pointer, the provider must assign a unique ID to the table.

cColumnDescs [in]

The number of DBCOLUMNDESC structures in the *rgColumnDescs* array.

rgColumnDescs [in/out]

An array of DBCOLUMNDESC structures that describe the columns of the table.

```
typedef struct tagDBCOLUMNDESC {
    LPOLESTR     pwszTypeName;
    ITypeInfo *  pTypeInfo;
    DBPROPSET *  rgPropertySets;
    CLSID *      pclsid;
    ULONG        cPropertySets;
    ULONG        ulColumnSize;
    DBID         dbcid;
    DBTYPE       wType;
    BYTE         bPrecision;
    BYTE         bScale;
} DBCOLUMNDESC;
```

The elements of this structure are used as follows. The consumer generally decides the values to use in the non-properties elements of this structure based on values from the PROVIDER_TYPES schema rowset.

Element	Description
pwszTypeName	The provider-specific name of the data type of the column. This name corresponds to a value in the TYPE_NAME column in the PROVIDER_TYPES schema rowset. In most cases, there is no reason for a consumer to specify a value for *pwszTypeName* that is different from the values listed in the PROVIDER_TYPES schema rowset.
pTypeInfo	If *pTypeInfo* is not a null pointer, then data type the column is an abstract data type (ADT) and values in this column are actually instances of the type described by the type library. *wType* may be either DBTYPE_BYTES with a length of at least 4, or it may be DBTYPE_IUNKNOWN. The instance values are required to be COM objects derived from **IUnknown**.
rgPropertySets	An array of DBPROPSET structures containing properties and values to be set. The properties specified in these structures must belong to the Column property group. If the same property is specified more than once in *rgPropertySets*, then it is provider-specific which value is used. If *cPropertySets* is zero, this argument is ignored. For information about the properties in the Column property group that are defined by OLE DB, see "Column Properties" in Appendix C. For information about the DBPROPSET and DBPROP structures, see "DBPROPSET Structure" and "DBPROP Structure" in Chapter 11.
pclsid	If the column contains OLE objects, a pointer to the class ID of those objects. If more than one class of objects can reside in the column, *pclsid* is set to IID_NULL.
cPropertySets	The number of DBPROPSET structures in *rgPropertySets*. If this is zero, the provider ignores *rgPropertySets*.
ulColumnSize	If *wType* is DBTYPE_STR or DBTYPE_WSTR, this is the maximum length in characters for values in this column. If *wType* is DBTYPE_BYTES, this is the maximum length in bytes for values in this column. For all other values of *wType*, this is ignored.
dbcid	The column ID of the column.
wType	The type indicator for the data type of the column. This name corresponds to a value in the DATA_TYPE column in the PROVIDER_TYPES schema rowset. In most cases, there is no reason for a consumer to specify a value for *wType* that is different from the values listed in the PROVIDER_TYPES schema rowset.

Element	Description
bPrecision	The maximum precision of data values in the column when *wType* is the indicator for a numeric type; it is ignored for all other data types. This must be within the limits specified for the type in the COLUMN_SIZE column in the PROVIDER_TYPES schema rowset. For information about the precision of numeric data types, see "Precision of Numeric Data Types" in Appendix A.
bScale	The scale of data values in the column when *wType* is DBTYPE_NUMERIC or DBTYPE_DECIMAL; it is ignored for all other data types. This must be within the limits specified for the type in the MINIMUM_SCALE and MAXIMUM_SCALE columns in the PROVIDER_TYPES schema rowset.

riid [in]

The IID of the interface to be returned for the resulting rowset; this is ignored if *ppRowset* is a null pointer.

cPropertySets [in]

The number of DBPROPSET structures in *rgPropertySets*. If this is zero, the provider ignores *rgPropertySets*.

rgPropertySets [in/out]

An array of DBPROPSET structures containing properties and values to be set. The properties specified in these structures must belong to the Rowset property group, for properties that apply to the rowset returned in **ppRowset*, or the Table property group, for properties that apply to the table. If the same property is specified more than once in *rgPropertySets*, then it is provider-specific which value is used. If *cPropertySets* is zero, this argument is ignored.

For information about the properties in the Rowset and Tables property groups that are defined by OLE DB, see "Rowset Properties" and "Table Properties" in Appendix C. For information about the DBPROPSET and DBPROP structures, see "DBPROPSET Structure" and "DBPROP Structure" in Chapter 11.

ppTableID [out]

A pointer to memory in which to return the DBID of the newly created table. If *ppTableID* is a null pointer, no DBID is returned.

ppRowset [out]

A pointer to memory in which to return the requested interface pointer on an empty rowset opened on the newly created table. If *ppRowset* is a null pointer, no rowset is created.

Return Code

S_OK
The method succeeded and the table is created and opened. In all DBPROP structures passed to the method, dwStatus is set to DBPROPSTATUS_OK.

DB_S_ERRORSOCCURRED
The table was created and the rowset was opened, but one or more properties—for which the *dwOptions* element of the DBPROP structure was DBPROPOPTIONS_SETIFCHEAP—were not set. The consumer checks *dwStatus* in the DBPROP structures to determine which properties were not set. The method can fail to set properties for a number of reasons, including:

- The property was not supported by the provider.
- The property was not in the Column, Rowset, or Table property group.
- The property set was not supported by the provider.
- It was not cheap to set the property.
- *colid* in the DBPROP structure was not DB_NULLID.
- The data type in *vValue* in the DBPROP structure was not the data type of the property or was not VT_EMPTY.
- The value in *vValue* in the DBPROP structure was invalid.
- The property's value conflicted with an existing property.

E_FAIL
A provider-specific error occurred.

E_INVALIDARG
pTableID and *ppTableID* were both null pointers.

cColumns was zero or *rgColumnDescs* was a null pointer.

cPropertySets was not zero and *rgPropertySets* was a null pointer.

In an element of *rgPropertySets*, *cProperties* was not zero and *rgProperties* was a null pointer.

In an element of *rgColumnDescs*, *cProperties* was not zero and *rgProperties* was a null pointer.

In an element of *rgColumnDescs*, *cPropertySets* was not zero and *rgPropertySets* was a null pointer.

DB_E_BADCOLUMNID
dbcid in an element of *rgColumnDescs* was an invalid column ID.

DB_E_BADTABLEID
*pTableID was an invalid table ID.

DB_E_BADPRECISION
The precision in an element of *rgColumnDescs* was invalid.

DB_E_BADPROPERTYVALUE
> The value of a property was invalid.

DB_E_BADSCALE
> The scale in an element of *rgColumnDescs* was invalid.

DB_E_BADTYPE
> The *wType, pwszTypeName*, or *pTypeInfo* element in an element of *rgColumnDescs* was invalid.

DB_E_DUPLICATECOLUMNID
> *dbcid* was the same in two or more elements of *rgColumnDescs.*

DB_E_DUPLICATETABLEID
> The specified table already exists in the current data source.

DB_E_ERRORSOCCURRED
> The table was not created and no rowset was returned because one or more properties—for which the *dwOptions* element of the DBPROP structure was DBPROPOPTIONS_REQUIRED or an invalid value—were not set. The consumer checks *dwStatus* in the DBPROP structures to determine which properties were not set. None of the satisfiable properties are remembered. The method can fail to set properties for any of the reasons specified in DB_S_ERRORSOCCURRED except the reason that states that it was not cheap to set the property.

DB_E_NOAGGREGATION
> *pUnkOuter* was not a null pointer and the rowset being created does not support aggregation.

DB_SEC_E_PERMISSIONDENIED
> The consumer did not have sufficient permission to create the table.

Comments

If *ppRowset* is not a null pointer, an empty rowset is opened on the newly created table. If **CreateTable** returns any errors, the table is not created.

See Also

IDBProperties::GetPropertyInfo, ITableDefinition::AddColumn, ITableDefinition::DropColumn, ITableDefinition::DropTable

ITableDefinition::DropColumn

This method drops a column from the base table.

HRESULT DropColumn(
    DBID* *pTableID*,
    DBID* *pColumnID*);

Parameters

pTableID [in]
    A pointer to the DBID of the table from which to drop the column.

pColumnID [in]
    A pointer to the DBID of the column to drop.

Return Code

S_OK
    The method succeeded and the column was dropped from the base table.

E_FAIL
    A provider-specific error occurred.

E_INVALIDARG
    pTableID or *pColumnID* was a null pointer.

DB_E_BADCOLUMNID
    The column specified in **pColumnID* does not exist in the specified table.

DB_E_NOTABLE
    The specified table does not exist in the current data source.

DB_E_TABLEINUSE
    The specified table was in use.

DB_SEC_E_PERMISSIONDENIED
    The consumer did not have sufficient permission to drop the column.

Comments

If **DropColumn** returns any errors, the column is not dropped.

See Also

ITableDefinition::AddColumn

ITableDefinition::DropTable

Drops a base table in the data source.

HRESULT DropTable (
   DBID * *pTableID*)**;**

Parameters

pTableID [in]
   A pointer to the DBID of the base table to drop.

Return Code

S_OK
   The method succeeded and the table is dropped.

E_FAIL
   A provider specific error occurred.

E_INVALIDARG
   pTableID was a null pointer.

DB_E_NOTABLE
   The specified table does not exist in the current data source.

DB_E_TABLEINUSE
   The specified table was in use.

DB_SEC_E_PERMISSIONDENIED
   The consumer did not have sufficient permission to drop the table.

See Also

ITableDefinition::CreateTable

ITransaction

The **ITransaction** interface is used to commit, abort, and obtain status information about transactions. For more information about transactions, see Chapter 12, "Transactions."

Method	Description
Abort	Aborts a transaction.
Commit	Commits a transaction.
GetTransactionInfo	Returns information about a transaction.

ITransaction::Abort

Aborts a transaction.

HRESULT Abort(
    BOID * *pboidReason*,
    BOOL *fRetaining*,
    BOOL *fAsync*);

Parameters

pboidReason [in]

A pointer to a BOID that indicates why the transaction is being aborted. If this is a null pointer, no reason is provided.

fRetaining [in]

Whether the abort is retaining or non-retaining.

fAsync [in]

When *fAsync* is TRUE, an asynchronous abort is performed and the caller must use **ITransactionOutcomeEvents** to learn the outcome of the transaction.

Return Code

S_OK

The transaction was successfully aborted.

XACT_S_ABORTING

An abort operation was already in progress. This call was ignored.

XACT_S_ASYNC

An asynchronous abort was specified. The abort operation has begun but its outcome is not yet known. When the transaction is complete, notification will be sent by **ITransactionOutcomeEvents**.

E_FAIL

The transaction failed to abort for an unspecified reason.

E_UNEXPECTED

An unexpected error occurred. The transaction status is unknown.

XACT_E_ALREADYINPROGRESS

A commit operation was already in progress. This call was ignored.

XACT_E_CANTRETAIN

A retaining abort is not supported or a new unit of work could not be created. The abort succeeded and the session is in auto-commit mode.

XACT_E_CONNECTION_DOWN

The connection to the transaction manager failed. The transaction state is unknown.

XACT_E_INDOUBT

The transaction status is in doubt. A communication failure occurred or a transaction manager or resource manager has failed.

XACT_E_NOTRANSACTION

The transaction cannot be aborted because it already had been implicitly or explicitly committed or aborted. This call was ignored.

XACT_E_NOTSUPPORTED

fAsync was TRUE on input and asynchronous abort operations are not supported.

Comments

The following table shows how the values of *fRetaining* and DBPROP_ABORTPRESERVE affect the rowset state and transaction mode:

DBPROP_ ABORT PRESERVE	*fRetaining*	Rowset state after abort	Resulting transaction mode of session
FALSE	FALSE	zombie	implicit / auto-commit
FALSE	TRUE	zombie	explicit / manual
TRUE	FALSE	preserved	implicit / auto-commit
TRUE	TRUE	preserved	explicit / manual

See Also

ITransaction::Commit

ITransaction::Commit

Commits a transaction.

HRESULT Commit(
    BOOL   *fRetaining*,
    DWORD *grfTC*,
    DWORD *grfRM*);

Parameters

fRetaining [in]

Whether the commit is retaining or non-retaining.

grfTC [in]

Values taken from the enumeration XACTTC. Values that may be specified in *grfTC* are as follows. These values are mutually exclusive.

Flag	Description
XACTTC_ ASYNC	When this flag is specified, an asynchronous commit is performed.
XACTTC_ SYNC_ PHASEONE	When this flag is specified, the call to **Commit** returns after phase one of the two-phase commit protocol.
XACTTC_ SYNC_ PHASETWO	When this flag is specified, the call to **Commit** returns after phase two of the two-phase commit protocol.
XACTTC_ SYNC	Synonym for XACTTC_SYNC_PHASETWO.

grfRM [in]

Must be zero.

Return Code

S_OK

The transaction was successfully committed.

XACT_S_ASYNC

An asynchronous commit was specified. The commit operation has begun but its outcome is not yet known. When the transaction is complete, notification will be sent by **ITransactionOutcomeEvents**.

E_FAIL

A provider-specific error occurred. The transaction was aborted.

E_UNEXPECTED

An unexpected error occurred. The transaction status is unknown.

XACT_E_ABORTED

The transaction was aborted before **Commit** was called.

XACT_E_ALREADYINPROGRESS

A commit or abort operation was already in progress. This call was ignored.

XACT_E_CANTRETAIN

Retaining commit is not supported or a new unit of work could not be created. The commit succeeded and the session is in auto-commit mode.

XACT_E_COMMITFAILED

The transaction failed to commit for an unknown reason. The transaction was aborted.

XACT_E_CONNECTION_DOWN

The connection to the transaction manager failed. The transaction was aborted.

XACT_E_INDOUBT

The transaction status is in doubt. A communication failure occurred or a transaction manager or resource manager has failed.

XACT_E_NOTRANSACTION

Unable to commit the transaction because it had already been implicitly or explicitly committed or aborted. This call was ignored.

XACT_E_NOTSUPPORTED

An invalid combination of commit flags was specified or *grfRM* was not equal to zero. This call was ignored.

Comments

The following table shows how values of the *fRetaining* parameter and DBPROP_COMMITPRESERVE affect the rowset state and transaction mode:

DBPROP_ COMMIT PRESERVE	*fRetaining*	Rowset state after commit	Resulting transaction mode of session
FALSE	FALSE	zombie	implicit / auto-commit
FALSE	TRUE	zombie	explicit / manual
TRUE	FALSE	preserved	implicit / auto-commit
TRUE	TRUE	preserved	explicit / manual

If **Commit** fails for any reason that results in an aborted transaction, the session is left in auto-commit mode.

See Also

ITransaction::Abort

ITransaction::GetTransactionInfo

Returns information regarding a transaction.

HRESULT GetTransactionInfo(
XACTTRANSINFO **pInfo*);

Parameters

pInfo [out]

A pointer to the caller-allocated XACTTRANSINFO structure in which the method
returns information about the transaction. *pInfo* must not be a null pointer.

```
typedef struct XACTTRANSINFO {
    XACTUOW  uow;
    ISOLEVEL isoLevel;
    ULONG    isoFlags;
    DWORD    grfTCSupported;
    DWORD    grfRMSupported;
    DWORD    grfTCSupportedRetaining;
    DWORD    grfRMSupportedRetaining;
} XACTTRANSINFO;
```

The elements of this structure are used as follows.

Element	Description
uow	The unit of work associated with this transaction.
isoLevel	The isolation level associated with this transaction. ISOLATIONLEVEL_UNSPECIFIED indicates that no isolation level was specified. For more information, see **ITransactionLocal::StartTransaction**.
isoFlags	Will be zero.
grfTCSupported	This bitmask indicates the XACTTC flags that this transaction implementation supports.
grfRMSupported	Will be zero.
grfTCSupportedRetaining	Will be zero.
grfRMSupportedRetaining	Will be zero.

Return Code

S_OK

The method succeeded.

E_FAIL

A provider-specific error occurred.

E_INVALIDARG

pInfo was a null pointer.

E_UNEXPECTED

An unknown error occurred. No information is returned.

XACT_E_NOTRANSACTION

Unable to retrieve information for the transaction because it was already completed. No information is returned.

ITransactionJoin

ITransactionJoin is exposed only by providers that support distributed transactions. The consumer calls **QueryInterface** for **ITransactionJoin** to determine whether the provider supports coordinated transactions. For more information, see "Coordinated Transactions" in Chapter 12.

Method	Description
GetOptionsObject	Returns an object that can be used to specify configuration options for a subsequent call to **JoinTransaction**.
JoinTransaction	Requests that the session enlist in a coordinated transaction.

ITransactionJoin::GetOptionsObject

Returns an object that can be used to specify configuration options for a subsequent call to **JoinTransaction**.

HRESULT GetOptionsObject (
    ITransactionOptions ** * *ppOptions*);**

Parameters

ppOptions [out]
> A pointer to memory in which to return a pointer to the object that can be used to set extended transaction options.

Return Code

S_OK
> The method succeeded.

E_FAIL
> An unknown error occurred.

E_INVALIDARG
> *ppOptions* was a null pointer.

E_OUTOFMEMORY
> Unable to allocate memory.

See Also

ITransactionOptions::GetOptions

ITransactionJoin::JoinTransaction

Requests that the session enlist in a coordinated transaction.

HRESULT JoinTransaction (
    IUnknown *   *punkTransactionCoord,*
    ISOLEVEL   *isoLevel,*
    ULONG   *isoFlags,*
    ITransactionOptions *   *pOtherOptions*);

Parameters

punkTransactionCoord [in]

A pointer to the controlling **IUnknown** of the transaction coordinator. **QueryInterface** can be called for the transaction coordinator for **ITransaction**.

isoLevel [in]

The isolation level to be used with this transaction. For more information, see **ITransactionLocal::StartTransaction**.

isoFlags [in]

Must be zero.

pOtherOptions [in]

Optionally a null pointer. If this is not a null pointer, then it is a pointer to an object previously returned from **GetOptionsObject** called on this session.

Return Code

S_OK

The method succeeded.

E_FAIL

An unknown error occurred.

E_INVALIDARG

punkTransactionCoord was a null pointer.

E_UNEXPECTED

An unknown provider-specific error occurred.

XACT_E_CONNECTION_DOWN

The connection to the transaction manager failed.

XACT_E_CONNECTION_REQUEST_DENIED

The transaction manager did not accept a connection request.

XACT_E_ISOLATIONLEVEL

Neither the requested isolation level, nor a strengthening of it, can be supported by this transaction implementation or *isoLevel* was not valid.

XACT_E_LOGFULL

Unable to begin a new transaction because the log file is full.

XACT_E_NOENLIST

A transaction coordinator was specified, but the new transaction was unable to enlist therein.

XACT_E_NOISORETAIN

The requested semantics of retention of isolation across retaining commit and abort boundaries cannot be supported by this transaction implementation or *isoFlags* was not equal to zero.

XACT_E_NOTIMEOUT

A time-out was specified, but time-outs are not supported.

XACT_E_TMNOTAVAILABLE

Unable to connect to the transaction manager or the transaction manager is unavailable.

XACT_E_XTIONEXISTS

This session can handle only one extant transaction at a time, and there is presently such a transaction.

Comments

The provider of the session will generally first register its **ITransactionOutcomeEvents** notification sink with the transaction coordinator, so that it can be notified of the outcome of the coordinated events, and will then enlist with the transaction coordinator using the interfaces defined in OLE Transactions. It is important that the provider first register with the outcome events so that it can be advised of any failures which may occur between enlistment registration of the outcome events.

See Also

ITransactionLocal::StartTransaction

ITransactionLocal : ITransaction

ITransactionLocal is an optional interface on sessions. It is used to start, commit, and abort transactions on the session. For more information, see "Simple Transactions" in Chapter 12.

Method	Description
GetOptionsObject	Returns an object that can be used to specify configuration options for a subsequent call to **StartTransaction**.
StartTransaction	Begins a new transaction.

ITransactionLocal::GetOptionsObject

Returns an object that can be used to specify configuration options for a subsequent call to **StartTransaction**.

HRESULT GetOptionsObject (
    **ITransactionOptions ** *ppOptions*);

Parameters

ppOptions [out]

A pointer to memory in which to return a pointer to the object that can be used to set extended transaction options.

Return Code

S_OK

The method succeeded.

E_FAIL

A provider-specific error occurred.

E_INVALIDARG

ppOptions was a null pointer.

E_OUTOFMEMORY

Unable to allocate memory.

E_UNEXPECTED

An unknown error occurred and the method failed.

See Also

ITransactionLocal::StartTransaction, ITransactionOptions::SetOptions

ITransactionLocal::StartTransaction

Begins a new transaction.

HRESULT StartTransaction (
ISOLEVEL	*isoLevel,*
ULONG	*isoFlags,*
ITransactionOptions *	*pOtherOptions,*
ULONG *	*pulTransactionLevel);*

Parameters

isoLevel [in]

The isolation level to be used with this transaction. For more information, see "Isolation Levels" in Chapter 12.

Value	Description
ISOLATIONLEVEL_ UNSPECIFIED	Applicable only to **ITransactionJoin::JoinTransaction**. Invalid for **ITransactionLocal** or for setting isolation level while in auto-commit mode.
ISOLATIONLEVEL_ CHAOS	Cannot overwrite the dirty data of other transactions at higher isolation levels.
ISOLATIONLEVEL_ READUNCOMMITTED	Read Uncommitted.
ISOLATIONLEVEL_ BROWSE	Synonym for ISOLATIONLEVEL_READUNCOMMITTED.
ISOLATIONLEVEL_ READCOMMITTED	Read Committed.
ISOLATIONLEVEL_ CURSORSTABILITY	Synonym for ISOLATIONLEVEL_READCOMMITTED.
ISOLATIONLEVEL_ REPEATABLEREAD	Repeatable Read.
ISOLATIONLEVEL_ SERIALIZABLE	Serializable.
ISOLATIONLEVEL_ ISOLATED	Synonym for ISOLATIONLEVEL_SERIALIZABLE.

isoFlags [in]

Must be zero.

pOtherOptions [in]

Optionally a null pointer. If this is not a null pointer, it is a pointer to an object previously returned from **GetOptionsObject** called on this session instance.

pulTransactionLevel [out]

A pointer to memory in which to return the level of the new transaction. The value of the top-level transaction is one. If *pulTransactionLevel* is a null pointer, the level is not returned.

Return Code

S_OK

The method succeeded.

E_FAIL

A provider-specific error occurred.

E_UNEXPECTED

An unknown error occurred and the method failed.

XACT_E_CONNECTION_DENIED

This session could not create a new transaction at the present time due to unspecified capacity issues.

XACT_E_CONNECTION_DOWN

This session is having communication difficulties with its internal implementation.

XACT_E_ISOLATIONLEVEL

Neither the requested isolation level nor a strengthening of it can be supported by this transaction implementation or *isoLevel* was not valid.

XACT_E_LOGFULL

A transaction could not be created because this session uses logging to a device which lacks available space.

XACT_E_NOISORETAIN

The requested semantics of retention of isolation across retaining commit and abort boundaries cannot be supported by this transaction implementation or *isoFlags* was not equal to zero.

XACT_E_NOTIMEOUT

A non-infinite time-out value was requested, but time-outs are not supported by this transaction.

XACT_E_XTIONEXISTS

This session can only handle one extant transaction at a time, and there is presently such a transaction.

See Also

ITransactionOptions::SetOptions

ITransactionObject

ITransactionObject enables consumers to obtain the transaction object associated with a particular transaction level. For more information, see "Transaction Objects" in Chapter 12.

Method	Description
GetTransactionObject	Returns an interface pointer on the transaction object.

ITransactionObject::GetTransactionObject

Returns an interface pointer on the transaction object.

HRESULT GetTransactionObject (
    ULONG   *ulTransactionLevel*,
    ITransaction ** *ppTransactionObject*);

Parameters

ulTransactionLevel [in]
    The level of the transaction.

ppTransactionObject [out]
    A pointer to memory in which to return a pointer to the returned transaction object.

Return Code

S_OK
    The method succeeded.

E_FAIL
    A provider-specific error occurred.

E_INVALIDARG
    ulTransactionLevel was zero or *ppTransactionObject* was a null pointer.

E_UNEXPECTED
    An unknown error occurred and the method failed.

ITransactionOptions

ITransactionOptions gets and sets a suite of options associated with a transaction.

Method	Description
GetOptions	Gets a suite of options associated with a transaction.
SetOptions	Sets a suite of options associated with a transaction.

ITransactionOptions::GetOptions

Gets a suite of options associated with a transaction.

HRESULT GetOptions(
    XACTOPT * *pOptions*);

Parameters

pOptions [in/out]

A pointer to an XACTOPT structure in which to return the options for this transaction. The consumer allocates this structure. For more information, see **SetOptions**.

Return Code

S_OK

Success.

E_FAIL

A provider-specific error occurred.

E_INVALIDARG

pOptions was a null pointer.

E_UNEXPECTED

An unknown error occurred; the method failed.

Comments

This method can be called at any time. **GetOptions** does not make any logical changes to the state of any open transactions.

See Also

ITransactionOptions::SetOptions, ITransactionJoin::GetOptionsObject, ITransactionLocal::GetOptionsObject

ITransactionOptions::SetOptions

Sets a suite of options associated with a transaction.

HRESULT SetOptions(
    XACTOPT * *pOptions***);**

Parameters

pOptions [in]

A pointer to an XACTOPT structure containing the options to be set in this transaction. This cannot be a null pointer.

```
typedef struct XACTOPT {
    ULONG         ulTimeout;
    unsigned char szDescription[MAX_TRAN_DESC];
} XACTOPT
```

The elements of this structure are used as follows.

Element	Description
ulTimeout	The amount of real-time in milliseconds before the transaction is to be aborted automatically. Zero indicates an infinite timeout. If no options have been previously set, *ulTimeout* is zero.
szDescription	A pointer to a textual description associated with this transaction. This string is appropriate for display in various end-user administration tools that might monitor or log the transaction. If no options have been previously set, *szDescription* is an empty string.

Return Code

S_OK

The method succeeded.

E_FAIL

A provider-specific error occurred.

E_INVALIDARG

pOptions was a null pointer.

E_UNEXPECTED

An unknown error occurred; the method failed.

See Also

ITransactionOptions::GetOptions, **ITransactionLocal::StartTransaction**

Appendixes

Data Types

This appendix describes data types in OLE DB. For information about how consumers and providers use data types, see Chapter 10, "Data Types in OLE DB."

Type Indicators

A type indicator indicates a data type. For more information, see Chapter 10, "Data Types in OLE DB."

```
typedef WORD DBTYPE;

enum DBTYPEENUM {
    // The following values exactly match VARENUM in OLE Automation
    // and may be used in VARIANT
    DBTYPE_EMPTY = 0,
    DBTYPE_NULL,
    DBTYPE_I2,
    DBTYPE_I4,
    DBTYPE_R4,
    DBTYPE_R8,
    DBTYPE_CY,
    DBTYPE_DATE,
    DBTYPE_BSTR,
    DBTYPE_IDISPATCH,
    DBTYPE_ERROR,
    DBTYPE_BOOL,
    DBTYPE_VARIANT,
    DBTYPE_IUNKNOWN,
    DBTYPE_DECIMAL,
    DBTYPE_UI1 = 17,
    DBTYPE_ARRAY = 0x2000,
    DBTYPE_BYREF = 0x4000,
```

```
// The following values exactly match VARENUM in OLE Automation
// but cannot be used in VARIANT
DBTYPE_I1 = 16,
DBTYPE_UI2 = 18,
DBTYPE_UI4,
DBTYPE_I8,
DBTYPE_UI8,
DBTYPE_GUID = 72,
DBTYPE_VECTOR = 0x1000,
DBTYPE_RESERVED = 0x8000,

// The following values are not in VARENUM in OLE
DBTYPE_BYTES = 128,
DBTYPE_STR = 129,
DBTYPE_WSTR,
DBTYPE_NUMERIC,
DBTYPE_UDT,
DBTYPE_DBDATE,
DBTYPE_DBTIME,
DBTYPE_DBTIMESTAMP
};
```

The following table describes each type indicator, including the C data type it corresponds to.

Type indicator	Description
DBTYPE_EMPTY	No value was specified. This indicator is valid only in a VARIANT structure and exists only to match the VT_EMPTY value in the VARENUM enumerated type in OLE. It does not correspond to any C data type.
DBTYPE_NULL	A NULL value. This indicator is valid only in a VARIANT structure and exists only to match the VT_NULL value in the VARENUM enumerated type in OLE. It does not correspond to any C data type.
DBTYPE_ RESERVED	Reserved for future use by OLE. This indicator does not correspond to any C data type.
DBTYPE_I1	A one-byte, signed integer: `signed char`
DBTYPE_I2	A two-byte, signed integer: `SHORT`
DBTYPE_I4	A four-byte, signed integer: `LONG`
DBTYPE_I8	An eight-byte, signed integer: `LARGE_INTEGER`

Type indicator	Description
DBTYPE_UI1	A one-byte, unsigned integer: `BYTE`
DBTYPE_UI2	A two-byte, unsigned integer: `unsigned short`
DBTYPE_UI4	A four-byte, unsigned integer: `unsigned int`
DBTYPE_UI8	An eight-byte, unsigned integer: `ULARGE_INTEGER`
DBTYPE_R4	A single-precision floating point value: `float`
DBTYPE_R8	A double-precision floating point value: `double`
DBTYPE_CY	A currency value: `LARGE_INTEGER` Currency is a fixed point number with four digits to the right of the decimal point. It is stored in an eight-byte signed integer, scaled by 10,000.
DBTYPE_ DECIMAL	An exact numeric value with a fixed precision and fixed scale, stored in the same way as in OLE Automation:

```
typedef struct tagDEC {
    USHORT wReserved;
    union {
        struct {
            BYTE scale;
            BYTE sign;
        };
        USHORT signscale;
    };
    ULONG Hi32;
    union {
        struct {
            ULONG Lo32;
            ULONG Mid32;
        };
        ULONGLONG Lo64;
    };
} DECIMAL;
```

Type indicator	Description
DBTYPE_ DECIMAL (*continued*)	The elements of this structure are used as follows: • *wReserved*—Reserved. Should be 0. • *scale*—The scale specifies the number of digits to the right of the decimal point and ranges from 0 to 28. • *sign*—The sign: 0 if positive, 0x80 if negative. • *Hi32*—The high part of the integer (32-bit aligned). • *Mid32*—The middle part of the integer (32-bit aligned). • *Lo32*—The low part of the integer (32-bit aligned). For example, to specify the number 12.345, the scale is 3, the sign is 0, and the number stored in the 12-byte integer is 12345. For information about what precision and scale the provider uses when accessing DECIMAL structures, see "Conversions Involving DBTYPE_NUMERIC or DBTYPE_DECIMAL" later in this appendix.
DBTYPE_ NUMERIC	An exact numeric value with a fixed precision and scale: ```\ntypedef struct tagDB_NUMERIC {\n BYTE precision;\n BYTE scale;\n BYTE sign;\n BYTE val[16];\n} DB_NUMERIC;\n``` The elements of this structure are used as follows: • *precision*—The maximum number of digits in base 10. • *scale*—The number of digits to the right of the decimal point. • *sign*—The sign: 1 for positive numbers, 0 for negative numbers. • *val*—A number stored as a 16-byte scaled integer, with the least-significant byte on the left. For example, to specify the base 10 number 20.003 with a scale of 4, the number is scaled to an integer of 200030 (20.003 shifted by four tens digits), which is 30D5E in hexadecimal. The value stored in the 16-byte integer is 5E 0D 03 00 00 00 00 00 00 00 00 00 00 00 00 00, the precision is the maximum precision, the scale is 4, and the sign is 1. For information about what precision and scale the provider uses when accessing DB_NUMERIC structures, see "Conversions Involving DBTYPE_NUMERIC or DBTYPE_DECIMAL" later in this appendix.
DBTYPE_DATE	A date stored in the same way as in OLE Automation: ```\nDATE\n``` A DATE is a double, the whole part of which is the number of days since December 30, 1899, and the fractional part of which is the fraction of a day. For example, the number 2.25 represents the datetime January 1, 1900 6:00 AM.

Type indicator	Description
DBTYPE_BOOL	A Boolean value stored in the same way as in OLE Automation: `VARIANT_BOOL` 0 means false and ~0 (bitwise, the value is not 0; that is, all bits are set to 1) means true.
DBTYPE_BYTES	A binary data value. That is, an array of bytes: `BYTE[length]` The length of the array is specified by *cbMaxLen* in the DBBINDING structure if DBTYPE_BYTES is used by itself. It is specified by the bound length value if DBTYPE_BYTES is combined with DBTYPE_BYREF. For columns containing binary data, the provider reports the data type as DBTYPE_BYTES and the maximum length as the true maximum length of the binary data (assuming there is one). For small, fixed-length binary data, such as a column in an SQL database of type BINARY(1000), the consumer generally binds the column as DBTYPE_BYTES. For small, variable-length binary data, such as a column in an SQL database of type VARBINARY(1000), the consumer generally binds the column as DBTYPE_BYTES | DBTYPE_BYREF, so no space is wasted and no data is truncated. For long binary data, the consumer generally binds the column as DBTYPE_IUNKNOWN and uses a storage interface such as **ISequentialStream** to manipulate the data. For more information, see "Accessing BLOB Data" in Chapter 7. When null-terminated string data is converted to or from DBTYPE_BYTES, the null termination character is not included in the length count or the data transferred.
DBTYPE_BSTR	A pointer to a BSTR, as in OLE Automation: `typedef WCHAR * BSTR;` A BSTR is a pointer to a null-terminated character string in which the string length (in bytes) is stored as a DWORD in the memory location preceding the actual string. Because the length precedes the string, BSTR variables can contain embedded null characters. The length of a BSTR is a count of bytes that does not include the null termination character or the space for the count. In Win32 (the environment for OLE DB) a BSTR contains Unicode. Consumers are responsible for freeing the memory used by BSTRs. Failure to free such memory is a common cause of memory leaks. For example, if a consumer calls **IRowset::GetData** to retrieve a BSTR, the provider allocates memory for the BSTR and returns a pointer to it in the memory pointed to by *pData*. A memory leak occurs when the consumer

Type indicator	Description
DBTYPE_BSTR (*continued*)	calls **GetData** again with the same value of *pData* without first freeing the memory for the BSTR. In this case, the provider allocates new memory for the BSTR and overwrites the pointer to the old BSTR with the pointer to the new BSTR. The old BSTR is still allocated, but the pointer to it is lost. For more information, see "Memory Management" in Chapter 6 and the *OLE Programmer's Reference, Volume 2*.
DBTYPE_STR	A null-terminated ANSI character string: `char[length]` If DBTYPE_STR is used by itself, the number of bytes allocated for the string, including the null termination character, is specified by *cbMaxLen* in the DBBINDING structure. If DBTYPE_STR is combined with DBTYPE_BYREF, the number of bytes allocated for the string, including the null termination character, is at least the length of the string plus one. In either case, the actual length of the string is determined from the bound length value. If a locale is applicable, it is indicated first by the column metadata, or if none is available then by table metadata, or if none is available then by the database locale.
DBTYPE_WSTR	A null-terminated Unicode character string: `wchar_t[length]` If DBTYPE_WSTR is used by itself, the number of bytes allocated for the string, including the null termination character, is specified by *cbMaxLen* in the DBBINDING structure. If DBTYPE_STR is combined with DBTYPE_BYREF, the number of bytes allocated for the string, including the null termination character, is at least the length of the string plus two. In either case, the actual length of the string is determined from the bound length value. Note that the maximum length of the string is the number of allocated bytes divided by **sizeof(wchar_t)** and truncated to the nearest integer.
DBTYPE_ VARIANT	An OLE Automation VARIANT: `VARIANT` The DBTYPE values that do not match OLE Automation VARENUM values represent data types that cannot be stored in a VARIANT. If the VARIANT structure contains a pointer to the data, then the buffer for that data is allocated separately.
DBTYPE_ IDISPATCH	A pointer to an **IDispatch** interface on an OLE object: `IDispatch *` For more information, see the *OLE Programmer's Reference, Volume 2*.

Type indicator	Description
DBTYPE_IUNKNOWN	A pointer to an **IUnknown** interface on an OLE object: `IUnknown *` For columns containing OLE objects, the provider reports the data type as DBTYPE_IUNKNOWN. The consumer specifies the interface to use through the *pObject* element of the DBBINDING structure. For more information, see "IPersist* Objects" in Chapter 7.
DBTYPE_GUID	A globally unique identifier (GUID): `GUID` GUIDs are also known as universally unique identifiers (UUIDs) and are used as class identifiers (CLSIDs) and interface identifiers (IIDs). For more information, see the OLE documentation.
DBTYPE_ERROR	A 32-bit error code: `SCODE` For more information, see the OLE documentation.
DBTYPE_BYREF	A pointer to data: `void *` DBTYPE_BYREF must be combined with another type indicator. This indicates that the data in the consumer's buffer is a pointer to the other type. For example, DBTYPE_STR	DBTYPE_BYREF means that the data is a pointer to an ANSI string and DBTYPE_I2	DBTYPE_BYREF means that the data is a pointer to a two-byte integer. DBTYPE_BYREF is commonly used to return pointers to variable-length data. It is used with provider-owned bindings to return pointers to the data in the rowset's copy of a row. When DBTYPE_BYREF is used, the data in the consumer's buffer can be a null pointer only when the corresponding status value is DBSTATUS_S_ISNULL. When setting a column value, if the data in the consumer's buffer is a null pointer and the status is not DBSTATUS_S_ISNULL, the provider returns a conversion error. DBTYPE_BYREF is mutually exclusive with the DBTYPE_ARRAY and DBTYPE_VECTOR modifiers and cannot be combined with the following values: DBTYPE_EMPTY DBTYPE_NULL DBTYPE_RESERVED For information about how DBTYPE_BYREF values are allocated, see "Memory Management" in Chapter 6.

Type indicator	Description
DBTYPE_ARRAY	A pointer to a SAFEARRAY: `SAFEARRAY *` DBTYPE_ARRAY must be combined with another type indicator. This indicates that the data in the consumer's buffer is a pointer to a SAFEARRAY of the other type. For example, DBTYPE_I2 | DBTYPE_ARRAY means that the data is a pointer to a SAFEARRAY of two-byte integers. When DBTYPE_ARRAY is used, the data in the consumer's buffer can be a null pointer only when the corresponding status value is DBSTATUS_S_ISNULL. When setting a column value, if the data in the consumer's buffer is a null pointer and the status is not DBSTATUS_S_ISNULL, the provider returns a conversion error. DBTYPE_ARRAY is mutually exclusive with the DBTYPE_BYREF and DBTYPE_VECTOR modifiers and cannot be combined with indicators for variable-length data types because there is no way to determine the length of each element of the array. DBTYPE_ARRAY can be combined with DBTYPE_BSTR because DBTYPE_BSTR is a fixed-length data type: A BSTR is a pointer to a separately allocated string that contains its own length. For information about how SAFEARRAYs are allocated, see "Memory Management" in Chapter 6. For more information about SAFEARRAYs, see the OLE documentation.

DBTYPE_ VECTOR	A DBVECTOR structure:
	
	`typedef struct tagDBVECTOR {`
	`    void * ptr;`
	`    ULONG  size;`
	`} DBVECTOR;`
	
	DBTYPE_VECTOR must be combined with another type indicator. This indicates that the data in the consumer's buffer is a DBVECTOR structure, which contains a pointer to an array of the other type. For example, DBTYPE_I2 | DBTYPE_VECTOR means that the data is a DBVECTOR structure that contains a pointer to an array of two-byte integers.
	
	When DBTYPE_VECTOR is used, the pointer in the DBVECTOR structure can be a null pointer only when the corresponding status value is DBSTATUS_S_ISNULL. When setting a column value, if the pointer is a null pointer and the status is not DBSTATUS_S_ISNULL, the provider returns a conversion error.
	
	DBTYPE_VECTOR is mutually exclusive with the DBTYPE_BYREF and DBTYPE_ARRAY modifiers and cannot be combined with indicators for variable-length data types because there is no way to determine the length of each element of the array.
	
	For information about how the memory pointed to by DBVECTOR structures is allocated, see "Memory Management" in Chapter 6.

Type indicator	Description
DBTYPE_UDT	A user-defined data type of variable length. In future versions, OLE DB may define the use of type libraries to support user-defined data types. This indicator does not correspond to any C data type.
DBTYPE_ DBDATE	A date structure: ```typedef struct tagDBDATE {\n SHORT year;\n USHORT month;\n USHORT day;\n} DBDATE;``` The elements of this structure are used as follows: • *year*—The year: 0-9999 measured from 0 A.D. • *month*—The month: 1–12. • *day*—1–*n* where *n* is the number of days in the month.
DBTYPE_ DBTIME	A time structure: ```typedef struct tagDBTIME {\n USHORT hour;\n USHORT minute;\n USHORT second;\n} DBTIME;``` The elements of this structure are used as follows: • *hour*—The hour: 0–23. • *minute*—The minute: 0–59. • *second*—The second: 0–59.
DBTYPE_ DBTIMESTAMP	A timestamp structure: ```typedef struct tagDBTIMESTAMP {\n SHORT year;\n USHORT month;\n USHORT day;\n USHORT hour;\n USHORT minute;\n USHORT second;\n ULONG fraction;\n} DBTIMESTAMP;```

Type indicator	Description
DBTYPE_ DBTIMESTAMP (*continued*)	The elements of this structure are used as follows: • *year*—The year: 0-9999 measured from 0 A.D. • *month*—The month: 1–12. • *day*—1–*n* where *n* is the number of days in the month. • *hour*—The hour: 0–23. • *minute*—The minute: 0–59. • *second*—The second: 0–59. • *fraction*—Billionths of a second: 0–999,999,999.

Precision of Numeric Data Types

The following OLE DB data types are used to represent numeric values. Each type has a corresponding maximum precision value that indicates the maximum number of base 10 digits that it can store. The radix of the precision for all numeric types is 10. The maximum precision returned by the provider in the COLUMN_SIZE column of the PROVIDER_TYPES schema rowset is the maximum possible precision for the data type that is supported by the data source. For example, if a data source can only support a maximum precision of 28 for a DBTYPE_NUMERIC column, the provider returns 28, not 38, as the maximum precision.

Type indicator	Maximum precision
DBTYPE_I1	3
DBTYPE_I2	5
DBTYPE_I4	10
DBTYPE_I8	19
DBTYPE_UI1	3
DBTYPE_UI2	5
DBTYPE_UI4	10
DBTYPE_UI8	20
DBTYPE_R4	7
DBTYPE_R8	16
DBTYPE_CY	19
DBTYPE_DECIMAL	28
DBTYPE_NUMERIC	38

Fixed-Length Data Types

The following type indicators are for fixed-length data types. For more information, see "Fixed- and Variable-Length Data Types" in Chapter 10.

DBTYPE_I1	DBTYPE_BSTR
DBTYPE_I2	DBTYPE_IDISPATCH
DBTYPE_I4	DBTYPE_ERROR
DBTYPE_I8	DBTYPE_BOOL
DBTYPE_UI1	DBTYPE_VARIANT
DBTYPE_UI2	DBTYPE_IUNKNOWN
DBTYPE_UI4	DBTYPE_GUID
DBTYPE_UI8	DBTYPE_NUMERIC
DBTYPE_R4	DBTYPE_DECIMAL
DBTYPE_R8	DBTYPE_DBDATE
DBTYPE_CY	DBTYPE_DBTIME
DBTYPE_DATE	DBTYPE_DBTIMESTAMP

Variable-Length Data Types

The following type indicators are for variable-length data types. For more information, see "Fixed- and Variable-Length Data Types" in Chapter 10.

DBTYPE_STR	DBTYPE_WSTR
DBTYPE_BYTES	

Data Type Conversion Rules

For information about the conversions providers are required to support and how consumers determine what these conversions are, see "Data Type Conversion" in Chapter 10. Providers that support optional conversions should follow the guidelines listed in this section.

Conversion Tables

The tables in this section describe most additional conversions. They use the following symbols:

- **S** = A safe conversion is possible.
- **T** = Conversion with truncation of non-significant digits is possible.
- **E** = An error due to truncation of significant digits is possible.
- **–** = The conversion is not supported.

To ⇒ From ⇓	I1	I2	I4	I8	UI1
I1	S	S	S	S	S, E
I2	S, E	S	S	S	S, E
I4	S, E	S, E	S	S	S, E
I8	S, E	S, E	S, E	S	S, E
UI1	S, E	S	S	S	S
UI2	S, E	S, E	S	S	S, E
UI4	S, E	S, E	S, E	S	S, E
UI8	S, E	S, E	S, E	S, E	S, E
R4	S, T, E	S, T, E	S, T	S, T	S, T, E
R8	S, T, E	S, T, E	S, T, E	S, T	S, T, E
CY	S, T, E	S, T, E	S, T, E	S, T	S, T, E
DEC	S, T, E	S, T, E	S, T, E	S, T, E	S, T, E
NUM	S, T, E	S, T, E	S, T, E	S, T, E	S, T, E
BOOL	–	–	–	–	–
DATE	–	–	–	–	–
DBDATE	–	–	–	–	–
DBTIME	–	–	–	–	–
DBTIMESTAMP	–	–	–	–	–
BYTES	S, E	S, E	S, E	S, E	S, E
BSTR	S, T, E	S, T, E	S, T, E	S, T, E	S, T, E
STR	S, T, E	S, T, E	S, T, E	S, T, E	S, T, E
WSTR	S, T, E	S, T, E	S, T, E	S, T, E	S, T, E
DISP	–	–	–	–	–
UNK	–	–	–	–	–
GUID	–	–	–	–	–

To ⇒ From ⇓	UI2	UI4	UI8	R4	R8
I1	S, E	S, E	S, E	S	S
I2	S, E	S, E	S, E	S	S
I4	S, E	S, E	S, E	S	S
I8	S, E	S, E	S, E	S, E	S, E
UI1	S	S	S	S	S
UI2	S	S	S	S	S
UI4	S, E	S	S	S, E	S
UI8	S, E	S, E	S	S, E	S, E
R4	S, T, E	S, T, E	S, T, E	S	S
R8	S, T, E	S, T, E	S, T, E	S, E	S
CY	S, T, E	S, T, E	S, T, E	S, E	S, E
DEC	S, T, E	S, T, E	S, T, E	S, E	S, E
NUM	S, T, E	S, T, E	S, T, E	S, E	S, E
BOOL	–	–	–	–	–
DATE	–	–	–	–	–
DBDATE	–	–	–	–	–
DBTIME	–	–	–	–	–
DBTIMESTAMP	–	–	–	–	–
BYTES	S, E	S, E	S, E	S, E	S, E
BSTR	S, T, E	S, T, E	S, T, E	S, T, E	S, T, E
STR	S, T, E	S, T, E	S, T, E	S, T, E	S, T, E
WSTR	S, T, E	S, T, E	S, T, E	S, T, E	S, T, E
DISP	–	–	–	–	–
UNK	–	–	–	–	–
GUID	–	–	–	–	–

To ⟹ From ⟓	CY	DEC	NUM	BOOL	DATE
I1	S	S	S	–	–
I2	S	S	S	–	–
I4	S	S	S	–	–
I8	S, E	S	S	–	–
UI1	S	S	S	–	–
UI2	S	S	S	–	–
UI4	S	S	S	–	–
UI8	S, E	S	S	–	–
R4	S, T	S	S	–	–
R8	S, T	S	S	–	–
CY	S	S	S	–	–
DEC	S, E	S	S	–	–
NUM	S, E	S, T, E	S	–	–
BOOL	–	–	–	S	–
DATE	–	–	–	–	S
DBDATE	–	–	–	–	S
DBTIME	–	–	–	–	S
DBTIMESTAMP	–	–	–	–	S, T
BYTES	S, E	S, E	S, E	S, E	S, E
BSTR	S, T, E	S, T, E	S, T, E	S, E	S, T, E
STR	S, T, E	S, T, E	S, T, E	S, E	S, T, E
WSTR	S, T, E	S, T, E	S, T, E	S, E	S, T, E
DISP	–	–	–	–	–
UNK	–	–	–	–	–
GUID	–	–	–	–	–

To ⇒ From ⇓	DBDATE	DBTIME	DBTIME STAMP	BYTES	BSTR
I1	–	–	–	S	S, E
I2	–	–	–	S, E	S, E
I4	–	–	–	S, E	S, E
I8	–	–	–	S, E	S, E
UI1	–	–	–	S	S, E
UI2	–	–	–	S, E	S, E
UI4	–	–	–	S, E	S, E
UI8	–	–	–	S, E	S, E
R4	–	–	–	S, E	S, E
R8	–	–	–	S, E	S, E
CY	–	–	–	S, E	S, E
DEC	–	–	–	S, E	S, E
NUM	–	–	–	S, E	S, E
BOOL	–	–	–	S	S, E
DATE	S, T, E	S, T	S, T, E	S, E	S, E
DBDATE	S	–	S	S, E	S, E
DBTIME	–	S	S	S, E	S, E
DBTIMESTAMP	S, T	S, T	S	S, E	S, E
BYTES	S, E	–	S	S, E	S, E
BSTR	S, T, E	S, T, E	S, T, E	S, E	S
STR	S, T, E	S, T, E	S, T, E	S, E	S
WSTR	S, T, E	S, T, E	S, T, E	S, E	S
DISP	–	–	–	S, E	–
UNK	–	–	–	S, E	–
GUID	–	–	–	S, E	S, E

To ⇒ From ⇓	STR	WSTR	DISP	UNK	GUID
I1	S, E	S, E	–	–	–
I2	S, E	S, E	–	–	–
I4	S, E	S, E	–	–	–
I8	S, E	S, E	–	–	–
UI1	S, E	S, E	–	–	–
UI2	S, E	S, E	–	–	–
UI4	S, E	S, E	–	–	–
UI8	S, E	S, E	–	–	–
R4	S, T, E	S, T, E	–	–	–
R8	S, T, E	S, T, E	–	–	–
CY	S, T, E	S, T, E	–	–	–
DEC	S, T, E	S, T, E	–	–	–
NUM	S, T, E	S, T, E	–	–	–
BOOL	S, E	S, E	–	–	–
DATE	S, T, E	S, T, E	–	–	–
DBDATE	S, T, E	S, T, E	–	–	–
DBTIME	S, T, E	S, T, E	–	–	–
DBTIMESTAMP	S, T, E	S, T, E	–	–	–
BYTES	S, E	S, E	S, E	S, E	S, E
BSTR	S, T	S, T	–	–	S, E
STR	S, T	S, T	–	S, E	S, E
WSTR	S, T	S, T	–	S, E	S, E
DISP	–	–	S	S	–
UNK	–	–	–	S	–
GUID	S, E	S, E	–	–	S

Conversions Involving Strings

The following formats are used for conversions to and from strings. Note that only non-trivial formats are listed.

Type indicator	Format
DBTYPE_BYTES	When strings are converted to and from binary data, each byte of binary data is represented as two ASCII characters. These characters are the ASCII character representation of the number in its hexadecimal form. For example, a binary 00000001 is converted to "01" and a binary 11111111 is converted to "FF".
DBTYPE_CY	"...*cccc.cccc*"
DBTYPE_BOOL	"True" and "False"
DBTYPE_DATE	As in OLE Automation: "*mm/dd/yy hh*:*mm*:*ss* {AM|PM}"
DBTYPE_DBDATE	As in ODBC: "*yyyy-mm-dd*"
DBTYPE_DBTIME	As in ODBC: "*hh*:*mm*:*ss*"
DBTYPE_ DBTIMESTAMP	As in ODBC: "*yyyy-mm-dd hh*:*mm*:*ss.f*..." where "*f*..." is fractions of a second (up to nine digits may be used).
DBTYPE_GUID	As represented in the registry: "{*xxxxxxxx-xxxx-xxxx-xxxx-xxxxxxxxxxxx*}" where *x* is a hexadecimal digit.
DBTYPE_STR DBTYPE_WSTR DBTYPE_BSTR	Conversion between strings of different locale IDs (LCIDs) is not supported. Conversion between ANSI and Unicode strings of the same LCID are required. In converting a Unicode string to ANSI, information may be lost as the Unicode range is greater. Lost characters are represented in the ANSI string by a special character and the conversion is considered to be a truncation. When mixing character sets, conversion to Unicode is the preferred solution. If conversion to ANSI is needed to use ANSI strings with the user interface, and the LCID of the user interface is different from the LCID of some columns, then the consumer is responsible for the conversion. The LCID of a column is returned in the DBCOLUMN_COLLATING_SEQUENCE column returned by **IColumnsRowset::GetColumnsRowset**.

Conversions Involving Numeric Values

Conversions involving numeric values use the following general guidelines:

- Except for the most significant digit, all digits in floating point numbers are considered to be less significant. Thus, floating point numbers can always be converted (possibly with truncation) to integers, numerics, or strings as long as they don't overflow the integer, numeric, or string.

  For example, 1.234567E2 is truncated to 123 when converted to an integer, to 123.4 when converted to a NUMERIC(4, 1), to 120 when converted to a NUMERIC(4, −1), assuming the provider supports negative scale (many do not), to "123\0" when converted to a four-byte ANSI string, and to "123.4\0" when converted to a six byte ANSI string. It cannot be converted to an ANSI string of three or fewer bytes as such a conversion would overflow the string.

- In DBTYPE_NUMERIC and DBTYPE_DECIMAL, digits to the right of the decimal point are considered less significant and can be truncated; digits to the left of the decimal point are considered significant and cannot be truncated. For example, 123.4567 is truncated to 123 when converted to an integer and to "123.4\0" when converted to a six-byte ANSI string.

- In strings that represent numbers, digits to the right of the decimal pointer are considered less significant and can be truncated; digits to the left of the decimal point are considered significant and cannot be truncated. For example, "123.45\0" is truncated to 123 when converted to an integer and 123.4 when converted to a NUMERIC(4, 1). "1234.5\0" cannot be converted to a one-byte integer.

- It is provider-specific whether negative numbers are truncated up or down. Thus, −1.99 might be truncated to −1 or to −2 when converted to an integer.

Conversions Involving DBTYPE_NUMERIC or DBTYPE_DECIMAL

When retrieving data from a DB_NUMERIC or DECIMAL structure, the provider uses the maximum precision and scale stored in that structure. When storing data in a DB_NUMERIC or DECIMAL structure, the provider uses the maximum precision and scale in the metadata for that structure. For consumer structures, these are in the binding structure. For provider structures, these are in the DBCOLUMNINFO structure returned by **IColumnsInfo::GetColumnInfo** or the DBPARAMINFO structure returned by **ICommandWithParameters::GetParameterInfo**.

The following table shows the maximum precision and scale used by the provider when accessing data in a DB_NUMERIC or DECIMAL structure in the consumer's buffer.

Consumer structure	Getting or setting data	Maximum precision	Scale
DB_NUMERIC	getting	*precision* element of DB_NUMERIC structure	*scale* element of DB_NUMERIC structure
DB_NUMERIC	setting	*bPrecision* element of DBBINDING structure	*bScale* element of DBBINDING structure
DECIMAL	getting	28	*scale* element of DECIMAL structure
DECIMAL	setting	28	*bScale* element of DBBINDING structure

The following table shows the maximum precision and scale used by the provider when accessing data in a DB_NUMERIC or DECIMAL structure in the provider.

Provider structure	Getting or setting data	Maximum precision	Scale
DB_NUMERIC	getting	*precision* element of DB_NUMERIC structure	*scale* element of DB_NUMERIC structure
DB_NUMERIC	setting	*bPrecision* element of DBCOLUMNINFO or DBPARAMINFO structure	*bScale* element of DBCOLUMNINFO or DBPARAMINFO structure
DECIMAL	getting	28	*scale* element of DECIMAL structure
DECIMAL	setting	28	*bScale* element of DBCOLUMNINFO or DBPARAMINFO structure

Conversions Involving VARIANTs

The following table describes conversions to and from VARIANTs. Type indicator X can be modified by DBTYPE_ARRAY or DBTYPE_BYREF. No conversions are supported when it is modified by DBTYPE_VECTOR.

Source type indicator	Target type indicator	Notes
X	DBTYPE_VARIANT	If X is a valid VARENUM value (that is, it is a type indicator that can be used in a VARIANT), the provider sets *vt* in the target VARIANT to X and transfers the data to the corresponding element of the union.
		If X is not a valid VARENUM value, it is provider-specific whether the provider supports the conversion and what type it uses in the VARIANT. Any such conversions must follow the rules in this appendix.
DBTYPE_VARIANT	X	If the type indicator specified in the source VARIANT is X, the provider transfers the data.
		If the type indicator specified in the VARIANT is not X, it is provider-specific whether the provider supports the conversion. Any such conversions must follow the rules in this appendix.
DBTYPE_VARIANT	DBTYPE_VARIANT	The provider sets *vt* in the target VARIANT to the same value as *vt* in the source VARIANT. It transfers the data from the union element in the source VARIANT to the same element in the target VARIANT.

Conversions Involving DBTYPE_BYREF

The following table describes conversions to and from types modified by DBTYPE_BYREF. Type indicators X and Y are unmodified by DBTYPE_BYREF.

Source type indicator	Target type indicator	Notes
X	Y | DBTYPE_BYREF	If Y is a variable-length data type and the provider supports a conversion from X to Y, the provider must support this conversion.
		If Y is not a variable-length data type, it is provider-specific whether this conversion is supported. Any such conversions must follow the rules in this appendix.
		For information about further restrictions when memory is provider-owned, see the description of *dwMemOwner* in "DBBINDING Structures" in Chapter 6.
X | DBTYPE_BYREF	Y	If X equals Y, the provider must support this conversion.

Source type indicator	Target type indicator	Notes
X | DBTYPE_BYREF (*continued*)	Y	If X is not equal to Y, the provider supports this if and only if it supports a conversion from X to Y. Any such conversions must follow the rules in this appendix.
X | DBTYPE_BYREF	Y | DBTYPE_BYREF	The provider must support this conversion if it supports a conversion from X to Y | DBTYPE_BYREF. Any such conversions must follow the rules in this appendix.

Conversions Involving DBTYPE_ARRAY

The following table describes conversions to and from types modified by DBTYPE_ARRAY. Type indicators X and Y are unmodified; when combined with DBTYPE_ARRAY, they cannot be DBTYPE_EMPTY or DBTYPE_NULL.

Source type indicator	Target type indicator	Notes
X	Y | DBTYPE_ARRAY	It is provider-specific whether this is supported.
X | DBTYPE_ARRAY	Y	It is provider-specific whether this is supported.
X | DBTYPE_ARRAY	Y | DBTYPE_ARRAY	If the provider supports a conversion from X to Y, and the provider supports both X | DBTYPE_ARRAY and Y | DBTYPE_ARRAY, it must support this conversion. Any such conversions must follow the rules in this appendix.
X | DBTYPE_VECTOR	Y | DBTYPE_ARRAY	Not supported.
X | DBTYPE_ARRAY	Y | DBTYPE_VECTOR	Not supported.

Conversions Involving DBTYPE_VECTOR

The following table describes conversions to and from types modified by DBTYPE_VECTOR. Type indicators X and Y are unmodified.

Source type indicator	Target type indicator	Notes
X	Y | DBTYPE_VECTOR	It is provider-specific whether this is supported.
X | DBTYPE_VECTOR	Y	It is provider-specific whether this is supported.
X | DBTYPE_VECTOR	Y | DBTYPE_VECTOR	If the provider supports a conversion from X to Y, and the provider supports both X | DBTYPE_VECTOR and Y | DBTYPE_VECTOR, it must support this conversion. Any such conversions must follow the rules in this appendix.
X | DBTYPE_ARRAY	Y | DBTYPE_VECTOR	Not supported.
X | DBTYPE_VECTOR	Y | DBTYPE_ARRAY	Not supported.

Schema Rowsets

The schema information specified in OLE DB is based on the assumption that providers support the concepts of a catalog and a schema. The ANSI SQL '92 specification defines them as follows:

- A *catalog* contains one or more schemas, but always contains a schema named INFORMATION_SCHEMA which contains the views and domains of the information schema. In Microsoft SQL Server and Microsoft Access terms, a catalog is a database; in ODBC 2.*x* terms, a catalog is a qualifier.

- A *schema* is a collection of database objects which are owned or have been created by a particular user. In Microsoft SQL Server and ODBC 2.*x* terms, a schema is an owner; there is no equivalent to a schema in a Microsoft Access database.

Schema information in OLE DB is retrieved using predefined schema rowsets; this appendix lists the contents of each schema rowset.

Schema rowsets are retrieved with **IDBSchemaRowset::GetRowset**. **GetRowset** allows consumers to specify simple restrictions, such as returning all the columns in a particular table. Each schema rowset is guaranteed to return all of the columns in the order shown in the section detailing that rowset. In addition, providers can return provider-specific columns after the last column defined by OLE DB.

In implementing **IDBSchemaRowset**, it is suggested that providers pay particular attention to rowset construction and data retrieval performance, because these commands will be frequently used by consumers.

This information schema also defines a minimum content of the system schema. It is assumed that consumers will prepare and store the specialized commands used for things like command planning and execution-time plan validation, and storage engines may have specialized optimizations associated with those plans. Consumers can also look at the schema tables in the schema, and thus discover other schema tables and attributes beyond the minimum set.

Logical Information Schema Rowsets

This section details each schema rowset in the logical information schema. These schema rowsets are primarily concerned with the logical database metadata and are a superset of the information presented by the INFORMATION_SCHEMA views defined in ANSI SQL '92, with the exception of the COLUMNS and DOMAINS rowsets, which contain subsets of this information. The INFORMATION_SCHEMA schema exists in all ANSI SQL '92 catalogs.

Although the ANSI SQL '92 views define some columns as NOT NULLABLE, OLE DB does not enforce this restriction. Therefore, consumers should check the metadata for a particular column with **IColumnsInfo::GetColumnInfo** or **IColumnsRowset::GetColumnRowset** to determine if it is nullable.

The following rowsets are in the logical information schema. All providers that support **IDBSchemaRowset** must support the TABLES and COLUMNS schema rowsets. Support for other schema rowsets in the logical information schema is optional.

ASSERTIONS	PROCEDURE_PARAMETERS
CHARACTER_SETS	PROCEDURES
CHECK_CONSTRAINTS	REFERENTIAL_CONSTRAINTS
COLLATIONS	SCHEMATA
COLUMN_DOMAIN_USAGE	SQL_LANGUAGES
COLUMN_PRIVILEGES	TABLE_CONSTRAINTS
COLUMNS	TABLE_PRIVILEGES
CONSTRAINT_COLUMN_USAGE	TABLES
CONSTRAINT_TABLE_USAGE	TRANSLATIONS
FOREIGN_KEYS	USAGE_PRIVILEGES
KEY_COLUMN_USAGE	VIEW_COLUMN_USAGE
PRIMARY_KEYS	VIEW_TABLE_USAGE
PROCEDURE_COLUMNS	VIEWS

Physical Information Schema Rowsets

This section details the contents of each schema rowset in the physical information schema. These schema rowsets are primarily concerned with the physical database metadata. The contents of such metadata is not defined in ANSI SQL '92; all definitions in this section are OLE DB extensions to ANSI SQL '92.

The following rowsets are in the physical information schema. All providers that support **IDBSchemaRowset** must support the PROVIDER_TYPES schema rowset. Support for other schema rowsets in the physical information schema is optional.

CATALOGS   PROVIDER_TYPES

INDEXES   STATISTICS

ASSERTIONS Rowset

The ASSERTIONS rowset identifies the assertions defined in the catalog that are owned by a given user.

The ASSERTIONS rowset contains the following columns:

Column name	Type indicator	Description
CONSTRAINT_CATALOG	DBTYPE_WSTR	Catalog name. NULL if the provider does not support catalogs.
CONSTRAINT_SCHEMA	DBTYPE_WSTR	Unqualified schema name. NULL if the provider does not support schemas.
CONSTRAINT_NAME	DBTYPE_WSTR	Constraint name.
IS_DEFERRABLE	DBTYPE_BOOL	VARIANT_TRUE—The assertion is deferrable. VARIANT_FALSE—The assertion is not deferrable.
INITIALLY_DEFERRED	DBTYPE_BOOL	VARIANT_TRUE—The assertion is initially deferred. VARIANT_FALSE—The assertion is initially immediate.
DESCRIPTION	DBTYPE_WSTR	Human-readable description of the column.

Default Sort Order: CONSTRAINT_CATALOG, CONSTRAINT_SCHEMA, CONSTRAINT_NAME

CATALOGS Rowset

The CATALOGS rowset identifies the physical attributes associated with catalogs accessible from the DBMS. For some systems, such as Microsoft Access, there may be only one catalog. For Microsoft SQL Server, this rowset would enumerate all catalogs (databases) defined in the system database.

The CATALOGS rowset contains the following columns:

Column name	Type indicator	Description
CATALOG_NAME	DBTYPE_WSTR	Catalog name.
DESCRIPTION	DBTYPE_WSTR	Human-readable description of the table.

Default Sort Order: CATALOG_NAME

CHARACTER_SETS Rowset

The CHARACTER_SETS rowset identifies the character sets defined in the catalog that are accessible to a given user.

The CHARACTER_SETS rowset contains the following columns:

Column name	Type indicator	Description
CHARACTER_SET_ CATALOG	DBTYPE_WSTR	Catalog name. NULL if the provider does not support catalogs.
CHARACTER_SET_ SCHEMA	DBTYPE_WSTR	Unqualified schema name. NULL if the provider does not support schemas.
CHARACTER_SET_NAME	DBTYPE_WSTR	Character set name.
FORM_OF_USE	DBTYPE_WSTR	Name of form-of-use of the character set.
NUMBER_OF_ CHARACTERS	DBTYPE_I8	Number of characters in the character repertoire.
DEFAULT_COLLATE_ CATALOG	DBTYPE_WSTR	Catalog name containing the default collation. NULL if the provider does not support catalogs or different collations.
DEFAULT_COLLATE_ SCHEMA	DBTYPE_WSTR	Unqualified schema name containing the default collation. NULL if the provider does not support schemas or different collations.
DEFAULT_COLLATE_ NAME	DBTYPE_WSTR	Default collation. NULL if the provider does not support different collations.

Default Sort Order: CHARACTER_SET_CATALOG,
CHARACTER_SET_SCHEMA, CHARACTER_SET_NAME

CHECK_CONSTRAINTS Rowset

The CHECK_CONSTRAINTS rowset identifies the check constraints defined in the
catalog that are owned by a given user.

The CHECK_CONSTRAINTS rowset contains the following columns:

Column name	Type indicator	Description
CONSTRAINT_ CATALOG	DBTYPE_WSTR	Catalog name. NULL if the provider does not support catalogs.
Column name	**Type indicator**	**Description**
CONSTRAINT_SCHEMA	DBTYPE_WSTR	Unqualified schema name. NULL if the provider does not support schemas.
CONSTRAINT_NAME	DBTYPE_WSTR	Constraint name.
CHECK_CLAUSE	DBTYPE_WSTR	The **WHERE** clause specified in the **CHECK** clause.
DESCRIPTION	DBTYPE_WSTR	Human-readable description of the column.

Default Sort Order: CONSTRAINT_CATALOG, CONSTRAINT_SCHEMA,
CONSTRAINT_NAME

COLLATIONS Rowset

The COLLATIONS rowset identifies the character collations defined in the catalog
that are accessible to a given user.

The COLLATIONS rowset contains the following columns:

Column name	Type indicator	Description
COLLATION_CATALOG	DBTYPE_WSTR	Catalog name. NULL if the provider does not support catalogs.
COLLATION_SCHEMA	DBTYPE_WSTR	Unqualified schema name. NULL if the provider does not support schemas.
COLLATION_NAME	DBTYPE_WSTR	Character set name.
CHARACTER_SET_ CATALOG	DBTYPE_WSTR	Catalog name containing the character set on which the collation is defined. NULL if the provider does not support catalogs or different character sets.

Column name	Type indicator	Description
CHARACTER_SET_SCHEMA	DBTYPE_WSTR	Unqualified schema name containing the character set on which the collation is defined. NULL if the provider does not support schema or different character sets.
CHARACTER_SET_NAME	DBTYPE_WSTR	Character set name on which the collation is defined. NULL if the provider does not support different character sets.
PAD_ATTRIBUTE	DBTYPE_WSTR	"NO PAD"—The collation being described has the **NO PAD** attribute. "PAD SPACE"—The collation being described has the **PAD SPACE** attribute.

Default Sort Order: COLLATION_CATALOG, COLLATION_SCHEMA, COLLATION_CATALOG, CHARACTER_SET_CATALOG, CHARACTER_SET_SCHEMA, CHARACTER_SET_NAME

COLUMN_DOMAIN_USAGE Rowset

The COLUMN_DOMAIN_USAGE rowset identifies the columns defined in the catalog that are dependent on a domain defined in the catalog and owned by a given user.

The COLUMN_DOMAIN_USAGE rowset contains the following columns:

Column name	Type indicator	Description
DOMAIN_CATALOG	DBTYPE_WSTR	Catalog name. NULL if the provider does not support catalogs.
DOMAIN_SCHEMA	DBTYPE_WSTR	Unqualified schema name. NULL if the provider does not support schemas.
DOMAIN_NAME	DBTYPE_WSTR	View name.
TABLE_CATALOG	DBTYPE_WSTR	Catalog name in which the table is defined. NULL if the provider does not support catalogs.
TABLE_SCHEMA	DBTYPE_WSTR	Unqualified schema name in which the table is defined. NULL if the provider does not support schemas.
TABLE_NAME	DBTYPE_WSTR	Table name.
COLUMN_NAME	DBTYPE_WSTR	Column name. This column, together with the COLUMN_GUID and COLUMN_PROPID columns, forms the column ID. One or more of these columns will be NULL depending on which elements of the DBID structure the provider uses.

Column name	Type indicator	Description
COLUMN_GUID	DBTYPE_GUID	Column GUID.
COLUMN_PROPID	DBTYPE_UI4	Column property ID.

Default Sort Order: DOMAIN_CATALOG, DOMAIN_SCHEMA, DOMAIN_NAME, TABLE_CATALOG, TABLE_SCHEMA, TABLE_NAME, COLUMN_NAME, COLUMN_GUID, COLUMN_PROPID

COLUMN_PRIVILEGES Rowset

The COLUMN_PRIVILEGES rowset identifies the privileges on columns of tables defined in the catalog that are available to or granted by a given user.

The COLUMN_PRIVILEGES rowset contains the following columns:

Column name	Type indicator	Description
GRANTOR	DBTYPE_WSTR	User who granted the privileges on the table in TABLE_NAME.
GRANTEE	DBTYPE_WSTR	User name (or "PUBLIC") to whom the privilege has been granted.
TABLE_CATALOG	DBTYPE_WSTR	Catalog name in which the table is defined. NULL if the provider does not support catalogs.
TABLE_SCHEMA	DBTYPE_WSTR	Unqualified schema name in which the table is defined. NULL if the provider does not support schemas.
TABLE_NAME	DBTYPE_WSTR	Table name.
COLUMN_NAME	DBTYPE_WSTR	Column name. This column, together with the COLUMN_GUID and COLUMN_PROPID columns, forms the column ID. One or more of these columns will be NULL depending on which elements of the DBID structure the provider uses.
COLUMN_GUID	DBTYPE_GUID	Column GUID.
COLUMN_PROPID	DBTYPE_UI4	Column property ID.
PRIVILEGE_TYPE	DBTYPE_WSTR	Privilege type. One of the following: "SELECT" "DELETE" "INSERT" "UPDATE" "REFERENCES"

Column name	Type indicator	Description
IS_GRANTABLE	DBTYPE_BOOL	VARIANT_TRUE—The privilege being described was granted with the **WITH GRANT OPTION** clause. VARIANT_FALSE—The privilege being described want not granted with the **WITH GRANT OPTION** clause.

Default Sort Order: TABLE_CATALOG, TABLE_SCHEMA, TABLE_NAME, COLUMN_NAME, COLUMN_GUID, COLUMN_PROPID, PRIVILEGE_TYPE

COLUMNS Rowset

The COLUMNS rowset identifies the columns of tables defined in the catalog that are accessible to a given user.

The COLUMNS rowset contains the following columns:

Column name	Type indicator	Description
TABLE_CATALOG	DBTYPE_WSTR	Catalog name. NULL if the provider does not support catalogs.
TABLE_SCHEMA	DBTYPE_WSTR	Unqualified schema name. NULL if the provider does not support schemas.
TABLE_NAME	DBTYPE_WSTR	Table name.
COLUMN_NAME	DBTYPE_WSTR	The name of the column; this might not be unique. If this cannot be determined, a NULL is returned. This column, together with the COLUMN_GUID and COLUMN_PROPID columns, forms the column ID. One or more of these columns will be NULL depending on which elements of the DBID structure the provider uses. If possible, the resulting column ID should be persistent. However, some providers do not support persistent identifiers for columns. The column ID of a base table should be invariant under views.
COLUMN_GUID	DBTYPE_GUID	Column GUID.
COLUMN_PROPID	DBTYPE_UI4	Column property ID.
ORDINAL_POSITION	DBTYPE_UI4	The ordinal of the column. Columns are numbered starting from one. NULL if there is no stable ordinal value for the column.

Column name	Type indicator	Description
COLUMN_HASDEFAULT	DBTYPE_BOOL	VARIANT_TRUE—The column has a default value. VARIANT_FALSE—The column does not have a default value or it is unknown whether the column has a default value.
COLUMN_DEFAULT	DBTYPE_WSTR	Default value of the column. A provider may expose DBCOLUMN_DEFAULTVALUE but not DBCOLUMN_HASDEFAULT (for SQL '92 tables) in the rowset returned by **IColumnsRowset::GetColumnsRowset**. If the default value is the NULL value, COLUMN_HASDEFAULT is VARIANT_TRUE, and the COLUMN_DEFAULT column is a NULL value.
COLUMN_FLAGS	DBTYPE_UI4	A bitmask that describes column characteristics. The DBCOLUMNFLAGS enumerated type specifies the bits in the bitmask. For information about DBCOLUMNFLAGS, see **IColumnsInfo::GetColumnInfo**. This column cannot contain a NULL value.
IS_NULLABLE	DBTYPE_BOOL	VARIANT_TRUE—The column might be nullable. VARIANT_FALSE—The column is known not to be nullable.
DATA_TYPE	DBTYPE_UI2	The indicator of the column's data type. If the data type of the column varies from row to row, this must be DBTYPE_VARIANT. For a list of valid type indicators, see "Type Indicators" in Appendix A.
TYPE_GUID	DBTYPE_GUID	The GUID of the column's data type.
CHARACTER_ MAXIMUM_LENGTH	DBTYPE_UI4	The maximum possible length of a value in the column. For character, binary, or bit columns, this is one of the following: • The maximum length of the column in characters, bytes, or bits, respectively, if one is defined. For example, a CHAR(5) column in an SQL table has a maximum length of 5. • The maximum length of the data type in characters, bytes, or bits, respectively, if the column does not have a defined length. • 0 if neither the column nor the data type has a defined maximum length. NULL for all other types of columns.

Column name	Type indicator	Description
CHARACTER_OCTET_LENGTH	DBTYPE_UI4	Maximum length in octets (bytes) of the column, if the type of the column is character or binary. A value of zero means the column has no maximum length. NULL for all other types of columns.
NUMERIC_PRECISION	DBTYPE_UI2	If the column's data type is numeric, this is the maximum precision of the column. The precision of columns with a data type of DBTYPE_DECIMAL or DBTYPE_NUMERIC depends on the definition of the column. For the precision of all other numeric data types, see "Precision of Numeric Data Types" in Appendix A. If the column's data type is not numeric, this is NULL.
NUMERIC_SCALE	DBTYPE_I2	If column's type indicator is DBTYPE_DECIMAL or DBTYPE_NUMERIC, this is the number of digits to the right of the decimal point. Otherwise, this is NULL.
DATETIME_PRECISION	DBTYPE_UI4	Datetime precision (number of digits in the fractional seconds portion) of the column if the column is a datetime or interval type.
CHARACTER_SET_CATALOG	DBTYPE_WSTR	Catalog name in which the character set is defined. NULL if the provider does not support catalogs or different character sets.
CHARACTER_SET_SCHEMA	DBTYPE_WSTR	Unqualified schema name in which the character set is defined. NULL if the provider does not support schemas or different character sets.
CHARACTER_SET_NAME	DBTYPE_WSTR	Character set name. NULL if the provider does not support different character sets.
COLLATION_CATALOG	DBTYPE_WSTR	Catalog name in which the collation is defined. NULL if the provider does not support catalogs or different collations.
COLLATION_SCHEMA	DBTYPE_WSTR	Unqualified schema name in which the collation is defined. NULL if the provider does not support schemas or different collations.
COLLATION_NAME	DBTYPE_WSTR	Collation name. NULL if the provider does not support different collations.
DOMAIN_CATALOG	DBTYPE_WSTR	Catalog name in which the domain is defined. NULL if the provider does not support catalogs or domains.

Column name	Type indicator	Description
DOMAIN_SCHEMA	DBTYPE_WSTR	Unqualified schema name in which the domain is defined. NULL if the provider does not support schemas or domains.
DOMAIN_NAME	DBTYPE_WSTR	Domain name. NULL if the provider does not support domains.
DESCRIPTION	DBTYPE_WSTR	Human-readable description of the column. For example, the description for a column named Name in the Employee table might be "Employee name."

Default Sort Order: TABLE_CATALOG, TABLE_SCHEMA, TABLE_NAME

CONSTRAINT_COLUMN_USAGE Rowset

The CONSTRAINT_COLUMN_USAGE rowset identifies the columns used by referential constraints, unique constraints, check constraints, and assertions, defined in the catalog and owned by a given user.

The CONSTRAINT_COLUMN_USAGE rowset contains the following columns:

Column name	Type indicator	Description
TABLE_CATALOG	DBTYPE_WSTR	Catalog name in which the table is defined. NULL if the provider does not support catalogs.
TABLE_SCHEMA	DBTYPE_WSTR	Unqualified schema name in which the table is defined. NULL if the provider does not support schemas.
TABLE_NAME	DBTYPE_WSTR	Table name.
COLUMN_NAME	DBTYPE_WSTR	Column name. This column, together with the COLUMN_GUID and COLUMN_PROPID columns, forms the column ID. One or more of these columns will be NULL depending on which elements of the DBID structure the provider uses.
COLUMN_GUID	DBTYPE_GUID	Column GUID.
COLUMN_PROPID	DBTYPE_UI4	Column property ID.
CONSTRAINT_CATALOG	DBTYPE_WSTR	Catalog name. NULL if the provider does not support catalogs.

Column name	Type indicator	Description
CONSTRAINT_SCHEMA	DBTYPE_WSTR	Unqualified schema name. NULL if the provider does not support schemas.
CONSTRAINT_NAME	DBTYPE_WSTR	Constraint name.

Default Sort Order: TABLE_CATALOG, TABLE_SCHEMA, TABLE_NAME, COLUMN_NAME, COLUMN_GUID, COLUMN_PROPID, CONSTRAINT_CATALOG, CONSTRAINT_SCHEMA, CONSTRAINT_NAME

CONSTRAINT_TABLE_USAGE Rowset

The CONSTRAINT_TABLE_USAGE rowset identifies the tables that are used by referential constraints, unique constraints, check constraints, and assertions defined in the catalog and owned by a given user.

The CONSTRAINT_TABLE_USAGE rowset contains the following columns:

Column name	Type indicator	Description
TABLE_CATALOG	DBTYPE_WSTR	Catalog name in which the table is defined. NULL if the provider does not support catalogs.
TABLE_SCHEMA	DBTYPE_WSTR	Unqualified schema name in which the table is defined. NULL if the provider does not support schemas.
TABLE_NAME	DBTYPE_WSTR	Table name.
CONSTRAINT_CATALOG	DBTYPE_WSTR	Catalog name. NULL if the provider does not support catalogs.
CONSTRAINT_SCHEMA	DBTYPE_WSTR	Unqualified schema name. NULL if the provider does not support schemas.
CONSTRAINT_NAME	DBTYPE_WSTR	Constraint name.

Default Sort Order: TABLE_CATALOG, TABLE_SCHEMA, TABLE_NAME, CONSTRAINT_CATALOG, CONSTRAINT_SCHEMA, CONSTRAINT_NAME

FOREIGN_KEYS Rowset

The FOREIGN_KEYS rowset identifies the foreign key columns defined in the catalog by a given user. This schema rowset is built upon several SQL '92 schema views as a convenience to the non-SQL programmer, and, if supported, this must be synchronized with the related SQL '92 views (REFERENTIAL_CONSTRAINTS and CONSTRAINT_COLUMN_USAGE).

The FOREIGN_KEYS rowset contains the following columns:

Column name	Type indicator	Description
PK_TABLE_CATALOG	DBTYPE_WSTR	Catalog name in which the primary key table is defined. NULL if the provider does not support catalogs.
PK_TABLE_SCHEMA	DBTYPE_WSTR	Unqualified schema name in which the primary key table is defined. NULL if the provider does not support schemas.
PK_TABLE_NAME	DBTYPE_WSTR	Primary key table name.
PK_COLUMN_NAME	DBTYPE_WSTR	Primary key column name. This column, together with the PK_COLUMN_GUID and PK_COLUMN_PROPID columns, forms the column ID. One or more of these columns will be NULL depending on which elements of the DBID structure the provider uses.
PK_COLUMN_GUID	DBTYPE_GUID	Primary key column GUID.
PK_COLUMN_PROPID	DBTYPE_UI4	Primary key column property ID.
FK_TABLE_CATALOG	DBTYPE_WSTR	Catalog name in which the foreign key table is defined. NULL if the provider does not support catalogs.
FK_TABLE_SCHEMA	DBTYPE_WSTR	Unqualified schema name in which the foreign key table is defined. NULL if the provider does not support schemas.
FK_TABLE_NAME	DBTYPE_WSTR	Foreign key table name.
FK_COLUMN_NAME	DBTYPE_WSTR	Foreign key column name. This column, together with the FK_COLUMN_GUID and FK_COLUMN_PROPID columns, forms the column ID. One or more of these columns will be NULL depending on which elements of the DBID structure the provider uses.
FK_COLUMN_GUID	DBTYPE_GUID	Foreign key column GUID.
FK_COLUMN_PROPID	DBTYPE_UI4	Foreign key column property ID.
ORDINAL	DBTYPE_UI4	The order of the column names (and GUIDs and property IDs) in the key. For example, a table might contain several foreign key references to another table. The ordinal starts over for each reference; for example, two references to a three-column key would return 1, 2, 3, 1, 2, 3.)

Column name	Type indicator	Description
UPDATE_RULE	DBTYPE_WSTR	If an <update rule> was specified then the UPDATE_RULE value is one of the following:
		"CASCADE"—A <referential action> of **CASCADE** was specified.
		"SET NULL"—A <referential action> of **SET NULL** was specified.
		"SET DEFAULT"—A <referential action> of **SET DEFAULT** was specified.
		"NO ACTION"—A <referential action> of **NO ACTION** was specified.
DELETE_RULE	DBTYPE_WSTR	If a <delete rule> was specified then the DELETE_RULE value is one of the following:
		"CASCADE"—A <referential action> of **CASCADE** was specified.
		"SET NULL"—A <referential action> of **SET NULL** was specified.
		"SET DEFAULT"—A <referential action> of **SET DEFAULT** was specified.
		"NO ACTION"—A <referential action> of **NO ACTION** was specified.

Default Sort Order: FK_TABLE_CATALOG, FK_TABLE_SCHEMA, FK_TABLE_NAME

INDEXES Rowset

The INDEXES rowset identifies the indexes defined in the catalog that are owned by a given user.

The INDEXES rowset contains the following columns:

Column name	Type indicator	Description
TABLE_CATALOG	DBTYPE_WSTR	Catalog name. NULL if the provider does not support catalogs.
TABLE_SCHEMA	DBTYPE_WSTR	Unqualified schema name. NULL if the provider does not support schemas.
TABLE_NAME	DBTYPE_WSTR	Table name.
INDEX_CATALOG	DBTYPE_WSTR	Catalog name. NULL if the provider does not support catalogs.

Column name	Type indicator	Description
INDEX_SCHEMA	DBTYPE_WSTR	Unqualified schema name. NULL if the provider does not support schemas.
INDEX_NAME	DBTYPE_WSTR	Index name.
PRIMARY_KEY	DBTYPE_BOOL	Whether the index represents the primary key on the table. NULL if this is not known.
UNIQUE	DBTYPE_BOOL	Whether index keys must be unique. One of the following: VARIANT_TRUE—The index keys must be unique. VARIANT_FALSE—Duplicate keys are allowed.
CLUSTERED	DBTYPE_BOOL	Whether an index is clustered. One of the following: VARIANT_TRUE—The leaf nodes of the index contain full rows, not bookmarks. This is a way to represent a table clustered by key value. VARIANT_FALSE—The leaf nodes of the index contain bookmarks of the base table rows whose key value matches the key value of the index entry.
TYPE	DBTYPE_UI2	The type of the index. One of the following: DBPROPVAL_IT_BTREE—The index is a B+-tree. DBPROPVAL_IT_HASH—The index is a hash file using, for example, linear or extensible hashing. DBPROPVAL_IT_CONTENT—The index is a content index. DBPROPVAL_IT_OTHER—The index is some other type of index.
FILL_FACTOR	DBTYPE_I4	For a B+-tree index, this property represents the storage utilization factor of page nodes during the creation of the index. The value is an integer from 1 to 100 representing the percentage of use of an index node. For a linear hash index, this property represents the storage utilization of the entire hash structure (the ratio of used area to total allocated area) before a file structure expansion occurs.
INITIAL_SIZE	DBTYPE_I4	The total amount of bytes allocated to this structure at creation time.

Column name	Type indicator	Description
NULLS	DBTYPE_I4	Whether null keys are allowed. One of the following:
		DBPROPVAL_IN_DISALLOWNULL—The index does not allow entries where the key columns are NULL. If the consumer attempts to insert an index entry with a NULL key, then the provider returns an error.
		DBPROPVAL_IN_IGNORENULL—The index does not insert entries containing NULL keys. If the consumer attempts to insert an index entry with a NULL key, then the provider ignores that entry and no error code is returned.
		DBPROPVAL_IN_IGNOREANYNULL—The index does not insert entries where some column key has a NULL value. For an index having a multi-column search key, if the consumer inserts an index entry with NULL value in some column of the search key, then the provider ignores that entry and no error code is returned.
SORT_BOOKMARKS	DBTYPE_BOOL	How the index treats repeated keys. One of the following:
		VARIANT_TRUE—The index sorts repeated keys by bookmark.
		VARIANT_FALSE—The index does not sort repeated keys by bookmark.
AUTO_UPDATE	DBTYPE_BOOL	Whether the index is maintained automatically when changes are made to the corresponding base table. One of the following:
		VARIANT_TRUE—The index is automatically maintained.
		VARIANT_FALSE—The index must be maintained by the consumer through explicit calls to **IRowsetChange**. Ensuring consistency of the index as a result of updates to the associated base table is the responsibility of the consumer.

Column name	Type indicator	Description
NULL_COLLATION	DBTYPE_I4	How NULLs are collated in the index. One of the following: DBPROPVAL_NC_END—NULLs are collated at the end of the list, regardless of the collation order. DBPROPVAL_NC_START—NULLs are collated at the start of the list, regardless of the collation order. DBPROPVAL_NC_HIGH—NULLs are collated at the high end of the list. DBPROPVAL_NC_LOW—NULLs are collated at the low end of the list.
ORDINAL_POSITION	DBTYPE_UI4	Ordinal position of the column in the index, starting with one.
COLUMN_NAME	DBTYPE_WSTR	Column name. This column, together with the COLUMN_GUID and COLUMN_PROPID columns, forms the column ID. One or more of these columns will be NULL depending on which elements of the DBID structure the provider uses.
COLUMN_GUID	DBTYPE_GUID	Column GUID.
COLUMN_PROPID	DBTYPE_UI4	Column property ID.
COLLATION	DBTYPE_I2	One of the following: DB_COLLATION_ASC—The sort sequence for the column is ascending. DB_COLLATION_DESC—The sort sequence for the column is descending. NULL—A column sort sequence is not supported.
CARDINALITY	DBTYPE_I4	Number of unique values in the index.
PAGES	DBTYPE_I4	Number of pages used to store the index.
FILTER_CONDITION	DBTYPE_WSTR	The **WHERE** clause identifying the filtering restriction.

Default Sort Order: UNIQUE, TYPE, INDEX_CATALOG, INDEX_SCHEMA, INDEX_NAME, ORDINAL_POSITION

KEY_COLUMN_USAGE Rowset

The KEY_COLUMN_USAGE rowset identifies the columns defined in the catalog that are constrained as keys by a given user.

The KEY_COLUMN_USAGE rowset contains the following columns:

Column name	Type indicator	Description
CONSTRAINT_CATALOG	DBTYPE_WSTR	Catalog name. NULL if the provider does not support catalogs.
CONSTRAINT_SCHEMA	DBTYPE_WSTR	Unqualified schema name. NULL if the provider does not support schemas.
CONSTRAINT_NAME	DBTYPE_WSTR	Constraint name.
TABLE_CATALOG	DBTYPE_WSTR	Catalog name in which the table containing the key column is defined. NULL if the provider does not support catalogs.
TABLE_SCHEMA	DBTYPE_WSTR	Unqualified schema name in which the table containing the key column is defined. NULL if the provider does not support schemas.
TABLE_NAME	DBTYPE_WSTR	Table name containing the key column.
COLUMN_NAME	DBTYPE_WSTR	Name of the column participating in the unique, primary key, or foreign key. This column, together with the COLUMN_GUID and COLUMN_PROPID columns, forms the column ID. One or more of these columns will be NULL depending on which elements of the DBID structure the provider uses.
COLUMN_GUID	DBTYPE_GUID	Column GUID.
COLUMN_PROPID	DBTYPE_UI4	Column property ID.
ORDINAL_POSITION	DBTYPE_UI4	Ordinal position of the column in the constraint being described. If the constraint being described is a key of cardinality one, the value of ORDINAL_POSITION is always one.

Default Sort Order: CONSTRAINT_CATALOG, CONSTRAINT_SCHEMA, CONSTRAINT_NAME, TABLE_CATALOG, TABLE_SCHEMA, TABLE_NAME, ORDINAL_POSITION

PRIMARY_KEYS Rowset

The PRIMARY_KEYS rowset identifies the primary key columns defined in the catalog by a given user. This schema rowset is built upon an SQL '92 schema view as a convenience to the non-SQL programmer, and, if supported, must be synchronized with the related SQL '92 view (CONSTRAINT_COLUMN_USAGE).

The PRIMARY_KEYS rowset contains the following columns:

Column name	Type indicator	Description
TABLE_CATALOG	DBTYPE_WSTR	Catalog name in which the table is defined. NULL if the provider does not support catalogs.
TABLE_SCHEMA	DBTYPE_WSTR	Unqualified schema name in which the table is defined. NULL if the provider does not support schemas.
TABLE_NAME	DBTYPE_WSTR	Table name.
COLUMN_NAME	DBTYPE_WSTR	Primary key column name. This column, together with the COLUMN_GUID and COLUMN_PROPID columns, forms the column ID. One or more of these columns will be NULL depending on which elements of the DBID structure the provider uses.
COLUMN_GUID	DBTYPE_GUID	Primary key column GUID.
COLUMN_PROPID	DBTYPE_UI4	Primary key column property ID.
ORDINAL	DBTYPE_UI4	The order of the column names (and GUIDs and property IDs) in the key.

Default Sort Order: TABLE_CATALOG, TABLE_SCHEMA, TABLE_NAME

PROCEDURE_COLUMNS Rowset

The PROCEDURE_COLUMNS rowset returns information about the columns of rowsets returned by procedures.

The PROCEDURE_COLUMNS rowset contains the following columns:

Column name	Type indicator	Description
PROCEDURE_CATALOG	DBTYPE_WSTR	Catalog name. NULL if the provider does not support catalogs.
PROCEDURE_SCHEMA	DBTYPE_WSTR	Unqualified schema name. NULL if the provider does not support schemas.
PROCEDURE_NAME	DBTYPE_WSTR	Table name.

Column name	Type indicator	Description
COLUMN_NAME	DBTYPE_WSTR	The name of the column; this might not be unique. If this cannot be determined, a NULL is returned. This column, together with the COLUMN_GUID and COLUMN_PROPID columns, forms the column ID. One or more of these columns will be NULL depending on which elements of the DBID structure the provider uses.
COLUMN_GUID	DBTYPE_GUID	Column GUID.
COLUMN_PROPID	DBTYPE_UI4	Column property ID.
ROWSET_NUMBER	DBTYPE_UI4	Number of the rowset containing the column. This is greater than one only if the procedure returns multiple rowsets.
ORDINAL_POSITION	DBTYPE_UI4	The ordinal of the column. Columns are numbered starting from one. NULL if there is no stable ordinal value for the column.
IS_NULLABLE	DBTYPE_BOOL	VARIANT_TRUE—The column might be nullable. VARIANT_FALSE—The column is known not to be nullable.
DATA_TYPE	DBTYPE_UI2	The indicator of the column's data type. If the data type of the column varies from row to row, this must be DBTYPE_VARIANT. For a list of valid type indicators, see "Type Indicators" in Appendix A.
TYPE_GUID	DBTYPE_GUID	The GUID of the column's data type.
CHARACTER_MAXIMUM_ LENGTH	DBTYPE_UI4	The maximum possible length of a value in the column. For character, binary, or bit columns, this is one of the following: • The maximum length of the column in characters, bytes, or bits, respectively, if one is defined. For example, a CHAR(5) column in an SQL table has a maximum length of 5. • The maximum length of the data type in characters, bytes, or bits, respectively, if the column does not have a defined length. • 0 if neither the column nor the data type has a defined maximum length. NULL for all other types of columns.

Column name	Type indicator	Description
CHARACTER_OCTET_LENGTH	DBTYPE_UI4	Maximum length in octets (bytes) of the column, if the type of the column is character or binary. A value of zero means the column has no maximum length. NULL for all other types of columns.
NUMERIC_PRECISION	DBTYPE_UI2	If the column's data type is numeric, this is the maximum precision of the column. The precision of columns with a data type of DBTYPE_DECIMAL or DBTYPE_NUMERIC depends on the definition of the column. For the precision of all other numeric data types, see "Precision of Numeric Data Types" in Appendix A. If the column's data type is not numeric, this is NULL.
NUMERIC_SCALE	DBTYPE_I2	If column's type indicator is DBTYPE_DECIMAL or DBTYPE_NUMERIC, this is the number of digits to the right of the decimal point. Otherwise, this is NULL.
DESCRIPTION	DBTYPE_WSTR	Human-readable description of the column. For example, the description for a column named Name in the Employee table might be "Employee name."

Default Sort Order: PROCEDURE_CATALOG, PROCEDURE_SCHEMA, PROCEDURE_NAME

PROCEDURE_PARAMETERS Rowset

The PROCEDURE_PARAMETERS rowset returns information about the parameters and return codes of procedures.

The PROCEDURE_PARAMETERS rowset contains the following columns:

Column name	Type indicator	Description
PROCEDURE_CATALOG	DBTYPE_WSTR	Catalog name. NULL if the provider does not support catalogs.
PROCEDURE_SCHEMA	DBTYPE_WSTR	Schema name. NULL if the provider does not support catalogs.
PROCEDURE_NAME	DBTYPE_WSTR	Procedure name.
PARAMETER_NAME	DBTYPE_WSTR	Parameter name. NULL if the parameter is not named.
ORDINAL_POSITION	DBTYPE_UI2	If the parameter is an input, input/output, or output parameter, this is the one-based ordinal position of the parameter in the procedure call. If the parameter is the return value, this is zero.

Column name	Type indicator	Description
PARAMETER_TYPE	DBTYPE_UI2	One of the following:
		DBPARAMTYPE_INPUT—The parameter is an input parameter.
		DBPARAMTYPE_INPUTOUTPUT—The parameter is an input/output parameter.
		DBPARAMTYPE_OUTPUT—The parameter is an output parameter.
		DBPARAMTYPE_RETURNVALUE—The parameter is a procedure return value. For example, in the following ODBC SQL statement to call a procedure, the question mark marks a procedure return value:
		`{? = call GetNextOrderID}`
		If the provider cannot determine the parameter type, this is NULL.
PARAMETER_HASDEFAULT	DBTYPE_BOOL	VARIANT_TRUE—The parameter has a default value.
		VARIANT_FALSE—The parameter does not have a default value or it is unknown whether the parameter has a default value.
PARAMETER_DEFAULT	DBTYPE_WSTR	Default value of parameter.
		If the default value is the NULL value, COLUMN_HASDEFAULT is VARIANT_TRUE, and the COLUMN_DEFAULT column is a NULL value.
IS_NULLABLE	DBTYPE_BOOL	VARIANT_TRUE—The parameter is nullable.
		VARIANT_FALSE—The parameter is not nullable.
DATA_TYPE	DBTYPE_UI2	The indicator of the parameter's data type. For a list of valid type indicators, see "Type Indicators" in Appendix A.
CHARACTER_MAXIMUM_LENGTH	DBTYPE_UI4	The maximum possible length of a value in the parameter. For character, binary, or bit parameters, this is one of the following:
		• The maximum length of the parameter in characters, bytes, or bits, respectively, if one is defined. For example, a CHAR(5) parameter has a maximum length of 5.
		• The maximum length of the data type in characters, bytes, or bits, respectively, if the parameter does not have a defined length.

Column name	Type indicator	Description
CHARACTER_MAXIMUM_LENGTH (*continued*)	DBTYPE_UI4	• 0 if neither the parameter nor the data type has a defined maximum length. NULL for all other types of parameters.
CHARACTER_OCTET_LENGTH	DBTYPE_UI4	Maximum length in octets (bytes) of the parameter, if the type of the parameter character or binary. A value of zero means the parameter has no maximum length. NULL for all other types of parameters.
NUMERIC_PRECISION	DBTYPE_UI2	If the parameter's data type is numeric, this is the maximum precision of the parameter. The precision of parameters with a data type of DBTYPE_DECIMAL or DBTYPE_NUMERIC depends on the definition of the parameters. For the precision of all other numeric data types, see "Precision of Numeric Data Types" in Appendix A. If the parameter's data type is not numeric, this is NULL.
NUMERIC_SCALE	DBTYPE_I2	If column's type indicator is DBTYPE_DECIMAL or DBTYPE_NUMERIC, this is the number of digits to the right of the decimal point. Otherwise, this is NULL.
DESCRIPTION	DBTYPE_WSTR	Human-readable description of the parameter. For example, the description of a parameter named Name in a procedure that adds a new employee might be "Employee name."

Default Sort Order: PROCEDURE_CATALOG, PROCEDURE_SCHEMA, PROCEDURE_NAME

PROCEDURES Rowset

The PROCEDURES rowset is an OLE DB extension, based on SQL 3. It identifies the procedures defined in the catalog that are owned by a given user.

The PROCEDURES rowset contains the following columns:

Column name	Type indicator	Description
PROCEDURE_CATALOG	DBTYPE_WSTR	Catalog name. NULL if the provider does not support catalogs.
PROCEDURE_SCHEMA	DBTYPE_WSTR	Unqualified schema name. NULL if the provider does not support schemas.
PROCEDURE_NAME	DBTYPE_WSTR	Procedure name.

Column name	Type indicator	Description
PROCEDURE_TYPE	DBTYPE_I2	DB_PT_UNKNOWN—It is not known whether there is a return value.
		DB_PT_PROCEDURE—Procedure; there is no returned value.
		DB_PT_FUNCTION—Function; there is a returned value.
PROCEDURE_DEFINITION	DBTYPE_WSTR	Procedure definition.
DESCRIPTION	DBTYPE_WSTR	Human-readable description of the procedure.

Default Sort Order: PROCEDURE_CATALOG, PROCEDURE_SCHEMA, PROCEDURE_NAME

PROVIDER_TYPES Rowset

The PROVIDER_TYPES rowset identifies the (base) data types supported by the data provider.

The PROVIDER_TYPES rowset contains the following columns:

Column name	Type indicator	Description
TYPE_NAME	DBTYPE_WSTR	Provider-specific data type name.
DATA_TYPE	DBTYPE_UI2	The indicator of the data type.
COLUMN_SIZE	DBTYPE_UI4	The length of a non-numeric column or parameter refers to either the maximum or the defined length for this type by the provider. For character data, this is the maximum or defined length in characters.
		If the data type is numeric, this is the upper bound on the maximum precision of the data type. For the maximum precision of all numeric data types, see "Precision of Numeric Data Types" in Appendix A.
LITERAL_PREFIX	DBTYPE_WSTR	Character or characters used to prefix a literal of this type in a text command.
LITERAL_SUFFIX	DBTYPE_WSTR	Character or characters used to suffix a literal of this type in a text command.

Column name	Type indicator	Description
CREATE_PARAMS	DBTYPE_WSTR	The creation parameters are specified by the consumer when creating a column of this data type. For example, the SQL data type DECIMAL needs a precision and a scale. In this case, the creation parameters might be the string "precision,scale". In a text command to create a DECIMAL column with a precision of 10 and a scale of 2, the value of the TYPE_NAME column might be DECIMAL() and the complete type specification would be DECIMAL(10,2).
		The creation parameters appear as a comma separated list of values, in the order they are to be supplied, with no surrounding parentheses. If a creation parameter is length, maximum length, precision, or scale, "length", "max length", "precision", and "scale" should be used, respectively. If the creation parameters are some other value, it is provider-specific what text is used to describe the creation parameter.
		If the data type requires creation parameters, "()" generally appears in the type name. This indicates the position at which to insert the creation parameters. If the type name does not include "()", the creation parameters are enclosed in parentheses and appended to the end of the data type name.
IS_NULLABLE	DBTYPE_BOOL	VARIANT_TRUE—The data type is nullable.
		VARIANT_FALSE—The data type is not nullable.
		NULL—It is not known whether the data type is nullable.
CASE_SENSITIVE	DBTYPE_BOOL	VARIANT_TRUE—The data type is a character type and is case sensitive.
		VARIANT_FALSE—The data type is not a character type or is not case sensitive.
SEARCHABLE	DBTYPE_UI4	If the provider supports **ICommandText**, then this column is an integer indicating the searchability of a data type, otherwise this column is NULL. One of the following:
		DB_UNSEARCHABLE—The data type cannot be used in a **WHERE** clause.
		DB_LIKE_ONLY—The data type can be used in a **WHERE** clause only with the **LIKE** predicate.
		DB_ALL_EXCEPT_LIKE—The data type can be used in a **WHERE** clause with all comparison operators except **LIKE**.

Column name	Type indicator	Description
SEARCHABLE (*continued*)	DBTYPE_UI4	DB_SEARCHABLE—The data type can be used in a **WHERE** clause with any comparison operator.
UNSIGNED_ATTRIBUTE	DBTYPE_BOOL	VARIANT_TRUE—The data type is unsigned. VARIANT_FALSE—The data type is signed. NULL—Not applicable to data type.
FIXED_PREC_SCALE	DBTYPE_BOOL	VARIANT_TRUE—The data type has a fixed precision and scale. VARIANT_FALSE—The data type does not have a fixed precision and scale.
AUTO_UNIQUE_VALUE	DBTYPE_BOOL	VARIANT_TRUE—Values of this type can be autoincrementing. VARIANT_FALSE—Values of this type cannot be autoincrementing.
LOCAL_TYPE_NAME	DBTYPE_WSTR	Localized version of TYPE_NAME. NULL is returned if a localized name is not supported by the data provider.
MINIMUM_SCALE	DBTYPE_I2	If the type indicator is DBTYPE_DECIMAL or DBTYPE_NUMERIC, this is the minimum number of digits allowed to the right of the decimal point. Otherwise, this is NULL.
MAXIMUM_SCALE	DBTYPE_I2	If the type indicator is DBTYPE_DECIMAL or DBTYPE_NUMERIC, this is the maximum number of digits allowed to the right of the decimal point. Otherwise, this is NULL.
GUID	DBTYPE_GUID	The GUID of the type. All types supported by a provider are described in a type library, so each type has a corresponding GUID.
TYPELIB	DBTYPE_WSTR	The type library containing the description of this type. All types supported by a provider, including those in Appendix A, are described in one or more type libraries.
VERSION	DBTYPE_WSTR	The version of the type definition. Providers may wish to version type definitions. Different providers may use different version schemes, such as a timestamp or number (integer or float). NULL if not supported.

Column name	Type indicator	Description
IS_LONG	DBTYPE_BOOL	VARIANT_TRUE—The data type is a BLOB that contains very long data; the definition of very long data is provider-specific.
		VARIANT_FALSE—The data type is a BLOB that does not contain very long data or is not a BLOB.
		This value determines the setting of the DBCOLUMNFLAGS_ISLONG flag returned by **GetColumnInfo** in **IColumnsInfo** and **GetParameterInfo** in **ICommandWithParameters**. For more information, see **GetColumnInfo**, **GetParameterInfo**, and "Accessing BLOB Data" in Chapter 7.
BEST_MATCH	DBTYPE_BOOL	VARIANT_TRUE—The data type is the best match between all data types in the data source and the OLE DB data type indicated by the value in the DATA_TYPE column.
		VARIANT_FALSE—The data type is not the best match.
		For each set of rows in which the value of the DATA_TYPE column is the same, the BEST_MATCH column is set to VARIANT_TRUE in only one row.

Default Sort Order: DATA_TYPE

REFERENTIAL_CONSTRAINTS Rowset

The REFERENTIAL_CONSTRAINTS rowset identifies the referential constraints defined in the catalog that are owned by a given user.

The REFERENTIAL_CONSTRAINTS rowset contains the following columns:

Column name	Type indicator	Description
CONSTRAINT_CATALOG	DBTYPE_WSTR	Catalog name. NULL if the provider does not support catalogs.
CONSTRAINT_SCHEMA	DBTYPE_WSTR	Unqualified schema name. NULL if the provider does not support schemas.
CONSTRAINT_NAME	DBTYPE_WSTR	Constraint name.
UNIQUE_CONSTRAINT_ CATALOG	DBTYPE_WSTR	Catalog name in which the unique or primary key constraint is defined. NULL if the provider does not support catalogs.

Column name	Type indicator	Description
UNIQUE_CONSTRAINT_SCHEMA	DBTYPE_WSTR	Unqualified schema name in which the unique or primary key constraint is defined. NULL if the provider does not support schemas.
UNIQUE_CONSTRAINT_NAME	DBTYPE_WSTR	Unique or primary key constraint name.
MATCH_OPTION	DBTYPE_WSTR	"NONE"—No <match type> was specified. "PARTIAL"—A <match type> of **PARTIAL** was specified. "FULL"—A <match type> of **FULL** was specified.
UPDATE_RULE	DBTYPE_WSTR	If an <update rule> was specified then the UPDATE_RULE value is one of the following: "CASCADE"—A <referential action> of **CASCADE** was specified. "SET NULL"—A <referential action> of **SET NULL** was specified. "SET DEFAULT"—A <referential action> of **SET DEFAULT** was specified. "NO ACTION"—A <referential action> of **NO ACTION** was specified.
DELETE_RULE	DBTYPE_WSTR	If a <delete rule> was specified then the DELETE_RULE value is one of the following: "CASCADE"—A <referential action> of **CASCADE** was specified. "SET NULL"—A <referential action> of **SET NULL** was specified. "SET DEFAULT"—A <referential action> of **SET DEFAULT** was specified. "NO ACTION"—A <referential action> of **NO ACTION** was specified.
DESCRIPTION	DBTYPE_WSTR	Human-readable description of the column.

Default Sort Order: CONSTRAINT_CATALOG, CONSTRAINT_SCHEMA, CONSTRAINT_NAME, UNIQUE_CONSTRAINT_CATALOG, UNIQUE_CONSTRAINT_SCHEMA, UNIQUE_CONSTRAINT_NAME

SCHEMATA Rowset

The SCHEMATA rowset identifies the schemas that are owned by a given user.

The SCHEMATA rowset contains the following columns:

Column name	Type indicator	Description
CATALOG_NAME	DBTYPE_WSTR	Catalog name. NULL if the provider does not support catalogs.
SCHEMA_NAME	DBTYPE_WSTR	Unqualified schema name.
SCHEMA_OWNER	DBTYPE_WSTR	User that owns the schemas.
DEFAULT_CHARACTER_SET_CATALOG	DBTYPE_WSTR	Catalog name of the default character set for columns and domains in the schemas. NULL if the provider does not support catalogs or different character sets.
DEFAULT_CHARACTER_SET_SCHEMA	DBTYPE_WSTR	Unqualified schema name of the default character set for columns and domains in the schemas. NULL if the provider does not support different character sets.
DEFAULT_CHARACTER_SET_NAME	DBTYPE_WSTR	Default character set name. NULL if the provider does not support different character sets.

Default Sort Order: CATALOG_NAME, SCHEMA_NAME, SCHEMA_OWNER

SQL_LANGUAGES Rowset

The SQL_LANGUAGES rowset identifies the conformance levels, options, and dialects supported by the SQL-implementation processing data defined in the catalog.

The SQL_LANGUAGES rowset contains the following columns:

Column name	Type indicator	Description
SQL_LANGUAGE_SOURCE	DBTYPE_WSTR	Should be "ISO 9075" for standard SQL.
SQL_LANGUAGE_YEAR	DBTYPE_WSTR	Should be "1992" for ANSI SQL '92 compliant SQL.
SQL_LANGUAGE_CONFORMANCE	DBTYPE_WSTR	One of the following: "ENTRY" "INTERMEDIATE" "FULL"
SQL_LANGUAGE_INTEGRITY	DBTYPE_WSTR	"YES"—Optional integrity feature is supported. "NO"—Optional integrity feature is not supported.

Column name	Type indicator	Description
SQL_LANGUAGE_ IMPLEMENTATION	DBTYPE_WSTR	NULL for "ISO 9075" implementation.
SQL_LANGUAGE_ BINDING_STYLE	DBTYPE_WSTR	"DIRECT" for C/C++ callable direct execution of SQL.
SQL_LANGUAGE_ PROGRAMMING_ LANGUAGE	DBTYPE_WSTR	NULL.

Default Sort Order: SQL_LANGUAGE_SOURCE

STATISTICS Rowset

The STATISTICS rowset identifies the statistics defined in the catalog that are owned by a given user.

The STATISTICS rowset contains the following columns:

Column name	Type indicator	Description
TABLE_CATALOG	DBTYPE_WSTR	Catalog name. NULL if the provider does not support catalogs.
TABLE_SCHEMA	DBTYPE_WSTR	Unqualified schema name. NULL if the provider does not support schemas.
TABLE_NAME	DBTYPE_WSTR	Table name.
CARDINALITY	DBTYPE_I4	Cardinality (number of rows) of the table.

Default Sort Order: TABLE_CATALOG, TABLE_SCHEMA, TABLE_NAME

TABLE_CONSTRAINTS Rowset

The TABLE_CONSTRAINTS rowset identifies the table constraints defined in the catalog that are owned by a given user.

The TABLE_CONSTRAINTS rowset contains the following columns:

Column name	Type indicator	Description
CONSTRAINT_CATALOG	DBTYPE_WSTR	Catalog name. NULL if the provider does not support catalogs.
CONSTRAINT_SCHEMA	DBTYPE_WSTR	Unqualified schema name. NULL if the provider does not support schemas.
CONSTRAINT_NAME	DBTYPE_WSTR	Constraint name.

Column name	Type indicator	Description
TABLE_CATALOG	DBTYPE_WSTR	Catalog name in which the table is defined. NULL if the provider does not support catalogs.
TABLE_SCHEMA	DBTYPE_WSTR	Unqualified schema name in which the table is defined. NULL if the provider does not support schemas.
TABLE_NAME	DBTYPE_WSTR	Table name.
CONSTRAINT_TYPE	DBTYPE_WSTR	Constraint type. One of the following: "UNIQUE" "PRIMARY KEY" "FOREIGN KEY" "CHECK"
IS_DEFERRABLE	DBTYPE_BOOL	VARIANT_TRUE—The table constraint is deferrable. VARIANT_FALSE—The table constraint is not deferrable.
INITIALLY_DEFERRED	DBTYPE_BOOL	VARIANT_TRUE—The table constraint is initially deferred. VARIANT_FALSE—The table constraint is initially immediate.
DESCRIPTION	DBTYPE_WSTR	Human-readable description of the column

Default Sort Order: CONSTRAINT_CATALOG, CONSTRAINT_SCHEMA, CONSTRAINT_NAME, TABLE_CATALOG, TABLE_SCHEMA, TABLE_NAME, CONSTRAINT_TYPE

TABLE_PRIVILEGES Rowset

The TABLE_PRIVILEGES rowset identifies the privileges on tables defined in the catalog that are available to or granted by a given user.

The TABLE_PRIVILEGES rowset contains the following columns:

Column name	Type indicator	Description
GRANTOR	DBTYPE_WSTR	User who granted the privileges on the table in TABLE_NAME.
GRANTEE	DBTYPE_WSTR	User name (or "PUBLIC") to whom the privilege has been granted.
TABLE_CATALOG	DBTYPE_WSTR	Catalog name in which the table is defined. NULL if the provider does not support catalogs.
TABLE_SCHEMA	DBTYPE_WSTR	Unqualified schema name in which the table is defined. NULL if the provider does not support schemas.

Column name	Type indicator	Description
TABLE_NAME	DBTYPE_WSTR	Table name.
PRIVILEGE_TYPE	DBTYPE_WSTR	Privilege type. One of the following: "SELECT" "DELETE" "INSERT" "UPDATE" "REFERENCES"
IS_GRANTABLE	DBTYPE_BOOL	VARIANT_TRUE—The privilege being described was granted with the **WITH GRANT OPTION** clause. VARIANT_FALSE—The privilege being described was not granted with the **WITH GRANT OPTION** clause.

Default Sort Order: TABLE_CATALOG, TABLE_SCHEMA, TABLE_NAME, PRIVILEGE_TYPE

TABLES Rowset

The TABLES rowset identifies the tables defined in the catalog that are accessible to a given user.

The TABLES rowset contains the following columns:

Column name	Type indicator	Description
TABLE_CATALOG	DBTYPE_WSTR	Catalog name. NULL if the provider does not support catalogs.
TABLE_SCHEMA	DBTYPE_WSTR	Unqualified schema name. NULL if the provider does not support schemas.
TABLE_NAME	DBTYPE_WSTR	Table name.
TABLE_TYPE	DBTYPE_WSTR	Table type. One of the following or a provider-specific value. "ALIAS" "TABLE" "SYNONYM" "SYSTEM TABLE" "VIEW" "GLOBAL TEMPORARY" "LOCAL TEMPORARY"

Column name	Type indicator	Description
TABLE_GUID	DBTYPE_GUID	GUID that uniquely identifies the table. Providers that do not use GUIDs to identify tables should return NULL in this column.
DESCRIPTION	DBTYPE_WSTR	Human-readable description of the table.

Default Sort Order: TABLE_TYPE, TABLE_CATALOG, TABLE_SCHEMA, TABLE_NAME

TRANSLATIONS Rowset

The TRANSLATIONS rowset identifies the character translations defined in the catalog that are accessible to a given user.

The TRANSLATIONS rowset contains the following columns:

Column name	Type indicator	Description
TRANSLATION_CATALOG	DBTYPE_WSTR	Catalog name. NULL if the provider does not support catalogs.
TRANSLATION_SCHEMA	DBTYPE_WSTR	Unqualified schema name. NULL if the provider does not support schemas.
TRANSLATION_NAME	DBTYPE_WSTR	Character set name.
SOURCE_CHARACTER_SET_CATALOG	DBTYPE_WSTR	Catalog name containing the source character set on which the translation is defined. NULL if the provider does not support catalogs.
SOURCE_CHARACTER_SET_SCHEMA	DBTYPE_WSTR	Unqualified schema name containing the source character set on which the translation is defined. NULL if the provider does not support schemas.
SOURCE_CHARACTER_SET_NAME	DBTYPE_WSTR	Source character set name on which the translation is defined.
TARGET_CHARACTER_SET_CATALOG	DBTYPE_WSTR	Catalog name containing the target character set on which the translation is defined. NULL if the provider does not support catalogs.
TARGET_CHARACTER_SET_SCHEMA	DBTYPE_WSTR	Unqualified schema name containing the target character set on which the translation is defined. NULL if the provider does not support schemas.
TARGET_CHARACTER_SET_NAME	DBTYPE_WSTR	Target character set name on which the translation is defined.

Default Sort Order: TRANSLATION_CATALOG, TRANSLATION_SCHEMA, TRANSLATION_NAME

USAGE_PRIVILEGES Rowset

The USAGE_PRIVILEGES rowset identifies the USAGE privileges on objects defined in the catalog that are available to or granted by a given user.

The USAGE_PRIVILEGES rowset contains the following columns:

Column name	Type indicator	Description
GRANTOR	DBTYPE_WSTR	User who granted the privileges on the object in OBJECT_NAME.
GRANTEE	DBTYPE_WSTR	User name (or "PUBLIC") to whom the privilege has been granted.
OBJECT_CATALOG	DBTYPE_WSTR	Catalog name in which the object is defined. NULL if the provider does not support catalogs.
OBJECT_SCHEMA	DBTYPE_WSTR	Unqualified schema name in which the object is defined. NULL if the provider does not support schemas.
OBJECT_NAME	DBTYPE_WSTR	Object name.
OBJECT_TYPE	DBTYPE_WSTR	Object type. One of the following: "DOMAIN" "CHARACTER SET" "COLLATION" "TRANSLATION"
PRIVILEGE_TYPE	DBTYPE_WSTR	Privilege type. One of the following: "USAGE"
IS_GRANTABLE	DBTYPE_BOOL	VARIANT_TRUE—The privilege being described was granted with the **WITH GRANT OPTION** clause. VARIANT_FALSE—The privilege being described was not granted with the **WITH GRANT OPTION** clause.

Default Sort Order: OBJECT_CATALOG, OBJECT_SCHEMA, OBJECT_NAME, OBJECT_TYPE, PRIVILEGE_TYPE

VIEW_COLUMN_USAGE Rowset

The VIEW_COLUMN_USAGE rowset identifies the columns on which viewed tables, defined in the catalog and owned by a given user, are dependent.

The VIEW_COLUMN_USAGE rowset contains the following columns:

Column name	Type indicator	Description
VIEW_CATALOG	DBTYPE_WSTR	Catalog name. NULL if the provider does not support catalogs.
VIEW_SCHEMA	DBTYPE_WSTR	Unqualified schema name. NULL if the provider does not support schemas.
VIEW_NAME	DBTYPE_WSTR	View name.
TABLE_CATALOG	DBTYPE_WSTR	Catalog name in which the table is defined. NULL if the provider does not support catalogs.
TABLE_SCHEMA	DBTYPE_WSTR	Unqualified schema name in which the table is defined. NULL if the provider does not support schemas.
TABLE_NAME	DBTYPE_WSTR	Table name.
COLUMN_NAME	DBTYPE_WSTR	Column name. This column, together with the COLUMN_GUID and COLUMN_PROPID columns, forms the column ID. One or more of these columns will be NULL depending on which elements of the DBID structure the provider uses.
COLUMN_GUID	DBTYPE_GUID	Column GUID.
COLUMN_PROPID	DBTYPE_UI4	Column property ID.

Default Sort Order: VIEW_CATALOG, VIEW_SCHEMA, VIEW_NAME, TABLE_CATALOG, TABLE_SCHEMA, TABLE_NAME, COLUMN_NAME, COLUMN_GUID, COLUMN_PROPID

VIEW_TABLE_USAGE Rowset

The VIEW_TABLE_USAGE rowset identifies the tables on which viewed tables, defined in the catalog and owned by a given user, are dependent.

The VIEW_TABLE_USAGE rowset contains the following columns:

Column name	Type indicator	Description
VIEW_CATALOG	DBTYPE_WSTR	Catalog name. NULL if the provider does not support catalogs.

Column name	Type indicator	Description
VIEW_SCHEMA	DBTYPE_WSTR	Unqualified schema name. NULL if the provider does not support schemas.
VIEW_NAME	DBTYPE_WSTR	View name.
TABLE_CATALOG	DBTYPE_WSTR	Catalog name in which the table is defined. NULL if the provider does not support catalogs.
TABLE_SCHEMA	DBTYPE_WSTR	Unqualified schema name in which the table is defined. NULL if the provider does not support schemas.
TABLE_NAME	DBTYPE_WSTR	Table name.

Default Sort Order: VIEW_CATALOG, VIEW_SCHEMA, VIEW_NAME, TABLE_CATALOG, TABLE_SCHEMA, TABLE_NAME

VIEWS Rowset

The VIEWS rowset identifies the viewed tables defined in the catalog that are accessible to a given user.

The VIEWS rowset contains the following columns:

Column name	Type indicator	Description
TABLE_CATALOG	DBTYPE_WSTR	Catalog name. NULL if the provider does not support catalogs.
TABLE_SCHEMA	DBTYPE_WSTR	Unqualified schema name. NULL if the provider does not support schemas.
TABLE_NAME	DBTYPE_WSTR	View name.
VIEW_DEFINITION	DBTYPE_WSTR	View definition. This is a query expression.
CHECK_OPTION	DBTYPE_BOOL	Check option. One of the following: VARIANT_TRUE—Local update checking only. VARIANT_FALSE—Cascaded update checking.
IS_UPDATABLE	DBTYPE_BOOL	VARIANT_TRUE—The view is updatable. VARIANT_FALSE—The view is not updatable.
DESCRIPTION	DBTYPE_WSTR	Human-readable description of the view.

Default Sort Order: TABLE_CATALOG, TABLE_SCHEMA, TABLE_NAME

OLE DB Properties

This appendix lists the properties in each property group that are defined by OLE DB.

Column Properties

The DBPROPSET_COLUMN property set contains the following properties. All of these properties are in the Column property group. Providers can define additional column properties.

Important The "Typical R/W" value for each property specifies whether that property can typically be read or written. Whether a particular property can actually be read or written is provider-specific and is returned in the *dwPropFlags* element of the DBPROPINFO structure.

Property ID	Description
DBPROP_COL_AUTOINCREMENT	Type: VT_BOOL Typical R/W: R/W Description: Autoincrement Whether the values of the column are autoincrementing. One of the following: VARIANT_TRUE—The values of the column are autoincrementing. VARIANT_FALSE—The values of the column are not autoincrementing.
DBPROP_COL_DEFAULT	Type: Any Typical R/W: R/W Description: Default A VARIANT specifying the default value for an object—typically a domain or column. If the default value is a string, the string must be quoted so it can be distinguished from an object of the same name. For example, 'Salary' is a string, Salary is an object, such as a column.

Property ID	Description	
DBPROP_COL_DESCRIPTION	Type:	VT_BSTR
	Typical R/W:	R/W
	Description:	Description
	A string specifying a human-readable description of the specified column.	
DBPROP_COL_FIXEDLENGTH	Type:	VT_BOOL
	Typical R/W:	R/W
	Description:	Fixed Length
	Whether a column is fixed- or variable-length.	
	If the value of this property is VARIANT_TRUE, the column is fixed length and *ulColumnSize* in the DBCOLUMNDESC structure contains the fixed length value. If the value of this property is VARIANT_FALSE or is not specified, the column is variable-length and *ulColumnSize* represents the maximum size of the column. For information about the DBCOLUMNDESC structure, see **ITableDefinition::CreateTable**.	
DBPROP_COL_NULLABLE	Type:	VT_BOOL
	Typical R/W:	R/W
	Description:	Nullable
	Whether a column can contain a NULL value. One of the following:	
	VARIANT_TRUE—The column can contain NULL values.	
	VARIANT_FALSE—The column cannot contain NULL values.	
DBPROP_COL_PRIMARYKEY	Type:	VT_BOOL
	Typical R/W:	R/W
	Description:	Primary Key
	Whether the column is part of the primary key. One of the following:	
	VARIANT_TRUE—The column is part of the primary key of the table.	
	VARIANT_FALSE—The column is not part of the primary key of the table.	
DBPROP_COL_UNIQUE	Type:	VT_BOOL
	Typical R/W:	R/W
	Description:	Unique
	Whether values of the column must be unique in the table. One of the following:	
	VARIANT_TRUE—The values of the column must be unique within the table.	
	VARIANT_FALSE—The values of the column can be repeated within the table.	

Data Source Properties

The DBPROPSET_DATASOURCE property set contains the following properties. All of these properties are in the Data Source property group. Providers can define additional data source properties.

Important The "Typical R/W" value for each property specifies whether that property can typically be read or written. Whether a particular property can actually be read or written is provider-specific and is returned in the *dwPropFlags* element of the DBPROPINFO structure.

Property ID	Description	
DBPROP_CURRENTCATALOG	Type:	VT_BSTR
	Typical R/W:	R/W
	Description:	Current Catalog
	The name of the current catalog. The consumer can use the CATALOGS schema rowset to enumerate catalogs.	

Data Source Creation Properties

OLE DB does not define any data source creation properties. Providers can define their own data source creation properties.

Data Source Information Properties

The DBPROPSET_DATASOURCEINFO property set contains the following properties. All of these properties are in the Data Source Information property group. Providers can define additional data source information properties. These properties are read-only in all providers and constitute a set of static information about the provider and data source.

Important The "Typical R/W" value for each property specifies whether that property can typically be read or written. Whether a particular property can actually be read or written is provider-specific and is returned in the *dwPropFlags* element of the DBPROPINFO structure.

Property ID	Description	
DBPROP_ACTIVESESSIONS	Type:	VT_I4
	Typical R/W:	R
	Description:	Active Sessions
	The maximum number of sessions that can exist at the same time. If this property is set to zero, there is no limit on the number of sessions that can exist at one time.	

Property ID	Description
DBPROP_ASYNCTXNABORT	Type: VT_BOOL Typical R/W: R Description: Asynchable Abort Whether transactions can be aborted asynchronously.
DBPROP_ASYNCTXNCOMMIT	Type: VT_BOOL Typical R/W: R Description: Asynchable Commit Whether transactions can be committed asynchronously.
DBPROP_BYREFACCESSORS	Type: VT_BOOL Typical R/W: R Description: Pass By Ref Accessors Whether the provider supports the DBACCESSOR_PASSBYREF flag in **IAccessor::CreateAccessor**. This applies to both row and parameter accessors.
DBPROP_CATALOGLOCATION	Type: VT_I4 Typical R/W: R Description: Catalog Location The position of the catalog name in a qualified table name in a text command. One of the following: DBPROPVAL_CL_START—The catalog name is at the start of the fully qualified name. For example, a dBASE® provider returns DBPROPVAL_CL_START because the directory (catalog name) is at the start of the table name, as in \EMPDATA\EMP.DBF. DBPROPVAL_CL_END—The catalog name is at the end of the fully qualified name. For example, an ORACLE server provider returns DBPROPVAL_CL_END because the catalog name is at the end of the table name, as in ADMIN.EMP@EMPDATA.
DBPROP_CATALOGTERM	Type: VT_BSTR Typical R/W: R Description: Catalog Term The name the data source uses for a catalog. For example, "catalog", "database", or "directory". This is used for building user interfaces.

Property ID	Description
DBPROP_CATALOGUSAGE	Type: VT_I4 Typical R/W: R Description: Catalog Usage A bitmask specifying how catalog names can be used in text commands. A combination of zero or more of the following: DBPROPVAL_CU_DML_STATEMENTS—Catalog names are supported in all Data Manipulation Language statements. DBPROPVAL_CU_TABLE_DEFINITION—Catalog names are supported in all table definition statements. DBPROPVAL_CU_INDEX_DEFINITION—Catalog names are supported in all index definition statements. DBPROPVAL_CU_PRIVILEGE_DEFINITION—Catalog names are supported in all privilege definition statements.
DBPROP_COLUMNDEFINITION	Type: VT_I4 Typical R/W: R Description: Column Definition A bitmask defining the valid clauses for the definition of a column. A combination of zero or more of the following: DBPROPVAL_CD_NOTNULL—Columns can be created non-nullable.
DBPROP_CONCATNULLBEHAVIOR	Type: VT_I4 Typical R/W: R Description: NULL Concatenation Behavior How the data source handles the concatenation of NULL valued character data type columns with non-NULL valued character data type columns. One of the following: DBPROPVAL_CB_NULL—The result is NULL valued. DBPROPVAL_CB_NON_NULL—The result is the concatenation of the non-NULL–valued column or columns.
DBPROP_DATASOURCENAME	Type: VT_BSTR Typical R/W: R Description: Data Source Name The name of the data source. This might be used during the connection process.
DBPROP_DATASOURCEREADONLY	Type: VT_BOOL Typical R/W: R Description: Read-Only Data Source VARIANT_TRUE—The data source is read-only. VARIANT_FALSE—The data source is updatable.

Property ID	Description	
DBPROP_DBMSNAME	Type:	VT_BSTR
	Typical R/W:	R
	Description:	DBMS Name
	The name of the product accessed by the provider. For example, "ORACLE Server" or, for Microsoft Excel, "Excel".	
DBPROP_DBMSVER	Type:	VT_BSTR
	Typical R/W:	R
	Description:	DBMS Version
	The version of the product accessed by the provider. The version is of the form ##.##.####, where the first two digits are the major version, the next two digits are the minor version, and the last four digits are the release version. The provider must render the product version in this form but can also append the product-specific version as well. For example, "04.01.0000 Rdb 4.1".	
DBPROP_DSOTHREADMODEL	Type:	VT_I4
	Typical R/W:	R
	Description:	Data Source Object Threading Model
	The threading model of the data source object. One of the following:	
	DBPROPVAL_RT_FREETHREAD	
	DBPROPVAL_RT_APTMTTHREAD	
	DBPROPVAL_RT_SINGLETHREAD	
DBPROP_GROUPBY	Type:	VT_I4
	Typical R/W:	R
	Description:	GROUP BY Support
	The relationship between the columns in a **GROUP BY** clause and the non-aggregated columns in the select list. One of the following:	
	DBPROPVAL_GB_EQUALS_SELECT—The **GROUP BY** clause must contain all non-aggregated columns in the select list. It cannot contain any other columns. For example, **SELECT DEPT, MAX(SALARY) FROM EMPLOYEE GROUP BY DEPT**.	
	DBPROPVAL_GB_CONTAINS_SELECT—The **GROUP BY** clause must contain all non-aggregated columns in the select list. It can contain columns that are not in the select list. For example, **SELECT DEPT, MAX(SALARY) FROM EMPLOYEE GROUP BY DEPT, AGE**.	
	DBPROPVAL_GB_NO_RELATION—The columns in the **GROUP BY** clause and the select list are not related. The meaning of non-grouped, non-aggregated columns in the select list is data source–dependent. For example, **SELECT DEPT, SALARY FROM EMPLOYEE GROUP BY DEPT, AGE**.	

Property ID	Description	
DBPROP_HETEROGENEOUSTABLES	Type:	VT_I4
	Typical R/W:	R
	Description:	Heterogeneous Table Support
	A bitmask specifying whether the provider can join tables from different catalogs or providers. A combination of zero or more of the following:	
	DBPROPVAL_HT_DIFFERENT_CATALOGS	
	DBPROPVAL_HT_DIFFERENT_PROVIDERS	
DBPROP_IDENTIFIERCASE	Type:	VT_I4
	Typical R/W:	R
	Description:	Identifier Case Sensitivity
	How identifiers treat case. One of the following:	
	DBPROPVAL_IC_UPPER—Identifiers in SQL are case insensitive and are stored in upper case in system catalog.	
	DBPROPVAL_IC_LOWER—Identifiers in SQL are case insensitive and are stored in lower case in system catalog.	
	DBPROPVAL_IC_SENSITIVE—Identifiers in SQL are case sensitive and are stored in mixed case in system catalog.	
	DBPROPVAL_IC_MIXED—Identifiers in SQL are case insensitive and are stored in mixed case in system catalog.	
DBPROP_MAXINDEXSIZE	Type:	VT_I4
	Typical R/W:	R
	Description:	Maximum Index Size
	The maximum number of bytes allowed in the combined columns of an index. If there is no specified limit or the limit is unknown, this value is set to zero.	
DBPROP_MAXROWSIZE	Type:	VT_I4
	Typical R/W:	R
	Description:	Maximum Row Size
	The maximum length of a single row in a table. If there is no specified limit or the limit is unknown, this value is set to zero.	
DBPROP_MAXROWSIZEINCLUDESBLOB	Type:	VT_BOOL
	Typical R/W:	R
	Description:	Maximum Row Size Includes BLOB
	VARIANT_TRUE—The maximum row size returned for the DBPROP_MAXROWSIZE property includes the length of all BLOB data.	
	VARIANT_FALSE—The maximum row size does not include the length of all BLOB data.	

Property ID	Description	
DBPROP_MAXTABLESINSELECT	Type:	VT_I4
	Typical R/W:	R
	Description:	Maximum Tables in SELECT
	The maximum number of tables allowed in the **FROM** clause of a **SELECT** statement. If there is no specified limit or the limit is unknown, this value is set to zero.	
DBPROP_MULTIPLEPARAMSETS	Type:	VT_BOOL
	Typical R/W:	R
	Description:	Multiple Parameter Sets
	VARIANT_TRUE—The provider supports multiple parameter sets.	
	VARIANT_FALSE—The provider does not support multiple parameter sets.	
DBPROP_MULTIPLERESULTS	Type:	VT_I4
	Typical R/W:	R
	Description:	Multiple Results
	A bitmask specifying whether the provider supports multiple results objects and what restrictions it places on these objects. A combination of zero or more of the following:	
	DBPROPVAL_MR_SUPPORTED—The provider supports multiple results objects.	
	DBPROPVAL_MR_CONCURRENT—More than one rowset created by the same multiple results object can exist concurrently. If this bit is not set, the consumer must release the current rowset before calling **IMultipleResults::GetResult** to get the next result.	
	If multiple results objects are not supported, DBPROPVAL_MR_NOTSUPPORTED is returned. For more information about multiple results, see "Multiple Results" in Chapter 3.	
DBPROP_MULTIPLESTORAGEOBJECTS	Type:	VT_BOOL
	Typical R/W:	R
	Description:	Multiple Storage Objects
	VARIANT_TRUE—The provider supports multiple, open storage objects at the same time.	
	VARIANT_FALSE—The provider supports only one open storage object at a time. Any method that attempts to open a second storage object returns a status of DBSTATUS_E_CANTCREATE for the column on which it attempted to open the second storage object, regardless of whether the objects are constructed over the same column, different columns in the same row, or different rows.	

Property ID	Description
DBPROP_MULTITABLEUPDATE	Type: VT_BOOL Typical R/W: R Description: Multi-Table Update VARIANT_TRUE—The provider can update rowsets derived from multiple tables. VARIANT_FALSE—The provider cannot update rowsets derived from multiple tables.
DBPROP_NULLCOLLATION	Type: VT_I4 Typical R/W: R Description: NULL Collation Order Where NULLs are sorted in a list. One of the following: DBPROPVAL_NC_END—NULLs are sorted at the end of the list, regardless of the sort order. DBPROPVAL_NC_HIGH—NULLs are sorted at the high end of the list. DBPROPVAL_NC_LOW—NULLs are sorted at the low end of the list. DBPROPVAL_NC_START—NULLs are sorted at the start of the list, regardless of the sort order.
DBPROP_OLEOBJECTS	Type: VT_I4 Typical R/W: R Description: OLE Object Support A bitmask specifying the ways in which the provider supports access to BLOBs and OLE objects stored in columns. A combination of zero or more of the following: DBPROPVAL_OO_BLOB—The provider supports access to BLOBs as structured storage objects. A consumer determines what interfaces are supported through DBPROP_STRUCTUREDSTORAGE. DBPROPVAL_OO_IPERSIST—The provider supports access to OLE objects through **IPersistStream**, **IPersistStreamInit**, or **IPersistStorage**.
DBPROP_ORDERBYCOLUMNSINSELECT	Type: VT_BOOL Typical R/W: R Description: ORDER BY Columns in Select List VARIANT_TRUE—Columns in an **ORDER BY** clause must be in the select list. VARIANT_FALSE—Columns in an **ORDER BY** clause are not required to be in the select list.

Property ID	Description
DBPROP_OUTPUTPARAMETERAVAILABILITY	Type: VT_I4 Typical R/W: R Description: Output Parameter Availability The time at which output parameter values become available. One of the following: DBPROPVAL_OA_NOTSUPPORTED—Output parameters are not supported. DBPROPVAL_OA_ATEXECUTE—Output parameter data is available immediately after **ICommand::Execute** returns. DBPROPVAL_OA_ATROWRELEASE—If a command returns a single result that is a rowset, output parameter data is available at the time the rowset is completely released. If a command returns multiple results, output parameter data is available when **IMultipleResults::GetResult** returns DB_S_NORESULT or the multiple results object is completely released, whichever occurs first. Before the output parameter data is available, the consumer's bound memory is in an indeterminate state. For more information about multiple results, see "Multiple Results" in Chapter 3.
DBPROP_PERSISTENTIDTYPE	Type: VT_I4 Typical R/W: R Description: Persistent ID Type An integer specifying the type of DBID that the provider uses when persisting DBIDs for tables, indexes, and columns. This is generally the type of DBID that the provider considers to be the most permanent under schema changes and physical data reorganizations. One of the following: DBPROPVAL_PT_GUID_NAME DBPROPVAL_PT_GUID_PROPID DBPROPVAL_PT_NAME DBPROPVAL_PT_GUID
DBPROP_PREPAREABORTBEHAVIOR	Type: VT_I4 Typical R/W: R Description: Prepare Abort Behavior How aborting a transaction affects prepared commands. One of the following: DBPROPVAL_CB_DELETE—Aborting a transaction deletes prepared commands. The application must re-prepare commands before executing them. DBPROPAL_CB_PRESERVE—Aborting a transaction preserves prepared commands. The application can re-execute commands without re-preparing them.

Property ID	Description
DBPROP_PREPARECOMMITBEHAVIOR	Type: VT_I4 Typical R/W: R Description: Prepare Commit Behavior How committing a transaction affects prepared commands. One of the following: DBPROPVAL_CB_DELETE—Committing a transaction deletes prepared commands. The application must re-prepare commands before executing them. DBPROPAL_CB_PRESERVE—Committing a transaction preserves prepared commands. The application can re-execute commands without re-preparing them.
DBPROP_PROCEDURETERM	Type: VT_BSTR Typical R/W: R Description: Procedure Term A character string with the data source vendor's name for a procedure; for example, "database procedure", "stored procedure", or "procedure". This is used for building user interfaces.
DBPROP_PROVIDERNAME	Type: VT_BSTR Typical R/W: R Description: Provider Name The filename of the provider. For example, "MYPRVDR.DLL".
DBPROP_PROVIDEROLEDBVER	Type: VT_BSTR Typical R/W: R Description: OLE DB Version The version of OLE DB supported by the provider. The version is of the form ##.##, where the first two digits are the major version and the next two digits are the minor version. For this version of OLE DB, this is "01.00".
DBPROP_PROVIDERVER	Type: VT_BSTR Typical R/W: R Description: Provider Version The version of the provider. The version is of the form ##.##.####, where the first two digits are the major version, the next two digits are the minor version, and the last four digits are the release version. The provider can append a description of the provider. This is the same as DBPROP_DBMSVER if the DBMS is the same as the provider; that is, if the DBMS supports OLE DB interfaces directly. It is different if the provider is separate from the DBMS, such as when the provider accesses the DBMS through ODBC.

Property ID	Description	
DBPROP_QUOTEDIDENTIFIERCASE	Type:	VT_I4
	Typical R/W:	R
	Description:	Quoted Identifier Sensitivity
	How quoted identifiers treat case. One of the following:	
	DBPROPVAL_IC_UPPER—Quoted identifiers in SQL are case insensitive and are stored in upper case in system catalog.	
	DBPROPVAL_IC_LOWER—Quoted identifiers in SQL are case insensitive and are stored in lower case in system catalog.	
	DBPROPVAL_IC_SENSITIVE—Quoted identifiers in SQL are case sensitive and are stored in mixed case in system catalog.	
	DBPROPVAL_IC_MIXED—Quoted identifiers in SQL are case insensitive and are stored in mixed case in system catalog.	
DBPROP_ROWSETCONVERSIONSONCOMMAND	Type:	VT_BOOL
	Typical R/W:	R
	Description:	Rowset Conversions on Command
	VARIANT_TRUE—Callers to **IConvertType::CanConvert** can inquire on a command about conversions supported on rowsets generated by the command.	
	VARIANT_FALSE—Callers can inquire on a command only about conversions supported by the command.	
DBPROP_SCHEMATERM	Type:	VT_BSTR
	Typical R/W:	R
	Description:	Schema Term
	The name the data source uses for a schema. For example, "schema" or "owner". This is used for building user interfaces.	
DBPROP_SCHEMAUSAGE	Type:	VT_I4
	Typical R/W:	R
	Description:	Schema Usage
	A bitmask specifying how schema names can be used in text commands. A combination of zero or more of the following:	
	DBPROPVAL_SU_DML_STATEMENTS—Schema names are supported in all Data Manipulation Language statements.	
	DBPROPVAL_SU_TABLE_DEFINITION—Schema names are supported in all table definition statements.	
	DBPROPVAL_SU_INDEX_DEFINITION—Schema names are supported in all index definition statements.	
	DBPROPVAL_SU_PRIVILEGE_DEFINITION—Schema names are supported in all privilege definition statements.	

Property ID	Description
DBPROP_SQLSUPPORT	Type: VT_I4 Typical R/W: R Description: SQL Support A bitmask specifying the level of support for SQL. A combination of zero or more of the following: DBPROPVAL_SQL_NONE—SQL is not supported. DBPROPVAL_SQL_ODBC_MINIMUM DBPROPVAL_SQL_ODBC_CORE DBPROPVAL_SQL_ODBC_EXTENDED—These levels correspond to the levels of SQL conformance defined in ODBC version 2.5. These levels are cumulative. That is, if the provider supports one level, it also sets the bits for all lower levels. For example, if the provider sets the DBPROPVAL_SQL_ODBC_CORE bit, it also sets the DBPROPVAL_SQL_ODBC_MINIMUM bit. DBPROPVAL_SQL_ESCAPECLAUSES—The provider supports the ODBC escape clause syntax. DBPROPVAL_SQL_ANSI92_ENTRY DBPROPVAL_SQL_FIPS_TRANSITIONAL DBPROPVAL_SQL_ANSI92_INTERMEDIATE DBPROPVAL_SQL_ANSI92_FULL—These levels correspond to the levels in ANSI SQL 92. These levels are cumulative. That is, if the provider supports one level, it also sets the bits for all lower levels. DBPROPVAL_SQL_ANSI89_IEF—The provider supports the ANSI 89 Integrity Enhancement Facility.
DBPROP_STRUCTUREDSTORAGE	Type: VT_I4 Typical R/W: R Description: Structured Storage A bitmask specifying what interfaces the rowset supports on storage objects. A combination of zero or more of the following: DBPROPVAL_SS_ISEQUENTIALSTREAM DBPROPVAL_SS_ISTREAM DBPROPVAL_SS_ISTORAGE DBPROPVAL_SS_ILOCKBYTES
DBPROP_SUBQUERIES	Type: VT_I4 Typical R/W: R Description: Subquery Support A bitmask specifying the predicates in text commands that support subqueries. A combination of zero or more of the following: DBPROPVAL_SQ_CORRELATEDSUBQUERIES DBPROPVAL_SQ_COMPARISON

Property ID	Description
DBPROP_SUBQUERIES (*continued*)	DBPROPVAL_SQ_EXISTS DBPROPVAL_SQ_IN DBPROPVAL_SQ_QUANTIFIED The DBPROPVAL_SQ_CORRELATEDSUBQUERIES bit indicates that all predicates that support subqueries support correlated subqueries.
DBPROP_SUPPORTEDTXNDDL	Type: VT_I4 Typical R/W: R Description: Transaction DDL Whether Data Definition Language (DDL) statements are supported in transactions. One of the following: DBPROPVAL_TC_NONE—Transactions are not supported. DBPROPVAL_TC_DML—Transactions can only contain Data Manipulation Language (DML) statements. DDL statements within a transaction cause an error. DBPROPVAL_TC_DDL_COMMIT—Transactions can only contain DML statements. DDL statements within a transaction cause the transaction to be committed. DBPROPVAL_TC_DDL_IGNORE—Transactions can only contain DML statements. DDL statements within a transaction are ignored. DBPROPVAL_TC_ALL—Transactions can contain DDL and DML statements in any order.
DBPROP_SUPPORTEDTXNISOLEVELS	Type: VT_I4 Typical R/W: R Description: Isolation Levels A bitmask specifying the supported transaction isolation levels. A combination of zero or more of the following: DBPROPVAL_TI_CHAOS DBPROPVAL_TI_READUNCOMMITTED DBPROPVAL_TI_BROWSE DBPROPVAL_TI_CURSORSTABILITY DBPROPVAL_TI_READCOMMITTED DBPROPVAL_TI_REPEATABLEREAD DBPROPVAL_TI_SERIALIZABLE DBPROPVAL_TI_ISOLATED For more information, see "Isolation Levels" in Chapter 12.

Property ID	Description
DBPROP_SUPPORTEDTXNISORETAIN	Type: VT_I4 Typical R/W: R Description: Isolation Retention A bitmask specifying the supported transaction isolation retention levels. A combination of zero or more of the following: DBPROPVAL_TR_COMMIT_DC—The transaction may either preserve or dispose of isolation context across a retaining commit. DBPROPVAL_TR_COMMIT—The transaction preserves its isolation context (that is, preserve its locks, if that is how isolation is implemented) across a retaining commit. DBPROPVAL_TR_COMMIT_NO—The transaction is explicitly not to preserve isolation across a retaining commit. DBPROPVAL_TR_ABORT_DC—The transaction may either preserve or dispose of isolation context across a retaining abort. DBPROPVAL_TR_ABORT—The transaction preserves its isolation context across a retaining abort. DBPROPVAL_TR_ABORT_NO—The transaction is explicitly not to preserve isolation across a retaining abort. DBPROPVAL_TR_DONTCARE—The transaction may preserve or dispose of isolation context across a retaining commit or abort. This is the default. DBPROPVAL_TR_BOTH—Isolation is preserved across both a retaining commit and a retaining abort. DBPROPVAL_TR_NONE—Isolation is explicitly not to be retained across either a retaining commit or abort. DBPROPVAL_TR_OPTIMISTIC—Optimistic concurrency control is to be used. If DBPROPVAL_TR_OPTIMISTIC is specified, then whatever isolation technology is in place (such as locking), it must be the case that other transactions' ability to make changes to the data and resources manipulated by this transaction is not in any way affected by the data read or updated by this transaction. That is, optimistic control is to be used for all data in the transaction. For more information, see **ITransactionLocal::StartTransaction**.
DBPROP_TABLETERM	Type: VT_BSTR Typical R/W: R Description: Table Term The name the data source uses for a table. For example, "table" or "file". This is used for building user interfaces.

Property ID	Description	
DBPROP_USERNAME	Type:	VT_BSTR
	Typical R/W:	R
	Description:	User Name
	A character string with the name used in a particular database, which can be different than a login name.	

Index Properties

The DBPROPSET_INDEX property set contains the following properties. All of these properties are in the Index property group. Providers can define additional index properties.

Important The "Typical R/W" value for each property specifies whether that property can typically be read or written. Whether a particular property can actually be read or written is provider-specific and is returned in the *dwPropFlags* element of the DBPROPINFO structure.

Property ID	Description	
DBPROP_INDEX_AUTOUPDATE	Type:	VT_BOOL
	Typical R/W:	R/W
	Description:	Auto-Update
	Whether the index is maintained automatically when changes are made to the corresponding base table. One of the following:	
	VARIANT_TRUE—The index is automatically maintained.	
	VARIANT_FALSE—The index must be maintained by the consumer through explicit calls to **IRowsetChange**.	
	Ensuring consistency of the index as a result of updates to the associated base table is the responsibility of the consumer.	
DBPROP_INDEX_CLUSTERED	Type:	VT_BOOL
	Typical R/W:	R/W
	Description:	Clustered
	Whether an index is clustered.	
	VARIANT_TRUE—The leaf nodes of the index contain full rows, not bookmarks. This is a way to represent a table clustered by key value.	
	VARIANT_FALSE—The leaf nodes of the index contain bookmarks of the base table rows whose key value matches the key value of the index entry.	

Property ID	Description	
DBPROP_INDEX_FILLFACTOR	Type:	VT_I4
	Typical R/W:	R/W
	Description:	Fill Factor
	For a B+-tree index, this property represents the storage utilization factor of page nodes during the creation of the index. The value is an integer from 1 to 100 representing the percentage of use of an index node. For a linear hash index, this property represents the storage utilization of the entire hash structure (the ratio of the used area to the total allocated area) before a file structure expansion occurs.	
DBPROP_INDEX_INITIALSIZE	Type:	VT_I4
	Typical R/W:	R/W
	Description:	Initial Size
	The total number of bytes allocated to this structure at creation time.	
DBPROP_INDEX_NULLCOLLATION	Type:	VT_I4
	Typical R/W:	R/W
	Description:	NULL Collation
	How NULLs are collated in the index. One of the following:	
	DBPROPVAL_NC_END—NULLs are collated at the end of the list, regardless of the collation order.	
	DBPROPVAL_NC_START—NULLs are collated at the start of the list, regardless of the collation order.	
	DBPROPVAL_NC_HIGH—NULLs are collated at the high end of the list.	
	DBPROPVAL_NC_LOW—NULLs are collated at the low end of the list.	
DBPROP_INDEX_NULLS	Type:	VT_I4
	Typical R/W:	R/W
	Description:	NULL Keys
	Whether NULL keys are allowed. One of the following values:	
	DBPROPVAL_IN_DISALLOWNULL—The index does not allow entries where the key columns are NULL. If the consumer attempts to insert an index entry with a NULL key, then the provider returns an error.	
	DBPROPVAL_IN_IGNORENULL—The index does not insert entries containing NULL keys. If the consumer attempts to insert an index entry with a NULL key, then the provider ignores that entry and no error code is returned.	

Property ID	Description
DBPROP_INDEX_NULLS (*continued*)	DBPROPVAL_IN_IGNOREANYNULL—The index does not insert entries where some column key has a NULL value. For an index having a multi-column search key, if the consumer inserts an index entry with NULL value in some column of the search key, then the provider ignores that entry and no error code is returned.
DBPROP_INDEX_PRIMARYKEY	Type: VT_BOOL Typical R/W: R/W Description: Primary Key Whether the index represents the primary key on the table.
DBPROP_INDEX_SORTBOOKMARKS	Type: VT_BOOL Typical R/W: R/W Description: Sort Bookmarks How the index treats repeated keys. One of the following: VARIANT_TRUE—The index sorts repeated keys by bookmark. VARIANT_FALSE—The index does not sort repeated keys by bookmark.
DBPROP_INDEX_TEMPINDEX	Type: VT_BOOL Typical R/W: R/W Description: Temporary Index Whether the index is temporary. One of the following: VARIANT_TRUE—The index is destroyed when the session is released. VARIANT_FALSE—The index is created permanently.
DBPROP_INDEX_TYPE	Type: VT_I4 Typical R/W: R/W Description: Index Type The type of the index. One of the following: DBPROPVAL_IT_BTREE—The index is a B+-tree. DBPROPVAL_IT_HASH—The index is a hash file using linear or extensible hashing. DBPROPVAL_IT_CONTENT—The index is a content index. DBPROPVAL_IT_OTHER—The index is some other type of index.

Property ID	Description
DBPROP_INDEX_UNIQUE	Type: VT_BOOL Typical R/W: R/W Description: Unique Whether index keys must be unique. VARIANT_TRUE: The index keys must be unique. VARIANT_FALSE: Duplicate keys are allowed.

Initialization Properties

The DBPROPSET_DBINIT property set contains the following properties. All of these properties are in the Initialization property group. Providers can define additional initialization properties.

Important The "Typical R/W" value for each property specifies whether that property can typically be read or written. Whether a particular property can actually be read or written is provider-specific and is returned in the *dwPropFlags* element of the DBPROPINFO structure.

Property ID	Description
DBPROP_AUTH_CACHE_AUTHINFO	Type: VT_BOOL Typical R/W: R/W Description: Cache Authentication VARIANT_TRUE—The data source object or enumerator is allowed to cache sensitive authentication information such as a password in an internal cache. VARIANT_FALSE—The data source object or enumerator is not allowed to cache sensitive authentication information.
DBPROP_AUTH_ENCRYPT_ PASSWORD	Type: VT_BOOL Typical R/W: R/W Description: Encrypt Password VARIANT_TRUE—The consumer requires that the password be sent to the data source or enumerator in an encrypted form. This property specifies a stronger form of masking than DBPROP_AUTH_MASKPASSWORD; it uses cryptographic techniques. VARIANT_FALSE—The password can be sent in an unencrypted form.

Property ID	Description	
DBPROP_AUTH_INTEGRATED	Type:	VT_BSTR
	Typical R/W:	R/W
	Description:	Integrated Security
	A string containing the name of the authentication service used by the server to identify the user using the identity provided by an authentication domain. If the BSTR is a null pointer, the default authentication service should be used. When this property is used, no other DBPROP_AUTH* properties are needed and, if provided, their values are ignored.	
DBPROP_AUTH_MASK_PASSWORD	Type:	VT_BOOL
	Typical R/W:	R/W
	Description:	Mask Password
	VARIANT_TRUE—The consumer requires that the password be sent to the data source or enumerator in a masked form.	
	VARIANT_FALSE—The password can be sent in an unmasked form.	
DBPROP_AUTH_PASSWORD	Type:	VT_BSTR
	Typical R/W:	R/W
	Description:	Password
	The password to be used when connecting to the data source or enumerator. When the value of this property is retrieved with **IDBProperties::GetProperties**, the provider might return a mask such as "******" or an empty string instead of the actual password. Note that the password is still set internally and is used when **IDBInitialize::Initialize** is called.	
DBPROP_AUTH_PERSIST_ENCRYPTED	Type:	VT_BOOL
	Typical R/W:	R/W
	Description:	Persist Encrypted
	VARIANT_TRUE—The consumer requires that the data source object persist sensitive authentication information such as a password in encrypted form.	
	VARIANT_FALSE—The data source object can persist sensitive authentication information in unencrypted form.	
DBPROP_AUTH_PERSIST_SENSITIVE_AUTHINFO	Type:	VT_BOOL
	Typical R/W:	R/W
	Description:	Persist Security Info
	VARIANT_TRUE—The data source object is allowed to persist sensitive authentication information such as a password along with other authentication information.	
	VARIANT_FALSE—The data source object cannot persist sensitive authentication information.	

Property ID	Description	
DBPROP_AUTH_USERID	Type:	VT_BSTR
	Typical R/W:	R/W
	Description:	User ID
	The user ID to be used when connecting to the data source or enumerator.	
DBPROP_INIT_DATASOURCE	Type:	VT_BSTR
	Typical R/W:	R/W
	Description:	Data Source
	The name of the database or enumerator to connect to.	
DBPROP_INIT_HWND	Type:	VT_I4
	Typical R/W:	R/W
	Description:	Window Handle
	The window handle to be used if the data source object or enumerator needs to prompt for additional information.	
DBPROP_INIT_IMPERSONATION_ LEVEL	Type:	VT_I4
	Typical R/W:	R/W
	Description:	Impersonation Level

The level of impersonation that the server is allowed to use when impersonating the client. This property applies only to network connections other than Remote Procedure Call (RPC) connections; these impersonation levels are similar to those provided by RPC. The values of this property correspond directly to the levels of impersonation that can be specified for authenticated RPC connections, but can be applied to connections other than authenticated RPC. One of the following:

DB_IMP_LEVEL_ANONYMOUS—The client is anonymous to the server. The server process cannot obtain identification information about the client and cannot impersonate the client.

DB_IMP_LEVEL_IDENTIFY—The server can obtain the client's identity. The server can impersonate the client for ACL checking but cannot access system objects as the client.

DB_IMP_LEVEL_IMPERSONATE—The server process can impersonate the client's security context while acting on behalf of the client. This information is obtained when the connection is established, not on every call.

DB_IMP_LEVEL_DELEGATE—The process can impersonate the client's security context while acting on behalf of the client. The server process can also make outgoing calls to other servers while acting on behalf of the client.

Property ID	Description
DBPROP_INIT_LCID	Type: VT_I4 Typical R/W: R/W Description: Locale Identifier The locale ID of preference for the consumer. Consumers specify the LCID at initialization. This provides a method for the server to determine the consumer's LCID of choice in cases where it can use this information. This property does not guarantee that all text returned to the consumer will be translated according to the LCID. Providers may wish to set the *dwOptions* of the DBPROP structure for this property to DBPROPOPTIONS_SETIFCHEAP.
DBPROP_INIT_LOCATION	Type: VT_BSTR Typical R/W: R/W Description: Location The location of the data source or enumerator to connect to. Typically, this will be a server name.
DBPROP_INIT_MODE	Type: VT_I4 Typical R/W: R/W Description: Mode A bitmask specifying access permissions. A combination of zero or more of the following: DB_MODE_READ—Read-only. DB_MODE_WRITE—Write-only. DB_MODE_READWRITE—Read/write (DB_MODE_READ | DB_MODE_WRITE). DB_MODE_SHARE_DENY_READ—Prevents others from opening in read mode. DB_MODE_SHARE_DENY_WRITE—Prevents others from opening in write mode. DB_MODE_SHARE_EXCLUSIVE—Prevents others from opening in read/write mode (DB_MODE_SHARE_DENY_READ | DB_MODE_SHARE_DENY_WRITE). DB_MODE_SHARE_DENY_NONE—Neither read nor write access can be denied to others.

Property ID	Description
DBPROP_INIT_PROMPT	Type: VT_I2 Typical R/W: R/W Description: Prompt Whether to prompt the user during initialization. One of the following values: DBPROMPT_PROMPT—Always prompt the user for initialization information. DBPROMPT_COMPLETE—Prompt the user only if more information is needed. DBPROMPT_COMPLETEREQUIRED—Prompt the user only if more information is needed. Do not allow the user to enter optional information. DBPROMPT_NOPROMPT—Do not prompt the user.
DBPROP_INIT_PROTECTION_LEVEL	Type: VT_I4 Typical R/W: R/W Description: Protection Level The level of protection of data sent between client and server. This property applies only to network connections other than RPC connections; these protection levels are similar to those provided by RPC. The values of this property correspond directly to the levels of protection that can be specified for authenticated RPC connections, but can be applied to connections other than authenticated RPC. One of the following: DB_PROT_LEVEL_NONE—Performs no authentication of data sent to server. DB_PROT_LEVEL_CONNECT—Authenticates only when the client establishes the connection with the server. DB_PROT_LEVEL_CALL—Authenticates the source of the data at the beginning of each request from the client to the server. DB_PROT_LEVEL_PKT—Authenticates that all data received is from the client. DB_PROT_LEVEL_PKT_INTEGRITY—Authenticates that all data received is from the client and that it has not been changed in transit. DB_PROT_LEVEL_PKT_PRIVACY—Authenticates that all data received is from the client, that it has not been changed in transit, and protects the privacy of the data by encrypting it.

Property ID	Description	
DBPROP_INIT_PROVIDERSTRING	Type:	VT_BSTR
	Typical R/W:	R/W
	Description:	Extended Properties
	A string containing provider-specific, extended connection information. Use of this property implies that the consumer knows how this string will be interpreted and used by the provider. Consumers should use this property only for provider-specific connection information which cannot be explicitly described through the property mechanism.	
DBPROP_INIT_TIMEOUT	Type:	VT_I4
	Typical R/W:	R/W
	Description:	Connect Timeout
	The amount of time (in seconds) to wait for initialization to complete.	

Rowset Properties

The DBPROPSET_ROWSET property set contains the following properties. All of these properties are in the Rowset property group. Providers can define additional rowset properties. The Column? designation states whether the property can be set on individual columns or only on the rowset as a whole.

Important The "Typical R/W" value for each property specifies whether that property can typically be read or written. Whether a particular property can actually be read or written is provider-specific and is returned in the *dwPropFlags* element of the DBPROPINFO structure.

Property ID	Description	
DBPROP_ABORTPRESERVE	Column?	N
	Type:	VT_BOOL
	Typical R/W:	R/W
	Description:	Preserve on Abort
	VARIANT_TRUE—After an abort that preserves, the rowset remains active. That is, it is possible to fetch new rows, update, delete, and insert rows, and so on.	
	VARIANT_FALSE—After an abort or abort that preserves, the only operations allowed on a rowset are to release row and accessor handles and to release the rowset.	

Property ID	Description
DBPROP_APPENDONLY	Column? N Type: VT_BOOL Typical R/W: R/W Description: Append-Only Rowset A rowset opened with this property set to VARIANT_TRUE will be initially empty. If the rowset was obtained by **IOpenRowset::OpenRowset**, this is equivalent to positioning the start of the rowset at the end of the table; if it was obtained by executing a command, it is equivalent to placing the start of the rowset at the end of the command's results. A rowset opened with DBPROP_APPENDONLY set to VARIANT_TRUE will be populated only by those rows inserted in it. DBPROP_APPENDONLY set to VARIANT_TRUE implies: • DBPROP_IRowsetChange is VARIANT_TRUE. • DBPROP_OWNINSERT is VARIANT_TRUE. • DBPROP_UPDATABILITY has the flag DBPROPVAL_UP_INSERT set. • DBPROP_OTHERINSERT is VARIANT_FALSE.
DBPROP_BLOCKINGSTORAGE-OBJECTS	Column? N Type: VT_BOOL Typical R/W: R/W Description: Blocking Storage Objects Whether storage objects might prevent use of other methods on the rowset. VARIANT_TRUE—Instantiated storage objects might prevent the use of other methods on the rowset. That is, after a storage object is created and before it is released, methods other than those on the storage object might return E_UNEXPECTED. VARIANT_FALSE—Instantiated storage objects do not prevent the use of other methods.
DBPROP_BOOKMARKS	Column? N Type: VT_BOOL Typical R/W: R/W Description: Use Bookmarks Whether the rowset supports bookmarks. One of the following: VARIANT_TRUE—The rowset supports bookmarks. Column 0 is the bookmark for the rows. Getting this column obtains a bookmark value which can be used to reposition to the row. VARIANT_FALSE—The rowset does not support bookmarks. The rowset is sequential and the values of the DBPROP_LITERALBOOKMARKS and DBPROP_ORDEREDBOOKMARKS properties are ignored.

Property ID	Description
DBPROP_BOOKMARKS (*continued*)	The value of this property is automatically set to VARIANT_TRUE if the value of DBPROP_IRowsetLocate, DBPROP_LITERALBOOKMARKS, or DBPROP_ORDEREDBOOKMARKS is set to VARIANT_TRUE.

DBPROP_BOOKMARKSKIPPED

Column?	N
Type:	VT_BOOL
Typical R/W:	R/W
Description:	Skip Deleted Bookmarks

Whether the rowset allows **IRowsetLocate::GetRowsAt** to continue if a bookmark row was deleted, is a row to which the consumer does not have access rights, or is no longer a member of the rowset. One of the following:

VARIANT_TRUE—**GetRowsAt** skips the bookmark row and continues with the next row.

VARIANT_FALSE—**GetRowsAt** returns DB_E_BADBOOKMARK.

DBPROP_BOOKMARKTYPE

Column?	N
Type:	VT_I4
Typical R/W:	R/W
Description:	Bookmark Type

The bookmark type supported by the rowset. One of the following:

DBPROPVAL_BMK_NUMERIC—The bookmark type is numeric. Numeric bookmarks are based upon a row property that is not dependent on the values of the row's columns. For instance, they can be based on the absolute position of the row within rowset, or on a row ID that the storage engine assigned to a tuple at its creation. The validity of numeric bookmarks is not changed by modifying the row's columns.

DBPROPVAL_BMK_KEY—The bookmark type is key. Key bookmarks are based on the values of one or more of the row's columns; these values form a unique key for each row. A key bookmark may be left dangling if the key values of the corresponding row are changed.

For more information, see "Bookmark Types" in Chapter 4.

DBPROP_CACHEDEFERRED

Column?	Y
Type:	VT_BOOL
Typical R/W:	R/W
Description:	Cache Deferred Columns

VARIANT_TRUE—The provider caches the value of a deferred column when the consumer first gets a value from that column. When the consumer later gets a value from the column, the provider returns

Property ID	Description
DBPROP_CACHEDEFERRED (*continued*)	the value in the cache. The contents of the cache can be overwritten by **IRowsetChange::SetData** or **IRowsetResynch::ResynchRows**. The cached value is released when the row is released.
	Consumers should set the value of this property to VARIANT_TRUE rather sparingly, as it might require substantial memory use in the provider. Such use might limit the number of rows that can be held at one time. Setting the value of this property to VARIANT_TRUE automatically sets the value of the DBPROP_DEFERRED property to VARIANT_TRUE.
	VARIANT_FALSE—The provider does not cache the value of a deferred column and multiple calls to **IRowset::GetData** for the column can return different values.

Property ID	Description	
DBPROP_CANFETCHBACKWARDS	Column?	N
	Type:	VT_BOOL
	Typical R/W:	R/W
	Description:	Fetch Backwards

Whether the rowset can fetch backwards.

VARIANT_TRUE—*cRows* in **IRowset::GetNextRows**, **IRowsetLocate::GetRowsAt**, and **IRowsetScroll::GetRowsAtRatio** can be negative. When it is negative, these methods fetch rows backward from the specified row.

VARIANT_FALSE—*cRows* must be non-negative.

Property ID	Description	
DBPROP_CANHOLDROWS	Column?	N
	Type:	VT_BOOL
	Typical R/W:	R/W
	Description:	Hold Rows

VARIANT_TRUE—The rowset allows the consumer to retrieve more rows or change the next fetch position while holding previously fetched rows with pending changes.

VARIANT_FALSE—The rowset requires pending changes to be transmitted to the data source and all rows to be released before fetching additional rows, inserting new rows, or changing the next fetch position.

Property ID	Description	
DBPROP_CANSCROLLBACKWARDS	Column?	N
	Type:	VT_BOOL
	Typical R/W:	R/W
	Description:	Scroll Backward

Whether the rowset can scroll backward.

VARIANT_TRUE—*lRowsOffset* in **IRowset::GetNextRows** or **IRowsetLocate::GetRowsAt** can be negative.

VARIANT_FALSE—*lRowsOffset* must be non-negative.

Property ID	Description
DBPROP_CANSCROLLBACKWARDS (*continued*)	If the rowset supports **IRowsetLocate**, then the value of this property is VARIANT_TRUE, as this method supports backward scrolling by definition.
DBPROP_CHANGEINSERTEDROWS	Column? N Type: VT_BOOL Typical R/W: R/W Description: Change Inserted Rows VARIANT_TRUE—The consumer can call **IRowsetChange::DeleteRows** or **IRowsetChange::SetData** for newly inserted rows. VARIANT_FALSE—If the consumer calls **DeleteRows** or **SetData** for newly inserted rows, **DeleteRows** returns a status of DBROWSTATUS_E_NEWLYINSERTED for the row and **SetData** returns DB_E_NEWLYINSERTED. A newly inserted row is defined to be a row for which the insertion has been transmitted to the data source, as opposed to a pending insert row. For some providers this property may imply other properties.
DBPROP_COLUMNRESTRICT	Column? N Type: VT_BOOL Typical R/W: R Description: Column Privileges VARIANT_TRUE—Access rights are restricted on a column-by-column basis. If the rowset exposes **IRowsetChange**, **IRowsetChange::SetData** cannot be called for at least one column. A provider must not execute a query which would specify a column for which the consumer has no read access rights. VARIANT_FALSE—Access rights are not restricted on a column-by-column basis. If the rowset exposes **IRowsetChange**, **SetData** can be called for any column in the rowset. If access is restricted both by row and by column, then individual columns of particular rows might have their own stricter access rights: the consumer might not even be permitted to read such columns. The column values will be NULL. If a NULL value is contrary to schema rules (NULLs not permitted) then the rowset should not count or return any rows which would have this condition. For more information, see DBPROP_ROWRESTRICT.
DBPROP_COMMANDTIMEOUT	Column? N Type: VT_I4 Typical R/W: R/W Description: Command Time Out The number of seconds before a command times out. A value of 0 indicates an infinite timeout.

Property ID	Description
DBPROP_COMMITPRESERVE	Column? N Type: VT_BOOL Typical R/W: R/W Description: Preserve on Commit VARIANT_TRUE—After a commit that preserves, the rowset remains active. That is, it is possible to fetch new rows, update, delete, and insert rows, and so on. VARIANT_FALSE—After a commit or commit that preserves, the only operations allowed on a rowset are to release row and accessor handles and to release the rowset.
DBPROP_DEFERRED	Column? Y Type: VT_BOOL Typical R/W: R/W Description: Defer Column VARIANT_TRUE—The data in the column is not fetched until an accessor is used on the column. VARIANT_FALSE—The data in the column is fetched when the row containing it is fetched. The value of this property is automatically set to VARIANT_TRUE if the value of the DBPROP_CACHEDEFERRED property is set to VARIANT_TRUE.
DBPROP_DELAYSTORAGEOBJECTS	Column? N Type: VT_BOOL Typical R/W: R/W Description: Delay Storage Object Updates In delayed update mode, if the value of this property is VARIANT_TRUE then storage objects are also used in delayed update mode. In particular: • Changes to the object are not transmitted to the data source until **IRowsetUpdate::Update** is called, • **IRowsetUpdate::Undo** undoes any pending changes, and • **IRowsetUpdate::GetOriginalData** retrieves the original value of the object; that is, the object's value when the row was last fetched or updated and excluding any changes made since then. In delayed update mode, if the value of this property is VARIANT_FALSE then storage objects are used in immediate update mode. In particular: • Changes to the object are immediately transmitted to the data source, • **Update** has no effect on the object,

Property ID	Description
DBPROP_DELAYSTORAGEOBJECTS (*continued*)	• **Undo** does not undo changes made to the object since the row was last fetched or updated, and
	• **GetOriginalData** retrieves the current value of the object, including changes made since the row was last fetched or updated.
	In immediate update mode, this property has no effect on storage objects.

Property ID	Description

DBPROP_IAccessor
DBPROP_IColumnsInfo
DBPROP_IColumnsRowset
DBPROP_IConnectionPointContainer
DBPROP_IConvertType
DBPROP_IRowset
DBPROP_IRowsetChange
DBPROP_IRowsetIdentity
DBPROP_IRowsetInfo
DBPROP_IRowsetLocate
DBPROP_IRowsetResynch
DBPROP_IRowsetScroll
DBPROP_IRowsetUpdate
DBPROP_ISupportErrorInfo
	Column? N
	Type: VT_BOOL
	Typical R/W: R/W (except as noted below)
	Description: IAccessor
	      IColumnsInfo
	      IColumnsRowset
	      IConnectionPointContainer
	      IConvertType
	      IRowset
	      IRowsetChange
	      IRowsetIdentity
	      IRowsetInfo
	      IRowsetLocate
	      IRowsetResynch
	      IRowsetScroll
	      IRowsetUpdate
	      ISupportErrorInfo

If the value of any of these properties is set to VARIANT_TRUE, the rowset supports the specified interface. These properties are primarily used to request interfaces through **ICommandProperties::SetProperties**.

The values of the DBPROP_IRowset, DBPROP_IAccessor, DBPROP_IColumnsInfo, DBPROP_IConvertType, and DBPROP_IRowsetInfo properties are read-only and are always VARIANT_TRUE. They cannot be set to VARIANT_FALSE. If the consumer does not set the value of any of these properties to true, the resulting rowset supports **IRowset**, **IAccessor**, **IColumnsInfo**, **IConvertType**, and **IRowsetInfo**.

Setting DBPROP_IRowsetLocate to VARIANT_TRUE automatically sets DBPROP_BOOKMARKS to VARIANT_TRUE. Setting DBPROP_IRowsetUpdate to VARIANT_TRUE automatically sets DBPROP_IRowsetChange to VARIANT_TRUE.

Property ID	Description	
DBPROP_ILockBytes DBPROP_ISequentialStream DBPROP_IStorage DBPROP_IStream	Column? Type: Typical R/W: Description:	Y VT_BOOL R/W ILockBytes ISequentialStream IStorage IStream

If the value of this property is set to VARIANT_TRUE, the specified column is treated as storage object that exposes the specified interface.

If this property is set on all columns, the provider must be capable of exposing all columns of the rowset as storage objects.

Property ID	Description	
DBPROP_IMMOBILEROWS	Column? Type: Typical R/W: Description:	N VT_BOOL R/W Immobile Rows

VARIANT_TRUE—The rowset will not reorder inserted or updated rows. For **IRowsetChange::InsertRow**, rows will appear at the end of the rowset.

VARIANT_FALSE—If the rowset is ordered, then inserted rows and updated rows (where one or more of the columns in the ordering criteria are updated) obey the ordering criteria of the rowset. If the rowset is not ordered, then inserted rows are not guaranteed to appear in a determinate position and the position of updated rows is not changed.

This property is meaningful only if DBPROP_OWNINSERT is VARIANT_TRUE.

Property ID	Description	
DBPROP_LITERALBOOKMARKS	Column? Type: Typical R/W: Description:	N VT_BOOL R/W Literal Bookmarks

VARIANT_TRUE—Bookmarks can be compared literally. That is, they can be compared as a sequence of bytes. Furthermore, if the bookmarks are ordered (as specified by the DBPROP_ORDEREDBOOKMARKS property), the bytes are guaranteed to be ordered so that an arithmetic comparison as their scalar type yields the same result as a call to **IRowsetLocate::Compare**. Setting the value of this property to VARIANT_TRUE automatically sets the value of DBPROP_BOOKMARKS to VARIANT_TRUE.

VARIANT_FALSE—Bookmarks can only be compared with **IRowsetLocate::Compare**.

Property ID	Description	
DBPROP_LITERALIDENTITY	Column?	N
	Type:	VT_BOOL
	Typical R/W:	R
	Description:	Literal Row Identity
	VARIANT_TRUE—The consumer can perform a binary comparison of two row handles to determine whether they point to the same row.	
	VARIANT_FALSE—The consumer must call **IRowsetIdentity::IsSameRow** to determine whether two row handles point to the same row.	
	Whether the handle of a newly inserted row can be successfully compared to another handle is specified by the DBPROP_STRONGIDENTITY property.	
	For more information about row identity, see "Uniqueness of Rows in the Rowset" in Chapter 4.	
DBPROP_MAXOPENROWS	Column?	N
	Type:	VT_I4
	Typical R/W:	R
	Description:	Maximum Open Rows
	The maximum number of rows that can be active at the same time. This limit does not reflect resource limitations such as RAM, but does apply if the rowset implementation uses some strategy which results in a limit. If there is no limit, the value of this property is zero.	
DBPROP_MAXPENDINGROWS	Column?	N
	Type:	VT_I4
	Typical R/W:	R
	Description:	Maximum Pending Rows
	The maximum number of rows that can have pending changes at the same time. This limit does not reflect resource limitations such as Random Access Memory (RAM), but does apply if the rowset implementation uses some strategy which results in a limit. If there is no limit, this value is zero.	
DBPROP_MAXROWS	Column?	N
	Type:	VT_I4
	Typical R/W:	R/W
	Description:	Maximum Rows
	The maximum number of rows that can be returned in a rowset. If there is no limit, this value is zero.	

Property ID	Description

DBPROP_MAYWRITECOLUMN

Column?	Y
Type:	VT_BOOL
Typical R/W:	R/W
Description:	Column Writeable

Whether a particular column is writeable or not. Note that this property can be set implicitly through the command used to create the rowset. For example, if the rowset is created by the SQL statement **SELECT A, B FROM MyTable FOR UPDATE OF A**, then this property is VARIANT_TRUE for column A and VARIANT_FALSE for column B.

DBPROP_MEMORYUSAGE

Column?	N
Type:	VT_I4
Typical R/W:	R/W
Description:	Memory Usage

This property estimates the amount of memory that can be used by the rowset. If it is 0, the rowset can use unlimited memory. If it is between 1 and 99 inclusive, the rowset can use the specified percentage of total available virtual memory (physical and page file). If it is greater than or equal to 100, the rowset can use up to the specified number of kilobytes of memory.

DBPROP_NOTIFICATIONGRANULARITY

Column?	N
Type:	VT_I4
Typical R/W:	R/W
Description:	Notification Granularity

DBPROPVAL_NT_SINGLEROW—For methods that operate on multiple rows and generate multi-phased notifications, the provider calls **IRowsetNotify::OnRowChange** separately for each phase for each row. A cancellation affects a single row; it does not affect the other rows and notifications are still sent for these rows.

DBPROPVAL_NT_MULTIPLEROWS—For methods that operate on multiple rows and generate multi-phased notifications, then for each phase, the provider calls **OnRowChange** once for all rows that succeed and once for all rows that fail. This separation can occur at each phase where a change can fail. For example, if **IRowsetChange::DeleteRows** deletes some rows and fails to delete others during the Preliminary Work phase, it calls **OnRowChange** twice: once with DBEVENTPHASE_SYNCHAFTER and the array of handles of rows that it deleted and once with DBEVENTPHASE_FAILEDTODO and the array of handles of rows it failed to delete. A cancellation affects all rows with handles that were passed to **OnRowChange**.

DBPROP_NOTIFICATIONGRANULARITY does not affect how providers return notifications about events that affect columns or the entire rowset.

Property ID	Description	
DBPROP_NOTIFICATIONPHASES	Column?	N
	Type:	VT_I4
	Typical R/W:	R
	Description:	Notification Phases
	A bitmask specifying the notification phases supported by the provider. A combination of two or more of the following:	
	DBPROPVAL_NP_OKTODO DBPROPVAL_NP_ABOUTTODO DBPROPVAL_NP_SYNCHAFTER DBPROPVAL_NP_FAILEDTODO DBPROPVAL_NP_DIDEVENT	
	The DBPROPVAL_NP_FAILEDTODO and DBPROPVAL_NP_DIDEVENT bits must be returned by all providers that support notifications.	
DBPROP_NOTIFYCOLUMNSET DBPROP_NOTIFYROWDELETE DBPROP_NOTIFYROWFIRSTCHANGE DBPROP_NOTIFYROWINSERT DBPROP_NOTIFYROWRESYNCH DBPROP_NOTIFYROWSETRELEASE DBPROP_NOTIFYROWSETFETCH- POSITIONCHANGE DBPROP_NOTIFYROWUNDOCHANGE DBPROP_NOTIFYROWUNDODELETE DBPROP_NOTIFYROWUNDOINSERT DBPROP_NOTIFYROWUPDATE	Column?	N
	Type:	VT_I4
	Typical R/W:	R
	Description:	Column Set Notification Row Delete Notification Row First Change Notification Row Insert Notification Row Resynchronization Notification Rowset Release Notification Rowset Fetch Position Change Notification Row Undo Change Notification Row Undo Delete Notification Row Undo Insert Notification Row Update Notification
	A bitmask specifying whether the notification phase is cancelable. A combination of zero or more of the following:	
	DBPROPVAL_NP_OKTODO DBPROPVAL_NP_ABOUTTODO DBPROPVAL_NP_SYNCHAFTER	
DBPROP_ORDEREDBOOKMARKS	Column?	N
	Type:	VT_BOOL
	Typical R/W:	R/W
	Description:	Bookmarks Ordered
	VARIANT_TRUE—Bookmarks can be compared to determine the relative position of their associated rows in the rowset. Setting the value of this property to VARIANT_TRUE automatically sets the value of DBPROP_BOOKMARKS to VARIANT_TRUE.	
	VARIANT_FALSE—Bookmarks can only be compared for equality.	

Property ID	Description
DBPROP_ORDEREDBOOKMARKS (*continued*)	Whether bookmarks can be compared byte-by-byte or must be compared with **IRowsetLocate::Compare** depends on the value of the DBPROP_LITERALBOOKMARKS property.

Property ID	Description

DBPROP_OTHERINSERT	Column? N
	Type: VT_BOOL
	Typical R/W: R/W
	Description: Others' Inserts Visible
	
	VARIANT_TRUE—The rowset can see rows inserted by someone other than a consumer of the rowset. That is, if someone other than a consumer of the rowset inserts a row, any consumer of the rowset can see that row the next time it fetches a set of rows containing it. Note that this includes rows inserted by other parties in the same transaction, as well as rows inserted by parties outside the transaction.
	
	The transaction isolation level does not affect the ability of the rowset to see rows inserted by other parties in the same transaction, such as other rowsets in the same session. However, it does restrict the ability of the rowset to see rows inserted by parties outside the transaction.
	
	VARIANT_FALSE—The rowset cannot see rows inserted by others.
	
	For programmers accustomed to the cursor model in ODBC, the DBPROP_OTHERUPDATEDELETE and DBPROP_OTHERINSERT properties correspond to ODBC cursors as follows:
	
	Static cursor:
	    DBPROP_OTHERINSERT = VARIANT_FALSE
	    DBPROP_OTHERUPDATEDELETE = VARIANT_FALSE
	
	Keyset-driven cursor:
	    DBPROP_OTHERINSERT = VARIANT_FALSE
	    DBPROP_OTHERUPDATEDELETE = VARIANT_TRUE
	
	Dynamic cursor:
	    DBPROP_OTHERINSERT = VARIANT_TRUE
	    DBPROP_OTHERUPDATEDELETE = VARIANT_TRUE
	
	Furthermore, the DBPROP_OWNUPDATEDELETE and DBPROP_OWNINSERT properties correspond to the values returned by the SQL_STATIC_SENSITIVITY information type in **SQLGetInfo** in ODBC.
	
	For a description of how these properties relate to transaction isolation level, see "Visibility of Other Changes" in Chapter 5.

Property ID	Description
DBPROP_OTHERUPDATEDELETE	Column? N Type: VT_BOOL Typical R/W: R/W Description: Others' Changes Visible VARIANT_TRUE—The rowset can see updates and deletes made by someone other than a consumer of the rowset. That is, suppose someone other than a consumer of the rowset updates the data underlying a row or deletes the row. If the row is released completely, any consumer of the rowset will see that change the next time it fetches the row. Note that this includes updates and deletes made by other parties in the same transaction, as well as updates and deletes made by parties outside the transaction. The transaction isolation level does not affect the ability of the rowset to see updates or deletes made by other parties in the same transaction, such as other rowsets in the same session. However, it does restrict the ability of the rowset to see updates or deletes made by parties outside the transaction. VARIANT_FALSE—The rowset cannot see updates and deletes made by others. For information about how this relates to the cursor types in ODBC, see the DBPROP_OTHERINSERT property.
DBPROP_OWNINSERT	Column? N Type: VT_BOOL Typical R/W: R/W Description: Own Inserts Visible VARIANT_TRUE—The rowset can see its own inserts. That is, if a consumer of a rowset inserts a row, any consumer of the rowset can see that row the next time it fetches a set of rows containing it. This ability is independent of the transaction isolation level, because all consumers of the rowset share the same transaction. VARIANT_FALSE—The rowset cannot see rows inserted by consumers of the rowset, unless the command is re-executed. For information about how this relates to the SQL_STATIC_SENSITIVITY information type in ODBC, see the DBPROP_OTHERINSERT property.
DBPROP_OWNUPDATEDELETE	Column? N Type: VT_BOOL Typical R/W: R/W Description: Own Changes Visible VARIANT_TRUE—The rowset can see its own updates and deletes. That is, suppose a consumer of the rowset updates or deletes a row. If the row is released completely, any consumer of the rowset will see the update or delete the next time it fetches that row.

Property ID	Description
DBPROP_OWNUPDATEDELETE (*continued*)	This ability is independent of the transaction isolation level, because all consumers of the rowset share the same transaction.
	VARIANT_FALSE—The rowset cannot see updates and deletes made by consumers of the rowset, unless the command is re-executed.
	For information about how this relates to the SQL_STATIC_SENSITIVITY information type in ODBC, see the DBPROP_OTHERINSERT property.
DBPROP_QUICKRESTART	Column? N Type: VT_BOOL Typical R/W: R/W Description: Quick Restart
	VARIANT_TRUE—**IRowset::RestartPosition** is relatively quick to execute. In particular, it does not re-execute the command that created the rowset.
	VARIANT_FALSE—**RestartPosition** is expensive to execute and requires re-executing the command that created the rowset.
	Although the value of this property can be set to VARIANT_TRUE, the provider is not required to honor it. The reason for this is that the provider does not know what the command is at the time the property is set; in particular, the consumer can set this property and then change the command text. However, the provider can fail this property if it is never able to quickly restart the next fetch position. Thus, if a consumer successfully sets this property, it must still check this flag on the rowset to determine if the next fetch position can be quickly set.
DBPROP_REENTRANTEVENTS	Column? N Type: VT_BOOL Typical R/W: R Description: Reentrant Events
	VARIANT_TRUE—The provider supports reentrancy during callbacks to the **IRowsetNotify** interface. The provider might not support reentrancy on all rowset methods. These methods return DB_E_NOTREENTRANT.
	VARIANT_FALSE—The provider does not support such reentrancy. The provider returns DB_E_NOTREENTRANT on methods called during the notification.
	Regardless of this flag, all providers must support **IRowset::GetData** and **IRowset::ReleaseRows** calls during notifications, so long as the columns being accessed do not include deferred columns.

Property ID	Description	
DBPROP_REMOVEDELETED	Column?	N
	Type:	VT_BOOL
	Typical R/W:	R/W
	Description:	Remove Deleted Rows

If the value of this property is VARIANT_TRUE, the provider removes rows it detects as having been deleted from the rowset. That is, fetching a block of rows that formerly included a deleted row does not return a handle to that row.

Which rows the rowset detects as having been deleted is determined by the DBPROP_OWNUPDATEDELETE and DBPROP_OTHERUPDATEDELETE properties; whether the rowset removes these rows is determined by this property.

Note that this property is independent of the transaction isolation level. While the transaction isolation level in some cases determines whether the rowset can detect a row as having been deleted, it has no effect on whether or not the rowset removes that row.

For programmers accustomed to the cursor model in ODBC, this value of this property is always VARIANT_TRUE for rowsets implemented through dynamic cursors; that is, dynamic cursors always remove deleted rows. Whether static and keyset-driven cursors remove deleted rows depends on the value of this property.

Property ID	Description	
DBPROP_REPORTMULTIPLE-CHANGES	Column?	N
	Type:	VT_BOOL
	Typical R/W:	R
	Description:	Report Multiple Changes

VARIANT_TRUE—An update or delete can affect multiple rows and the provider can detect that multiple rows have been updated or deleted. This happens when a provider cannot uniquely identify a row. For example, the provider might use the values of all the columns in the row to identify the row; if these columns do not include a unique key, an update or delete might affect more than one row.

VARIANT_FALSE—An update or delete always affects a single row or the provider cannot detect whether it affects multiple rows.

Property ID	Description	
DBPROP_RETURNPENDING-INSERTS	Column?	N
	Type:	VT_BOOL
	Typical R/W:	R
	Description:	Return Pending Inserts

VARIANT_TRUE—The methods that fetch rows, such as **IRowset::GetNextRows**, can return pending insert rows; that is, rows that have been inserted in delayed update mode but for which **IRowsetUpdate::Update** has not yet been called.

VARIANT_FALSE—The methods that fetch rows cannot return pending insert rows.

Property ID	Description	
DBPROP_ROWRESTRICT	Column?	N
	Type:	VT_BOOL
	Typical R/W:	R
	Description:	Row Privileges
	VARIANT_TRUE—Access rights are restricted on a row-by-row basis. If the rowset supports **IRowsetChange**, **IRowsetChange::SetData** can be called for some but not all rows. A rowset must never count or return a handle for a row for which the consumer does not have read access rights.	
	VARIANT_FALSE—Access rights are not restricted on a row-by-row basis. If the rowset supports **IRowsetChange**, **SetData** can be called for any row.	
	For more information, see DBPROP_COLUMNRESTRICT.	
DBPROP_ROWTHREADMODEL	Column?	N
	Type:	VT_I4
	Typical R/W:	R/W
	Description:	Row Threading Model
	The threading model of the rowsets generated by the command. One of the following:	
	DBPROPVAL_RT_FREETHREAD DBPROPVAL_RT_APTMTTHREAD DBPROPVAL_RT_SINGLETHREAD	
DBPROP_SERVERCURSOR	Column?	N
	Type:	VT_BOOL
	Typical R/W:	R/W
	Description:	Server Cursor
	If the value of this property is set to VARIANT_TRUE with **ICommandProperties::SetProperties**, the cursor underlying the rowset (if any) must be materialized on the server.	
	If the value of this property is not set with **SetProperties**, it is up to the provider to decide where to materialize the cursor.	
	The consumer can determine where the cursor was materialized by checking the value of this property on the rowset.	

Property ID	Description

DBPROP_STRONGIDENTITY	Column? N Type: VT_BOOL Typical R/W: R Description: Strong Row Identity
	VARIANT_TRUE—The handles of newly inserted rows can be compared as specified by DBPROP_LITERALIDENTITY.
	VARIANT_FALSE—There is no guarantee that the handles of newly inserted rows can be compared successfully. In this case, **IRowsetIdentity::IsSameRow** might return DB_E_NEWLYINSERTED.
	A newly inserted row is defined to be a row for which an insertion has been transmitted to the data source, as opposed to a pending insert row. For more information, see "Uniqueness of Rows in the Rowset" in Chapter 4.
DBPROP_TRANSACTEDOBJECT	Column? Y Type: VT_BOOL Typical R/W: R/W Description: Objects Transacted
	VARIANT_TRUE—Any object created on the specified column is transacted. That is, data made visible to the data source through the object can be committed with **ITransaction::Commit** or aborted with **ITransaction::Abort**.
	VARIANT_FALSE—Any object created on the specified column is not transacted. That is, all changes to the object are permanent once they are made visible to the data source.
	If this property is set on a column that does not contain an object, it is ignored.
DBPROP_UPDATABILITY	Column? N Type: VT_I4 Typical R/W: R/W Description: Updatability
	A bitmask specifying the supported methods on **IRowsetChange**. A combination of zero or more of the following:
	DBPROPVAL_UP_CHANGE—**SetData** is supported.
	DBPROPVAL_UP_DELETE—**DeleteRows** is supported.
	DBPROPVAL_UP_INSERT—**InsertRow** is supported.
	DBPROP_UPDATABILITY should be used in conjunction with DBPROP_IRowsetChange. If DBPROP_IRowsetChange is VARIANT_TRUE and DBPROP_UPDATABILITY is not set, then it is provider-specific what methods are supported on **IRowsetChange**.

Session Properties

The DBPROPSET_SESSION property set contains the following properties. All of these properties are in the Session property group. Providers can define additional session properties.

Important   The "Typical R/W" value for each property specifies whether that property can typically be read or written. Whether a particular property can actually be read or written is provider-specific and is returned in the *dwPropFlags* element of the DBPROPINFO structure.

Property ID	Description
DBPROP_SESS_AUTOCOMMIT-ISOLEVELS	Type: VT_I4 Typical R/W: R/W Description: Autocommit Isolation Levels A bitmask specifying the transaction isolation level while in auto-commit mode. The values that can be set in this bitmask are the same as those that can be set for DBPROP_SUPPORTEDTXNISOLEVELS.

Table Properties

The DBPROPSET_TABLE property set contains the following properties. All of these properties are in the Table property group. Providers can define additional table properties.

Important   The "Typical R/W" value for each property specifies whether that property can typically be read or written. Whether a particular property can actually be read or written is provider-specific and is returned in the *dwPropFlags* element of the DBPROPINFO structure.

Property ID	Description
DBPROP_TBL_TEMPTABLE	Type: VT_BOOL Typical R/W: R/W Description: Temporary Table Whether the table is temporary. One of the following: VARIANT_TRUE—The table is destroyed when the session is released. VARIANT_FALSE—The table is created permanently.

CoTypes, Structures, and Enumerated Types

This appendix lists the CoTypes, structures, and enumerated types defined by OLE DB.

OLE DB CoTypes

Enumerators:

```
CoType TEnumerator {
    [mandatory] IParseDisplayName;
    [mandatory] ISourcesRowset;
    [optional]  IDBInitialize;
    [optional]  IDBProperties;
    [optional]  ISupportErrorInfo;
}
```

Data Source Objects:

```
CoType TDataSource {
    [mandatory] interface IDBCreateSession;
    [mandatory] interface IDBInitialize;
    [mandatory] interface IDBProperties;
    [mandatory] interface IPersist;
    [optional]  interface IDBDataSourceAdmin;
    [optional]  interface IDBInfo;
    [optional]  interface IPersistFile;
    [optional]  interface ISupportErrorInfo;
}
```

Sessions:

```
CoType TSession {
    [mandatory] interface IGetDataSource;
    [mandatory] interface IOpenRowset;
    [mandatory] interface ISessionProperties;
    [optional]  interface IDBCreateCommand;
    [optional]  interface IDBSchemaRowset;
    [optional]  interface IIndexDefinition;
    [optional]  interface ISupportErrorInfo;
    [optional]  interface ITableDefinition;
    [optional]  interface ITransactionJoin;
    [optional]  interface ITransactionLocal;
    [optional]  interface ITransactionObject;
}
```

Commands:

```
CoType TCommand {
    [mandatory] interface IAccessor;
    [mandatory] interface IColumnsInfo;
    [mandatory] interface ICommand;
    [mandatory] interface ICommandProperties;
    [mandatory] interface ICommandText;
    [mandatory] interface IConvertType;
    [optional]  interface IColumnsRowset;
    [optional]  interface ICommandPrepare;
    [optional]  interface ICommandWithParameters;
    [optional]  interface ISupportErrorInfo;
}
```

Multiple Results Objects:

```
CoType TMultipleResults {
    [mandatory] interface IMultipleResults;
}
```

Rowsets:

```
CoType TRowset {
    [mandatory] interface IAccessor;
    [mandatory] interface IColumnsInfo;
    [mandatory] interface IConvertType;
    [mandatory] interface IRowset;
    [mandatory] interface IRowsetInfo;
    [optional]  interface IColumnsRowset;
    [optional]  interface IConnectionPointContainer;
    [optional]  interface IRowsetChange;
    [optional]  interface IRowsetIdentity;
    [optional]  interface IRowsetLocate;
    [optional]  interface IRowsetResynch;
    [optional]  interface IRowsetScroll;
    [optional]  interface IRowsetUpdate;
    [optional]  interface ISupportErrorInfo;
}
```

Indexes:

```
CoType TIndex {
    [mandatory] interface IAccessor;
    [mandatory] interface IColumnsInfo;
    [mandatory] interface IConvertType;
    [mandatory] interface IRowset;
    [mandatory] interface IRowsetIndex;
    [mandatory] interface IRowsetInfo;
    [optional]  interface IRowsetChange;
    [optional]  interface ISupportErrorInfo;
};
```

Transactions:

```
CoType TTransaction {
    [mandatory] interface IConnectionPointContainer;
    [mandatory] interface ITransaction;
    [optional]  interface ISupportErrorInfo;
};
```

Transaction Options:

```
CoType TTransactionOptions {
    [mandatory] interface ITransactionOptions;
    [optional]  interface ISupportErrorInfo;
};
```

Errors:

```
CoType TErrorObject {
    [mandatory] interface IErrorInfo;
    [mandatory] interface IErrorRecords;
}
```

Custom Errors:

```
CoType TCustomErrorObject {
    [optional]  interface ISQLErrorInfo;
}
```

OLE DB Structures and Enumerated Types

Type	Defined in	Used in

`typedef DWORD DBACCESSORFLAGS;`
 	
 `enum DBACCESSORFLAGSENUM {`
   `DBACCESSOR_INVALID,`
   `DBACCESSOR_PASSBYREF,`
   `DBACCESSOR_ROWDATA,`
   `DBACCESSOR_PARAMETERDATA,`
   `DBACCESSOR_OPTIMIZED`
 `};`
	IAccessor::
	 CreateAccessor
		IAccessor::CreateAccessor
		 IAccessor::GetBindings

Type	Defined in	Used in

```typedef struct tagDBBINDEXT {```
 ``` BYTE * pExtension;```
 ``` ULONG ulExtension;```
 ```} DBBINDEXT;```
	"DBBINDING Structures" in Chapter 6	DBBINDING

```typedef struct tagDBBINDING {```
 ``` ULONG   iOrdinal;```
 ``` ULONG   obValue;```
 ``` ULONG   obLength;```
 ``` ULONG   obStatus;```
 ``` ITypeInfo * pTypeInfo;```
 ``` DBOBJECT * pObject;```
 ``` DBBINDEXT * pBindExt;```
 ``` DBPART   dwPart;```
 ``` DBMEMOWNER dwMemOwner;```
 ``` DBPARAMIO   eParamIO;```
 ``` ULONG   cbMaxLen;```
 ``` DWORD   dwFlags;```
 ``` DBTYPE   wType;```
 ``` BYTE   bPrecision;```
 ``` BYTE   bScale;```
 ```} DBBINDING;```
	"DBBINDING Structures" in Chapter 6	**IAccessor::CreateAccessor**
		 IAccessor::GetBindings

```typedef DWORD DBBINDSTATUS;```
 	
 ```enum DBBINDSTATUSENUM {```
 ``` DBBINDSTATUS_OK```
 ``` DBBINDSTATUS_BADORDINAL```
 ``` DBBINDSTATUS_UNSUPPORTEDCONVERSION```
 ``` DBBINDSTATUS_BADBINDINFO```
 ``` DBBINDSTATUS_BADSTORAGEFLAGS```
 ``` DBBINDSTATUS_NOINTERFACE```
 ```};```
	IAccessor:: CreateAccessor	**IAccessor::CreateAccessor**

```typedef enum tagDBBOOKMARK {```
 ``` DBBMK_INVALID,```
 ``` DBBMK_FIRST,```
 ``` DBBMK_LAST```
 ```} DBBOOKMARK;```
	"Standard Bookmarks" in Chapter 4	

```typedef struct tagDBCOLUMNDESC {```
 ``` LPOLESTR   pwszTypeName;```
 ``` ITypeInfo * pTypeInfo;```
 ``` DBPROPSET * rgPropertySets;```
 ``` CLSID   * pclsid;```
 ``` ULONG   cPropertySets;```
 ``` ULONG   ulColumnSize;```
 ``` DBID   dbcid;```
 ``` DBTYPE   wType;```
 ``` BYTE   bPrecision;```
 ``` BYTE   bScale;```
 ```} DBCOLUMNDESC;```
	ITableDefinition:: CreateTable	**ITableDefinition::CreateAddColumn**
		 ITableDefinition::CreateTable

Type	Defined in	Used in

`typedef DWORD DBCOLUMNFLAGS;`
 	
`enum DBCOLUMNFLAGSENUM {`
  `DBCOLUMNFLAGS_ISBOOKMARK,`
  `DBCOLUMNFLAGS_MAYDEFER,`
  `DBCOLUMNFLAGS_WRITE,`
  `DBCOLUMNFLAGS_WRITEUNKNOWN,`
  `DBCOLUMNFLAGS_ISFIXEDLENGTH,`
  `DBCOLUMNFLAGS_ISNULLABLE,`
  `DBCOLUMNFLAGS_MAYBENULL,`
  `DBCOLUMNFLAGS_ISLONG,`
  `DBCOLUMNFLAGS_ISROWID,`
  `DBCOLUMNFLAGS_ISROWVER,`
  `DBCOLUMNFLAGS_CACHEDEFERRED`
`};`
	IColumnsInfo::
	GetColumnInfo
		DBCOLUMNINFO

`typedef struct tagDBCOLUMNINFO {`
  `LPOLESTR       pwszName;`
  `ITypeInfo *    pTypeInfo;`
  `ULONG          iOrdinal;`
  `DBCOLUMNFLAGS  dwFlags;`
  `ULONG          ulColumnSize;`
  `DBTYPE         wType;`
  `BYTE           bPrecision;`
  `BYTE           bScale;`
  `DBID           columnid;`
`} DBCOLUMNINFO;`
	IColumnsInfo::
	GetColumnInfo
		IColumnsInfo::GetColumnInfo

`typedef DWORD DBCOMPARE;`
 	
`enum DBCOMPAREENUM {`
  `DBCOMPARE_LT,`
  `DBCOMPARE_EQ,`
  `DBCOMPARE_GT,`
  `DBCOMPARE_NE,`
  `DBCOMPARE_NOTCOMPARABLE`
`};`
	IRowsetLocate::
	Compare
		IRowsetLocate::Compare

`typedef DWORD DBCONVERTFLAGS;`
 	
`enum DBCONVERTFLAGSENUM {`
  `DBCONVERTFLAGS_COLUMN,`
  `DBCONVERTFLAGS_PARAMETER`
`};`
	IConvertType::
	CanConvert
		IConvertType::CanConvert

`typedef struct tagDBDATE {`
  `SHORT  year;`
  `USHORT month;`
  `USHORT day;`
`} DBDATE;`
	"Type Indicators" in
	Appendix A	

Type	Defined in	Used in

typedef DWORD DBEVENTPHASE;
 	
enum DBEVENTPHASEENUM {
  DBEVENTPHASE_OKTODO,
  DBEVENTPHASE_ABOUTTODO,
  DBEVENTPHASE_SYNCHAFTER,
  DBEVENTPHASE_FAILEDTODO,
  DBEVENTPHASE_DIDEVENT
};
	IRowsetNotify	**IRowsetNotify::OnFieldChange**
		IRowsetNotify::OnRowChange
		IRowsetNotify::OnRowsetChange

typedef struct tagDBID {
  union {
    GUID   guid;
    GUID * pguid;
  } uGuid;
  DBKIND eKind;
  union {
    LPOLESTR pwszName;
    ULONG   ulPropid;
  } uName;
} DBID;
	"Column IDs" in Chapter 4	DBCOLUMNDESC
		DBCOLUMNINFO
		DBINDEXCOLUMNDESC
		DBPROP
		IColumnsInfo::MapColumnIDs
		**IColumnsRowset::
		GetAvailableColumns**
		**IColumnsRowset::
		GetColumnsRowset**
		IIndexDefinition::CreateIndex
		IIndexDefinition::DropIndex
		IOpenRowset::OpenRowset
		ITableDefinition::AddColumn
		ITableDefinition::CreateTable
		ITableDefinition::DropColumn
		ITableDefinition::DropTable

typedef DWORD DBINDEXCOLORDER;
 	
enum DBINDEX_COL_ORDERENUM {
  DBINDEX_COL_ORDER_ASC,
  DBINDEX_COL_ORDER_DESC
};
	**IIndexDefinition::
	CreateIndex**
		DBINDEXCOLUMNDESC

typedef struct tagDBINDEXCOLUMNDESC { DBID * pColumnID; DBINDEXCOLORDER eIndexColOrder; } DBINDEXCOLUMNDESC;	**IIndexDefinition:: CreateIndex**	**IIndexDefinition::CreateIndex** **IRowsetIndex::GetIndexInfo**

Type	Defined in	Used in
| ```
typedef DWORD DBKIND;

enum DBKINDENUM {
  DBKIND_GUID_NAME,
  DBKIND_GUID_PROPID,
  DBKIND_NAME,
  DBKIND_PGUID_NAME,
  DBKIND_PGUID_PROPID,
  DBKIND_PROPID,
  DBKIND_GUID
};
``` | "Column IDs" in Chapter 4 | DBID |
| ```
typedef DWORD DBLITERAL;

enum DBLITERALENUM {
  DBLITERAL_INVALID,
  DBLITERAL_BINARY_LITERAL,
  DBLITERAL_CATALOG_NAME,
  DBLITERAL_CATALOG_SEPARATOR,
  DBLITERAL_CHAR_LITERAL,
  DBLITERAL_COLUMN_ALIAS,
  DBLITERAL_COLUMN_NAME,
  DBLITERAL_CORRELATION_NAME,
  DBLITERAL_CURSOR_NAME,
  DBLITERAL_ESCAPE_PERCENT,
  DBLITERAL_ESCAPE_UNDERSCORE,
  DBLITERAL_INDEX_NAME,
  DBLITERAL_LIKE_PERCENT,
  DBLITERAL_LIKE_UNDERSCORE,
  DBLITERAL_PROCEDURE_NAME,
  DBLITERAL_QUOTE,
  DBLITERAL_SCHEMA_NAME,
  DBLITERAL_TABLE_NAME,
  DBLITERAL_TEXT_COMMAND,
  DBLITERAL_USER_NAME,
  DBLITERAL_VIEW_NAME
};
``` | **IDBInfo::GetLiteralInfo** | **IDBInfo::GetLiteralInfo** |
| ```
typedef DWORD DBMEMOWNER;

enum DBMEMOWNERENUM {
  DBMEMOWNER_CLIENTOWNED,
  DBMEMOWNER_PROVIDEROWNED
};
``` | "DBBINDING Structures" in Chapter 6 | DBBINDING |
| ```
typedef struct tagDB_NUMERIC {
  BYTE precision;
  BYTE scale;
  BYTE sign;
  BYTE val[16];
} DB_NUMERIC;
``` | "Type Indicators" in Appendix A | |

Type	Defined in	Used in
```typedef struct tagDBOBJECT { DWORD dwFlags; IID iid; } DBOBJECT;```	"DBBINDING Structures" in Chapter 6	DBBINDING
```typedef struct tagDBPARAMBINDINFO { LPOLESTR pwszDataSourceType; LPOLESTR pwszName; ULONG ulParamSize; DBPARAMFLAGS dwFlags; BYTE bPrecision; BYTE bScale; } DBPARAMBINDINFO;```	**ICommandWith-Parameters:: SetParameterInfo**	**ICommandWithParameters:: SetParameterInfo**
```typedef DWORD DBPARAMFLAGS; enum DBPARAMFLAGSENUM { DBPARAMFLAGS_ISINPUT, DBPARAMFLAGS_ISOUTPUT, DBPARAMFLAGS_ISSIGNED, DBPARAMFLAGS_ISNULLABLE, DBPARAMFLAGS_ISLONG };```	**ICommandWith-Parameters:: GetParameterInfo**	DBPARAMBINDINFO DBPARAMINFO
```typedef struct tagDBPARAMINFO { DBPARAMFLAGS dwFlags; ULONG iOrdinal; LPOLESTR pwszName; ITypeInfo * pTypeInfo; ULONG ulParamSize; DBTYPE wType; BYTE bPrecision; BYTE bScale; } DBPARAMINFO;```	**ICommandWith-Parameters:: GetParameterInfo**	**ICommandWithParameters:: GetParameterInfo**
```typedef DWORD DBPARAMIO; enum DBPARAMIOENUM { DBPARAMIO_NOTPARAM, DBPARAMIO_INPUT, DBPARAMIO_OUTPUT };```	"DBBINDING Structures" in Chapter 6	DBBINDING
```typedef struct tagDBPARAMS { void * pData; ULONG cParamSets; HACCESSOR hAccessor; } DBPARAMS;```	**ICommand::Execute**	**ICommand::Execute**

Type	Defined in	Used in

`typedef DWORD DBPART;`
 	
`enum DBPARTENUM {`
  `DBPART_INVALID,`
  `DBPART_VALUE,`
  `DBPART_LENGTH,`
  `DBPART_STATUS`
`};`
	"DBBINDING Structures" in Chapter 6	DBBINDING

`typedef DWORD DBPENDINGSTATUS;`
 	
`enum DBPENDINGSTATUSENUM {`
  `DBPENDINGSTATUS_NEW,`
  `DBPENDINGSTATUS_CHANGED,`
  `DBPENDINGSTATUS_DELETED,`
  `DBPENDINGSTATUS_UNCHANGED,`
  `DBPENDINGSTATUS_INVALIDROW`
`};`
	IRowsetUpdate:: GetPendingRows	**IRowsetUpdate::GetPendingRows**
		IRowsetUpdate::GetRowStatus

`typedef struct tagDBPROP {`
  `DBPROPID      dwPropertyID;`
  `DBPROPOPTIONS dwOptions;`
  `DBPROPSTATUS  dwStatus;`
  `DBID          colid;`
  `VARIANT       vValue;`
`} DBPROP;`
	"DBPROP Structure" in Chapter 11	DBPROPSET

`typedef DWORD DBPROPFLAGS;`
 	
`enum DBPROPFLAGSENUM {`
  `DBPROPFLAGS_NOTSUPPORTED,`
  `DBPROPFLAGS_COLUMN,`
  `DBPROPFLAGS_DATASOURCE,`
  `DBPROPFLAGS_DATASOURCECREATE,`
  `DBPROPFLAGS_DATASOURCEINFO,`
  `DBPROPFLAGS_DBINIT,`
  `DBPROPFLAGS_INDEX,`
  `DBPROPFLAGS_ROWSET,`
  `DBPROPFLAGS_TABLE,`
  `DBPROPFLAGS_COLUMNOK,`
  `DBPROPFLAGS_READ,`
  `DBPROPFLAGS_WRITE,`
  `DBPROPFLAGS_REQUIRED,`
  `DBPROPFLAGS_SESSION`
`};`
	"DBPROPFLAGS Enumerated Type" in Chapter 11	DBPROPINFO

Type	Defined in	Used in
``typedef struct tagDBPROPIDSET {
DBPROPID * rgPropertyIDs;
ULONG   cPropertyIDs;
GUID   guidPropertySet;
} DBPROPIDSET;```	"DBPROPIDSET Structure" in Chapter 11	**ICommandProperties:: GetProperties** **IDBDataSourceAdmin:: GetCreationProperties** **IDBProperties::GetProperties** **IDBProperties::GetPropertyInfo** **IRowsetInfo::GetProperties** **ISessionProperties::GetProperties**
``typedef struct tagDBPROPINFO {
LPOLESTR   pwszDescription;
DBPROPID   dwPropertyID;
DBPROPFLAGS dwFlags;
VARTYPE   vtType;
VARIANT   vValues;
} DBPROPINFO;```	"DBPROPINFO Structure" in Chapter 11	DBPROPINFOSET
``typedef struct tagDBPROPINFOSET {
DBPROPINFO * rgPropertyInfos;
ULONG   cPropertyInfos;
GUID   guidPropertySet;
} DBPROPINFOSET;```	"DBPROPINFOSET Structure" in Chapter 11	**IDBDataSourceAdmin:: GetCreationProperties** **IDBProperties::GetPropertyInfo**
``typedef DWORD DBPROPOPTIONS;

enum DBPROPOPTIONSENUM {
  DBPROPOPTIONS_REQUIRED,
  DBPROPOPTIONS_SETIFCHEAP
};``` | "DBPROPOPTIONS Enumerated Type" in Chapter 11 | DBPROP |
| ```typedef struct tagDBPROPSET {
  DBPROP * rgProperties;
  ULONG   cProperties;
  GUID   guidPropertySet;
} DBPROPSET;``` | "DBPROPSET Structure" in Chapter 11 | DBCOLUMNDESC
IColumnsRowset:: GetColumnsRowset

ICommandProperties:: GetProperties

ICommandProperties:: SetProperties

IDBDataSourceAdmin:: CreateDataSource

IDBDataSourceAdmin:: ModifyDataSource

IDBProperties::GetProperties

IDBProperties::SetProperties |

Type	Defined in	Used in
DBPROPSET (*continued*)	"DBPROPSET Structure" in Chapter 11	**IDBSchemaRowset::GetRowset** **IIndexDefinition::CreateIndex** **IOpenRowset::OpenRowset** **IRowsetIndex::GetIndexInfo** **IRowsetInfo::GetProperties** **ISessionProperties::GetProperties** **ISessionProperties::SetProperties** **ISourcesRowset::GetSourcesRowset** **ITableDefinition::CreateTable**

typedef DWORD DBPROPSTATUS;
 	
enum DBPROPSTATUSENUM {
  DBPROPSTATUS_OK,
  DBPROPSTATUS_NOTSUPPORTED,
  DBPROPSTATUS_BADVALUE,
  DBPROPSTATUS_BADOPTION,
  DBPROPSTATUS_BADCOLUMN,
  DBPROPSTATUS_NOTALLSETTABLE,
  DBPROPSTATUS_NOTSETTABLE,
  DBPROPSTATUS_NOTSET,
  DBPROPSTATUS_CONFLICTING
};
	"DBPROPSTATUS
	Enumerated Type" in
	Chapter 11
		DBPROP

typedef DWORD DBRANGE;
 	
enum DBRANGEENUM {
  DBRANGE_INCLUSIVESTART,
  DBRANGE_INCLUSIVEEND,
  DBRANGE_EXCLUSIVESTART,
  DBRANGE_EXCLUSIVEEND,
  DBRANGE_EXCLUDENULLS,
  DBRANGE_PREFIX,
  DBRANGE_MATCH
};
	**IRowsetIndex::
	SetRange**
		IRowsetIndex::SetRange

Type	Defined in	Used in

`typedef DWORD DBREASON;`
 	
`enum DBREASONENUM {`
`  DBREASON_ROWSET_FETCHPOSITIONCHANGE,`
`  DBREASON_ROWSET_RELEASE,`
`  DBREASON_ROWSET_CHANGED,`
`  DBREASON_COLUMN_SET,`
`  DBREASON_COLUMN_RECALCULATED,`
`  DBREASON_ROW_ACTIVATE,`
`  DBREASON_ROW_RELEASE,`
`  DBREASON_ROW_DELETE,`
`  DBREASON_ROW_FIRSTCHANGE,`
`  DBREASON_ROW_INSERT,`
`  DBREASON_ROW_RESYNCH,`
`  DBREASON_ROW_UNDOCHANGE,`
`  DBREASON_ROW_UNDOINSERT,`
`  DBREASON_ROW_UNDODELETE,`
`  DBREASON_ROW_UPDATE`
`};`
	IRowsetNotify	**IRowsetNotify::OnFieldChange**
		IRowsetNotify::OnRowChange
		IRowsetNotify::OnRowsetChange

`typedef DWORD DBROWSTATUS;`
 	
`enum DBROWSTATUSENUM {`
`  DBROWSTATUS_S_OK,`
`  DBROWSTATUS_S_MULTIPLECHANGES,`
`  DBROWSTATUS_S_PENDINGCHANGES,`
`  DBROWSTATUS_E_CANCELED,`
`  DBROWSTATUS_E_CANTRELEASE,`
`  DBROWSTATUS_E_CONCURRENCYVIOLATION,`
`  DBROWSTATUS_E_DELETED,`
`  DBROWSTATUS_E_PENDINGINSERT,`
`  DBROWSTATUS_E_NEWLYINSERTED,`
`  DBROWSTATUS_E_INTEGRITYVIOLATION,`
`  DBROWSTATUS_E_INVALID,`
`  DBROWSTATUS_E_MAXPENDCHANGESEXCEEDED,`
`  DBROWSTATUS_E_OBJECTOPEN,`
`  DBROWSTATUS_E_OUTOFMEMORY,`
`  DBROWSTATUS_E_PERMISSIONDENIED,`
`  DBROWSTATUS_E_LIMITREACHED,`
`  DBROWSTATUS_E_SCHEMAVIOLATION`
`};`
	"Arrays of Errors" in Chapter 13	**IRowset::AddRefRows**
		IRowset::ReleaseRows
		IRowsetChange::DeleteRows
		IRowsetLocate:: GetRowsByBookmark
		IRowsetLocate::Hash
		IRowsetResynch::ResynchRows
		IRowsetUpdate::Undo
		IRowsetUpdate::Update

`typedef DWORD DBSEEK;`
 	
`enum DBSEEKENUM {`
`  DBSEEK_INVALID,`
`  DBSEEK_FIRSTEQ,`
`  DBSEEK_LASTEQ,`
`  DBSEEK_GE,`
`  DBSEEK_GT,`
`  DBSEEK_LE,`
`  DBSEEK_LT`
`};`
	IRowsetIndex::Seek	**IRowsetIndex::Seek**

Type	Defined in	Used in

`typedef DWORD DBSOURCETYPE;`
 	
`enum DBSOURCETYPEENUM {`
`  DBSOURCETYPE_DATASOURCE,`
`  DBSOURCETYPE_ENUMERATOR`
`};`
	ISourcesRowset::
	GetSourcesRowset
		ISourcesRowset::GetSourcesRowset

`typedef DWORD DBSTATUS;`
 	
`enum DBSTATUSENUM {`
`  DBSTATUS_S_OK,`
`  DBSTATUS_E_BADACCESSOR,`
`  DBSTATUS_E_CANTCONVERTVALUE,`
`  DBSTATUS_S_ISNULL,`
`  DBSTATUS_S_TRUNCATED,`
`  DBSTATUS_E_SIGNMISMATCH,`
`  DBSTATUS_E_DATAOVERFLOW,`
`  DBSTATUS_E_CANTCREATE,`
`  DBSTATUS_E_UNAVAILABLE,`
`  DBSTATUS_E_PERMISSIONDENIED,`
`  DBSTATUS_E_INTEGRITYVIOLATION,`
`  DBSTATUS_E_SCHEMAVIOLATION,`
`  DBSTATUS_E_BADSTATUS,`
`  DBSTATUS_S_DEFAULT`
`    };`
	"Status" in Chapter 6	

`typedef struct tagDBTIME {`
`  USHORT hour;`
`  USHORT minute;`
`  USHORT second;`
`} DBTIME;`
	"Type Indicators" in
	Appendix A	

`typedef struct tagDBTIMESTAMP {`
`  SHORT   year;`
`  USHORT month;`
`  USHORT day;`
`  USHORT hour;`
`  USHORT minute;`
`  USHORT second;`
`  ULONG  fraction;`
`} DBTIMESTAMP;`
	"Type Indicators" in
	Appendix A	

Type	Defined in	Used in

`typedef WORD DBTYPE;`
 	
`enum DBTYPEENUM {`
`  DBTYPE_EMPTY,`
`  DBTYPE_NULL,`
`  DBTYPE_I2,`
`  DBTYPE_I4,`
`  DBTYPE_R4,`
`  DBTYPE_R8,`
`  DBTYPE_CY,`
`  DBTYPE_DATE,`
`  DBTYPE_BSTR,`
`  DBTYPE_IDISPATCH,`
`  DBTYPE_ERROR,`
`  DBTYPE_BOOL,`
`  DBTYPE_VARIANT,`
`  DBTYPE_IUNKNOWN,`
`  DBTYPE_DECIMAL,`
`  DBTYPE_UI1,`
`  DBTYPE_ARRAY,`
`  DBTYPE_BYREF,`
`  DBTYPE_I1,`
`  DBTYPE_UI2,`
`  DBTYPE_UI4,`
`  DBTYPE_I8,`
`  DBTYPE_UI8,`
`  DBTYPE_GUID,`
`  DBTYPE_VECTOR,`
`  DBTYPE_RESERVED,`
`  DBTYPE_BYTES,`
`  DBTYPE_STR,`
`  DBTYPE_WSTR,`
`  DBTYPE_NUMERIC,`
`  DBTYPE_UDT,`
`  DBTYPE_DBDATE,`
`  DBTYPE_DBTIME,`
`  DBTYPE_DBTIMESTAMP`
`};`
	"Type Indicators" in Appendix A	DBBINDING
		DBCOLUMNINFO
		DBPARAMINFO
		DBCOLUMNDESC
		IConvertType::CanConvert

`typedef struct tagDBVECTOR {`
`  ULONG  size;`
`  void * ptr;`
`} DBVECTOR;`
	"Type Indicators" in Appendix A	

Type	Defined in	Used in
| ```c
typedef struct tagDEC {
   USHORT wReserved;
   union {
      struct {
         BYTE scale;
         BYTE sign;
      };
      USHORT signscale;
   };
   ULONG Hi32;
   union {
      struct {
         ULONG Lo32;
         ULONG Mid32;
      };
      ULONGLONG Lo64;
   };
} DECIMAL;
``` | "Type Indicators" in Appendix A | |
| ```c
typedef struct tagERRORINFO {
   HRESULT hrError;
   DWORD   dwMinor;
   CLSID   clsid;
   IID     iid;
   DISPID  dispid;
} ERRORINFO;
``` | "Error Records" in Chapter 13 | **IErrorRecords::AddErrorRecord**<br>**IErrorRecords::GetBasicErrorInfo** |

Interface Summary

This appendix lists the prototypes of all interfaces in OLE DB.

```
interface IAccessor {
  HRESULT AddRefAccessor (
        HACCESSOR    hAccessor,
        ULONG *      pcRefCount);

  HRESULT CreateAccessor (
        DBACCESSORFLAGS    dwAccessorFlags,
        ULONG              cBindings,
        const DBBINDING    rgBindings[],
        ULONG              cbRowSize,
        HACCESSOR *        phAccessor,
        DBBINDSTATUS       rgStatus[]);

  HRESULT GetBindings (
        HACCESSOR            hAccessor,
        DBACCESSORFLAGS *    pdwAccessorFlags,
        ULONG *              pcBindings,
        DBBINDING **         prgBindings);

  HRESULT ReleaseAccessor (
        HACCESSOR    hAccessor,
        ULONG *      pcRefCount);
};


interface IColumnsInfo {
  HRESULT GetColumnInfo (
        ULONG *            pcColumns,
        DBCOLUMNINFO **    prgInfo,
        OLECHAR **         ppStringsBuffer);

  HRESULT MapColumnIDs (
        ULONG        cColumnIDs,
        const DBID   rgColumnIDs[],
        ULONG        rgColumns[]);
};
```

```
interface IColumnsRowset {
  HRESULT GetAvailableColumns (
        ULONG *  pcOptColumns,
        DBID **  prgOptColumns);

  HRESULT GetColumnsRowset (
        IUnknown *  pUnkOuter,
        ULONG       cOptColumns,
        const DBID  rgOptColumns[],
        REFIID      riid,
        ULONG       cPropertySets,
        DBPROPSET   rgPropertySets[],
        IUnknown ** ppColRowset);
};


interface ICommand {
  HRESULT Cancel();

  HRESULT Execute (
        IUnknown *  pUnkOuter,
        REFIID      riid,
        DBPARAMS *  pParams,
        LONG   *    pcRowsAffected,
        IUnknown ** ppRowset);

  HRESULT GetDBSession (
        REFIID      riid,
        IUnknown ** ppSession);
};


interface ICommandPrepare {
  HRESULT Prepare (
        ULONG cExpectedRuns);

  HRESULT Unprepare();
};


interface ICommandProperties {
  HRESULT GetProperties (
        const ULONG      cPropertyIDSets,
        const DBPROPIDSET rgPropertyIDSets[],
        ULONG *          pcPropertySets,
        DBPROPSET **     prgPropertySets);

  HRESULT SetProperties (
        ULONG       cPropertySets,
        DBPROPSET   rgPropertySets[]);
};
```

```
interface ICommandText : ICommand {
  HRESULT GetCommandText (
        GUID *       pguidDialect,
        LPOLESTR *   ppwszCommand);

  HRESULT SetCommandText (
        REFGUID    rguidDialect,
        LPCOLESTR  pwszCommand);
};


interface ICommandWithParameters {
  HRESULT GetParameterInfo (
        ULONG *        pcParams,
        DBPARAMINFO ** prgParamInfo,
        OLECHAR **     ppNamesBuffer);

  HRESULT MapParameterNames (
        ULONG            cParamNames,
        const OLECHAR *  rgParamNames[],
        LONG             rgParamOrdinals[]);

  HRESULT SetParameterInfo (
        ULONG                 cParams,
        const ULONG           rgParamOrdinals[],
        const DBPARAMBINDINFO  rgParamBindInfo[]);
};


interface IConvertType {
  HRESULT CanConvert (
        DBTYPE          wFromType,
        DBTYPE          wToType,
        DBCONVERTFLAGS dwConvertFlags);
};


interface IDBCreateCommand {
  HRESULT CreateCommand(
        IUnknown *  pUnkOuter,
        REFIID      riid,
        IUnknown ** ppCommand);
};


interface IDBCreateSession {
  HRESULT CreateSession (
        IUnknown *  pUnkOuter,
        REFIID      riid,
        IUnknown ** ppDBSession);
};
```

```
interface IDBDataSourceAdmin {
  HRESULT CreateDataSource(
        ULONG       cPropertySets,
        DBPROPSET   rgPropertySets[],
        IUnknown *  pUnkOuter,
        REFIID      riid,
        IUnknown ** ppSession);

  HRESULT DestroyDataSource ();

  HRESULT GetCreationProperties (
        ULONG              cPropertyIDSets,
        const DBPROPIDSET  rgPropertyIDSets[],
        ULONG *            pcPropertyInfoSets,
        DBPROPINFOSET **   prgPropertyInfoSets,
        OLECHAR **         ppDescBuffer);

  HRESULT ModifyDataSource (
        ULONG       cPropertySets,
        DBPROPSET   rgPropertySets[]);
};


interface IDBInfo {
  HRESULT GetKeywords(
        LPOLESTR *  ppwszKeywords);

  HRESULT GetLiteralInfo(
        ULONG             cLiterals,
        const DBLITERAL   rgLiterals[],
        ULONG *           pcLiteralInfo,
        DBLITERALINFO **  prgLiteralInfo,
        OLECHAR **        ppCharBuffer);
};


interface IDBInitialize {
  HRESULT Initialize();

  HRESULT Uninitialize();
};


interface IDBProperties {
  HRESULT GetProperties (
        ULONG             cPropertyIDSets,
        const DBPROPIDSET rgPropertyIDSets[],
        ULONG *           pcPropertySets,
        DBPROPSET **      prgPropertySets);
```

```
    HRESULT GetPropertyInfo(
        ULONG               cPropertyIDSets,
        const DBPROPIDSET   rgPropertyIDSets[],
        ULONG *             pcPropertyInfoSets,
        DBPROPINFOSET **    prgPropertyInfoSets,
        OLECHAR **          ppDescBuffer);

    HRESULT SetProperties (
        ULONG       cPropertySets,
        DBPROPSET   rgPropertySets[]);
};


interface IDBSchemaRowset {
    HRESULT GetRowset (
        IUnknown *      punkOuter,
        REFGUID         rguidSchema,
        ULONG           cRestrictions,
        const VARIANT   rgRestrictions[],
        REFIID          riid,
        ULONG           cPropertySets,
        DBPROPSET       rgPropertySets[],
        IUnknown **     ppRowset);

    HRESULT GetSchemas (
        ULONG *  pcSchemas,
        GUID **  prgSchemas,
        ULONG**  prgRestrictionSupport);
};


interface IErrorInfo {
    HRESULT GetDescription (
        BSTR *pbstrDescription);

    HRESULT GetGUID (
        GUID *pguid);

    HRESULT GetHelpContext (
        DWORD *  pdwHelpContext);

    HRESULT GetHelpFile (
        BSTR *pbstrHelpFile);

    HRESULT GetSource (
        BSTR *pbstrSource);
};
```

```
interface IErrorLookup {
   HRESULT GetErrorDescription (
         HRESULT          hrError,
         DWORD            dwLookupID,
         DISPPARAMS *     pdispparams,
         LCID             lcid,
         BSTR *           pbstrSource,
         BSTR *           pbstrDescription);

   HRESULT GetHelpInfo (
         HRESULT   hrError,
         DWORD     dwLookupID,
         LCID      lcid,
         BSTR *    pbstrHelpFile,
         DWORD *   pdwHelpContext);

   HRESULT ReleaseErrors (
         const DWORD dwDynamicErrorID);
};


interface IErrorRecords {
   HRESULT AddErrorRecord (
         ERRORINFO *      pErrorInfo,
         DWORD            dwLookupID,
         DISPPARAMS *     pdispparams,
         IUnknown *       punkCustomError,
         DWORD            dwDynamicErrorID);

   HRESULT GetBasicErrorInfo (
         ULONG        ulRecordNum,
         ERRORINFO * pErrorInfo);

   HRESULT GetCustomErrorObject (
         ULONG        ulRecordNum,
         REFIID       riid,
         IUnknown ** ppObject);

   HRESULT GetErrorInfo (
         ULONG         ulRecordNum,
         LCID          lcid,
         IErrorInfo ** ppErrorInfo);

   HRESULT GetErrorParameters (
         ULONG          ulRecordNum,
         DISPPARAMS *   pdispparams);

   HRESULT GetRecordCount (
         ULONG *  pcRecords);
};
```

```
interface IGetDataSource {
  HRESULT GetDataSource (
        REFIID       riid,
        IUnknown ** ppDataSource);
};


interface IIndexDefinition {
  HRESULT CreateIndex(
        DBID *                  pTableID,
        DBID *                  pIndexID,
        ULONG                   cIndexColumnDescs,
        const DBINDEXCOLUMNDESC rgIndexColumnDescs[],
        ULONG                   cPropertySets,
        DBPROPSET               rgPropertySets[],
        DBID **                 ppIndexID);

  HRESULT DropIndex(
        DBID *pTableID,
        DBID *pIndexID);
};


interface IMultipleResults {
  HRESULT GetResult(
        IUnknown *  pUnkOuter,
        LONG        lReserved,
        REFIID      riid,
        LONG *      pcRowsAffected,
        IUnknown ** ppRowset);
};


interface IOpenRowset {
  HRESULT OpenRowset(
        IUnknown *  pUnkOuter,
        DBID *      pTableID,
        DBID *      pIndexID,
        REFIID      riid,
        ULONG       cPropertySets,
        DBPROPSET   rgPropertySets[],
        IUnknown ** ppRowset);
};


interface IRowset {
  HRESULT AddRefRows(
        ULONG       cRows,
        const HROW  rghRows[],
        ULONG       rgRefCounts[],
        DBROWSTATUS rgRowStatus[]);
```

```
      HRESULT GetData (
            HROW         hRow,
            HACCESSOR    hAccessor,
            void *       pData);

      HRESULT GetNextRows (
            HCHAPTER hReserved,
            LONG     lRowsOffset,
            LONG     cRows,
            ULONG *  pcRowsObtained,
            HROW **  prghRows);

      HRESULT ReleaseRows (
            ULONG          cRows,
            const HROW     rghRows[],
            DBROWOPTIONS   rgRowOptions[]
            ULONG          rgRefCounts[],
            DBROWSTATUS    rgRowStatus[]);

      HRESULT RestartPosition (
            HCHAPTER hReserved);
};


interface IRowsetChange {
   HRESULT DeleteRows (
         HCHAPTER     hReserved,
         ULONG        cRows,
         const HROW   rghRows[],
         DBROWSTATUS  rgRowStatus[]);

   HRESULT InsertRow (
         HCHAPTER     hReserved,
         HACCESSOR    hAccessor,
         void *       pData,
         HROW   *     phRow);

   HRESULT SetData (
         HROW         hRow,
         HACCESSOR    hAccessor,
         void *       pData);
};


interface IRowsetIdentity {
   HRESULT IsSameRow (
         HROW   hThisRow,
         HROW   hThatRow);
};
```

```
interface IRowsetIndex {
  HRESULT GetIndexInfo (
        ULONG *              pcKeyColumns,
        DBINDEXCOLUMNDESC **  prgIndexColumnDesc,
        ULONG *              pcIndexProperties,
        DBPROPSET **         prgIndexProperties);

  HRESULT Seek (
        HACCESSORhAccessor,
        ULONG       cKeyValues,
        void *      pData,
        DBSEEK      dwSeekOptions);

  HRESULT SetRange (
        HACCESSORhAccessor,
        ULONG       cStartKeyColumns,
        void *      pStartData,
        ULONG       cEndKeyColumns,
        void *      pEndData,
        DBRANGE     dwRangeOptions);
};


interface IRowsetInfo {
  HRESULT GetProperties (
        const ULONG       cPropertyIDSets,
        const DBPROPIDSET rgPropertyIDSets[],
        ULONG *           pcPropertySets,
        DBPROPSET **      prgPropertySets);

  HRESULT GetReferencedRowset (
        ULONG       iOrdinal,
        REFIID      riid,
        IUnknown ** ppReferencedRowset);

  HRESULT GetSpecification (
        REFIID      riid,
        IUnknown ** ppSpecification);
};


interface IRowsetLocate : IRowset {
  HRESULT Compare (
        HCHAPTER       hReserved,
        ULONG          cbBookmark1,
        const BYTE *   pBookmark1,
        ULONG          cbBookmark2,
        const BYTE *   pBookmark2,
        DBCOMPARE *    pComparison);
```

```
HRESULT GetRowsAt (
        HWATCHREGION    hReserved1,
        HCHAPTER        hReserved2
        ULONG           cbBookmark,
        const BYTE *    pBookmark,
        LONG            lRowsOffset,
        LONG            cRows,
        ULONG *         pcRowsObtained,
        HROW **         prghRows);

HRESULT GetRowsByBookmark (
        HCHAPTER        hReserved,
        ULONG           cRows,
        const ULONG     rgcbBookmarks[],
        const BYTE *    rgpBookmarks[],
        HROW            rghRows[],
        DBROWSTATUS     rgRowStatus[]);

HRESULT Hash (
        HCHAPTER        hReserved,
        ULONG           cBookmarks,
        const ULONG     rgcbBookmarks[],
        const BYTE *    rgpBookmarks[],
        DWORD           rgHashedValues[],
        DBROWSTATUS     rgBookmarkStatus[]);
};


interface IRowsetNotify {
    HRESULT OnFieldChange (
        IRowset*        pRowset,
        HROW            hRow,
        ULONG           cColumns,
        ULONG           rgColumns[],
        DBREASON        eReason,
        DBEVENTPHASE    ePhase,
        BOOL            fCantDeny);

    HRESULT OnRowChange (
        IRowset*        pRowset,
        ULONG           cRows,
        const HROW      rghRows[],
        DBREASON        eReason,
        DBEVENTPHASE    ePhase,
        BOOL            fCantDeny);

    HRESULT OnRowsetChange (
        IRowset*        pRowset,
        DBREASON        eReason,
        DBEVENTPHASE    ePhase,
        BOOL            fCantDeny);
};
```

```
interface IRowsetResynch {
  HRESULT GetVisibleData (
        HROW         hRow,
        HACCESSOR    hAccessor,
        void *       pData);

  HRESULT ResynchRows (
        ULONG         cRows,
        const HROW    rghRows[],
        ULONG*        pcRowsResynched,
        HROW**        prghRowsResynched,
        DBROWSTATUS** prgRowStatus);
};


interface IRowsetScroll : IRowsetLocate {
  HRESULT GetApproximatePosition (
        HCHAPTER      hReserved,
        ULONG         cbBookmark,
        const BYTE *  pBookmark,
        ULONG *       pulPosition,
        ULONG *       pcRows);

  HRESULT GetRowsAtRatio (
        HWATCHREGION  hReserved1,
        HCHAPTER      hReserved2,
        ULONG         ulNumerator,
        ULONG         ulDenominator,
        LONG          cRows,
        ULONG *       pcRowsObtained,
        HROW **       prghRows);
};


interface IRowsetUpdate : IRowsetChange {
  HRESULT GetOriginalData (
        HROW         hRow,
        HACCESSOR    hAccessor,
        void *       pData);

  HRESULT GetPendingRows (
        HCHAPTER              hReserved,
        DBPENDINGSTATUS       dwRowStatus,
        ULONG *               pcPendingRows,
        HROW **               prgPendingRows,
        DBPENDINGSTATUS **     prgPendingStatus);

  HRESULT GetRowStatus(
        HCHAPTER              hReserved,
        ULONG                 cRows,
        const HROW            rghRows[],
        DBPENDINGSTATUS       rgPendingStatus[]);
```

```
        HRESULT Undo (
                HCHAPTER        hReserved,
                ULONG           cRows,
                const HROW      rghRows[],
                ULONG *         pcRows,
                HROW **         prgRows,
                DBROWSTATUS ** prgRowStatus);

        HRESULT Update (
                HCHAPTER    /   hReserved,
                ULONG           cRows,
                const HROW      rghRows[],
                ULONG *         pcRows,
                HROW **         prgRows,
                DBROWSTATUS**   prgRowStatus);
};


interface ISessionProperties {
   HRESULT GetProperties (
                ULONG             cPropertyIDSets,
                const DBPROPIDSET rgPropertyIDSets[],
                ULONG *           pcPropertySets,
                DBPROPSET **      prgPropertySets);

   HRESULT SetProperties (
                ULONG       cPropertySets,
                DBPROPSET   rgPropertySets[]);
};


interface ISourcesRowset {
   HRESULT GetSourcesRowset(
                IUnknown    pUnkOuter,
                REFIID      riid,
                ULONG       cPropertySets,
                DBPROPSET   rgPropertySets[],
                IUnknown ** ppSourcesRowset);
};


interface ISQLErrorInfo {
   HRESULT GetSQLInfo (
                BSTR *pbstrSQLState,
                LONG *plNativeError);
};


interface ISupportErrorInfo {
   HRESULT InterfaceSupportsErrorInfo (
                REFIID   riid);
};
```

```
interface ITableDefinition {
   HRESULT AddColumn(
        DBID *        pTableID,
        DBCOLUMNDESC * pColumnDesc,
        DBID **       ppColumnID);

   HRESULT CreateTable(
        IUnknown *    pUnkOuter,
        DBID *        pTableID,
        ULONG         cColumnDescs,
        DBCOLUMNDESC  rgColumnDescs[],
        REFIID        riid,
        ULONG         cPropertySets,
        DBPROPSET     rgPropertySets[],
        DBID **       ppTableID,
        IUnknown **   ppRowset);

   HRESULT DropColumn(
        DBID* pTableID,
        DBID* pColumnID);

   HRESULT DropTable (
        DBID *pTableID);
};


interface ITransaction {
   HRESULT Abort(
        BOID *   pboidReason,
        BOOL     fRetaining,
        BOOL     fAsync);

   HRESULT Commit(
        BOOL  fRetaining,
        DWORD grfTC,
        DWORD grfRM);

   HRESULT GetTransactionInfo(
        XACTTRANSINFO *   pInfo);
};


interface ITransactionJoin {
   HRESULT GetOptionsObject (
        ITransactionOptions ** ppOptions);

   HRESULT JoinTransaction (
        IUnknown *              punkTransactionCoord,
        ISOLEVEL                isoLevel,
        ULONG                   isoFlags,
        ITransactionOptions *   pOtherOptions);
};
```

```
interface ITransactionLocal : ITransaction {
  HRESULT GetOptionsObject (
        ITransactionOptions ** ppOptions);

  HRESULT StartTransaction (
        ISOLEVEL              isoLevel,
        ULONG                 isoFlags,
        ITransactionOptions * pOtherOptions,
        ULONG *               pulTransactionLevel);
};


interface ITransactionObject {
  HRESULT GetTransactionObject (
        ULONG              ulTransactionLevel,
        ITransaction **    ppTransactionObject);
};


interface ITransactionOptions {
  HRESULT GetOptions(
        XACTOPT *   pOptions);

  HRESULT SetOptions(
        XACTOPT *   pOptions);
};
```

Glossary

A

Abort To return the values changed by a transaction to their original state.

Accessor A collection of information that describes how data is stored in the consumer's buffer. The provider uses this information to determine how to transfer data to and from this buffer. *See also* reference accessor.

Accessor handle A handle that identifies an accessor.

Auto-commit mode A transaction commit mode in which all actions taken in a transaction are committed immediately after they are performed.

B

Binary large object (BLOB) Any binary or character data over a certain number of bytes, such as 255. Typically much longer. Such data is generally sent to and retrieved from the data source in parts. Also known as *long data*.

Binding As a verb, the act of associating a column in a rowset or a parameter in a text command with a consumer variable. As a noun, the association or the DBBINDING structure that describes the association.

Bookmark A value that identifies a row in a rowset. Bookmarks are saved by the consumer and used later in the life of the rowset to retrieve a particular row.

Buffer A piece of memory used to pass information, usually data, between the consumer and provider.

C

Catalog A database object that contains one or more schemas.

Change To update, delete, or insert a row of data.

Class ID A globally unique identifier (GUID) associated with an OLE class object. If a class object will be used to create more than one instance of an object, the associated server application should register its CLSID in the system registry so that clients can locate and load the executable code associated with the object(s). Every OLE server or container that allows linking to its embedded objects must register a CLSID for each supported object definition.

Client/server A database access strategy in which one or more clients access data through a server. The clients generally implement the user interface while the server controls database access.

Column The container for a single item of information in a row. Also known as *field*.

Column ID A structure used to identify a column, primarily in a command where there are no stable ordinals or column names.

COM object An object that conforms to the OLE Component Object Model (COM). A COM object is an instance of an object definition, which specifies the object's data and one or more implementations of interfaces on the object. Clients interact with a COM object only through its interfaces. *See also* Component Object Model and interface.

Command An OLE DB object that encapsulates a command.

Command text The text command associated with a command object. Although it is not required to be, this is usually an SQL statement.

Commit To make the changes in a transaction permanent.

Component An object that encapsulates both data and code, and provides a well-specified set of publicly available services.

Component Object Model (COM) The OLE object-oriented programming model that defines how objects interact within a single process or between processes. In COM, clients have access to an object through interfaces implemented on the object. *See also* interface.

Concurrency The ability of more than one transaction to access the same data at the same time.

Consumer Software that calls OLE DB methods and interfaces.

Convert To change data from one type to another, such as from an integer to a string.

Coordinated transaction A transaction composed of multiple, subordinate transactions. All of the subordinate transactions must succeed for the coordinated transaction to succeed. Also known as a *distributed transaction*.

CoType A way to define a group of COM objects, such as rowsets or commands, that have similar characteristics. All COM objects that belong to a particular CoType must expose the mandatory interfaces in that CoType. In addition, they can expose the optional interfaces in the CoType and any interfaces not in the CoType.

D

Data The data for a parameter in a text command or a column in a row.

Data Definition Language (DDL) Those text commands that define, as opposed to manipulate, data. For example, the SQL statements **CREATE TABLE**, **CREATE INDEX**, **GRANT**, and **REVOKE**.

Data Manipulation Language (DML) Those text commands that manipulate, as opposed to define, data. For example, the SQL statements **INSERT**, **UPDATE**, **DELETE**, and **SELECT**.

Data part Data has three parts: the data value, the length of the data value, and the status of the data value.

Data provider A provider that directly exposes data, as opposed to a service provider.

Data source The data the user wants to access, such as the data in a database, file, or array. This is distinct from a data source object.

Data source object An OLE DB object that connects to a data source. This is distinct from the data source.

Data type The type of a piece of data. *See also* type indicator.

Database A discrete collection of data in a DBMS. Also a DBMS.

Database Management System (DBMS) A layer of software between the physical database and the user. The DBMS manages all access to the database. An OLE DB provider can be built directly on top of a DBMS or as a layer between the DBMS and the consumer.

Deferred column A column for which the data is not instantiated in the rowset until the consumer actually attempts to access that data.

Delayed update mode An update mode in which changes made through **IRowsetChange** are cached in the rowset and transmitted to the data source only when **IRowsetUpdate::Update** is called. *See also* immediate update mode.

Delete To remove an existing row of data from the data source.

Distributed transaction *See* coordinated transaction.

E

Empty string A zero-length string. *See also* null pointer and NULL value.

Enumerator An OLE DB object that searches for data sources and other enumerators. *See also* root enumerator.

Error A condition in which a fatal error occurred. Also used to refer to any error, regardless of whether it is fatal.

Error object An object that contains detailed information about an error. *See also* OLE Automation error object and OLE DB error object.

Event An action taken by a provider, such as changing a column value or deleting a row, of which the provider notifies the consumer.

Execution plan A plan generated by a query engine to execute a command. Equivalent to executable code compiled from a third-generation language such as C.

F

Fetch To retrieve one or more rows from the data source and instantiate them in a rowset.

Field *See* column.

Fixed-length data type A data type that is always stored in the same number of bytes, such as a two-byte integer. *See also* variable-length data type.

Foreign key A column or columns in a table that match the primary key in another table.

G

Getting data Transferring data from the provider to the consumer, as in getting column or output parameter data.

Globally Unique Identifier (GUID) A 16-byte value that uniquely identifies something, usually the software that implements one or more COM objects or an interface on one of those objects. Also known as a *UUID (Universally Unique Identifier)*.

H

Handle A value that uniquely identifies something such as a row or an accessor. Handles are meaningful only to the software that creates and uses them, but are passed by other software to identify things.

HRESULT An opaque result handle defined to be zero for a successful return from a function and nonzero if error or status information is returned.

I

Interface Identifier (IID) A globally unique identifier (GUID) associated with an interface. Some functions take IIDs as parameters to allow the caller to specify which interface pointer should be returned.

Immediate update mode An update mode in which changes made through **IRowsetChange** are immediately transmitted to the data source. *See also* delayed update mode.

Index rowset A rowset built over an index. Each row in an index rowset contains a bookmark that points to a row in a rowset built over the corresponding table.

Initialize To change the state of an enumerator or data source object so it can be used to access data. For example, initializing a data source object might require the provider to open a data file or connect to a database.

Input parameter A parameter in a text command for which the consumer supplies a value to the provider.

Input/output parameter A parameter in a text command for which the consumer supplies a value to the provider and the provider returns a value to the consumer.

Insert To add a new row of data to the data source.

Instantiate To create an instance of a COM object.

Interface A group of semantically related functions that provide access to a COM object. Each OLE interface defines a contract that allows objects to interact according to the Component Object Model (COM). While OLE provides many interface implementations, most interfaces can also be implemented by developers designing OLE applications. *See also* Component Object Model and COM object.

IPersist* object An OLE object that supports **IPersistStream**, **IPersistStreamInit**, or **IPersistStorage**.

Isolation level *See* transaction isolation level.

J

Join An operation in a relational database that links the rows in two or more tables by matching values in specified columns.

K

Key A column or columns whose values identify a row. *See also* primary key and foreign key.

Key value bookmark A bookmark that uses a unique key to identify a row. *See also* numeric bookmark.

L

Length The length of a data value. *See also* data part, value, and status.

Listener A consumer that has requested that a provider send it notifications of various events.

Long data *See* BLOB.

M

Manual-commit mode A transaction commit mode in which transactions must be explicitly committed or aborted by calling **ITransaction::Commit** or **ITransaction::Abort**.

Maximum precision The maximum number of base 10 digits that can be stored in a particular data type. *See also* precision.

Metadata Data that describes a parameter in a text command or a column in a rowset. For example, the data type, length, and updatability of a column.

Method A function in an interface.

Multiple results object An OLE DB object created by executing a command and through which multiple results (rowsets or row counts) can be retrieved.

N

Next fetch position The position of the next row that will be fetched by a call to **IRowset::GetNextRows**.

Notification A call from a provider to a consumer, in which the provider notifies the consumer that a particular event is occurring.

Null pointer A pointer with a value of zero. It is an error to dereference a null pointer. *See also* empty string and NULL value.

NULL value Having no explicitly assigned value. In particular, a NULL value is different from a zero or a blank. *See also* empty string and null pointer.

Numeric bookmark A bookmark that uses a unique number to identify a row. *See also* key value bookmark.

O

Object In OLE, a programming structure encapsulating both data and functionality that are defined and allocated as a single unit and for which the only public access is through the programming structure's interfaces. A COM object must support, at a minimum, the **IUnknown** interface, which maintains the object's existence while it is being used and provides access to the object's other interfaces. *See also* Component Object Model and interface.

OLE Microsoft's object-based technology for sharing information and services across process and machine boundaries.

OLE Automation error object An error object that conforms to the standards specified for such objects by OLE Automation. *See also* OLE DB error object.

OLE DB A set of interfaces that expose data from a variety of data sources using COM.

OLE DB error object An error object used by OLE DB objects to return an error. OLE DB error objects are an extension of OLE Automation error objects.

OLE DB object A COM object defined by OLE DB. The COM objects defined by OLE DB are enumerators, data source objects, sessions, commands, rowsets, multiple results objects, OLE DB error objects, transaction objects, and transaction options objects.

OLE DB Software Development Kit (SDK) A collection of redistributable software, header files, tools, sample code, and documentation to be used by developers of OLE DB consumers and providers.

OLE object In OLE DB, a COM object that is stored in a column. In OLE, a COM object.

Optimistic concurrency A strategy to increase concurrency in which rows are not locked. Instead, before they are updated or deleted, a rowset checks to see if they have been changed since they were last read. If so, the update or delete fails. *See also* pessimistic concurrency.

Ordinary bookmark A bookmark whose value is defined by the provider. *See also* standard bookmark.

Output parameter A parameter in a text command for which the provider returns a value to the consumer.

P

Parameter A variable in a text command. A parameter can be an input, input/output, or output parameter.

Pending change A change that has been cached in a rowset and not yet transmitted to the data source. *See also* delayed update mode and immediate update mode.

Persist To save the current state of a COM object, such as to a file. Currently, only data source objects can be persisted.

Pessimistic concurrency A strategy for implementing serializability in which rows are locked so that other transactions cannot change them. *See also* optimistic concurrency.

Phase A step in a sequence of notifications caused by a single event. The sequence of notifications is similar to the phases in a two-phase commit protocol.

Precision The number of base 10 digits in a number. *See also* maximum precision.

Prepare To compile a command. An execution plan is created by preparing a command.

Primary key A column or columns that uniquely identifies a row in a table.

Procedure A group of one or more precompiled commands (generally SQL statements) that are stored as a named object in a database.

Property Attributes of an OLE DB object. For example, the maximum number of rows in a rowset that can be active at one time.

Property group The set of all properties that apply to a particular OLE DB object.

Property set A property is identified by a GUID and an integer (the property ID). A property set is the set of all properties that share the same GUID.

Provider Software that implements OLE DB methods and interfaces.

Q

Query A text command. Sometimes used to mean a text command that creates a rowset.

R

Reason The specific event that occurred, such as changing a row value or deleting a row.

Record *See* row.

Reference counting Keeping a count of each interface pointer held on an object to ensure that the object is not destroyed before all references to it are released. In OLE DB, rows and accessors are also reference counted.

Reference accessor An accessor that enables a consumer to get rowset data directly from the provider's buffer. Support for reference accessors is optional.

Release To decrease the reference count on a row, accessor, or COM object. When the reference count reaches zero, the provider generally releases the resources used by the row, accessor, or COM object.

Result A row count or rowset created by executing a command. *See also* multiple results object.

Resynchronize To update the data in a rowset with the data in the data source that is visible to the current transaction according to its isolation level.

Return code The value returned by an OLE DB method.

Root enumerator An enumerator shipped in the OLE DB SDK that enumerates the data sources and enumerators listed in the registry. *See also* enumerator.

Row A set of related columns that describe a specific entity. Also known as a *record*.

Row handle A handle used to identify a row.

Rowset An OLE DB object that contains a set of rows, each of which has columns of data.

S

Scale The number of digits in a number that are to the right of the decimal point.

Schema A database object that contains one or more tables, often created by a single user.

Schema rowset A predefined rowset that provides information about the structure of a database.

Self bookmark A bookmark, stored in column 0 of a row, that is used to return to that row.

Serializability Whether two transactions executing simultaneously produce a result that is the same as the serial (or sequential) execution of those transactions. Serializable transactions are required to maintain database integrity.

Service provider A provider that does not directly expose data, but instead provides a service, such as query processing. Used in conjunction with data providers.

Session An OLE DB object that serves as the context for a transaction.

Setting data Transferring data from the consumer to the provider, as in setting column or input parameter data.

SQL Structured Query Language. A language used by relational databases to query, update, and manage data. Text commands often use SQL.

Standard bookmark A bookmark whose value is defined by OLE DB. *See also* ordinary bookmark.

Status The status of a data value. *See also* data part, value, and length.

Storage interface An interface used to access data in a storage object: **ISequentialStream**, **IStream**, **IStorage**, or **ILockBytes**.

Storage object A COM object that implements a storage interface. Storage objects are used to access BLOB data and OLE objects stored in a column.

Success A condition in which no errors occurred.

T

Table A collection of rows in the data source.

Text command A text string, usually an SQL statement, that defines a command.

Transaction An atomic unit of work. The work in a transaction must be completed as a whole; if any part of the transaction fails, the entire transaction fails.

Transaction isolation The act of isolating one transaction from the effects of all other transactions.

Transaction isolation level A measure of how well a transaction is isolated.

Transaction object An OLE DB object used to support transactions.

Transaction options object An OLE DB object used to define various options for a transaction.

Transfer To move data between the consumer's and provider's buffers. The provider, not the consumer, transfers data. *See also* getting data and setting data.

Transmit To send changes made through **IRowsetChange** to the data source. *See also* delayed update mode and immediate update mode.

Transmitted change A change that has been sent to the data source. *See also* pending change.

Truncate To discard one or more bytes of variable-length data or non-significant digits of numeric data. Truncation results in a warning condition when getting data and an error condition when setting data.

Type indicator An integer value passed to or returned from an OLE DB method to indicate the data type of a consumer variable, a parameter, or a column.

U

Uninitialize To change the state of an enumerator or data source object so it cannot be used to access data. For example, uninitializing a data source object might require the provider to close a data file or disconnect from a database.

Unprepare To discard the current execution plan.

Update To change an existing row of data in the data source. Also, to transmit pending changes to the data source.

User The end user, which is a generally a person, as opposed to the consumer, which is a piece of software.

V

Value   A data value. *See also* data part, length, and status.

Variable-length data type   A data type for which the length of the data can vary, such as a string. *See also* fixed-length data type.

Visibility   Whether data values can be detected by a rowset. Refers both to the visibility of data in a data source and data cached in a rowset.

W

Warning   A condition in which a nonfatal error occurred.

Z

Zombie   A state in which the only valid consumer action on a COM object is generally to release that object.

Index

A

Abort 487–488
    coordinated transactions 142
    nested transactions 141
    OLE objects 606
    prepared commands 576
    retaining transactions 140
    storage objects 90, 98
    transaction objects 141
    transmitted changes 51
Aborting transactions 16, 140–141
    asynchronous 487, 570
    from transaction object 141
    local transactions 16
    method for 487
    notifications 142
    prepared commands 576
    reason for 487
    rowsets 140, 590
    transaction isolation 581
    transaction retention 140, 488
Abstract data types 85, 114
    creating tables 480
    future use 85
    type indicator 517
Access control *See* Authorization
Access rights *See* Permissions
Accessor handles
    See also HACCESSOR
    creating 178
    null 66
    releasing 186
Accessors 13, 66–68, 173–174
    See also Null accessors; Parameter accessors;
      Reference accessors; Reference counting,
      accessors; Row accessors
    bindings 69
    creating 66, 176
    efficient row copy 73

Accessors (*continued*)
    getting bookmarks 45
    inheriting 66, 173
    invalid with some methods 430, 445
    invalid, status of 62, 64
    multiple 67, 344
    null 177
    on command or rowset 66, 173
    optimizing 67, 177
    overview 57
    parameter 66
    properties 176–177
    reference 67–68, 176–177
    reference count 173
    releasing 66, 173, 174, 186
    releasing command, effect of 173
    releasing rowset, effect of 173
    RestartPosition, effect of 359
    row 66
    threading 173, 175, 186
    use by other rowsets 173
    validating 182
        delayed 62, 64
        errors 178
        not validated by GetData 343
        revalidating 359, 420
        when getting data 77
        when setting data 80
ACID 15
ACL checking 587
AddColumn 86, 477–478
AddErrorRecord 155, 315–316
Adding columns 477
AddRef
    notification for 422
    on data source objects, restricted 26
    on enumerators, restricted 25
    on storage objects 95
AddRefAccessor 175
    threading 173
    using 173

L

ISBN 1-55615-843-2, 1232 pages with one CD, $49.95
($67.95 Canada)

INSIDE OLE provides both a clear tutorial and a strong set of sample programs, giving you the tools to incorporate OLE into your own development projects. Written by a member of the Microsoft® OLE team, this book truly gives you the insider's perspective on the power of OLE for creating the next generation of innovative software.

INSIDE OLE provides detailed coverage of and reference material on:

- OLE and object fundamentals: objects and interfaces, connectable objects, custom components and the Component Object Model, and Local/Remote Transparency

- Storage and naming technologies: structured storage and compound files, persistent objects, and naming and binding

- Data transfer, viewing, and caching: Uniform Data Transfer, viewable objects, data caching, OLE Clipboard, and OLE Drag and Drop

- OLE Automation and OLE Properties: automation controllers; property pages, changes, and persistence

- OLE Documents: OLE Documents and embedding containers, OLE Documents and local embedding servers, in-process object handlers and servers, linking containers, and in-place activation (visual editing) for containers and objects

- OLE Controls and the future of OLE: OLE Controls, future enhancements, and component software

If you're interested in fully exploring and understanding OLE and component software, there's no better source than INSIDE OLE.

VALUABLE INFORMATION INCLUDED ON CD!
CD includes 75 source code examples (more than 100,000 lines of code) that demonstrate how to create components and how to integrate OLE features into applications.

Harness
the power of
ActiveX™ controls.

ActiveX controls are an important ingredient in Microsoft's emerging "object model" approach to the Internet, applications, development tools, and operating systems. Written by a former data management consultant and current program manager at Microsoft in the Visual Languages group, ACTIVEX CONTROLS INSIDE OUT is an in-depth guide for C++ and Microsoft® Visual Basic® programmers who want to build powerful custom controls and "componentware" using Microsoft's new tools and revolutionary COM (Component Object Model) technology. A comprehensive update to the successful first edition, *OLE Controls Inside Out,* this book contains the latest on MFC, changes to OLE, and Visual Basic and Microsoft Internet Explorer support for hosting ActiveX controls. It is an indispensable resource for all those programming for Windows® and the Internet.

U.S.A.	**$39.95**
U.K.	£37.49 [V.A.T. included]
Canada	$54.95
ISBN 1-57231-350-1	

Microsoft®*Press*

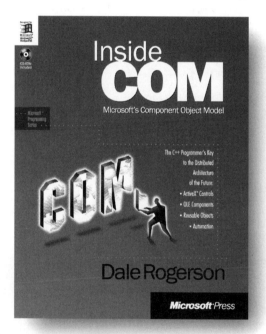

IMPORTANT—READ CAREFULLY BEFORE OPENING SOFTWARE PACKET(S). By opening the sealed packet(s) containing the software, you indicate your acceptance of the following Microsoft License Agreement.

MICROSOFT LICENSE AGREEMENT

(Book Companion CD)

This is a legal agreement between you (either an individual or an entity) and Microsoft Corporation. By opening the sealed software packet(s) you are agreeing to be bound by the terms of this agreement. If you do not agree to the terms of this agreement, promptly return the unopened software packet(s) and any accompanying written materials to the place you obtained them for a full refund.

MICROSOFT SOFTWARE LICENSE

1. GRANT OF LICENSE. Microsoft grants to you the right to use one copy of the Microsoft software program included with this book (the "SOFTWARE") on a single terminal connected to a single computer. The SOFTWARE is in "use" on a computer when it is loaded into the temporary memory (i.e., RAM) or installed into the permanent memory (e.g., hard disk, CD-ROM, or other storage device) of that computer. You may not network the SOFTWARE or otherwise use it on more than one computer or computer terminal at the same time.

2. COPYRIGHT. The SOFTWARE is owned by Microsoft or its suppliers and is protected by United States copyright laws and international treaty provisions. Therefore, you must treat the SOFTWARE like any other copyrighted material (e.g., a book or musical recording) except that you may either (a) make one copy of the SOFTWARE solely for backup or archival purposes, or (b) transfer the SOFTWARE to a single hard disk provided you keep the original solely for backup or archival purposes. You may not copy the written materials accompanying the SOFTWARE.

3. OTHER RESTRICTIONS. You may not rent or lease the SOFTWARE, but you may transfer the SOFTWARE and accompanying written materials on a permanent basis provided you retain no copies and the recipient agrees to the terms of this Agreement. You may not reverse engineer, decompile, or disassemble the SOFTWARE. If the SOFTWARE is an update or has been updated, any transfer must include the most recent update and all prior versions.

4. DUAL MEDIA SOFTWARE. If the SOFTWARE package contains more than one kind of disk (3.5", 5.25", and CD-ROM), then you may use only the disks appropriate for your single-user computer. You may not use the other disks on another computer or loan, rent, lease, or transfer them to another user except as part of the permanent transfer (as provided above) of all SOFTWARE and written materials.

5. SAMPLE CODE. If the SOFTWARE includes Sample Code, then Microsoft grants you a royalty-free right to reproduce and distribute the sample code of the SOFTWARE provided that you: (a) distribute the sample code only in conjunction with and as a part of your software product; (b) do not use Microsoft's or its authors' names, logos, or trademarks to market your software product; (c) include the copyright notice that appears on the SOFTWARE on your product label and as a part of the sign-on message for your software product; and (d) agree to indemnify, hold harmless, and defend Microsoft and its authors from and against any claims or lawsuits, including attorneys' fees, that arise or result from the use or distribution of your software product.

DISCLAIMER OF WARRANTY

The SOFTWARE (including instructions for its use) is provided "AS IS" WITHOUT WARRANTY OF ANY KIND. MICROSOFT FURTHER DISCLAIMS ALL IMPLIED WARRANTIES INCLUDING WITHOUT LIMITATION ANY IMPLIED WARRANTIES OF MERCHANTABILITY OR OF FITNESS FOR A PARTICULAR PURPOSE. THE ENTIRE RISK ARISING OUT OF THE USE OR PERFORMANCE OF THE SOFTWARE AND DOCUMENTATION REMAINS WITH YOU.

IN NO EVENT SHALL MICROSOFT, ITS AUTHORS, OR ANYONE ELSE INVOLVED IN THE CREATION, PRODUCTION, OR DELIVERY OF THE SOFTWARE BE LIABLE FOR ANY DAMAGES WHATSOEVER (INCLUDING, WITHOUT LIMITATION, DAMAGES FOR LOSS OF BUSINESS PROFITS, BUSINESS INTERRUPTION, LOSS OF BUSINESS INFORMATION, OR OTHER PECUNIARY LOSS) ARISING OUT OF THE USE OF OR INABILITY TO USE THE SOFTWARE OR DOCUMENTATION, EVEN IF MICROSOFT HAS BEEN ADVISED OF THE POSSIBILITY OF SUCH DAMAGES. BECAUSE SOME STATES/COUNTRIES DO NOT ALLOW THE EXCLUSION OR LIMITATION OF LIABILITY FOR CONSEQUENTIAL OR INCIDENTAL DAMAGES, THE ABOVE LIMITATION MAY NOT APPLY TO YOU.

U.S. GOVERNMENT RESTRICTED RIGHTS

The SOFTWARE and documentation are provided with RESTRICTED RIGHTS. Use, duplication, or disclosure by the Government is subject to restrictions as set forth in subparagraph (c)(1)(ii) of The Rights in Technical Data and Computer Software clause at DFARS 252.227-7013 or subparagraphs (c)(1) and (2) of the Commercial Computer Software — Restricted Rights 48 CFR 52.227-19, as applicable. Manufacturer is Microsoft Corporation, One Microsoft Way, Redmond, WA 98052-6399.

If you acquired this product in the United States, this Agreement is governed by the laws of the State of Washington.

Should you have any questions concerning this Agreement, or if you desire to contact Microsoft Press for any reason, please write: Microsoft Press, One Microsoft Way, Redmond, WA 98052-6399.

Register Today!

Return this
*Microsoft® OLE DB 1.1 Programmer's
Reference and Software Development Kit*
registration card for
a Microsoft Press® catalog

U.S. and Canada addresses only. Fill in information below and mail postage-free. Please mail only the bottom half of this page.

1-57231-612-8A   *MICROSOFT® OLE DB 1.1 PROGRAMMER'S*   *Owner Registration Card*
REFERENCE AND SOFTWARE DEVELOPMENT KIT

NAME

INSTITUTION OR COMPANY NAME

ADDRESS

CITY   STATE   ZIP

Microsoft®*Press*
Quality Computer Books

For a free catalog of
Microsoft Press® products, call
1-800-MSPRESS

BUSINESS REPLY MAIL
FIRST-CLASS MAIL   PERMIT NO. 53   BOTHELL, WA

POSTAGE WILL BE PAID BY ADDRESSEE

NO POSTAGE
NECESSARY
IF MAILED
IN THE
UNITED STATES

MICROSOFT PRESS REGISTRATION
MICROSOFT® OLE DB 1.1 PROGRAMMER'S
REFERENCE AND SOFTWARE DEVELOPMENT KIT
PO BOX 3019
BOTHELL WA   98041-9946